Defining the Struggle

Defining the Struggle

National Organizing for Racial Justice,
1880–1915

SUSAN D. CARLE

OXFORD
UNIVERSITY PRESS

OXFORD
UNIVERSITY PRESS

Oxford University Press is a department of the University of Oxford.
It furthers the University's objective of excellence in research, scholarship,
and education by publishing worldwide.

Oxford   New York
Auckland   Cape Town   Dar es Salaam   Hong Kong   Karachi
Kuala Lumpur   Madrid   Melbourne   Mexico City   Nairobi
New Delhi   Shanghai   Taipei   Toronto

With offices in
Argentina   Austria   Brazil   Chile   Czech Republic   France   Greece
Guatemala   Hungary   Italy   Japan   Poland   Portugal   Singapore
South Korea   Switzerland   Thailand   Turkey   Ukraine   Vietnam

Oxford is a registered trademark of Oxford University Press
in the UK and certain other countries.

Published in the United States of America by
Oxford University Press
198 Madison Avenue, New York, NY 10016

© Oxford University Press 2013

Library of Congress Cataloging-in-Publication Data
Carle, Susan D.
Defining the struggle : national organizing for racial justice, 1880–1915 / by Susan D. Carle.
pages cm
Includes bibliographical references and index.
ISBN 978-0-19-994574-0 (hardback : alk. paper)   1. African Americans—Legal status, laws,
etc.—History.   2. Civil rights movements—United States.—History.   3. Civil rights lawyers—
United States.—History.   I. Title.
KF4757.C37 2013
323.1196'073009034—dc23
2013020647

1 3 5 7 9 8 6 4 2
Printed in the United States of America
on acid-free paper

For Henry S. Friedman

CONTENTS

ABBREVIATIONS KEY

Organizations

AAC	National Afro-American Council
AAL	National Afro-American League
AFL	American Federation of Labor
ACLU	American Civil Liberties Union
AME	African Methodist Episcopal Church
CIICN	Committee for Improving the Industrial Condition of Negroes
CUCN	Committee on Urban Conditions among Negroes
GERC	Georgia Equal Rights Convention
ICSS	Institutional Church and Social Settlement
NAACP	National Association for the Advancement of Colored People
NACW	National Association of Colored Women
NAWSA	National American Women's Suffrage Association
NBL	National Negro Business League
NCWL	National Colored Women's League
NESA	National Ex-Slave Mutual Relief, Bounty and Pension Association
NFAAW	National Federation of Afro-American Women
NLPCW	National League for the Protection of Colored Women
NNAPL	National Negro American Political League
NUL	National League on Urban Conditions among Negros or National Urban League
NNC	National Negro Congress
WCTU	Women's Christian Temperance Union

Newspapers and Periodicals

AC	*Atlanta Constitution*
CT	*Chicago Tribune*
CG	*Cleveland Gazette*
CA	*Colored American*
DP	*Plaindealer* (Detroit)
IF	*Indianapolis Freeman*
NACWN	*National Association (of Colored Women) Notes*
NYA	*New York Age*
NYF	*New York Freeman*
NYG	*New York Globe*
NYT	*New York Times*
WB	*Washington Bee*
WP	*Washington Post*
WE	*Woman's Era*
VN	*Voice of the Negro*

Manuscript Collections

ASP	Arthur Spingarn Papers, Library of Congress
BLSP	Bethel Literary Society Papers, Moorland-Spingarn Research Center, Howard University
FHMMP	Freeman Henry Morris Murray Papers, Moorland-Spingarn Research Center, Howard University
GHP	George Edmund Haynes Papers, Special Collections Library, Fisk University
JMP	John E. Milholland Papers, Ticonderoga Historical Society
JSP	Joel Spingarn Papers, Moorland-Spingarn Research Center, Howard University
LHWP	L.Hollingsworth Wood Papers, Special Collections Library, Haverford College
MCTPLOC	Mary Church Terrell Papers, Library of Congress
MCTPMS	Mary Church Terrell Papers, Moorland-Spingarn Research Center, Howard University
NAACPP	Papers of the NAACP, Library of Congress
NACWP	Papers of the National Association of Colored Women (NACW), Library of Congress
NULP	Papers of the National Urban League, Library of Congress

OGVP   Oswald Garrison Villard Papers, Harvard University, Houghton
            Special Collections
TTFP   T. Thomas Fortune Papers, Schomburg Center for Research in Black
            Culture, New York Public Library
VMP   Victoria Earle Matthews Papers, Schomburg Center for Research in
            Black Culture
WEBDBP   The W.E.B. Du Bois Papers, W.E.B. Du Bois Library, University of
            Massachusetts at Amherst
WRMP   White Rose Mission Papers, Schomburg Center for Research in
            Black Culture

PREFACE

A multidisciplinary perspective frames my inquiry here. As a law professor who focuses on the development of American conceptions of "public interest" lawyering, I am highly influenced by contemporary trends in legal scholarship, especially the many outstanding works on the legal history of the civil rights movement cited throughout the book.[1] My questions are derived from legal civil rights historians' work, as well as the work of contemporary human rights theorists who query the division between civil and political rights and economic and social welfare issues.[2] Those debates undergird my exploration of the ways in which nineteenth-century American jurists' notions of "civil" rights affected national organization-building activists' work. I am also influenced by the literature on democratic experimentalism, the movement in legal scholarship that emphasizes the importance of local experimentation with quasi-legal forms of governance that mix public and private activity and produce forms of law other than statutes, regulations, and cases.[3]

I draw on social movement theory when it is applicable as well. I take to heart historians' caution that the "social movement" label should not be slapped on to all instances of social change activism, lest that term lose its specific meaning in referring to relatively short-lived, mass social phenomena. What I have found most helpful in social movement theory are its insights about organizations that seek to bring about social change through methods other than business-as-usual politics. I especially share the theoretical commitments of some social movement scholars to a form of analysis sometimes referred to as "interactionism" (or "symbolic interactionism"), which seeks to interpret social phenomena by studying the cultural meaning produced through interactions among social, political, legal, and historical conditions, individual personalities, and collective action initiatives.[4] I have more fully articulated elsewhere my theoretical commitments in this regard; for now it suffices to point out that interactionism (a social science methodology first sketched by philosophers such as John Dewey, who happens to be a peripheral actor in this narrative as well) emphasizes the importance of appreciating human agency, under even limited space to maneuver, as a factor in understanding social change.[5] This is a theme to which I repeatedly return in this project: Even in the face of social and political conditions including lynching, political disfranchisement, Jim Crow segregation, and massive structural subordination in employment, education, housing and health, the organizations and leaders I examine here found ways to exercise agency to oppose racial injustice.

This project arises out of articles I wrote a decade and a half ago on lawyering within the early NAACP. My interest in late nineteenth-century racial justice activism started with those articles and was further piqued by discovering the foundational work by Emma Lou Thornbrough on T. Thomas Fortune, the National Afro-American League, and the National Afro-American Council; the autobiography of Mary Church Terrell; and an unpublished dissertation by Patrick H. Carroll on the ideological commitments of the members of the Niagara Movement.[6] I later found the work of a contemporary group of what I refer to as "revisionist" historians, including Shawn Leigh Alexander, Cornelius L. Bynum, Jay Driskell, Blair L. M. Kelley, Robert J. Norrell, R. Volney Riser, and others who are developing modified accounts of civil rights activism in the late nineteen and early twentieth centuries.[7] My questions are different from theirs, and I sometimes disagree with them, but I reflect my debt to their expert work in my citations.

A different literature generated by historians of African American women's experiences, including Bettye Collier-Thomas, Paula Giddings, Elizabeth Higginbotham, Dorothy Roberts, Dorothy Salem, Deborah Gray White, and others also greatly inspired and educated me. Glenda Gilmore's classic *Gender and Jim Crow* showed the benefits of synthesizing civil rights and women's history, as did Tomiko Brown-Nagin's prize-winning account of later civil rights and social welfare activism in Atlanta.[8]

A very important source of material support for this book's completion comes from the Ruth Landes Memorial Fund. Ruth Schlossberg Landes was an important American anthropologist (1908–1991) whose research interests spanned questions including gender and sexuality, race and ethnicity, immigration patterns, and social identity. Landes, in other words, pioneered traditions of social inquiry from which this book draws deep support, not only materially but also intellectually.

Defining the Struggle

Introduction

When President Lyndon Johnson signed the Civil Rights Act of 1964 in an oval office ceremony days before the nation's Fourth of July celebrations that year, the room was crowded with representatives of national civil rights organizations. Few present that day remembered the long line of leaders of national organizations, stretching back to the nineteenth century, whose racial justice activism had begun the push for this legislation. That early activism had used both court-based and legislative initiatives to push for enforcement of the promises contained in Reconstruction-era constitutional amendments to grant equal rights to all citizens in voting and other aspects of civic participation regardless of race. In 1965, Congress passed the Voting Rights Act, another federal statute that reinstated Reconstruction-era promises of equal voting rights for all citizens. That statute, too, had its origins in turn-of-the-century national organizations' struggles against racial disfranchisement, again using strategies that included both test case litigation and federal legislative proposals. Few today remember that this struggle began so long ago.[1]

The leaders of these early national racial justice organizations include figures as diverse as T. Thomas Fortune, the law-trained journalist who founded the National Afro-American League (AAL) in 1890, and Reverdy C. Ransom, an African Methodist Episcopal minister who was active in the social gospel movement, which believed that religious ethics mandated social reform advocacy during one's time on earth. Ransom was the earliest leader of the radical civil rights contingent within the National Afro-American Council (AAC), founded in 1898. Mary Church Terrell, who stood at the head of African American high society in Washington, DC, was another deeply committed social reformer, who served as the first president of the National Association of Colored Women (NACW), founded in 1895, and then sat on the NAACP's founding committee and early governing board. In 1905, the great twentieth-century intellectual W.E.B. Du Bois started another national organization dedicated to racial justice, known as the Niagara Movement after the place of its birth, and he also became a member of the NAACP's inner circle of founding leaders. Mary White Ovington, a white social worker who lived in African American settlement houses in New York City, was yet another founding member of the NAACP, as was New York City high school principal William Lewis Bulkley. Bulkley pioneered blending public and private resources to provide vocational training for African American youth, and also helped found and served on the governing board of the early National Urban League.

The Nadir Period

These activists created a first generation of national nonpartisan organizations intended to have long-term status.[2] They did this work during the decades following the end of Reconstruction, a period commonly referred to as the "nadir" because racial conditions in the United States were at their worst since the abolition of slavery.[3] Frequent outbreaks of racial violence included race riots, labor unrest with racial dimensions, and gruesome lynchings, sometimes totaling more than one hundred persons per year. Rather than curtailing such acts, law aided the construction of a repressive racial order, as Southern states enacted Jim Crow statutes mandating segregation in transportation and public accommodations and adopted new constitutions disfranchising African American male voters through a variety of legally inscribed devices. The U.S. Supreme Court issued opinions invalidating federal civil rights statutes and explicitly approving legally sanctioned Jim Crow. In the economic sphere, African Americans were forced out of desirable occupations, blocked from employment mobility, and lost ground in the professions. Laborers in the South faced tenancy farming and peonage labor and, if they moved North, encountered housing and employment discrimination. Schools for African Americans were segregated and drastically underfunded, as were hospitals and other health care services. As a wide range of new social welfare institutions, including municipal services, kindergartens, recreational facilities, and public libraries, emerged in the so-called Progressive era, African American communities found themselves excluded from these benefits.

Contemporary scholarship on civil rights history often uses the framework of social movements theory, which predicts that such unrelentingly dismal conditions would suppress political activism.[4] Indeed, the nadir period is commonly viewed as an "age of accommodationism," dominated by conservative race leader Booker T. Washington. Washington, the director of a vocational training institute for African American youth in Tuskegee, Alabama, publicly preached that African Americans should "accommodate" white racial prejudice and forgo protesting for equal civil and political rights in favor of working patiently on economic advancement. In light of these conditions involving both abysmal racial conditions and Booker T. Washington's accommodationist philosophy, legal scholars have assumed that racial justice activism during the late nineteenth- and early twentieth-century period had little significance.

This book shows that such assumptions are incorrect—that path-setting, law-related activism took place in the period surrounding the turn of the twentieth century, along with the founding of ambitious new national organizations. Washington certainly did broker relations between powerful white industrialists and politicians, on the one hand, and African American aspirants to the benefits this racially defined power structure could dispense, on the other. But he was far from successful in his attempts to suppress energetic civil rights activism. A host of largely forgotten leaders engaged in a wide range of racial justice initiatives, from which they gained experiences they then passed on to later organizations.

To be sure, most of these initiatives fell short of success. This is perhaps another reason that legal scholars who focus on civil rights history have not bothered to closely examine these first national organizations: They have assumed that nothing important resulted from the efforts of organizations whose projects did not achieve fruition. Indeed, as already noted, social movement theory predicts that such repeated failures would produce a social movement's death. But I will show that precisely the opposite result occurred: Failure led to even more determined efforts, producing increasingly sophisticated strategies and, eventually, organizing models that had the staying power to prevail over nearly insurmountable odds. This book shows, in other words, that much can be learned from studying early national organizations' "failed" efforts because these failures forged the ideas that produced later, seemingly almost miraculous, successes.[5]

Reevaluating the Origins of National Legal Civil Rights Organizing

Legal history scholarship emphasizes the origins of modern civil rights activism in NAACP initiatives starting in the 1920s and 1930s.[6] A similar focus can be seen in political science scholarship, especially scholarship in the burgeoning field of social movement theory. This literature, too, starts with the third and fourth decades of the twentieth century in understanding the later mass civil rights movement—understandably enough since this is the period in which racial justice activism first started to exhibit the characteristics of what theorists generally define as a "social movement," including mass membership mobilization and some discernible policy success.[7] Prior to that, as some experts in African American history have cautioned, racial justice activism should not be described as a social movement at all. This is because there was, first, not yet a broad-scale citizen mobilization (in other words, no mass "social" phenomenon), and, second, no significant change (in other words, no "movement").[8] Indeed, in his leading work examining the historical origins of the U.S. civil rights movement, Doug McAdam dates its immediate historical antecedents to the 1930s, but not earlier. McAdam argues that the extreme hostility against African Americans on the judicial, legislative, and political fronts, as shown by the slew of anti–civil rights cases the Supreme Court handed down during the nadir period, as well as a host of other political, legislative, and executive branch develop- ments, "communicated to blacks the virtual impossibility of successful group action to combat discrimination."[9] My study casts doubt on the political opportunities hypothesis insofar as it seeks to predict the existence of activist organizing efforts. The hypothesis that rising political opportunity predicts the emergence of activism is belied not only by the NAACP's rapid growth in the face of adverse conditions well before the 1930s, but also by the work of the predecessor national organiza- tions that I examine here. My study of these organizations shows that insistent activ- ist strategies were being pursued on a national level even in the decades prior to the NAACP's founding. Political opportunities strongly influenced the directions this activism took, as I will show. But the lack of political opportunity did not extinguish activism; instead, it led to creative experimentation. This work generated lessons that activists transmitted to the early NAACP, giving that organization its successful start in the face of the adverse conditions it set out to oppose at the height of the nadir period.[10]

To be sure, most of this early activism should not be characterized as a "social movement" under a traditional definition of that term (although the African American women's club movement is correctly termed as such, given its depth and breadth, as discussed in chapter 7).[11] But this definitional question need not detain us. This study shows that coordinated, national-level activism was taking place even though it had not at the time spawned a modern "movement." Moreover, this activ- ism created organizations and resources on which the next generations would draw. The transmission of ideas from generation to generation was by no means continu- ous or uninterrupted over the course of the twentieth century. Nonetheless, key foundational ideas were transmitted from one generation to the next in the cen- tury's first years.

Experts in African American history have long been aware that late nineteenth- and early twentieth-century organizations provided the ideas underlying the NAACP's founding, but these earlier organizations are surprisingly little known among nonspecialists.[12] No legal scholar has yet examined what ideas about the use of law these earlier national racial justice advocacy organizations transmitted to the early NAACP, and to the National Urban League (NUL) as well, or how these flag- ship early twentieth-century organizations took up these ideas. That is the task this book undertakes; it examines the role of early advocates and the organizations they led in shaping the direction of twentieth-century activists' work to bring law-related strategies to bear on the problem of racial injustice. To do so, it explores a series of questions: First, who were these activists, and how did their backgrounds and beliefs propel their activist work? Second, how did their ideas and concerns shape their decisions about what issues to prioritize and what strategies to pursue? Third, what initiatives did these largely forgotten leaders and organizations attempt, and what lessons did they draw from their efforts? Fourth, what ideas did they have about the relationship between social-change activism and law—and, equally importantly, about the limits of law-focused strategies as a means of social change within their particular social, political, and historical milieu? Finally, which of these ideas about law did this forerunner generation pass on to future generations, most directly to the NAACP and National Urban League, and how did this transmission occur?[13]

Reevaluating the Objectives of Early National Racial Justice Organizing

Modern legal commentators have criticized the so-called civil rights movement for having focused unduly on civil and political rights issues—especially on formal equality under the law, sometimes referred to as "legal liberalism"—at the alleged expense of the economic and social welfare concerns that could make real, material differences to people's everyday lives.[14] In so doing, these law-focused critics have made the mistake of scrutinizing only the civil and political rights aspects of prior generations of race justice activists' law-related work. Not only does the legal liberalist critique ignore legal campaigns to combat peonage, convict leasing, and lynching, but it also ignores a huge swath of early activism focused on improving the material conditions of people's lives through self-help and voluntary institution building in the private sphere. Activists of the era called these projects race "uplift" work, and they did not describe it as part of a campaign to change law per se. But I will argue that this work, too, must be seen as a part of a comprehensive racial justice agenda related to law reform.

In so doing, I am joining other legal scholars and civil rights historians who have responded to the legal liberalist critique of the civil rights movement by generating a new literature analyzing the myriad strategies racial justice advocates used as the twentieth century progressed—strategies that spanned both political and civil rights *and* economic and social welfare goals.[15] So far this literature has not reached back to the founding generation of national organization builders of the late nineteenth and early twentieth centuries to explore the significance of their work in influencing the paths these later, richly diverse activist campaigns would take. This project seeks to fill this hole in the existing literature.

This book's goals, however, are not merely descriptive in this sense. My study advances a two-part argument: First, it insists, with copious supporting detail, on a new appreciation of the importance of the transmission of ideas about law-related racial justice activism from a founding generation of leaders involved in the AAL, AAC, NACW, and Niagara Movement to the NAACP and NUL. It argues that the NAACP's ideas did not emerge full blown from the minds of those who happened to found it, as often supposed, but drew from decades of prior racial justice activism. Second, this book argues that these ideas and strategies about law and racial justice activism were of a specific, previously incompletely understood, nature.

I support the first argument by showing how the AAL transmitted to the NAACP, through the intermediary of the Niagara Movement, particular principles for a nonpartisan national organization devoted to racial justice activism. These principles included a commitment to test case litigation and an underlying democratic socialist allegiance to economic fairness and social welfare reform. The AAC's contributions differed somewhat: That organization transmitted to the NAACP a pragmatic substantive issue agenda, including a priority focus on test cases to challenge Southern disfranchisement, legislation and litigation to combat Jim Crow, and a legislative and public education campaign to combat lynchings. The AAC further contributed strategies for building organizational resources, in several respects. First, it experimented with the potential synergy between raising funds for test cases and simultaneously building membership enthusiasm, using methods such as mass turnout meetings and nationally coordinated days for church sermons and other public events focusing attention on specific aspects of racial injustice. Second, it used its Washington, DC, members to generate a lobbying presence at the federal legislative level. Third, it began cultivating legal expertise, such as advisor Albert Pillsbury, who worked with the AAC on its antidisfranchisement initiatives and later transferred his efforts to the early NAACP.

In turn, the Niagara Movement passed on its publication, *The Horizon,* which retained much of its design and content emphasis in becoming *The Crisis,* as well as a deeply committed, courageous, and experienced cadre of local activists who had severed their allegiance to Booker T. Washington and were primed to mount an outspoken national racial justice campaign. These particular activists—many of whom were also leaders in the NACW—soon became the core leaders of the NAACP's biggest early branches, which propelled the organization's rapid grassroots growth.

Most important, the early NAACP benefited from the insights of key leaders of forerunner organizations. For example, AAC and Niagara Movement leaders advised this new effort to eschew the "letterhead top-heavy" organizing models of traditional national Progressive-era organizations. Instead, these experienced leaders urged the NAACP to adopt an organizational design that would help build grassroots strength by empowering local chapters. Likewise, I will show, albeit in less detail, how the National Urban League drew on the experiments of organizations like the NACW's affiliates and Reverdy Ransom's social settlement experiments in developing its organizational mission and strategies.

My second argument, concerning the content of the ideas and strategies passed from the late nineteenth to the early twentieth century through these specific, documented lines of transmission, is equally important: I will show that these ideas and strategies contemplated a multifaceted racial justice agenda that spanned political and civil rights issues *and* economic and social welfare concerns. All these aspects of racial justice organizing coexisted in a fairly undifferentiated way in the AAL's founding platform. A decade later the AAC focused more exclusively on a civil and political rights agenda. This, I will show, was not because its leaders believed that these issues were of a higher priority than economic and social welfare concerns, but instead because they were stymied from tackling a broader agenda because of their vastly different visions of economic and overall social justice.

The AAC relied on its so-called sister organization, the NACW, to address social welfare concerns. I will argue that the NACW's strategies, though often omitted from accounts of legal civil rights reform because they are thought to have been merely about "social" or charity work, require inclusion in any attempt to understand the law reform strategies of early twentieth-century civil rights activism. The NACW's strategies *were* law related, albeit in a less direct or traditional way. What the NACW movement sought to do was, first, to start building a new reality "on the ground," so to speak, by constructing private institutions to perform the functions of the nascent, Progressive-era social welfare state from which African Americans were being excluded. Second, it requested that the functions these institutions were performing be taken over, or at least supported, by the public institutions of government. To be sure, these women reformers were usually unsuccessful in achieving this latter objective. But the existence of this strategy, the reasons for it, and its difference from the legislative and litigation tactics of white women reformers seeking protective legislation at the same time, require far more attention than they have previously received. These differences had important consequences to the subsequent building of the New Deal welfare state.

This book thus advances a several-part argument. It does so, however, primarily by telling a story, and I have let the story speak for itself until the book's conclusion. In other words, although theoretical questions of interest to legal and other scholars motivate this project, its foremost aim is to recount from a new perspective an important but generally forgotten historical narrative. Accordingly, to avoid disturbing the narrative flow of the chapters that follow, I reserve most of my explicit theoretical dialogue with other scholars for footnotes intended to be of use to other scholars. For these scholars' benefit I have outlined my intellectual debts and underlying theoretical commitments in this book's preface. For the more general reader, I promise to save further explicitly theoretical discussion for the conclusion. Throughout the book, I have focused on aspects of the historical record that remain underexplored, and I thus give less emphasis to matters that are well documented in other historical accounts. For this reason I devote more chapters to the law-related work of the AAL, AAC, and Niagara Movement, for example, than to the similar work of the NACW, NUL, and NAACP—not because I think these latter organizations are less important but because they are already quite well researched. In contrast, the former group of organizations' contributions to early twentieth-century racial justice organizing remain less well appreciated, and I therefore explore them in more detail. Another important limiting decision concerned the choice of organizations to which to devote chapters. I made those decisions based on my assessments as to which organizations most strongly transmitted their organizing philosophies into the early twentieth century, based on which specific organizational leaders I could document transmitting ideas across organizations, and thus across generations as well.[16]

Summary of Chapters

This book's chapters are organized as follows: Chapter 1 explores the connections between personal background and social, political, historical, and legal milieus by introducing the sometimes intersecting and sometimes contrasting backgrounds of five key figures within the leadership ranks of the national racial justice organizations this project explores. Many more figures eventually require discussion as this narrative unfolds, but focusing on a smaller handful at the outset introduces some main characters who help anchor the complex story of turn-of-the-century race activism. The characters selected are those mentioned at the opening of this introduction and meet the criteria of having been central but understudied figures whose race activism spanned many years and included active participation in at least several of the organizations this project considers.

Chapter 2 begins to explore the National Afro-American League. The AAL was the earliest substantial national organization-building effort aimed at establishing a nonpartisan institution with permanent status to oversee national racial justice activism. The AAL thus marked a break from prior postabolition national organizing efforts, which focused on periodic conventions and groups with electoral party affiliations. In contrast, T. Thomas Fortune's idea was to create an organization that would have more permanent status and would eschew affiliation with electoral parties. To further explore the organizing philosophy underlying the Afro-American League, chapter 2 closely examines the young Fortune's political thought, as reflected in his many writings throughout the 1880s, and then traces in detail the connections between Fortune's views and his organizational vision for the AAL.

Chapter 3 looks at the efforts of Fortune and others within the AAL to put these ideas into action, assesses the available evidence concerning the AAL's law-related work, and explores the political and legal perspectives of lawyers whose ideas were key to the AAL's activity. These leaders ended up transmitting to the NAACP, through successor organizations, many of the original features of the AAL's organizing philosophy, including its long-term social justice vision influenced by the tenets of democratic socialism, its interest in pursuing coalition-based politics with more progressive elements within the U.S. labor movement, and a pragmatic short-term action agenda blending both test case litigation and federal and state legislative reform initiatives. The AAL's experiments in fostering a synergetic relationship between local test case initiatives, fund-raising, and national organization building also forged a path the NAACP would later pursue. At the same time, some aspects of the AAL's vision dropped away from the NAACP's priorities in its earliest years, especially the young Fortune's sense of a tight interconnection between short-term goals and long-term vision. By the time of the NAACP's early work several decades after the AAL folded, a trend toward organizational specialization would lead the NAACP to focus more exclusively on law-related strategies. It did not abandon, but put off for another day, many of its leaders' longer-term social justice aspirations related to democratically achieved, structural economic reform.

Chapter 4 turns to the turn-of-the-twentieth-century organizing efforts of the AAL's successor organization, the National Afro-American Council (AAC). It first focuses on the sociopolitical background that illuminates the reasons for the split between the two groups of activists within the AAC, who are frequently referred to as the "radicals," on the one hand, and the "accommodationists" or conservatives, on the other. Earlier generations of historians discounted the AAC as an insignificant organization dominated by Booker T. Washington and thus incapable of civil rights militancy. But primary materials and more recent scholarship reveal that, to the contrary, the AAC's key leaders steadfastly emphasized the importance of demanding gains in civil and political rights.[17] Indeed, as has long been known, Washington himself sponsored test case litigation to this end, but did so in highest secrecy to avoid damaging his accommodationist public persona. Chapter 4 argues that the internal conflict that marked the AAC's decade-long existence had its origins, not in any significant disagreement about the short-term importance of pushing a political and civil rights agenda, but in its leaders' clashing visions of ultimate social justice. The radicals tended to favor long-term fundamental political reform, especially in redistributing wealth through democratic reform. They envisioned coalition organizing with the labor movement to achieve these goals. In contrast, the so-called accommodationists supported the capitalist system underlying the economic status quo and envisioned African Americans advancing, through race-based interest group politics, to become allies of the capitalist class, as pitted *against* labor unions. Chapter 4 develops this argument by contrasting the life trajectories and ideas of two central figures: Reverdy Ransom and Booker T. Washington, who best embody this ideological split within the AAC. Ransom and other so-called radicals within the AAC favored a democratic, labor-based, coalition-organizing approach, as inherited from the young Fortune (who had since gone over to the Bookerite camp). In contrast, the Bookerite accommodationist approach endorsed a far more conservative, racial interest group or power-brokering model of racial progress.

Chapter 5 focuses on the AAC's decade-long organizational history. It first sketches the worsening social and political conditions of the 1890s that led the AAC's founders to undertake a new national organization-building effort at the decade's end, and then broadly sketches the AAC's tumultuous internal politics. It argues that this internal bickering led the AAC to focus on an action agenda that was based on a pragmatic civil rights consensus—in other words, to focus primarily on pressing threats to African Americans' constitutionally protected political and civil rights because these were matters about which the AAC's members could all agree. The AAC thus concentrated its organizational resources primarily on test case litigation and proposals for federal legislative reform that addressed political and civil rights issues. Even though all AAC members, including Washington, regarded social welfare and economic advancement concerns as at least equally important to political and civil rights progress, their differing underlying political philosophies led them to leave these matters to other organizations—in particular, to the National Association of Colored Women, which the AAC viewed somewhat as its "sister" organization. Chapter 6 explores the law-based initiatives the AAC undertook, which included two kinds of test case litigation and five areas of proposed federal legislative reform, and shows why these efforts, despite being unsuccessful, were crucial to developing the specific set of ideas and strategies the AAC passed on to the NAACP.

Chapter 7 then turns to the National Association of Colored Women's social welfare work and argues that this work, too, must be seen as a critical part of the foundational law-related strategies of the national organization-building generation. The NACW put aside its sometimes significant internal disagreements in favor of its own pragmatic consensus, one based on supporting a vast array of local experiments aimed at delivering social welfare and economic supports to struggling African American communities. The NACW's national leaders explicitly eschewed ideological litmus tests in favor of practical activity, and this organizing model produced more successful organizational growth than that of the AAC. At the same time, the NACW was far from apolitical (despite some earlier mistaken accounts), and it endorsed many political and civil rights stances similar to those of the AAC. Its priority action agenda, however, concentrated on institution building in the private sphere through voluntary efforts. Both men and women undertook this work in forums such as churches and social settlements, as well as local and regional civic clubs. I note how these institution-building achievements sometimes led leaders to request private-public partnerships, including state support or assumption of state responsibility for institutions created through private voluntary effort. The NACW's place in civil rights history thus needs rethinking, both to better appreciate its highly important role and to revisit assumptions about the scope of the political and social reform objectives early racial justice organizers held.

With the broad scope and agenda of turn-of-the-century national racial justice organizing thus laid out, I move on to consider other national organization-building efforts in the later years of the new century's first decade as dissatisfaction with the AAC's limits grew. Chief among these efforts was the 1905 founding of the Niagara Movement by Ransom, Du Bois, and other radicals, including key AAC civil rights lawyer Fredrick McGhee. Chapter 8 traces in detail the Niagara Movement's internal structure and issue agenda and resurrects where possible the biographies of the men (and only men at the Niagara Movement's founding because it initially excluded women from membership) who dared incur Washington's wrath by participating in this explicitly anti-Washington organization.

Chapter 9 explores the Niagara Movement's work after its stirring 1906 meeting at Harper's Ferry. It explores the biographies of the Niagara Movement's new women members, including Washington, DC, writer Barbara E. Pope, who served as the Niagara Movement's plaintiff in its only test case, filed to challenge Jim Crow train car segregation in Virginia. It explores this and other Niagara Movement attempts under McGhee's leadership to generate a civil rights test case agenda, as well as the lessons McGhee and other Niagara Movement leaders learned from this effort. Those lessons included the need for full-time, paid staff as it became obvious that a part-time, all-volunteer effort could not maintain a hard-pressing civil rights operation at the level of consistent intensity that would be required. Relatedly, it became clear that such an operation required far more major funding support than a small organization proved able to generate.

Chapter 9 also analyzes the lessons about national organization building Du Bois learned from the Niagara Movement and took with him to the NAACP after the Niagara Movement began to lose momentum toward the end of the decade. These lessons included Du Bois's growing understanding of his own great strengths, which were in long-term strategizing and articulating the organization's compelling vision, and his weaknesses, which were in managing the personal-relations aspect of organization building. His prior Niagara Movement leadership experience directed him into just the right role in the early NAACP as the editor who built its powerful publication, *The Crisis*. From the Niagara Movement's publication, *The Horizon*, Du Bois also took a winning aesthetic and format. At its start, *The Crisis*, with its focus on accurate, intelligible legal reporting mixed with political, organizational, and general news of race interest, in effect was a continuation of *The Horizon* under another name.

Chapter 10 looks at local conditions and organizing activities in two different urban areas, New York City and Atlanta. It examines how local conditions led to different priorities and how those priorities shaped local activism, which in turn influenced varying national organizing models. It then traces the National Urban League's creation through the merger of a set of prior New York City organizations. In 1911, the new NUL and NAACP agreed to divide the vast field of racial injustice issues. They agreed that the NAACP, which was already amassing a national legal committee of leading lawyers, would handle political and civil rights issues, and the NUL, staffed primarily by social workers, would focus on social welfare and economic concerns using voluntarist strategies inherited from predecessor organizations.

Finally, chapters 12 and 13 provide the denouement to the story, tracing in detail how people and ideas moved from the national organizations described earlier to found the NAACP's leadership ranks and issue agenda. A conclusion then situates this story within the broader scope of social movement theory and legal civil rights history, closing with the argument that civil rights activism in the early twenty-first century should include in its broad charge the important but not yet fully achieved goals of economic and social welfare reform that motivated founding activists a century ago. Although largely forgotten today, these activists pioneered visions and strategies that blended demands for formal civil and political equality with a wide variety of experimentalist strategies to bring about more comprehensive racial and social justice reform as well.

1

A New Generation of
Post-Reconstruction Leaders

The American generation born right around the Civil War years lived through the end of slavery and the promise of the Reconstruction period, during which the nation seemed to be trying, however imperfectly, to give birth to a more racially just society. But by the time this generation came of age in the 1880s, the Reconstruction experiment had collapsed. Lynchings and instances of mob rule took place with increasing frequency, yet the country did nothing. Public and private actors alike violated the dictates of the Reconstruction-era constitutional amendments with impunity. A generation of young people emerged into adulthood to confront a world becoming more violent, more racially oppressive, and seemingly utterly defeated of the will to strive for racial justice. By early adulthood, the members of this generation had already lived through several major historical transformations—namely, the abolition of slavery, the rise and fall of Reconstruction, and the emergence of the oppressive conditions of the nadir period. These experiences informed the approaches the leaders of this generation would forge as racial justice activists. Born into vastly diverse circumstances but at a profoundly important, shared historical moment, these leaders would work to develop strategies to reverse the direction of a country in the grips of a downward spiral of increasing racism and injustice. At the century's conclusion, these leaders would hone and then deliver a well-developed template for civil rights organizing to the next generation of leaders, who would in the following decade take up the major national organization-building efforts of the early twentieth century. This chapter introduces five central leaders of the forerunner generation by briefly exploring the formative years of their sometimes intertwining and sometimes vastly disparate early lives. Each of these figures played a central leadership role in founding the organizations this book explores: T. Thomas Fortune, born in 1856, founded the Afro-American League; Reverdy C. Ransom, born in 1861, was the earliest, most outspoken leader of the so-called radical wing of the Afro-American Council and was later a participant in the founding phases of both the NAACP and National Urban League (NUL); Mary Church Terrell, born in 1863, was the founding president of the National Association of Colored Women and played an important role in founding the NAACP. Born in 1865, Mary White Ovington, a white social worker in African American communities, helped found the NAACP and organizations that became the NUL; and William Bulkley, born the same year, also played an important role in founding both of these national organizations.

T. Thomas Fortune

The end of Reconstruction came early and violently to Florida with the rise of the Ku Klux Klan there in 1868. In the small town of Marianna, seat of Jackson County in the midst of the bogs and pine-covered hills of the Florida Panhandle, the Klan murdered 150 citizens between 1868 and 1871. Its purpose was to drive newly elected Republican state legislators such as T. Thomas Fortune's father, Emanuel Fortune, out of office, and it succeeded in doing so. After holding out for several years, Emanuel Fortune decided in the spring of 1871 to leave Marianna with his wife and family, relinquishing both his seat in the Florida legislature and his small farm and livestock to begin a new life in Jacksonville.

Figure 1.1 T. Thomas Fortune, circa 1891 (New York Public Library).

Emanuel's friend John Q. Dickinson, a white carpetbagger from Vermont who served as the county justice of the peace, was less lucky; with his murder later in 1871 the Florida Klan succeeded in eradicating the last Republican officeholder elected in the county.[1]

Timothy, as T. Thomas Fortune was known in his childhood, was fifteen at the time of his family's flight from Marianna, and the violence he witnessed in his hometown had, in the words of his biographer, "a lasting influence on the development of the sensitive and imaginative boy."[2] Later, when Fortune had grown up to become a leading intellectual among African American activists and founding leader of the National Afro-American League, he would sometimes call for African American men to fight back with arms against violence inflicted upon them, but he never romanticized lawless violence as a means to lasting political and social change. Like other members of his generation of post-Reconstruction activists, Fortune's personal experience with the results of violent change was too immediate to allow him to place faith in revolution as a means of overcoming injustice. He and a number of other leading African American intellectuals of his generation were instead socialists of the mild democratic, Fabian, or religiously inspired sort; they were not revolutionaries and explicitly set themselves apart from the German, or "foreign," strands of socialist thinking also popular during the decades immediately surrounding the turn of the century. Like his father, Emanuel, Fortune placed his faith in the process of democratically induced change, despite the cynicism he soon developed about electoral party politics in the country.

The Fortune family started a new life two hundred miles away in the state capital. Fortune's mother died soon after the family's move, suffering from an illness exacerbated by the extreme stress of the family's circumstances in Marianna. Emanuel used skills he had learned during slavery to gain work as a laborer and also remained active in Republican politics. Timothy's political connections allowed him to obtain a job as a page at the state capitol, where he watched the machinations of Florida state politics firsthand and began to develop his deeply held skepticism about the motives of white politicians who purported to have African Americans' interests at heart.

Despite having started his life in slavery when he was born in 1856 in the Florida Panhandle, Timothy never forgot his roots in what he remembered as the idyllic natural landscape there. On emancipation his father, Emanuel, received farmland from his former "owner," who had been a close childhood friend, and acquired livestock. These resources allowed the Fortune family to make their living off the land until they were forced to abandon their property without payment on their flight from the Klan. Fortune's earliest childhood memories focused on harvesting the bounty of the land through hunting and fishing. He also gained a basic education at a local Freedmen's Bureau school. Fortune learned to "stick" type in the offices of the local newspaper, which would provide him with a skill essential to his future journalism career.

Indeed, Timothy inherited a number of assets during his childhood that would stand him in good stead in his future career: He shared his father's facility with words and love for political debate, he obtained a basic education, and he acquired a manual trade.[3] Fortune's early life experiences further taught him that connections to sources of political power provided a route to chances in life. At the age of seventeen Fortune was eager to get out of the South and make his way on his own. He again made use of his father's political connections to obtain a job in New Jersey as a postal carrier. That job allowed him to earn enough money to enroll in 1876 at Howard University, a flagship educational institution for a newly freed generation of African Americans, which had been established by the Freedmen's Bureau in Washington, DC.

The vagaries of congressional appropriations, chronic lack of funding, and text-book and other resource constraints made Howard University's mission difficult. It nevertheless produced many of the leaders whose work this book investigates, especially those with training in law. Fortune was one of them. He first took a year or so of preparatory classes at Howard to fill in gaps in his elementary education and then completed its classics-focused college program. To augment his small savings Fortune worked in the offices of an African American weekly in Washington, DC, called the *People's Advocate.* He also found employment as an assistant or runner in Congress, again absorbing all the practical learning he could in both of those jobs. His work at the *People's Advocate* exposed him to the vibrant political and cultural life among African American political and civic leaders in the city. Fortune enjoyed opportunities to meet and hear speeches by figures such as Frederick Douglass and John Mercer Langston, who was serving as dean of Howard Law School during Fortune's enrollment as an undergraduate student.

Inspired in part by Langston, Fortune decided to continue his studies at Howard by enrolling in law classes there. He attended law classes for a year and a half, cover-ing most of the two-year curriculum required at the time for a law degree. In this way, Fortune absorbed the jurisprudence Langston and other classic abolitionist jurists espoused—a jurisprudence that would greatly influence his, and others', later analysis of legal and political issues, as explored further in chapter 3. Fortune's law school training thus gave him a basic orientation to political and civil rights mat-ters that he would draw on frequently in his future career. Even though he did not complete his law degree, Fortune would retain a lifelong interest in and facility for writing about law as part of his work as a journalist and an activist.

A bank crisis in 1876 caused Fortune to lose all of his savings and led him to dis-continue his law studies a semester short of graduation. He left Howard and married his childhood sweetheart, Carrie Smiley, who would later become active in women's club work. The couple returned to Florida, where Fortune became a schoolteacher. But the oppressive political conditions and inadequate resources for education he encountered in his home state led him, in his words, to seek alternative employ-ment outside the South "four dark and arduous years later."[4] Through a connection from his prior work for the *People's Advocate,* Fortune heard about a print-setting job at a small, white-owned religious newspaper in New York City. He and Carrie set out for New York City in 1881 and never returned to live in Florida. Fortune often drew on his childhood memories of Florida's land and natural beauty in his political thought, as explored further in chapter 2. For the time being, we will leave Fortune in New York City, poised on the verge of beginning his career as a journalist, intellectual, and national organization builder, and return to an in-depth focus on his developing political and legal thought in chapter 2.

Reverdy C. Ransom

Fortune shared both deeply remembered rural origins and a racial justice ideology rooted in the tenets of democratic socialism with another important but largely forgotten post-Reconstruction racial justice activist, Reverdy C. Ransom. Ransom spent his adult life as a minister within the African Methodist Episcopal (AME) Church. He also served as a founding member of a host of significant turn-of-the-twentieth-century organizations devoted to racial justice, including his own African American settlement house in Chicago, known as the Institutional Church and Social Settlement or ICSS, as well as the AAC, the Niagara Movement, the NAACP, and the NUL.[5]

Figure 1.2 Reverdy C. Ransom, from "Centennial Oration to William Lloyd Garrison," Faneuil Hall, Boston, 1905 (Rubenstein Library, Duke University).

Ransom was born in 1861 in a log cabin in rural Ohio to a single mother and an unknown biological father speculated to have been Irish because of Ransom's red hair. Ransom avoided slavery, but he did not escape rural poverty. In later years, he was fond of painting vivid images of an early childhood spent among matriarchs who smoked corncob pipes and drank homemade whiskey before breakfast, and he based his social justice ministry on his personal knowledge of the suffering entailed in being very poor.[6] Ransom's mother, Harriet, determined to obtain an education for her son, moved with him to the town of Cambridge, Ohio, when he reached school age. There she married, and her husband became Ransom's stepfather. Like many other women of her race and class, Harriet found work as a domestic servant and also took in washing on the side to support herself and her son as Reverdy attended the town's mediocre public schools. In turn, Ransom supplemented his education through reading he was able to do while working in a white household. Through these efforts Ransom achieved the level of educational success necessary to present himself as a promising college candidate.

In 1881, at the age of twenty, Ransom entered Wilberforce University, in central western Ohio. The Methodist Church had established Wilberforce in 1856 as an institution to which white planters could send their mixed-race children for higher education. The economic devastation of the Civil War forced it to close, but a far-sighted AME leader took advantage of the opportunity to buy the property and bring it under AME control. After the Civil War Wilberforce served as the oldest African American–controlled site offering higher education, and it also played a special role as the primary site for educating future AME clergy.[7]

Ransom found Wilberforce's strict approach to both discipline and theology too constraining.[8] Its rigid rules forbade drinking, most forms of entertainment, and all but the most closely chaperoned social intermixing between the sexes. The next year, Oberlin College offered Ransom a scholarship, and he decided to transfer there. Ransom attended Oberlin only for the 1882–83 academic year, however. Although the college was one of the few predominantly white liberal arts colleges to admit African American students, it was not free of race prejudice.[9] A campaign began to require African American female students to eat at a separate table in the school dining hall. Ransom showed already strong instincts for speaking out against injustice when he joined protests against this initiative. As a result, he reported, his scholarship was not renewed.[10]

Ransom then reenrolled in Wilberforce and completed his education there. He still found the institution constraining, but he later attributed his learning of discipline and a prodigious work ethic to his education there.[11] Wilberforce was not all drudgery for Ransom in any event. He gained many important assets there that would help him in his later professional life. Most important, Ransom developed a close relationship with a prominent figure in the AME Church, Rev. Benjamin W. Arnett, who would serve as a mentor to Ransom at many crucial points in his career. Arnett was an adherent of the social gospel movement, which preached the importance of carrying out God's word by seeking to improve social conditions for the poor on earth.[12] Ransom took this social gospel message to heart, and it would serve as his guiding philosophy as he undertook a wide variety of activist commitments throughout his adult life. He also reputedly read every book in the institution's library, thus starting a lifetime habit of voracious reading that kept him abreast of wide-ranging trends in social and political thought.[13] Ransom also benefited from Wilberforce's debating club, the Sodalian Society, where he practiced the oratorical skills for which he would later become renowned.[14] Ransom's formative educational experiences thus allowed him to benefit from a combination of educational influences: the progressive political theory being taught at Oberlin, the ideas of the social gospel movement, and traditional classics and theology offered in Wilberforce's curriculum.

Ransom's experiences at Wilberforce also guided him in his choice of career, leading him to abandon early aspirations to a career in law for life as a member of the AME clergy instead.[15] After ending an ill-advised early marriage, Ransom married Emma S. Connor, who would go on to play an important role as Ransom's partner in ministry while she also pursued independent work within the African American women's social reform movement.[16] The two worked together throughout the early years of Ransom's ministry career on their shared commitment to an anti-poverty religious ministry. Ransom was first assigned to a series of small churches in Pennsylvania and Ohio, and the couple sought to set up social and church programs to benefit the congregations and communities they encountered. As he later recalled, "the need for social service came to me as my wife and I almost daily went through the alleys and climbed the dark stairways of the wretched tenements, or walked out on the planks to the shanty boats where our people lived on the river."[17]

Ransom's superiors soon began to notice his talents in oratory, fund-raising, and congregation building, and he started receiving appointments to progressively larger pastorates.[18] In 1893 Ransom was appointed to St. John's AME Church in Cleveland, Ohio. St. John's was the first parish that offered the Ransoms enough resources to implement their ideas about creating a social justice ministry through the church. Ransom again displayed his talent for increasing the size of his congregation while persuading its members to donate extra funds for such work. The parish began offering a variety of social programs, including infant education classes for mothers, a free kindergarten, various men's groups, and a literary society, which Emma Ransom led. Ransom also set up the AME's first deaconess program, which trained women to provide religiously based social welfare services to their communities.[19]

Cleveland was a hub of African American political and intellectual activity, and Ransom became involved in political action work. He became friends with Harry C. Smith, editor of the Cleveland Gazette.[20] Smith had been a founding member of the AAL and would go on to become a charter member of the Niagara Movement and of the NAACP's Committee of 100 as well.[21] In 1892 Smith had won election to the state legislature and would succeed in having the state pass an improved civil rights bill in 1894. In 1896 he shepherded into law one of the first state antilynching statutes in the country, later known as the Smith Act in his honor.[22] Ransom and Smith shared similar political sympathies and worked collaboratively on a number of racial justice issues (though the two would later have a falling out over Smith's continued allegiance to the Republican Party). Ransom invited Ida Wells to come to St. John's to speak, and her visit led to the formation of a Cleveland antilynching league, in which Ransom became president and Smith was also involved.[23]

The Chicago World's Fair took place in the summer of 1893, and Ransom eagerly attended. There he took part in the World Parliament of Religions, a huge ecumenical gathering of denominations from around the world. He attended programs on the social mission of the church and methods of instituting church programs devoted to social problems. At these meetings he encountered ministers from both the United States and overseas who were involved in the social gospel movement. Many of them were also involved in the growing transatlantic movement to set up social settlement houses in a variety of ethnic neighborhoods to aid the poor and help with the assimilation of new immigrant groups to city life.[24] Chicago was home to the iconic settlement houses popular history best remembers, whose leaders included Jane Addams of Hull House and Rev. Graham Taylor of the Chicago Commons.[25] Ransom met both of these figures at the World's Fair, and they would soon become important supporters of his work.[26] Ida Wells was there, too, and she and Ransom had discussions; she, too, would soon become a collaborator and friend.

At the World's Fair Ransom also attended a wide variety of other gatherings of social reformers discussing poverty, juvenile delinquency, and the prevention of crime; a Congress of Women, where Susan B. Anthony and others spoke; and the African American exhibition, where he heard speeches by Frederick Douglass and local leaders such as Charles E. Bentley, a prominent dentist and later a member of Ransom's congregation, who would join with him in becoming a founding member of the Niagara Movement.

Three years later, Emma and Reverdy moved to Chicago. Ransom had been assigned to be pastor of the Bethel AME Church, home of a prestigious congregation made up of many of that city's most prominent African Americans. Located on Chicago's South Side, Bethel was also close to the area in which growing numbers of African Americans were settling as the result of a still slow but steady migration from the South. In the face of the housing discrimination practiced in most parts of the city, this area of Chicago was becoming an African American enclave, and the Ransoms were excited about the opportunity to bring their social gospel model of ministry, based on the well-off helping the less fortunate, to this fertile arena for social change activism. We will thus leave the Ransoms poised at the start of their ambitious experiment in combining civil rights activism and social ministry and return to a more in-depth study of Ransom's interrelated activism and thought in chapter 4.

Mary Church Terrell

Ransom was a staunch supporter of women's rights, both within the church and in the broader society, and his social settlement work in Chicago and later in New York City took place in close cooperation with the African American women's club movement. Such associations began early in Ransom's life; as it happened, the year he spent at Oberlin overlapped with the college years at Oberlin of Mary Church Terrell.[27] Neither figure wrote about knowing each other at Oberlin; it is likely that Church Terrell reserved her social attentions for those closer to her in their more privileged upbringings. Nor did Church Terrell apparently confront the campus segregation Ransom protested—at least, she did not write about it in her autobiography, though she did reminisce about the protests she lodged against Oberlin's residential segregation when her daughter enrolled there in 1914.[28]

Both Church Terrell's mother and father were born enslaved but later rose to business success. Her father could boast of becoming one of the first African American millionaires, while her mother, Louisa Ayers, was a successful, independent businesswoman. Born in 1839, Robert Church became a saloon owner after emancipation in Memphis, Tennessee. In 1866 white rioters destroyed African American

Figure 1.3 Mary Church Terrell, n.d. (Moorland Spingarn Research Center, Howard University).

neighborhoods of that city. They shot Church and left him for dead on the floor of his saloon, but he recovered and began astutely purchasing property at distressed prices, first after the 1866 riots and then again after a yellow fever epidemic swept the area in 1878. Through such shrewd real estate speculation Church gradually amassed a fortune that made him one of the richest African American men in the South during his lifetime.[29]

Born in Memphis in 1863, Church Terrell obtained most of her precollege education at Ohio boarding schools and through private tutoring so she could avoid having to attend the segregated public schools of that city. She attended Oberlin as a paying student and excelled in her language studies there. Her father may have been a business pioneer, but when it came to his daughter he held deeply traditional views. He was happy to support her studies to attain bachelor's and master's degrees in languages at Oberlin and then to fund a period of travel in Europe, during which she perfected her German and practiced her French and Italian. But when she returned to the United States, Church strongly opposed his daughter's desire to enter into professional work, to the point of temporarily severing contact with her when she accepted a teaching job at Wilberforce. After only a year there, Church Terrell moved to Washington, DC, to accept a position teaching German and Latin in the city's segregated high schools. There she met her future husband, Robert Terrell, then serving as a school principal, and the two married in 1891. Under the school district policies in place at the time, marriage required her to resign from her teaching position. She turned her energies instead to writing, public speaking, and leadership of the city's African American "high society."[30]

This African American society in Washington, DC, had a long, proud history stretching back to a small free black community that lived in Georgetown at the end of the eighteenth century. The District and the nearby city of Alexandria, Virginia, were major centers of slave trading, and draconian black codes required free persons of color to carry certificates of freedom, imposed curfews, and prohibited the granting of shop licenses to persons of African descent. Washington's free black community nevertheless organized its own schools, churches, charitable organizations, and social clubs.[31] After the Civil War, the need to maintain a clear line between Washington's preexisting African American society and the "ignorant, penniless, ragged, dirty, and hungry" freed slaves who were crowding into the city led Washington's older free black families to organize exclusive clubs confined to the "leading" members of the community. Washington society became renowned for its activity and refinement. The existence of white-collar federal government jobs for educated African American men, in positions such as typists, transcribers, clerks, and librarians, offered economic security and status, and Howard University produced teachers for Washington's segregated public schools, as well as doctors, lawyers, and ministers. The most financially lucrative business positions for African American men were in real estate and life insurance companies, and some

Washingtonians managed to accumulate considerable wealth through these business enterprises as well.[32]

Church Terrell and her husband, Robert, stood near the apex of Washington, DC, society. The two had a happy public partnership: Robert Terrell was a supporter of women's suffrage and, from all evidence, fully supported his wife's involvement in civic affairs, giving her sage political advice and encouraging her charitable and public service activities. She, in turn, was instrumental in helping her husband obtain appointment as superintendent of DC's African American schools (over W.E.B. Du Bois, who also wanted the job) and then working through Booker T. Washington to obtain Terrell's appointment as DC's first African American municipal judge. The two also enjoyed attending DC social events, which included formal dress balls, musical recitals, and literary discussion groups, all of which required full formal dress, including floor-length evening gowns for women.

Church Terrell frequently contributed columns to African American papers on topics such as "Christmas at the White House," in which she described a visit there during the early years of the Roosevelt administration. Other articles she wrote described Washington, DC, high society life, reporting that it consisted of many different clubs of people who wished to associate with each other, but "no apex"— something of a gracious understatement since she probably stood at this apex herself. Always concerned with respectability, Church Terrell happily reported that "no bore or moral leper could obtain social recognition among the educated, refined colored people of Washington"; instead, one could "see women tastefully arrayed," "refined," "correct in their use of the English language," and "graceful in carriage," while among men one could meet graduates of Harvard, Yale, and Cornell. Church Terrell further reported that "[w]hile the colored people of Washington believe that all work and no play makes Jill as well as Jack very stupid and dull, they have a serious side which presents itself in many ways."[33]

Church Terrell's serious side led her to contribute incisive articles on the political and social reform developments of her day. She wrote scholarly work on the subject of peonage, marshaling facts and arguing eloquently for reform.[34] She displayed her biting wit and a clear-sighted sense of outrage about race discrimination in articles such as "Service Which Should Be Rendered the South." Opening this article by describing in general terms the need for missionaries in this underprivileged region of the country, she then delivered her punch line, explaining that such missionaries were needed not for the freedmen but to free "the white South from the thralldom of its prejudices, emancipating it from the slavery of its petty, narrow views which choke the good impulses and throttle the better nature of even its worthiest citizens." Thus, she argued, it was the "average white man [who] dwells in a state of mental and moral darkness." Turning the tables on conventional stereotypes, she concluded that it would take "men and women strong in intellect, lofty of purpose and stout of heart to undertake this work among the white people of the South."[35]

Church Terrell's firm and deserved sense of her own social superiority, on grounds of education, intelligence, refinement and worldliness, gave her a source of strength in opposing the race prejudice she endured. Those experiences were frequent, and in her autobiography she frankly described the many indignities she endured throughout her lifetime, including the difficulties she and Robert experienced in purchasing a home to their liking in Washington, DC; and many incidents of humiliation in seeking to travel on Pullman cars, such as conductors selling her tickets for the wrong lines, leaving her stranded in strange locations where she could not obtain overnight accommodations, and even being pulled from her seat when she was a tiny child by a conductor using racial epithets after her father temporarily left her unguarded to take a smoke in the smoking car. Church Terrell likewise recounted discrimination in the provision of health services, including lack of access to an incubator for her prematurely born infant, which probably resulted in its death.[36]

Church Terrell's interest in race—and gender—justice stemmed from her dual sense of outrage at race oppression, some of it personally experienced despite her economic and social advantages, and of her own social superiority. This duality produced the belief that motivated her life's work—namely, that her relative privilege gave her a special duty to help the less fortunate. Unapologetic in this regard, Church Terrell argued in another clever piece favoring "meddlers" that it was wrong that "those who are educated and cultured do not as a matter of habit ask about habits and conditions of the unwashed, the unlettered and the unkempt," or that "the literate do not interfere sufficiently with the illiterate."[37] In this respect she sounded every bit like Jane Addams, who wrote similar unapologetic justifications of her work based in the need for the superior to help the less fortunate.[38]

Church Terrell was a master political operative who gracefully navigated the difficult political waters of turn-of-the-century race organization politics both within and across the race divide. She used these skills not only on behalf of her husband's career but also for her own advancement into leadership positions within the many organizations with which she was involved, including her founding and several-term presidency of the NACW. Chapter 7 takes up a more in-depth analysis of Church Terrell's and the NACW's contributions to shaping the agenda of early twentieth-century, law-related racial justice activism.

Mary White Ovington

Church Terrell was one of the few African American women who helped found and then served on the earliest board of directors of the NAACP. Another early female NAACP leader with a long history of work on racial justice issues was Mary White Ovington, a white woman born in 1865, just a few years after Church Terrell. Like Church Terrell, Ovington's father was a businessman, and Ovington's financial records show that she lived in part off earnings from investment income,

Figure 1.4 Mary White Ovington, circa 1890–1900 (University of Massachusetts at Amherst Library).

though these were modest.[39] Unlike Church Terrell, however, Ovington was born in the North, in Brooklyn Heights, New York, and her awareness of racial oppression began only after she became an adult and decided to pursue a career in social work. After hearing Booker T. Washington lecture, Ovington became inspired to devote her energies to African American communities. She helped found African American settlement houses in New York City and became a friend and ally of Du Bois. An unusually egalitarian white race progressive for her times, Ovington once caused a news scandal after photographers captured her dining in a restaurant elbow-to-elbow with African American men—despite the fact that they were accompanied by their wives as well. Ovington was the only female member of the NAACP's innermost leadership core, and her social location reflects other currents of activism that flowed into that organization's birth.

Of all the whites involved in the NAACP's founding, Ovington displayed the most long-standing and sincere commitment to racial equality (along with a very small handful of others such as the Spingarn brothers, whose involvement did not begin until shortly after the organization's founding). Some of the NAACP's white founders, such as Oswald Garrison Villard, expressed open race prejudice, as when he wrote, as late as 1947, about African Americans' general suitability for domestic servant jobs.[40] Others, such as wealthy Southern writer and socialist William English Walling, who convened and served as secretary at

the NAACP's founding proceedings, dabbled in progressive race politics during the early years of the new century, only to then move on to new intellectual
amusements—joining with Gompers to assist in his leadership of the increasingly racially prejudiced AFL, for example, in much the same way as he dabbled
with radical politics in marrying but then discarding into poverty his exotic, radical Russian wife, Anna Strunsky, and the three children he fathered with her.[41]
Both Villard and Walling had been born and raised in the South and never rid
themselves of their unwillingness, approaching aversion, to engaging in social
relations with African Americans. Ovington, on the other hand, relished opportunities to gently stick white America in its collective eye for its race prejudice, as
in the dining scandal just described. She sometimes verged on race essentialism
in her romantic generalizations about the talents of the African race, a habit of
thought she acquired in part under Du Bois's tutelage. But Ovington led the way
in forging a stance of well-meaning, if sometimes clumsily misaimed, solidarity
work undertaken by white race progressives who sought to support the cause of
African American equality.[42]

Ovington was born to a family with social capital and moderate wealth and
proudly counted prominent abolitionists among her ancestors. Her father was
a china and glassware merchant with a Fifth Avenue store, but both her parents
were political radicals. Like many white middle-class women who shared her
social and historical location, Ovington obtained a substantial education, consisting of elite private schooling followed by two years at Radcliffe College, only to
find herself positioned in early adulthood as an overeducated but unemployable
young woman with a strong public service ethic but very few professional paths
open to her. Like many others in this position, Ovington turned to the social settlement movement as an outlet for her energies. She never married (though she
did, according to her biographer, probably have a steamy romance with the married John Milholland, founder of the biracial Constitution League, whom we will
meet in chapter 5). Eschewing the conventional life of middle-class white women
of her time, Ovington lived in New York City settlement houses serving African
American communities and later lived in a modest residential hotel while working full time in the NAACP's offices at modest or no pay. She served the NAACP
continuously in various capacities from 1910 until her retirement in 1939 at the
age of seventy-four.[43]

Ovington thus represents yet another strand of social justice activism that
came together in the founding of the NAACP and its sister organization, the
NUL. At their beginnings these organizations melded the law-related civil
rights experiments of a host of African American racial justice leaders, including Fortune, Ransom, and other leaders of the AAL and the AAC; the social
welfare work of women and men such as Church Terrell, the Ransoms, and
many other activists located in African American women's, church, and educational institutions of the period; and, in the first decade of the new century, the

backing and financial resources of a small group of white race progressives and social reformers.

In the first years of the new century, Ovington sought out Atlanta University professor W.E.B. Du Bois as her tutor on race matters. Through a mix of sincere flattery catering to the great man's ego; modest financial contributions to his sociological research projects conducted at Atlanta University, with promises of more fund-raising to come; and an amply demonstrated willingness to learn, Ovington succeeded in winning Du Bois's intellectual attentions. The two kept up a lively correspondence in the years before Du Bois moved to New York City, during which Ovington urged Du Bois to share her socialist commitments and Du Bois helped Ovington gain greater sophistication in her perspectives on race. Du Bois permitted Ovington to attend as a purported journalist—and sole white person at—the second annual meeting of his Niagara Movement.[44] Later, after Du Bois resigned from Atlanta University in 1910 to become editor of *The Crisis* magazine, Ovington took on the role of NAACP national secretary and then chair of the board of that organization, and the two worked closely together within the NAACP's New York City offices, where they continued to be allies and friends. Indeed, Ovington appears to have been one of the only white leaders of the early NAACP (along with former academic Joel Spingarn, the NAACP's board chair after Villard's resignation in 1914), whom Du Bois trusted. Without Ovington, Du Bois would have had an even harder time enduring his intense personality conflict with NAACP board chair and later treasurer, Villard.[45] As we will see further in chapter 11, Ovington performed other important, albeit sex stereotypic, work in massaging these men's egos through the period of the NAACP's birth and infancy.

Of course, no introductory discussion of the leadership generation whose work laid the groundwork for the founding of the NAACP and the NUL can leave out the great twentieth-century intellectual and race activist Dr. W.E.B. Du Bois, about whom many excellent intellectual and personal biographies have already been written.[46] This book focuses its lens somewhat away from Du Bois, however, in order to highlight lesser-known leaders whose work was also important in the turn-of-the-century period. Du Bois was born in Great Barrington, Massachusetts, in 1865. By the end of his long life, spanning nearly an entire century, he indisputably stood as the most important thinker on race issues of the twentieth century. Not only a great thinker but also a doer, Du Bois threw his energies into a variety of institution-building projects during the turn-of-the-century period. Like his near contemporary Ransom, Du Bois was involved in many of the predecessor organizations whose ideas and experiments provided the undergirding without which the NAACP could not have been successfully built. Today Du Bois is correctly perceived as the mastermind of many of those ideas, but in taking a more fine-grained view, Du Bois emerges as having come to the ideas of the so-called civil rights radicals relatively late in the game. As the twentieth century dawned, other figures led the way, including the young Fortune and, after his exit from the vanguard of civil rights radicalism following his enlistment with the Washington camp, the slightly younger Ransom, along with other figures who will be introduced as this narrative further unfolds.

William Lewis Bulkley

Although journalists and lawyers made up the majority of civil rights radicals who opposed Washington's accommodationism, some social workers and educators played this role as well. Many of these figures have faded from historical memory, but their work, too, requires attention in order to resurrect the social and economic welfare side of the vision of this founding generation of race activists. Leaders such as William Lewis Bulkley exemplify this strand of turn-of-the-century racial justice work. Born in 1861 in Greenville, South Carolina, to free parents of partial African descent, Bulkley remembered his first school experiences in a rundown frame building with a curriculum consisting solely of a Webster's spelling book, overseen by an elderly African American schoolmaster who maintained discipline through the use of a hickory switch. Bulkley later attended a school run by Northern missionaries and began serving as a public school teacher at the age of sixteen. He then enrolled in Claflin University, newly founded by the Methodist Episcopal Church (now the United Methodist Church) to educate African American youth in Orangeburg,

Figure 1.5 William. L. Bulkley, 1899 (New York Public Library).

South Carolina. Bulkley's father, who had become a Methodist Episcopal clergyman after the Civil War, helped in Claflin's founding, and William emerged as the school's first college graduate in 1882. After teaching there for two years, Bulkley entered Wesleyan University in Connecticut. His father then died, and Bulkley returned to South Carolina and taught languages at Claflin for a time, becoming a vice president of that institution. Bulkley also undertook a year and a half of travel and study of languages in Europe. By 1893 Bulkley had accomplished the distinction of becoming the first African American to receive a PhD in Latin, which he obtained from Syracuse University after completing his course of study there in absentia.[47]

By 1900 Bulkley had moved to New York City with his growing family, consisting of his wife, née Mary Fisher Carroll, also a Claflin graduate, and four girls. As he explained to a newspaper interviewer, he saw himself as a Southerner who had left his home only because "every right dear to any full man has been ruthlessly torn from our grasp." He found work as a public school teacher and soon received appointment as the first African American principal within the city's newly consolidated school system. As principal of Public School No. 80, Bulkley used his control over that school's facilities to pioneer experiments in vocational training for African American youth. Using classrooms that stood empty after the end of the regular school day, Bulkley established evening classes aimed at helping African American teenage boys learn the skills necessary for office jobs and employment in the skilled trades. He also organized efforts to convince employers to hire these trainees. Bulkley sometimes found time to write about his work, reflecting on his views about the role and limits of law in solving the problem of racial subordination in employment and other areas of privately generated social resources. In 1909 he was appointed, over teacher protests, as the first principal of a predominantly white school. Bulkley took time to reflect in writing about the lessons his work was teaching him, and these writings provide important insights into the views that motivated his activism.[48]

Bulkley took his education-related activism and reflective analysis with him in deciding to join the Niagara Movement as well. Like Booker T. Washington, Bulkley cared most deeply about vocational education—albeit in an urban, Northern setting rather than in a rural, Southern one. Bulkley nevertheless strongly disagreed with the Tuskegean's race advancement philosophy. Publicly opposing Washington and daring to join the explicitly anti-Tuskegee Niagara Movement took courage for a person in Bulkley's position. Bulkley lacked independent financial means but wanted to advance his professional career in New York City, which was viewed as a Tuskegee machine stronghold, and many of his peers in similar positions tried to curry favor with Washington. Bulkley, like his fellow Niagara Movement members, chose to put political convictions ahead of pragmatic personal interests in signing on with the Niagara Movement, where he most actively participated in its work on educational issues.

Bulkley devoted himself to a host of other civil rights and social welfare activities as well. He helped found and direct the Committee for Improving the Industrial Condition of Negroes (CIICN), an organization that sought to persuade employers to voluntarily dismantle their discriminatory employment practices. The CIICN was one of several organizations that gradually fused to become the National Urban League. After that merger, Bulkley served as a founding board member of the NUL. He also served on the founding committee that established the NAACP. There he not only lent his experience and contacts to that fledging effort but also served as one of a handful of African Americans invited to deliver a prepared speech at the NAACP's founding conference. In short, the long-forgotten activist William Lewis Bulkley, like many others, deserves renewed historical attention.

Each of the five central figures presented here—T. Thomas Fortune, Reverdy C. Ransom, Mary Church Terrell, Mary White Ovington, and William L. Bulkley—played a central leadership role in an activist organization this book examines in detail. Although this book is organized around these organizations—namely, the Afro-American League, the Afro-American Council, the National Association of Colored Women, the Niagara Movement, and then the early NAACP and National Urban League, respectively—the story it presents is at bottom the story of these key but often forgotten figures. It is the story of a founding generation of national organization builders whose efforts laid the groundwork for twentieth-century national racial justice activism but whose work has largely faded from popular memory today.

The earliest of the organizations this book examines in detail was the Afro-American League—an organization that, not surprisingly, few remember today in light of its relatively short national duration more than a century ago. The AAL's importance to the history of racial justice activism far exceeded its relatively short life, however, as I will show. In his vision for the AAL, T. Thomas Fortune did nothing less than propose the basic strategic and substantive template that the NAACP would follow on its founding more than two decades later.

The Legal and Political Vision of
T. Thomas Fortune, Founder of the
Afro-American League, 1880–1890

Unlike the other organizations this book examines, the National Afro-American League (AAL) arose largely from the vision of a single actor—journalist and racial justice advocate T. Thomas Fortune. Fortune's vision for the AAL entailed many important breaks from the past. It was both inspired by and sought to move beyond the episodic national and regional meetings of the National Convention Movement, in which African American activists gathered periodically, starting well before Emancipation in the North, to address both civil rights and economic issues. These meetings dispersed without establishing a permanent organizational structure between gatherings.

In contrast, Fortune called for a permanent organization. In order to prevent leaders from using the national organization as a launching pad for personal political ambitions, he also insisted on a separation between party politics and the national organization he envisioned. Instead he foresaw creating a synergistic dynamic between a national association that would sponsor civil rights test cases in courts and statutes in legislatures, on the one hand, and undertake efforts to build organizational enthusiasm, increase membership, and develop financial resources through grassroots fund-raising, on the other. Fortune believed a national organization could have both immediate, pragmatic priorities and a long-term vision that would seek economic as well as racial justice and would work for democratically achieved, radical political transformation. Those bigger goals would be tackled someday in the future, when coalition-based political organizing rendered the conditions ripe for major structural changes brought about through majoritarian political processes.

What is most striking about this introductory summation of the AAL's distinctive character as compared to what came before it is the following plain but neglected fact: Fortune's vision for the AAL in essence defined the essential features of the NAACP's design and purposes even though that organization did not get off

Figure 2.1 Men at the meeting of the Colored National Convention held at Nashville, Tennessee, April 1876 (New York Public Library).

the ground for several more decades. Imperfect as he was in executing his vision and despite being unable to sustain his commitment to it in his later life, Fortune invented the idea for the NAACP.

But no ideas spring full blown from nothing out of someone's head. This chapter examines the sources of Fortune's specific ideas about what shape a national organization devoted to racial justice advocacy should take. Those specific ideas were the following: (1) to grow a strong, national, permanent organization that would be (2) nonpartisan and separated from electoral politics, (3) focused on sponsoring and funding test case litigation, and (4) aimed at exploiting the potential synergies arising between law-related action campaigns, membership growth, and broad-based fund-raising. The longer-term aims of the organization would be to pursue (5) a broader justice-seeking agenda that would be (6) politically progressive in ideological orientation, with an interest in (7) working in coalition with other progressive interest groups, especially the labor movement. Finally, Fortune believed that (8) members of the race who were the intended beneficiaries of the organization should also be the ones to run it. Turn-of-the-century race leaders would have to forfeit this last idea for pragmatic reasons in the short term when they took part in founding the NAACP.

Fortune's educational experiences, especially his years in law school, present the most obvious place to look first for the source of Fortune's ideas about the relationship between law and racial justice organizing. He got that education at Howard

University, where African American abolitionist John Mercer Langston had just resigned from the position of dean. Many lawyer-activists involved in national organization building at the turn of the century, including both Fortune and the AAL's first official legal counsel, David Augustus Straker, attended Howard Law School and learned the fundamentals of civil rights jurisprudence there, either directly or more indirectly from the law department's intellectual leader Langston. Langston had been a leader of the earlier national convention movement and had electoral political aspirations, so he did not become deeply involved in either the AAL or the AAC, because both organizations had rules against their leaders holding political office. But even though Langston kept himself at the periphery of these organizations, his ideas remained important. He had thought deeply about constructing an African American version of abolitionist civil rights theory, and he taught these views to his students, who in turn transformed them to fit the changing political conditions their generation faced. A striking number of Howard alums became leading racial justice advocates during the late nineteenth century and the turn-of-the-century period, including not only Fortune and Straker of the AAL but also Jesse Lawson and George H. White of the AAC.

Langston often discussed his jurisprudential orientation in his speeches and writings, leaving a clear record of what his ideas were.[1] Exploring them helps illuminate the mindset of the lawyer activists who directed the AAL's legal work. His ideas arose from his own historical context as an antebellum black legal intellectual. Langston was born in Virginia in 1829 to a mother of African American and Indian heritage and a wealthy white plantation owner father. He lost both his parents to separate illnesses in 1834 but inherited substantial financial resources, which allowed his guardian to arrange for him to go to private school in Ohio. Langston eventually enrolled in both a preparatory and a college program at Oberlin College and graduated in 1849. He wanted to attend law school but was denied admission on account of race from all schools to which he applied. A college advisor suggested that Langston enroll in Oberlin's theology school as an alternative means of preparing himself to practice law. He did so and obtained his master's degree in theology from Oberlin in 1853. Langston later wrote that he believed this theological training had prepared him well for law because the "intricate and profound system of hermeneutics and exegesis as taught and applied to our sacred writings" was closely analogous to the "hardest and most difficult tasks" of solving intellectual problems in law.[2]

After obtaining this advanced degree, Langston read for the bar in the offices of a white abolitionist lawyer and then sat for and was admitted to the Ohio bar—but only after the chief justice committed the subterfuge of declaring that Langston met the state bar requirement that only "white" men be admitted.[3] Langston practiced law and became active in the abolitionist movement in Ohio; helped recruit African American soldiers for the Union army during the Civil War; and, after the war, became a Freedmen's Bureau official. At the same time he carried out civic work aimed at promoting the Republican Party in African American communities.[4] In return for his loyalty, Langston obtained an appointment in 1868 as professor of law at Howard. He became dean of the law school in 1870 but resigned in 1875 after he was passed over for the permanent position of university president.[5] He later served as a U.S. congressman from Virginia for six months between 1890 and 1891 after winning a challenge to the election results. Langston delivered many speeches at Howard and elsewhere in which he explained his jurisprudence, and those speeches undoubtedly inspired Fortune and other law-trained African American legal intellectuals as they thought about their advocacy work in the post-Reconstruction period.

Just as other nineteenth-century jurists did, Langston believed in the concept of natural rights. Like other jurists of his age, Langston divided "rights" into three categories: (1) political rights; (2) legal or civil rights; and (3) social rights, which were in fact not rights reachable by law at all. Most important in the category of political rights was the right to "free and untrammeled use of the ballot."[6] On this all African American civil rights lawyers agreed, and their commitment to voting as the fundamental political right and priority would only become stronger as Southern states began to adopt new disfranchising state constitutions in the last decade of the nineteenth century.

The second set of rights in Langston's and other late nineteenth-century jurists' taxonomy involved civil or legal rights. Late nineteenth-century conceptions of

Figure 2.2 Illustration from John Mercer Langston's autobiography picturing him sitting for admission to the Ohio Bar, 1854 (New York Public Library).

these terms differed from modern understanding of these concepts. In the nine-teenth century, civil or legal rights referred to a quite limited set of privileges con-sidered fundamental to all citizens' relationship to the federal government.[7] These were the rights discussed in the *Slaughterhouse Cases,* the opinion in which the U.S. Supreme Court rejected a business owner's challenge to a public health regulation on constitutional rights-based grounds. The Court there held that the privileges and immunities constitutionally granted to all U.S. citizens involved only matters such as rights to jury service, protection of property, access to the courts, petitioning of the government, protection on the high seas, and other similar rights, which it did not fully enumerate.[8] In this late nineteenth-century legal tradition, it was only these limited rights that constitutional law should guarantee. This was part of the reasoning behind the Court's opinion in the 1883 *Civil Rights Cases,* which invali-dated important provisions of Congress's Reconstruction-era legislation aimed at granting persons of African descent equal rights to public accommodations and transportation: The Court did not view the right to nondiscrimination in access to quasi-public goods and services as among the constitutionally protected set of core "civil" rights.[9]

Langston disagreed with the Court about which rights fit within this narrow cat-egory, although he agreed with the standard legal thought of his era in understand-ing civil or legal rights as involving only a limited set of core citizenship principles applicable to the relationship between the individual and the federal government. To Langston and other classical abolitionist lawyers, these core legal or civil rights included:

> the right to bring a suit in any and all the courts of the country, to be a wit-ness of competent character therein, to make contracts, under seal or oth-erwise, to acquire, hold, and transmit property, to be liable to none other than the common and usual punishment for offences committed by him, to have the benefit of trial by a jury of his peers, to acquire and enjoy with-out hindrance education and its blessings, ... and to be subjected by law to no other restraints and qualifications, with regard to personal rights, than such as are imposed upon others.[10]

The abolitionists' position thus differed from that of most jurists of the late nine-teenth century on two important issues. First, the abolitionists, but not the Court, viewed the right of equal access to public transportation and accommodations as a core civil right; second, they viewed the right to nondiscriminatory public schooling as such a right, as the preceding passage reflects. Conventional jurists, on the other hand, classified interactions among persons utilizing public transportation or other facilities and among students in educational settings—even public schools—as involving "social" rights—in other words, matters pertaining to free and voluntary associations among persons in what was deemed, at this time, the private sphere.

According to the dominant view, such "social" matters neither could nor should be subject to government regulation through law.

This jurisprudential carving of the realm of rights into civil or legal rights, requiring recognition and protection in law, and social rights, which were not properly subject to the reach of law, posed a major problem to post-Reconstruction civil rights jurisprudence. Linda Przybyszewski has helpfully discussed how this jurisprudence guided the judicial reasoning of Supreme Court Justice John Marshall Harlan. Although he was the sole dissenter in several key opinions in which the Court retreated from the Reconstruction-era agenda, Justice Harlan failed to dissent in other key cases, including *Cumming v. Board of Education of Richmond County*, upholding segregation in public education, and *Pace v. Alabama*, upholding a state law that imposed more severe penalties for unmarried cross-race sexual relations than for such relationships between members of the same race. According to Przybyszewski, Harlan's thinking stumbled in these cases because he categorized the rights at issue—namely, the right to attend nonsegregated public schools and the right to engage in intimate relationships across race lines—as social rather than civil rights.[11]

In contrast, Langston and the pupils he inspired faced no such analytic conundrum because they viewed the rights at issue as core legal or civil rights. Although, by the end of the nineteenth century, many race leaders had retreated from the abolitionist insistence on banning segregation in public education, as we will see, civil rights radicals continued to adhere to a staunch nonsegregation principle in the provision of all public and quasi-public services, including education, public accommodations, and transportation. Thus in one 1874 speech Langston called for the abolition of "[t]wo separate school systems, tolerating discriminations in favor of one class against another."[12] In another speech he delivered at Howard University during Fortune's years there, Langston reported that Charles Sumner had charged the first class of Howard law graduates with the following professional mission:

> I do not doubt that every denial of equal rights, whether in the school-room, the jury-box, the public hotel, the steamboat, or the public conveyance, by land or water, is contrary to the fundamental principles of republican government, and therefore to the Constitution itself, which should be corrected by the courts, if not by Congress. See to it that this is done.[13]

Continuing this same speech cast through Sumner's reported words, Langston urged as follows:

> Insist, also, that the public conveyances and public hotels, owing their existence to law, shall know no discrimination unknown to the Constitution....

> Insist upon equal rights everywhere; make others insist upon them....
> I hold you to this allegiance: first, by the race from which you are sprung;
> and secondly, by the profession which you now espouse.[14]

In short, Langston espoused a noncompromising, abolitionist, equal rights rhetoric on education, public transportation, and public accommodations. He saw the securing of these equal legal rights as the mission of African American lawyers as a matter of both race allegiance and professional role. This perspective became that of lawyer activists like Fortune and Straker as well, though they would amend it somewhat to respond to changing circumstances.

The classic abolitionists' jurisprudential view that certain civil rights were fundamental as a matter of natural law undoubtedly contributed to late nineteenth-century legal activists' insistence on pursuing test cases. They particularly wanted to advance the principle of nondiscrimination in public accommodations despite the negative precedent set by the U.S. Supreme Court in the 1883 *Civil Rights Cases* and later in *Plessy v. Ferguson*, decided in 1896.[15] From an abolitionist perspective, these equality principles should be pressed through litigation even in the face of strong contrary precedent because the Court's opinions were simply wrong. These early civil rights lawyers fully appreciated that the justices who sat on the Court were deeply flawed, swayed by political influences, and thus highly untrustworthy figures. Nonetheless, these advocates retained a belief that the institution of the judiciary, guided by principles of inalienable civil and political rights, would eventually recognize the correctness of their claims. This faith in law undergirded early civil rights lawyers' resolve in continuing to bring test cases to the courts despite the judicial hostility and evasion they repeatedly met. Their tenacity is otherwise difficult to explain. Civil rights advocates—lawyers and nonlawyers alike (and indeed sometimes nonlawyers seemed to have greater faith than lawyers in the corrective justice power of the courts)—believed that law could, and eventually would, correctly apply the principles of equality contained in the nation's founding documents.[16]

This focus on achieving legal recognition of the principle of nonsegregation in education, transportation, public accommodations, and other public goods was far from the only or main objective of late nineteenth-century race activists, but it was the one that natural law jurists could readily see as capable of vindication through the courts. For other objectives such as economic redistribution and the provision of social welfare supports, classically law-trained race activists did not see court-based strategies as a likely—or even an appropriate—strategy. Instead, leaders such as Fortune and Straker believed in the transformative power of democratically induced legislative change. Fortune figured out his approach to those ideas as a young journalist and intellectual who edited the nation's leading newspaper focused on topics of particular interest to an African American reading audience. His newspaper writing thus provides a portal into Fortune's developing political thought as he began his journalistic career.

Fortune's Journalistic Launch

Fortune's background qualified him for his role as founding leader of the AAL in ways he could not have anticipated when he set off for New York City with his wife, Carrie, at the age of twenty-four. He took from Florida assets the Klan could not take away when it drove his family from their home. He had obtained a basic education at a Freedmen's Bureau school, and, already intellectually precocious and interested in journalism, he had acquired typesetting skills by working on the local newspaper, which provided him with the manual trade that would support his intellectual activities. He had also developed a passionate, albeit cynical, interest in politics from observing his father's impressive but short-lived political career, the machinations of the Florida state legislature, the workings of Congress, and the oratory of political figures like Langston.

The move to New York City in 1881 disappointed Fortune in some ways, as his biographer has observed. Conditions were better than in Florida in some but not all respects: African Americans could vote without fear of physical intimidation, and educational opportunities were better, but Fortune discovered that his presence at the small white religious paper that had hired him had become grounds for a work stoppage. White workers frequently used this tactic as part of a race-based job protection scheme in the North as well as the South, and at Fortune's employer's newspaper his white colleagues walked off the job to protest the hiring of two African Americans.[17] Fortune's employer did not fire him, but this experience must have left Fortune feeling uncomfortable in his work environment. He and his fellow African American coworker, who had been the one to initially tell Fortune about the job opening, soon began working for another African American paper at night. There Fortune met a Howard alum who had studied under Langston, a lawyer named John H. Quarles. Recognizing Fortune's talents, Quarles mentored Fortune, teaching him the skills required for newspaper publishing, and in 1883 Quarles turned over his newspaper to Fortune.[18] Fortune renamed the newspaper the *New York Globe* and assumed responsibility as publisher and editor. He quickly turned it into the leading paper covering national and regional political news, along with social and cultural affairs of interest to African Americans. The name of Fortune's paper changed as different business partnerships formed and dissolved, so that it sequentially bore the names *New York Globe* (until November 1884), *New York Freeman* (until October 1887), and then *New York Age* until Fortune's breakdown in 1907 and Booker T. Washington's secret assumption of financial control. Until then, Fortune ran the paper himself, except for a year and a half during which Fortune's brother and another partner assumed editorial responsibility. Fortune used his paper to present politically independent, sharp, and often witty analyses of the events of his time. His work offered fresh and creative perspectives that still sound on point in many of their critical analyses.

In format, Fortune's papers typically offered hard news and political analysis on the front page, along with columns submitted by regional correspondents reporting on local developments and happenings. Internal editorial pages carried opinion pieces, frequently but not always drafted by Fortune, along with snippets of information and opinion and often letters responding to pieces run in prior weeks. These letters were often quite critical, thus giving Fortune's papers, at least through the early 1890s, the feel of an open forum for disagreement and debate. Copies of his newspaper printed between 1892 and 1905 have unfortunately been lost to history, leaving an incomplete record of Fortune's arguably changing views as his increasingly dire financial situation and changing priorities in middle age affected his viewpoints. Nevertheless, the rich record left by his newspaper and other writings in the period extending through 1892 provides a clear window into his thought and activities leading up to and immediately following his formal call for the founding of the AAL in 1890.

A survey of the most frequent topics in Fortune's papers reveals what Fortune regarded as the key issues of his time. These topics included federal aid for education, maltreatment of African Americans on common carriers and in places of public accommodations and amusement, and, with increasing frequency as the 1880s wore on, reports of "outrages" in the form of lynchings and other acts of violence against African Americans (and also other groups, such as Italians, about which Fortune also reported).[19] Fortune published many exposés of the peonage labor and the convict-leasing systems in the South and wrote in support of the nonracially discriminatory policies of the Knights of Labor, the then-growing labor organization that sought to unite workers across race lines in both the North and the South.[20] He also wrote passionate editorials on the need for African American and white workers to recognize their common class interests.

Fortune staunchly championed women's rights, and his papers usually carried a weekly women's column, written by Gertrude Mossell, a journalist and club woman from Philadelphia who later assumed a leadership position in the AAC.[21] Fortune also befriended and mentored Ida Wells Barnett, whom he described as one who "handles a goose quill with diamond point as handily as any of us men in newspaper work." This took place in the early 1890s, when Wells started off as part owner of a small printing press and newspaper in Memphis called the *Memphis Free Speech*. After her friend Tom Moss was lynched there, she wrote a pithy condemnation in her paper. Angry whites retaliated by breaking into her printing press offices and smashing her equipment, forcing her to flee from that city under threat to her life. Fortune took her in as an employee and part owner of *The Age*, thus giving her a writing platform from which she began to develop a national reputation as a journalist. Fortune's paper carried regular reporting on the women's suffrage movement and the work of advocates such as Susan B. Anthony, whom he praised for her work on behalf of African American civil rights. He also regularly highlighted the accomplishments of African American women in the professions.[22]

Fortune liked to follow the political struggles of other traditionally excluded groups, including people of color around the world and Jews, whom he saw as experiencing discrimination in the United States and Russia similar to that facing African Americans.[23] Fortune's favorite analogy looked to the political struggles of the Irish, whose experiences provided particular inspiration for his vision for the Afro-American League as a race-based, justice-seeking interest group formation.[24]

Fortune's Early Political Ideology

In 1884 Fortune wrote *Black and White,* a book that outlined the underlying political and economic philosophy that guided his activism in the 1880s. This book influenced other activists and lawyers of the time, including D. Augustus Straker, a Michigan lawyer active in the AAL, as well as the progressive political independent Archibald Grimké.[25] Fortune's political outlook started with a natural law theory of human beings' inherent rights. These included the political and civil rights enshrined in the Declaration of Independence, which Fortune, like many other law-trained civil rights advocates of the time, cited with great frequency. But these rights also included, on Fortune's analysis, rights to basic subsistence resources, including air and water. This was a version of the agrarian radicalism thinkers like English protosocialist John Ruskin and American single-taxer Henry George espoused. Both of these political theorists developed ideas that remained important in progressive thought in the United States during the years of the country's transition from a predominantly agrarian to a predominantly industrial economy, and Fortune and other progressive African American activists, such as Ransom, shared this generally held progressive enthusiasm. Ruskin's ideas included extending the principles of biblical teachings about caring for the poor into economic relationships by adopting laws to impose just wages, prevent the exploitation of workers, and protect the destitute. George, an enormously popular writer, argued that the roots of economic injustice and other social problems of the nineteenth-century lay in the private ownership of land and proposed a single tax on land as a way of equalizing wealth.[26]

Drawing from these ideas about the importance of rights in land, Fortune argued that the right to land was a natural human right. To Fortune, solving problems of poverty, inequality, and vice required granting all citizens basic subsistence rights to cultivate land.[27] Fortune extended this basic analysis to the class oppression African American and white workers shared. He argued that social injustice arose from great wealth concentrating in the hands of the few, along with the wealthy exploiting working people's labor. These political convictions pointed to the labor movement as a potentially positive political force for social and economic change. Fortune wrote of his hope that, in the South and elsewhere, workers would soon unite across race lines to become a political force calling for redistributing society's wealth. Foreseeing a time when racism would be less prevalent, Fortune argued that even then class oppression would undoubtedly persist. These conditions, even in a world in which race discrimination had abated, would not present true conditions for justice in Fortune's view. Instead, Fortune's powers of sympathetic identification led him to a political vision based on reducing both racial and general economic injustice. He argued that poverty was the true touchstone of injustice regardless of race. Thus he stated the following in his preface to *Black and White:* "My purpose is to show that poverty and misfortune make no invidious distinctions of 'race, color, or previous condition,' but that wealth unduly centralized oppresses all alike."[28]

Fortune developed other themes in *Black and White* that would be important to how people thought in this period. He cogently argued that African Americans should stay politically independent from both major electoral parties, and he weighed in on the debate about classical versus "industrial" education.[29] But Fortune arguably contributed the most in his 1880s' intellectual work through his ideas about racial justice activism, government, and law. On these topics, he showed a deeply cynical but also passionately justice-seeking sensibility. He laid out the analytic underpinnings of his late nineteenth-century radical vision of racial justice and strategies for its achievement.

Fortune believed that racial justice posed a deep and multifaceted problem and that its solution required change in many spheres, especially education and economics. He did not believe that court-made law would solve the problem of racial injustice, but he did think that such law mattered. Fortune frequently reported on incidents of discriminatory treatment and violence against African Americans, including against himself and his friends. To oppose these dignitary harms he championed test cases, on which he reported as lawyers filed them in many parts of the country on a variety of legal theories.[30]

Along with his fellow legal intellectuals such as Langston and Straker, Fortune often espoused a natural rights, abolitionist-influenced jurisprudence. Natural law theory sees certain rights as inherent in law, so natural law theory at least sees a potential for court-made law to reach just results on issues of civil and political rights equality. By the same token, however, Fortune had nothing but negative views about most sitting members of the judiciary. His pithy descriptions of the members of the U.S. Supreme Court as "deficient in legal acumen," "swayed by colorphobia," and "biased by powerful corporate influences" convey his attitude.[31] At the same time, it would grossly distort Fortune's views to claim that he had no faith in law at all. He powerfully advocated for court-focused strategies as one part of a multidimensional racial justice agenda, even despite the many setbacks the Court delivered to the cause of racial justice during the post-Reconstruction period.

When the courts, and especially the U.S. Supreme Court, returned adverse opinions that set back the racial justice cause, Fortune's legal training allowed him to write with sophisticated understanding and critical insight about the consequences. In 1883 alone, the Court issued three important civil rights decisions, *United States v. Harris,* the *Civil Rights Cases,* and *Alabama v. Pace,* all with devastating results for the reach of the Reconstruction-era amendments and the federal civil rights statutes passed under them. Fortune wrote passionate denunciations of each of those decisions, and understanding these cases and Fortune's reaction to them helps puts the AAL's law-related strategies in their legal context.

The 1883 Cases and Fortune's Analysis

The U.S. Supreme Court's post-Reconstruction civil rights jurisprudence focused on interpreting the three Reconstruction-era constitutional amendments: the Thirteenth Amendment, which abolished slavery; the Fourteenth Amendment, which provided that "[n]o State shall make or enforce any law which shall abridge the privileges or immunities of citizens of the United States; nor...deprive any person of life, liberty, or property, without due process of law; nor deny to any person within its jurisdiction the equal protection of the laws"; and the Fifteenth Amendment, which provided that the "right of citizens of the United States to vote shall not be denied or abridged by the United States or by any State on account of race, color, or previous condition of servitude." In a complex line of cases, the Court narrowed the reach of these amendments by drawing a line between public or government action on the one hand and private action on the other. The Court then held that the language of the Fourteenth and Fifteenth Amendments just quoted reached government or state action only.

Fortune's critique attacked this public-private dichotomy and pointed out the ways in which the Court's reasoning eviscerated the protections promised by the Reconstruction amendments and civil rights statutes enacted under them. Fortune pointed out that state inaction had the result of denying inherent political and civil rights on account of race just as profoundly as might acts of state action, as—for example, in barring states from prosecuting private parties for terrorizing freedmen through acts of violence to prevent them from exercising their newly won right to vote in *United States v. Harris;*[32] or permitting common carriers to prohibit persons of African American descent from moving freely on public transportation or availing themselves of public accommodations in the *Civil Rights Cases;*[33] or refusing legal recognition to interracial romantic unions and to children born of such unions in *Pace v. Alabama.*[34] In this respect, Fortune presaged the critical legal studies and critical race studies critiques of the public-private distinction many decades later.

To fully appreciate the legal context in which Fortune's and other activists' ideas and strategies developed, it is helpful to understand the import of these cases. *Harris* represented the culmination of a line of cases that started with *United States v. Cruikshank,*[35] which arose out of the 1873 massacre of fifty African American freedmen in Colfax, Louisiana, described as the "bloodiest single instance of racial carnage in the Reconstruction era."[36] In the facts underlying *Cruikshank,* federal prosecutors indicted some of the whites involved in the massacre under Section 6 of the federal Enforcement Act of May 31, 1870. The U.S. Supreme Court held, how-ever, that each of the thirty-two counts of the indictment had a fatal, often highly technical, flaw. For example, even though the indictment had specifically recited that the citizens at issue were "of African descent and persons of color," the Court held that "[t]here is no allegation that [the violation alleged] was done *because* of the race or color of the persons conspired against." Likewise, the allegations that the defendants had intended to "hinder and prevent the citizens named, being of African descent, and colored," from exercising "their several and respective right and privilege to vote at any election" was insufficient because the Fifteenth Amendment protected, not the right to vote, but only "exemption from *discrimination* in the exer-cise of the elective franchise on account of race, color, or previous condition of ser-vitude." The Court proceeded in a similar vein through all of the allegations in the indictment, eventually concluding that the prosecutions were invalid and unconsti-tutional and must be dismissed.[37] In a companion opinion in *United States v. Reese,* the Court declared Section 6 of the 1870 Enforcement Act unconstitutional alto-gether. *Reese* involved an indictment against inspectors of a municipal election in Kentucky for refusing to receive and count the vote of "a citizen of the United States of African descent." The facts thus involved state action, but this did not persuade the Court to reach a different result. Instead, the Court reiterated its statement in *Harris* that the Fifteenth Amendment "does not confer the right of suffrage on any one" and held that Section 6 of the Enforcement Act was too broad because it *could* be applied more broadly than the Fifteenth Amendment allowed.[38]

The facts in *Harris,* one of the Court's opinions Fortune most abhorred, involved prosecutors in Tennessee who had applied the Ku Klux Klan Act of 1861 to indict R. G. Harris and nineteen other whites on charges of conspiring to prevent African American citizens from voting through acts of violence.[39] The Court, relying on *Reese* and *Cruikshank,* first held that the Fifteenth Amendment could not support the prosecutors' indictment on the ground that the Fifteenth Amendment pro-vided only for an "exemption from discrimination in the enjoyment of the elective franchise on account of race, color, or previous condition of servitude" and not the right to vote itself. The Court then rejected arguments that the statutory provision at issue could be supported under the Fourteenth Amendment, holding that this Amendment covered only state action, and also refused to apply the language of the Thirteenth Amendment, which clearly contained no state action requirement and thus reached private conduct. Using reasoning similar to that in *Reese* and *Cruikshank,* the Court performed this sleight of hand by focusing on the possibil-ity that the Act could potentially be used to reach conspiracies "between two free white men against another free white man."[40] To this Court, it did not matter that this specter of overbroad application was not present on the facts of the case before it, which *did* involve the deprivation of political rights to African American citizens. (Today the Court generally would not engage in such specious reasoning but would interpret a statute only as broadly as the facts before it required.)

As Fortune well understood, the Court's line of cases culminating in *Harris* essentially killed federal government Reconstruction-era efforts to protect African Americans' voting rights in the South. It signaled that Southern states could experiment with curtailing voting rights, essentially without worrying about federal court interference. It thus heralded a coming age of impunity, and Fortune clearly understood this. He did not even pause to parse the Court's bad logic but bluntly identified the consequences of the Court's decision: It meant that although African Americans could in theory have the ballot, the Court had stripped the federal government of the power to protect the exercise of it. Fortune understood the principles of federalism that led to the result but critiqued the way the Court had applied them, pointing out the ill effects of holding that Reconstruction-era statutes could offer no protection against private violence to the country's newly enfranchised citizens. Fortune also presciently saw that African Americans should not expect future protection from law: "Having been made equal before the law by a spasmodic outburst of goodness, we have got to settle down to that earnest and successful competition which equality of citizenship imposes." Fortune warned against looking to the Court for help; conditions instead demanded self-help and intrarace solidarity. These would be admonitions activists would do well to heed in general terms as they planned post-Reconstruction strategies.[41]

Later the same year, the Court dealt another severe blow to efforts to use federal legislation enacted under the Reconstruction amendments to protect civil rights, further confirming Fortune's predictions about what the future held. In the *Civil Rights Cases,* the Court invalidated the Civil Rights Act of 1875. That Act stated that all citizens of the United States "shall be entitled to the full and equal enjoyment of the accommodations, advantages, facilities, and privileges of inns, public conveyances on land or water, theaters, and other places of public amusement; subject only to the conditions and limitations...applicable alike to citizens of every race and color." The Court consolidated five cases involving the statute for joint review, including four criminal prosecutions of hotels and theaters for denying access on grounds of race and one lawsuit an African American couple filed against a railroad company that had refused the wife access to the ladies' car.[42]

Again, the Court struck down the quoted language of the 1875 Act as unconstitutional. Analyzing the statute under the Fourteenth Amendment, the Court held that, like the statute in *Harris,* it impermissibly sought to regulate action beyond that of the state itself by laying "down rules for the conduct of individuals in society towards each other."[43] Because it had disposed of the issue on this ground, the Court declined to decide whether the right to enjoy equal accommodations and privileges in places of public accommodations, entertainment, and transportation "is one of the essential rights of the citizen which no State can abridge."[44] Turning to the Thirteenth Amendment, which, the Court acknowledged, "clothes Congress with power to pass all laws necessary and proper for abolishing all badges and incidents of slavery in the United States," the Court implausibly asserted that discrimination on public transportation and in places of public accommodation and entertainment had "nothing to do with slavery." The Court noted that the black codes that had existed during slavery similarly barred inns and public conveyances from receiving African Americans but asserted that these had been "merely a means of preventing" escapes of enslaved persons and "no part of the servitude itself." The Court argued that Congress had not intended through the Thirteenth Amendment to go so far as to "adjust what may be called the social rights of men and races in the community." Just as free persons of color before the abolition of slavery had enjoyed the "essential rights" of free white citizens but still were subjected to discrimination in public accommodations and transportation, the Court reasoned, "[m]ere discriminations on account of race or color were not regarded as badges of slavery" and thus could not be prohibited under the authority of the Thirteenth Amendment.[45]

In dissent, Justice Harlan pointed out that slavery had been an institution that "rested wholly upon the inferiority, as a race, of those held in bondage," and thus "their freedom necessarily involved immunity from, and protection against, all discrimination against them, because of their race, in respect of such civil rights as belong to freemen of other races." In Harlan's eyes, the rights to free movement on common carriers and in places of public accommodation or entertainment were *civil* rights, not social rights as the majority opinion would have it.[46] Harlan further disputed the line the Court had drawn between public and private action, arguing that Congress's power to legislate to remove badges of inferiority left from slavery should extend to "at least, such individuals and corporations as exercise public functions and wield power and authority under the State." As Harlan noted, corporations such as railroads are granted special powers under law to carry out public purposes and are subject to state control for public benefit, and as such it followed that the right of a person of color to use the public services provided by such corporations on equal terms is a fundamental right of civil freedom.[47]

Fortune, needless to say, agreed with Harlan's analysis. In the days following the Court's ruling, Fortune wrote that the *Globe* was "profoundly grateful" to "our friends" but prepared to return to "our enemies…scorn for scorn."[48] Noting that "only a few months ago" the Court in *Harris* had declared the United States "powerless to protect its citizens in the enjoyment of life, liberty, and the pursuit of happiness," Fortune asked, "What sort of Government is that which openly declares it has no power to protect its citizens from ruffianism, intimidation and murder!" Fortune's critique of the *Civil Rights Cases* followed the same lines as those being offered by other African American statesmen.[49] As Fortune wrote:

> [T]he Supreme Court now declares that we have no civil rights—declares that railroad corporations are free to force us into smoking cars or cattle cars; that hotel keepers are free to make us walk the streets at night; that theatre managers can refuse us admittance…it has reaffirmed the infamous

decision of the infamous Chief Justice Taney [in *Dred Scott*] that a "black man has no rights that a white man is bound to respect."[50]

These rulings set the course for efforts to improve the citizenship status of African Americans through the courts. The reality of race discrimination by common carriers and places of public accommodations severely curtailed mobility and thus civil freedom. As court-driven law protected these practices, it also necessarily defined the strategies required for opposing them. The civil right to enjoy free movement in transportation, public accommodations, and public entertainment would continue as a special focus of reporting in Fortune's papers throughout the decade and would also become an important tenet in Fortune's platform for the Afro-American League. This was not because Fortune thought civil liberty was the complete, or even most important, component of the solution to the problem of racial justice. Instead, discrimination in transportation and public accommodations became a key issue because it imposed significant material burdens on immediate lived experience and thus presented a concrete issue around which to organize resistance. Fortune and other race activists sought to reverse the Court's rulings on these matters as one set of tangible goals within a much broader overall agenda.

Of the Court's three major civil rights decisions in 1883, the one that arguably troubled Fortune the most was a less remembered one, *Pace v. Alabama*. In that case, a unanimous Court upheld the constitutionality of an Alabama statute that made it illegal for any " 'white person' " and any person of "negro descent" to marry or live together in " 'adultery or fornication,' " punishable by imprisonment or hard labor for two to seven years. Another section of the Alabama Code prescribed less severe penalties for adultery and fornication involving persons of the same race. The plaintiff, Tony Pace, an African American man, and his wife, Mary Cox, a white woman, had been convicted and sentenced to two years imprisonment under the statutory provision that applied to interracial couples, and Pace filed a Fourteenth Amendment challenge, arguing that the state denied him equal protection of the laws because it punished him more severely than it would a white person for the same conduct.[51]

The Court rejected Pace's claim. Prefiguring its later decision in *Plessy v. Ferguson*,[52] the Court reasoned that the Alabama statutes did not violate the Fourteenth Amendment's equal protection mandate because the state had treated the races equally: Both African Americans and whites who engaged in intimate relations across race lines were punished more severely than persons of either race engaged in impermissible sexual relations within the same race.[53]

Fortune's critique focused on two aspects of the decision, invoking the vocabularies of both social facts and natural rights. Fortune foresaw the harm both *Harris* and *Pace* would do to the race as a whole, the former by denying the law's protection against violence and the latter by denying the legality, and thus undermining the stability, of the relationships into which many children assigned African American identities would be born. Fortune also described the issue as one of natural rights, noting that "it cannot be overlooked, that when a law prohibits a black man from marrying a white woman, because of his color, it strikes at the root of natural liberty."[54]

In some ways Fortune seemed more troubled by this case than any other of the year. With sophisticated critical-legal insight, he pointed out how the Court's logic undermined families and defiled African Americans' striving for respectability. The law's prohibition on marriage between the parents of children conceived through interracial sexual unions meant that fathers could not restore respectability to their children's mothers even if they wanted to and thus all but instructed fathers to abandon their children. Fortune saw that law, in shaping the acts of private individuals, was creating future generations of children who would be forced to struggle with the absence of their paternal parent. Through its power to shape the rules governing social relations, Fortune observed, the Court had relegated countless children, far into the future, into mandatory illegitimacy.

Fortune would return to these decisions repeatedly during the course of the year, tying their results to the politics of the Court and the nation generally. No legal formalist, Fortune placed the blame for the Court's opinions squarely on the national political parties. According to Fortune, the opinions were the result of partisan politics and no more and heralded the abandonment of African Americans by both political parties.[55]

For all of his antiparty rhetoric, Fortune was an inveterate political junkie; the pages of his papers were always full of national political analysis. Hardheaded and cynical, Fortune called on African Americans to engage in self-help strategies—to help themselves through their own efforts and to distrust outsiders purporting to have friendly or sympathetic intentions, especially institutions tied to party politics, including the courts. This theme would soon undergird his vision for the Afro-American League, involving a nonpartisan, black-led advocacy organization with multidimensional goals.

Fortune's National Legislative Efforts

Although Fortune had no trust in white political or legal figures to provide genuine help in the struggle for racial justice, he and many other law-focused activists in this period showed more faith in the actual *system* of government established by the U.S. Constitution. Indeed, Fortune saw in the Constitution a promise of a government that would provide all citizens with the basic personal assets necessary to support a productive human life. Because education provides the most important personal asset defining the course of a person's life, Fortune viewed the federal government's responsibilities as extending to ensure adequate and effective education for new generations of citizens. Thus, Fortune's papers throughout the 1880s paid special attention to a decade-long, eventually unsuccessful, initiative to obtain federal aid for education. Commonly referred to as the "Blair education bill" because its chief sponsor was Republican senator Henry W. Blair of New Hampshire, this bill proposed to provide federal aid to states in proportion to their respective illiteracy rates in order to improve basic education.[56] Various versions of this proposal passed the Senate several times, but each time the House of Representatives blocked the measures.[57]

According to historians who have researched the Blair bill in depth, opposition to it did not line up on regional or party grounds. Southern states wanted the appropriation, arguing that since Northerners had forced enfranchisement of African Americans, they should help bear the costs of educating the freedmen. The key issues that blocked enactment involved opponents' wariness about Republican pro-tariff policies and concerns about locking treasury surpluses into expensive new appropriations commitments. Other concerns invoked federalism, or constitutional limits on federal involvement in and oversight of state matters. To counter these objections, later versions of the proposed bill called for joint federal and state oversight or even left supervision of expenditures completely up to the states. Even these compromises did not satisfy opponents, however. Opponents also questioned whether federal funding would eventually lead to demands for nonsegregated education. In an attempt to allay these fears, the bill's sponsors eventually drafted language permitting the continuation of dual education systems, but even this step failed to result in its enactment.[58]

Politicians accepted these compromise proposals, and even many African American leaders consulted on the matter said they were willing to compromise on the nonsegregation principle in the interests of obtaining more resources for African American education.[59] Not surprisingly, however, Fortune and other abolitionist radicals found continued segregation unacceptable. Fortune also opposed proposals to reduce federal oversight of appropriations to the states. As he pointed out, Southern states already invested far more funds in white schools than in African American ones and would continue to do so with additional funds if allowed.[60] Thus, throughout the 1880s, Fortune wrote in favor of the Blair initiative but against these compromise proposals.

In 1883 Fortune testified before the Senate Committee on Labor and Education on the bill. He argued that the national government should guarantee the social resources necessary to prepare citizens for effective citizenship: "[T]he education of the people is a legitimate function of Government and is not in any sense a feature of centralization, but is eminently a feature of self-preservation." Like national defense, education should be among the services the national government provides without controversy: "We make lavish appropriations for harbors, forts, the navy and the army for the common defense, but illiteracy is a more insidious foe from within than any that can or will assail us from without." Fortune further proposed creating a federal Bureau of Education to assume responsibility for education.[61]

In short, to Fortune writing in the 1880s, the federal government should protect the fundamental well-being and proper development of its citizens. This responsibility included guaranteeing a right to adequate and effective education not only for African Americans but also for "ignorant foreigners" and uneducated whites.[62] He saw an important connection between education and racial justice that included not only a negative right to be free of state-sponsored discrimination and school segregation but also the positive right to an adequate and effective education.

In his congressional testimony, Fortune tied his analysis of the federal government's duty to guarantee education to his critique of peonage and convict labor in the South and the need to provide means for African Americans to improve their economic situation. He worked in some of his ideas about basic rights to subsistence guaranteed by government through access to commonly owned land as well. Not one to mince words in front of any audience, he included rhetoric on the evils of concentrating wealth in the hands of the few.[63]

This was another topic to which Fortune returned repeatedly in his writing, and his view on the government's role in regulating economic relations further reveals his perspective on the relationships between racial and economic justice and law. Second only to the right to education guaranteed by the national government, Fortune's favorite topic in his writings involved the relationship of race oppression to systems of economic production. Fortune was especially interested in how the operation of law maintained oppressive production systems, especially in the institutions of peonage and convict labor, as well as in the exploitation of labor generally.[64] As Fortune wrote, the "poorer classes of the South are systematically victimized through the medium of legislation," and these "laws are systematically framed in the interest of the capitalist."[65]

Fortune on Labor and Economics

Fortune also reported with enthusiasm about the growth of the Knights of Labor and its racially inclusive organizing model and membership policies.[66] Fortune saw in the Knights of Labor hopeful signs of the potential for development of a unified, majoritarian, class-based political movement. Unlike electoral party politics, about which he was unremittingly cynical, Fortune continued through the end of the 1880s to retain optimism about the white working class's potential for racial enlightenment.[67] In this position, Fortune disagreed with his close friend and fellow activist, T. McCants Stewart. Stewart was a minister, professor, and lawyer who often wrote for or was featured in Fortune's newspapers. Stewart shared Fortune's progressive analysis of the evils of unrestrained capitalism and the need to reduce the disparity between the rich and the poor, but Stewart's thinking focused more exclusively on within-race advancement. Stewart eschewed what he saw as Fortune's romantic notions of majoritarian class solidarity across lines of race. Indeed, Stewart even agreed with the position that "black men [should] combine and apply for the places made vacant by the strikers.... [I]f we fail to apply and then growl about not having an opportunity to compete with the whites, the fault will be with us."[68] In retort, Fortune countered that he thought it a shame to see "so good a man as [Stewart] go wrong." Fortune argued that "colored laborers...cannot afford to antagonize white laborers when the latter are on strike for whatever cause" and that Stewart's doctrine encouraging African American strike breaking was a "pernicious practice" that "would intensify the antagonism between white and colored labor."[69]

On this issue, Fortune and Stewart disagreed. More often the two friends' views were not far apart. In one editorial Stewart wrote about ideas he had been advancing on the lecture circuit about the necessity of intrarace cooperation. Stewart emphasized the importance of developing "race pride." He criticized what he saw as the unduly great dependence on "wealthy white people" of successful African American businessmen "north of the Mason Dixon line." Stewart wrote of the importance of instead developing what he called "industrial cooperation," just as "other races do." In response to criticism of this position, Fortune supported Stewart, writing "we must support our men." It was time to "wake up and let our race stand by our pioneers. Money is power and we must get power."[70]

Embedded in Fortune and Stewart's argument are the ideas of racial self-help and intraracial advancement that many race leaders—including both Washington and Du Bois in their very different ways—would begin to press further by the turn of the century. These were ideas that would continue to influence race activists' ideology far into the twentieth century, as Kenneth Mack and others have explored. The reasons for this turn in race activists' thinking has complex roots, but a salient one, as August Meier observed, involved the changing social and economic conditions of the late nineteenth century. Stewart had correctly described the predominantly white, or often mixed race, clientele of many successful African American businessmen in Northern cities in the 1880s, as well as in cities in the South, such as Atlanta, during the 1870s, when African American businesses such as barber shops catered to a rich white clientele. But these regional pictures changed at various paces and in different degrees as the attitudes associated with Jim Crow spread, leading to increasing segregation in the North and an upsurge in lynchings and the destruction of African American businesses and property in the South, border regions, and even sometimes in the North.[71]

Along with these developments came ideas that African Americans should concentrate on taking care of their own. These ideas arose first and most forcefully in communities like Atlanta, where Jim Crow emerged soonest and with the most virulence. The argument was that African Americans should forego abolitionist-style, race blind, equal rights talk and instead concentrate on intragroup advancement just as other ethnic groups, such as the Irish, had done successfully in monopolizing certain employment sectors and acting shrewdly in politics. Stewart's and Fortune's thought clearly reflected this trend, and it would provide an important motivating idea underlying the founding of the Afro-American League.

Fortune and Stewart thus agreed about intrarace advancement, if not on cross race labor organizing. And Fortune saw that his romantic vision of cross-racial political cooperation was not necessarily where the labor movement was heading in the late nineteenth century. Fortune championed a strong labor movement, but he was not a booster of all of its activities. He wanted a labor movement that would amass political power in order to change the fundamental structure of government, as the Knights of Labor envisioned. He did not espouse a model for the labor movement that aimed to settle industrial relations through contests of private power, as trade unionism endorsed.[72]

An unsigned editorial written a few days after the Haymarket riot of May 4, 1886, explained these views.[73] The editorial disapproved of the growing phenomenon of labor strikes aimed at securing higher wages and the eight-hour workday. At first glance, this might appear a strange position for an editorial in Fortune's paper, given Fortune's usual pro-union views. In context, however, the opinions expressed in the editorial are consistent with Fortune's vision of the role of government in protecting its citizens and setting the conditions for a just society.

The editorial argued that it was counterproductive to the true aims of the working class to seek shorter hours and higher wages through industrial confrontation rather than through government reform. This was because the laws of economics dictated that higher wages and shorter hours would cause employers' manufacturing costs to go up, which employers would pass on to consumers in the form of higher prices. Through this cycle, working people would find themselves no better off because their wages would buy less. Thus, private ordering of economic relations through a battle between labor and capital would not accomplish the goal of greater economic justice; only government could do that:

> [P]hilosophers of the labor movement will still have to seek the proper remedy through the intricate and tortuous machinery of legislation [in order to]...curtail[] to some extent the enormous and pernicious aggregation of capital in the hands of a limited number of men, to the danger and disadvantage of the masses of society.[74]

As with Fortune's views on education, the position expressed in this editorial places responsibility for reform squarely on the government's shoulders. In Fortune's view, government could best be directed through appropriate legislation, which would be achieved through coalition building uniting a majority holding similar economic interests.

A concern about the dangers of lawless violence surely influenced this argument in favor of government intervention rather than the private ordering of industrial relations through contests between labor and capital. In context, it is not difficult to understand why. Not only had the deaths resulting from the Haymarket riot occurred just days before this editorial came out, following waves of strikes marked by increasing violence, but anarchists were gaining strength within the labor movement at the time, and strikers' rhetoric and actions sounded increasingly in revolutionary tones. To Fortune, who had lived through the violence that brought about the end of Reconstruction in Florida, such rhetoric and the violence that went with it must have been disconcerting, to say the least. At the same time, Fortune was watching lawless race-related violence rise as lynchings and other outrages against African Americans increased.[75] He could not have failed to make a connection between this violence and the labor violence taking place at the same time, especially as employers' increasing use of African American strikebreakers directly connected the two forms of violence through white laborers' attacks on African American "scabs."[76] Although Fortune refrained from engaging in blanket condemnations of the labor movement for its growing Jim Crowism, he seemed unable to convince himself that the path to greater racial and economic justice lay with the private ordering of relations between labor and capital. He wanted legislative reform instead.

Fortune was no pacifist—he often called on African American men to exert their masculinity through violent self-defense where circumstances warranted.[77] But at bottom he believed in orderly regulation through government, as might be expected of a child of the Reconstruction era. Disillusioned though Fortune was by what he had lived through during those years, he had witnessed his father sacrifice material well-being and physical safety to participate in bringing about a new, more just society ordered through law. Fortune had followed a path similar to his father's in his idealism, material sacrifice, and commitment to reasoned public debate. That commitment reflects a central theme in Fortune's political thought.

Fortune on Majoritarian Government

In sum, to Fortune the achievement of racial and economic justice depended centrally on government reform through democratic processes. This vision in turn required faith in a means by which democratic processes could bring about such reform. To Fortune, that means was the creation of majoritarian pressure organized through coalition politics across lines of race and within the common interests of the working class. When Fortune set out to found the Afro-American League, all of these carefully thought out, long-considered views came into play in his ideas for the organization's platform and founding mission. Fortune saw the AAL as a national, nonpartisan organization that could bring together African Americans much the way in which the Irish had organized in the United Kingdom to protect their political interests. At the same time, Fortune's long-term vision was not one of interest group pluralism but instead a more idealistic vision of democratic reform leading to economic fairness. He foresaw a beneficent government charged with ensuring social welfare by protecting fundamental positive rights to education and adequate basic subsistence for all. His vision for an organization that could work along these lines toward both short- and long-term goals far exceeded what was reasonably possible given the severe resource constraints this first national experiment at permanent institution building for racial justice faced. Nevertheless, the founding of the AAL was significant in putting in motion core ideas that would be transmitted to many future organizations.

|| 3 ||

The National Afro-American League's Founding and Law-Related Work, 1887–1895

Fortune's position as editor of what he had developed into the nation's leading African American newspaper gave him an excellent vantage point from which to observe and analyze political developments. The national scope of his paper's reporting gave him detailed knowledge of events throughout the country. As he reported on the many state, regional, and national civil rights meetings and initiatives that were taking place in various regions, he had an opportunity to reflect on their significance. At the same time, his legal training gave him a sophisticated analytical approach to law, which allowed him to join with others in theorizing about the relationship between law and race activism. Because he controlled a newspaper of relatively large circulation and excellent reputation, his arguments mattered to African American public opinion. Fortune's newspaper thus gave him an ideal platform from which to engage in the dual projects of national-level organization building and theorizing about visions of racial justice and strategies to bring it about. He did so most concretely by proposing that activists found the national Afro-American League and by describing the directions he thought such an organization should take.

Founding the AAL

Over the years, Fortune occasionally suggested in his newspapers that a national civil rights organization should be formed; in the spring of 1887, Fortune published a detailed, well-thought-out call for the formation of a national organization to be called the Afro-American League.[1] Its foremost motivating issue would be "mob law in the South," and its strategy would be to "take hold of the matter ourselves, as the Irish have done" and "[l]et the entire race ... organize into a Protective League ... on the same plan that the Irish National League is."[2]

A month later Fortune listed six issues a national league should immediately address—namely, (1) the "almost universal suppression of our ballot in the South"; (2) the South's "reign of lynch and mob law"; (3) the "unequal distribution of school funds"; (4) the "odious and demoralizing penitentiary system of the South, with its chain-gangs" and "convict leases"; (5) the "almost universal tyranny of common carrier corporations in the South...in which the common rights of colored men and women are outraged and denied"; and (6) "the general policy of those who conduct places of public accommodation," involving "matters [which] reach down in the very life of a people."[3] Fortune hoped (unrealistically, as it turned out) that the South would be the "stronghold" for such an organization because that was where these forms of injustice were "most glaring and oppressive."[4] It was in the South, for example, that the "colored laboring masses of that section are fast falling into a condition not unlike...chattel slavery," and "employers of such labor" operated with impunity, "backed up by ample legislation and by all the machinery of the law."[5]

Fortune's idea for the Afro-American League occurred in the context of and in competition with a huge outpouring of organizational efforts; the league was just one of many organizing ideas in play at the time. Periodic national African American conventions had started taking place several decades before emancipation in the North. This organizing energy had reached high levels by the 1880s in many parts of the country, including the South. Fortune reported on the call for one such national convention in Louisville in 1883, and there were statewide conventions as well, such as the one called the Chicago Committee (held in Pittsburgh, Pennsylvania) that same year by Harry C. Smith, the editor of the *Cleveland Gazette,* and prominent Republican lawyer Ferdinand Barnett (best known for his later marriage to Ida Wells). This call had followed from the Court's decision in the *Civil Rights Cases* and urged "loyal men of the race" to gather in a nonpartisan setting to consider how to hold the nation's political parties and its courts accountable for protecting "our rights as citizens."[6]

New England was another frequent site of such meetings. An 1886 Boston meeting opened with comparisons to the struggle of the Irish in England: The "8,000,000 colored Americans of the United States...know what it is to be oppressed, [and] send a hearty greeting to Irish people in Ireland, who are struggling to be free from the oppressive policy of the English government."[7] Its theme was that help for the people must come from within: Just as the "Irishman depends upon the brainy men of his race for leadership," so, too, should the African American stop "pin[ning] his hopes to some slimy, oily, trickey [sic] white man for leadership." Ohio, too, formed an "equal rights league" that year, organized against "laws...degrading to colored people" on the statute books of various states.[8]

In Baltimore, the Brotherhood of Liberty was formulating test case litigation strategies that Fortune would soon incorporate into his list of priorities for the AAL. An alliance between Baptist minister Harvey Johnson and several civil rights lawyers led to the founding of the Brotherhood in response to the 1883 *Civil Rights Cases*. The organization adopted a multipronged civil rights organizing strategy, pursuing test case litigation to protest transportation segregation and state bas-tardy laws, as well as a successful legislative effort to prohibit discrimination in bar admissions. Another Brotherhood initiative took up a community defense cam-paign that provided legal representation for the defendants charged in an upris-ing of exploited African American guano miners that took place on a Caribbean Island against the Navassa Phosphate Company in 1889, leading to the case of *Jones v. United States*.[9] In Baltimore and elsewhere, Northern activists mobilized to campaign for state civil rights statutes that would do some of the work that the 1875 federal Civil Rights Act, struck down by the Court in its 1883 *Civil Rights Cases*, had aimed to do.[10]

The push to focus the AAL on test case litigation appears to have come first from Baltimore lawyer and Brotherhood of Liberty leader Joseph Davis. Explaining that he was drawing on ideas that he and fellow lawyer Everett Waring had begun to develop through test case litigation in that city, Davis wrote to the *New York Freeman* urging the AAL to give high priority to removing statutes that "should be declared unconstitutional and void." Such test litigation, Davis argued, either must lead the Constitution to "assert itself or it must confess its weakness and receive the contempt it may merit from the honest men of all nationalities." Davis spelled out the elements necessary for test case litigation to work. It would be nec-essary to "follow such cases as are suitable from the station house to the Supreme Court," and it would require "the best legal talent attainable," which would require well-paid lawyers. To support this plan, Davis envisioned an organization that would have to have a big membership and, with it, the "sum[s] of money needed in the legitimate prosecution of its [objectives]."[11] With these words, written in 1887, Davis in essence outlined the test case litigation strategy the NAACP would begin to pursue on its founding almost a quarter century later. At the time, however, this intensively court-focused—and expensive—strategy was only one of many ideas in play.

Organizing AAL Chapters

Fortune's columns soon began reporting on organizing meetings of local and state leagues around the country, usually in regions where race activists had already engaged in substantial organizing. Activists organized local meetings in Boston, Baltimore, Philadelphia, the District of Columbia, and Cleveland. Meetings took place at the state level as well, in Kansas, Rhode Island, and New York.[12] Along with others, lawyer Fredrick McGhee (later an AAC legal director and the person whom Du Bois would credit with the idea for the Niagara Movement) called for founding a league in Minnesota.[13] In late 1889 Fortune announced that this local and regional organizing called for holding a national convention and scheduled it for January 1890 in Chicago, using the *Freeman* to generate turnout to this important event.[14]

But cracks in the unified front Fortune was trying to generate soon became apparent.[15] One involved how the league should deal with organizations not specifically organized as leagues. Fortune wanted such groups to declare themselves affiliated with the AAL, but longtime local activists sometimes had other ideas, wanting to preserve their local independence and cooperate when they chose on an issue by issue basis. Another point of contention concerned the organization's name. Looking to Irish self-help analogy, Fortune liked the connotations of an "Afro-American" league. But others liked the race-neutral, abolitionist-style emphasis on "equal rights" and wanted to use that phrase in the organization's title. Along with this difference in the connotations embedded in the organization's name came differences in focus. Some activists protested Fortune's idea that the organization's members should be primarily African Americans. To this Fortune responded that it was not the organization that was drawing the color line; rather "[t]he color line is unmistakably and cruelly drawn already."[16]

Fortune found himself explaining in *The Age* what was special about the AAL organizing model as opposed to other possibilities. Quickly picking up on the idea of forcing legal equality as one key distinguishing feature of the league, Fortune promised that the AAL would not be just "passing…resolutions" or endorsing political parties, as had previous national conventions, but instead would have a "corner-stone…contention [of] absolute justice under State and Federal constitutions."[17]

The AAL's First National Convention

Fortune's Afro-American League convened in Chicago in January 1891 as planned. According to newspaper accounts, the meeting boasted a large attendance and delegates whose enthusiasm bordered on boisterousness. Fortune presided. Hampered by his lack of experience in running large meetings, Fortune resorted to an umbrella in place of a gavel in an attempt to call the delegates to order.[18]

Once they finally settled down to business, the delegates achieved their goal of setting the basic structure for a new national organization. They endorsed Fortune's proposed substantive platform basically as written. Their most heated debate took place on the Blair education bill, with the delegates in the end passing a resolution that endorsed solely "the principle of Federal aid for education."[19] The delegates also adopted a multilevel organizational structure—which later would be criticized for being too unwieldy—and elected heads of a large number of subcommittees. In another choice Fortune insisted on even though it was unpopular with electorally ambitious African American political leaders, the AAL declared that members who held elected office would be ineligible for organizational leadership positions. Fortune and others who supported this rule viewed it as necessary to prevent the

AAL from becoming a pawn in electoral politics. But this policy also had the effect of lessening interest in the AAL of rising African American politicians such as then U.S. congressman John Mercer Langston from Virginia. League supporters had initially floated Langston's name as a potential leader for the league, but its nonpartisanship rule required other possibilities to be considered instead. In the end, he did not even attend the Chicago meeting. Instead, delegates to the founding convention elected respected Southern educator J. C. Price as AAL president. Leading Chicago lawyer Edward H. Morris was elected attorney of the league.

Perhaps because of the AAL's nonpartisanship rule for organizational officeholders, many prominent leaders with political aspirations chose to lend their weight to other organizational options.[20] Just one month after the league's founding convention, an alternative large meeting to form an "Equal Rights League" took place in Washington, DC.[21] This meeting's character differed even though its attendance overlapped quite a bit with that of the Chicago AAL Convention. The meeting focused on the theme of equal rights and featured a different list of speakers, drawn far more heavily from the African American political elite in Washington, DC, as well as from leaders with strong political party ties and histories of holding political office. Langston attended and spoke, and delegates easily endorsed the Blair education bill as well as resolutions urging Congress to pass legislation to protect Southern national elections from fraud and to prevent murders of African Americans for political reasons. But still the lines between the AAL and other organizations remained fluid. An AAL committee took advantage of being in DC while attending the Equal Rights League conference to meet with President Harrison and present him with the AAL's address to the nation, which the Chicago delegates had endorsed, along with a letter outlining conditions for African Americans in the South.[22]

After the initial flurry of effort and enthusiasm surrounding the AAL's first national convention, Fortune faced the difficult task of sustaining a national organization for the long haul. Reports in *The Age* testified to his uphill efforts to keep the league's momentum going. Fortune understood that there had to be a synergy that sustained a national infrastructure while generating activity at the local and state levels, but no one had yet worked out exactly how to get this kind of dynamic going. Nonetheless, state and local activity clearly was taking place, and some state leagues reported real progress in regional initiatives. Recognizing its importance, Fortune was quick to report on the successes, focusing especially on New York State, where he could witness exciting legal developments first-hand.

New York Initiatives

The AAL in Albany, working in conjunction with other groups, focused primarily on championing passage of state legislation. Standard accounts of civil rights history rarely focus on these early state successes, aimed at fighting back against the

1883 *Civil Rights Cases.* They should be emphasized far more because they show that activists were not quiescent even in the face of declining national political conditions.

In New York these successes involved enacting legislation to strengthen that state's already existing civil rights legislation, which the 1883 *Civil Rights Cases,* addressing federal legislative efforts only, could not dismantle. New York activists also successfully enacted a little-remembered state law ban on discrimination in insurance.[23] Mutual efforts by a number of organizations proved key to these state legislative successes, though Fortune's reports, not surprisingly, emphasized the AAL state chapter's role. In early 1890, an Albany-based AAL boasted sixty-eight members.[24] Its first state convention that spring took place in a room "tastefully ornamented with American flags," with about seventy-five persons present, a third of whom were official delegates. Fortune took part, and records show a young Rev. Alexander Walters of the AME Zion Church in New York City also emerging as a vocal participant. The delegates debated the national AAL's prohibition against state leagues engaging in political activity, with Walters speaking against it and Fortune rising to its defense. The delegates elected Fortune state league president and lawyer T. McCants Stewart as the league's attorney. Walters received a position on the executive board. The delegates voted to demand a speedy settlement of the then pending challenge to Langston being seated in Congress and to support the passage of state civil rights legislation. Fortune and others spoke about the "benefits of the ladies as members of the society" and praised the work of a female delegate.[25] Writing in the aftermath of his appointment as official state league counsel, Stewart outlined his sense of the organization's priority agenda, emphasizing the need to work for an insurance nondiscrimination statute modeled after one already enacted in Ohio and also for a civil rights statute that would include punitive provisions for discrimination in places of public accommodations, including public schools, inns, and conveyances.[26]

With the Albany chapter taking the lead, AAL members testified before the state senate on the insurance nondiscrimination bill.[27] In the spring of 1891, they won its passage, and Fortune planned the next state convention to follow in the wake of this victory.[28] When the governor signed the measure, Stewart provided an analysis, noting that no legislator of either party had voted against it and that African American political power, spread across both parties, had produced this result.[29]

At the same time, Fortune fortuitously stumbled into an incident that gave rise to the facts to support undertaking a test case of his own. In June of 1890 Fortune had been refused service in a pub in New York City, and when he protested that this was the result of illegal race discrimination, a police officer had forcibly ejected him and booked him for disorderly conduct at the police station.[30] Fortune retained his friend and fellow activist T. McCants Stewart to file a case against the hotel that had ejected him under New York's state law banning discrimination in places of public accommodations, seeking $10,000 in damages.[31] Fortune covered the matter at length in *The Age,* and African American newspapers in other regions picked up the story and began to call for making it into a "test case."[32] Soon the front pages of Fortune's papers began to feature calls for contributions to Fortune's legal defense fund, endorsed by well-known leaders such as Price and Terrell.[33] The money that came in was modest, but Fortune foresaw much greater potential, writing in *The Age* of the need "[n]ot to raise deadly weapons against your fellow man, but to raise a fund of a million dollars that we may carry these outrages, cruelties and insults to the highest courts of the land until we obtain justice."[34]

The next year the front pages of *The Age* were full of reports of Stewart's arguments in Fortune's case and then the successful verdict he obtained in it. A jury awarded Fortune the sum of $1,016, including costs. Fortune and Stewart won again on appeal, and Langston, Washington, and others wrote to *The Age* to congratulate Fortune and Stewart on their great victory.[35] At the same time, some note of uneasiness can be detected in members' responses to the Fortune test case initiative. People applauded Fortune's victory but seemed a bit skeptical of fund-raising that could end up so directly in Fortune's pockets. To Fortune, financially maintaining himself and his family at the very meager material standard at which they lived, while at the same sustaining his newspaper and the expenses involved in running the national AAL, were all one and the same project. But those loose financial standards left him vulnerable to criticism and may have contributed to his inability to generate long-term momentum for his national organizing initiative.

Other State-Level AAL Activity

At the same time that the New York chapter was experimenting with a mix of legislative and test case initiatives, other state chapters were involved in a wide variety of activities of their own. Boston's group, which called itself an Equal Rights League, sent reports of meetings and resolutions supporting federal elections legislation and taking other stands.[36] The District of Columbia, also still adhering to its National Equal Rights Association model, reported on large meetings that weighed in on federal elections legislation proposals such as the Lodge bill, which sought to protect African American voting rights in the South. Many other initiatives were taking place at the state level in other regions as well, although it is often difficult to distinguish which aspects of this work can legitimately be attributed to the AAL and which aspects would have taken place anyway due to the existence of state and local civil rights organizations that predated the AAL's founding. These initiatives usually involved a combination of state legislative and test case campaigns.

In Ohio, *Cleveland Gazette* publisher Harry Smith championed several important pieces of civil rights legislation on lynching and public accommodations. He successfully organized against an 1890 state legislative proposal that would have segregated Ohio's public schools.[37] A year later Smith wrote urging that a test case lawsuit be filed to protest a hotel's ill treatment of a prominent African American state senator and complained, "It is a pity that the state Afro-American League has been allowed to die."[38]

In Michigan, a large group met in Detroit to found a local chapter.[39] David Augustus Straker, AAL founding member and state chapter representative, led this effort. Straker at the same time continued to pursue a case he had previously filed under the caption *Ferguson v. Gies*, which challenged, under Michigan's state statute prohibiting discrimination in public accommodations, a restaurant's denial of equal accommodations to two African American patrons, including print shop owner and AAL member William Ferguson. The trial court rejected Straker's theory on the grounds that Ferguson had been offered a substantially similar table in another section of the restaurant. This reasoning portended the separate but equal rationale the U.S. Supreme Court would later adopt in *Plessy v. Ferguson*. On appeal to Michigan's highest court, however, Straker successfully argued for reversal, convincing the court of the following:

> [I]n Michigan there must be and is an absolute, unconditional equality of white and colored men before the law. The white man can have no rights or privileges under the law that [are] denied to the black man. Socially people may do as they please within the law, and whites may associate together, as may blacks, and exclude whom they please from their dwellings and private grounds; but there can be no separation in public places between people on account of their color alone which the law will sanction.[40]

This success led Straker and others to propose the creation of a legal defense fund to finance additional cases, which they formed as the Detroit Afro-American League.[41]

Another lawsuit challenging the denial of public accommodations, *Howell v. Litt*, took place in Milwaukee, Wisconsin, and prompted activists to form a local equal rights league that sent a delegate to the AAL's first national convention.[42] Howell had used a messenger to purchase a main-floor ticket to see a play at the opera house, but on his arrival the usher had refused to admit him and tried to send him to the gallery instead. Howell won a directed verdict from the judge, who instructed the jury that the Reconstruction amendments "render unlawful every discrimination in account of color or race." The jury awarded $100 in damages plus costs.[43]

The Milwaukee group also pushed a state initiative for an improved civil rights bill. One of its leaders, William T. Green, at the time a law student in his midtwenties, led this effort and testified in 1891 before the state legislature's judiciary committee on the proposed legislation. The Democrats gutted the proposal by restricting the bill's coverage to exclude most places of public accommodations other than inns, but four years later Green, now practicing law in partnership with a white lawyer, worked with legislators to pass a better bill, which the governor signed in April 1895. This measure prohibited racial discrimination in a long list of public accommodations and imposed civil and criminal fines for violations.[44]

The AAL thus was more than a large annual gathering at which delegates adopted a platform expressing their collective viewpoints, as the earlier national convention meetings had been. It clearly helped spawn some ambitious and ongoing local activist activities, which were at least somewhat united under the umbrella of a national organization and often also publicized nationally in *The Age*. But despite Fortune's efforts, the AAL's ongoing national infrastructure was faint at best. The AAL's presence waxed and waned at the national level in sync with its two conventions and their aftermath. Developing a permanent national organization required creating an administrative infrastructure that could keep the desired national functions going on a more consistent basis. That would require more resources, and figuring out how to obtain these would lie farther in the future. In the early 1890s the desire for a permanent national organization would propel the AAL through only two national conventions.

The AAL's Second National Convention

The second of the AAL's national meetings took place in 1891, when the organization decided to hold its annual convention in Knoxville, Tennessee. This decision to hold its convention in the South was a purposeful one, intended to put into action the AAL's plans to make Southern organizing a priority. As an additional consideration, Tennessee had just passed a separate-cars law, and the AAL's leaders wanted to take a stand against it and possibly generate test cases by showing up in the state despite this hostile gesture. These hopes did not play out as successfully as the organizers wanted. Fewer delegates attended the Knoxville convention than the Chicago one, as some delegates decided against facing the hostile conditions of Jim Crow travel. Two test cases did materialize, though neither gave rise to the principled court victory the lawyer activists desired. The convention did generate lively proceedings as various speakers presented their remarks and the delegates debated the issues of the day. Of particular note was the speech a young Ida B. Wells, then editor of the Memphis *Free Speech,* delivered. As Fortune reported, Wells was "eloquent, logical, and dead in earnest" and "kept the audience in a bubble of excitement and enthusiasm."[45]

As expected, delegates traveling to or from Knoxville encountered humiliating Jim Crow treatment. William Heard, an AME minister traveling from Philadelphia, found himself ejected from his first-class sleeper berth on a Pullman Company interstate train as he traveled back from the convention. Heard had won an earlier case before the Interstate Commerce Commission and decided to file a lawsuit against the Pullman Company and the Nashville, Chattanooga, and St. Louis Railroads.

Captain Judson W. Lyons of Augusta, Georgia (later an active AAC member), handled the suit. Fortune coordinated it for the AAL.[46]

To draw attention to the case and to Tennessee's legislation, AAL members in New York City called a rally at Walters's church in New York City, where Walters and others spoke. Later that month, Fortune settled the Heard suit against the Pullman Company for $250 and a promise that the offending conductor be fired.[47] In a news report Fortune initially vowed that a suit against the Nashville, Chattanooga, and St. Louis railroad would continue, but this never happened. Fortune later explained: "There is no money in the league treasury, and it is simple tomfoolery to institute suit against a railroad without money to prosecute it."[48]

Opinions were generally favorable though somewhat divided about the resolution of the Heard case. Smith's *Cleveland Gazette* initially wrote in favor of the settlement with Pullman, a company it regarded as "friendly to our race." Such actions, Smith hoped, would "strengthen the league with our people and do much to extend its influence."[49] Somewhat more skeptically, the Detroit *Plaindealer* wondered whether the funds received actually made it into the AAL's treasury (a point the *Gazette* had also raised about Fortune's damages award in his lawsuit around the same time).[50] Other newspapers joined in the criticism, pointing out, for example, that Pullman had not given its word that "ejection will not again occur."[51] *The Age* swiftly responded with a letter signed by august legal figures such as Langston and Terrell, affirming that the "victory was signal, rapid and complete, and is a splendid example of the potentiality of your organization and a noble vindication of the plan and purpose of your League."[52]

The Minnesota league became one of the critical voices raising doubts about the strategy of settlement. Its leadership, including St. Paul, Minnesota, lawyer Fredrick McGhee, vowed to pursue a test case to victory in the courts, so that new legal principles could be established.[53] A Minnesota Civil Rights Committee, which operated at least informally as that state's AAL affiliate, decided to move forward independently on a test case of its own. With McGhee serving as lead counsel, the group pursued this challenge through a case Samuel E. Hardy of St. Paul filed. Hardy had been a Minnesota delegate at the AAL's Knoxville convention. On his way to the convention, conductors had forbidden Hardy to ride in the regular passenger car even though he had paid full fare. They instead forced him into an inferior coach intended for passengers who paid a lower fare. On his way home, Hardy had tried to buy a second-class ticket but was not permitted to do that, either. A large meeting convened at the Shiloh Baptist Church in St. Paul heard from Hardy about these experiences and listened to letters from Fortune and Ida B. Wells urging the state group to act. The group adopted resolutions condemning the Tennessee separate-cars law and authorized a committee that McGhee chaired to bring suit and to raise funds to pursue it. Attendees at the meeting gave or promised funds totaling $150 and issued a call for more.

In his initial court filings, McGhee advanced both constitutional rights and breach of contract and intentional infliction of emotional distress claims on Hardy's behalf. However, this case, too, appears not to have been pursued to a litigated judgment. McGhee's biographer surmises that McGhee dropped it for lack of funding or other similar reasons.[54] Indeed, McGhee's biographer documents this lawyer dropping many cases for lack of funds or lack of success, a practice that appears to have been common and perfectly acceptable in the late nineteenth century prior to the advent of strict ethics regulation, though it would run afoul of professional responsibility dictates today.[55]

McGhee's biographer traces this lawyer's political commitments, which switched between the two major national parties as McGhee became disenchanted with both the Republicans and the Democrats based on their dismal records on racial justice issues. McGhee also spoke on occasion for Populist candidates and thus appears to have been fairly politically progressive though personally conservative as a teetotaler and a Catholic. McGhee made this choice of religious affiliation based on what he saw as the Catholic Church's relatively better stand on principles of racial equality.[56] McGhee was too busy with a highly successful criminal defense practice in St. Paul, Minnesota, to write about his overarching vision linking politics, national organizing, and racial justice advocacy. But his fellow AAL lawyer-activist, David Augustus Straker, who was leading state chapter litigation efforts in the neighboring state of Michigan, did write extensively on these questions. These writings help illuminate what at least one deeply committed AAL lawyer activist thought about the relationships between activism, politics, and law. Straker's views help fill out this examination of the AAL's vision not because they are necessarily representative of

Figure 3.1 David Augustus Straker, 1887 (New York Public Library).

the views of others but because they serve as an example of why at least one other major AAL lawyer-activist was drawn to Fortune's vision and motivated to give his time and efforts to the AAL.

David Augustus Straker's Vision of Racial Justice Advocacy

Straker served as chair of the AAL's 1890 convention and was active in its early national and Michigan activities, as already described. He also led other activist organizations of the period, including the short-lived National Federation of Colored Men, which he founded in 1895.[57] Straker had been born in the West Indies in 1842. In 1868 he moved to Kentucky, where he made his living as a schoolteacher. He then enrolled in Howard Law School in 1869 and graduated from its two-year program with his law degree in 1871, six years before Fortune started there and at the height of Langston's influence. After graduating, Straker served for a short time as a postal clerk and began writing for Frederick Douglass's *New National Era*. He then joined a law firm in Charleston, South Carolina, and ran for and won elections for state legislative office several times. Each time, however, the South Carolina Redeemer Democrats refused Straker his seat on the grounds that he was not an American citizen even though he had been naturalized long before. Straker eventually appealed all the way to President McKinley on the matter but never succeeded in obtaining his seat. Between 1882 and 1887 Straker served as dean at Allen University's law school in Columbia, South Carolina. In 1887, having abandoned hope that the political situation or racial conditions would improve in the South, he moved his law practice to Detroit, Michigan. From this location he joined the call for founding the AAL and rapidly became involved in its protest and test case litigation activities.[58]

Straker was a generation younger than Langston and fourteen years older than Fortune. His jurisprudential commitments, much like Fortune's, reflect a blending of the classic abolitionist tradition learned from Langston at Howard with the democratic socialist political theory espoused by Fortune, Ransom, and a number of other late nineteenth-century progressives. This blending of abolitionist-influenced, rights-based jurisprudence with Fortune-style democratic progressive political theory can be seen in the writing of other law-trained activists of his generation as well, including Archibald Grimké, another prolific writer on legal topics, but one who carefully guarded his independence, reputation, and diplomatic career prospects and never became involved in the AAL, AAC, or Niagara Movement (but later led the NAACP's powerhouse Washington, DC, branch).[59] These law-trained leaders often acknowledged the influence on their thought of both Fortune's book, *Black and White,* and Henry George's book, *Poverty and Progress.* Legally, their jurisprudence reflected a creative synthesis of principles drawn from traditional nineteenth-century jurisprudence where helpful, with modifications as required to fit these principles into the pressing demands of a changing political situation.

Straker offered his most comprehensive discussion of these views regarding political economy, blended with his jurisprudential commitments and strategic ideas for race justice activism, in his 1888 work, *The New South Investigated,* which he published based on speeches he had delivered after settling in Michigan.[60] This work's central focus was on the political economy of the South, and Straker's anger and disappointment about his Southern homeland was evident throughout. Straker's education and class status allowed him to assume a position of superiority in explaining race prejudice as due to the ignorance and lack of education of the whites who held such views. A second aspect, in Straker's view, was the capitalist economic system of production.[61]

Straker's central point depicted the South's economic backwardness as integrally linked to race oppression.[62] Straker believed the most important remedy for this condition was improving education in the South for poor whites and African Americans alike, and he championed passage of the Blair bill to accomplish this objective.[63] Like Fortune and Langston, Straker saw the guarantee of a right to an adequate education as a fundamental responsibility of national government; according to Straker, "[t]he national government is duty bound to supply this need."[64]

Like Fortune, much of Straker's argument focused on labor and class-based analysis. Frequently referring to Henry George's work, Straker highlighted injustice in the relations of production as a key aspect of economic injustice, linking the South's economic woes to the labor-related subordination of poor whites and African Americans alike.[65] Again like Fortune, Straker's economic radicalism had no sympathy for left-wing elements that advocated the use of violence or the overthrow of existing government to achieve such change. Straker explained that he liked radical ideas based in democratic theory, as opposed to the "foreign" or revolutionary type.[66] To post–Reconstruction era African American progressives like Straker and Fortune, the reality of lawless mob action hit far too close to home to entertain romantic notions about violent revolution.

Another key aspect of Straker's analysis focused on labor-related discrimination against African American workers. He described and critiqued the problem of the structural economic subordination of African Americans as related both to racial injustice and to the South's laggard economic development and saw this as a key problem requiring attention. Straker articulated a discrimination-based view of this problem, although he did not propose antidiscrimination law as its solution (as indeed, no one would for several more decades):

> It is not an unusual thing to see a white and a black mechanic, who although doing the same work, yet receive different wages. Discrimination is introduced even into the precincts of the schoolhouse. A first-class colored teacher never receives the equal salary as a first-class white teacher.... The

professional, on account of caste prejudice, is shut out from equal opportunity of securing an equal patronage with his white fellow, because of his
color [and further is seen] the closing of the doors of industry, few as they
are in the South, to the colored brother because of his color, and shutting
them against him in every vocation in life which is not strictly menial.[67]

Straker attacked labor organizations' discrimination as well, asserting that "[t]he
folly of trades unions, or the spirit which denies colored persons admission to the
workshops in the South, is the chief cause of Southern depression in trade."[68] But
again Straker did not advance a legal strategy for attacking labor discrimination;
instead, his vision for how to advance the employment and thus economic status of
African Americans relied exclusively on self-help:

> [T]he solution ... is to be found in the colored people themselves. We first
> need *unity*, then action, in this direction. Let us commence in our schools
> and colleges to learn our youth the arts of industrious life. Let us, ourselves,
> by mutual help and mutual confidence, create for ourselves the opportu-
> nity for engaging in industrious pursuits of life.[69]

Straker described the kinds of cooperative economic activity he envisioned, including savings and loan banks, mutual life insurance associations, and industrial cooperatives.[70] Drawing on analogies to the Germans, Irish, and French Americans,
Straker argued for "race pride," through which African Americans would "stand
together and uplift one another."[71] In this way "the social condition of the colored
people of the South must receive a change within themselves. They must seek to
occupy positions in life which will demand respect and recognition from the selfish
standpoint of reciprocal benefit."[72]

Straker also discussed at length transportation and accommodations discrimination, as well as lynchings, again tying these practices to the South's economic and
cultural backwardness: "Another social feature of the South which blurs its progress
and is a relic of the past, is the unjust discrimination of passengers on railroads."[73]
Here, however, in contrast to matters involving economics and private employment, Straker fully envisioned legal strategies as key to dismantling Jim Crow. Like
Langston and other abolitionist-inspired jurists, Straker's taxonomy of political,
civil, and legal rights supported both legislation and litigation strategies to oppose
transportation and public accommodations segregation. Such segregation violated
the right to personal liberty, defined as "the power of locomotion where one's incli-
nation may direct without interference except as restrained by due process of law."
Straker also saw civil rights as encompassing the guarantee of inalienable rights to
personal security and private property.[74]

Similarly, Straker argued for the fundamental importance of suffrage, defined as
"the exercise of the privilege to vote" and "the foundation of free government" and

argued that disfranchisement—of both African American men and all women—required both political and legal assault. Like Fortune, Straker saw clear connections between the denial of suffrage on race and gender grounds: "I advocate rights for women because the rights of my race ha[ve] been denied upon no better foundation, and 'A fellow feeling makes us wondrous kind.' "[75]

Finally, Straker carefully distinguished the demand of racial justice advocates for equality as to political, civil, and legal rights from the frequently raised "bugbear called social equality." Most major written works of race activists during the period included a careful recitation of this point, namely, that, contrary to their opponents' incessant assertions, the demand for equality in political, civil, and legal rights did *not* reflect a desire to mingle in private social relations in circles in which one was unwelcome.[76]

In sum, Straker's views proposed a primary focus on democratically achieved, fundamental economic restructuring to enhance the fairness of U.S. society, coupled with a legalist approach to achieve a limited set of core political, civil, and legal rights, including adequate education, nondiscrimination in public and quasi-public goods and services (such as transportation and public accommodations), bodily security, and unimpeded rights to vote and otherwise take part in the political process.

Straker's personal story of national activism essentially ended with his unsuccessful 1895 effort to launch the National Federation of Colored Men. When that failed to produce a lasting national organization, Straker did not transfer any particularly noteworthy level of energy to the AAC. Perhaps he, like many other progressive race reformers, was wary of Booker T. Washington's influence over that organization. Straker died in 1908, two years before the NAACP began, though his ideas sounded similar to those of the many activists who took part in that initiative. Like Fortune, Straker sounds like an economic radical to modern ears. In the parlance of late nineteenth- and early twentieth-century thought, however, these views were quite mainstream, shared by religious figures such as Ransom and other social gospel adherents, as well as by Du Bois and most of the white progressives who eventually became involved in the founding of the NAACP, including Ovington, Russell, and Walling. All of these racial justice advocates saw the long-term goal of their reform crusade as restructuring the economic system to ensure greater fairness in the distribution of social resources for all.

To progressive African American race advocates of the period, however, this long-term goal had to be accompanied by a shorter-term goal of organizing internally in order to present a strong, cohesive group identity. Although this focus on intrarace advancement in many respects resembled the interest-group brokering model of race advancement endorsed by more conservative, Bookerite race leaders, there was a different valence to the progressives' ideas. The progressives' end goal was a cross-race democratic movement for economic reform, and their emphasis on organizing within the race was aimed at creating the political power required to command respect and cooperation from other interest groups such as the white-dominated trade union movement.

Thus the progressive race activists' political ideas differed in subtle but important respects from the power-brokering model for race uplift Booker T. Washington
espoused, which focused on cultivating wealthy and powerful figures to bestow
benefits on the African American community.[77] Booker T. Washington's version of
intragroup solidarity and self-help did not seek to challenge the underlying structural conditions of inequality, of which racial injustice was a part. In contrast, the
young Fortune and other political progressives such as Straker and Ransom, and
later Du Bois, espoused a politically progressive, economic radicalism view. That
approach focused on intracommunity uplift and organization building as a means
of creating a coalition-based political movement for economic reform. To be sure,
Straker, Fortune, and Ransom were no integrationists; they believed that African
Americans should focus on building their own communities. But their long-term
political vision was one of class- and coalition-based democratic change.

Jurists' and activists' views varied, and I do not offer Straker's views as representative of lawyers of his period or of the activists who supported the AAL. Economic
radicalism characterized only some lawyers' and other activists' views. Others, such
as Booker T. Washington's personal lawyer, Wilford Smith, whose deep personal
cautiousness and professional prudence led him to steer clear of all such organizing
efforts, were either exclusively focused on law without any stated beliefs or held conservative views similar to Washington's on economic matters. Nonetheless, themes
of economic radicalism integrated with law-based discussions of civil and political
rights matters are noticeably frequent in the writings, political activities, and other evidence of the underlying motivation of the more progressive group of lawyer-activists
in the 1880s and early 1890s. Other examples include Fortune's friend and lawyer
T. McCants Stewart and St. Paul lawyer Fredrick McGhee, who sometimes took time
from his busy criminal defense practice to give speeches for race-progressive Populist
Party candidates. Archibald Grimké, too, frequently wrote progressive analyses of the
labor relations problem.[78] To late nineteenth-century lawyers and law-trained racial
justice advocates who saw economic issues as a key to reform, progressive political
theory helped explain how such goals could be met despite a civil rights jurisprudence
that saw court-made law as reaching only a limited set of equality rights.

Fortune had blazed the path for this kind of analysis. By the mid 1890s, however, the burdens of middle age were beginning to wear down Fortune's youthful
idealism. His national role as a visionary founding leader essentially ended with the
death of the national AAL.

The AAL's National Collapse

By 1892 the AAL had begun to collapse at the national level, although local
efforts continued longer. Even before the organization's second annual convention, Fortune had begun to complain in *The Age* that state leagues were

failing to transmit sufficient funds into the national league treasury to pay the expenses of running a national operation. Fortune desperately urged state vice presidents to organize and send in their payment of one dollar per person to the national office, as he as secretary could not "carry the League on his shoulders."[79] Soon there was no money for postage.[80] Reports still came in of some organizing efforts in the Midwest and New England, and the New York organizations' efforts to enact and strengthen that state's civil rights protective legislation continued.

Even Fortune could find little positive news to report about organizing in the South. After the 1891 Knoxville annual meeting, Fortune continued to insist that the league was not dead, but issued another urgent call for local leagues to report to the general secretary that winter.[81] In 1892 the AAL held no national convention, and by August 1893 even Fortune was prepared to announce the AAL's demise as a national organization.[82]

The organization had collapsed for reasons that are not surprising in retrospect: To remain viable it needed to meet expectations based in the earlier national convention movement. Those expectations required the AAL to show that it could mobilize annually a large group of nationally prominent leaders for a show of enthusiasm and unity. But many of those leaders had other agendas, especially concerning national party politics, and failed to demonstrate the strong show of support a new organization required. At the same time, to maintain constant activity, the AAL needed to steadily raise funds that would go to support its national-level work. But the techniques for doing this—such as issuing special calls in connection with high-profile, promising test case initiatives, as Fortune tried to do for his own case—were still in the early stages of development. Finally, and no less important in my view, were the problems of perception that arose because Fortune was on such a shoestring budget personally. Lines between personal material sustenance and the organization's treasury did not exist, and without such lines a national organizing effort was vulnerable to criticisms that it was serving its leader's personal benefit— much the same way as Fortune worried that electoral political involvement would taint organizational leaders' motives for becoming prominent in the AAL. There is no evidence that Fortune was in any way a corrupt leader, but he often was a very materially desperate one, and supporting oneself informally from organizational fund-raising rather than drawing a defined salary had drawbacks. In contrast, the AAC's top leader, Bishop Walters, received a salary from his church and never faced criticism based on funds intended for the AAC going for his material support. Instead, the AME Zion church in effect provided an indirect, material subsidy to the AAC's operation by allowing Walters to work on the AAC's affairs on church "time," so to speak. Fortune had no such financially secure location from which to operate. He was attempting to support a newspaper, a national organization, and a family through individual effort, and that model did not prove viable for the long term.

Thus, the national AAL's effective existence ended a few years after it began even though civil rights organizing continued at the local and regional levels in many areas of the country.[83]

The enthusiastic rise followed by the rapid demise of the Afro-American League is sometimes described as an unfortunate failure, but history proves otherwise. Organizations dedicated to race advancement came and went with great frequency during the period, creating many loosely coordinated local and initiative-based efforts that ebbed and flowed as outrages occurred and other local developments demanded, and as new energetic activists emerged as leaders but then moved on to other preoccupations. Fortune had founded the AAL specifically to impose more national and permanent coordination on these efforts, but that difficult goal would take a long time to achieve. Nonetheless, even in this nascent stage of coordinated national civil rights organizing, sporadic organizational efforts helped build an experience base without which further steps could not have occurred. Just as the AAL followed from prior national equal rights conventions, the organizing efforts leading to the AAL laid the groundwork for the later efforts of the AAC and the Niagara Movement.

Fortune's Changing Role

Throughout the 1890s Fortune continued to edit *The Age* and remained involved in activist work in New York State. When Bishop Alexander Walters issued his call for reviving a national civil rights organization at the end of that decade, Fortune took part in the dialogue and activities that led to that organization's founding. By the late 1890s, however, Fortune's always high-strung temperament became increasingly erratic, for reasons historians debate. It may be that Fortune suffered from a mental illness that medical experts would today label manic depression (which might also explain his overwhelming output the decade before). It may be that he struggled with alcohol dependency, as his contemporaries sometimes accused. It may be that he came increasingly under the financial influence of Booker T. Washington, as Fortune's biographer argues, though a more recent biographer argues that in his political views Fortune changed hardly at all.[84] It is especially difficult to piece together how and why Fortune changed as the twentieth century dawned because copies of his newspapers for the period between 1892 and 1902 no longer exist. What is clear is that after the early 1890s Fortune no longer wrote the abstract, left-wing political theory that had inspired others such as Straker and Grimké on reading *Black and White*. By the end of the 1890s Fortune had fallen away from the vanguard of radical racial justice advocacy. The newly emerging "radical" contingent of racial justice advocates, which would start to make its voice heard through protests within the AAC starting in 1899, regarded Fortune as an enemy.

This generation largely forgot that it was Fortune who first staked the territory they would occupy. But one thoughtful reflection from Du Bois remembered the change from the younger to the older Fortune—and its causes based on his relationship to Washington—in these vivid terms:

> I remember first knowing the man. It was about 1883, while I was a lad in the High School. I became an agent for his paper and wrote crude little news notes from our town. He wrote me an encouraging letter—a good long sympathetic letter. That letter I shall not forget.... He worked on. His fierce brave voice made men of the nation hearken, even while it scared them.... Then his voice became bitter, wild and strained... Temptations gathered... The Arch-Tempter came, smooth-tongued and cynical, with gold: "I have a commission from the Gods-that-be to buy your soul." And the man, bitter at those who had criticized and deserted and refused to support him, mortgaged his Soul and Home to Hell. His slavery began— a bitter, cringing, maddening serfdom.... [T]he fault is ours as well as his....Who refused his wiser youthful leadership? Who withheld the money and bread and clothes due him and his suffering Family? We did.[85]

Whether Fortune indeed "sold out" in the context of the AAC depends on the viewpoint of the observer. Fortune did, to be sure, often but not always side with Washington and the Tuskegee machine as the AAC became the testing ground for deep ideological disputes. Those disputes would fracture the national activist community on many questions but also channel it, at least for a time, in the direction of political and civil rights advocacy, especially as short-term, defensive pragmatic issues became increasingly urgent as the conditions of the nadir period continued to decline.

4

The Dispute between the "Radicals" and the "Accommodationists" within the Afro-American Council: Reverdy Ransom and Booker T. Washington's Contrasting Visions of Racial Justice, 1895–1902

This chapter begins an examination of the national organization that took the AAL's place, which activists named the National Afro-American Council (AAC). Alexander Walters, a bishop of the AME Zion church, took the lead in founding the AAC in 1898 along with Fortune. An earlier generation of civil rights historians often discounted the AAC's importance because of Booker T. Washington's perceived control over it, but the following three chapters examining the AAC argue that, for several reasons, the AAC is far more important in understanding legal civil rights history than previously supposed. First, the debates that took place within the AAC expose the deep ideological fissures underlying the AAC's efforts to define the path forward for civil rights activism—fissures that remained important well into the twentieth century. Second, through trial and error, and much more often through failure rather than success, the AAC's leaders drew lessons about the ingredients necessary to sustain a national organization devoted to racial justice activism. Third and no less importantly, the AAC's work refined a substantive agenda of issue priorities, which it then transmitted to the new century through its leaders' involvement in founding the NAACP. Chapters 4, 5, and 6 take up each of these topics in turn.

Although the AAC was the AAL's direct successor and many of the same figures, including Fortune, participated in both organizations, the AAC differed markedly from the AAL in a number of respects. First, the national AAC survived longer, continuing for a full decade, and engaged in much more activity at the national level than did the AAL. The AAC's executive board usually met at least biannually to oversee a number of national-level projects, including both test case litigation and legislative work. Another important difference involved resources. The AAC's elected president throughout most of its existence, AME Zion bishop Alexander Walters, enjoyed the security of a reasonably well-compensated, high-level church position, which allowed him to devote considerable time to the AAC's affairs without extreme financial sacrifice. Walters never came across as desperate for personal funds in the way Fortune sometimes did.

Other differences stemmed from Booker T. Washington's growing national influence, which began in the mid-1890s. This development did not render the AAC inconsequential, as an earlier generation of scholars of African American civil rights history often argued, but it did result in some marked differences in tone between the AAL and the AAC. The AAC's language sounded less militant, and its long-term vision was less radical than the AAL's. Another difference concerned the two organizations' internal workings. The young Fortune's radical views caused many political moderates and those with electoral political ambitions to keep the AAL at arm's length. In contrast, Walters wanted to create a stronger, larger organization in the AAC and favored an organizing model that could embrace a broad spectrum of political views. Debates about the direction of race justice activism therefore took place over the next decade within the AAC. These debates often stymied the AAC and dragged down its potential momentum, but serve to illuminate the key disagreements that characterized turn-of-the-century racial justice advocacy.

The ideological split within the AAC caused it to break into factions, often labeled as the "radicals," on the one hand, and the conservatives or "accommodationists," on the other. Booker T. Washington played the public figurehead role as the "great accommodationist." AME social gospel minister Reverdy Ransom quickly emerged as the AAC's earliest, most outspoken "radical." As the first to raise his voice publicly against Washington within the AAC, Ransom forged a path on which others, including Du Bois, McGhee, and William Monroe Trotter, would later join him in founding the Niagara Movement in 1905.[1]

As I argue later, neither the so-called radicals nor the accommodationists were exactly what these labels imply. Both groups supported assertively pressing the case for equality in civil rights through test case litigation and national legislative initiatives (Washington just wanted to keep his involvement in this activity secret). And both groups strongly believed in the priority of intragroup efforts at economic and social welfare advancement. Nor did either group envision a *legal* agenda as a means to advance economic and social welfare goals as an aspect of their short- or even midterm strategy. Instead, both groups believed that these goals should be tackled largely through self-help measures in African American communities, with some outreach to sympathetic whites for voluntary assistance. I will show that the difference between the groups lay in their long-term visions of racial justice. The so-called civil rights radicals' real radicalism was in their long-term democratic socialist political vision. Washington's real accommodationism was in his embrace of capitalism as the best system through which to advance African Americans' economic interests. The traditional labels that describe this division between two groups of racial justice activists at the turn of the century capture the fact that they were distinctly different and often at odds with each other, but the nature of their fundamental disagreement differed from what is commonly assumed.

Booker T. Washington, the Great Accommodationist

The year 1895 marked a watershed in the history of racial justice organizing due to two important events. First, in Washington, DC, the great abolitionist Frederick Douglass died, on the very same day he had sat on stage next to his long-time friend and ally Susan B. Anthony and other white suffragists at a National Women's Suffrage Association meeting in the nation's capital.[2] The second event that captured the nation's attention that year portended the new direction African American race leadership would take with Douglass's passing. In an early example of the virtually overnight creation of a national media celebrity, Booker Taliaferro Washington, the thirty-five-year-old principal of a school for the "industrial education" of African American students in the tiny town of Tuskegee, Alabama, rose to national prominence as the result of a speech he delivered at the Atlanta Exposition. Washington was known half facetiously as the "Wizard" of Tuskegee. His Tuskegee Institute for Industrial Training prepared young African Americans for jobs in the manual trades and farming. But even before his rise to national fame, Washington had made himself into a well-respected figure in the field of African American education by impressing Northern white philanthropists with his ambition and efficiency. Washington had developed a reputation as a reliable and compelling speaker at events requiring a leading but safely conservative African American leader to deliver remarks. He also occasionally contributed articles, such as one opposing peonage labor, to Fortune's *Age*.[3]

Washington delivered his famous speech at the Atlanta Exposition in 1895 to an audience of several thousand. Whites dressed in their special-occasion finery sat in the preferred central seating areas of the huge auditorium, while African Americans were relegated to segregated seating areas on the sides. Washington used his speech to appease white Americans anxious about African Americans' growing demands for political participation and citizenship equality. He used his speech to project a fantasy image of a nonthreatening black man willing to eschew political and civil rights demands and instead continue to patiently play the role of hardworking laborer and subordinate. Thus Washington started his speech by denigrating African Americans' political aspirations, apologizing that "Ignorant and inexperienced, it is not strange that...a seat in Congress or the State Legislature was more sought than real estate or industrial skill; that the political convention or stump-speaking had more attractions than starting a diary-farm or truck-garden." Of course, African Americans' development of economic strength would prove threatening to whites just as their acquisition of political power would, as later events in Atlanta would prove. But Washington glossed over all of those points as he attempted to convince white Americans of the benefits of supporting African Americans' energetic economic activity.

In a series of metaphors that would endure in public consciousness, Washington called on both African Americans and whites in the South to "cast down your bucket where you are." For African Americans, Washington urged recognition that "the masses of us are to live by the productions of our hands"—a reassuring image to whites accustomed to the subordination of African Americans in lower-status occupations. For whites, Washington carried a message urging recognition that African Americans "have, without strikes and labor wars, tilled your fields, cleared your forests, builded your railroads and cities,... and your families will be surrounded by the most patient, faithful, law-abiding, and unresentful people that the world has seen." Thus Washington, always a foe of organized labor, contrasted the image of immigrant laborers, ready to strike or otherwise foment labor unrest, with the image of the loyal, subservient African American workers on whom U.S. businesses could count for uncomplaining cooperation.

Washington's second metaphor continued a focus on economic relations. He invoked the image of separate fingers on the same hand, promising whites that in "all things that are purely social we can be as separate as the fingers, yet one as the hand in all things essential to mutual progress." In so stating, Washington suggested that his version of race self-help would not protest Jim Crow segregation. This promise to "accommodate" white social prejudice prompted whites in the packed auditorium to burst into wild applause.[4]

African Americans, not surprisingly, had far more complex and ambivalent responses. Du Bois, then a new professor at Wilberforce University, wrote favorably about the speech, a fact he later regretted. But many older hands, such as Harry Smith of the *Cleveland Gazette,* were appalled. Describing the performance of "Prof. B. T. or Bad Taste Wash," Smith wrote that, although the "white press style Prof. Bad Taste the new Negro," if "there is anything in him except the most servile type of the old Negro we fail to find it in any of his last acts." Another writer, this one publishing a report from Texas in the *Woman's Era,* explained "[h]ow proud we have all felt over the achievement of our great orator, Mr. Booker T. Washington" but felt compelled to add the following in gently phrased criticism: "Of course, some of us do not agree altogether with some of his utterances.... For instance, Mr. Washington warns us against trying to spend our dollar in an opera house ... yet I can't see why we should be debarred from spending our money... which we have earned, in any harmless way we may see fit."[5]

Washington's offer to abandon civil and political rights protest in favor of a focus on economic advancement hit just the right note with whites fearful of African

Figure 4.1 Booker T. Washington and Margaret Murray Washington, posing with some of the teachers and trustees of the Tuskegee Institute, including Andrew Carnegie, 1906 (New York Public Library).

Americans' demands for citizenship equality. The white press covered and praised his speech widely.[6] Washington fully recognized the great boon this reception to his speech could be to his work. Making no missteps, he skillfully cultivated this reputation he had gained with whites as the African American leader who could be counted on to be "reasonable" on civil rights matters in order to increase both his political influence and his ability to fund-raise for the Tuskegee Institute and many other African American educational institutions.[7] He developed connections with wealthy industrialists, including Andrew Carnegie, who would eventually donate the huge fortune for its day of $600,000 to Tuskegee, plus $150,000 for Washington's personal use (later revised to an undetermined sum to avoid public criticism).[8]

Washington also cultivated his fame and reputation to develop important alliances with white politicians, through which he became the broker between the white political class and aspiring African Americans desiring political appointments. Washington's success in this arena started with President William McKinley, though McKinley always continued to listen to a range of African American advisers, including AME bishop Arnett.[9] After McKinley's assassination in 1901, Washington even more successfully and exclusively asserted himself as the premier informal advisor on African American appointments and affairs with President Theodore Roosevelt, at least for a time. The two would dine at the White House soon after Roosevelt took office, to the indignant outcries of some sectors of the public, especially in the South—just a little more than a century before a man of African descent would become president and start issuing the White House invitations himself.

Washington also told derogatory "darky" jokes before white—and sometimes even African American—audiences. Today, and to many African Americans and even a few whites at the time, these messages seem quite appalling. It is important, however, as a new generation of scholars of African American history have pointed out, not to portray Washington as a nemesis of civil rights progress without a more nuanced appreciation of his role. Underneath Washington's accommodationist public persona created to cater to the white public, the man held far more complex views. While he sought to reassure powerful and wealthy whites of their continuing racial superiority as a means of manipulating their patrician impulses, he also worked behind the scenes to promote several types of test case litigation, as well as to push other civil rights initiatives. These facts have long been known, but a new generation of revisionist historians has taken a far more sympathetic and often more accurate view of the complexities of Washington's role in promoting racial progress. What remains largely unexplored but also undisputed is the fact of Washington's general political stance, which favored a race-based, interest-group, power-brokering model of African American progress under a capitalist economic system. This underlying political model often clashed with broader justice-seeking goals.

Washington's cynical, realpolitik political vision was one thing, but his tactics in seeking to retain control over the direction of civil rights work were quite another. These ruthless tactics, which civil rights history revisionists sometimes ignore, must factor into any overall account of the Tuskegean's role in turn-of-the-century racial reform efforts. While the evidence establishes that Washington did genuinely and intensely want to end the civil and political disfranchisement of African Americans and that he did secretly devote substantial effort and financing to these goals, it also shows that he even more resolutely wanted to squelch opposition to his leadership, regardless of the consequences of doing so. He especially wanted to maintain his role as the central power broker between African American political ambition and the white-controlled political system. He did so through many ruthless means. Most simply, he used his political connections to reward supporters and punish critics. Second, he secretly obtained control over a number of leading African American newspapers of the time, including T. Thomas Fortune's *Age*, in which Washington secretly purchased a controlling share in 1907 while Fortune was suffering from nervous exhaustion. Washington then unceremoniously dumped the unemployed Fortune onto the street, severing his so-called friend from all connection with the publication he had devoted his entire life to building. Washington also provided secret financing in order to control two Boston-area publications, the *Colored American Magazine* and *Alexander's Magazine,* hoping to use his control over these publications as a means of countering his critics in that city. He assigned his agents to work within other prominent publications, such as the well-respected, Atlanta-based *Voice of the Negro* as well.[10]

Third, Washington recruited prominent African Americans to inform him about what his opponents were doing and saying about him; he turned people, in other words, into "spies." Washington's personal secretary, Emmett J. Scott, helped him organize these efforts to control the politics of race activism, and it is somewhat ironically due to Scott's loyal fastidiousness in saving and cataloging Washington's correspondence that we know so much about the extent of Washington's iniquity in suppressing opposition to his reign. Washington destroyed promising careers, started vicious and untrue rumor campaigns, pressured funders to turn against hardworking advocates, and even had his enemies imprisoned and subjected to threats of lynching.

Some of the classical historians of African American race activism, including Louis Harlan, August Meier, Elliot Rudwick, and Emma Lou Thornbrough, thus not unfairly adopted largely negative viewpoints of Washington and his activities, including his attempts to control the AAC. For this reason, historians have until recently largely overlooked or downplayed the AAC's contributions to the development of civil rights activism in the United States, dismissing the AAC as a weak organization captured by the Tuskegee machine. More recently, revisionist historians have offered a more positive view of both Washington and the AAC. Washington's involvement in the AAC, they suggest, does not diminish the AAC's importance. Some of these historians continue to regard Washington as a major force and the AAC as a quite disorganized and peripheral presence, whereas others see the AAC as far more important than previously assumed and Washington's role as less important than the classical historians portrayed.[11] There is merit to both views: The AAC was far more than a Washington puppet, and at the same time Washington was certainly influential in its workings.

In the end, evaluating the AAC's contribution to early racial justice activism in the United States requires taking a normative position on Washington's involvement, if only because that topic so centrally preoccupied the AAC's members themselves. Although the AAC's executive board continued apace to plan activities, including its legal work, largely unaffected by the organization's political fireworks, its annual meetings often did involve pyrotechnics as its radicals and conservatives clashed. At each of a series of increasingly fractious annual meetings, the so-called civil rights radicals within the AAC—most notably, Ransom, Wells Barnett, and Trotter, joined a bit later by McGhee, Du Bois, and others—agitated against Washington and the principles they believed he stood for. By the early years of the twentieth century, the perception that Washington was suppressing the AAC's potential civil rights militancy had led to an internal crisis, and the AAC began to lose members and momentum. Bishop Walters, the figure who resolutely stood at the head of the organization for most of the ten years of its existence, was staunchly in favor of public civil rights advocacy and persevered by urging members to continue focusing their immediate, consensus-based, and pragmatic strategy on civil rights.

The perspective on Washington one chooses in assessing his role within the AAC and turn-of-the-century civil rights activism depends a great deal on one's views about Washington's underlying political philosophy rather than his stands on particular civil rights topics. There simply was not nearly as much difference as commonly supposed between the issue-specific views of Washington and Du Bois, who is usually cast as Washington's chief nemesis in classical accounts. Washington did support civil rights litigation to obtain voting and other civil rights (he just wanted to keep his support secret), and the differences between Washington and Du Bois supporters on the question of higher education versus manual or vocational training have likewise been far overstated; both camps fully acknowledged the importance of both projects at every opportunity but accused each other of striking the wrong balance between these two priorities. Moreover, Washington and Du Bois agreed on the need to develop African American business and to promote intracommunity solidarity and self-help. The idea for Washington's National Negro Business League grew out of Du Bois's 1899 Atlanta conference titled "The Negro in Business," for example, and Du Bois served as the first director of the AAC's business bureau. Indeed, all race leaders staunchly believed in the importance of prioritizing community self-help and internal capacity-building efforts. They saw civil and political rights agitation as yet another aspect of, not a substitute for or a higher priority than, attention to economic advancement.

The real differences between Washington and the civil rights radicals came not from their views about short-term priorities but instead from their views of what a just society would look like in the long term. Many of the so-called radicals wanted fundamental economic restructuring as their ultimate goal.[12] In contrast, those more closely aligned with the Bookerite version of a racial self-help philosophy favored the advancement of African Americans under a conventional capitalist model. The radicals, exemplified in the AAL in the young Fortune, in the early AAC by Ransom, and then even later by Du Bois in leaving the AAC to found the Niagara Movement, favored coalition building between a well-organized and thus empowered African American community joined with the more progressive, politically oriented, and less racist sectors of the labor movement in the United States. Washington and other like-minded economic conservatives argued instead for building an alliance between African Americans and the white capitalist class.

This clash between the underlying political-economy views of Washington and the radicals within the AAC can best be illustrated by examining the contrast between Washington and Ransom. Ransom was Washington's first and most outspoken opponent within the AAC. To an extent not yet sufficiently appreciated, Ransom was an important turn-of-the-century intellectual force. He worked out his passionately held ideas by testing them through social welfare activist experimentation. Well educated and widely read in many trends of the emerging political and social thought of his day, the enormously energetic Ransom managed to place himself at many key transmission sites for turn-of-the-century ideas about racial justice activism, including the founding of the Niagara Movement, the NAACP, and the National Urban League.

Lives Compared

We have already met Ransom and reviewed the trajectory of his life up to the early 1900s in chapter 1. In many respects, Washington's and Ransom's early lives were strikingly similar. The two men were both born prior to emancipation to young single mothers and unidentified, probably white fathers. Both entered the world into conditions of rural poverty. Ransom was not born enslaved as Washington was, but both young boys faced expected lives of hard physical labor—Booker in Alabama salt and coal mines and Reverdy in the Ohio timber industry. Both men escaped these likely fates because of their mothers' strong support, as well as their good fortune in securing positions and educational advantages by working in the homes of well-to-do whites. In these settings both pursued their academic skills while obtaining a basic formal education in nearby Freedmen's Bureau schools. Washington's biographers describe the mistress of the house for whom Booker worked, Mrs. Viola Ruffner, as a stern Yankee taskmaster who felt out of place in the Southern home to which she had moved as a governess and then as the second wife of a leading local businessman and politician.[13] Ruffner instilled in the young Booker an almost obsessive preoccupation with the values of efficiency, cleanliness, Puritanism, and hard work, all of which he would later strive to promote at the Tuskegee Institute, much to the approval of the white philanthropists who provided that institution's funding.

From such similar beginnings, the two men's lives would begin to diverge as they pursued different paths to higher education. Ransom began a curriculum focused on classical academic training at Oberlin and Wilberforce, while Washington attended the Hampton Normal and Agricultural Institute in Virginia, a school that combined some academic training with a heavy dose of instruction in manual and vocational arts. But interesting similarities between the two men's life trajectories persisted. Both of them owed much of their later success to the strong mentoring relationships they each cultivated with leadership figures at their respective schools: Bishop Arnett at Wilberforce, on Ransom's part, and the white philanthropist and educator Gen. Samuel Chapman Armstrong, head of the Hampton Institute, on the part of Washington. Armstrong would later recommend Washington to head the newly founded Tuskegee Institute in response to a request for a recommendation of a "teacher or some other white man" who had absorbed the general's ideas about African American education.[14] Armstrong recommended Washington despite his race, and the board of the Tuskegee Institute benefited from more than thirty years of Washington's leadership, during which he developed the school from one that lacked even a physical plant to an institution that controlled hundreds of acres of land and attracted tens of thousands of dollars in philanthropic donations per year.

Both of the young men even flirted briefly with ideas about pursuing careers in law, though they then decided that their true callings were in other directions. Nevertheless, the two men retained an interest in and appreciation for the significance of law as a social institution of key relevance to their chosen life projects of improving the conditions confronting their race. At the same time, their views about how to advance these shared goals could not have been more different.

Ransom's early interest in law is apparent in his sermons, in which he frequently spoke about, and usually railed against, constitutional law developments on civil rights issues. In contrast, Washington generally remained publicly silent about these developments. Washington's public silence reflected his cagey attempt to avoid alienating whites, but also had the adverse effect of alienating African Americans who saw him as kowtowing to a racial caste system. This result produced a particularly ironic state of affairs, given that, behind the scenes in highest secrecy, Washington was financing the most successful test case litigation in this period, a story recounted in more detail in chapter 6.

Washington combined his outer face of accommodationism with intense interest in promoting intrarace economic advancement through the promotion of African American business activity and fund-raising for African American educational institutions. He clearly detested the civil rights retrogression taking place during the 1890s, but his style of response involved secret rather than openly confrontational attacks. He worked with organizations that shared his intrarace self-help goals, but he was wary of efforts he could not control, especially anything smacking of public civil rights militancy.

Ransom's approach to race self-help had a very different political valence. Stimulated by his World's Fair experiences, Ransom was in the mid-1890s reading widely in the developing literature on the social gospel and socialist movements. His taste in reading included writers such as John Ruskin, an English art and social critic who wrote in opposition to the free-market liberal individualism of philosophers such as J. S. Mill. Ruskin argued for extending biblical teachings about social justice and caring for the poor into economic relationships, and he advocated the passage of laws to impose just wages and prevent the exploitation of workers by their bosses, as well as social legislation to protect the destitute.[15] These ideas influenced the English democratic socialists, who then influenced some strains of U.S. progressivism. Henry George, for example, a favorite of both Ransom and the young Fortune, argued in his popular 1879 book, *Poverty and Progress*, that access to basic sustenance through the tilling of land was a fundamental right. Progressive American academic Richard Ely, a frequent visitor at Jane Addams's Hull House, the famous Chicago settlement, studied in depth and wrote favorably about the potential of democratic or "English-style" socialism in the United States. These were the authors Ransom was fond of quoting in his sermons and speeches.[16]

By 1896 Ransom was prepared to endorse democratic socialism as the most promising political path for African Americans. He did so in a speech delivered to the Ohio Federation of Labor that summer. As Ransom declared, his was a socialism "that believes in the republican form of government in a democratic state"; socialists of his ilk "do not seek the overthrow of the government, but to gain their ends through existing governments." Much like Fortune writing a decade before, Ransom saw this version of socialism as holding powerful appeal because the "American Negro belongs almost wholly to the proletarian or industrial class. He constitutes a large and important factor in the development of this country and the production of its wealth."[17]

Ransom was writing after the implosion in the late 1880s of the Knights of Labor, a politically focused, national labor-organizing effort that had included both whites and African Americans (but at the same time excluded persons who were Chinese). In contrast, the American Federation of Labor (AFL) offered a different model of business unionism focused on organizing skilled laborers by craft and advancing members' economic interests while eschewing broader political objectives. By the 1890s Jim Crow attitudes were growing within the AFL as within the country as a whole, and Ransom sought in his speech before Ohio labor activists to counter this trend through reasoned argument and dialogue. Noting the exclusion of African Americans from many of the nation's labor unions, Ransom explained that this was why the "Negro has little sympathy with and takes little interest in the cause of organized labor." However, Ransom argued:

> [These] old relations of men, entrenched behind centuries of custom, will
> not be able to beat back the rising tide. The battles of socialism are not [to]
> be fought by white men, for the benefit of white men. It is not, as we have
> said, a question of race, it is the question of man. So far as America is con
> cerned, the question cannot be settled without the Negro's aid. The cause
> of labor, of the industrial army, is one.[18]

Thus, Ransom optimistically believed, as did Fortune and other labor-oriented progressive African American leaders of this era, the assertion of political and economic power by African Americans would lead to changes in the attitudes of white-led labor organizations and eventually to an appreciation on both sides of the race divide of the need for unity and class solidarity as a political strategy.

Ransom expressed these ideas in a Thanksgiving sermon he delivered in Chicago in 1896 as Bethel's new pastor. Speaking at the end of a year that had seen a harsh national recession, Ransom started by invoking botanical images that evoked Ruskin's naturalistic socialism and George's focus on rights in land. Ransom's theme, appropriately enough for a Thanksgiving sermon, emphasized God's abundance in stocking the earth generously with plentiful natural resources. Ransom argued that God had given human beings a great bounty but that human beings, through their badly managed interpersonal relations, had destroyed these gifts. Invoking a Populist rhetoric, Ransom pointed his finger at the cause of this misery: "[T]he earth which God has given to His children has become the possession of idle aristocracy, the plaything of corporations and syndicates." Next Ransom opposed the claims of the laissez-faire economists, arguing that "poverty is not natural"; just as slavery had existed for centuries, so, too, the fact that other conditions have existed for centuries "does not argue that they are right; that of itself does not make them divine."[19]

Only after laying this groundwork by talking about justice and plenty for all people did Ransom introduce the topic of racial injustice, moving to discuss "the social and industrial condition of our race in this land." His analysis focused first on African Americans' economic situation: Although in "the years that are past and gone," as well as in the present, "we have played a marked part in the industrial development of this country," race caste had been used to shove African Americans down to the lowest rungs of the economic class ladder:

> [W]e have been forced in the north, in Chicago, as well as in the south, into a condition that may truly be termed industrial serfdom. In other words, it is the unwritten law in almost every avenue of life, that the Negro shall perform those tasks and engage in those enterprises which are distasteful to white men, and whenever the Negro aspires to a position in life which is thought desirable by white men he is felt to be an intruder, to be aspiring out of his place and above his plane.[20]

Ransom presciently pointed out the reversal in African American economic progress as a sign of a coming era of regression in race relations. Implicitly criticizing the integrationist hopes of some of his congregation members, he pointed out that "[w]e used to have the barber business of the country...but [if] you go into the better shops...you will find the Negro blacking boots [instead]; the white people have chased him way back in the corner." Similarly, the African American tradition of skilled cooks seemed to be on the decline, and Ransom worried the hotel industry would be next. He noted the searing hypocrisy of those who would argue that African Americans should simply work hard to overcome race barriers and break into more economically advantaged class statuses:

> We are accused of being poor, but no man can ever become wealthy or save money until he makes money. The only way to accumulate money is that we first earn it before we accumulate it, and we cannot accumulate wealth or comfortable homes, [unless] we are permitted to have a place or part in the wealth producing industries of the country.[21]

Ransom then moved to the problem of African American political rights, articulating what he saw as an inextricable connection between economic and political concerns. He condemned both the lack of African American voting rights despite the guarantees of the Fifteenth Amendment and the U.S. Supreme Court's *Plessy v. Ferguson* decision of that year, which had upheld the "separate but equal" principle in transportation.[22] Thus Ransom saw a political and civil rights agenda as crucial to racial justice advocacy and at the same time saw economic issues as at least as crucial. His disagreements with Washington did not arise from differences about substantive priorities but from dissimilar approaches to long-term goals. Even on short-term priorities on economic issues, Ransom and Washington shared some points of agreement. For example, both advocated self-help within African American communities, with minimal involvement from the state. The key difference was that Ransom envisioned these short-term strategies eventually flowing into a broad-based democratic movement for greater economic fairness, while Washington foresaw interest group politics advancing the status of his own racially defined identity group within an existing political system. These dissimilarities need not even have mattered that much since either view required essentially the same within-group "uplift" priorities, to use the term activists of the era adopted. But Ransom viscerally opposed Washington's indirect, often Machiavellian, political style, and from that difference sprang the bitter opposition that would first pit the two men against each other, and then a growing group of radicals against the Tuskegee machine.

Reverdy Ransom, Outspoken Social Settlement Activist

Ransom's initiatives at Bethel put into practice both the short-term priorities and the long-term ideals about which he so often preached. When they moved to Chicago in 1896, Reverdy and Emma Ransom quickly established programs and activities through which less well-off members of the congregation received resources that better-off members contributed. These so-called elite members of Ransom's congregation contributed not only financially but also through their social connections and status.[23] His congregation included many leading members of Chicago's African American high society, including Charles Bentley and Dr. Daniel Hale Williams, still famous as the first doctor in the United States to successfully suture a human heart.[24] Williams took part in Bethel's men's club when his busy schedule allowed, while his wife, Alice Williams, chaired the women's committee that oversaw all of the Institutional Church and Social Settlement's social programs and led fund-raising efforts for it.[25] Alice's commitment to charitable social self-help work did not signal egalitarian tendencies on her part. The Williamses believed in the social superiority of the upper class, like fellow church members Ida Wells Barnett and her husband,

Ferdinand Barnett, and the Ransoms did. Other Chicago figures dedicated to charitable self-help, such as Jane Addams, held similar views as well.[26]

Ida and Ferdinand Barnett had married at Bethel the year before in a grand affair featuring orange blossoms and chiffon, and they soon counted themselves among Ransom's most ardent supporters.[27] Ferdinand sat on Bethel's board of directors, while Ida jumped with great energy into supporting Bethel's programs and activities, delighted to find in Ransom an ally with a similarly uncompromising approach.[28] On moving to Chicago in 1893, Wells Barnett had faced disapproval when she proposed opening a kindergarten for African American children whom the white-led kindergarten movement of the era were not serving. Established community leaders at the time, still committed to integrationist strategies that had seemed to serve their professional interests in the past, opposed her proposal, but Ransom defended Wells Barnett's position, and such a kindergarten began operating at Bethel.[29] Ransom and Wells Barnett would continue to serve as mutual allies throughout Ransom's years in Chicago and beyond.

In addition to a kindergarten, Bethel offered many other classes and programs aimed at bringing both economic and cultural self-help opportunities to the residents of its surrounding neighborhood. These programs resembled those beginning to take place in other parts of the country, both in settlement houses for white immigrants and in the women's club work African American women led.[30] Although such settlement house work was taking place on both sides of the race divide, little of it spanned the racial chasm that characterized civil society in this period.[31] African American charitable work had been occurring for decades— indeed, it was Jane Addams's participation in African American mission house work that lifted her from a depression she fell into during her early adult years and provided her with a vision for how she could pursue a meaningful life of service to others.[32] But Addams had decided to focus her efforts on acculturating the many (white) immigrant "races" arriving in the United States, and Hull House sat in the midst of white immigrant neighborhoods. Hull House quite explicitly did not serve African Americans.[33] During the years in which the Ransoms were in Chicago, their social justice ministry work rivaled all other programs addressed to the needs of African Americans in that city.

Bethel's programs drew heavily upon the ideas and efforts of the African American women's club movement. In keeping with those ideas, the programs offered at Bethel, as elsewhere around the country, catered both to economic needs and to so-called cultural self-help. With women conducting the lion's share of organizing work, Bethel offered vocational training and an employment bureau to help community members looking for work as cooks, maids, launderers, waiters, porters, butlers, and stenographers. It offered classes in dressmaking, cooking, and catering, all aimed at teaching employment skills. At the same time, Bethel offered infant classes, boys' groups, separate men's and women's clubs, a literary society, and voice, piano, and choral arts classes.[34] Bethel also offered classes to inculcate improved—that is, middle-class—parenting and housekeeping norms, as well as to expose interested members of the surrounding neighborhood to higher culture and the arts. This mix of objectives did not substantially differ from those of white settlement houses such as Hull House, except that the African American women who helped in African American settlement houses perceived themselves as sharing a racial identity with the intended beneficiaries of their work in a way that white settlement house women, who saw immigrants as racially distinct, did not.

In addition, Bethel offered a forum for political discussion and organizing that was specifically focused on African American civil rights. The building frequently hosted well-attended evening events targeted at protesting lynching and demanding civil rights equality. African American "social" work would later become professionalized and arguably depoliticized as well. But in the 1890s its aim of social self-help more closely resembled a form of political activism, at least in settings like Ransom's congregation.[35]

Ransom promoted a civil rights agenda in other ways as well, such as by hosting a selective organization of Midwestern interracial couples of " 'high moral and intellectual standing' " called the Manasseh Society. Interracial marriage was a sensitive subject within African American society, as historian Willard Gatewood has written about in examining the so-called "black elite" of the late nineteenth and early twentieth century. Many of this African American elite had lighter skin tones (though often because of white on black sexual assault rather than intermarriage), but couples who married interracially found themselves in an uncomfortable position, accepted by neither whites nor blacks. Ransom, always one to champion the outcast, performed many interracial marriage ceremonies in his church.[36]

The first years of the twentieth century marked the apex of Ransom's youthful radicalism. The year 1900, when Ransom turned thirty-eight, saw not only his retreat from the AAC after becoming fed up with fighting for more militant stands, but also his resignation from his relatively comfortable sinecure at Bethel AME. Ransom resolved to take on the challenging project of building a new social gospel settlement house only eight blocks down from Bethel. It is not clear why he made this move; the two institutions were similar, and the personal cost to Ransom of having to raise independent funds for a new start-up institution would weigh heavily on him. But for whatever reasons, Ransom undertook to become pastor and superintendent of a new social settlement experiment, to be called the Institutional Church and Social Settlement (ICSS), four years after he started at Bethel.[37] Funding to purchase the large building that housed the ICSS came from Bishop Arnett, who sat on the AME Church's Finance Committee at the time.[38] Professional help came by way of an assistant pastor, Richard R. Wright Jr., a graduate of the University of Chicago Divinity School, who would later join Ransom as a founding Niagara Movement member and then would serve on the NAACP's Committee of 100.[39]

Figure 4.2 Reverdy C. Ransom and Emma Ransom in front of the Institutional Church and Social Settlement, 1902 (Chicago History Museum).

The AME church charged Ransom with raising the funds for the ICSS's entire operating budget, and he did so by motivating his congregation's leadership, as well as by reaching out to others involved in the social gospel movement in Chicago. These included Bishop Samuel Fallows, a white Episcopal minister who shared Ransom's commitment to social justice ministry and spoke at the ICSS's opening ceremonies,[40] and Frank W. Gunsaulus, a Congregational Church pastor and social gospel adherent whose oratory inspired Chicago's wealthy meat-packer family to fund the Armour Institute, devoted to Chicago's civic improvement, and to install Gunsaulus as its head.[41] Other supporters included Graham Taylor, the white minister who had opened a social settlement house in a racially mixed community near the University of Chicago; and Hull House leader Jane Addams, the grand matriarch of the U.S. branch of the multinational social settlement house movement, who also spoke at the ICSS's opening.[42] In Addams, Ransom reported, he found a significant ally, and her papers verify that she lent her important fund-raising and political contacts to the ICSS project.[43] Other key white donors included wealthy Chicago industrialists, many of whom, notably, had been or would be involved in industrial strikes during which African American strikebreaking became an issue. These included figures such as Mrs. George Pullman, widow of the founder of the Pullman Railroad Company; Robert L. Lincoln, President Lincoln's son and current president of the Pullman Company; P. D. Armour, wife of J. Ogden Armour of the Armour Packing Company; and the wife of Gustavus Franklin Swift, head of another major Midwestern meat-packing empire.[44]

With financial backing from a combination of well-to-do ICSS congregation members, including Ida Wells Barnett, Ferdinand Barnett, and the Bentleys; white Chicago progressives; and wealthy industrialists, the Ransoms and the ICSS congregation developed an impressive array of social programs at the ICSS. The church offered day care, recreational activities, educational programs, religious services, and a Sunday school. A free kindergarten, which Emma Ransom oversaw, boasted of a paid principal and two assistants and served sixty-two children, a quarter of whom were white.[45] An employment bureau helped place applicants in domestic service jobs. Fund-raising produced substantial donations from well-to-do individuals and many businesses for a total budget of $3,500, enough to cover expenses, though no salary was paid to Ransom himself.[46] By 1904 the new church boasted three hundred members and packed worship services.

As he had at Bethel, Ransom offered the ICSS as a forum for discussion and lectures on progressive topics.[47] Clarence Darrow, one of the few white Chicago attorneys known as a supporter of African American causes, was a great friend of Ransom's and frequent speaker at both Bethel and the ICSS.[48] The ICSS was the site of several mass meetings to protest lynchings and other civil rights outrages.[49] Ransom also sought, according to his self-report, to play a role in mediating Chicago's labor strife, which was becoming intertwined with growing racial animosity among Chicago's white workers as industrialists used the very African American workers they would not otherwise hire to break labor strikes. Ransom offered the ICSS as a site for mediation between striking workers and African American strikebreakers—who had assumed jobs they would otherwise have been excluded from by unions, employers, or both. Striking workers bitterly resented and attacked these replacement workers and others who racially resembled them, without caring that their own exclusionary rules created a class of workers who often had little sympathy for such hypocritical principles of labor "solidarity."[50]

In the same period, Ransom attempted to take on Chicago's crime bosses, calling a mass meeting at ICSS to denounce "policy gambling," a type of numbers playing through which bettors could participate with coins of small denomination.[51] Ransom asked the crime bosses responsible for this game, such as Irishman Patsy King, to withdraw it from African American neighborhoods.[52] This form of gambling was attractive to men earning low wages because it required little money to play, and it sprang up in groceries and similar venues all over Chicago's State Street area, where the ICSS was located. The games were reportedly lively spectacles, complete with systems of runners who took funds back and forth to "hubs," or facilities run by crime bosses who provided banking services to small-time policy game operators in return for taking a large portion of their profits. According to a historian who has studied this phenomenon, in the early 1900s these hub leaders were either whites or African Americans partnered with whites; African American syndicate bosses did not emerge until the 1920s.[53] Nonetheless, the front men who ran the games in the State Street area were all African American, as was their clientele.

Ransom was incensed with the negative influence policy gambling exerted on the ICSS neighborhood and began denouncing the syndicate leaders in his Sunday lectures, calling on the mob bosses to leave the neighborhood and take with them the vice they brought. He further escalated his attacks by organizing an interracial coalition of clergymen to speak out against the policymakers' presence. In retaliation, unknown persons dynamited the ICSS in May 1903. The explosion shattered windows and blew out a door just minutes after Ransom had finished preaching a Sunday sermon.[54] Still undeterred, Ransom preached the next week, carrying a gun under his Bible and continuing to urge ministers of white denominations to cooperate, pointing out that the battle being fought "belongs to the white sections of the city as well."[55]

In the end, Ransom's attempts to bring the crime bosses to justice failed.[56] His failure was due in part to the criminal defense work of African American lawyer Edward H. Morris, who served as lead counsel, on a $100 a month retainer, to the syndicate bosses. Ransom never forgave Morris for this role. Even many years later, Ransom's failed attempt to combat the vice he saw as damaging the ICSS neighborhood left him with the bitter memory that it had been none other than Chicago's leading African American attorney Morris who had successfully defended these Chicago crime figures against state prosecution.

Morris's practice spanned business law for white-owned corporations and civil rights test cases for African American plaintiffs who could have paid little or no fees.[57] He had run successfully for the state House and was serving in that position during the policy gambling trials.[58] Morris was Catholic and thus unlikely to have been a regular visitor to Bethel AME or ICSS, but Morris and Ransom clearly moved in similar circles and knew each other.[59] Along with Ferdinand Barnett, Morris had been one of the two Chicago lawyers who issued the founding call for the AAL in 1889, and Morris had served as legal counsel for that organization as well. Morris had been an early professional mentor to AAC legal affairs director and later Niagara Movement founder Fredrick McGhee, who practiced in Morris's firm in Chicago until he and Morris's brother relocated to St. Paul, Minnesota, where McGhee became a prominent criminal defense lawyer in his own right.[60]

As McGhee's legal specialty of criminal defense attests, Morris's representation of the gambling syndicate leaders did not violate professional standards. Ransom's friend Clarence Darrow was certainly building his career and reputation by taking high-profile criminal cases, and it was well accepted—within the bar at least—that acceptance of a client was not an endorsement of the client's moral views or legal objectives and that all persons, including or especially criminal defendants, deserved zealous legal representation. Ransom could have viewed the choice of Morris to represent white crime leaders as a form of compliment to an African

American attorney who, in the face of race discrimination, had to seize business opportunities where he could get them, just as African Americans seeking employment in other sectors had to do.

But to Ransom none of these explanations bore any weight. Even half a century later, Ransom excoriated Morris for his lack of loyalty to the project of racial self-help, stating that "so far as I know [Morris] took little, or no unselfish interest in the welfare of his people. He had great political influence and power in the city government. I know of no instance in which he used this influence and power usefully according to the standards of colored people."[61] Such harsh words were on balance unfair; Morris had a distinguished record as a civil rights activist and litigator and was also an outspoken opponent of the Tuskegee machine, just as Ransom was. To Ransom, however, the defense of white criminal bosses seeking to prey on poor African Americans for profit by promoting vice was inexcusable. In this instance as in others, Ransom was not a person prone to appreciating moral complexity: One was either on the side of justice or on the other side.

Morris, in contrast, stood as a figure who made choices that sometimes required him to ally himself with white power structures that provided lucrative business prospects. Like a number of other AAL attorney activists such as Straker, Morris largely dropped out of national race justice activism after the AAL, concentrating instead on his business and local civic involvements.[62] Pragmatism among leading African American professional men took many forms, and Morris's focus on his career in the face of the declining business prospects of the nadir period reflected one such option. Professional advancement often conflicted with race justice activism. The very different approach of Morris's mentee, Fredrick McGhee, who worked himself to an early death in his attempts to balance a heavy criminal defense case load with intense activity for both the AAC and then the Niagara Movement, attests to the self-punishing consequences of heavy altruistic commitments.[63]

Ransom suffered from the consequences of such commitments as well. By mid-1904, he had left the ICSS and Chicago altogether. He had, not surprisingly, created many enemies among fellow AME ministers in the area, who resented Ransom's dynamism and also disapproved of his radical politics.[64] When Ransom's mentor, Bishop Arnett, relocated from the Midwest to take charge of an AME district in the East, Ransom's enemies apparently convinced Arnett's successor to remove Ransom from the ICSS. A new minister took over the ICSS, and Ransom moved, with Arnett's help, to a pastorate in New Bedford, Massachusetts. There he would meet future fellow Niagara Movement member radical Edwin B. Jourdain, one of the few civil rights radicals who joined and advocated for more militancy within the National Negro Business League.[65]

Ransom soon moved again from New Bedford to the more prestigious and high-visibility pastorate at the Charles Street AME in Boston, where he met still other new acquaintances whose paths soon intertwined, including fellow Niagara Movement founding member William H. Scott, a Baptist minister and social gospel advocate who presided over the proceedings during Ransom's acclaimed oratories at Faneuil Hall.[66]

From this location Ransom delivered a number of important sermons that received national attention, including his denunciation of Booker T. Washington's ideology after the 1906 Atlanta race riots. In that speech Ransom pointed out the fundamental problem with Washington's publicly stated philosophy of African American business development without corresponding political rights: The lack of political rights left one helpless to protect economic interests and property, because such legal protection could be ensured only if one had the right to exercise political power to hold the government accountable for protecting one's rights.[67]

By 1908 the Ransoms had moved to New York City, where Reverdy opened a new social settlement for prostitutes and other social outcasts, which he patterned on the ICSS.[68] He took part in social self-help organizations that eventually became the National Urban League and lent his oratorical gifts to the NAACP's founding convention as well.[69] Emma continued her reform work, including leading a successful campaign to transform the YWCA into an interracial organization. There the couple remained until Ransom was called into the higher reaches of the church's hierarchy on his appointment to bishop in 1924.[70] By then Ransom's church duties had taken him far from the radical path he had forged within the AAC in the early 1900s, though others, including McGhee and Du Bois, continued to pursue it through the AAC's tumultuous ten years of national activity between 1989 and 1908. That internal turmoil very much shaped what the AAC was and was not able to accomplish in terms of national racial justice activism, and I therefore turn to a broad analysis of the AAC's internal history below.

The Afro-American Council's Internal History, 1898–1908

The Afro-American Council began in late 1898, when Bishop Alexander Walters, the young rising star within the AME Zion church, published an open letter in *The Age*, addressed to its editor, Fortune. Walters pointed out with great alarm how badly racial conditions were deteriorating throughout the country, noting the recent murders of two African American postmasters, as well as the "determined effort on the part of white labor unions of the country to exclude the Negro from industrial avenues in which he can make an honest living." He urged Fortune to call a meeting of race leaders to consider these worsening conditions and to deliberate about how to respond to them. He also proposed re-creating the national organizing effort Fortune had started with the AAL. In subsequent letters published in *The Age* and other newspapers Walters repeated his call, appending a growing list of prominent figures who concurred. Eventually this list included the names of more than one hundred men and women.[1]

Fortune replied in his own public letter published in *The Age*, explaining that he fully agreed with Walters's view about the urgent need for national organization but that his prior experiences had led him to conclude that African Americans were not yet ready to throw their full support behind such an effort. In the course of further exchanges with Walters, Fortune eventually relented. With public interest heightened by the drama of their public debate, the two men jointly agreed to schedule a meeting to consider a revival of the AAL.[2]

The Worsening Conditions of the Nadir Period

Walters's call focused on the dramatic worsening of the country's racial conditions in the years following the national AAL's collapse. This deterioration was occurring on a number of fronts. Wells Barnett's research showed that lynchings and other incidents of racial violence were on the rise throughout the country. Totaling more

Figure 5.1 Bishop Alexander Walters, 1895 (New York Public Library).

than one hundred deaths per year throughout the 1890s, these incidents included the murders of the two African Americans selected for U.S. government positions as postmasters in Hogansville, Georgia, and Lake City, South Carolina, as mentioned in Walters's call.[3] State laws mandating Jim Crow were spreading as well. Although it was not uncommon for railroads and steamboats to impose segregation after the Civil War, Reconstruction had initially aborted states' plans to encode such practices into law. By 1892, however, nine Southern states had enacted laws mandating Jim Crow segregation on trains. These were Florida in 1887; Mississippi in 1888; Texas in 1889; Louisiana in 1890; Alabama, Arkansas, Georgia, and Tennessee in 1891; and Kentucky in 1892.[4] In 1890 a divided U.S. Supreme Court upheld Mississippi's separate-cars statute, with Justices Harlan and Bradley dissenting. The Court based its decision on somewhat obscure commerce clause grounds, reasoning that the Mississippi courts' interpretation of the statute as regulating travel solely within the state meant that the law fell outside the scope of matters reserved exclusively for congressional regulation under the U.S. Constitution's interstate commerce clause.[5] The Court concluded that, for this reason, the state was free to regulate race relations in intrastate transportation without federal court intervention.

In 1896, in *Plessy v. Ferguson,* the Court revisited this question as to whether a state could constitutionally enact a Jim Crow statute that purported to apply only to passengers in intrastate commerce. This time the Court pulled no punches in announcing its "separate but equal" doctrine. Citing the *Civil Rights Cases,* the *Plessy* Court held that "the enforced separation of the races, as applied to the internal commerce of the state, neither abridges the privileges or immunities of the colored man, deprives him of his property without due process of law, nor denies him the equal protection of the laws, within the meaning of the fourteenth amendment." This time, Justice Harlan was the sole voice in dissent.[6]

In the years prior to the *Plessy* decision, the Interstate Commerce Commission (ICC), which Congress established in 1887, had upheld several challenges African American clergymen had filed to protest separate-car seating. These decisions found that the complaining passengers had not received "equal" accommodations when railroads forced them to sit in Jim Crow cars.[7] *Plessy* in effect reversed these decisions by declaring that such separate cars could be "equal." But the actual conditions of Jim Crow cars belied the abstract legal fiction on which *Plessy* rested. African American passengers who were traveling on first-class tickets but then ordered to move into Jim Crow cars encountered dingy, dirty conditions, lacking amenities provided to first-class passengers, such as cold water. Most problematically, a rowdy male element frequently traveled in these second-class cars. Their presence led to unpleasant traveling conditions for African American men subject to harassment from them but even more risk of danger to African American women passengers, who faced white male cultural norms that regarded all women of color as sexually available.[8]

Throughout the South, African American plaintiffs, usually women, along with some male clergymen, defied state Jim Crow train car laws by refusing to move to second-class accommodations. Quite often, conductors forcibly ejected such resisters.[9] A long tradition supported filing lawsuits to challenge such treatment. Such suits included Ida Wells's 1884 suit after being ejected from a train in Memphis (during the course of which she managed to bite the conductor as he tried to push her out of the train); an 1885 suit by women on the steamboat *The Sue*, which the Maryland Brotherhood of Liberty sponsored; and even suits stretching back to the antebellum period in the North.[10] Although these suits rarely ended in victory, activists resolved to continue them as an expression of resistance to the human dignity violation Jim Crow involved. Activists saw that organizing at the national level could provide a means of coordinating and funding these efforts.

Racial justice advocates would have faced a more than ample national organizing agenda in seeking to combat lynching and the spread of Jim Crow laws. But an even more troubling legal phenomenon, going to the very heart of political citizenship, was occurring simultaneously, which even more urgently required action. This phenomenon again involved encoding racial subordination into the very foundations of public law as Southern states sought new ways to strip African American men of the right to vote that the Reconstruction-era constitutional amendments purportedly promised. Along with Jim Crow railroad legislation, Southern states undertook a wave of disfranchisement initiatives aimed at more effectively eliminating African American males from voter registration rolls.[11] (Women of all races, of course, still remained disfranchised in most states.)

The impulse to find effective ways to diminish African Americans' political power in the South after the initial grant of citizenship rights under the Reconstruction-era constitutional amendments was far from new, but the devices to accomplish such disfranchisement had evolved. As the facts in *Cruikshank, Reese,* and other cases involving Ku Klux Klan terror campaigns show, interference with African Americans' exercise of the franchise had been a significant and ongoing problem since emancipation. The prevalence of voter fraud, voter manipulation, and failure to properly count votes also attested to the broadscale effort to combat the potential strength of African American electoral power.[12] But these informal practices had proved insufficiently effective, and African Americans' block voting presented an increasingly potent and unpredictable factor in Southern elections. Southern politicians accordingly resolved to wipe out African American electoral influence even more effectively through wider-reaching laws. The Reconstruction-era amendments explicitly prohibited this, of course. But the defeat of the Lodge (or "Force") bill, which would have strengthened federal oversight of state elections in the interests of protecting Fourteenth and Fifteenth Amendment rights, coupled with the Court's refusal to enforce those constitutional dictates in cases like *Cruikshank* and *Reese*, emboldened Southern legislators. They settled on new disfranchisement strategies that could be embedded in the very foundations of public law—namely, in states' constitutions themselves.

Racial Disfranchisement

These disfranchising techniques involved amending state constitutions to embed new broadly exclusionary voting requirements in them. The most blatantly discriminatory of these provisions were "grandfather" clauses. Grandfather clauses limited the right to vote to the male descendants of men who either had been able to vote before, or had fought during, the Civil War. Since virtually no African American men in the South voted before or fought in the Civil War, this clause quite obviously excluded them from the franchise. Another device involved variations on what were called "understanding" clauses, which granted voter registrars the discretion to decide whether applicants sufficiently "understood" the principles of government to be entitled to exercise the franchise. Still another was known as the "character" clause, which gave registrars the discretion to decide whether applicants possessed sufficiently high character to be granted the privilege of voting. Other provisions required voters to prove they could read or that they owned substantial property; these requirements were often unequally enforced against blacks but not whites. (Another extremely effective disfranchising device, which was among the earliest used and did not require constitutional amendments, imposed steep cumulative poll taxes that male citizens had to remit before voting.[13])

Mississippi was the first of what eventually would become ten Southern states to enact state constitutional measures to achieve broadscale, legally entrenched racial disfranchisement. It amended its state constitution in 1890 to add a literacy qualification, a property ownership alternative, and an understanding clause to its voter qualification requirements.[14] No organized constituency offered resistance, and the

Mississippi Supreme Court "swatted away" a challenge an unsuccessful white political candidate mounted.[15] The Mississippi measure then stood as an example to other
states, and South Carolina soon followed Mississippi's lead. George Washington
Carver, one of the last African American politicians to hold elected federal office in
the South, filed a lawsuit to challenge that state's constitution, but it ended in defeat,
as did another challenge to the Mississippi constitutional measure that African
American lawyer Cornelius J. Jones mounted. Jones lost his case before the U.S.
Supreme Court in 1898 in *Williams v. Mississippi*, in which the Court held that Jones
had failed to create a sufficient factual record to prove the discriminatory intent he
alleged.[16] Mississippian John Roy Lynch, another African American U.S. congressman who watched his electoral career end with disfranchisement (after which he
became Robert Terrell's law partner in Washington, DC), tried a hybrid political
and litigation challenge, but that failed as well.[17]

By 1896 more Southern states had joined the movement to design legal strategies to more permanently and broadly ensure African American disfranchisement.
Louisiana adopted a grandfather clause in 1898. In 1899 North Carolina followed
suit. By 1901 Booker T. Washington's home state of Alabama had adopted this
device as well. Race leaders of all political stripes, including Washington, perceived
the fundamental threat disfranchisement posed to any vision of African American
progress in the United States. A lack of voting rights stripped away the ability to
protect property, economic interests—and, indeed, life itself. Without voting rights
African American constituencies had no means of enforcing political accountability
in public officials. No one, even Washington, would have argued to the contrary,
at least under conditions allowing for private candor. The question was what to do
about the situation, and again, to all major leaders, organizing at the national level,
as well as locally and regionally, appeared increasingly imperative.

A First Organizing Meeting

Against this backdrop, Fortune could hardly oppose the arguments Walters was
making in favor of a new attempt to build a national organization. Still an organizer
at heart, Fortune relented from his first pessimistic reaction to Walters's call and proposed a meeting for Rochester, New York, timed to coincide with a long-planned
ceremony to unveil a monument to Frederick Douglass.[18] In September 1898 this
meeting took place as planned. Although the AAC's founders later boasted about
the large and prestigious group that attended, most of the people who gathered in
Rochester came for the Douglass memorial event. A smaller group took part in the
meetings to discuss the formation of a new national organization to be called the
National Afro-American Council.

This meeting's attendance may have been small, but its composition was
indisputably select. The list of well-known figures who took part signaled the

continuation of a long-standing racial justice protest tradition that spanned both gender and race divides. Prominent public leaders from many sectors of civil society showed up, including many well-known clergy, elected and appointed African American political figures, and prominent African American club women. Susan B. Anthony, Frederick Douglass's longtime friend, addressed the group to urge its success.[19]

The attendees adopted a statement of principles substantially similar to the AAL's, though more moderate in tone. The AAC listed its objectives in an order different from those of the AAL, but the ten objectives the AAC included in its constitution and bylaws included all six of the AAL's: namely, (1) combating lynching; (2) "testing the constitutionality of laws which are made for the express purpose of oppressing the Afro-American"; (3) "securing legislation which in the individual States shall secure to all citizens the rights guaranteed them by the 13th, 14th and 15th Amendments to the Constitution"; (4) "Prison Reform"; (6) "both industrial and higher education"; and (10) "urg[ing] the appropriation [of] school funds by the Federal Government to provide education for citizens who are denied school privileges by discriminating State laws."[20] One participant, as if to test the limits of the organization's fundamental organizing philosophy, requested a ruling on whether his membership would be welcome if he favored separate schools and disapproved of interracial marriage. Fortune, presiding as temporary chair, quickly ruled that these views barred the inquirer from membership.[21]

Although the AAC's and AAL's founding platforms remained substantially similar, differences can be detected, too. The main shift involved greater focus on constitutional test case litigation. The AAC's emphasis on the oppressive "purpose" of these laws also signaled a slight shift or refinement of the theory under which such cases would be pursued. The legal theory for challenges to discrimination had become more exclusively rooted in constitutional theory rather than referring to contract- and tort-based doctrines requiring "common carriers" to serve all passengers as had the AAL's. The priority the AAC gave to test cases had shifted as well: The council listed this as its second priority, right under ending lynching, whereas the AAL had listed this goal last.[22]

The AAC's founding platform also sounded less militant in tone than had the AAL's. Fortune's call for attention to fair wages had switched to a call for "promot[ing] business enterprises," and instead of emphasizing organizing in the South, the AAC "recommend[ed] a healthy migration from terror-ridden sections of our land to States where law is respected and maintained." The AAC's objectives placed greater emphasis on African American communities engaging in self-help and working to encourage education and to "inaugurate and promote plans for the moral elevation of the Afro-American people." In place of the AAL's demand to immediately end all lynchings and other forms of racial oppression, the AAC's founding platform spoke of investigating and making "an impartial report of all lynchings," as well as working to "educate sentiment on all lines that specially affect our race."[23]

The assembled group also elected its first leaders. Attendees first endorsed Fortune for president, but after Wells Barnett questioned whether it was wise to elect a leader who had expressed reservations about the new organization's viability, Fortune declined the position. The delegates voted to approve Bishop Walters for the leadership post instead. Well-known figures filled other top offices as well, including as vice president John C. Dancy, collector of customs in Wilmington, North Carolina, and as treasurer Wells Barnett. These figures, along with four more, including Ransom's mentor, AME bishop Arnett, became the national executive committee.[24]

The Rochester founding meeting in the midst of the Douglass celebration gave the AAC an auspicious start. Walters, displaying his characteristic organization-building savvy, sought to take advantage of this momentum by calling the AAC's first annual meeting only a few months later, at the close of the year. Seeking to draw big-name delegates while at the same time making the organization's presence known to federal officials, Walters chose Washington, DC, for the gathering's location.[25]

A First Annual Meeting in Washington, DC

The scheduling of a high-visibility Washington, DC, meeting for the AAC's first official gathering did not please everyone; Washington quickly begged off attending. But an otherwise very well-attended meeting received ample publicity in both the African American and the white press.[26] News reports focused especially on the lengthy address to the nation the delegates adopted, which a committee that included Fortune, Wells Barnett, and others had drafted. Among many other topics, the address called attention to Southern disfranchisement. Pointing in particular at the grandfather clause device, these delegates insisted that the new constitutions of Mississippi, South Carolina, and Louisiana had as both their "intent and consequence" the disfranchisement of citizens on the basis of race and called on the courts to "quickly consider" these restrictions. In a move that Walters and the radicals favored but that Washington and other more conservative members of the council opposed, the delegates called on Congress to reduce the federal electoral representation of disfranchising states pursuant to the explicit language of Section 2 of the Fourteenth Amendment, which states that the calculation of federal electoral representation "shall be reduced in the proportion which the number of [nonvoting] male citizens shall bear to the whole number of male citizens twenty-one years of age in such State.[27] Finally, the AAC's address to the nation urged African Americans "everywhere to resist by all lawful means the determination to deprive them of their suffrage rights" and threatened that African Americans might split their vote between the national parties if this proved necessary to accomplish their purpose. Other sections of the address protested Southern separate-cars laws, urged passage of the Blair education bill, championed reform of the penal system in the South, and protested President McKinley's silence in the face of rising incidents of lynchings and other forms of racial violence throughout the country.[28]

At the end of the meeting, a contingent composed of nationally known figures secured a meeting with President McKinley in the White House to present the address.[29] This delegation's members included prominent clergy, former and current elected and appointed officials, educators, and newspaper editors. Representatives of major churches included AME bishop Arnett and two AME Zion bishops, Walters and George Clinton, who was another social gospel adherent and champion of women's rights.[30] Current and former elected officials included Pinckney B. S. Pinchback, former lieutenant governor and then briefly governor of Louisiana, who later studied law at Straight University and participated in the citizens' committee that engineered *Plessy v. Ferguson* as a test case. Others included Henry Plummer Cheatham, a former U.S. congressman who was now recorder of deeds in Washington, DC, as well as then-current U.S. Congressman George H. White of North Carolina, the last African American from the South to hold federal legislative office between Reconstruction and passage of the 1965 Voting Rights Act.[31]

Prominent political appointees who attended the McKinley meeting included Judson Whitlocke Lyons, register of the U.S. Treasury and an 1884 Howard Law School graduate who was initially a Bookerite conservative but lost his federal appointment after he expressed sympathy for radical Boston activist William Monroe Trotter in 1903; and customs collector John C. Dancy, who played a variety of institutional roles within the AAC during its early years.[32] Newspaper editors included John Mitchell Jr., of Richmond, Virginia, editor of the *Richmond Planet,* a radical civil rights paper at the time; Benjamin Pelham, editor of the Detroit *Plaindealer;* and John Quincy Adams, National Negro Press leader, brother of AAC secretary and internal historian Cyrus Adams and editor of the St. Paul–based *Western Appeal,* which would long continue frequent and favorable coverage of the AAC.[33] Newspaper accounts initially reported that Fortune had also attended, but he wrote back to state that he had refused to go because he opposed "the obsequious and truckling efforts of the office-holders to secure an [e]ndorsement of the treacherous and ungrateful policy of the President toward the Afro-American people."[34]

Still others who attended the meeting with President McKinley and would continue to play key roles within the AAC included lawyer and assistant librarian of Congress Daniel A. Murray, as well as sociologist and lawyer Jesse Lawson of New Jersey. These two men would soon become the AAC's Washington, DC, lobbying arm, serving as officers of its legal and legislative affairs bureau and testifying before Congress on a range of legislative matters important to the AAC's agenda.

The delegates at this first annual meeting continued the task of organization building as well. They expanded the national executive committee to include many of the big-name delegates just listed who had agreed to attend the McKinley meeting. They structured this committee to include three delegates from each represented state and, in a strikingly modern gesture, decided that each state's executive committee of three must include one woman. This led to a total of twenty-five women representatives on the organization's initial governing body.[35] In subsequent years, women's representation on the executive committee would decline, but at least a good handful of women always held leadership positions.

Additional organization building created new "bureaus" within the AAC's internal structure. These bureaus included a legal and legislative bureau, headed by Murray and later by McGhee,[36] as well as bureaus for matters labeled as industrial; financial, which Lawson initially headed; and antilynching, initially spearheaded by Wells Barnett.[37]

The AAC sought to avoid the AAL's difficulties in organizing new local affiliates by adopting a membership policy that allowed delegates to establish their right to vote in national meetings in a wide variety of ways. A delegate could claim the right to vote in annual AAC meetings by showing that he or she represented a duly accredited local council *or* any other organization that held similar plans and purposes and was cooperating with the council. Delegates could also establish AAC voting credentials if they represented religious or secular organizations "working for the mental and moral elevation of the race"; served as editors of African American newspapers; or held appointment as school or college principals. Through this more expansive means of defining official representatives, the AAC astutely sought to encourage leaders to participate in its affairs as representatives of a broad range of African American communities and groups. It hoped in this way to develop a national organization rooted in preexisting local strength. This allowed the AAC to avoid undertaking the monumental task of building new affiliate organizations on a community-by-community basis—a goal the AAL had attempted but failed to accomplish. Later, the NAACP's success would result from such grassroots building of new local chapters. But its ability to succeed in this way rested on the preexisting organizational infrastructure predecessor organizations, including the AAC and the Niagara Movement, had built.

The AAC sought to further learn from the AAL's experiences by establishing a firmer financial base. Rather than having membership dues per se, it required all delegates and organizations sponsoring delegates to pay a five-dollar annual credential fee in order to obtain delegate status at annual meetings.[38] This requirement aimed to avoid the problem of chronically unpaid annual dues by creating an incentive to pay at the time of the organization's key annual event in order to gain participation rights. And, indeed, although the AAC faced incessant demands on its limited funds, especially to help finance test case litigation, it did maintain steady accounts and a positive bank balance in its early years, at least through the last cumulative financial report secretary Adams published in 1902.[39]

Partly because of the lessons activists learned from the AAL's demise, the AAC's momentum did not lag after its initial flurry of activity during its founding year. The AAC continued to hold credible annual meetings for the next decade and undertook a host of activities on a wide range of law-related racial justice matters. Walters, who served as the AAC's president for seven of its ten active years, clearly deserves the credit for the monumentally difficult task of holding the organization together despite its members' many differences.

Bishop Walters's Pragmatic Organizing Vision

A pragmatist rather than an adherent to any particular ideological perspective, Walters emphasized three pressing political and civil rights issues: voting, Jim Crow, and lynching. Like other figures of the era who took strong civil rights stands while managing to avoid clashing with the Tuskegee machine, Walters avoided direct criticism of Washington. But primary sources show that Walters did consistently advocate a strong civil rights agenda. Some earlier historians portrayed him as vacillating or wavering in response to Washington's influence, but a review of Walters's many public addresses as AAC president show him to have been resolute on these civil rights issues throughout the AAC's existence.[40]

There was something, however, that made Walters unusual among the members of his generation who would rise to the top of national race leadership—namely, that Walters, unlike most such leaders, had received no formal higher education whatsoever.[41] Born enslaved in 1858 in Kentucky to a household that ran a hotel, Walters obtained some lower-school education at segregated schools after emancipation and then started what he viewed as his real education, which he got working in hotels and traveling widely as a crew member on steamboats passing through Louisville, Kentucky, which he adopted as his home base. Walters's mother had been deeply involved in the AME Zion church, and Walters became active there, too. Under its auspices he first became an itinerant pastor, and then, as his multi-faceted talents at speaking, administration, and fund-raising became apparent, he began quickly rising through its ranks, much as Ransom had done within a sister church, the AME.[42]

The AAC tested Walters's strong political and organizational skills to their very limits, and he clearly deserves much recognition for his accomplishments as the AAC's leader. Despite minuscule funds and perennial internecine clashes between the anti-Washington radicals and Washington's defenders, Walters managed to avoid the organization's collapse throughout a key decade leading into the twentieth century. He even brought the AAC back from the verge of suffocation after Washington temporarily succeeded in suppressing most of its activity by forcing through his choices for the position of organizational president between 1902 and 1906. Walters's genius, as Shawn Alexander has persuasively argued, lay in his vision for the AAC as an umbrella organization that could hold within it activists espousing a wide range of viewpoints. This model had both benefits and drawbacks, but without it there most likely would not have been one central national organization devoted to civil rights advocacy as the twentieth century began—an organizing ideal leaders then transmitted as the objective for founding the NAACP.[43]

Yet even Walters's strengths in pragmatic leadership did not prevent the AAC from becoming the battleground for debilitating disputes between anti- and pro-Bookerite forces. These disputes highlight what I have argued in chapter 4 were the real underlying philosophical cleavages within the AAC. Internal clashes often stymied forward momentum even on the urgent matters about which everyone agreed, which involved combating the growing assaults on African Americans' civil, economic, and political status. Although Walters and other AAC leaders valiantly strived to push forward a nationally coordinated agenda, they achieved far less than they aspired to accomplish. A triumphal account of the AAC's history is thus inapt, though greater appreciation of the groundwork the AAC's efforts laid is surely long overdue.

A portrayal of the AAC's decade of existence can easily become a dizzying recitation of dates, names, and places accompanied by variations on the theme of bitter internal disputes and distrust over the extent of Washington's influence over the council. Two detailed treatments of the AAC's organizational history are now available, one by historian and Afro-American studies professor Shawn Leigh Alexander and one by freelance writer Benjamin Justesen.[44] These accounts reconstruct the AAC's complex organizational history in great detail, allowing me to focus on a different task—namely, understanding the flavor of the underlying differences that marked these debates, which in turn fed into the organization's plans for its law-related work. This legal work sometimes proceeded in tandem with, but at other times was surprisingly independent of, the vagaries of the AAC's organizational highs and lows, and chapter 6 focuses on the as-yet unexplored topic of the relationship between the AAC's organizational vision and its law-related campaigns. Here a relatively brief summary of the main phases of the AAC's internal history will set the stage for doing so. Those phases involved (1) the early rumblings of radicals' dissatisfaction with Washington's attempts to influence the AAC (1899–1901), followed by (2) Washington's temporary success in achieving control of the AAC's presidency through surrogates (1902–1906), leading the radicals to defect to the Niagara Movement in 1905, and ending with (3) Walters's promising efforts to pull the AAC back to its democratically defined civil rights objectives, which ended with the beginnings of a new effort to unite all civil rights factions into a new national organization, which would become the NAACP.

Stage One: Rumbling Dissent by the AAC's Radicals

Walters soon discovered that the success of the AAC's first annual meeting in December 1898 in Washington, DC, would be hard to repeat. In August 1899 the AAC took its national annual meeting to Chicago, and there the first public rumblings of ideologically driven dissent within the AAC became audible. The AAC's radical wing sought to push from the floor for a pro-labor agenda and at the same time openly denounced Washington before the white press. For his part, Washington stayed away from the meeting site but remained holed up in a nearby hotel, summoning his supporters to him to plan strategy as if he controlled them like puppets on a string. This meeting set in motion the widening of a chasm between the radicals and the Bookerites that even Walters's considerable political skills never managed to halt.

The AAC delegates gathered in Chicago just a few days after the NACW's annual meeting concluded there.[45] Many married couples took part in both events, and the programs for the two organizations' meetings not surprisingly contained many similar topics. Issue priorities on the AAC's agenda included investigating lynchings and pushing for federal antilynching legislation; testing the constitutionality of laws made for the purpose of oppressing African Americans; lobbying for legislation to secure for all citizens their constitutional rights; prison reform; "migration out of terror-ridden sections of our land"; encouraging both industrial and higher education; lobbying for federal school funding; and, finally, promoting business enterprises, education, and the moral elevation of the African American people.[46] Another topic, introduced by *Age* women's affairs columnist and Philadelphia club woman leader Gertrude Mossell, involved public health. Crime was also a topic on the agenda. Harry Smith spoke of his success in securing passage of his Ohio antilynching bill, and Wells Barnett presented the facts concerning the rising numbers of lynchings. An evening public meeting produced overflow crowds to hear Du Bois speak on "The Business Enterprises of the Race and How to Foster Them," along with remarks from AME bishop Arnett and other speakers.[47]

The lineup of AAC officers read like a who's who of leading African American activists. Bishop Walters was president, and Ransom's mentor, AME bishop Arnett, was one of several vice presidents.[48] Robert H. Terrell, Mary Church Terrell's husband, served as legal counselor.[49] Wells Barnett, who had previously been active in the AAL and had been elected AAC secretary at its annual meeting in Washington, DC, in 1898, spearheaded an AAC antilynching campaign. Her presence probably drew Ransom into the organization's work.

Wells Barnett took part in local planning for the Chicago meeting. She used her influence to promote the organization's more radical wing, selecting Bethel for the opening session, for example, so that Ransom could set the meeting's opening tone in a welcoming speech. She also ensured that the program would include other radicals, such as her Cleveland-based antilynching collaborator, Harry Smith.[50] But scheduled speakers included a wide array of leading representatives of various schools of thought on strategies for racial progress, including both men and women. Women's club leaders were easy to secure since they were still in town. Their speeches emphasized the need to work for concrete improvements in local communities, and this theme united the AAC's male speakers' messages as well. Du

Bois's paper on the importance of African American business, for example, which was a product of his research project on that topic at Atlanta University, agreed with Washington's emphasis on intracommunity uplift and building economic strength. Other topics were far more controversial. Reverend Henry McNeal Turner argued for emigration from the United States to Africa, for example, but discussion of this topic ended in the AAC's passage of a resolution rejecting this idea.[51]

The delegates adopted a number of consensus resolutions, including one emphasizing the importance of enforcing the Fifteenth Amendment and another urging passage of federal antilynching legislation. Lawyer-sociologist Jesse Lawson drafted this year's AAC address to the nation. It called for creating a commission to investigate the conditions of African Americans in the country, as well as repeating in strong terms the standard list of the AAC's many issue priorities.

But the radicals wanted the organization to move further than this. The fact that many Bookerites had gotten wind of likely militancy at the conference and stayed away helped the radicals' attempts to dominate the convention. Washington had absented himself, as had his more cautious acolytes such as Judson Lyons.[52] When the general convention proceedings opened, Ransom, Wells Barnett, and others pushed from the floor for a series of strong resolutions the meeting would vote on endorsing. One such resolution, which Ransom introduced, would have condemned McKinley for his silence on lynching.[53] Another, introduced by a different delegate, would have resolved that the council was in favor of starting a new political party and would henceforth oppose all politicians who did not support protection for African American voters in the South.[54] Neither resolution carried, but the council did issue a statement disapproving all public officials who had "not used their station to voice the best conscience of the nation in regard to mob violence and the fair treatment of just deserving men."[55]

Ransom made yet another, even bolder though again unsuccessful parry; he moved from the floor that the council vote to condemn Booker T. Washington himself. Washington's absence from the meeting had followed the advice of strategists, including Fortune,[56] who feared that the Tuskegean's attendance would tarnish his carefully guarded national reputation for moderation. In a similarly distancing gesture, Mary Washington, in town for the NACW convention, sent a last-minute note asking to be excused from giving her scheduled speech before the AAC.[57] That evening Ransom called for a debate on the floor on Washington's philosophy and leadership failings. According to one often-quoted newspaper account, Ransom argued as follows: "No such man ought to claim to be our leader. We want the country to know he is nothing to us. We hold him in contempt. He is trying to hold us in line. From his room in the Palmer House, he says, 'Sh!, Sh!,' but he's afraid to come in. I move that Mr. Washington's name be stricken from the roll."[58] Ransom's resolution failed, but in committee he did successfully block a resolution to endorse Washington instead.

Ransom also succeeded in getting a resolution passed that called for building alliances between the council and the leaders of organized labor. Echoing similar language Fortune had placed in the AAL's founding documents, Ransom introduced a resolution that called for a two-part strategy to bring such an alliance into being. First, according to Ransom's proposal, the council should "confer with leaders of organized labor in the United States to impress upon them the mutual benefits that would accrue to laborers regardless of race and [the importance that] overt discrimination be set aside to bring about a spirit of fraternity and cooperation among American workers of every grade, regardless of race or section."[59] Second, the council should "meet with the National Labor Bureau to lay before it the conditions of Negro laborers in the United States and to keep them informed in regard to the same, and to have them appoint, if possible, a subcommittee to cooperate with the national bureau."[60] In the end, the council passed a milder version of Ransom's resolution, thus putting itself on record as siding with the prolabor radicals rather than the antilabor Bookerites.

The meeting thus ended with ambiguous results for the AAC radicals. Wells Barnett remained secretary, and Ransom had been elected as the eighth of nine council vice presidents.[61] The assembled body had arrived at many consensus points, including endorsing proposed federal antilynching legislation and listening, with approval from all, to Du Bois's speech on the need to promote African American business enterprises.[62] Washington's followers attempted to reassure their leader that no real damage had been done by the media coverage of the opposition to him at the AAC meeting. In an interview with the *New York Times*, Washington claimed that the meeting had gone very smoothly, with only a bit of protest by inconsequential attendees.[63] Du Bois, who had attended the convention and opposed Ransom from the floor, took advantage of the opportunity to curry favor with Washington by going on record scolding Ransom for his outbursts.[64] (Du Bois was at the time considering a possible move to become a professor at Washington's Tuskegee Institute.[65]) In the end Ransom issued an apology to Washington.[66]

The next year, the AAC's annual meeting took place in Indianapolis. Again, fighting between the organization's radicals and pro-Washington members dominated the meeting. Ransom served on the Committee on Resolutions, and Walters was reelected to a third term as president, Wells Barnett to the position of national organizer, McGhee to direct the Legislative Bureau, and Du Bois to head the Business Bureau. The boisterous Chicago meeting had only increased Washington's distrust of a new national organization that would govern itself through democratic processes. He seemed to be scheming to undermine the AAC's success when he scheduled a national meeting for his new National Business League (NBL) in Boston shortly before the AAC's event so as to make attendance at both meetings difficult. Du Bois had been the intellectual force behind the founding idea for the NBL, which had grown out of his 1899 Atlanta conferences on the topic of "The Negro in Business." However, Washington planned to, and did, exercise a firm hand over this organization, and only a few radicals remained members for long. When Washington issued a call for the NBL's organizing meeting to be held in Boston shortly before the AAC meeting was to convene, newspapers and other commentators queried whether this was an attempt to sabotage the AAC.[67] Just days before the Indianapolis meeting Washington had been far away at his new National Negro Business League's meeting, but he managed to make an appearance on the last day of the AAC meeting to assuage his critics nonetheless.

The meeting's agenda of scheduled speakers again attempted to balance differing perspectives. Ransom delivered the opening prayer; Du Bois, representing the AAC's Business Bureau, delivered a talk on "The Negro as a Producer and Consumer"; Wells Barnett gave a speech on behalf of the Anti-Lynching Bureau; Lawson spoke about "The Relations between the Races"; and Washington capped off the agenda with a final speech titled "The Negro and the Industrial Problem."[68] But this approach was not enough for Ransom. The Indianapolis meeting was his last; by 1901 Ransom had resigned from the organization out of disgust with Washington's involvement. As he saw it, the AAC had proved itself "useless as a weapon, toward, or in favor of political and social justice."[69] Other radicals stayed in the AAC, hoping to work within its broad umbrella. It would not be until a few years later that Du Bois would begin to break publicly with Washington in his thoughtful and balanced critique of the Tuskegean's respective virtues and demerits in a chapter of his 1903 book, *The Souls of Black Folk*, titled "Of Mr. Booker T. Washington and Others."[70] Ransom, upon reading the essay, would invite Du Bois to come to Chicago to speak. Afterward, in a meeting at Bentley's home, discussions about forming the Niagara Movement began.[71]

But in 1900 all of this remained several years in the future. The AAC's 1900 gathering in many ways proved a promising success even in the eyes of many of the radicals. It had produced the largest revenue from delegates' fees to date.[72] The finance committee reported on its work in raising funds for a test case challenge to disfranchisement in the South. In response the delegates voted in support of a motion to keep "all moneys collected for the purpose of testing the validity of laws" separate from general funds, "to be used for no other purpose."[73] Even Washington's apparent effort to diminish the AAC's success by suppressing turnout had backfired; with some of Washington's closest supporters missing, dissident voices could again become stronger. The *New York Times* reported rumors "that trouble will be made by some of the Afro-Americans who are angry with the administration."[74] More cautious and politically ambitious leaders concerned about the political consequences of attending again stayed away. The radicals once more pushed for strong language denouncing President McKinley for his continued failure to take a strong stand against lynching and other race-related violence, and the delegate resolutions stated the following quite forcefully: "Resolved, That we are heartily grieved that the president of the United States and those in authority have not from time to time used their high station to voice the best conscience of the nation in regard to mob violence and the fair treatment of justly deserving men."[75]

The 1900 meeting marked the apex of the radicals' ability to influence the AAC—at least until they began putting pressure on it from outside by founding the Niagara Movement. The AAC's annual meeting the next year was held in Philadelphia. The meeting was calmer but also less well attended.[76] This time some of the radicals, including Du Bois and Wells Barnett, stayed away, and Washington's close associate Scott took over from Du Bois as head of the AAC's Business Bureau. Important organizational business took place, as reported by AAC secretary Gertrude Mossell, the journalist and former *Age* columnist who was a very active club woman and championed women's entry into the professions.[77] Lawson reported on the receipt of test case funding from a generous anonymous donor (Washington himself, though very few knew this), which caused the audience to erupt in cheers.[78] The delegates voted that all affiliated organizations should set aside one day a month to collect money to aid the work of the council and endorsed resolutions calling for national legislation to make the government answerable for the lynching of U.S. citizens just as for foreigners. Other resolutions opposed the federal government engaging in race discrimination in selecting Americans to represent the country in its newly acquired possessions and asked Congress to appoint a commission to inquire into the status of the Afro-American race.[79]

Although the AAC was perceptibly shifting toward Washington, it continued to maintain an insistent tone in its public statements. This made the Tuskegee machine unhappy. Washington's chief lieutenant, Scott, worried that opposition to disfranchisement had been "too violently expressed" and had been covered in the white press.[80] The radicals, however, failed to foresee the much more dramatic tilting in the organization's delicately maintained balance that was about to occur. The next year, at the organization's fifth annual meeting, held in July 1902 in St. Paul, Minnesota, the radicals had a local base. This was the hometown of Ransom's and Du Bois's ally McGhee, and he agreed to serve as chair of the local organizing committee. Still an AAC loyalist, McGhee devoted himself to planning a fair and balanced meeting. A lawyer known for his abundant energy, attention to detail, and volubility, McGhee intended to host an impressive, even ornate, meeting. As his biographer details, McGhee's plans included classical music programs, special stationery designed for the event, and a formal dress ball to cap off the last day of the proceedings.[81]

The St. Paul meeting achieved a respectable attendance of fifty authorized delegates, plus many more who turned out for the public meeting programs. Its organizers again strived to achieve balance in political perspective. Josephine Yates, president of the NACW, delivered one of the principal evening addresses, urging unity of purpose and organization and espousing the Tuskegean message that African Americans should focus on working hard and abandon attempts to influence politics or legislation. Du Bois spoke from a different perspective on the problem of work, agreeing with Washington and Yates about the importance of economic and labor issues but not their ideas about strategy. Washington attended and delivered a speech emphasizing the need for patience and hard work and thanking

Figure 5.2 Fredrick McGhee, attorney and counselor at law, from 1903 Washington Conference on the Race Problem in the United States (New York Public Library).

the race's "white friends."[82] Lawson, as chair of the AAC's legal bureau, reported on its test case litigation challenging the grandfather clause in Louisiana's new constitution. He also highlighted pending national legislation on which the AAC was working. One proposal the AAC developed would create a commission for investigating the condition of African Americans, while another would amend the Interstate Commerce Act to prohibit common carriers from discriminating against interstate passengers on the basis of race.[83]

In its substantive aspects the meeting thus continued to be productive, offering the promise that concerted political and legal activity on pressing pragmatic concerns could continue despite obvious disagreements on underlying philosophies and long-term goals. The major players could have continued to agree to disagree had not major trouble broken out during the business meeting. These troubles signaled the beginning of the end of the radicals' willingness to work through the AAC toward shared pragmatic political and civil rights goals.

Stage Two: Washington Attempts to Seize Control

The trouble at the 1902 meeting involved procedural maneuvers that ended with Fortune's surprise election as the AAC's next president. The radicals viewed Fortune, probably correctly, as now deeply under Washington's influence. In turn, Fortune had become a publicly outspoken foe of the radicals within the AAC. Erratic and cantankerous as well, Fortune was in the radicals' eyes one of the least acceptable AAC leaders. But behind-the-scenes work of William Pledger, a former Georgia politician and soldier who was also known as a Washington loyalist, with assistance from Fortune and Scott, produced a patently rigged scheme that managed to install a figurehead president through which Washington apparently believed he would be able to control the AAC.

This coup, as both Justesen and Alexander tell the tale, apparently went down this way: During the middle of the business proceedings, when most of the delegates were absent to take part in a late lunch break, the few remaining delegates received a report from the nominating committee that recommended switching Walters and Fortune in their respective leadership posts. Fortune was at the time serving as chair of the executive committee, so this recommendation would install him as president. Although the presentation of the nominating committee report had been scheduled for later on the conference agenda, the delegates in the room were asked to vote to approve the report. They were then informed that their vote had been not merely to approve the nominating committee's report for transmission to the full delegate assembly but also to complete the act of electing the organization's officers.[84] The delegates returning from lunch arrived to the startling news that Fortune had been elected president during their lunch break, and he now assumed the gavel to preside over the rest of the meeting. Attempts to protest Fortune's asserted election met with Fortune vigorously gaveling the dissenters out of order, stating that he was willing to entertain only motions to adjourn. The next day opponents of the election results again sought to protest the procedural irregularities of the preceding day but failed to reverse the course of events. The radicals had been surprised and outmaneuvered, and the election results stood.[85]

The results thrilled Washington's acolytes. As Scott wrote in the aftermath of the meeting, "we control the Council now...It was wonderful to see how completely your personality dominated everything at St. Paul."[86] But a number of delegates who had previously held their tongue about the AAC's failings, including Du Bois and McGhee, publicly protested what had taken place in comments to the press covering the event.[87] McGhee continued his work on behalf of the AAC for at least another year; Du Bois decided on the basis of what had happened in St. Paul not to attend any future AAC meetings.[88] Wells Barnett withdrew her participation from the AAC as well. Even Edward Cooper, the editor of Colored American, previously a reliable Tuskegee ally, was fed up, describing the meeting as a "roaring farce."[89] Washington Bee editor Calvin Chase, long an irascible and erratic commentator on the AAC as well as other organizations, used the most vivid imagery of any commentator in describing the 1902 meeting. As he described it, Washington's "satellites were in the saddle.... They trotted and pranced as he pulled the reins and his ticket was elected and his namby-pamby policy...was incorporated into the address, which was noth- ing more than a pronouncement of his Nibs, the boss of Negro beggars."[90]

What had been a delicately managed balance among competing viewpoints and philosophies had developed into an all-out war, and the AAC's organizational health would suffer as a result. Far less public activity took place over the rest of that year, prompting further grumblings in the African American press. The *Colored American* queried, "The question is often asked, What is the National Afro-American Council doing now-a-days? Does its function end in holding national conventions, or has it other work to do? There is plenty of work for a national race organization to do. Has brother McGhee laid aside the harness...?"[91] The *Broad Ax* opined that, although Fortune might in other circumstance not be a bad choice, "viewed in light of present events it is about as bad a calamity as could have befallen the organization"—in part because Fortune appeared to be desperately seeking a political appointment at the time.[92]

This newspaper's prediction proved prescient. By the year's end, Fortune had convinced President Roosevelt to send him as a special envoy to study labor conditions in Hawaii and the Philippines. Accordingly, AAC president Fortune suddenly announced plans to be absent from the country for the next half year. But before departing, he left behind for others to execute his ideas on how to generate greater membership for the council. Joining in the negative chorus about the AAC, he began by asserting that the "official board of the organization really constitutes the only members of the National Council from the adjournment of one annual convention to the assembling of another." As a remedy Fortune called for the formation of at least five hundred local councils of at least ten persons each by the time of the AAC's next annual meeting. He added, "I am reasonably certain that the women of the race will take hold of the work."[93] With the future organizing success of the AAC thus delegated to "the women of the race," Fortune departed, leaving Pledger to fill in for him in his absence.

But again Washington's attempt to control the AAC fell short of success. The swap of Fortune and Walters in their respective AAC leadership positions left Walters with opportunities for new tactics because he now headed the AAC's very active executive committee. With Fortune out of the country, Walters went on the lecture circuit to urge African Americans to protest disfranchisement.[94] The executive committee came together for its regular meeting in January 1903, at which it issued an updated address to the nation that sounded very much like those drafted under Walters's presidency. The address continued to hit on many of the same insistent demands, calling for an end to disfranchisement and praising local efforts to combat disfranchisement in Virginia, Alabama, and Louisiana. It also protested the South's peonage system and Jim Crow train car laws and urged passage of legislation to investigate the social and economic conditions of African Americans throughout the country.[95] It decided to take its disfranchisement campaign to the Republican Party as well. The executive committee worked on strategies to combat so-called lily whitism within the Republican Party and issued a formal public statement urging the party's next national convention to support suffrage rights for African Americans.[96]

In short, even though the AAC's top leadership now included many Bookerite loyalists, it was not possible for Washington to steer the organization so that it would take a sharp turn in a more conservative direction. Washington could not suppress the voices of activists like Walters, who never attacked Washington personally but continued to make strong civil rights statements. The Tuskegee machine's pressure tactics did not work on figures in Walters's situation, who held secure positions within independent institutions that Washington could not threaten with a cutoff of funds.[97]

Another factor that contributed to the AAC's continued militancy even after Washington's attempted coup was the presence of external pressure from an alternative antidisfranchisement organizing effort that Boston radical William Monroe Trotter and Virginia civil rights lawyer James Hayes had begun. A public meeting held in conjunction with the AAC's 1903 executive committee meeting featured a speech by Hayes, who was one of the lawyers handling litigation efforts in his state to challenge its new constitution's disfranchising provisions. A report in the *Washington Post* quoted Hayes as having used incendiary rhetoric in which, to enthusiastic applause, he allegedly "declared that the negro has now reached the limit of his endurance, and advocated the sword and the torch as a means for the negro to maintain his manhood." This kind of speaking went beyond anything the AAC had previously endorsed and quickly led to an outpouring of refutations, responses, and commentary.[98] The direction in which national antidisfranchisement efforts would head thus remained murky and would become only more so at the AAC's next annual meeting.

The AAC's next convention, held in Louisville in July 1903, again became a site of controversy as Fortune, newly returned from the Philippines, won reelection as president after "stormy debate" about the nominating committee's report recommending Fortune's reelection. Trotter and others also vociferously protested after Washington's loyalists put his portrait on the stage of the meeting auditorium.[99] The white press amply covered a lengthy speech Washington delivered, in which he urged calm and the avoidance of violence, after which the delegates adopted resolutions endorsing these sentiments.[100] A large crowd attended the evening public meeting, but a dissenting group walked out to attend the meeting Trotter and Hayes had scheduled nearby to discuss the formation of an organization to be called the National Afro-American Suffrage Convention.[101] Longtime AAC leaders such as McGhee, who was at the time serving as national financial secretary, tried to put a good face on the meeting, emphasizing the important work done in calling on President Roosevelt to recommend to Congress the passage of a voting rights law, as well as federal anti–Jim Crow and antilynching legislation.[102] McGhee would later report, however, that he had privately remonstrated with Walters late into the night about the need to be more responsive to Hayes and his fellow dissenters' disfranchisement work. He also complained about how a "secret cabal" in control of the organization had practiced "bad faith" and "treachery" that cast a lie on his and others' years of "hard service" to the organization. McGhee explained that at this point he had begun to believe in the need for a new organization to stand for "the accomplishment of good, helpful and profitable ends." This view would soon lead him into the discussions with Du Bois, Ransom, and others that resulted in the founding of the Niagara Movement.[103]

The 1903 meeting produced similar conclusions in the minds of other AAC radicals as well. Harry Smith editorialized in his *Cleveland Gazette* that " '[m]uch as we regret to say it, the Council seems to have outlived its usefulness' due to 'the questionable methods of the Wizard of Tuskegee' and his anti-citizen and anti-civil rights propaganda."[104] Walters and others committed to the AAC continued to coop-erate with efforts to get a nationally coordinated antidisfranchisement campaign off the ground. Haynes spoke at mass meetings and cast his new antidisfranchisement effort as one being undertaken in coordination with, but not under the auspices of, the AAC.[105] In short, the AAC seemed to be losing its place at the forefront of civil rights leadership, even though Walters was trying mightily to maintain its relevance despite what was going on internally.

The AAC's seventh annual convention, held in St. Louis in September 1904, was the most conservative of all. Fortune had precipitously resigned from the presidency earlier that year following a major falling out with Washington. Their argument had apparently occurred after Fortune revealed to civil rights attorney Douglas Wetmore—who would soon take over the AAC's legal department—the highly guarded secret information that Washington had been involved in the Alabama test case litigation.[106] At this point Washington's patience with Fortune snapped completely, and he began to scheme to divest Fortune of his ownership of *The Age.*

Gone as well by 1904 was Walters's "delicate balance between the moderate and radical racial philosophies."[107] In its place emerged a Bookerite organizing model that sought to tightly control the AAC's public profile to avoid any grounds for the white press to engage in alarmist reporting about African American political mil-itancy. The call for the 1904 meeting thus announced that all speakers would be limited to twenty minutes and all speeches must be submitted in manuscript form prior to the meeting "in view of the fact that a portion of the Caucasian press of the country is ever ready to misrepresent the words of Afro-Americans."[108] This effort to put on an orchestrated show fell flat; few newspapers, African American or white, even reported on the meeting's occurrence.

At this point the AAC's continued relevance hung in serious doubt. But Walters was not one to give up easily. Acting in his capacity as chair of the executive com-mittee, he published an open letter in *The Age* in late July 1905, seeking to rally what he referred to as the AAC's "old guard." In this open letter Walters indirectly invoked his first letter that had gotten the AAC started, only this time he listed by name many high-profile figures now absent from the organization who had been active in the AAC's earlier years. In this list he included Wells Barnett, Fortune, Pinchback,

White, Arnett, Clinton, Dancy, Lyons, Murray, McGhee, Mossell, Lawson, and many others. Walters called on these prominent figures to return to a newly revived organization in order to continue working together to address the increasingly adverse conditions facing the nation's African Americans.[109]

Walters's call came too late; by the time he published it, Du Bois, McGhee, Trotter, Ransom, and several dozen others had already received considerable press attention for pulling off the Niagara Movement's founding in mid-July 1905.[110] The radicals were winning the public relations war. As one newspaper put it, on the one hand, "[t]he old apologetic Afro-American council is dying of inanity, the Booker T. Washington 'lay low and keep dark' policy has nauseated the manly Negro, and the lack of proper leadership was falling like a pall upon the race." On the other hand, however, Du Bois does not "tickle" with derogatory anecdotes but instead stands "as earnest as Garrison, as cultured as Sumner, and as unyielding as Douglass."[111]

Stage Three: Reviving the AAC

Thus the tide of enthusiasm was receding from the AAC, but still Walters persevered. Staking his reputation on the project, he continued throughout the year to promote the AAC and the need for unity in national organizing around the pressing political and civil rights issues confronting the race. In August 1905 an AAC annual meeting took place in Detroit, spurred by Walters's call.[112] Only a limited number of delegates attended. In what must have felt like a collective burst of relief, they reelected Walters to the position of president. The delegates took other steps to revitalize the organization as well, appointing up-and-coming litigator Judson Douglas Wetmore of Florida, who was pursuing test case litigation against Jim Crow streetcar legislation in that state, as the new head of the legal and legislative bureau. Wetmore had gained a measure of notoriety in activist circles for his role in engineering an exciting but short-lived victory against a 1905 Florida statute known as the Avery Law, which mandated the physical separation of the races on streetcars in the state. Born in 1870 and raised in Florida by two parents of partial African descent, Wetmore had attended a year of formal law school education at the University of Michigan Law School. There, he later told friends, he had passed as white.[113] He then returned to Jacksonville and gained admission to the bar without the problems that beset his darker African American colleagues. Wetmore opened a law practice with the young James Weldon Johnson, who later would become an important Harlem Renaissance writer as well a key national staffer for the NAACP. Wetmore and Johnson had been childhood friends, and Wetmore (disguised as a figure referred to as "D.—") serves as a significant character in the chapters of Johnson's autobiography that recount his younger years, offering an opportunity to gain some insights into this elusive figure's personality. According to Johnson, the young Wetmore was handsome and cynical and possessed a "rough and tumble style" that made him an effective speaker. He had successes in business and local politics, always followed by predictable lows.[114] In 1905 Wetmore won a seat on the city council for a term, but the deteriorating political prospects for African Americans in the state were obvious, and, like many other African American lawyers of his generation in the South, Wetmore eventually decided to head North, moving to New York City in 1908.

Before making this decision, however, Wetmore tried another strategy designed to enhance African American civil rights prospects in his hometown. With fellow African American lawyer Isaac Lawrence Purcell, Wetmore undertook to engineer a test case strategy much like the one the Citizens' Committee had used in the *Plessy* litigation. Wetmore and Purcell worked with the local streetcar company, which disliked the additional expense imposed by the Avery bill, to stage a test case through which their chosen plaintiff, the fifty-year-old Andrew Patterson, would be arrested for refusing to comply with the segregation mandate. The streetcar line had a predominantly African American ridership, and it had complied with the segregation mandate by screening off a few seats in the *back* of the car for whites. Newspaper reports noted the confusion and irony caused when Patterson insisted on sitting in those seats to bring about his arrest. Delivered by streetcar right to the courthouse, Patterson declined to post bail at his arraignment, and Wetmore filed a writ of habeas corpus alleging that the arrest had been illegal because the law under which it had been made was unconstitutional.[115]

Wetmore and Purcell's strategy focused on a technical flaw in the Florida statutory system: Rather than using formally equivalent or race-neutral terms to define an exemption from the separate-seating mandate for African American nurses attending white adult patients or children, the Avery Law specified that only "colored" nurses attending whites were exempted from the mandate that they sit in segregated seating. Wetmore argued that this race-specific language violated the privileges and immunities language of the Fourteenth Amendment's Equal Protection Clause. He won on this argument before the lower court, and the state appealed but lost. In a classic illustration of formalist reasoning detached from the reality of the world outside the courthouse walls, the Florida court held that the statute was unconstitutional on the grounds that it discriminated against *whites*. The court reasoned that, by allowing African American nurses the right to attend patients in either kind of cars but not "the African mistress the equal right to have her child attended in the African department of the car by its Caucasian nurse," the statute withheld "from the Caucasian nurse the same privilege." The court further accepted Wetmore's argument that the rest of the Avery statute had to be struck down because the invalid provision affected the legislature's overall intent.[116]

Patterson I was thus a victory, and the residents of Jacksonville reveled in it, riding conspicuously in the city's streetcars to show they knew and appreciated the significance of the Avery Law's invalidation. The victory was short lived, how-ever; the next year several Florida municipalities simply drafted new ordinances that contained appropriately "formally equal" language exempting nurses of either race who were administering to the needs of different-race children or invalid patients.[117]

Wetmore and Purcell staged two more test cases to challenge these new ordi-nances. This time, however, the state's highest court, in an opinion written by the same judge who had drafted *Patterson I*, rejected the plaintiff's lawyers' expanded set of arguments. The court ruled that now there was no constitutional flaw in the municipalities' Jim Crow ordinances because they ostensibly gave "equal" treat-ment to both races of nurses attending cross-race clients. Wetmore and Purcell tried to pursue the court's reasoning in *Patterson I* by pointing out that the Florida statute denied African Americans—but not whites—the seat of their choice on streetcars, but the court brushed this argument aside with the statement that "a passenger has no right to any particular seat."[118] In short, the court's focus on for-mal equality ignored the socially understood meaning of the practice under chal-lenge. African American women could ride in first-class cars only as servants or caretakers of whites and not as femininely gendered citizens deserving of civility and respect.[119]

The U.S. Supreme Court ended the *Patterson* test case challenges when it denied Wetmore's appeal from the Florida high court decisions. But *Patterson I* neverthe-less stood as one of only a few state supreme court victories on Jim Crow issues during the era. Wetmore emerged with an enhanced national profile and reputa-tion and professed his continuing determination to seek new avenues for test case challenges.[120]

Given his promising, even if ultimately unsuccessful, track record in civil rights litigation, Wetmore was an excellent pick to head a newly revived AAC Legal Affairs Bureau. He was well known, had succeeded in a civil rights case before his state's highest court despite the great odds against such a result, and had energy, ambition, and plans to do more. Wetmore represented a particular type of AAC lawyer-activist, one who focused on civil and political rights, viewed the courts as the primary vehicle for pursuing those rights, and insisted on relentlessly pursuing formal equality principles through this route. He became something of a folk hero, with one editor writing that his victory against Jim Crow in Jacksonville "will be heard down the ages" and that civil rights organizations should hire only lawyers like Wetmore and McGhee, rather than white lawyers, to begin systematically test-ing the unconstitutionality of all discriminatory Southern laws.[121]

Wetmore had also, by 1905, begun to alienate Washington, who viewed him as having "too high an opinion of himself" and "lacking in good breeding and com-mon sense." Wetmore was bold and brash and something of an entrepreneur who attempted to play both sides in the conflict between Washington's supporters and opponents, not realizing that observers were reporting his actions to Washington.

Wetmore did not last long as a leading civil rights lawyer—and, indeed, "crossed over" to live as white in New York City in his later years. But at the time of his appointment he seemed to exemplify the AAC's hopes for a future that would include bolder test case litigation. [122]

Wetmore's appointment was but one indication of the AAC's delegates' determination to rally around Walters's renewed call for political and civil rights activism. The returning delegates hoped for the revival of an AAC united around a common platform of formal civil and political rights equality. The meeting's list of speakers and elected officers again exhibited a balance in both ideological perspectives and gender composition, including a speech by Mary Church Terrell and her reelection to one of nine vice president positions and to head of the antilynching bureau, as well as a speech and reappointment to the literary bureau of prominent Chicago club woman and Washington supporter Fannie B. Williams.

As the meeting opened, *The Age* signaled that the AAC intended to return to its founding focus on constitutional test case litigation, declaring that the meeting's central purpose was "to put in motion the forces that will bring to a test in the highest courts of the nation the constitutionality of every law that aims to oppress and restrict the rights and privileges of the Afro-American citizen."[123] The tenor of the delegates' address to the nation, as reported by and probably drafted in substantial part by Fortune, continued to demand political and civil rights, including reemphasizing that the AAC's request was for "justice and fair play under the laws as a legal right, and for an 'open door of opportunity' in the effort we are making for moral, social and material betterment." The address further urged the African American people to contribute to testing in court all state laws that denied equal benefits of protection of government as guaranteed by the federal constitution and called for the end of the time in which African Americans would be the object of "class legislation" under laws that they had no part in making because of laws disqualifying them from voting. Rather than pushing for a reduction in electoral representation in the South as the AAC's previous addresses to the nation had done, this 1905 address merely noted the South's comparatively unfair advantage on this score. Finally, the address pointed to the grave problem of employment discrimination in the North as African Americans moved there from the South.[124]

The next summer, *The Age* announced that the AAC's next scheduled annual meeting would continue with these goals. As *The Age* declared:

> The AAC at its meeting in New York next October will make a vigorous effort to organize a financial campaign for raising the funds necessary to employ one of the most famous lawyers in the country to put the issue of disfranchisement up to the Supreme Court. This purpose should enlist the instant support of the whole Afro-American people. The great churches, led by such bishops as [Henry McNeal] Turner and Walters, should use their centralized organizations to command the financial support of the

great masses whom the churches only are able to reach with effectiveness and promptitude.[125]

With greater ideological balance and, along with it, a more vibrant organization reemerging, the 1906 AAC annual meeting, held in October in New York City, lived up to the impression organizers were hoping for—namely, that the AAC was continuing on an upswing. The meeting saw an increase in attendance along with another set of addresses from a balanced list of both African American and white civil rights spokespersons. Newspapers reported that attendees raised a thousand dollars at the meeting, adding to the six hundred dollars already collected to set the AAC on its way toward its goal of amassing a great defense fund to "test the disfranchising and 'jim crow' car laws that oppress the Negro race in this land of ours." Walters delivered a speech that "was unquestionably one of the ablest presentations of the case of the Negro that this generation has ever listened to," in which he made a "manly plea for justice," urged the federal government to become involved in stopping mob violence, attacked the grandfather clause, and urged federal aid for education. Other speakers included Fortune, Wetmore, Church Terrell, William Bulkley, and Washington, resulting in a session "characterized by a harmony and good fellowship that speaks well for the future."[126] The speakers' list also included figures who would soon lead the call for founding a new biracial organization. One of these was Oswald Garrison Villard, the New York City publisher of *The Nation* and the *New York Evening Post,* who also held the distinction of being the grandson of the great abolitionist William Lloyd Garrison. Villard would become chair of the NAACP just a few years later. He would import to that project the ideas about ambitious test case litigation he heard the AAC discussing at its 1906 convention.

In his 1906 speech before the AAC convention, Villard praised it for its work in attempting to mount legal cases to test the principles of citizenship equality: "I am here merely to add, for what it is worth, my word of approval to the aims of the Afro American Council, whose cry is: 'Organize, organize, organize.' " Villard described what he had learned about the AAC's agenda and envisioned an even grander future: "The Afro American Council asks for a fund to carry to the Supreme Court the question of the ballot in the South. It ought to have a national defence [*sic*] fund reaching into the hundreds of thousands of dollars for a hundred different purposes.... It should be able to fight in the courts every unjust discrimination, to protect and aid threatened or injured colored schools, and to generally supervise the welfare of the race." Three years later Villard would recycle almost these same words in describing the founding objectives of the NAACP.[127]

Another speaker at the 1906 AAC meeting was John Milholland, founder of a biracial, primarily New York–based organization named the Constitution League. Milholland had made a substantial fortune as the inventor of a pneumatic tube method for sending messages between city buildings via underground air tunnels. He, too, would go on to play a role in founding the NAACP, and his organization, whose contribution consisted primarily of offering substantial funding for a number of public meetings and other well-timed acts of assistance, would help show the way in which racial justice activism might develop in more biracial directions.[128]

1906 Civil Rights Outrages: Tipping Point

The year 1906 saw two major civil rights outrages that would turn out to be the tipping point in race justice activists' patience with talk of incrementalist strategies. In September 1906 the city of Atlanta exploded in a race riot precipitated by false rumors spread in the white press of black on white sexual violence. Race leaders spoke with wrath from various parts of the country, but Washington and his allies, including Fortune writing in *The Age,* criticized these speeches as the hypocritical talk of Northerners who lacked the bravery to face conditions in the South.[129] In addition, just one month earlier, a group of decorated African American soldiers stationed near Brownsville, Texas, had been accused of being involved in an incident in which an unidentified group had fired from a distance on a saloon, resulting in the killing of a white person. The entire regiment of 165 African American men had been dishonorably discharged without a trial and despite evidence pointing to their innocence. President Roosevelt had refused to intercede on the soldiers' behalf, and Washington had remained characteristically silent about the matter, not wishing to criticize the president, on whom his patronage power depended.

The especially sharp injustice of the Brownsville incident, in which decorated African American soldiers were treated dishonorably and with no due process, spurred moderate race leaders like Mary Church Terrell to greater militancy. Washington's refusal to join in the efforts of Church Terrell and others to encourage Roosevelt to act on the soldiers' behalf became the tipping point in her and other previously cautious race leaders' willingness to criticize the Tuskegean.

Church Terrell had been one of the cofounders and incorporators of the Constitution League in 1905. When John Milholland called Church Terrell to ask her to request a meeting with Secretary of War Taft, she readily agreed to do so. She quickly secured the interview, during which Taft agreed to bring the matter up with Roosevelt, although to no avail as things turned out. As one scholar has aptly noted, in her quick response Church Terrell seemed to surprise herself as well as Milholland; this act became an important step in her individual journey toward a greater boldness in action even when it meant potentially damaging her high social standing and political connections.

The Constitution League allowed moderates to work on the Brownsville injustice and other matters without having to venture into the ideological wars that plagued other organizations. As she became more involved, Church Terrell began to speak and write openly of her anger at Roosevelt and in only slightly more veiled terms about her disapproval of Washington. Her husband, formerly regarded as a Bookerite in light of his indebtedness to Washington for his judicial appointment, seemed to agree with his wife.[130]

On a general collective level as well, the two fall 1906 incidents escalated a mood of indignation, as African American churches held coordinated meetings on the topics across the country and pastors preached about what had taken place.[131] Brownsville and Atlanta, in other words, helped destabilize the status quo; the events shook up settled assumptions in a way that led even moderates to rethink their views and gain a greater willingness to speak out in more militant terms.[132] A new era was on the verge of beginning.

The AAC's End

In its last years the AAC would play a key role in bringing about this transition to a new era, especially by transmitting its collective knowledge and experience to allow a new organization to take off from the ground previously achieved. By 1907 it was clear that a new stage was beginning, but it was not yet clear what the new arrangements would be. Lawyers certainly would play a role, but what that role would be was still being defined as various organizational models, ideas, and resources competed for future control. Drawing on its new lawyer talent, the AAC offered legal bureau chair Wetmore as counsel to represent the falsely accused Brownsville soldiers.[133] Wetmore boldly announced that his plan would include offering federal legislation to deprive the president and Secretary of War William Howard Taft of the power to discharge soldiers without trial.[134] Walters delivered perhaps his most incendiary address ever before an overflow crowd at Chicago's Bethel AME church, openly attacking Roosevelt and advocating that African Americans rebel against the government. Interspersed in this uncharacteristically strong talk, Walters set forth "the doctrines of the Afro-American Council."[135]

Walters also issued his strongest call yet for the organization's annual meeting, to be held in June 1907 in Baltimore. Reenthused, former critics saw a renewed possibility that the AAC "might accomplish some good in the future," provided that "its officers will refrain from permitting Booker T. Washington and the politicians to control its actions."[136] The Baltimore meeting saw fifty official delegates in attendance and a strong emphasis on unity and cooperation. Niagara Movement leader Lafayette Hershaw shared the podium with the AAC's leaders. Fortune debated with Church Terrell and Wells Barnett, who had also heeded Walters's call to return to the AAC's fold, as well as old AAC veterans Dancy and Clinton, about the challenges of developing a mass membership for a national organization. In addition, W. H. H. Hart became legal director, and Walters, Archibald Grimké, and others made many "vigorous and manly speeches."[137] In a later editorial, Fortune wrote about the difficulties of fund-raising at sufficient levels to sustain a national organization. He also found ways to praise the AAC and criticize the Niagara Movement.[138]

Walters's lengthy convention speech summarized the AAC's history and assessed which of its principles remained unchanged and which had shifted over the course of the decade. Noting that its ten core principles remained just as apposite as they had been at the organization's founding, Walters laid heavy emphasis on the need for fund-raising and continued pursuit of test case litigation "even if it should take 50 to 100 years to establish the principle that African Americans should be subject to the same treatment as all other citizens under law." He further noted the dire need for paid staff to undertake the work needed to accomplish such results.[139] Washington then took the podium to urge calm after the Atlanta riot, followed by Milholland of the Constitution League, who emphasized the way in which ill treatment of African Americans hurt the nation as a whole. In all, the event unfolded as a grand and unified display of both intra- and interracial solidarity.

At the same time, the real game was shifting to the attempt to form a new organization that would amalgamate the leadership of the AAC, Niagara Movement, and Constitution League. By now, other new organizing efforts were also in play. In 1908 Rev. J. Milton Waldron, formerly one of the most active leaders within the Niagara Movement, founded the National Negro American Political League (NNAPL). This organization's stated primary aim was to force more accountability from the Republican Party. Waldron was to be its chief officer, with support from a committee that included Walters, representing the AAC, and Trotter, representing the Niagara Movement. It was clear that, whatever shape future national organizing efforts might take, they were not going to remain under the AAC's control.[140]

The AAC never met again, but Walters's leadership role would continue with his participation in the NNAPL and then at the 1909 National Negro Conference, at which the NAACP would be born. He would serve as a member of that organization's steering committee and then transfer to the NAACP's founding board and serve as a local vice president in New York City. Walters's involvement in the early NAACP was short lived due to a clash with Villard, but before he resigned in 1913 he would transmit some of the wisdom he gained through his leadership of the AAC to a new generation of activists, especially as they struggled with the crucial issues of organizational design.

"Should Not a Nation Be Just to All of Her Citizens?": The Afro-American Council's Legal Work, 1898–1908

The story of the AAC's tumultuous organizational history can easily overshadow the important contributions its law-related experiments made to civil rights history. To be sure, the AAC often did look like a careening ship that had lost its rudder as battles took place on its deck for leadership control. And these battles did interfere with the AAC's ability to pursue its legal agenda despite the consensus within the organization about these goals. Nonetheless, the AAC managed to carry out experiments in both the test case litigation and federal legislative arenas that would shape the subsequent direction of national civil rights activism. This chapter examines what, precisely, those experiments were. Its aim is to lay a basis for later tracing with concrete particularity the transmission of ideas and experiences, through identifiable leaders, from the AAC to early twentieth-century organization-building efforts.

In short summary, the AAC attempted one major piece of test case litigation attacking disfranchisement in the South and cooperated in several others, pursued a variety of avenues for challenging Jim Crow legislation, and had an active Washington, DC, presence in opposing harmful federal legislation and supporting a number of affirmative measures. On the organization's top priority issue of combating disfranchisement, the only litigation challenge it managed to file specifically under its own auspices, which challenged the grandfather clause in Louisiana's 1898 constitution, failed miserably, in part because the outside white lawyers hired to handle the case bungled it.[1] Many other factors also contributed to this result, including the disruptive and counterproductive shift in the AAC's leadership from Walters to Fortune in 1902 and a more general problem of having too many top officers issuing conflicting directives. The AAC's perennial difficulty in raising funds, especially sufficient funds for costly litigation, posed another key problem. Its centerpiece test case litigation took place before the rise of norms for pro bono legal representation in complex civil rights litigation. Later, one of the prominent legal figures who lent his legal advice to the AAC, Boston lawyer and former Massachusetts attorney general Albert E. Pillsbury, would argue as a member of the NAACP's first national legal committee that lawyers with well-paying clienteles should feel duty bound to take on civil rights cases for free.[2]

The AAC's troubles raising funds to finance test case litigation increased its dependence on Booker T. Washington for financial contributions at crucial junctures. At first, the Tuskegean promised to secretly raise funds from his white philanthropist contacts in the North, and he did so. But Washington disagreed fundamentally with the AAC's model of building an inclusive, democratically managed national movement. His discomfort with the AAC soon led him to decide to covertly finance his own litigation to challenge Alabama's grandfather clause, in the case known as *Giles v. Harris*. Washington's personal lawyer, Wilford Smith, managed this and two other related test cases with strategic brilliance, though he, too, would ultimately lose before the U.S. Supreme Court on the key issue of dismantling disfranchisement— but not without forcing a merits consideration and winning at least a symbolic victory on race discrimination in jury selection.

Without sufficient financial backing at critical moments, the AAC's centerpiece litigation effort ended in defeat. Its leaders certainly wanted to mount other test case challenges and possibly could have done so under Wetmore's new leadership—if the direction of race justice activism had not taken a turn in 1909 toward organizing a new group to bring together all activist factions and add white reformers to the mix.[3]

In its legislative work at the national level, as in its test case initiative, the AAC failed to bring about legal change. One could hardly expect otherwise, given the lack of national African American political clout during the nadir period, made all the worse by disfranchisement in the South. But the AAC activists' work in designing legislative initiatives contributed new ideas, some of which would eventually see fruition more than half a century later in the major federal civil rights acts of the 1960s. Historians often overlook these legislative experiments in focusing primarily on early civil rights test case strategies. But these legislative initiatives are also important in revealing how AAC activists thought about the proper scope and use of law, what obstacles they encountered in seeking law-related solutions to racial subordination, and why they formed and passed on to future generations the particular foundational legal ideas they held.

Establishing a Legal Action Agenda

At its inception, the AAC announced as its highest priority a plan to pursue a litigation and legislative agenda. Walters delivered the charge to develop such an agenda to the AAC's legal and legislative bureau in 1899. He and others never wavered from this commitment to promote citizenship equality through law. Thus any objective assessment of the goals of racial justice activists of this generation cannot ignore their early and resolute focus on the courts and on law generally. At the same time, these activists were not "legal liberals" in the modern sense of that term, which tends to connote a naïve faith in the courts as the most important protectors of human rights. The AAC activists' agenda was far more complex than that, but it did insist on pressing constitutional rights issues before the federal and state judiciaries, along with other strategies. Indeed, the AAC's central national agenda devoted less attention to economic uplift and social welfare work than any of the other national organizations examined in this book. This was not because its leaders did not care about these issues; they all did see economic and social welfare issues as top priorities. But they differed in their views about how to make progress on these issues, as we have already seen. In addition, the AAC's leaders viewed their work as closely associated with and complementary to that of their "sister" organization, the NACW, which was engaging in rich experiments on social welfare matters during the same period, as further discussed in chapter 7.

The AAC emphasized its legal focus in its earliest public statements, and by 1900 it had announced ambitious plans to back antilynching legislation sponsored by AAC member George H. White, the last African American to serve in Congress in the post-Reconstruction era. It also announced its imminent filing of a test case to challenge Louisiana's grandfather clause disfranchisement provision, and it vowed to carry out a massive fund-raising effort to accomplish these and other legal objectives.[4] A subcommittee of prominent African American Republicans took on the task of pushing the Republican National Convention on antilynching and disfranchisement issues as well.[5] Lawyer Fredrick McGhee of Minnesota spoke as "the attorney for the Afro-American Council" at a meeting held at Ransom's Bethel AME Church in Chicago, which the AAC called to raise funds for a constitutional challenge to disfranchisement in the South. The AAC activists organized similar meetings in other locations as well.[6]

Once the AAC decided to hire counsel to initiate test case litigation, it faced the problem of having sufficient funds on hand to meet the periodic financial demands of such a litigation campaign. As well as holding mass meetings, it began a letter-writing fund-raising campaign, sending appeals for funds that would be specially dedicated to testing the Louisiana law in court.[7] Some money was raised in this way, though certainly far less than would be needed. A second possible avenue for fund-raising depended on reaching individuals with the ability to write large checks. That plan depended on Booker T. Washington's cooperation since he so carefully cultivated and guarded his contacts within the white race-progressive philanthropic community, where most such large pots of wealth that might be channeled to race work could be found. A volley of correspondence began between Jesse Lawson, representing the AAC's legislative and legal affairs bureau—or sometimes Walters, as AAC president—on the one hand, and Washington or his chief lieutenant, Emmett Scott, on the other. Lawson repeatedly assured Washington that the AAC was making progress on the litigation strategy it had chosen to pursue and that all it needed were crucial additional funds to continue with this work.[8] On Washington's side, replies at first consisted of checks in not insignificant amounts of one to two hundred dollars, along with promises to pursue more from his white contacts in the North. Washington's papers show that he did solicit for the AAC from these contacts, writing, for example, to Francis Jackson Garrison, son of abolitionist William Lloyd Garrison, for a contribution.[9]

At the AAC's 1901 annual meeting, organizers announced these substantial contributions as having come from an anonymous donor, "Mr. X.Y.Z.," eliciting huge applause from the audience.[10] Some of the delegates may have had an inkling as to who this generous benefactor was, but most of the audience was cheering simply because they approved the legal bureau's fund-raising success. In the broader sphere of the African American community, including its press outlets, Washington's support for antidisfranchisement litigation remained unknown. Indeed, somewhat ironically, Washington's public insistence on remaining disassociated from the AAC's antidisfranchisement campaign produced the harshest critiques African American journalists leveled against him.[11] What these critics did not know was that, by 1902, Washington was secretly sponsoring test cases of his own.

Washington began this effort after his attempts to work behind the scenes in his home state to head off disfranchisement failed. Even after he and all other African Americans were disinvited from an 1899 Montgomery conference organized to discuss the future of African American voting in the state, Washington continued to maintain polite relations with the well-meaning but "racist and Southern sectionalist" leader of the initiative to exclude African Americans from the franchise.[12] This initiative succeeded, with the state deciding to adopt new constitutional provisions, including a grandfather clause, that Washington clearly saw for their blatantly racially exclusionary intent. But Washington still said nothing publicly against the convention delegates' actions—and prudently could not have done so, given the precarious position of his school in a state whose white majority was not known for friendly feelings toward African Americans generally.[13]

Secretly, however, Washington was impressively bold, using money, possibly gained from Andrew Carnegie's increasingly generous bequests, to sponsor a frontal attack on the constitutionality of the discriminatory provisions of the new constitution.[14] Unlike the AAC's case, Smith's challenges made it all the way to the U.S. Supreme Court. There Smith suffered defeat on his suffrage challenge, though a related challenge to the exclusion of African Americans from juries prevailed.

Attacking the Specifics of Disfranchisement

The disfranchising provisions of each Southern state's revised constitutions varied in their particulars but embodied a similar overall design. Their grandfather clause provisions were usually temporary measures that provided a short-term chance

for whites to register before new educational and property ownership requirements came into effect, purportedly to raise the general standards of the electorate.
Louisiana's scheme, for example, worked through several sections of Article 197 in
its 1898 amended constitution. Section 3 provided that an elector would henceforth have to demonstrate his ability to read and write when he applied for a voter
registration certificate, while Section 4 provided that, in the alternative, an elector
would be entitled to register if he showed that he was the bona fide owner of property valued at three hundred dollars or more.

In an approach many scholars now criticize in hindsight, not only the AAC but
many race leaders at the time accepted the legitimacy of heightened education and
property clauses provided they were fairly applied to all. These leaders bought into
a Progressive-era rhetoric that supported raising the quality of the electorate even
if doing so had a vastly disparate impact on African American voters. Race leaders
frequently urged African Americans to raise themselves up to the new standards
imposed rather than complain about them.[15]

The problem with Southern states' new constitutions in turn-of-the-century race
leaders' eyes had to do with the provisions that plainly did not accord equal treatment to white and African American voters who were similarly situated in their lack
of literacy or property. Thus the AAC's attack on the Louisiana constitution focused
solely on its grandfather clause contained in Section 5 of Article 197. That section
suspended for three and a half months, from May 16, 1898, to August 31, 1898,
the education and property qualifications in sections 3 and 4 for two categories of
voters: those who had been recently naturalized (thus ensuring that foreign-born
whites could vote) and those who on January 1, 1867, or before were entitled to
vote in any state of the union as well as their sons and grandsons over twenty-one
years of age.[16] That provision was race neutral in only the most transparently illegitimate sense since men formerly enslaved had not been entitled to vote prior to
the specified date. It was this patently race-based treatment that the AAC wanted
to attack.

To the AAC's credit, it managed to mount such a challenge, an impressive feat
in its own right. Less positively, it did so to disappointing results. The progress
and disposition of the case were full of the arcane legal and procedural technicalities typical of litigation during this era, but its ultimate, merits-related disposition
was clear: There would be no relief forthcoming because the case was purportedly
wrongly pled.

The AAC's Louisiana Challenge

More than a year passed between the AAC's announcement of its intention to file a
Louisiana test case as its top organizational priority and the actual filing of its petition in court. For reasons that remain unclear, the AAC representatives in charge of

the project—and it was often difficult to tell exactly who was in charge—decided to hire two white lawyers to pursue the case: Arthur A. Birney, who had helped found and then served as a longtime lecturer at Howard Law School and was a partner in a Washington, DC, law firm, and Armand Romain, a politically ambitious Republican lawyer from New Orleans, who was to serve as local counsel.[17] In litigation styled *Ryanes v. Gleason*, these lawyers presented David J. Ryanes as plaintiff and requested from the civil district court for the Orleans parish a writ of mandamus (in essence, an order of the court directing a public official to perform a specific duty) to order Jeremiah M. Gleason, the supervisor of voter registration for the parish, to instate Ryanes's name on the state's voter registration rolls.

Ryanes averred that he and all of his ancestors were of the African race, that he had been a voter in Louisiana for the past thirty years, that he could not read or write and owned no real property, and that neither he nor his father nor grandfather had been entitled to vote in 1867. He further alleged that when he presented himself to the Orleans parish registrar in July 1901 to apply to vote under the new system created by the 1898 amended constitution, he had been refused registration. Ryanes argued that his experience showed that the new system disfranchised only poor and illiterate persons of the African race but not similarly situated poor and illiterate whites, and for this reason it violated the Fourteenth and Fifteenth Amendments.[18]

Gleason responded by arguing that the court was without jurisdiction to hear the case and that the petition contained no valid cause of action. In August 1901 the Orleans parish court ruled in favor of Gleason, holding that no valid cause of action had been pled.[19] Although it was necessary to file a notice of appeal within a short deadline in order to preserve the option to appeal, Ryanes's lawyers did nothing for nine months after the decision, possibly because they lacked additional funds to proceed. Birney reported to the AAC that the case had been "subject to many delays and complications, arising from local and legal causes," and again the AAC issued an urgent appeal for more money to carry on the legal contest.[20] In April 1902 Romain filed a motion with the court asking that the July 1901 case be "discontinued" and at the same time filed a new petition making all the same allegations as the first but adding some general information on voter statistics. Gleason countered with the obvious argument that the case was *res judicata*—meaning that it had already been decided and thus could not be brought again. Gleason correctly noted that all the same parties and same elements were being alleged in the new case so that this doctrine properly applied to bar a second chance in court.

At this point the court held a brief hearing and took testimony from Ryanes, which included detailed documentary evidence showing the dramatic change in registration figures that had taken place after the 1898 constitution went into effect.[21] In July 1902 a different parish district court judge sustained Gleason's exception on *res judicata* grounds. This result was entirely to be expected because the Ryanes team in fact had filed and then abandoned its case the first time. This time the AAC seemed more prepared to proceed to an appeal. To do so it needed to produce additional funds of $100 to post an appeal bond, and it managed to do this on August 7, 1902. Two years later, by order of April 25, 1904, the Supreme Court of Louisiana disposed of this appeal by granting Gleason's motion to dismiss, agreeing with an argument Gleason had made that the court lacked jurisdiction over the appeal on state procedural law grounds.[22]

This disposition solely on state law procedural grounds barred Ryanes from seeking review by the U.S. Supreme Court, which does not review cases in which no question of federal law is presented. The AAC's first test case challenge to disfranchisement thus failed, leaving the AAC's litigation strategy in disarray: As McGhee put it in seeking to persuade Washington to attend the organization's 1902 annual meeting in St. Paul prior to the strategy's ultimate defeat, "[a]side from the Louisiana case, the Council has no well-defined course."[23] But the will to find a way to reach the merits of Southern states' disfranchising constitutions remained, despite the AAC lawyers' inability to find a litigation handle with which to hold on to the slippery legal issues involved.

At the same time that Washington was writing to Lawson about the AAC's need for funding for the *Ryanes* litigation, he was also communicating with white Boston lawyer Albert E. Pillsbury about this case. Pillsbury was a former Republican legislator and then attorney general of Massachusetts who, like many other white race progressives of his generation, counted abolitionists in his family background. He was something of an expert on the Commerce Clause, having argued and won, against expectations, a case defending the constitutionality of a Massachusetts statute that regulated the sale of oleomargarine. Retired from politics after he was passed over for his party's nomination for governor, Pillsbury described himself as maintaining a law practice "chiefly in connection with large corporate interests." He would also for many years contribute his services to racial justice causes, usually by advocating in writing and congressional testimony for federal antilynching legislation and serving as a consultant on litigation.

Pillsbury had agreed to assist in such a consultant capacity on the Louisiana test case.[24] Writing to Washington in July 1901, just as the initial petition in *Ryanes v. Gleason* was being filed, Pillsbury presciently worried that the court "may say that even if the Grandfather clause is void for unlawful discrimination between the races, it is separable from the educational and property qualifications…so that he is not entitled to vote whether the Grandfather clause is or is not unconstitutional."[25] Pillsbury further advised that the key would be to get the court to declare the entire scheme of suffrage qualifications unconstitutional. He warned, however, that "in view of the character of the subject and the disposition of the court to evade precipitating political issues by judicial decision," this could prove hard to accomplish. Pillsbury would turn out to be right about this, too, as Washington and his lawyer, Wilford Smith, would discover in their independent, top-secret attempt to mount a challenge to Alabama's disfranchising constitution a short time later.

Washington's Challenge to Disfranchisement in Alabama

Alabama's 1902 disfranchising provisions worked much like Louisiana's. As in Louisiana, Alabama's new constitution contained education and property quali-fications clauses: To be eligible to vote after January 1, 1903, a person had to be able to read and write any article of the U.S. Constitution, or either own or be the husband of an owner of forty acres of land or real or personal property assessed at $300 or more in the state. Moreover, as in Louisiana, Alabama's revised consti-tution added a grandfather clause to protect whites who were illiterate or lacked property from being knocked off the new voter registration rolls. Alabama's grand-father clause applied to all who had served honorably in the enumerated wars of the United States, including those on either side of the "war between the states," as well as all lawful descendants of persons who had so served.[26] Its constitution contained an understanding and character clause as well, which allowed registrars to include on voter rolls all persons who are "of good character and understand the duties and obligations of citizenship under a republican form of government." Both the grandfather and character and understanding clause provisions were to do their work during a brief and temporary effective period: Once registered under the new constitution but prior to January 1, 1903, a voter would remain eligible to vote for the rest of his life, whereas men who had been unable to qualify to vote prior to that date had to obtain registration subject to the property and education qualifications.[27]

Like most race leaders at the time, Washington did not object to education and property qualifications for voters. Instead, he wanted to attack the blatantly dis-criminatory purpose underlying Alabama's grandfather and character clauses. He especially wanted to mount a challenge in Alabama since this was his home turf. Moreover, his efforts to reason with legislators in connection with the state's con-stitutional convention had been summarily rebuffed.[28] This was a clear instance in which Washington's care to appear reasonable to whites had produced no benefits. However, Washington knew it would be a mistake to speak out publicly against the new Alabama constitution. This was for many reasons, not the least of which involved the safety of the Tuskegee Institute, located in rural Alabama with poten-tially hostile whites surrounding it. Washington thus opted for a supersecret opposi-tion strategy. Consulting with virtually no one other than his trusted assistant Scott, Washington hired a stellar African American lawyer who had no affiliation with the AAC, Wilford H. Smith, to mount a challenge to Alabama's constitution. Smith had recently moved to New York City from his prior practice in Galveston, Texas, and readily agreed to Washington's plan.

An 1883 graduate of Boston University School of Law, Smith was an impeccably dressed man with a long, well-groomed mustache and the starched, stand-up col-lar shirts and thin ties befitting a gentleman lawyer of his times. His first law prac-tice had been in the "Black Belt" of the Mississippi Delta. He then relocated to the city of Galveston, Texas, where he built a thriving practice out of a mix of personal injury, criminal defense, and insurance litigation against African American fraternal organizations. Two of his criminal cases involved the defense of representatives of an African American newspaper that had attacked unnamed Irish streetcar conductors for the rough handling of an African American female passenger. His clients had used intemperate language referring to "irish snides," a "mangy ape," and "pimps... descendants of Oscar Wilde; greasy curs, foul smelling scavengers [who] are imported to this country to insult and humiliate." Smith lost after the judge held that these words amounted to group libel against the city's railway conductors. The newspaper's editor was sentenced to a year in jail, while its business manager, also the article's author, paid a $100 fine.[29]

In other cases Smith had more success. These cases included the U.S. Supreme Court win in 1900, which earned him a national reputation and brought him to Washington's attention. That case involved a civil rights action Smith managed to sustain all the way to the U.S. Supreme Court, a huge accomplishment in itself during this judicial period, in which courts used every procedural device possible to avoid considering the merits of civil rights claims. Even more impressively, Smith had won before the Court in one of the very few decisions it rendered in favor of an African American civil rights litigant during this era. The case was *Carter v. Texas*, and in it the Court held that systematic exclusion of African Americans from a grand jury violated the Fourteenth Amendment's equal protection guarantee.[30] The Court reached this conclusion while adhering to its limited definition of the set of "civil rights" covered by the Fourteenth Amendment's privileges and immunities clause. As the Court saw it, discrimination on the basis of race on jury lists denied African Americans equal protection of the laws and was thus unconstitutional.[31] Although this win did not produce actual change in courts' practices, which continued to routinely discriminate in jury selection on racial grounds, it was an enormous symbolic gain.

Smith was first suggested to Washington by Emmett Scott, but Washington thoroughly vetted Smith in person before deciding to retain him. It was a match to Washington's long-term liking. Smith would remain Washington's personal lawyer throughout his lifetime, handling his most sensitive matters until the Tuskegean's death.[32] Washington appears to have trusted Smith for several reasons. First and most impressive was Smith's successful civil rights litigation record. Second, Smith appears to have had little or no interest in abstract matters of political theory and certainly none in the kinds of radical ideology that Washington deplored. Third, Smith had the circumspect, shrewd, and cool-headed manner that Washington respected. Indeed, the two men had similar personal styles and thus could understand and "read" each other in an environment in which much of what one thought and desired had to remain coded to avoid giving whites offense.

This side of Smith's personality is on display in his writing to a general audience. A lengthy piece Smith authored at around the same time that he was pursuing the

Alabama disfranchisement cases considered the topic of "Negroes and the Law." Smith's analysis reveals his jurisprudential commitments to a classic "civil rights" perspective. This was the term Smith used throughout his essay to summarize the legal matters at stake. Arguing that the Reconstruction-era amendments were adopted to secure "equal civil rights," Smith defined those rights fairly narrowly, with the key questions being whether "the negro can secure a fair and impartial trial in the courts, and can be secure in his life and liberty and property, so as not to be deprived of them except by due process of law, and can have a voice in the making and administration of the law…" Smith also mentioned and criticized Jim Crow segregation. Unlike Fortune, however, Smith did not place the right to marry across race lines in this category of civil rights, stating instead that he believed both whites and African Americans generally supported prohibitions against intermarriage.[33] Civil rights radicals, such as Ransom, who made a point of welcoming interracial couples to marry in his church, took a very different view, as would the NAACP, starting in its early work. Smith's lack of support made him a conservative along this spectrum of civil rights advocacy viewpoints.

Nevertheless, he was savvy about how law worked to deny African Americans' legal rights. Smith's legal experience led him to see clearly that "it is mainly in the enforcement, or the administration of the laws, however fair and equal they may appear on their face, that the constitutional rights of negroes to equal protection and treatment are denied, not only in the South but in many Northern states." Smith displayed a special appreciation for the particularly detrimental ways in which rights were denied African American defendants in criminal cases. Here Smith was reflecting on lessons he had learned in his own practice in Galveston. He was also, as it turned out, foreshadowing the first legal issues the infant NAACP would take on, which pertained to criminal justice procedural rights, as further described in chapter 12. As it further turned out, Smith and the fledgling NAACP forecast the direction in which constitutional law protections for African Americans would first begin to develop, as Michael Klarman describes in his account how doctrinal change in civil rights law finally got under way.[34]

Smith interspersed in his savvy legal analysis a series of anecdotes apparently intended to exert a subtle didactic influence on whites. Some described incidents in which whites who were initially hostile to the legal rights of an African American individual then realized the individual's worth and proceeded to bring about the just results, such as by allowing the voter registration of one worthy African American who had fought for the Confederacy. Other anecdotes told of the tragic outcome of failing to reach this realization in time, such as whites' regrets about stoning to death an African American who had paid a poor white boy to carry his satchel.[35] Smith was a good lawyer. In these stories he appears to have been calculating how best to persuade his audience. What is striking is the similarity between Washington and Smith's choice of folksy storytelling as a rhetorical device. The pair clearly shared sympathetic personal styles.

The two men had in common a preference and a talent for extreme discretion as well. Because of Washington's fear of being discovered to have been supporting the militant strategy of contesting disfranchisement in court, even the private correspondence among Smith, Washington, and his personal secretary Scott went to elaborate lengths to disguise the correspondents' identities, using code terms to refer to Washington, Smith, and the sums of money being discussed.[36] With funding thus provided in top secret by Washington—and with no acknowledgement that Smith's efforts were associated with the Tuskegean or any nationally relevant enterprise—Smith mounted a complex three-part challenge to the grandfather and character clause provisions in the voter registration scheme of Alabama's 1901 constitution.

Smith filed his challenge in September 1902, several months after the Orleans parish court's second opinion in *Ryanes*. He strived to avoid the pitfalls the *Ryanes* lawyers had encountered. Smith chose as his plaintiff Jackson Giles, an educated, middle-class African American resident of Montgomery who worked as a post office clerk. Giles headed the Colored Men's Suffrage Association of Alabama, which had come together to challenge the state's disfranchising constitution and had raised substantial funds to this end.[37] To establish the facts for the test case, Giles and many of his fellow post office workers had attempted to register during the window period in which the character and grandfather clauses were applicable. They were all refused registration, purportedly because the registrar deemed them lacking in "good character" but really on the basis of their race.

Smith's suit on Giles's behalf alleged that Giles and many thousands of other African Americans similarly situated were refused registration in violation of the Fourteenth and Fifteenth Amendments. As relief Giles sought to have his and others' names added to the new voter registration list and further requested $5,000 in damages against the board of registrars for refusing to register Giles despite his qualifications.[38]

Smith lost before the Alabama courts, as he fully expected. As he quickly wrote to assure his benefactor, however, he had framed his case so as to preserve his right to appeal on the federal question that would allow him to reach the nation's highest court. In fact, as revisionist historian R. Volney Riser explains in his careful explication of these complicated cases, Smith decided to file three cases. Each raised only one federal question he wanted the U.S. Supreme Court to consider. This way Smith sought to be sure to get the Court to face his test case challenge quickly during its upcoming term. In his letter to Washington, Smith warned that the state constitution's defenders and the state courts meant "to resort to every possible device permissible under state practice, to avoid deciding the Federal question" and would "dismiss any one or all of our appeals for some informality" if they could. He confessed that "[t]his kind of a fight, quasi political, is entirely new to me" and that he had "no idea at first what such a case would require." He confidently predicted, however, that "we have only to get to Washington on the Federal question and our case will win itself; and with the proof I shall be able to put in the record, we will knock out both the temporary and permanent sections of that odious document." Smith concluded by asking for additional funds to bring his fee for the entire matter to $2,000. This would allow him to work full time on the challenge. Giles's local organization, Smith noted, would pick up the state court costs.[39]

Smith's confidence about the correct legal answer to the federal question his cases raised was not misplaced. But he gave too much credit to the justices in assuming that they would not resort to the same dodging tactics that the state courts used to avoid deciding civil rights challenges that were strong on their merits. Indeed, variations on the theme of "dodging the merits" sums up the basic theme of most courts' jurisprudence on civil rights challenges during this era. No case better illustrates this than *Giles v. Harris*, as Smith's main challenge came to be named.

In February 1904 the Court delivered its opinions in two of Smith's cases under this caption. Famous jurist Oliver Wendell Holmes, widely regarded as the father of legal realism—the movement in legal thought that argued that judges should look beyond mere formalities to the social reality reflected by facts in legal cases—wrote the majority opinion. Three justices, including Harlan, voted in dissent. Justice Holmes first rejected the argument that the Court lacked jurisdiction to hear the appeal, holding that the relevant Reconstruction-era statutory provision that extended jurisdiction to the federal courts to hear claims of deprivation of constitutional rights conferred such jurisdiction.[40] Nevertheless, Holmes held that the Court could issue no relief in the case for two reasons. First, he asserted that the Court could not order the basic relief Giles was requesting—namely, to be registered as a voter—because if Giles was correct in arguing that Alabama's voting scheme was unconstitutional and therefore void, the Court would be adding another voter to a fraudulent list. Holmes stated that the Court was expressing no opinion as to the alleged unconstitutionality of the state's scheme but that it simply was not willing to assume that the rest of the state's constitution was valid in the face of Giles's allegations to the contrary. For this reason, Holmes concluded, Giles's very allegations required the Court to decline to grant the main relief Giles wanted.

The Court did not discuss the option of declaring the grandfather clause provision unconstitutional but upholding the rest of the new voter registration scheme. Today it would necessarily have to consider doing so under the now well-settled severability doctrine, which mandates that a court should save as much of a state statute as possible if it must invalidate a certain provision as unconstitutional.[41] Thus Holmes's argument was too clever by half; the Court could have upheld all of the provisions of the constitution except the grandfather and character clauses and then ordered the defendant registrar to redo the voter registration lists without applying those discriminatory tests. But in 1903 this sensible doctrine was not as well developed, allowing Holmes grounds for dodging the important constitutional question presented.

Holmes's second ground for refusing to respond to Giles's allegation was an even broader and more devastating dodge: Holmes argued that the Court was without power to act because the question presented was a "political" one, in which courts should not intervene. This argument took precisely the path about which Pillsbury had been concerned. Holmes pointed out that Giles's suit "imports that the great mass of the white population intends to keep the blacks from voting" and that to counter such intent "something more than ordering the plaintiff's name to be inscribed upon the lists of 1902 will be needed. If the conspiracy and the intent exist, a name on a piece of paper will not defeat them." In other words, Holmes predicted—this time with a more valid basis—nothing short of the Court "undertaking to supervise" the entire voting system of the state would be required. Faced with this understandably intimidating prospect (one the Court would again face, this time more bravely, in seeking many decades later to supervise school boards' compliance with *Brown v. Board of Education*), Holmes concluded that "relief from a great political wrong, if done, as alleged by the people of a state and the state itself, must be given by them or by the legislative and political department of the government of the United States." In short, the Court announced, through its great, supposedly progressive jurist Holmes, it was without power to do anything about disfranchisement.[42]

The second case Smith was able to press all the way to the Court, *Giles v. Teasley*, focused on Giles's damages claim against the Montgomery County registrar. With Justice Day writing for the majority and Justice Harlan again in dissent, the Court dismissed this claim on the ground that the state court had disposed of it for reasons independent of the federal right claimed. As a further rationale, the Court again invoked the political question doctrine Holmes articulated in *Giles v. Harris*.[43] Thus Smith lost both prongs of his voting rights challenges to Alabama's revised constitution. But he had at least succeeded in forcing the Court to acknowledge and examine the constitutional claim that African American voting rights advocates were raising.

The third related case Smith filed challenging the effect of Alabama's disfranchising constitution produced a modest victory. Smith patterned this case after his win in *Texas v. Carter*. In a case styled *Rogers v. Alabama*, Smith filed a challenge to the composition of a grand jury that had indicted an African American defendant on a murder charge. Smith alleged that the list from which grand jurors had been selected excluded all persons of African descent because it relied on voter registration rolls that discriminated on the basis of race. The Alabama Supreme Court dismissed Smith's challenge on the specious ground that his motion had been "unnecessarily prolix." The U.S. Supreme Court overturned this ruling, however, easily discerning that a federal question was presented and that its answer was squarely controlled by Smith's earlier victory in *Carter v. Texas*.[44] This decision did not invalidate the disfranchising provision of the state's new constitution, but it at least held that these provisions led to constitutional rights violations. The victory, Washington assured Smith, "has given the colored people a hopefulness that means a great deal."[45]

Smith had achieved a symbolic and morale-boosting win, but one that had little practical effect.[46] Although *Rogers v. Alabama* articulated the limited constitutional principle that African Americans should not be tried by juries from which their racial peers had been excluded, this rule continued to be ignored in practice for many decades.[47] Moreover, Smith's victory in *Rogers v. Alabama* did nothing to address the denial of voting rights in the first place; it in no way compelled the state to allow African Americans to register to vote. Thus *Rogers* was far better than a defeat, but it certainly was not a significant win on the voting rights front.

After the Supreme Court's opinions came down, Smith wrote to Washington with ideas about how he could frame a follow-on test case that would at the least force the Court "to invent some new excuse to escape us."[48] The two corresponded for a time on the topic, but no such follow-on case ever took place.[49] The ever-shrewd Washington may have recognized that the chances for success were too slim to justify the expense involved.

Assessing the Results

After the *Giles* defeat, proponents of African American voting rights were despondent. Although they cheered the decision in *Rogers* and talked of plans to push it further by mounting local challenges to juries that had been unconstitutionally convened, they realized they had moved no closer to their central goal of restoring African Americans' voting rights. A period of blame shifting and finger pointing followed, in which some AAC leaders, perhaps out of sour grapes, blamed Smith for the defeat. They failed to realize, understandably enough given the technicalities of the cases, the significance of Smith's achievement in at least getting the questions at issue squarely presented before the U.S. Supreme Court.[50] This was a problem that would also stymie the Niagara Movement when it undertook test case litigation. Developing methods for framing test cases so that courts would be forced to consider their substantive merits would take decades of experimentation—as well as historical change resulting in a more receptive judiciary.

Other litigation efforts were taking place at the state level at around the same time as the *Giles* defeat. These cases produced no better results. Hayes's case in Virginia was one of these. In 1902 Virginia adopted a revised constitution, and Hayes, a Howard law school graduate, along with white lawyer John S. Wise, a former U.S. congressman who had joined the Constitution League, undertook to challenge its disfranchising provisions. They drew support from a state-level civil rights organization that had grown out of the Negro Educational and Industrial Association of Virginia.[51] The AAC lent its support and fund-raising efforts to Hayes as well, and it was Hayes whose reportedly incendiary remarks in conjunction with the December 1902 AAC gathering in Washington, DC, stirred up such controversy and opposition in the white press.

Hayes and Wise's case also met with rejection before the U.S. Supreme Court, which refused their request to invalidate the elections Virginia had held after the disfranchising provisions of its new constitution took effect.[52] Another Virginia voting rights case in which Wise was involved was likewise rejected on various grounds, including the political question doctrine.[53] With these defeats, the litigation campaign against voting disfranchisement entered a hiatus until the early NAACP took it up again.

As historians have pointed out, one of the most telling aspects of the multiple disfranchisement test case efforts undertaken in the period between 1898 and 1910 was the lack of accurate information about these efforts in the African American press.[54] Key case rulings were reported inaccurately, belatedly, and sometimes not at all.[55] An atmosphere of suspicion, distrust, and competition characterized relations among the various individuals and groups that had undertaken challenges to Southern states' disfranchising constitutions, and criticism of others' efforts abounded. Given the great difficulty of framing test cases in order to force courts to consider the constitutional principles at stake, even the best-trained lawyers in the land would probably have failed at the task at the time—and only a few from this tier of top litigators with Supreme Court experience, such as Smith and Pillsbury, were then on hand. This resource of elite litigators with experience and top reputations before the U.S. Supreme Court was one that the early NAACP would work hard to develop; within the AAC it was just emerging.[56]

In the late nineteenth century it is likely that the U.S. Supreme Court would have continued to refuse to consider the politically and institutionally problematic matter of states' disfranchising constitutions regardless of who litigated the test cases or how they were framed. Justice Holmes was right in a certain respect: The problem of broadscale Southern disfranchisement of African American voters would not be solved until Congress acted. Congress's passage of the 1965 Voting Rights Act, more than half a century after a founding generation of civil rights activists took up this challenge, finally put in place law that forced the end of most major, blatant racial disfranchisement schemes.[57]

In its newly revived final phase of organizational existence in the years between 1905 and 1908, the AAC had not given up its plans to continue test case litigation. In reporting on the AAC's 1906 meeting, *The Age* wrote with enthusiasm of such possibilities, but as history would have it, those plans would push forward under a new organizational structure. The AAC's ambition to obtain a legal pronouncement regarding the unconstitutionality of grandfather clauses would finally see fruition in the NAACP's first Supreme Court victory, in its challenge to Oklahoma's grandfather clause in the 1915 case *Guinn v. United States*.[58] *Guinn* declared grandfather clauses unconstitutional, providing the NAACP with an early victory that became an effective fund-raising hook and helped it to build membership by generating optimism on the basis of a Supreme Court win.[59] It had only very limited positive effects "on the ground," however; the state quickly adopted a new scheme that neither the NAACP nor the U.S. government sought to challenge.[60] But the AAC's Louisiana challenge—and Washington and Smith's separate and secretly sponsored, better conceived but also ultimately unsuccessful Alabama cases—laid the groundwork for this first, importantly symbolic national test case victory.

The AAC's inability to gain legal traction on the crucially important issue of voting presented a huge source of frustration to the AAC's leaders. Nevertheless, important experiences accrued. The AAC's leaders and spokespersons raised many thousands of dollars, most of them incrementally from waves of church and community gatherings called in the name of challenging voting rights restrictions. Women were highly significant contributors to this fund-raising work.[61] Both before and after the *Ryanes* defeat, local, state, and national organizations undertook such supportive efforts in large meetings that often produced overflow crowds. All of this work laid the foundation for future organizing that would take place throughout the early decades of the twentieth century.[62]

The failed litigation also taught important lessons. There clearly had been a great disparity between the degree of local energy called for and national results achieved. This fact highlighted the need for a more effective, professionally managed national organization; an all-volunteer movement could not achieve the needed results. Nor could an organization achieve these results if it depended for its staff on leaders who were also busy with other highly demanding "day jobs." Bishop Walters was a case in point, bearing responsibility not only for running the AAC but also for overseeing the affairs of a busy diocese of one of the nation's largest African American denominations. The AAC's organizational model, resting on a loose federation of big-name leaders who attended annual meetings but perhaps did little else for the rest of the year, simply could not produce the intense effort that hard experience proved would be required. To be sure, some of its leaders were active year-round on AAC business, especially those on its most active committees such as the executive and the legislation and legal affairs committees. And some local leaders produced impressive turnouts in response to Walters's periodic calls for local gatherings to respond to lynchings and other outrages as they occurred. But like many reform organizations of its era, the AAC was an organization propelled mainly by the stature of its big-name leaders rather than the work of many thousands of members. That model for national civil rights organizing would have to change under the NAACP—and it was none other than Walters, drawing on his AAC experience as a member of the NAACP's Committee on Organization, who would be among those who understood the importance of and successfully advocated for this organizational design change during the NAACP's first years.

The need for greater legal expertise also became apparent. If one learns one's greatest lessons from failures, then the AAC and the race activist community at large learned such lessons from the effort to stop disfranchisement. It became clearer that money raised at the local level had to end up quickly and reliably in fund-raising accounts for intended litigation campaigns, and that a disciplined cadre of accountable leaders had to oversee disbursements while making firm and informed decisions about when and how to pursue litigation. Recognition of how daunting the task was proving could well have led to a dissipation of effort; instead, it spurred further and more sophisticated work.

In sum, to describe the turn-of-the-century antidisfranchisement test case campaign as a failure is not to criticize the activists who undertook it. Perhaps more than in any other area of racial justice legal work, these activists were David pitted against the Goliath of Southern states that had encoded politically nullifying measures into the very foundations of their public law. To mount challenges required sophisticated constitutional strategizing in the face of dismal political and institutional odds and called on activists to reach the heart of federal/state and intergovernmental branch relations. Social movement theory might predict that such an impossible challenge would lead to a movement's demise, but it did not, even though it would take more than another half century of battling to resolve.

Challenging Jim Crow

A somewhat less challenging area for civil rights test case litigation presented itself in Jim Crow separate transportation statutes. Although the precedents here were also far from promising, the challenges of mounting cases were considerably lower: One simply had to find a willing prospective or already affronted plaintiff and then file a suit on that person's behalf. Numerous such cases had been filed, starting with the first Jim Crow measures undertaken in Northern states before the Civil War.[63] Indeed, *Plessy v. Ferguson,* which a citizens committee in Louisiana engineered, was the product of just such a test case. African American lawyer Louis Martinet led this organizing effort, and white lawyer and abolitionist Albion Tourgée argued the case to unsuccessful results before the Supreme Court.[64]

After its founding, the AAC considered, undertook, or assisted with several of these Jim Crow transportation cases, though none of them appear to have come to fruition, again because of a lack of funds and too many chiefs taking matters into their own hands in conflicting directions. As in the disfranchisement litigation, AAC figures who involved themselves in searching for and handling cases included the chair and members of the legal affairs and legislation committee, including McGhee and other lawyers who might volunteer to investigate or handle a case from their region, and the AAC's elected leadership, including Walters, as well as Fortune, who often seemed to insert himself in these matters even without formal authority to do so. Worse yet, there seems to have been no agreement about who, among all of these figures, was ultimately in charge of decision making about whether to take on potential cases and then whether to pursue, abandon, or settle them. This facet of coordinating test case litigation with organization building would also become far more streamlined by the mid-1910s, but an ungainly process of trial and error preceded the honing of this skill. The NAACP did not simply burst onto the scene with an effective test case litigation strategy fully formed as so often supposed.

Another key part of orchestrating the duet between test case litigation and organization building involved fund-raising. Both AAC representatives and sympathetic allies made numerous fund-raising appeals, and local activists—usually women—collected monies to support litigation expenses for anticipated Jim Crow test cases. They often targeted these fund-raising appeals to women, as when the editor of the *Broad Ax* published a front-page appeal on behalf of the Legal and Legislative Bureau of the AAC, noting that an upcoming annual meeting of the NACW would require "the women of our race" to engage special Pullman cars at extra expense or else endure the indignities of Jim Crow.[65]

The AAC considered a number of potential test cases. In 1902 Du Bois wrote to Washington reporting that he had been in communication with Wilford Smith about undertaking a test case to challenge a state law that purported to apply to interstate passengers. Smith had advised Du Bois that he believed the law was void and that the best strategy would be to "make a case before the United States Circuit court, and have it come directly to Washington," adding that he would need at least $2,000 plus expenses to take on such a matter. Du Bois told Washington that he regarded this fee as too steep and that he planned to ask Smith about bringing a case before the Interstate Commerce Commission instead.[66] Nothing more seems to have come of this tentative probe, but the AAC did commence at least one suit against the Pullman Company, filing it in state rather than federal court, contrary to Smith's advice. Reverend Harvey T. Johnson, the editor of the AME *Christian Recorder,* served as the plaintiff in this case after the Pullman Company had refused him first-class dining accommodations even though he held a first-class ticket. A jury returned a verdict awarding a small damages judgment to Rev. Johnson, but the trial court judge set it aside, ruling that the company had the right as a matter of law to deny accommodations on the basis of race. McGhee reported in a fund-raising appeal that the AAC had taken steps to appeal the case to the U.S. Supreme Court and that additional fund-raising appeals had been issued through newspapers, requests that ministers ask for contributions from their congregations, and AAC appearances at local associations and societies.[67] The final disposition of this case is murky; no subsequent case report appears to exist.

Washington's correspondence reflects numerous unsuccessful attempts to intervene with railroad executives more informally to improve traveling conditions for African American passengers. He especially tried to improve the Pullman Company's segregation policies by appealing to its president, Robert Todd Lincoln (son of the former president, ironically enough) through personal approaches, committee delegations, and indirect interventions through Long Island railroad president William

H. Baldwin Jr., who was a race progressive, friend of Washington's, and important Tuskegee Institute donor who would later help found the National Urban League. All of Washington's tactics failed, however, pointing to yet another area of stasis and frustration. True to form, Washington's public stance downplayed the problem by repeatedly claiming that African Americans were generally well treated once within a Pullman car even if they sometimes found it hard to purchase first-class tickets. This was a claim Washington well knew from firsthand reports was incorrect, but he apparently thought this stance better than publicly criticizing a major employer of African American workers, albeit in race-segregated jobs.[68]

Federal Legislative Initiatives

As well as exploring test case opportunities, the AAC's leaders energetically pursued federal legislative initiatives. The organization relied for this work on the Washington, DC–based leaders of its legal and legislative bureau. These figures often held federal government jobs, placing them in an excellent position to monitor what was happening in Congress. A common impression about turn-of-the-century race activism holds that activists turned to the courts and eschewed legislative strategies during the nadir period because it was so obvious that majoritarian political processes would produce no beneficial results. A careful assessment of the evidence belies this assumption, however; the AAC's leaders proposed federal legislation in a number of priority areas and in others engaged in defensive battles to prevent federal legislative initiatives inimical to civil rights interests. They used these campaigns to generate enthusiasm and turnout for AAC meetings in the nation's capital and elsewhere and hoped these showings of support would help them achieve their legislative goals. In retrospect, these efforts to achieve change through national legislation seem quixotic, given the political conditions of the era, but the future of national politics on racial justice issues was not yet clear from the vantage point of these leaders, who had experienced great change in their lifetimes and could not foretell how future change in a new century would unfold. The AAC's Washington, DC–based legislative advocates may also have shared a characteristic that social movements scholars have found in many social reform activists—namely, highly optimistic dispositions that led them to forge ahead rather than attempting to first gauge their prospects of success.[69]

And keep going was just what they did. At first, the leaders of this arm of the AAC's activities engaged in standard interest group lobbying, and they had success in heading off some negative legislative initiatives, such as federal Jim Crow transportation legislation. They had no success whatsoever on the affirmative legislative front, however, where they focused on at least five federal legislative proposals that tracked the AAC's programmatic priorities: federal aid for education, disfranchisement, Jim Crow transportation, antilynching, and the economic and social welfare development of the race. By 1903 one of the leaders of the AAC's Washington-based legislative arm had decided to organize a large gathering of race leaders to engage in collective self-analysis about more effective avenues for influencing public policy.[70] Historians have tended to overlook this conference even though it captured the changing legal sensibilities of a generation of race activists poised between the old legal ideologies of the nineteenth-century formalists and the new ideologies of the early twentieth-century protorealists or "sociological" jurisprudes.

To be sure, none of the affirmative legislation the AAC supported won enactment, but then its test cases also failed, so failure alone cannot account for why legal civil rights historians tend to ignore turn-of-the-century race justice activists' legislation-focused work. These efforts reveal the AAC's views about both the potential and the limits of federal statutory law as a means of bringing about change.

The first affirmative federal legislative proposal the AAC endorsed was the old Blair education bill, which would have provided federal funding to support and enhance basic elementary school education, especially in the South. The AAL had supported this bill under Fortune's leadership despite qualms when its congressional supporters gradually stripped from it the provisions designed to ensure racial fairness in allocating funding, all in an effort to make the bill more palatable to Southern politicians. By the time the AAC came on the scene, this legislative proposal simply provided for federal funding of basic education in regions of the country with high illiteracy rates. The AAC's willingness to accept these compromises reflected its pragmatism not only on civil and political rights but here in the area of social welfare spending as well. Although this bill passed the Senate three times, by 1890 it had met its final defeat with Blair's loss of his congressional seat. The AAC's leaders nevertheless championed its revival for many years.

A second federal legislative proposal the AAC endorsed in its early years was the Lodge bill (sometimes also called the "Force" bill because it was viewed as forcing Southern states' electoral policy). This legislation would have provided for federal law enforcement intervention to protect African American voters from fraud and intimidation in elections. By the early 1890s it, too, had stalled. The new disfranchisement strategies states were pursuing rendered this legislation no longer apposite to the developing problem anyway, and its supporters basically abandoned their efforts in 1891 even though the AAC endorsed it to the end.[71]

The Crumpacker Resolution

The developing legal landscape regarding disfranchisement gave rise to a third federal legislative initiative that was far more controversial within the AAC. This proposal was known as the Crumpacker resolution after its main sponsor, Republican Edgar D. Crumpacker of Indiana, and it emerged from inquiries the House of

Figure 6.1 Congress—14th Amendment, 2nd section, cartoon in *Washington Post,* Feb. 19, 1902 (Library of Congress).

Representatives' Census Committee had undertaken.[72] The Crumpacker resolution called on this Census Committee to "ascertain whether any of the States have denied or abridged the right of male inhabitants [to vote]" and, if so, to report out an apportionment bill that would reduce the electoral representation of those states in proportion to the percentage of their male population barred from voting, as provided for under the explicit language of Section 2 of the Fourteenth Amendment.[73] The proposal failed to gain traction in Congress, unsurprisingly enough, but continued to be a focus of debate and discussion both within and outside the AAC during the first years of the new century.[74]

Fortune and Washington were against the proposal, but Walters and others found appeal in the idea, seeing it as a tactic through which to threaten Southern states about the consequences of continuing to pursue mass race-based disfranchisement.[75] Like most voting rights advocates at the time, Crumpacker and the AAC accepted education-based disfranchisement rules, provided that these standards applied equally to the uneducated classes among both African Americans and whites.[76] What these advocates sought was the more modest objective of protecting the voting rights of those the polity deemed fit to exercise the franchise on grounds other than race. They hoped to use the Crumpacker resolution to give enforcement teeth to the non-self-executing rules in the Fourteenth Amendment, which the Court was repeatedly showing itself unwilling or unable to enforce. Although supporters of the Crumpacker resolution and related proposals could not have rationally believed they would succeed, they saw tactical advantage in pressing a proposal that forced attention to the language protecting voting rights in the U.S. Constitution.

The Republicans controlled Congress, but few of them resembled their radical abolitionist ancestors of the Reconstruction era. Crumpacker's idea, quite predictably, stalled in committee.[77] Stymied by Congress's failure to even take up the proposal, supporters turned to an alternative strategy to attempt to increase national awareness of the social, political, and economic situation African Americans faced. This strategy appears to have been the brainchild of Jesse Lawson and Daniel Murray and sought to chart a less direct route to congressional consideration of the consequences of disfranchisement. In 1902 the House Committee on Labor, chaired by decorated former Civil War Union officer Republican William R. Warnock of Ohio, reported on a new bill to create a body to be known as the Freedmen's Inquiry Commission. This commission was to undertake "a comprehensive investigation of the condition" of African Americans in the United States, including their educational progress, the "best means of promoting harmony between the races," and "the best manner of adjusting the troubles which now disturb the harmonious relations between the races." Thus couching its charge in the most soft-pedaled rhetoric possible, emphasizing harmony rather than rights, the report cited the need to acquaint African Americans "with their true condition" and to furnish information for sociological study. In rhetoric that strikes the ear quite oddly today and perhaps intentionally played to white stereotypes, the report invoked what it described as the negative consequences of Southern blacks leaving agriculture, to which pursuit they "seemed especially adapted," and flocking to large cities to live in unhealthy conditions and closed with the plea that the inquiry commission would be well worth setting up if it proved to African Americans "that it is to their advantage to remain on the farm and grow strong" because the federal government had decided to "make them secure in the enjoyment of their rights as American citizens."[78]

The minority response to Warnock's report bought none of this line of argument. Virginia Democrat Henry D. Flood drafted this response, using it to invoke the standard "special benefits" rhetoric directed at any race-specific legal proposal during the period. Flood argued as follows: "We see no reason why a special commission should be created to investigate the general condition of the negro race any more than that such a commission should be created for the purpose of investigating the general condition of every other race of people who are citizens of this Republic." Proceeding with the usual litany of points, Flood asserted that the "negro race can never reach its full development until it is permitted by the Government to work out its destiny as do the other races" and that treating African Americans as "wards of the nation" could only "retard the development of the manhood and independence of this race." Moreover, Flood's minority report opined, the true purpose of the proposed inquiry was to promote the Crumpacker resolution and to push for "promoting harmony between the races by turning over to the domination of the Negroes the government of every county, city, and State in the United States in which they are numerically in the majority."[79]

The few white press reports about the proposal were equally hostile. The *Richmond Times*, for example, accused the bill's advocates of asking "the government to enact some special class legislation in favor of the Negro because of the color of his skin" and depicted African Americans as already being too dependent on the federal government.[80] These were old arguments—and unfair ones. The U.S. Supreme Court had raised just such claims in its opinion in the *Civil Rights Cases*, for example, even though it was there reviewing legislation that imposed a rule of *equal* treatment. In both that context and the one presented by the proposed racial inquiry commission, charges of special legislation or special treatment were misdirected. Just as the Reconstruction-era legislation the Court invalidated in the *Civil Rights Cases* had called for a *non*discrimination principle—in other words, the *opposite* of special treatment—the national commission idea sought to look into how African Americans were being treated and whether they were being given the *same* rights and opportunities as others. However, the newspaper twisted the commission proposal, sarcastically characterizing it as an effort to ask the federal government to help African Americans "make a living and accumulate wealth." This argument that there was something untoward about addressing race specifically—even in the context of undoing explicit race discrimination—had power despite its illogic and has left a long heritage in national debates about race, as contemporary scholars such as Darren Hutchinson have shown.[81]

The bill's sponsor was Republican congressman Harvey S. Irwin from Kentucky, although reports attributed its actual drafting to Murray.[82] Murray and Lawson, working as a pair, became the primary force within the AAC championing the Irwin bill along with other federal legislative initiatives. Both reportedly testified before Congress urging the need for more attention to the conditions of African Americans with respect to "their educational, material, and sociological advancement."[83] At AAC meetings they repeatedly spoke about its virtues and ensured that the AAC included the proposal as a priority in its annual addresses to the nation.

The legislation did seek, as one of its primary motivations, to lend support to the flagging Crumpacker resolution, just as its opponents accused. But its scope and purpose were broader than this, and it stands as one of the first post-Reconstruction federal legislative proposals aimed at considering the particular, race-specific situation of persons of African descent within the United States. Lawson's professional identity, which spanned both sociology and law, undoubtedly had much to do with this approach. He had been born in Maryland in 1856 and educated at Howard University and then at its law school, like so many of his contemporaries engaged in

Figure 6.2 Jesse Lawson, president, National Sociological Society, from 1903 Washington Conference on the Race Problem in the United States (New York Public Library).

race activist work. He worked in the 1900s at the Bureau of Pensions in Washington, DC, as a legal examiner and was active in Republican Party politics. In 1889 he had represented Langston in contesting the Virginia electoral committee's refusal to recognize and seat him in Congress. Lawson also found time to edit the *Colored American* for two years (between 1895 and 1897), as well as chairing at various points AAC bureaus including finance and legal affairs. His peers, not surprisingly, described him as having boundless enthusiasm for projects. He also lectured on sociology at institutions in Washington, DC, earning the honorific "Professor."[84]

Lawson's 1903 Conference

In the early 1900s Lawson founded the National Sociological Society, dedicated to considering "the race problem."[85] Through its auspices Lawson convened what appears to have been the first and only conference of the society in Washington, DC, and charged it with gathering information in order to lay the issue of race relations before Congress and the public. Lawson published a volume memorializing these conference proceedings, and it provides a window into participants' evolving thoughts on the relationship between social facts and legal reform and between political power and law.[86] The ideas reflected in the conference proceeding remained inchoate and disparate, pointing to the still substantially unsettled status of strategic choices for a racial justice campaign for the new century. The participants largely agreed on some basic starting points, including that "[a]s solutions of the race problem we regard colonization, expatriation and segregation as unworthy of future consideration," and we "have abiding faith in the principles of human rights established in the Declaration of Independence and the national Constitution."[87] Beyond that, opinions varied widely.

Former congressman George White, the society's president, began with a speech noting the inextricable connection between voting rights and all else: "When the ballot is gone, incidentally schools and everything else will go with it."[88] In later discussion White proposed a "systematic thinning out" of African American presence in the South, along with provision of employment and temporary housing for migrants so they could have "new ideals, new and increased opportunities for education of their children, where they could be treated as men and women"—thus seeming to foresee the great migration soon to begin. White further proposed purchasing land tracts to form small colonies to "pave the way for home getting by our less fortunate brothers in the South."[89]

Lawson similarly took up the creative brainstorming challenge by suggesting that African Americans concentrate their presence in states where they could obtain majority voting power. This would presage the scheme for drawing electoral district boundaries to protect African American voting strength under the Voting Rights Act of 1965.[90] Lawson's AAC associate Murray held similar views, proposing a quasi-market-based paradigm that involved "inducing those affected by unjust laws to seek those sections of the country that offer the greatest inducement in the matter of just treatment."[91] Reverend Harvey Johnson, however, offered a dissenting voice, denouncing any proposal that appeared to accept segregation in any state in the country: "The sentiment that should go forth from this Conference is that we shall never yield an iota of anything that pertains to our manhood rights.... [G]oing wholesale into the North or West is as absurd as it would be detrimental."[92]

This exchange aptly captured the competing paradigms of two generations of race activists. The older one, represented by Johnson, was still steeped in legalist "equal rights" principles; the younger one, immersed in political conditions in which race was explicitly always on the table, saw the need for pragmatic political action through the means available—namely, the movement of disfranchised populations—in order to bring about a changed political environment.[93]

Washington appeared briefly to present "very short" remarks, urging, ironically enough, given his efforts to capture the AAC during this very period, the importance of promoting the flourishing of race organizations with multiple goals.[94] The brilliant lawyer and academician L. M. Hershaw, a prominent member of the National Negro Academy (and a foe of Washington's, soon to become a founding member of the Niagara Movement), observed that the movement of African Americans to cities reflected nothing unusual but was part of general worldwide trends among all peoples.[95]

By the end of this free-flowing exchange, the topic had returned to law, with Dancy and Pinchback bringing the audience back to a focus on the Constitution and "the necessity of seeing that these cases before the Supreme Court of the United States do not go by default."[96] A final resolution highlighted the matter of education and proposed pressing Congress to act wisely and discreetly on the facts with regard to "the proposal of a bill for general education throughout the South."[97] Careful about public relations, Lawson ensured that the upshot of the meeting the white press would cover was that the society's approach continued to insist on equal treatment under the laws; the group reportedly declared that the government's duty was "to afford adequate and equal protection to each and every citizen in the full enjoyment of every right guaranteed by the Constitution and by the law of the land."[98]

The 1903 conference met its goal of gathering leading political thinkers together to toss around future strategic visions, but beyond that it left no mark. Still no action took place in Congress. Instead, it became more obvious that state constitutional disfranchisement was likely to endure for the long term. The National Negro Suffrage Association Trotter and Haynes organized briefly arose and then suffered crashing defeat in the Virginia litigation. Despite Lawson's creative efforts to keep Congress's attention on the disfranchisement crisis and broader related issues, all attempted strategies appeared for a time to have hit dead ends. Enthusiasm for the Crumpacker proposal waned even among radicals. In his independent assessment of the issue published in 1906, for example, D. Augustus Straker argued that even if the Crumpacker proposal were enacted into federal law, it would serve only to further render African Americans permanently irrelevant to the electoral process.[99] By the time of Walters's resuscitation of the AAC, pronouncements supporting enforcement of the Fourteenth Amendment's representation reduction clause had waned. A shift in strategy was perceptibly under way as the focus of activists' rhetoric turned to enforcing the *Fifteenth* Amendment's prohibition against race discrimination in voting.

With legislative approaches to disfranchisement defeated, it appeared that challenges to political disfranchisement on the basis of race would have to be mounted through the courts. It was thus no coincidence that the idea of sponsoring test case litigation to challenge Southern disfranchisement emerged at the top of Oswald Garrison Villard's list of urgent priorities in calling for the 1909 National Negro Conference, as further discussed in chapter 11. The leaders of a precursor generation had imparted their experience with the antidisfranchisement struggle as a key aspect of the transfer of ideas from the AAC to the NAACP.

Anti–Jim Crow Legislation

A fifth federal legislative initiative the AAC supported would have prohibited Jim Crow train cars as a matter of federal law, thus abrogating *Plessy's* approval of state Jim Crow car statutes under the separate but equal doctrine. Republican representative Edward de V. Morrell of Pennsylvania first introduced this bill; in 1902 supporters attached it as an amendment to another statute addressing the Interstate Commerce Commission's powers to regulate interstate shipping rates. Daniel Murray, AAC legislative bureau member, reportedly drafted this language, and at congressional hearings on it in May 1902 AAC leaders Lawson, White, and Adams, among others, turned out to testify in favor of it, addressing not only this bill but other AAC-supported initiatives as well.[100]

Neither the Morrell bill nor the Murray amendment advanced from committee, but these efforts were far from an unmitigated failure. Large audiences packed meetings the AAC called to support the bill's passage at downtown Baptist churches in Washington, DC.[101] In this campaign the AAC found common ground to work with the Constitution League and Washington's "Committee of Twelve," which also supported the proposal, providing an experience in interorganizational cooperation that would soon prove valuable.

These benefits of working together across organizational divisions became obvious when the AAC and the recently formed Niagara Movement found themselves facing what both organizations viewed as an entirely wrongheaded new legislative initiative in 1906. Introduced by well-meaning but misdirected civil rights supporter Joseph B. Foraker, a Republican from Ohio, along with Republican senator William Warner of Missouri, this proposal would have mandated that the "separate" cars the *Plessy* Court permitted had to really be "equal," as measured by the amenities provided in them.[102] On Foraker's reasoning, the Morrell proposal banning separate cars had no chance of passing, but imposing the cost of maintaining two different systems of real first-class cars on railroads could indirectly attack Jim Crow by making segregation prohibitively expensive.

Foraker's strategy, however, overlooked the dignitary rights African American leaders viewed as fundamentally at stake. In one of their first jointly organized initiatives, representatives of both the AAC and the Niagara Movement, along with the Constitution League and members of the Committee of Twelve, succeeded in scuttling the Warner-Foraker proposal, though not until after it had passed the Senate.[103] Washington, true to character, remained publicly silent on the matter while working behind the scenes to discourage the legislation. Later he sought to have Grimké and Miller from his Committee of Twelve claim credit for defeating it.[104]

Antilynching Legislation

Yet another legislative initiative the AAC championed was Congressman White's federal antilynching bill, which he introduced in 1900 while serving in Congress.[105] White's antilynching proposal would have called for the protection of all persons born or naturalized in the United States from being "murdered, tortured, [or] burned to death by any and all organized mobs commonly known as 'lynching bees' " and would have imposed on such acts the federal penalties reserved for treason.[106] In offering his bill in

Figure 6.3 Hon. George H. White, from 1903 Washington Conference on the Race Problem in the United States (New York Public Library).

the House, White introduced into the record a lengthy letter from Albert Pillsbury analyzing and defending the constitutionality of this proposal. White noted the universal coverage of the bill, which would protect members of all races—including, for example, Italians, who were also sometimes subject to racially motivated lynching. White's biographer argues that, by this point in his congressional career, White had abandoned efforts to sound moderate on the civil rights issues closest to his heart, and he included all of the civil rights issues he cared most about in an impassioned speech on the House floor. In it White laid out the AAC's basic agenda without naming it as such:

> Should not a nation be just to all of her citizens…? There can be but one candid and fair answer to this inquiry, and that is in the affirmative. But, unfortunately for us, what should have been done has not been done, and to substantiate this assertion we have but to pause for a moment and make a brief survey of the manumitted Afro-American during the last thirty-five years. We have struggled on as best we could with the odds against us at every turn. Our constitutional rights have been trodden under foot; our right of franchise in most every one of the original slave States has been virtually taken away from us, and during the time of our freedom fully 50,000 of my race have been ignominiously murdered by mobs, not 1 percent of whom have been made to answer for their crimes in the courts of justice…[107]

White was at this point facing vicious and unfounded attacks from reactionary North Carolina press outlets, coupled with the loss of his voting base as North

Carolina's new discriminatory voter qualification rules took effect. These factors led him to decide not to run for reelection after serving in Congress for two terms (1896–1901).[108] Afterward, White sought to become the AAC's national president. He was unsuccessful in this goal, however; AAC insiders apparently worried that ex-congressman White, now jobless, would expect a salary for this work, and they realized the organization's budget could not support a paid national leader.[109] But White, a lawyer by both training and vocation, had sufficient commitment to the AAC's issues to remain active in the AAC's legislative and legal affairs until 1905 or so despite the personal affront he felt in losing his bid for its presidency. He remained in Washington, DC, and made his living as a lawyer. After that, according to his biographer, White decided to bow out of what he saw as the increasingly convoluted politics of national racial justice activism. He instead became involved in a local, intrarace community building project, moving to New Jersey to head an organization that was constructing a model community for African Americans, which it named Whitesboro in the former congressman's honor.[110]

Like other legislative proposals the AAC championed, the White antilynching bill went nowhere. Still, it set in motion a decades-long campaign by the NAACP for federal antilynching legislation. Those proposals, too, never won passage.[111] Although the NAACP's antilynching campaign was a legislative defeat, it was an organizing success, setting in motion decades of activism and, by the late 1940s, a dramatic reduction in this heinous practice.[112]

Opposing Ex-Slave Pensions

The AAC not only affirmatively championed legislation but also opposed initiatives on race matters that its leaders believed would harm African Americans' interests. In this defensive posture, it generally had better success. One such initiative was the Warner-Foraker proposal already discussed. Another involved proposals for ex-slave pensions the National Ex-Slave Mutual Relief, Bounty, and Pension Association (NESA) supported.[113] The AAC's leaders opposed these proposals.[114] As historian Mary Frances Berry has pointed out, the split between NESA and the African American middle class on this issue reflected deep schisms. Even within a generation often born into slavery, some had escaped to professional pursuits— such as Walters, Wells Barnett, Fortune, and others within the AAC's leadership ranks—whereas others remained in rural poverty on former plantations given over to tenancy farming. Moreover, U.S. government agencies, including the pension, treasury, and post offices—where, indeed, prominent AAC members such as Lyons and Lawson held positions—prosecuted NESA and some of its leaders on charges of mail fraud, alleging that NESA agents, or imposters pretending to be NESA agents, illegally collected funds from former slaves by falsely maintaining that ex-slave pension legislation had been enacted and that payment was required for this income to begin flowing. Some NESA activists ended up serving jail terms.[115] Contemporary advocates of the African American reparations movement view NESA as an ancestor. The AAC's opposition highlights its historical location as championing a kind of advocacy and a range of political commitments that often emphasized forward-looking, formal equality. Its leaders were not yet ready for a more historically focused, contextually race-specific approach—though Lawson's 1903 conference had started to move in these directions.

Other Law-Related Activities

The AAC's agenda did not concentrate solely on federal law-related strategies, of course. Leaders of the AAC engaged in public education and other state and locally focused activities to promote the AAC's issues as well. Wells Barnett, head of the AAC's antilynching bureau, published reports on the murder of Robert Charles, which set off the New Orleans race riot of 1900, in which dozens were killed, as well as many other incidents.[116] When Wells Barnett retreated from the AAC during its most conservative phase, Church Terrell took over her post, and she, too, frequently lectured and published on lynching as well as a host of other matters. Early in the organization's history, after postmaster Frazier Baker and his infant daughter were murdered in South Carolina, AAC leaders wrote letters to the U.S. postmaster general protesting both the incident and the proposed appointment of a white replacement for Baker.[117]

Walters called for a day of prayer and fasting to protest lynching following the Sam Hose lynching in Georgia in 1899—where a mob burned and then sliced up the body of its victim, displaying some body parts in store windows and attempting to deliver others to the governor. On numerous occasions he issued appeals to governors, legislatures, and judges in the South to prevent such lawlessness and provide the protection of the law to all citizens.[118] In response to a brutal 1901 lynching in Kansas, Walters called for AAC meetings around the country. These took place and included a very large gathering featuring an overflow crowd at a Washington, DC, Baptist facility.[119] After the 1906 Atlanta riots Walters again called for a national day of prayer, and gatherings were held in many communities across the country.[120]

The AAC's attempts to influence national policy reached into the executive branch and foreign relations as well. The AAC held three meetings in as many years with President McKinley, at each of which its representatives emphasized the need for strong presidential leadership to oppose lynching. The AAC's representatives held several meetings with President Roosevelt as well, though Roosevelt's racial retrenchment and close ties to Washington meant that the Tuskegean usually preempted this "race consultation" function, precluding it from being spread among a more representative group of leaders.[121] The AAC sent representatives to the Pan-African Council, to celebrations of the Haitian Republic, and to other gatherings promoting cross-national ties, and frequently invoked its sense of connection with other nations of people of color in its resolutions and platforms.[122]

The AAC participated in or lent its support to a range of state statutory and litigation initiatives as well. It supported streetcar boycotts and litigation in Virginia. In Washington, DC, the AAC Executive Committee, meeting in the home of Daniel Murray, adopted a resolution deploring discrimination at the city's new Grand Opera house and offered to help finance lawsuits on the matter; several were reported to be in the works. In Seattle it protested police discrimination, while in New York it supported a bill prohibiting school discrimination.[123]

The AAC sought to influence private action as well as public policy. It organized a letter-writing campaign to major railroad companies in the South to protest their institution of segregation practices that were not legally mandated.[124] Leaders of the AAC planned commemorative events to honor civil rights leaders of a past era, erect memorials, and celebrate John Brown. In all of these and other ways, they developed a base of supporters at a local level that, although not yet tightly organized, was primed to sign up for a nationally coordinated network. Without the AAC, the NAACP's field organizers would have found less fertile ground for their work. In the end it was the fact of local activity, however directed, as much as any specific issue campaign or political vision, that mattered most. Across the country, African American citizens from the middle and working classes were becoming increasingly angry and were expressing that anger by attending meetings and contributing their limited, individually small but amassable funds. Although this mobilization was not yet apparent under a national spotlight, it was beginning to occur; without it, later nationally coordinated organizing would have been slower and less successful.

Indeed, the nadir period produced far more dissenting activism than is generally acknowledged. As Blair Kelley argues in her book on local transportation segregation boycott campaigns, local and state legislative initiatives to bring Jim Crow segregation to streetcar transportation met with boycott campaigns in several Southern cities. These campaigns were usually short lived and unsuccessful. Sometimes they were defeated by ambitious local race leaders, who cut deals with government and corporate officials and then undermined calls for citizen action. But even though these boycott campaigns were unsuccessful, sporadic citizen mobilization contributed to building an activist tradition, which produced the fertile soil in which the seeds for later victories against all odds could grow.

"Unity in Diversity": The National Association of Colored Women's Dual Social Welfare and Civil Rights Agenda, 1895–1910

The AAC benefited greatly from women's involvement; a few assumed leadership positions, and many more performed much of the fund-raising work. But African American women also formed organizations of their own, and in 1895 they founded the National Association of Colored Women (NACW) to join these organizations under a nationwide umbrella. August Meier erred in dismissing this work as largely apolitical and not often effective in his classic 1963 investigation of turn-of-the-century African American thought. Later generations of research have put such misimpressions to rest; African American women's club work was important, highly effective as measured against resource constraints, and spanned both social welfare and civil and political rights goals.[1]

Even with Meier's misimpressions corrected through a generation of rich scholarship, however, many investigations of the late nineteenth-century history of civil rights organizing devote little attention to the NACW and its regional and local affiliates as political organizations. This chapter argues that recognizing these organizations' importance as sites of political reform activism changes the assessment of African American leaders' political priorities during this formative period. It does so by illuminating activists' embrace of a scope of concerns far broader than those related solely to so-called "political and civil rights" in the classic sense of those terms. The NACW's reform agenda, for example, put early childhood education at the top of its list of priorities and also emphasized vocational training, improved health and medical services and housing conditions, child care, and improved facilities and programs for recreation, arts, life skills, and youth engagement. This social welfare agenda reflects NACW political objectives that also must be figured into conceptions of the legacy early twentieth-century racial justice leaders inherited from a founding generation of national organization builders.

NACW-affiliated activists did not think about social welfare activism in law-related terms. None were lawyers or even trained in the law. But leaders like Church Terrell, Josephine Ruffin, and Wells Barnett certainly had ample exposure to "law talk" in their social context, and the NACW adopted many law-related resolutions on political and civil rights matters. On social welfare matters, the NACW emphasized voluntarist strategies in the private sphere, followed where possible by requests that public institutions take over or at least contribute to these endeavors. This presented a strategy that I argue should be seen as part of a multifaceted turn-of-the-century racial justice agenda.

The NACW members aimed to construct private institutions to fill in where public institutions were failing to meet their responsibilities to bestow the benefits of the Progressive era, nascent social welfare state on African American communities.[2] Where possible as a next step, these activists attempted to get public institutions to assume responsibility, or at least to share responsibility, for the social welfare functions being handled through the private institutions they had built. Put otherwise, African American women's club work sought to shift the boundaries of responsibility between the private and public realms and, in so doing, to lay where possible the groundwork for later reform through the government's assumption of responsibility for social welfare functions. This model for social change activism presented an alternative mode of social reform activism under conditions that did not present direct avenues for law reform.

The NACW members' social reform strategies arose from the political and social context they confronted. They arose not only from an instrumental assessment as to what options were feasible but also from a sense of what kind of work these reformers wanted to do and saw as effective. Unlike the white women reformers of the same time period who were litigating and lobbying for social welfare legislation, African American women wanted to build their own community support systems that would not depend on state beneficence. Law had far less appeal to activists who saw how it had been used against their communities for harmful, exclusionary purposes.

Founding the NACW

The National Association of Colored Women's organizing model involved amalgamating their many secular and religious social reform and social welfare organizations existing at the local and regional levels into a national federation.[3] This organization-building model based on uniting already existing organizations—rather than attempting to build anew at a national level, as did the AAL and the Niagara Movement—proved highly successful for the NACW. Indeed, in its burgeoning membership rolls and high activity levels the NACW looked much more like a true "social movement" than did the AAL, AAC, and Niagara Movement. Those latter organizations always remained small by their official national membership counts, which ranged in the hundreds rather than the many thousands. The NACW, in contrast, grew from approximately 100 clubs sending delegates to its first biennial convention in 1897; to 300 clubs in 1900; 400 in 1902; and then to more than a thousand delegate representatives, reflecting 50,000 members, by 1914, and even more beyond that.[4]

The by now well-known story of the NACW's founding begins with Josephine St. Pierre Ruffin, the widow of Judge George Lewis Ruffin (the first African American graduate of Harvard Law School), who called a conference in Boston to consider founding a national organization of African American women's clubs. Ruffin was at the time president of the vibrant Boston-based Woman's Era Club, which published the *Woman's Era,* a journal that richly captured middle-class African American women's views and concerns. A London antilynching committee had passed on to Ruffin a letter from a Missouri newsman named John Jacks, which attacked Wells Barnett in particular, and the morality of African American women in general, apparently in response to Wells Barnett's great success during an antilynching speaking tour she had conducted in Great Britain.[5]

Wells Barnett's contemporaries greatly admired her as a courageous public figure. Prominent women's clubs bore Wells Barnett's name, and her speaking engagements drew large audiences, with fund-raising proceeds to match. A tiny woman

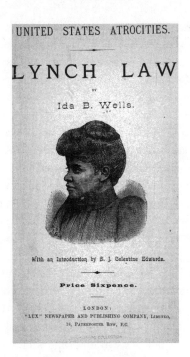

Figure 7.1 Title page from Ida B. Wells, *United States Atrocities: Lynch Law* (1892) (New York Public Library).

not more than five feet tall, Wells Barnett's determined face, framed by full white blouses with fancy lace trim worn atop modest floor-length dark skirts, attested to her intensity and resolve. The fact that Jacks would attack her morals in his scurrilous letter provided the emotional impetus for African American "club" women, as they called themselves, to band together nationally.

Other reasons to organize nationally included the increasingly alarming conditions of the nadir period and the race prejudice of white women's reform organizations, which were displaying the same racist attitudes as those infecting the country as a whole.[6] As NACW president Church Terrell would later explain in justifying the decision to form a women's organization defined by racial identity: "We denominate ourselves colored, not because we are narrow, and wish to lay special emphasis on the color of the skin … [but] because our peculiar status in this country at the present time seems to demand that we stand by ourselves in accomplishing the special work for which we have organized."[7]

The first national conference, held in Boston, was known as the National Colored Women's Conference and resulted in the formation of the National Federation of Afro-American Women (NFAAW). Alabama-based Margaret Murray Washington, Booker T. Washington's third wife, was elected as its head. Ruffin failed, however, to secure the buy-in of another competing federation of women's clubs known as the National Colored Women's League (NCWL). This was the Washington, DC–based club where Church Terrell was a leader. The NCWL had started in 1892, a year before Ruffin's New Era Club, and its affiliated clubs extended as far west as Missouri. Its members were teachers and other professionals and/or the wives of successful professional men, and it saw its primary goal as working to supplement gaps in DC's segregated school system by sponsoring night school classes to offer enrichment in subjects such as literature and foreign languages. Public school teachers or former teachers volunteered their services to teach these classes. According to Church Terrell, the NCWL's members took special pride in having sent some of the students participating in its programs to college and then into future teaching careers of their own. The NCWL also sponsored a model kindergarten serving forty children. Fifteen young women, who were training for teaching jobs under the supervision of a leading kindergarten instruction expert, taught in this program.[8]

With the organizing successes of the NCWL standing behind her, Church Terrell challenged Ruffin's claim to be the presumptive heir to national leadership of a women's club movement. Using her skills as a political strategist, Church Terrell held herself and some of her followers away from the NFAAW's founding convention. In this way, Church Terrell ensured that the next year another conference would be needed to discuss the conditions for "merging" the NFAAW and the NCWL, and she arranged that this conference would be held on her home turf, in Washington, DC. When the conference took place in July 1896, Church Terrell emerged as the elected leader of a new organization, much to Ruffin's disappointment and ongoing resentment. Ruffin was elected first vice president, while Margaret Murray

Washington became chair of the executive committee. Margaret Washington also became editor of the organization's newspaper, the *National Association Notes,* which she produced from the Tuskegee Institute with help from her students.

The new organization was to be called the NACW, reflecting the preference of some leaders, including Church Terrell and Ruffin, to emphasize their multiple ethnic roots through the term *colored* rather than their African descent through use of the term *Afro,* as in the name of the NFAACW. Margaret Washington, Fannie Barrier Williams, and others, who were influenced by T. Thomas Fortune's arguments as to terminology, preferred the Afro-American emphasis, but the contingent favoring the term *colored* outvoted them.

Church Terrell and Ruffin each stood at the apex of African American high society in their respective cities, both of which were long-standing centers of African American intellectual activity. We have already met Church Terrell in chapter 1 as she was growing up in socioeconomically privileged circumstances, obtained an advanced education in languages at Oberlin, engaged in European travel her father financed, became a teacher, and then married Robert Terrell, settling into a life as a leading member of Washington, DC, high society. Josephine St. Pierre Ruffin was considerably older than Church Terrell, having been born in 1842 in Boston, where her father, John St. Pierre, was a successful clothes merchant. John St. Pierre hailed originally from Martinique and was of African, French, and Indian descent; Ruffin's mother was from England. Married by the age of sixteen, Ruffin did not have the advanced liberal arts education about which Church Terrell could boast, but Ruffin, too, had received an elite education "in the best schools of Boston" and possessed a strong intellectual bent.[9] Just as Church Terrell was active in the DC Bethel Literary Society, Ruffin participated in Boston's literary and social clubs and was especially dedicated to organizations devoted to the arts.

In contrast to the college educations of men like Langston, Fortune, Straker, Du Bois, and Ransom, which had focused on political theory, theology, and/or law, both Ruffin and Church Terrell's educations centered on the humanities, and they came to their activism with a humanist ethic of helping others in need. This ethic helped unite the diversity within the NACW without creating the degree of tension about underlying political visions that affected the AAC.[10]

White women social reform activists started to go to law school in small but significant numbers by the early 1900s—Florence Kelley, for example, did so in 1893, and John Milholland's daughter, the iconic suffragette and racial justice advocate Inez Milholland, did so in 1910, graduating in 1912.[11] In contrast, African American women activists, facing the dual discriminatory barriers of gender and race, did not begin to attend law schools in appreciable numbers until the 1920s.[12] Instead, the most typical professional path for educated African American women was in either higher education or lower-school teaching, or sometimes medicine or nursing.[13] Thus none of the national leaders of the NACW in the turn-of-the-century period had training in law. Quite a few of them were involved in literary society circles in which legal topics were frequently discussed, however; both Church Terrell and Ruffin, as well as a number of other NACW figures such as Wells Barnett and Fannie Barrier Williams, were married to lawyers. These women absorbed—by social proximity to, if not by formal training in—strong appreciations for the role of law in shaping race conditions in the country.[14] Nevertheless, the dual barriers of race and sex discrimination that prevented African American women from gaining access to the law as a professional career also contributed to the ways in which they thought about strategies for social reform.[15] They were less interested in legal prescription and more interested in institutional construction than were the AAC's leaders (though at the same time both genders cared deeply about both projects). These divergent strategies each contributed to different but related facets of turn-of-the-century racial justice activism.

Church Terrell's NACW Leadership

Church Terrell's term as president of one of Washington, DC's elite literary societies, the Bethel Literary and Historical Association, or "Bethel Literary" for short, reveals the law-infused intellectual climate of which she was a part. She served in this role, as the society's internal historian reported, over some gender-based objections, but proved herself capable of presiding "with ease and grace, plan[ning] with foresight, and execut[ing] with vigor." Founded in 1880 under the AME, the group had grown from what this historian referred to as "the brothers and sisters in the 'amen corner' " to an organization dedicated to scholarly debate. A review of paper topics provides a window into the key controversies of the time: One "very well written paper" titled "Separate Schools" produced "the most lively discussion up to its time," with equal numbers of members speaking for and against the topic. Industrial education likewise posed a controversial topic, as "opposing forces" clashed after the presentation of a paper titled "The Trades or the Professions: Which Should Our Young Men Undertake?" A paper titled "Individual Development" led to more lively debate. The author argued that "in laying stress upon race pride we are apt to lose sight of individual development"; his critics argued that such a focus on individual accomplishment could lead "to indifference to the needs and conditions of the masses." Frederick Douglass frequently spoke at the society's gatherings, presenting on topics such as "The Philosophy and History of Reform," a paper that met "severe and eloquent criticisms and a battle royal" between Douglass and his opponent, in which "Greek met Greek with vigorous onslaught and heroic defense."[16]

Many of Bethel Literary's members were lawyers, including Everett J. Waring, the leading civil rights lawyer involved in the Brotherhood of Liberty in Baltimore who was one of the first to champion test case litigation as an organizing objective for the AAL. Another was Church Terrell's husband, Robert H. Terrell, a graduate of Harvard University and Howard Law School, who in 1910 became the first

African American municipal court judge in Washington, DC. Still another lawyer member was Lafayette M. Hershaw, who would later help Du Bois found the Niagara Movement and edit its newspaper and then would become one of a handful of African American speakers at the founding meeting for the NAACP. Fellow Niagara Movement member William Henry Harrison Hart, a Howard Law School professor, was yet another Bethel Literary member. Hart would represent himself in a successful lawsuit contesting Maryland's separate cars law in 1905. In 1904 dean of the Chicago African American bar, Edward H. Morris, visited Bethel Literary to deliver a diatribe against Booker T. Washington, in which he dubbed him a sham and a traitor to the race.[17] Other law-trained speakers at Bethel were more favorably inclined toward Washington, including T. Thomas Fortune and T. McCants Stewart, as well as Archibald Grimké, whose primary career was in diplomatic service and freelance political commentary. Washington himself appeared, though his telling of a "darky" joke during the talk he gave there in 1904 was not well received. Most presenters were men, but more than a handful were women. Women's suffrage was debated, and Belva Lockwood presented a paper titled "Is Marriage a Failure?" In 1894 Wells delivered her important work "Southern Outrages" at Bethel, and Church Terrell presented papers as well.[18]

Church Terrell can be better understood sociologically by comparing her to Wells Barnett. As history would have it, these two prominent clubwomen had been childhood acquaintances; Wells Barnett had been born in Memphis just one year before Church Terrell. But Wells Barnett's childhood reflected none of the social and economic privilege that characterized Church Terrell's. While Church Terrell attended private schools with special tutoring in German on the side, Wells Barnett's education was in far less lofty Freedmen's Aid Bureau schools, ending with one year of practical or industrial education at the newly founded Shaw University.[19] In 1878, when Wells Barnett was fifteen, both her parents died in the yellow fever epidemic—the same one in which Mary's father, Robert Church, amassed much of his real estate empire. This forced Wells Barnett to become her siblings' principal breadwinner through teaching and journalism work, with no chance for further education.[20]

Wells Barnett remembered meeting Church Terrell when both were young women in Memphis. As she wrote in her autobiography many decades later, Wells Barnett was highly impressed with Church Terrell, realizing "her ambitions seem so in consonance with mine."[21] Indeed, the two young women were strikingly similar in emerging as national leaders who pursued careers in education and civic involvement. Church Terrell, in contrast, never explicitly mentioned Wells Barnett in her own autobiographical writing. Instead, veiled references seem to indicate some feelings of rivalry as she found herself sometimes outshone by Wells Barnett's extraordinary speaking ability and growing fame as she pursued her antilynching crusade.[22]

Church Terrell, too, was involved in antilynching work, taking over Wells Barnett's position as chair of the AAC antilynching bureau when Wells Barnett resigned. Both women ascribed their commitment to the antilynching cause to the Memphis lynching in 1892 of their mutual friend Tom Moss, an up-and-coming African American businessman whom a white mob removed from jail and murdered, along with two of his employees, after a petty dispute between schoolchildren of different races in Moss's store escalated into another excuse for racial terrorism in that city.[23]

Wells Barnett and Church Terrell shared many other points of commonality as well. Both married prominent African American lawyers, and both husbands supported their wives' public activities.[24] Both women were proud of their dual roles as mothers and leading public figures, and both struggled but persevered in the difficulties of balancing those often inconsistent obligations. In these respects, Wells Barnett and Church Terrell shared an experience somewhat different from that of many white women settlement house and social reform workers of the same period. The latter often renounced long-term marriage in order to pursue lives devoted to their calling of social reform. Wells Barnett, Church Terrell, and many other (but not all) African American women's club leaders, on the other hand, maintained public commitments and marriages and motherhood. Under the narrow social norms of the period, the pairing of these latter two institutions applied with particular rigidity to African American women who wished to maintain their respectability.

This point of difference regarding the desirability of marriage and motherhood sometimes produced tension between African American and white women reformers. As Wells Barnett described, this tension led her to clash with white Chicago social reformer Celia Woolley, who founded and ran the Frederick Douglass Center in Chicago, where middle-class African Americans and whites gathered together for discussions on race and other issues of the day. Woolley had suggested that Wells Barnett serve as vice president of this organization, but Wells Barnett ended up resigning out of pique at what she saw as Woolley's race-superior attitudes. The incident that most irked Wells Barnett involved Woolley's condescension toward her when she spoke about the importance she placed on her motherhood role. Woolley interrupted Wells Barnett to point out that many women, such as Susan B. Anthony, led fulfilling lives without marriage and children. But from Wells Barnett's perspective, standing less than a generation away from slavery and facing social forces that denigrated African American women and deprived them of the opportunities for respectable marriage and child rearing that white women considered routine, performing the role of mother was to be cherished, not downgraded. To Church Terrell, too, connections between her role as mother and her work within the NACW were important to her worldview, and she, too, made this point with explicit reference to slavery's historical shadow.[25]

Ruffin and Church Terrell, as members of a very small group of African American women at the turn of the twentieth century who can truly be classified as "elite," were thus far from typical. The example of Wells Barnett shows a different path to national race justice leadership, one that did not involve starting from a place of social privilege. The general membership of the NACW, though typically "middle" class, likewise comprised women from a variety of social and economic origins.

Nor did Church Terrell's and Ruffin's membership in the small group of turn-of-the-century activists with socially elite origins produce an alliance or a friendship between these two women. Instead, Church Terrell and Ruffin were arch rivals (thus belying any gender essentialist claim that women leaders tend to have kinder or gentler leadership styles). Their rivalry started with Church Terrell's election as NACW president, if not before, and reached its apex when Church Terrell stood for a third two-year term as NACW president in 1899. A prior change to the NACW's constitution, which Ruffin's allies had engineered, arguably barred any president from serving for more than two terms. But the delegates supporting Church Terrell at the 1899 convention asserted that this provision had only prospective effect. Church Terrell then easily won reelection under a regularly conducted, seemingly fair vote. Ruffin and her largely New England–centered base were incensed and blasted Church Terrell in public media outlets, including in the NACW's own internal news organ.[26]

Personally hurt by these attacks, Church Terrell nonetheless carried on with her leadership role, and the tempest soon blew over within the NACW. Unlike the AAC, where the far more underhanded tactics of Washington's supporters in manipulating the 1902 officer election results almost brought about the organization's collapse, the NACW continued to prosper despite such internal political conflict. Indeed, the NACW's national organization-building success went so far beyond that of the AAC as to require further analysis. One of the features of the NACW that made it thrive, as Du Bois would rather enviously point out in his study of the differences between African American women's and men's organizations in this period, was its enormous capacity to tolerate differences in viewpoint because its focus was on an immediate action agenda of lending aid and support to the "less fortunate" members of the race.[27] The NACW functioned, as Collier-Thomas has aptly put it, as a kind of "think tank" for experimenting with and modeling a vast array of projects and strategies, which women's organizations with diverse local bases and resource capacities could adopt as they chose.[28]

The NACW's Organizing Model

To be sure, the NACW's rapid growth stemmed from many factors, including relatively privileged women's ability to devote time to club organizing tasks while their husbands worked at paying occupations. But a key factor involved the fact that, whereas men's organizations such as the AAC and the Niagara Movement became weighed down by controversy, frustration, and lack of success given external circumstances, the NACW thrived through an emphasis on activity that produced concrete results. An important force propelling its growth was its members' enthusiastic engagement with service-oriented work. Such work provided the satisfaction of accomplishment, which in turn spurred greater ambition and even higher levels of activity. This dynamic crucial to organization-building success did not occur to nearly the same extent in the male-dominated national civil rights groups of the same era. Those organizations became bogged down by their inability to achieve significant victories in the political and civil rights arena. Such victories would be forthcoming in future eras, but at the turn of the twentieth century this work suffered from the malaise of repeated frustration in obtaining core objectives. As that happened, men also began to more explicitly define civil and political rights activism as "men's" work and to develop a rhetoric that emphasized their masculine duty to protect the race.

The great variety in NACW affiliates' projects contributed to the success of its organizing model, which often emphasized a corresponding feminine duty to care for the race. This variation in projects related to a host of factors, including region, urban versus rural surroundings, local organizing history, and leadership personalities. One of the most militant local organizations was the Women's Loyal Union of New York and Brooklyn, headed by prominent club woman Victoria Earle Matthews, the journalist and writer who would also found the New York City White Rose Mission and serve as NACW national organizer. Explaining that "[a]mong our members we claim professional women, doctors, school teachers, literary women, writers of poetry and prose, tradeswomen, artists, home-makers and housekeepers," this club reported that its object "is the diffusion of accurate and extensive

Figure 7.2 Victoria Earle Matthews, circa 1893 (New York Public Library).

information relative to the civil and social status of the colored American citizen, that they may be directed to an intelligent assertion of their rights, and united in the employment of all lawful means to secure and retain the undisputed exercise of them."[29]

Toward the opposite end of the militancy spectrum were hundreds of local clubs in smaller communities scattered across the country that devoted their efforts to specific projects such as funding kindergartens and schools and helping the poor. The Married Ladies' Afternoon Club of Xenia, Ohio, reported at a regional gathering on its work raising funds to purchase art for the public schools, while the Phyllis Wheatley Club of Grand Rapids, Michigan, raised funds to help purchase medicines for the poor. Also typical of such reports was one from the Woman's Club of Jefferson City, Montana, which had opened a training school to give children Saturday instruction in sewing, followed by "short talks on temperance, truthfulness and honesty."[30]

The focus of affiliate organizations did not always depend on their settings in rural versus urban locations. The Ladies' Auxiliary Club of Washington, DC, led by Josephine B. Bruce (the wife of former Republican senator Blanche K. Bruce; Josephine Bruce later became a Tuskegee Institute teacher following her husband's death), devoted its work to helping the elderly by providing a warm gathering place and clothing. The Boston Woman's Era Club defined its very different mission as collecting "facts which show our true position to the world," "endeavoring to create sentiment against the proscriptions under which we suffer," and "awaken[ing] in our women an active interest in the events of the day [by] hearing and participating in the discussion of current topics." Some clubs, such as the Woman's Era, were secular in orientation; many others were religiously based, such as the large and highly organized Progressive Circle of the King's Daughters in Chicago, headed by Emma Ransom with Alice Williams as secretary, which defined its mission as "to accomplish all the good possible in His name." Five years later the Dearborn Center Women's Club would report as a "department" of Reverdy Ransom's ICSS.[31] Southern affiliates likewise varied in their orientation. Those in cities such as Atlanta embraced ambitious goals that would continue to fuel the construction of alternative social welfare institutions in that city for decades to come. More rural settings enjoyed fewer resources and usually expressed far more modest objectives, though in these regions, too, clubs varied greatly in their goals.[32] The NACW's objectives focused not only on social welfare goals but also on a range of political and civil rights issues similar to the AAC's priorities. In contrast to the AAC, where Booker T. Washington tried to squelch leaders' public outspokenness, the NACW did not seem to have faced a significant internal dilemma about how outspoken to be. The NACW instead spoke with a united and surprisingly militant voice on the key political and civil rights issues of the day.

Dorothy Salem and others long ago corrected August Meier's error in dismissing the African American women's club movement as only rarely political and thus not worth extensive attention in a study of turn-of-the-century African American thought. Nonetheless, a tradition of bifurcating study of African American activism in the late nineteenth and early twentieth centuries along gender lines arguably continues to distort understandings of the multifaceted objectives of that activism. The NACW's objectives spanned both the political and the civil rights goals to which the AAC attended *and* the social welfare objectives on which African American women and many men focused as well; these objectives were knitted in with classic political and civil rights advocacy. The NACW's political platforms show how social welfare and political and civil rights objectives fit together in turn-of-the-century activists' visions.[33]

When women club members convened in Washington, DC, in July 1896 to discuss merging the NFAAW and the NCWL, they charged a committee on resolutions with addressing matters such as "the Georgia convict system, lynching, and the Florida state law making it a crime to teach white and colored children" together. The resolutions this committee presented blended the NACW's social welfare concerns with many strong statements on political and civil rights issues. One resolution endorsed the dissenting opinion of Justice Harlan in *Plessy v. Ferguson* and gave "hearty thanks to the wise and upright judge," while another resolution deplored the majority's decision in that case. Still another resolution proclaimed that "the separate car law in operation in several of these United States perpetuates an unjust, un-American and unconstitutional discrimination against the Afro-American whose claim to American citizenship is second to that of no [other] race"; that "we must depend on ourselves in this matter"; and that "needless excursions" that added revenues "to enrich the railroads at our own expense" should be avoided.[34] Yet another set of resolutions voiced the delegates' "condemnation of Lynch Law and mob violence," resolved to "redouble our efforts to arouse public sentiment to the demand that the majesty of the law prevail . . . until every human being is guaranteed a fair trial by law," and commended the Republican Party for "at last insert[ing] in its platform a clause denouncing lynching." The next resolution addressed the convict lease system, describing it as a "shame and disgrace."[35] When the NACW's first executive committee met after the convention to adopt a plan of action for the organization's first year, it listed as its priorities "[t]o attack the chain gang system of the South [and] the separate car law," as well as "to do rescue work" in "the alleys and slums of our great cities" and for "the plantation woman and child," while at the same time founding homes for the indigent and generally showing "greater interest in the fallen and wayward."[36]

This attention to a range of political and civil rights issues blended with social welfare work continued well after the NACW's founding. An 1899 appeal in the *National Association Notes* implored women of all races to oppose separate cars laws in the South.[37] Church Terrell's report on the organization's activities at the end of the next year noted with approval the way in which women were agitating on "[q]uestions affecting our legal status as a race." She explained that in Tennessee and Louisiana "colored women have several times petitioned the legislature of their respective states to repeal the obnoxious Jim Crow car laws" and that the NACW had attempted "[i]n every way possible" to call "attention to the barbarity of the convict lease system." Church Terrell promised that against "the convict lease system, the Jim Crow car laws, lynchings and all other barbarities which degrade us, we shall protest with such force of logic and intensity of soul that those who oppress us [will be defeated]."[38] In her 1901 national address, Church Terrell similarly highlighted the problems of convict leasing and general prison reform and called for petitioning the legislatures of states for action against lynching.[39]

At the NACW's 1904 biennial convention, the more than two hundred official delegates in attendance (several times as many as the official delegate count at the AAC's convention that year) adopted renewed resolutions decrying lynchings and Jim Crow legislation and again called on women to unite "to induce our people to refrain from patronizing street cars."[40] This year's resolutions also saw the NACW's first mention of male disfranchisement in the South, when the NACW delegates commended the Republican Party for adopting a platform endorsing a reduction in congressional representation of states that disfranchised voters.[41]

Women's suffrage was also a priority issue for NACW members. Church Terrell saw a strong historical affinity between the NACW's work and that of the earlier Seneca Falls women's rights movement. In her last speech before stepping down from the NACW presidency, Church Terrell noted that "we have learned a valuable lesson from that great organization of women, to whose unremitting zeal, constant agitation against unjust restrictions imposed upon the weaker sex... every woman in this county [is] indebted for opportunities conferred and privileges conferred." She further observed that "we are cheated out of so much of our inheritance on account of prejudice that it is just as necessary for us to contend against injustice and battle with wrong as it was for our more favored sisters sixty years ago."[42] Church Terrell also recognized the need to work with the National American Women's Suffrage Association (NAWSA) and delivered a speech before that organization in 1900, in which she urged it to support universal suffrage regardless of race. The NAWSA and its predecessor organizations' record on race-based suffrage restrictions was a checkered one at best, but Church Terrell saw sufficient importance in that organization's goals to become a lifetime member.[43]

Interest in women's suffrage extended beyond Church Terrell and the NACW's other national leadership.[44] Women reporting on local chapter activities wrote about women's suffrage, as when Baptist women's leader S. Willie Layten of California reported on a Woman's Parliament held in Los Angeles, which discussed women's suffrage from the standpoint of the wife, the mother, the unmarried woman, the working woman, the professional woman, the business woman, and the politician. Layten concluded, "I am certain no woman listening to these logical arguments [any] longer questions the need of the ballot for women."[45] Women's suffrage was an especially favorite topic of the NACW affiliate in Colorado, where state law had granted women voting rights, to excellent effect as the Colorado state editor proudly explained.[46] Here as in other ways, the NACW's political stances reflected its members' awareness that they stood at the intersection of two discriminatory systems. As Church Terrell frequently put it, "not only are aspiring Colored women handicapped on account of sex, and just now it is evident that women all over the world consider the handicap of sex very heavy and serious indeed," but "they are everywhere baffled and mocked on account of their race" as well.[47]

Just as interest in women's suffrage extended beyond the national leadership ranks of the NACW, so activism in political and civil rights matters took place within some local clubs as well as at the national level. Local clubs most often adopted anti-lynching resolutions.[48] But local club activity aimed at influencing law went beyond passing resolutions. Some clubs supported litigation not only through fund-raising for the AAC, Niagara Movement, and other groups but also through independent initiatives. The Virginia Women's League proudly reported in the *Woman's Era* that its members had raised more than four hundred dollars to fund legal representation for three African American women accused of murdering a white woman. The state's highest court had issued a writ of error, and the club hoped this would result in a new trial for the defendants. The following month the Virginia League reported that it had generated interest in the case among both whites and African Americans and had circulated a petition praying that the presiding judge would move the defendants from jail in Richmond back to their local jurisdiction.[49] Later updates from Virginia continued to focus on criminal matters, reporting on prison conditions and the inequitable racial balance in that state's prison population, especially among women.[50] Two clubs Ida Wells Barnett organized in Chicago in 1910 similarly supported prisoners' rights litigation, and she would send the NAACP one of its first criminal defense cases.[51]

Other NACW political activity involved circulating petitions on both state and national legislation, as the New York City Woman's Loyal Union Club did when it organized a drive to support federal antilynching legislation and delivered the signatures it collected to federal lawmakers in Washington, DC. A number of clubs in the South sent petitions to their state legislatures opposing separate cars legislation.[52] Wells Barnett's new Chicago-area clubs protested discrimination in employment and public facilities through letter-writing campaigns and conferences.[53] Although such political work was not the mainstay of, or even included within, the scope of the work of all or even many clubs affiliated with the NACW, it was by the same token not absent from local organizations' activities—a fact too often overlooked as the result of tendencies to disregard the NACW's political dimensions.[54]

Scholars have sometimes assumed that the NACW's internal newspaper, the *National Association Notes*, was relatively tame due to Mary Murray Washington's central role as editor, but reading it produces a different conclusion. Mary Washington and her husband were quite different persons, and she does not seem to have attempted to damp down the NACW's political voice. Indeed, during the Ruffin/Church Terrell imbroglio in which she published the Woman's Era Club attack against Church Terrell on the front page of the *National Association Notes,* Mary Washington defended herself by explaining that she espoused a firm principle of printing whatever was properly submitted to the newspaper for publication.[55] The motto she sometimes included in the paper was "unity in diversity," and a close reading of her newspaper shows it to be notably varied in its perspectives.

Discussions in its pages frequently included promoting women's role in business and the professions. One Texas contributor questioned whether women should continue to desire marriage in light of the gender oppression frequently accompanying that arrangement—a point of view striking for women who had only a generation before been treated as chattel with no right to marry legally in that state.[56] To be sure, such occasional freethinking discussions appeared side by side with expressions of deeply Victorian views about the importance of women's roles in the home and in shaping the next generation of children. These ideas paralleled the classic separate spheres ideology prevalent at the time among female social reform activists of all races. As amply discussed in a now-abundant literature, this separate spheres ideology helped justify women's growing involvement in public affairs by explaining it as a matter of women attending to traditionally "feminine" concerns.[57] Women's participation in public affairs was acceptable because they were undertaking such a role in order to voice their insights into matters within their gendered purview, especially the welfare of children. In the case of African American women, this ideology came with a special twist, as Church Terrell observed in one of her frequent references to her awareness of the historical proximity of slavery in her own background. Church Terrell explained that her focus on caring for the children of the race was an extension of her realization that, not long before, "instead of possessing my only child, a little girl but six years old, I might be hunting her tonight, not knowing where or to whom she had been sold."[58]

Although a separate spheres ideology most certainly dominated NACW's members' justification for their multidimensional activism, they used it to define a broad scope for their public political participation. In her speeches as NACW president, Church Terrell typically began by emphasizing the importance of women protecting children and the home but then quickly switched to discussing women's responsibility for fostering beneficial social conditions for the next generation. She ranged far into other issues, such as prison reform and lynching, which related to women's relationship to children only to the extent that women's responsibility was to care for society's future well-being in general terms. These claims were an effective rhetorical strategy among women reformers of all races at the turn of the twentieth century, serving to legitimize women's activism in the public sphere prior to a general shedding of Victorian values, which viewed women's proper place as in the home. While the NACW was by no means at the vanguard of shifting conceptions of women's social roles at the turn of the twentieth century, its internal discourse reflected the general debate about women's changing status that was going on within society as a whole.

Reexamining the Respectability Critique

Scholars of African American women's experience have frequently noted the way in which African American women's club members were particularly concerned about projecting images of "respectability" to the broader white society. As Evelyn Higginbotham explains, advocates of the ideology of respectability believed that promoting middle-class norms within the race "would earn their people a measure of esteem from white America, and hence they strove to win the black lower classes' psychological allegiance to temperance, industriousness, thrift, refined manners, and Victorian sexual morals." Kevin Gaines points out that this ideology "also represented the struggle for a positive black identity in a deeply racist society, turning the pejorative designation of race into a source of dignity and self-affirmation through an ideology of class differentiation, self-help, and interdependence." Gaines further points out that the construction of class differences in African American communities had much less to do with differences in material assets, which were often not great in light of rampant employment discrimination, than with ideas of who lived in a respectable manner and who did not. Gaines and others have leveled criticism against this emphasis on respectability, noting that a focus on inculcating middle-class values among poorer women overlooked working-class African Americans' struggles to overcome far more immediate material problems.[59] This critique certainly has legitimacy, though there is of course no reason that middle-class African American leaders should be faulted for Victorian sensibilities any more than white activists of the same era.

But might too much criticism be directed to the NACW women's class bias in any case? Such bias certainly could be detected in the NACW's work to the extent that the small handful of truly privileged women of African descent sought to imagine how to provide aid and support to women who enjoyed far less privileged circumstances. Many important women's club leaders, however, hailed from modest economic circumstances. Such leaders include Margaret Murray Washington, born to a sharecropper family in 1865, and Lugenia Burns Hope, founder of the Atlanta Civil Association, who had worked as a dressmaker, bookkeeper, and secretary to help support her mother and siblings prior to her marriage.[60] In addition, class stratification among African American women was far shallower than among whites, so that the respectable middle class included many individuals toiling at working-class occupations. Even some women considered to reside at the apex of this shallower African American class structure, such as Church Terrell, were only a generation removed from slavery. All experienced much racial subordination in their own lifetimes, as Church Terrell recounts in her autobiography.[61] In these respects, the notion of a condescending African American socioeconomic "elite" at the turn of the century seems somewhat off base. Might not strong critiques as to these women's social distance and insensitivity to the situation of the poor be overstated?

Most importantly for the purposes of this project, it is important to note that moral uplift objectives constituted only a part of NACW women's efforts. Much of their work focused on providing key material supports, including constructing the architecture required for delivering social welfare services. In cities that could support fund-raising for expensive projects, women's groups built facilities for hospitals, orphanages, recreation centers, libraries, playgrounds, and the like. Other initiatives involved developing model programs such as kindergartens and free day nurseries to provide child care for working women, as well as promoting public health initiatives, including inoculation programs and health care clinics, and collecting detailed data on conditions in African American communities. In fact, NACW women pioneered methods the National Urban League would later professionalize. Such work included vocational training, vocational placement, and the provision of short-term housing for new migrants, especially women, who were moving from rural areas to cities.[62] Some of these programs remained largely in the "private" or voluntary sector, but even in the early years of the twentieth century much of this work took place at the border marking the so-called public/private divide. African American women's club activism pushed at the boundaries of what should be considered the responsibility of the state. Sometimes it did so in the very act of stepping in to fill the void left by African Americans' exclusion from the benefits of the social welfare state that public entities were in the process of constructing for white communities.

Pushing the Public/Private Boundary

A few examples illustrate these projects NACW activists developed and how they pushed the boundary between private and public social welfare responsibility. Many projects filled in where there were yawning public services gaps for African Americans under Jim Crow citizenship regimes. Fund-raising aimed to literally construct this missing material infrastructure of hospitals, orphanages, and "asylums" (a term used generally to describe facilities to house persons needing special protection).[63] One early priority was establishing facilities for seniors, including former slaves.[64] Another involved sheltering orphaned children.[65] Fancy-dress balls and other forms of entertainment such as plays and musical events had the serious underlying purpose of raising funds to further these goals.[66]

Other service work pioneered model programs such as free kindergartens, day nurseries for infants and toddlers whose mothers worked outside the home, and vocational training.[67] Vocational training programs included, at the most basic level, sewing classes. These were a popular offering because they required relatively few resources to set up, potentially provided women with a relatively well-paying

Figure 7.3 Photo collected by Du Bois, documenting a free class in home economics, circa 1900, where schools made no provision for domestic science for African American girls in New Orleans. Building was rented from "colored YMCA" and refurbished with cooking equipment at a cost of $1,700 (Du Bois Papers, Special Collections and University Archives, University of Massachusetts at Amherst Library).

occupation other than domestic service by responding to the market for fancy dresswork and, as a collateral benefit, produced clothes for those in need.[68] At a level that required more resources and expertise, organizations such as Victoria Earle Matthews's White Rose Mission in New York City sponsored training in the skills needed for paid domestic services work.[69]

The free kindergartens NACW affiliates established throughout the country stood as a centerpiece accomplishment. This was Church Terrell's special priority. Her background as a teacher made her especially interested in early education, and she pushed this project during her three terms as NACW president. Recognizing that the segregated and inferior education systems offered African American children were not benefiting from the educational reforms that were bringing early childhood education to white students, Church Terrell committed the NACW to a national campaign to found such kindergartens in the communities in which African American children lived. Officers of the NACW committed themselves to raising a kindergarten fund that could support sending out a national organizer to arouse the conscience of women and establish kindergartens around the country.[70]

Local club reports indicate that many of the NACW's several hundred local affiliates carried out kindergarten projects to considerable success at various levels of public resource commitment depending on local circumstances. In Kentucky NACW affiliates opened a kindergarten in a public school, furnished through donations and headed by a principal who had graduated from a teacher-training program. In Rome, Georgia, a kindergarten project started with students bringing supplies such as wooden blocks from home, while private donations provided tables and chairs. The city later took over this project.[71] By 1906 three such kindergartens existed in Atlanta, all of which were funded by private contributions and located in donated church facilities.[72] Church facilities housed many such projects, but other projects used public school facilities. Volunteers who served as staff were often trained teachers who donated time beyond their regular workdays. The NACW also pushed to recruit and pay specially trained teachers for these roles. In some jurisdictions these efforts went even further by effectively bringing pressure to bear on school districts not only to provide space and staff for, but sometimes also to entirely take over, these programs by incorporating them into the public education system.[73]

Another major initiative called for setting up free day nurseries for women forced to leave their children in order to work at paying occupations to support their families. These programs did not produce state-funded childcare—a goal still not achieved in the United States. But they did at least recognize a need that was obvious to African American women, many of whom were working outside the home due to financial need many decades before middle-class white women began to move into the paid workforce in large numbers.[74]

The NACW-affiliated activists also monitored developments in the juvenile justice system and especially emphasized the need to rehabilitate rather than condemn young offenders to punitive prison systems.[75] White women reformers were also engaged in juvenile justice work, but here as on a host of other issues African American women adopted a stance that was sometimes cooperative with but sometimes independent of white women's reform perspectives. Thus Anne Meis Knupfer explores the way in which African American women activists in Chicago, such as Elizabeth McDonald and Amanda Smith, at first performed unpaid work as probation officers and opened several homes for African American juvenile delinquents without support from the state. They then either sought and obtained state funding or turned these projects over to the state for operation. This was also an activity with which William H. H. Hart experimented in Washington, DC, as discussed in chapter 8. The results of these attempts at private-state cooperation were often unhappy: McDonald's school closed in 1920, Smith's was destroyed by fire, and Hart spent his retirement in bitter litigation against the federal government for funds owed him. Even so, these less than successful projects reflect early experiments aimed at filling voids left by the discriminatory and inadequate provision of social welfare services. Activists sought to exploit the limited avenues for social reform available to them at the time.[76]

Still another area of NACW affiliates' work involved initiatives in public health. Projects included health screenings and public education campaigns to stem the spread of tuberculosis (also a project Gertrude Mossell promoted within the AAC and one the health committee within the Niagara Movement pursued). The NACW collected statistics showing vastly different mortality rates among the races and promoted strategies to close this gap. Other projects included teaching hygiene, sponsoring nurse-training programs, and experimenting with a variety of methods to provide medical services to those too poor to pay for them.[77] The Woman's Improvement Club of Indianapolis, for example, established a tuberculosis treatment facility, one of the first of its kind, and urged movement "toward social reform grounded in scientific investigation, planning, and alteration of the environment."[78] Lugenia Burns Hope's work in Atlanta also sought to address the prevention of tuberculosis, along with other public health campaigns.[79]

Yet another extensive effort involved conducting surveys and collecting statistical information about African American health and other indices of community well-being. These concerns often led to collaboration with male activists with special interests in sociological studies, such as Du Bois and Lawson. This work in turn provided models for combining sociological data collection with social welfare work—approaches pursued by leaders of the early National Urban League.[80]

Another area of attention within the NACW involved the pernicious increase in labor and employment discrimination during the nadir era. Just as men interested in social welfare work, such as Reverdy Ransom in Chicago and William L. Bulkley in New York City, were sounding an alarm about the rising levels of structural employment subordination African American workers faced, both Ruffin and Church Terrell highlighted declining employment prospects as a priority issue in speeches to national gatherings. Ruffin listed the opening of occupations for the rising generation of boys and girls as her first priority in her 1895 speech convening a national meeting of women's clubs. Church Terrell continued this emphasis in speeches she delivered during her terms as NACW president, noting in 1899, for example, "the alarming rapidity with which [African American women] are losing ground in the world of labor." Church Terrell predicted that, with "[s]o many families...supported entirely by our women,...if this movement to withhold employment from them continues to grow, we shall soon be confronted with a...serious and disastrous" situation. Indeed, Church Terrell put the modern label of illegal "discrimination" on this phenomenon years before many lawyers, steeped in natural law notions of private-sector employment as an area of "freedom of contract," did so. Church Terrell frequently referred to both employer and labor union employment discrimination in addresses she gave to the NACW and to outside organizations, including white women's reform groups. The National Urban League and the NAACP would start to jointly pioneer strategies that depended on law rather than voluntarist methods to attack private-sector employment discrimination in the 1930s. The insights of this forerunner generation of activists, which included Church Terrell, Ransom, and Bulkley, paved that road by beginning to develop an analysis of pervasive employment subordination in the North as well as the South, as a key matter for racial justice activism.[81]

In conclusion, accurate assessment of the contributions of Progressive-era African American women's club work to racial justice organizing requires rethinking categories. African American women's activism spanned the divide between civil rights and social welfare advocacy. It did so through strategies that often were not aimed directly at law reform but at the same time sought to affect legal consciousness, especially conceptions of the boundaries between public and private social welfare responsibilities.[82] These strategies fit the limited spaces for exercising agency that African American women activists encountered in the face of the racialized social, legal, and political constraints of the period. The strategy of building parallel institutions was a purposeful one, designed for the political situation African American women activists confronted.[83]

There were strengths and drawbacks to the strategy of working to construct institutions to fill in resource gaps left by public institutions' discriminatory policies. On the one hand, this strategy avoided the racist dynamics of U.S. law; on the other hand, it left gains unprotected from destruction through either violence or simply the continuing operation of unjust law. But strategies and institutions designed to span the public/private divide have, as democratic experimentalist theorists remind us, important potential. They may be of particularly great relevance in political and economic environments that permit only modest commandeering of public resources. Those situations presented conditions calling for the NACW's strategies of pushing the boundaries between the public and the private by undertaking projects that began with a focus on voluntarist work in the private sphere and then called on public institutions to take over, join with, or otherwise support these projects.

While the women's club movement engaged in this work, the male-dominated civil rights focus sought new avenues for protest after the AAC became stymied by Washington's attempts to exert control. The outlet achieved was the Niagara Movement, which sought to blend civil rights and social welfare work. Soon many NACW activists would become involved in the Niagara Movement too, but not until it lifted its initial ban on women's membership. I turn to that organizing effort in Chapter 8.

8

Asserting "Manhood" Rights: The Niagara Movement's First Year, 1905

In July 1905 twenty-nine distinguished men dressed in dark suits and ties gathered at a tidy Victorian-style hotel on the Ontario, Canada, side of the Niagara Falls to form the Niagara Movement. They did so because they were fed up with Washington's efforts to squelch the Afro-American Council; they wanted a new, uncorrupted national organization that would speak out about the economic and social conditions of the nadir period in a brave, principled manner—in a "manly" way, as they often said. Their organization lasted only a few years, not surprisingly, given Washington's power to block it from all sources of funding support. But in taking the step of founding an explicitly anti-Washington national organization, the first members of the Niagara Movement irrevocably turned the direction of national racial justice organizing and set it on its early twentieth-century course of militant political and civil rights protest.

Accounts vary as to why the Niagara Movement's founders chose Canada as their first gathering place: They may have wanted to symbolize the lack of freedom they faced in the United States; they may have been forced to move from a hotel on the New York side of the border once its proprietor realized who was gathering there; or they may have switched locations at the last moment to confound Booker T. Washington's spies who were sent to scout out what was taking place. In all events, these men had traveled to Niagara Falls by train from eleven jurisdictions: Georgia, Virginia, Kansas, Minnesota, Illinois, Ohio, Pennsylvania, New York, Washington DC, Rhode Island, and Massachusetts, with the intent to found a new national African American civil rights organization. Their founding platform's demands included many of the AAC's but added some other ones as well and often stated them in more insistent tones. Thus the Niagara Movement demanded "full manhood suffrage," the "abolition of all caste distinctions based simply on race and color," the "recognition of the highest and best human training as the monopoly of no class or race," and a "belief in the dignity of manual toil."[1]

Opposing the Tuskegee Machine

Agreeing to lend one's name to the call for the Niagara Movement's founding meeting was no decision for cowards. Doing so signaled opposition to Booker T. Washington, and a significant number of the men who participated in the Niagara Movement's founding had already or would soon experience the adverse consequences of doing so. Boston civil rights radical journalist William Monroe Trotter had been attacking Washington from the pages of his newspaper, the *Boston Guardian*, since 1901. In 1903 Trotter found himself locked up in jail after he led the disruption of a meeting sponsored by the National Negro Business League at an AME Zion Church in Boston. Trotter and his allies hissed from the audience and then sprinkled cayenne pepper flakes on the podium of the speaker (who happened to be none other than T. Thomas Fortune), leading to a general melee and Trotter's arrest. Boston attorney William H. Lewis, who would later receive an appointment as the first African American assistant U.S. attorney with Washington's backing, prosecuted Trotter in a criminal trial that resulted in Trotter's conviction on disorderly conduct charges and sentence to a three-month jail term.[2]

Trotter would soon become a founding Niagara Movement member. Hailing from a relatively well-to-do family as the son of the nation's first African American postmaster general, James Monroe Trotter, William Trotter inherited substantial real estate holdings from his father. Along with his wife, the blue-eyed, fair-skinned Geraldine (or Deenie) Trotter (née Geraldine Louise Pindell), he could easily have settled into a life of financial comfort and high social prestige as a member of Boston's "society" of educated African Americans of elite social origins. But the Trotters chose a different path, dedicating themselves, at great financial loss, to a lifetime of civil rights work. They used their assets to finance the *Guardian* and labored together weekly to put it out. During Trotter's frequent absences to take part in the many local, state, and national civil rights organizations in which he became involved, Deenie assumed the full weight of the *Guardian*'s production work, enabling it to come out virtually without break for twenty-five years.[3]

Trotter was able to retain his independent, anti-Washington newspaper despite its inflammatory rhetoric because he started life with independent financial resources. Other journalists were not so fortunate. Although the young T. Thomas Fortune's radical ideas would live on in the Niagara Movement's underlying vision, the middle-aged Fortune would be nowhere near the new organization's founding meeting. Indeed, the Niagara Movement radicals viewed Fortune as an archenemy, and Fortune was neither invited to nor informed of this secret meeting. He had, after all, not long before participated in seizing control of the AAC's leadership with underhanded procedural tactics, acting in coordination with Washington. Historians debate how much independence Fortune relinquished as he moved into Washington's orbit, but it cannot be denied that the Niagara Movement's leaders, at

least, viewed Fortune as a Tuskegee machine operative despite the radical tendencies of his youth. Fortune's classic biographer, Emma Lou Thornbrough, explores
the complicated set of factors that drew Fortune to Washington, including extreme
financial necessity, personal ambition, and genuine feelings of admiration and
friendship toward the charismatic leader from Tuskegee. Fortune performed many
tasks for him, including ghostwriting and public speaking on Washington's behalf.
Nevertheless, Washington in the end decided that Fortune was too unreliable to
remain the editor of *The Age* and orchestrated Fortune's removal from the institution he had built through a lifetime's labor. This left Fortune and his wife Carrie with
no income during a period in which Fortune was suffering from an acute mental
disability. To blame Washington for destroying Fortune would be to give Fortune
too little agency in his own destiny, but to say that Washington left his former
friend Fortune destitute during a desperate personal crisis is to state a documented
historical fact.[4]

The Age was not the only highly respected African American publication whose
independence Washington destroyed. Niagara Movement member and Atlanta
journalist Jesse Max Barber also lost his publication, *The Voice of the Negro,* and was
driven out of Atlanta and then out of journalism altogether for defying Washington's
attempts to control his editorial pen. In 1903, as a condition of backing Barber as he
sought to raise the financing for this periodical, Washington installed Emmett Scott
as Barber's coeditor at the *Voice.* When Barber refused to accept Scott's interference, Scott quit his position in anger. Barber continued to edit the *Voice* on his own
and included balanced but sometimes critical reporting on Washington's activities.
Even worse in Washington's eyes, Barber included positive accounts of the Niagara
Movement's organizing activities in the *Voice.* This defied Washington's campaign
to suppress all reporting about the Niagara Movement in order to downplay its
significance.[5]

The Atlanta race riot's aftermath gave Washington his opportunity to punish
Barber for failing to take orders. The causes of the riot had roots in white resentment
about African Americans' economic progress and political participation demands.
In a four-day period in September 1906, whites, ostensibly angry about false reports
of several black-on-white rapes, went on a violent rampage that included murdering
approximately forty African Americans and destroying the downtown neighborhoods in which African American businesses and other properties were located.
The city's law enforcement officers merely stood by and let the rioters proceed.[6]

The Atlanta riot exposed the flaws in Washington's strategy of focusing on
economic progress without also publicly demanding protection of equal citizenship status and political rights. Reverdy Ransom would emphasize this point in an
important speech he delivered from Faneuil Hall in Boston in the aftermath of the
riot.[7] But Washington was not one to ruminate on such paradoxes; he instead used
the opportunity the Atlanta crisis presented to put Barber's very life in jeopardy.
After the Atlanta riot Barber had written an anonymous letter to the editor of a

New York newspaper, in which he condemned the politicians who had inflamed race hatred with false reports of rapes. The letter further argued that preventing future riots required "impartial enforcement of the laws" and public authorities who acted to "protect all the people." Washington soon discovered that Barber was the letter's author and disclosed his identity to Atlanta officials. They in turn presented Barber with the choice of leaving the city or risking lynching. Faced with this ominous warning, Barber fled to Chicago. Washington's agents then wrote articles accusing Barber of "cowardice" and Ransom of hypocrisy for criticizing the South from the comfort of the North.[8] Washington also blocked Barber's efforts to find a new publisher for his newspaper. After a number of failed attempts to get a new journal off the ground, including initiatives in cooperation with Du Bois, Barber eventually gave up on his journalistic ambitions and turned to dentistry as a substitute career. Moving to Philadelphia to practice this vocation, Barber later became a leader of that city's NAACP branch.[9]

Du Bois, too, found that his affiliation with the Niagara Movement created professional problems. Atlanta University had appointed him as professor of history and economics in 1899. Washington urged white funders of the university to withhold donations unless the institution disowned Du Bois, but Du Bois luckily found himself protected by the university's proud civil rights history. The oldest school in the country devoted to African American graduate education, Atlanta University was accustomed to the problems this mission could generate. It offered, for example, free college tuition to the children of its faculty members, and many of its professors, black and white, took advantage of this benefit. This prompted the Georgia legislature, which was appalled by "social mixing" of the races in college classrooms, to pass a statute in 1887 denying state funding to any mixed-race college. The university nevertheless refused to dismiss its white students, resulting in the loss of all of its state funding.[10] The threat of losing private funding by continuing to provide Du Bois with an intellectual home was thus par for the course for the university, and its president stood fast in supporting Du Bois. But Washington's pressure interfered with Du Bois's efforts to raise supplemental funding for the many research projects and conferences he was working on in Atlanta, and these stresses contributed to Du Bois's eventual decision in 1910 to leave academia to become editor of the NAACP's publication, *The Crisis*.[11]

Du Bois, born a free citizen in the North but lacking inherited wealth or social privilege, fell into the category of African American turn-of-the-century leaders who were most vulnerable to Washington's power to make or break professional careers. Until 1903 Du Bois exercised well-justified caution in his dealings with Washington, and even flirted with the benefits of being on Washington's good side, including a possible job offer at the Tuskegee Institute and unfulfilled hopes that Washington would support him in his 1900 bid to become assistant superintendent for Washington, DC's African American schools. Washington's endorsement instead went to Robert Terrell, who received effective behind-the-scenes help from his politically adept spouse, Mary Church Terrell. In 1901 Terrell left this job to become a municipal court judge, again with Washington's backing, and Du Bois tried again for the superintendent's post, though he never received it.[12] Du Bois thus spent a long, cautious decade attempting to work with Washington before he decided to publicly criticize him. He took this step in his balanced, thoughtful essay titled "On Washington and Others," included in his 1903 book, *The Souls of Black Folk*. Here Du Bois eloquently articulated his vision of how racial justice could be achieved through distinctively African American perspectives and effort.

By 1905 Du Bois had abandoned all hope of working productively with the Tuskegee machine. He had withdrawn from the Carnegie-funded Committee of Twelve effort, convinced that Washington would thoroughly control it, and quit the AAC for the same reason. That summer he took the bold step of calling for the Niagara Movement. This new organization, as its founding call proclaimed, would stand for "freedom of speech and criticism," "freedom of an unsubsidized press," and "efforts to realize these ideals under a leadership of courage and ideals"—all transparent criticisms of the Tuskegee machine.[13] Joining Du Bois in this call were fifty-nine others, many of them members of the AAC's radical contingent, including Trotter, Ransom, Bentley, McGhee, and Harry Smith.

Wells Barnett would very likely have been present at the Niagara Movement's founding as well except for one problematic fact: The Niagara Movement at its birth excluded women from membership or even attendance at its business meetings. This rule apparently resulted from Trotter's insistence that civil rights organizing should be the exclusive province of men.[14] In 1906 Du Bois would bow to women's pressure to organize a Women's Department within the Niagara Movement, but the organization's emphasis always remained on the assertion of "manly" or "manhood" rights—favorite phrases Du Bois and others used in discussing the Niagara Movement's central objectives.[15]

The Niagara Movement's Exclusionary Membership Rules

In its policies on gender, the Niagara Movement was anachronistic even for its own time. The 1890 Afro-American League had certainly permitted women members, as one would expect, given Fortune's staunch support for women's rights and professional success. The AAC, too, had many women members and even adopted a policy to promote women in leadership positions. But for all of its militancy—and, indeed, arguably in connection with that very militancy—the Niagara Movement's founding posture was to exclude women altogether. Its founding leaders believed the work that needed to be done involved "manly" duties. This work included defending African American women but granted women an inferior, nonparticipatory role. In this emphasis on "manly" battle, as in other respects, the Niagara Movement epitomized contradictions of the old and the new juxtaposed at the beginning of the twentieth century: Old Victorian gender stereotypes clashed with the reality of highly effective women activists, just as old notions of a class-based elite provided the membership principle for an organization that had pledged itself to dissolving all distinctions based on both race and class.

The Niagara Movement's gender exclusion seems particularly puzzling given that neither the AAL nor the AAC had such exclusionary rules. There are hints that some Niagara Movement leaders distrusted women's club movement activists because of their often more sympathetic stance toward Washington. Du Bois's correspondence reveals him to have been initially tepid in his response to women's objections to the Niagara Movement's exclusionary membership rule; he wrote back to one such objector proposing only small-scale modifications, involving a proposed "woman's auxiliary" that "shall grow from small beginnings as duties call it." He thus would start with "a small national committee of women under a secretary who will correspond with them." Most important in his mind was ensuring appointment to this committee of women of the highest "standing." Perhaps Du Bois was worried about women members leaking information to Washington or about alienating Trotter, whom he at the time appeared to regard as essential to the Niagara Movement's success. Time would prove both the Niagara Movement's exclusion of women members and Du Bois's attempts to mollify Trotter to have been bad ideas. In the Niagara Movement's first year, however, both men appeared to feel a need for a gender-exclusive space to plan their "manly" agitation, and that is what Du Bois, as the organization's secretary or chief officer, initially set out to create.[16]

A Talented Tenth Organizing Model

Du Bois's organizing model for the Niagara Movement corresponded to his "talented tenth" idea. What Du Bois wanted to do was to gather the male professional elite of the race into an exclusive organization that would lead the way forward as it determined best.[17] He believed that this natural leadership class could be counted on to wisely and effectively guide the broader masses in their shared project of racial advancement. Du Bois's views about the superiority of an elite social class were not unusual at the time. Most progressive reformers, including figures such as Jane Addams and her fellow settlement house workers, believed in the inherent superiority of the social elites of all "races" (or what we would today term ethnicities). Prevailing views about equality would evolve rapidly over the course of the early twentieth century, and Du Bois's views about effective organizing models would soon change as well, in part based on his experiences with the Niagara Movement. But as the new century opened Du Bois believed that an organization ideally suited to exercise race leadership could best be launched by gathering together a small elite group of African American professional men who had proved their mettle by being willing to stand openly against the Tuskegee machine.

Du Bois thus carefully handpicked the men he invited to attend the Niagara Movement's founding meeting. To his disappointment, not everyone he deemed of sufficiently high character to merit being invited to join the Niagara Movement shared Du Bois's regard for the worthiness of his new organizing project. Two leading intellectuals particularly disappointed Du Bois in steering clear of the Niagara Movement's founding: These were lawyer and diplomat Archibald Grimké and Howard University professor and sociologist Kelly Miller. These two figures had taken part in early brainstorming conversations about what a new organization might look like, and Du Bois had believed they would come with him to the Niagara Movement, but they did not.

These conversations had begun after the 1904 Carnegie-funded conference to assemble leading race leaders for discussion in New York City. Du Bois had briefly participated in this effort, engaging in tense negotiations about the proposed list of invitees, during which he attempted to add the names of persons who had either overtly expressed or whom he believed covertly harbored anti-Washington views. The meeting took place, but in its aftermath it became clear that Washington would dominate the leadership group that emerged from the conference, which was called the Committee of Twelve. When this became clear, Du Bois resigned.[18] Du Bois believed that Grimké and Miller, who had both participated in the Committee of Twelve and had reputations for being independent thinkers, would share his views about the need for a new, independent organization. Instead they chose to remain neutral, to his disappointment.[19]

Other leading male African American civil rights advocates weighed the risks and benefits of openly opposing Washington and did not join the Niagara Movement, either, even though their political sympathies appeared closer to the Niagara Movement's than to Washington's. These included Judge Terrell of Washington, DC, who had obtained his position as the first African American municipal judge in DC in 1902 through Washington's support but who sometimes gave public speeches in which he sounded every bit like a civil rights militant.[20] Terrell, like Grimké, was an astute political operator who believed it wise to stay out of the factional bickering of turn-of-the-century national civil rights advocacy. Indeed, given the political circumstances of the times, one had to have a very strong sense of principle—amounting even to rashness—to be willing to risk Niagara Movement membership. A tally of willing members as compared with cautious decliners reveals this important aspect of the Niagara Movement's brief existence: Those who voted with their feet by joining the Niagara Movement in its early years did so at significant personal risk. Doing so reflected an example of the many brave individual acts upon which the twentieth-century civil rights movement would be based.[21]

The Founding Meeting

In the end, of the fifty-nine men who signed the Niagara Movement's call, a smaller group of twenty-nine traveled to the Canadian border to take part in the organization's founding meeting. The intrigue that surrounded this meeting helped fuel the excitement of the moment. Prominent men such as Boston lawyer Clifford H. Plummer reduced themselves to working as spies for Washington in seeking to report to him about the Niagara Movement's organizing plans, which its organizers guarded in closest secrecy.[22]

The minutes of this meeting reflect the excitement and ambitious hopes that new beginnings allow. The founding platform focused on a combination of civil and political rights—such as "full manhood suffrage" and the "abolition of all caste distinctions based simply on race and color"—along with economic and social welfare issues. The meeting sought to put flesh on these founding objectives by developing a multifaceted, concrete action plan.[23] On the meeting's opening day, July 11, 1905, a packed agenda took the assembled men from 9 a.m. until late into the night. Du Bois gave a report as provisional secretary, and the assembled participants then proceeded through a series of sessions chaired by men who had been previously assigned the task of gathering information and formulating preliminary action plans. First among these were the Committees on Conditions and Needs and Economic Opportunity, followed by the Committees on Voting, Education, and, finally, "Crime Rescue and Reform." Meetings of the Finance Committee, Committee on Organization, and Committee on Legal Defense followed. At seven o'clock in the evening, the committees on Press and on Health gathered to formulate plans, and, finally, at 8 p.m., the men engaged in prayer led by Rev. Garnett R. Walker, a social gospel Baptist minister from Florida who emphasized the responsibility of religious institutions to work for social justice on earth. Still not finished for the day, Walker's prayer set the scene for an important late evening report to the assembly from the Committee on Organization.[24]

The next morning's meeting returned to the important matter of permanent organization, along with finance. In the afternoon the delegates considered reports from the Committee on Conditions and Needs, and, finally, Legal Defense. The final day focused on the reports each of these respective committees had prepared following their meetings during the preceding two days, sequenced in the following order: (1) economic opportunity, (2) "crime rescue" (meaning addressing the problem of crime and its causes), (3) education, and (4) health. A midafternoon break allowed the meeting attendees to visit the Niagara Falls, where a group photograph captured many of the twenty-nine founding members dapperly sporting light straw hats with contrasting fabric rim bands as they stood or sat solemnly before a false background depicting the grand Niagara Falls. Then it was on to the serious work of the final session, convening at 8 p.m. with reports on the Committees on Address to the Nation and the Press and the meeting's final adjournment.[25]

The initial meeting, accompanied by the secrecy and intrigue required to throw Washington's spies off track, inspired participants with a sense of newness and daring. But as other leaders of national civil rights organization-building efforts had discovered before, the real work of sustaining a fledgling organization past the charismatic moment of its kickoff required hard and often lonely labor with

Figure 8.1 Founding the Niagara Movement, 1905 (Special Collections and University Archives, University of Massachusetts at Amherst Library).

little immediate gratification or glory. That work fell to Du Bois, now officially installed as the Niagara Movement's general secretary. From his summer office in Massachusetts and then from his desk at Atlanta University, Du Bois sent regular entreaties to members reminding them of the duties they had assumed and the positions they had accepted. Du Bois urged members to continue devoting intense efforts to recruiting "an intelligent, upright membership of the very best class of Negro Americans." He further emphasized—repeatedly, thus suggesting also with some frustration—"above all, answer this letter quickly."[26] Other letters from Du Bois apprised members of plans to hold a coordinated series of Thanksgiving meetings and to piggyback on celebrations many churches and other organizations had planned to commemorate William Lloyd Garrison's one hundredth birthday. Du Bois urged members to see to it that at each such celebration a "Niagara Movement man speak" and emphasized the importance that each such meeting take "the practical turn of taking a firm stand for National aid to Negro education."[27]

Organizational Structure and Leaders

The Niagara Movement's founders adopted an organizational structure based on a system of state chapters. There were twenty-three such chapters, and a state secretary headed each one. Together these state secretaries constituted the Niagara Movement's national executive committee.[28] Under the organization's bylaws it was Du Bois's prerogative to appoint these state secretaries, and he tried to choose wisely in accordance with his talented tenth organizing model. He chose Clement G. Morgan, a Harvard-educated lawyer, to represent the Massachusetts chapter. Morgan had been born to enslaved parents in Virginia in 1859 and, after attending high school in Washington, DC, had initially become a barber. He later gained more preparatory education in Boston and then put himself through Harvard College, working as a barber to support himself. He became the third African American to receive his law degree from Harvard Law School and set up a law practice in Cambridge. Clement and his wife, Gertrude (née Wright, originally of Illinois), participated in the city's exclusive social clubs, such as the Omar Khayyam Circle, whose members devoted themselves to discussing the learned poets at evening gatherings to which they wore full evening dress, including floor-length gowns for the women. Like fellow Bostonian and Harvard alumnus William Trotter, Morgan was a staunch anti-Bookerite. Both men enjoyed the vantage point of elite educations in the North and exclusive social standing, and both believed that neither they nor African Americans generally should refrain from insisting on equal citizenship rights.[29]

Representing Georgia was Du Bois's close friend and colleague John Hope, president of Atlanta Baptist College (later called Morehouse College), a small liberal arts college dedicated to training African American youth for positions in the professions. Hope's father, James Hope, had been a Scottish merchant in New York City. He was white but began living with his brother's African American mistress, Mary Frances Butts, in Augusta, Georgia after his brother died and James began managing his brother's affairs. Mary Butts gave birth to John Hope in 1868.

Hope's early childhood had been one in which he felt little different from the whites in his extended family, until the Hamburg massacre of 1876 took place. The event occurred right across the river from Augusta and involved armed white men shooting and killing members of an African American militia in one of many incidents of racial violence that marked the end of Reconstruction in South Carolina. The event swept in the antiblack Redeemers and a new era of more oppressive race relations in Augusta. When Hope's father died soon afterward, the measures he had tried to take to provide for his mixed-race family were ignored. John and his mother and siblings found themselves suddenly transformed from wealthy, high-status Creoles to a fatherless, impoverished African American family. Hope dropped out of school to help take care of his family but later obtained his older brother's financial assistance to attend a New England preparatory school and then Brown University. Hope graduated in 1894 and then began his career as an educator, moving to Atlanta Baptist College as a professor in 1898 and taking over as president in 1906.[30]

Illinois was represented by Bentley, who was an anti-Bookerite radical within the AAC and an active member of Ransom's ICSS. Washington, DC, boasted as its state secretary the well-connected lawyer Lafayette M. Hershaw, who was widely regarded as one of his generation's most brilliant intellectuals. Born enslaved in North Carolina in 1863, Hershaw was of French and African descent and spoke and read French fluently. After attending Atlanta University, he became a teacher and then a principal in the Atlanta Public Schools. In 1890 he came to Washington, DC, as an executive in the U.S. civil service, serving as a land examiner at the Department of the Interior. In 1892 he received his law degree from Howard, after which he continued in various positions within the Department of the Interior, winning the admiration of both Republican and Democratic political appointees.[31]

Like Morgan in Boston, Hershaw was a leading force in Washington, DC's social and literary clubs, including Bethel Literary as well as an even more exclusive club Hershaw founded, known as the Pen and Pencil Club. That club was made up of forty leading African American men active in public affairs, who met regularly to debate the political and policy issues of the times. Washington and his associates viewed the club as a hotbed of anti-Washington, "radical" civil rights thinking, and he tried mightily but unsuccessfully to destroy Hershaw's career by having the African American newspapers and agents under his control attack Hershaw with accusations of disloyalty to Roosevelt. Bipartisan political connections cultivated through his decades of federal civil service allowed Hershaw to withstand these attacks, and he eagerly joined forces with other anti-Bookerites in the Niagara Movement.[32]

Hershaw's deep scholarly bent led him to a strong affinity with Du Bois, and Du Bois regarded him as one of his closest allies. Hershaw was a member of the American Negro Academy and published several articles in its prestigious set of publicly disseminated papers. One examined the citizenship status of free African Americans prior to 1860, while another analyzed laws that discriminated on the basis of race in labor. Through these scholarly contributions Hershaw sought to draw lessons from history that could help explain the nation's trend toward Jim Crow practices and legislation. With similar intent, another of his papers examined peonage.[33]

Hershaw became a coeditor and financial supporter of the Niagara Movement's short-lived publications, *The Moon* and *The Horizon*. In 1909 Hershaw would join Du Bois in trying to expose Washington's manipulation of the African American press to Oswald Garrison Villard, who soon afterward called the meeting that kicked off the NAACP's founding. Along with Du Bois, Ransom, and others, Hershaw was one of the handful of African Americans invited to speak at the NAACP's founding convention.

From Pennsylvania, Du Bois appointed yet another lawyer, George W. Mitchell. Mitchell was a relatively young Niagara Movement member who had earned his BA and law degrees from Howard University. He maintained a solo practice in Philadelphia, where he reportedly served a predominantly white clientele.[34] Indeed, an examination of the list of the Niagara Movement's Executive Committee members shows that a substantial number, although somewhat less than a majority, were lawyers.

Figure 8.2 The Original Twenty-Nine (with two missing) (Special Collections and University Archives, University of Massachusetts at Amherst Library).

The Niagara Movement's Legal Committee

Many lawyers served on the Niagara Movement's Legal Committee as well. Along with Morgan, Hershaw, and Mitchell, lawyers on the Legal Committee included Chicago-based Ferdinand Barnett and Edward H. Morris, both of whom have already been introduced, as well as Massachusetts lawyer Edmund B. Jourdain, who had descended from an old New Bedford abolitionist family that had made a fortune in whaling.[35] Another member was Butler R. Wilson, a graduate of Atlanta University and then Boston University's law school, who was a highly respected criminal defense lawyer in Boston (and who later became the head of the NAACP's Boston branch).[36]

Harrisburg, Pennsylvania, lawyer W. Justin Carter also sat on the Legal Committee; Carter had earned his law degree at Howard Law School in the 1890s and maintained a diverse general practice with both white and black clients. He successfully prosecuted at least one civil rights case against a hotel in 1898, and in 1904, after having been rejected for membership in the county bar association only months before, he delivered a speech to an all-white audience on citizenship rights that has been preserved as classic. Carter would later become a member of the NAACP's Committee of One Hundred.[37]

Perhaps the key lawyer who served on the Niagara Movement's Legal Committee was Fredrick L. McGhee, the former AAL and AAC legal department leader. McGhee ran a successful criminal defense practice in St. Paul, Minnesota and served the Niagara Movement both as state secretary for Minnesota and as Legal Committee chair. Du Bois later credited McGhee with the original idea to organize the Niagara Movement, and in the Niagara Movement's limited extant records McGhee stands out for the amount of work he performed on the organization's behalf, providing extensive reports on his region's activities and on legal matters even when many other officers could not find the time to do so.[38]

McGhee was a person who liked to take part in organizations, but he had developed an aversion to most of the white-led options for political involvement. At various times he had tried both Republican and Democratic party affiliations, but in the end he became disenchanted with both parties because of their lack of commitment to African American rights. He also on occasion lent his rhetorical talents to the third-party Populists.[39]

The painstaking research of McGhee's biographer provides valuable detail about McGhee's life in the law. Born in Mississippi several years before the Civil War, McGhee and his family appear after emancipation to have joined the exodus of freedmen who followed Union soldiers fleeing from Mississippi to Tennessee after defeat in ongoing battles with Southern forces in 1864. At the age of nineteen, McGhee joined his brother in the small but steady early trickle of freedmen from the South who migrated to the great city of Chicago. Working as a hotel porter during the day and attending law school at night, McGhee obtained his law degree from Northwestern University and took up practice with Chicago's leading African American lawyer, Edward H. Morris, in 1885.

McGhee had natural courtroom talent and a tall, handsome appearance, with intense eyes and a rugged square jaw, and he soon became a favorite within the African American high society set in Chicago. But like so many others of the social elite of his generation, McGhee chose a life devoted to civil rights struggle rather than one of more comfortable complacency. He decided to eschew a schedule of invitations to the events of the Chicago Autumn Club, which sponsored frequent fancy-dress balls, to take on harder challenges—though he always remained involved in society events and seems to have enjoyed them.

McGhee had a controlled but clearly discernible streak of adventurousness about him, which showed itself not only in his early career decisions but also in his willingness to throw his effort into the Niagara Movement. In 1889 he displayed his risk-taking bent when he decided to stake out new territory by moving to the young city of St. Paul, Minnesota, along with Morris's brother, William, to take his chances at opening a law practice there. McGhee's calculated risk paid off; he came to enjoy a fair measure of celebrity in St. Paul, earning a reputation as one of the city's best legal orators. Newspapers reported in complimentary fashion on his courtroom arguments without reference to his race, and audiences packed the courtroom to hear his closing speeches. McGhee concentrated his practice on criminal defense, and his clients were usually white, often prostitutes or lower-level operatives within organized crime groups. Edward Morris had his share of such work in Chicago as well, as we have already seen. It may be that this was the work with which McGhee had prior experience and was able to obtain in St. Paul, or it may be that he enjoyed it because of the opportunity it gave him for courtroom theatrics. In his personal life, however, McGhee was the very opposite of his clients: a teetotaler and a Catholic whose recreational interests focused on the arts.[40] McGhee's professional direction gave him a level of success in his legal career that was becoming increasingly unusual among African American lawyers due to the heightening effects of race prejudice during the nadir period. Through his work he was able to build a materially comfortable and socially successful life for his family, albeit a very busy, even harried, professional life for himself. He died in 1915 at the age of fifty, soon after helping found a St. Paul chapter of the NAACP, ostensibly of complications related to pneumonia, but in fact, his biographer concludes, from overwork.[41]

Still another lawyer among the Niagara Movement's founding members who was among the most active in its legal efforts was William H. H. Hart. Born in Eufaula, Alabama, in 1857, of an enslaved mother and a white slave-dealer father, Hart had supported the Radical Republicans in his youth. Like the Fortune family, Hart was forced to flee his home with the coming of the Redeemers. Hart reportedly walked, in stages, from Alabama to Washington, DC. There he enrolled at Howard University and eventually obtained several advanced law degrees. Earning his living as a law professor at Howard, Hart also founded the Farm School for Colored Boys in the city, an endeavor that caused him to clash with District of Columbia authorities after they took over his school as a public institution. Like many of these arrangements, such public-private cooperation often ended badly for the private actors involved. After government authorities failed to compensate Hart for his investments in the farm school project, Hart engaged in protracted litigation over the matter, reportedly leaving him bitter and bankrupt in his old age.[42]

Hart had a reputation for having a fierce temper as well as outstanding oratory skills. But his most important legacy was a legal case for which he was renowned at the time, namely, his victory in pursuing one of the first successful court challenges to segregation in interstate transportation. Hart filed this case on his own behalf in 1905, after he was thrown off a train in Maryland for refusing to move to a segregated car. He won the case in Maryland's highest court on the theory that the state's separate-cars statute imposed too great a burden on persons traveling across state boundaries to survive constitutional scrutiny under the interstate commerce clause. Although this novel approach did not gain traction for many decades, it eventually helped provide the constitutional basis for enactment of the federal Civil Rights Act of 1964.[43]

Like many Southern-born activists, including Wells Barnett, McGhee, Fortune, Morgan, Hershaw, and Walker, Hart was among many civil rights figures of the era who began their lives in slavery. Indeed, an analysis of the social backgrounds of the founding members of the Niagara Movement found that nine began life enslaved and almost 75% were born in the South of poor families. At the same time, close to 80% received college educations, and one third went on to earn graduate degrees, usually in law.[44] Thus most of the Niagara Movement men had achieved recognition as members of Du Bois's talented tenth through lifetimes of hard work rather than from any head start of inherited social privilege. These facts belie the common notion that early civil rights activism was the province of an elite who inherited their status through the lucky accident of birth into aristocratic light-skinned, mixed-race families. Although this latter description applies to the backgrounds of approximately half a dozen Niagara Movement founding members, the remaining men who were not born into slavery, including figures such as Ransom and Mitchell, hailed from backgrounds of extremely modest financial circumstances and limited early educational opportunity. These facts highlight the importance of refraining from slipping into stereotypic thinking about turn-of-the-century race leaders as a detached elite with experiences widely separated from those of most African Americans.

The racially segregated social context of turn-of-the-century life in the United States also affected the professional lives of the Niagara Movement men. McGhee, for example, can fairly be characterized as one of the leading civil rights litigators of his time, but he, like his mentor, Edward Morris, did not make his living primarily from pursuing civil rights cases. McGhee did on occasion take on such cases, often experimenting with contracts or torts-based claims, which were the kinds of civil law he most often encountered in his everyday practice; he did not necessarily head first into constitutional law terrain. Nor was McGhee's civil rights work and his other lawyering activity neatly separated into pro bono and fee-generating categories. McGhee pursued civil rights cases with hopes of fees and success but also a noticeable willingness to drop these cases when those hopes proved unlikely. This approach shaped the way his civil rights cases developed (or failed to do so), as in the examples of his handling of Jim Crow car cases for the AAL and the AAC.[45]

Because of this work for the AAL and the AAC, McGhee had more experience litigating civil rights cases than anyone else on the Niagara Movement's executive committee. He had been the head of the AAL's legal department and in this capacity had at least filed—though apparently not pursued to completion, for reasons not entirely discernible from the distance of history—several civil rights matters.[46] McGhee had also been a key member of the AAC's legal committee. Once he switched his allegiance to the Niagara Movement, he frequently delivered reports to its members about the status of state civil rights statutes, again focusing on explicit, concrete sources of civil rights law rather than simply expounding on lofty, abstract constitutional law principles.[47] It was probably his hardheaded familiarity with how civil rights cases might actually arise in practice that led McGhee to head the Niagara Movement's Legal Defense Committee, also called the Legal Department. With this position McGhee took on the duty of attempting to get off the ground legal "test cases" as one of a myriad of strategies, including legislative lobbying and public education, that the founding delegates committed themselves to pursuing.

Finding a First Test Case

In choosing a first test case for the organization, McGhee had to confront the Niagara Movement's lack of funds. It was all well and good for Washington to pay Wilford Smith to file lawsuits contesting political and civil disfranchisement of African Americans in the South, given Washington's access to sources of funding for such work. It was very much another thing for an organization with virtually no treasury to undertake such projects. To have a hope of succeeding, a Niagara Movement test case would have to have a number of features that would render Niagara Movement sponsorship feasible. First, it would have to involve a jurisdiction in a state in which the Niagara Movement had members—and preferably lawyer members who could serve as local counsel. Second, it would have to be relatively straightforward with regard to the law involved. Complicated constitutional law questions related to Southern states' efforts to disfranchise African Americans required lawyers highly experienced in constitutional law matters—who were usually white, given the legal profession's highly discriminatory occupational hierarchy at the time. (In this respect Wilford Smith was all the more outstanding as an exception proving the rule.) To turn to white lawyers to handle litigation would have contravened the Niagara Movement's organizing model, which focused on African Americans assuming leadership for the progress of the race.

The well-tried model for easily generated test case litigation stretched back to individual and group acts of resistance to the indignity of public accommodations segregation. Resisters had been refusing to move and then sometimes pursuing cases in court for as long as whites had been attempting to impose segregation. McGhee was very familiar with this history. His professional mentor, Edward H. Morris, had won a civil rights case before the Illinois Supreme Court in 1888 under an Illinois antidiscrimination statute based on the denial of first-class seating for an African American couple in a theater. McGhee undoubtedly knew about this case since he was working for Morris at the time.[48] Fortune had pursued and won a case under a similar New York statute in 1891 and had used this case as a last fund-raising rallying cry for the AAL. It thus made perfect sense for McGhee to look for a public accommodations or transportation matter to kick off the Niagara Movement's test case ambitions.

McGhee also had the state of the law to consider in evaluating how to direct the Niagara Movement's litigation efforts. On the one hand, it might make sense to pursue public accommodations and intrastate transportation cases under the state laws of jurisdictions that prohibited such discrimination. These were the state statutes that some Northern state civil rights groups had pursued to enactment in the wake of the U.S. Supreme Court's invalidation, in its 1883 opinion in the *Civil Rights Cases,* of the Reconstruction-era *federal* legislation that barred public accommodations discrimination. The *Civil Rights Cases* did not, however, bar *states* from prohibiting discrimination in public accommodations or intrastate transportation. Civil rights activists had exploited this "space for agency" left for antidiscrimination legislation in states where political conditions supported such strategies. Pursuing cases to enforce those statutes thus presented one highly winnable option, following the path the AAL had set several decades earlier. This strategy was not necessarily the one that promised the most impact, however, because those states with antidiscrimination statutes were the very ones that had at least expressed a nondiscrimination principle in their laws. Winning a case under those laws would not significantly expand the national bounds of antidiscrimination protection as the Niagara Movement delegates wanted to do.

Cases challenging segregation in *inter*state transportation on federal constitutional grounds thus seemed the best avenue for test case litigation that would be both relatively inexpensive and most broadly effective if won. These cases would arise under a backdrop of federal or national legal principles rather than state law and would, if successful, push those principles in directions that recognized core constitutional provisions addressing equality in citizenship rights. Moreover, there was some potentially relevant new law developing at the federal level through the Interstate Commerce Commission. The first version of the 1887 statute creating the ICC had contained a provision requiring that separate accommodations for African American passengers also had to be "equal," but this language did not survive in the version of the statute that finally passed. Nevertheless, the ICC had sometimes ruled that separate but equal facilities were required in interstate train transportation, articulating a concept the U.S. Supreme Court then upheld in 1896 in *Plessy v. Ferguson.*[49] Most Niagara Movement men, not surprisingly, vehemently opposed this separate but equal concept and were highly enthusiastic about bringing a challenge to it. Hart's 1905 win in Maryland's highest court, which declared race-based segregation in interstate transportation altogether unconstitutional on "burden to interstate commerce" grounds, provided an exciting precedent, handed down the very year the Niagara Movement was founded. *Hart v. State* suggested that segregated transportation in interstate commerce could be knocked out entirely rather than simply being made to conform to the strictures of *Plessy*. The problem was finding a case that could present the facts to push this theory.

As it turned out, McGhee did not have to wait long for facts giving rise to the kind of test case he was hoping to find. The organizing plans for the Niagara Movement's next annual meeting produced just the kind of simple but promising facts that the Niagara Movement's Legal Department required, when Barbara Pope, traveling from Washington, DC, to the Virginia countryside, found herself being hauled to the local courthouse after her train car passed into Virginia and she declined to change seats.

A Second Annual Meeting

Unlike the conspiratorial, "all business" first meeting of the Niagara Movement, to which "ladies" were emphatically and entirely "not allowed," the organizers of the Niagara Movement's second meeting hoped to set a very different tone. The mood they strove for was celebratory, with women and children affirmatively encouraged to attend—though women continued to be warned that they would not be permitted to attend the Niagara Movement's business meetings. The organizers especially encouraged couples and families to travel to the meeting's location, where they could enjoy the recreational opportunities provided on the mountain-ringed grounds of Storer College in Harper's Ferry, West Virginia. The location and date would also serve to highlight a historical event exemplifying the uncompromising demand for full citizenship rights to which the Niagara Movement was dedicated. The date chosen commemorated the fiftieth anniversary of John Brown's first antislavery uprising, and the conference organizers planned a tour for attendees of the nearby fort where Brown later maintained his last stand before being captured and executed. The organizers hoped in this way to inspire reflection on the continuing need to demand equal citizenship rights in uncompromising terms.

These more serious objectives were to take place between picnics and games of croquet. Invitations thus went out emphasizing the dual objectives of recreational opportunities combined with serious protest objectives: "Bring your opera glasses, tennis racquet, your hammock, some music and that instrument," and "come for inspiration and vacation." Expect weather that will be "cool and delightful," "but at the same time, "Plan to act—bring your brains." And remember, this time, "Women and children welcome."[50]

With this call to travel to West Virginia, the Niagara Movement may have put a test case in motion, just as the AAL's and the AAC's transportation test cases arose from travel to their conventions. It is not clear whether the test case the Niagara Movement developed in connection with the 1906 meeting did arise directly out of convention travel. The case began when Pope, a "cultured woman" hailing from Washington, DC, attempted to travel by train from her home to the Virginia countryside two weeks before the meeting. According to news reports, Pope was fond of vacationing in the country and had done so many times before. This time, however, she would meet with the indignity—and financial and physical harm—of being ejected en route and subjected to a criminal fine after she refused to move from her first-class car. Virginia had by 1904 enacted several Jim Crow transportation statutes, so this treatment could not have been unexpected. Lawyers Hart and Mitchell came to Pope's aid, handling the case for her in the initial proceedings with assistance from local counsel. But McGhee, recognizing a promising civil rights test case opportunity when he saw one, quickly urged the Niagara Movement to assume responsibility for it under its organizational auspices, launching what would end up being the Niagara Movement's central experience with civil rights test case litigation.

Pope's arrest occurred on August 7, 1906, and was widely reported in local papers. After being evicted from the train when she refused to move to a segregated car, Pope told the conductor that she was employed as a clerk at the ICC and was well aware of her rights. His response was to escort her to the nearby courthouse, where the mayor of Falls Church fined her ten dollars.[51] The timing was perfect, and Pope's case would become the rallying cry for the test case litigation aspect of the Niagara Movement's multifaceted action agenda at its second annual meeting.

The Beginnings of Twentieth-Century Protest in the Niagara Movement's Experience, 1906–1909

The Niagara Movement's 1906 meeting at Harper's Ferry ran for five late-summer days in a setting of "mountain scenery of unsurpassing beauty and grandeur." As J. Max Barber reported, the attendees found themselves surrounded by a "crimson banner" of sumac in fall colors and skies "exultant with the skylarks' wondrous melodies" as they took part in the meeting's many well-planned programs. This setting provided the delegates, both naturalistically and intellectually, with a range of vision "immense and majestic," providing a "wondrously set slate" for the work the delegates were setting out to do. Three public sessions, spread over the evenings of August 15 and 16 and the afternoon of August 17, featured musical entertainment and addresses from speakers including Trotter, Barber, McGhee, and Hart. Friday, August 17, was designated John Brown Day in honor of the fiftieth anniversary of John Brown's first antislavery raid in the Kansas Territory. At sunrise on that date the meeting attendees began a barefoot pilgrimage to the Harper's Ferry building where John Brown organized his last stand during his antislavery attack on the U.S. armory in that town. In the afternoon the public meeting continued to pursue the theme of Brown's significance to the ongoing racial justice struggle.

Ransom on John Brown's Legacy

The program featured an address by Du Bois and another one by Rev. James Robert Lincoln Diggs, a radical Baptist pastor who had a law degree and a PhD in sociology and had been one of the Niagara Movement's founding members. Reverdy Ransom followed with the keynote address. His speech was so stirring, according to Barber, that it "caused women to weep" and "men to shout and wave their hats." Already on their feet, the participants closed with a rousing choral rendition of the "Battle Hymn of the Republic." Ransom's speech cinched his reputation as a key Niagara Movement rhetorician. As Barber reported, it was simply "the most eloquent address I have ever listened to." William Ferris, later describing the many personalities involved in the Niagara Movement, claimed that "genius" flowed from Ransom's lips, "the most gifted orator...in recent years." Even the often critical editor of the *Washington Bee* called it "a rare masterpiece" and a "classic of effective and convincing oratory."[1]

In the speech Ransom invoked many of the themes he had been emphasizing for years, with some changes in emphasis to reflect the changing conditions of the new century's beginning. Ransom's central theme located the Niagara Movement in the long history of civil rights struggle, in which John Brown stood as an early martyr and hero: "Garrison could write and Beecher could preach, while the silver-toned voice of Phillips pleaded," but it was John Brown who "performed the *doing of it.*" After additional description of Brown, Ransom tied history to current concerns. Noting the increasing migration of African Americans to the North, Ransom insisted on a continuing need to fix civil rights conditions in the South: "Today Negroes are coming North in increasing numbers. But this does not change or modify a revised constitution in any southern state, abolish one Jim Crow car, or stop a single lynching." Next Ransom attacked the current president, just as he had done before the AAC in 1899. Now the president was Theodore Roosevelt, whom Ransom condemned for his silence on enforcing the Fifteenth Amendment. Ransom then placed the current state of the nation's politics in historical context:

> It is, indeed, paradoxical that a nation which has erected monuments of marble and bronze to John Brown, Frederick Douglass, William Lloyd Garrison, Charles Sumner, and other abolitionists ... now sits supinely down, silent and inactive, while work of the liberators is ignored, while those who fought to destroy the Niagara Movement, *regain in the halls of Congress the victories they lost on the field of battle,* while the Constitution is flouted and the Fifteenth Amendment brazenly trampled underfoot.

Pointing out that neither political party was a friend to African Americans, Ransom took up the question of what strategies fit these conditions. He painted a bright line between the Bookerites and the Niagara Movement. As Ransom saw it:

> Today two classes of Negroes, confronted by a united opposition, are standing at the parting of the ways. The one counsels patient submission to our present humiliations and degradations; it deprecates political activity, ignores or condones the usurpation and denial of our political and constitutional rights, and preaches the doctrine of industrial development and the acquisition of property, while it has no word of protest or

condemnation for those who visit upon us all manner of fiendish and inhuman indignities....

The other class believes that it should not submit to being humiliated, degraded, and remanded to an inferior place.... It believes in money and property, but it does *not believe in bartering its manhood for the sake of gain.* It believes in the gospel of work and in industrial efficiency, but it does *not believe in artisans being treated as industrial serfs,* and in laborers occupying the position of a peasant class. It does not believe that those who toil and accumulate will be free to enjoy the fruits of their industry and frugality, if they permit themselves to be shorn of political power.

Ransom closed by returning to his theme tracing the long historical trajectory from John Brown's rebellion to the Niagara Movement's birth: "The rifle shot at Harpers Ferry received defiant answer from the cannon fired upon Fort Sumter. This nation needs again to be aroused. The friends of truth and justice must be rallied. But men cannot be rallied without a rallying cry; and even with this upon their lips, there must be a lofty standard to which they may resort." The Niagara Movement, in Ransom's vision, was the organization that would restore the lofty standard of unbending civil rights protest lost in the Bookerite era.[2]

Getting Down to Business

With less fanfare, the members-only business meetings of the organization then took place, convening at the late hour of 9:30 p.m. following the conclusion of the public gathering. The Rev. Harvey Johnson of Baltimore, founder of the Baltimore Brotherhood of Liberty in 1883, delivered the meeting's convening invocation. John Hope, chair of the Committee on Education, presented the committee's recommendations that the Niagara Movement continue to push for federal legislation to improve school conditions in the South and to compensate for African American children's loss of educational opportunity due to discrimination. Ransom was active in the ensuing discussion, suggesting that the report be made broader to encompass conditions outside the South and to encourage well-equipped technical schools as well as classical curricular offerings. McGhee gave the health committee's report in the absence of its chair and focused on the work taking place on tuberculosis prevention and on Du Bois's study of African American health conditions undertaken under the auspices of Atlanta University.

Social gospel minister Rev. J. Milton Waldron spoke as well. Waldron was from Florida but would soon move to Washington, DC, to serve as pastor of the Shiloh Baptist Church. From this position he played an increasingly important role in the Niagara Movement until frustration with its elitist organizing model led him to focus on new organizational models as the century's first decade ended. Like many Niagara Movement leaders, Waldron became a leading activist in the early NAACP, serving as president of its DC branch until a clash with Hershaw, Grimké, and others led to his ouster in 1913. In his comments at his first national Niagara Movement meeting, Waldron emphasized the need for a multipronged approach that would stress "the gospel of cleanliness, water and air." The Rev. Richard R. Wright Jr., Ransom's successor at the ICSS in Chicago, sent in a report from the Committee on Suppression of Crime, which he chaired, and the committees on legal defense and civil rights delivered reports as well.[3]

The state branches also presented their work. According to Barber's later report, Illinois branch secretary Charles Bentley described local work in Chicago to block initiatives to institute racial segregation in Chicago schools. The local committee had worked to secure the appointment of men with compatible views on the body that set the city's education policies and collaborated with Jane Addams and other white reformers on this and other local issues. They had also worked to oppose the Warner-Foraker amendment to the rate bill and had succeeded in having a Niagara Movement member appointed as a municipal judge. The Massachusetts branch was similarly very active. In Maryland the state chapter had worked with suffrage organizations to block attempts to institute disfranchisement there. Minnesota, under McGhee's leadership, had held a large conference. Other states presenting local reports included Pennsylvania, Rhode Island, and New York.[4]

At the next morning's business meeting Barber presided, filling this role in Du Bois's absence. Du Bois had been called to a meeting with the Niagara Movement women attendees, who wanted to discuss their concerns about the Niagara Movement's sex discriminatory membership rules. In the meantime, Barber chaired a discussion of the delegates about a case in which one of these very women was serving as test plaintiff. This was the case of Barbara E. Pope, the woman from DC who had been arrested and fined in Virginia for refusing to occupy a Jim Crow car. The delegates voted to fund the expense of completing an appeal in Pope's case. Acting in his capacity as head of the Niagara Movement Legal Committee, McGhee then presented an overview of the status of African American civil rights in selected states as background to considering further test case strategies. At 9:30 p.m. that evening, following the gathering's last public meeting and program, the delegates reconvened their business meeting to wrap up their agenda.[5]

By the end of the meeting, the delegates had adopted three quite disparate priorities. First, they avowed a renewed commitment to "an effort to secure national aid to Negro education." Second, they resolved to work on health issues, with a particular focus on antituberculosis work. Third, on the recommendation of its Legal Department, the Niagara Movement would continue to pursue the Barbara E. Pope interstate travel case as a means of furthering the work the organization wanted to undertake against Jim Crow and, in the future, against disfranchisement as well. As Barber later elaborated, the plan was to "secure two or three significant court decisions," working in conjunction with "any organization or anybody who is honestly seeking to uproot these evils."[6]

The delegates also approved resolutions that highlighted the organization's philosophy and demands. Drafted by Du Bois and read to the delegates by Hershaw, these resolutions, titled "An Address to the Country," demonstrated the Niagara Movement's mix of civil rights militancy coupled with social welfare concerns, as well as socialist-leaning rhetoric coupled with a growing emphasis on law and due process rights. They also showed the organization's continuing vestiges of old-fashioned notions about gender, and finally, they reflected the approach of the Niagara Movement's Committee on Crime. As the Niagara Movement delegates stated:

> First we would vote; with the right to vote goes everything: freedom, manhood, the honor of our wives, the chastity of our daughters, the right to work, and the chance to rise...Second, we want discrimination in public accommodations to cease....Third. We claim the right of freemen to walk, talk and be with them who wish to be with us....Fourth. We want the laws enforced against rich as well as poor; against Capitalist as well as Laborer; against white as well as black. We are not more lawless than the white race, we are more often arrested, convicted, and mobbed. We want justice even for criminals and outlaws. We want the Constitution of the country enforced. We want Congress to take charge of the Congressional elections....Fifth. We want our children educated....We want the national government to step in and wipe out illiteracy in the south....We want our children trained as intelligent human beings should be and we will fight for all time against any proposal to educate black boys and girls simply as servants and underlings, or simply for the use of other people. They have a right to know, to think, to aspire.[7]

The Women's Membership Issue

The Niagara Movement delegates were clear on the list of demands they would present to the outside world, which distinctly echoed the AAL's list of demands from a decade and half earlier. They were less united on the internal issue of women's membership. The meeting organizers' enthusiastic invitation to women to attend the Harper's Ferry meeting meant that this issue could no longer be put off. By the end of the meeting, Du Bois's negotiations with the Harper's Ferry women attendees had produced a compromise plan, under which women could choose among several options for Niagara Movement affiliation. First, women could opt to pay the full dues men paid, of five dollars a year, in order to become full members. These women would be organized into a separate body headed by a national secretary for women. Du Bois had appointed Gertrude Morgan, the wife of Clement Morgan, chair of the Massachusetts men's chapter, to this position. The plan was to eventually appoint such "women's secretaries" for women members in each Niagara Movement state chapter, but this process would await women's joining in sufficient numbers to warrant this step. Women who wished to become full members would also have to contend with strict vetting procedures under the Niagara Movement's membership system. This system required each candidate for full membership to receive majority approval by vote of the state organization's members as well as a second confirming vote by the national executive committee. The cumbersome record-keeping requirements this system imposed would soon prove highly problematic for the organization's future. But no one foresaw these difficulties during the heady days of the Harper's Ferry meeting.

The negotiated compromise Du Bois reached with the Niagara Movement women members also offered an alternative route for women to associate themselves with the organization. This route avoided the more onerous requirements of becoming full members and allowed women to avoid paying the hefty full membership dues. Instead, women who "sympathize with the Niagara Movement" could pay a lower one-dollar associate membership fee, which would entitle them to attend annual meetings but not to vote in them. Finally, the plan Du Bois and the Harper's Ferry women attendees hammered out allowed women's clubs to affiliate with the Niagara Movement by paying a five-dollar annual affiliation fee per club. This option, too, would allow members of such affiliated clubs to attend annual meetings, though not as voting members, and would grant one delegate from each such club voting privileges at Niagara Movement business meetings. Only a few women's clubs appear to have chosen to affiliate in this manner.[8] It is not clear why this was so, given that many individual women involved in the club movement joined the Niagara Movement. Perhaps the individual membership option proved easier because it avoided potentially controversial group affiliation decisions.

With this plan before them, the Niagara Movement delegates voted their agreement that the organization would no longer discriminate on the basis of sex in membership. No one seems to have pointed out, however, that they had solved their gender issue by instituting their own form of "separate but equal." Nor did anyone seem to notice the irony of segregating women into their own division in an organization devoted to ending Jim Crow. The minutes merely announced, "Properly qualified persons may be admitted to the Niagara Movement without distinction of sex."

Although some aspects of the membership requirements would become formally equal, the high dues requirement for voting membership affected women and men differently; fewer women than men opted to pay the fee. Dues records show that almost all of the twenty-six women who became Niagara Movement members in 1906 opted for associate membership status at the one dollar per year rate. Four

stalwarts, including two unmarried women, chose to pay the five dollar dues obligation for full members, thus joining the ranks of the seventy-five male full members
who remained current on their dues. Later more women—especially, it appears
on the basis of very incomplete data, unmarried ones—opted for full membership
status. Still, there was always a disparity in the gender balance within the full membership ranks. Again, the irony of this arrangement in its similarities to "neutral"
poll tax requirements imposed to discourage African Americans from voting in
Southern states appears to have escaped everyone's attention.[9]

The Niagara Movement's New Women Members

Who were these women? Many of their names remain obscure, in part because of
the historical convention, so annoying to historians of women's experience, under
which women frequently identified themselves by appending "Mrs." to their husband's first and last names. But a number of women's names are unambiguously
recognizable, and it is worth investigating their biographies because this aspect of
uncovering the Niagara Movement's history remains incomplete.[10]

A brief survey provides much information about the general characteristics of
these female Niagara Movement members. Many of them were educators. Their
chief intellectual interests tended to focus on literature, through participation in
literary societies and also sometimes in publishing writing of their own. In their
class and status backgrounds they were typically, but not always, descendants of
the African American free elite. Many were married. Some in this group joined the
Niagara Movement even though their husbands did not. Others were single. In age
they varied widely. Most who are identifiable today played leadership roles in the
women's club movement, a fact that is probably due to the high rate of club movement involvement by middle-class African American women during this era. But
it is also true that the Niagara Movement and the NACW shared similar priorities,
because both organizations combined interest in civil rights issues with concerns
about social welfare matters such as public health and community uplift. This, too,
undoubtedly attracted women to the organization.

Like their male counterparts, the Niagara Movement women who are today identifiable had records of personal achievement. Medical pioneer Dr. Rebecca Cole, for
example, joined the Niagara Movement in 1906 as an associate member. Sixty years
old, Dr. Cole had surely reached a stage in her life when new activist commitments
were discretionary, but she was motivated to express her affinity with the Niagara
Movement's goals. Cole had been the second female African American graduate of
a U.S. medical school. She had pioneered the field of public health while serving in
various positions providing health care services to low-income populations, including in her 1899 appointment as superintendent of a home run by the Association for
the Relief of Destitute Colored Women and Children in Washington, DC. In earlier

Figure 9.1 Women members of the Niagara Movement at the Harper's Ferry meeting, including Delilah Murray (second from left), Ida D. Bailey (fourth from left), Charlotte Hershaw (far right), and Gertrude Morgan (seated), 1906 (F. H. M. Murray Papers, Moorland-Spingarn Research Center, Howard University).

work in Philadelphia she opened a women's center to provide medical and legal services to women and children without financial resources. When Du Bois attributed the high African American death rate from tuberculosis to ignorance about hygiene, Cole corrected him, pointing out that landlords who provided substandard housing shared the blame. Cole was probably attracted to the Niagara Movement because of her long acquaintanceship with Du Bois and their shared interest in public health issues including antituberculosis work.[11]

Another older woman who joined the Niagara Movement in 1906 as an associate member was Helen Appo Cook, the wife of DC tax collector John F. Cook Jr. Both members of this couple were descendants of distinguished free African American families. At sixty-nine years of age, Helen Cook was also well beyond the stage of life in which acquiring new organizational affiliations signaled either a sense of obligation or an ambition to advance to new leadership roles. Cook had been the founding and longtime president of the Washington, DC, Colored Women's League, in which capacity she wrote a "Washington Letter" for the *Woman's Era,* and she was active as a social reformer in many other ways as well. In 1898 she shared a speaking platform with Du Bois to denounce the attribution of negative behavior traits to the inborn tendencies of the race, pointing instead to the effects of poverty and prejudice. Cook may have been attracted to the Niagara Movement due to her shared affinity with its talented tenth concept of leadership and its dual emphasis on equal citizenship rights and social welfare goals.[12]

Two other Niagara Movement women with strong ties to women's clubs were younger, and both went on to assume important leadership roles in the early NAACP. Carrie Williams Clifford, forty-four years old, was one of the few women to join the Niagara Movement in 1906 as a full voting member. Clifford had been the founding president of the Ohio Federation of Colored Women's Clubs, one of the few women's groups to formally affiliate with the Niagara Movement. She had served as national NACW secretary in 1900 and in July 1906 ran unsuccessfully against Elizabeth C. Carter for national vice president at large. Clifford was not a close friend of Church Terrell, having once rejected Church Terrell's request for an invitation to speak before the Ohio Federation, but she was a close ally of Du Bois. Capable and ambitious, Clifford published several books of poetry and frequently contributed essays and poems to publications, including Barber's *Voice of the Negro,* the Niagara Movement's *Horizon,* and then the NAACP's *Crisis,* as well as the National Urban League's *Opportunity* magazine. In 1910 Clifford would move to Washington, DC, with her husband, William H. Clifford, a lawyer and Republican state legislator who was appointed as a war department auditor. From this location she became an important local leader of the NAACP's Washington, DC, branch.[13]

Clifford's opponent in the 1906 NACW national officers' election, Elizabeth Carter, also joined the Niagara Movement as an associate member. Carter had been president of the NACW's New Bedford, Massachusetts, chapter. Prior to that, she had been a founding member and recording secretary of the NFAAW and founding president of the Northeastern Federation of Colored Women's Clubs. Not surprisingly given her geographic allegiances, Carter was a Ruffin ally and had publicly criticized the outcome of the 1899 NACW convention after Church Terrell won reelection to a third term as national president. Carter had been elected as recording secretary at that meeting but soon resigned from that post for "unspecified personal reasons."[14] She had been the first African American to be appointed a public school teacher in New Bedford and in 1897 established a home for the aged in that city.

Carter was thirty-nine years old when she joined the Niagara Movement. Three years later she became the NACW's fourth national president. In 1910 she was appointed as a member of the NAACP's first national General Committee, which served as its advisory board, and also was active in its DC chapter, where her energy, along with Clifford's, helped establish that branch as one of the largest and most active in the country.[15]

Other female Niagara Movement members had been or were schoolteachers, often with strong interests in literature. These included Medora Gould, who was unmarried and a full voting member. Gould was the eldest daughter of African American Civil War soldier William B. Gould (an ancestor of Stanford law professor and highly respected former National Labor Relations Board chair William

B. Gould IV). She had been appointed a drawing teacher at Livingstone College in Salisbury, North Carolina, in 1890, though she does not appear to have spent her entire working life in this position. A prominent participant in literary societies, Gould had served as literary editor for the *Woman's Era,* where she reviewed publications ranging from traditional English classics to new works by African American women.[16] Another Niagara Movement member, F. Eva Lewis, was also unmarried and paid the full membership rate. Lewis left traces of her life as an active Bethel Literary member who enjoyed defending the "new novel" and published short stories in the *Woman's Era.*[17]

Maria L. Baldwin was a third female Niagara Movement member who was unmarried and joined at the full dues rate. A prominent Boston educator, Baldwin served as the principal of the Agassiz School (later renamed after her), where the Boston elite of both races sent their children. A lover of literature, Baldwin took classes at Harvard University, participated in the Omar Khayyam Circle, and lectured and taught widely. One of her pupils, e.e. cummings, would later laud her influence on him.[18]

Yet another full member was Mrs. Mattie Allen McAdoo, a contralto soloist who toured internationally with her husband, Orpheus, until his death in 1900. McAdoo continued to perform as a singer and later worked for the Phyllis Wheatley YMCA in Washington, DC. McAdoo escaped Gertrude Morgan's sex-segregated department to head the Niagara Movement's arts department, perhaps because of her special artistic talents.[19] Like others who joined, McAdoo was a close friend of Du Bois. Similarly, Du Bois invited Mary White Ovington to be a member after she sent in a five-dollar donation.[20]

Still another group of women affiliated with the Niagara Movement were married women. Some were far more active in the Niagara Movement than their husbands. Falling in this category was not only Carrie Clifford but also Annie E. Conn Cromwell, the second wife of John Wesley Cromwell, a Howard Law School–trained lawyer and civil service employee in Washington, DC. John Cromwell had been the editor of the *People's Advocate* (the DC publication at which Fortune had worked during law school) until he lost his job and his newspaper after Democrat Grover Cleveland's election as president. John Cromwell later became an educator and served as president of the American Negro Academy.[21] Annie Conn Cromwell affiliated herself as a Niagara Movement associate member in 1906 and retained this status in 1907. She came from Pennsylvania, and her stepdaughter described her as "a woman of the world" interested in clubs and parties, but little other biographical information is available about her.[22]

Still another woman important to the Niagara Movement, who first appears on the Niagara Movement's membership roster as a member of Morgan's women's committee in 1907, was test case plaintiff Barbara E. Pope. Pope was yet another woman of her era with a strong literary bent. An acclaimed short story author, Pope had worked for periods as a schoolteacher in Washington, DC, as well as a government clerk. Her family lived in Georgetown, and Pope had sufficient social status to have her recreational comings and goings reported on in the *Washington Bee,* as was common in the society pages of local African American papers.

Pope's short stories reveal her to have been very much the "new woman" about which *NACW National Notes* commentators debated. Her stories often gently poke fun at the manners of the members of "society." In one story, a social climber, Mrs. Fletcher, vacations in the country in the hopes of meeting another woman of higher social status who also vacationed at the same house. Mrs. Fletcher treats poorly a young woman who dresses and behaves in a plain, unassuming manner, only to discover that this young woman is the niece of the wealthy woman Mrs. Fletcher was aiming to impress. Another of Pope's stories explores the gradual decision of a young society woman to give up an engagement proposal from a man of great wealth after becoming enamored with a less wealthy but far more intelligent and interesting man, who in the end asks her to marry him. Still another story explores with ambivalence an experiment a landowner and his hired handyman undertake in sharing ownership of and responsibility for managing a farm. The two agree that all laborers hired to work on this land in the future must share in the ownership rights. In the end the hired hand is not willing to give up what he now owns to others, and the agreement collapses. Here Pope espouses views far from avid egalitarianism.

Most interesting is Pope's story titled "The New Woman," which examines the tensions within a new marriage. The wife, Margaret, is beautiful with a brownish yellow complexion, large black eyes, and raven hair; dresses in exquisite clothes; and has been brought up equally along with her brother to exercise both traditionally masculine and feminine skills. Margaret has always wanted to be a lawyer and wishes to attend the court proceedings of her attorney husband. The husband objects to this and other manifestations of his wife's desire to assume more masculine functions, protesting that the courtroom is no place for her delicate sensibilities. Margaret reminds her husband that he, too, has a sensitive and refined nature, so his logic would preclude him from his occupation as well. In a happy-ever-after ending, the differences between husband and wife gradually mellow—but without the wife ever achieving her desire to practice law. Perhaps here Margaret is a stand-in for Pope, or perhaps Pope was using her fiction writing to reconcile the "new woman" with the traditional expectations of conventional men.

In any event, Pope's life did not have the happy ending she was able to create for her characters. Although the African American press approvingly noted Pope's debut as an author, her tragic death from suicide several years after the end of her Niagara Movement test case received little attention.[23]

Another category of Niagara Movement women members were the wives of the Niagara Movement's male leaders, including Charlotte Hershaw, Gertrude Morgan, and Delilah Murray, the second wife of Niagara Movement founding member and *Horizon* editor Freeman Henry Morris Murray. Unlike some others, Delilah Murray had no claims to elite ancestry in her own background. She originally joined

Murray's family as a washerwoman with special skills as a seamstress, and cared for Murray's children after his first wife fell ill and then died of tuberculosis. Soon afterward, Delilah married Murray and continued to help him manage his large family.[24] It is likely that some of the other Niagara Movement women whose identities cannot be traced came from modest economic backgrounds as well; information about women who were not part of the era's social elite by either personal background or marriage is, not surprisingly, harder to uncover.

Charlotte Hershaw's leadership of the Niagara Movement's "Women's Circle No. 1" in the District of Columbia attests to her activist skills. She raised one of the highest local chapter fund-raising totals to support the *Pope* case and also sent letters thanking Senator Foraker for his support in the Brownsville affair.[25] Still another DC dynamo was Ida Dean Bailey, wife of Dr. Henry Bailey. Ida Bailey became what Du Bois would later characterize as the "lion" of the Niagara Movement's female membership. Du Bois gave Bailey what he viewed as the ultimate compliment when he wrote about her in *The Horizon* after her untimely death from an illness in 1908: "We think of women as things to be loved and wifed. We think of friendship as primarily masculine. But Ida Bailey was...a woman and a friend—a combination, rare but wonderful in its full realization."

Bailey's deathbed message, printed by several newspapers, delivered a charge to race activists to do the following: "Fight race discrimination"; "Fight the Jim Crow Cars"; "Lend a hand to Monroe Trotter; hold up his hands, for if you don't agree with all his methods, you know he is honest"; and "be brave men; be brave women." These values show Bailey's reasons for joining. Looking for an uncompromising protest organization, she found it in the Niagara Movement. This is perhaps the central commonality that unites the Niagara Movement women members across differences in class background and other identity markers: They shared a willingness to formally affiliate with the Niagara Movement as an expression of their commitment to its platform of forceful, principled protest.[26]

At this point, despite the internal organizational travails soon to come, the Niagara Movement had sown the seeds for a slow-growing but adamant protest movement. Women with well-developed leadership skills began organization building to support a principled, uncompromising national effort, and there would be no stopping the momentum such a protest-oriented national initiative could generate. The vessel to hold all that energy had not yet been built, but the general direction in which it would head had been set.

Du Bois clearly understood the power of women's organizing because he had written about it on previous occasions. Yet again somewhat ironically, he did not, even after his negotiations with the Niagara Movement's women attendees, seem to fully grasp the notion of complete gender equality within a protest organization established to attack status-based inequality. As one writer insightfully points out in a short essay on women in the Niagara Movement, Du Bois's announcement of women's inclusion in Niagara Movement membership in a circular following the

1906 meeting ended with the suggestion that "circles of women associated with the Niagara Movement be formed to aid such of these activities as they are especially interested in, by gathering information, raising funds, solicitations, letter writing, etc." Ironically for an organization whose platform emphasized the citizenship rights of laborers, the Niagara Movement's founder appreciated women's *labor* but gave far less thought to the idea that they should also assume leadership roles.[27] But women's labor was essential to generating the sustained activism that could give the organization vitality. It is no coincidence that many of the Niagara Movement's women activists quickly moved into similar roles within the NAACP.

1907 Activities

With the women's membership question resolved to his satisfaction at the conclusion of the 1906 Niagara Movement gathering, Du Bois plunged back into his organization-building work with energy and focus. By the spring of 1907 the Niagara Movement had further expanded its structure of committees, or departments as they were also called. Most of the Niagara Movement's lawyer members served on the Legal Committee, chaired by McGhee. The committee had twenty-two members in all, including Hart, Richards, Edward Morris, Barnett, Diggs, Jourdain, Carter, and a young Maryland lawyer named W. Ashbie Hawkins, who would soon begin litigating challenges to residential segregation ordinances for the early NAACP.[28]

Richard R. Wright Jr.'s Crime Committee had eleven members, and Dr. Marcus F. Wheatland, a prominent Rhode Island doctor who had been born in the West Indies and is believed to be the first African American radiology specialist, headed the seventeen-member health committee. New York educator William L. Bulkley headed an education committee, joined by fourteen members. The two largest committees were those dealing with suffrage and with civil rights. Ransom and Harry C. Smith sat on the latter of these two committees; almost thirty others focused on suffrage. Another committee focused on economics, while still other committees attended to the army and navy, ethics, arts, the press (chaired by Trotter), Pan-Africanism, and students. The membership roll had climbed to 380 in total, with 236 having full membership status. All but one of the women members holding committee positions did so under Gertrude Morgan's separate department, called simply "The Women," on which Clifford, Pope, Gould, and Bailey sat, among others.[29]

The Barbara Pope Case and Other Legal Matters

The most immediate and expensive initiative that required attention concerned the Barbara Pope case. Pope had filed a lawsuit challenging her criminal fine in October 1906. The trial court had affirmed the fine, and a jury subsequently returned a verdict assessing only one cent in damages.[30] The newspapers mocked Pope for this result, and the verdict was indeed insulting to a person who had initiated a lawsuit to insist on her dignity and equal status. The trial court's decision to uphold the fine was exactly what the Niagara Movement's lawyers hoped would happen, however, because it allowed them to pursue the case to the state's court of appeals. At this stage the state used a tactic that allowed it to avoid a test of the constitutionality of its criminal transportation segregation statute; it conceded before the appeals court that the statute's text did not allow for criminal fines and that the lower court's ruling was therefore in error. In an opinion dated January 9, 1907, the court of appeals agreed, reversing the trial court's judgment and remanding the case for a new trial (which the state, of course, never pursued).

This disposition technically amounted to a victory in Pope's favor. But this success was a mixed blessing at best. On the one hand, the Niagara Movement had won the case; on the other hand, the state and the Virginia court had managed to dodge the substantive issue the Niagara Movement wanted to test—namely, the constitutionality of a state statute that required the segregation of passengers who were engaged in interstate travel.

In his April 1907 membership letter, Du Bois chose to focus on the positive aspects of the Pope case. This opinion, Du Bois explained, "means that the NIAGARA MOVEMENT has established that under the present statute Virginia cannot fine an interstate passenger who refuses to be Jim-Crowed." But more needed to be done, Du Bois pointed out. The Niagara Movement now wanted to test whether a railway company could refuse to transport such a passenger. A new civil suit had been filed to test this proposition. Niagara Movement lawyers, including Morgan and Hawkins, would handle it. Still, such legal campaigns, Du Bois pointed out, were very expensive. The case had already cost $600, $240 of which was still due. "Will you help pay this promptly?" Du Bois implored.[31]

In the meantime, McGhee fully understood the necessity of finding another case to test the constitutional principle that interstate passengers should not be subject to segregation under state Jim Crow laws. Although he would try to do so and at times in the future would proclaim that he had knowledge of such a legal opportunity or that Niagara Movement involvement was in the works, no one has yet been able to track down such cases; perhaps they fizzled out or are otherwise lost to history due to a lack of records. What is clear is that the Niagara Movement kept up its protest of Jim Crow segregation in interstate commerce through other means, such as a letter Du Bois wrote protesting segregation by the Pullman Car Company. The Niagara Movement's legal department members were most preoccupied with the proposed Foraker amendment, which would have permitted separate facilities provided they were equal. As civil rights radical and Niagara Movement Legal Committee member Hershaw saw it, the Foraker amendment constituted "the most vicious and abominable surrender of our rights ever perpetrated." Morgan fully agreed.[32]

Moderates in the Niagara Movement's Civil Rights Department, however, seemed to have a different view. Connecticut lawyer George Crawford chaired this group and reported that it had adopted four projects or priorities. Two were uncontroversial and consistent with long-running goals of civil rights activists— namely, securing enactment of civil rights bills in Northern states by working with allies "like the Constitutional League," and achieving jury service in the South for African American men. Another objective, however, contravened the Niagara Movement Legal Department's stance by calling for work to improve traveling accommodations on local carriers in the South. Without explicitly addressing the differing viewpoints among Niagara Movement departments, the Civil Rights Department called for using litigation, or "a systematic bringing of suits," to enforce the federal court mandate that separate accommodations on public conveyances must be "equal in quality and convenience." The report further observed that administrative expenses and the sheer volume of work required could easily swamp the national organization, so that much of this work would need to be done at the state level, and closed by urging as follows: "Don't sit down and wait on the initiative of the overworked General Secretary"; instead, "Do something on your own initiative." But on its very terms this report reflected the flip side of encouraging enthusiastic local initiatives. These could easily contradict the national organization's agenda, leading the organization's branches to work at cross-purposes, such as by opposing separate but equal legislation while at the same time bringing lawsuits to enforce that very principle.[33]

Planning the 1907 Annual Meeting

Although the Niagara Movement's various departments and committees were thus generating energetic if somewhat uncoordinated activity by the middle of 1907, big troubles lay right around the corner. These troubles surfaced as the organization began planning for its 1907 annual meeting. After weighing a choice between Chicago or Boston as the location for this next meeting, Du Bois sent out a call announcing that the Niagara Movement's third annual meeting would be held in late August in Boston. This was a decision he would later regret because this choice of location served to highlight for the national membership a tempest brewing between Trotter and Morgan within the Massachusetts chapter.

The two men's interpersonal difficulties had several facets. One involved Trotter's allegations that Morgan, as Niagara Movement state secretary, had permitted certain persons to become members of the Massachusetts chapter without receiving a majority vote of approval from the state's membership body. Trotter especially opposed granting Niagara Movement membership to persons he found unacceptably close to Booker T. Washington. These included Maria Baldwin, the Boston educator, and Archibald Grimké. The former U.S. diplomat Grimké, a strong civil rights supporter in his frequent writings on disfranchisement and other civil rights matters, had at the same time been careful to maintain friendly relations with Washington and never directly attacked him or his views. Seeing this, Trotter developed intensely anti-Grimké views. To Trotter, a friend of an enemy was by definition an enemy. Trotter had thus protested Du Bois's earlier interest in recruiting Grimké to the Niagara Movement. Now Grimké had decided to join, and to Trotter this was akin to allowing the enemy to enter the Niagara Movement's walls.[34]

A second problem arose from the Massachusetts chapter's efforts to raise money for the Niagara Movement's legal defense fund. As usual, women had assumed responsibility for this function. In Boston Gertrude Morgan had proposed a children's play as a legal defense fund-raiser. Several relatively small matters arising from this play had upset William and Deenie Trotter. First, the Morgans had invited the Massachusetts governor, whom the Trotters regarded as insufficiently supportive of African American civil rights because he had failed to protest race segregation at the Jamestown Exposition, a 1907 World's Fair event. Second, the Trotters believed that Deenie Trotter had not been invited to help with the play preparations until late in the process, whereas George W. Forbes and his wife had been included from the outset. Forbes had once been Trotter's coeditor at the *Guardian,* but the two had a falling out after Forbes criticized Trotter as too crass in the way he had attacked Washington for his 1895 Atlanta address. Trotter in turn claimed that Forbes lacked the boldness and courage to take on Washington. As a result of this public exchange the two had not been on speaking terms for years. In response to the Trotters' complaints, the Morgans claimed that it was the Trotters who had boycotted and blocked arrangements for the play and pointed out that the event had succeeded in its objectives by raising $65 for the Niagara Movement's legal fund.[35]

Du Bois maintained strong personal friendships with both couples. He had been part of the same social circle as Deenie Trotter during his graduate school years at Harvard and obviously had great respect for the Morgans as well, having appointed Gertrude to be head of the Niagara Movement women's department after anointing her husband as head of the Massachusetts chapter. In fact, Du Bois had entrusted all of the leadership power within the Massachusetts branch to the Morgans. This fact must have fed the Trotters' growing pique about Niagara Movement affairs even if they were not admitting as much. In an effort to smooth over relations, Du Bois paid a visit to Boston and stayed with the Trotters, departing with assurances that their prior differences with the Morgans were forgotten. Soon afterward, however, the Trotters delivered to Du Bois a long communication that again demanded that Clement Morgan be reprimanded for his alleged transgressions. Deenie Trotter resigned her Niagara Movement membership and William Trotter resigned from his position on the local arrangements committee for the upcoming annual meeting. When he changed his mind a short time later, Morgan refused to allow him back on this committee. The Massachusetts branch's internal politics were, to put it plainly, a mess.

Meanwhile, Trotter's many supporters within the national membership heard about the Boston strife and sided with Trotter. These Trotter sympathizers tended to be among the organization's more radical members, who admired the brave *Guardian* editor's adherence to principle and his staunch anti-Washington advocacy. They also perhaps felt less warmly toward Morgan's more aristocratic personality.[36] Trotter's sympathizers went so far as to vow not to take part in any but the business parts of the proceedings planned for Boston. Du Bois was planning what he hoped would be large gatherings at Boston's famed Faneuil Hall as well as pilgrimages to sites related to abolitionism in Boston, all aimed at keeping the spirit generated at Harper's Ferry alive. But the dispute among the Niagara Movement's Boston leaders now contaminated the collective mood of the national membership. These problems festered throughout the summer and cast a pall on the emotional tone building for the upcoming meeting.

When the meeting did convene from August 26 to 28, 1907, Du Bois believed that the Trotter sympathizers had carried through on their boycott threat. Attendance was unexpectedly low at the planned public events, which had been intended to bolster another year of energetic organizing. Instead, delegates went into the business meetings in a sour frame of mind. Those meetings only further exacerbated the sudden and negative change in mood within the organization Du Bois had striven so hard to launch on an inspiring, upward trajectory.

This change seemed to taint not only the members' consideration of their internal difficulties but their evaluation of their substantive successes as well. The members were especially critical of the organization's progress—or lack thereof—on the central objective of fostering test case litigation, as adopted as a priority at the 1906 meeting. McGhee stepped down as head of the legal department—though he would soon return to this role—and Jourdain took over this position. McGhee's report for the legal department, which W. Justin Carter read out loud because McGhee had been unable to attend, dealt primarily with the Barbara Pope case. As McGhee reported to the general membership, the court had determined that the Virginia statute had not authorized fines against passengers who refused to move to separate cars and had disposed of the case on that ground. The Niagara Movement hoped, however, as McGhee explained, to go further in its next case to test the constitutional merits of legislating separation of interstate passengers by race.

When Ransom asked about the law in the case, Carter explained that the Niagara Movement's goal was "to put a case squarely before the Supreme Court of the United States" that would test whether passengers could be segregated when a passenger was traveling in interstate commerce. Another member asked why the organization was calling for more money in the Barbara Pope case, and Du Bois explained that, even though it turned out that this particular case could not be carried as far as the Niagara Movement wanted, "we have gained something" nevertheless in the state's admission of error in the fine. What the Niagara Movement wanted to do was to raise money to carry on such cases generally, apart and beyond the Pope matter.[37]

McGhee's report stated that he had found another case that might prove a good vehicle for the organization's goals (from Kentucky, although researchers have not yet been able to find evidence of it). Waldron stated his willingness to move to proceed with that case. But the delegates were not so ready to jump on the bandwagon once again. Ida Bailey advised "going slow" in proceeding with such cases since it appeared the organization had made a mistake in entering into the *Pope* matter. Du Bois again responded by counseling patience. Precisely the right case would not come along right away, Du Bois warned. The Niagara Movement might end up paying the expenses of five cases, for example, and if it met with defeat in four but got a good decision in the fifth, that "would be unusually lucky." Repeating his view that nothing had been lost in the *Pope* case and that he was "glad we did it," Du Bois tried again to redirect the discussion, arguing that we were "more successful than we had any right to expect."[38]

What no one mentioned in the discussion was the fate of the brave plaintiff who had put herself forward to receive the Virginia jury's insulting verdict of one cent in damages in response to her civil case. There was no talk of extending the Niagara Movement's gratitude to Pope. By the next year, she would be struggling from a painful condition that rendered her unable to sleep (possibly what would be diagnosed and treated as clinical depression today). Despite her friends' efforts to nurture her back to health, Pope tragically took her own life on September 5, 1908, at the age of fifty—by the particularly terrible method, in light of the lynching epidemic of her era, of hanging herself from a tree near her Georgetown home. Local press accounts reported her death, and the *Washington Bee* remembered her "remarkable intellect" and literary accomplishments. But neither the press nor the Niagara Movement appears to have taken note of her contribution in agreeing to serve as the Niagara Movement's centerpiece test case plaintiff.[39]

The difficulties of stepping up to serve as the public face of test case litigation were not new, of course. Jackson Giles no longer had a job at the post office after he agreed to be the test case plaintiff in *Giles v. Harris*, and countless others had in the past and would in the future experience similar adverse consequences from agreeing to take this step. The civil rights struggle would produce many personal casualties, often quickly forgotten by others. Suicides and mental health breakdowns were not infrequent: Fortune had a so-called nervous collapse in 1907, and in 1915 McGhee suffered an untimely death from overwork. Trotter would be another casualty in 1934, following his apparent suicide in a fall from the roof of his house after a period of sleeplessness and agitation. To this list Barbara Pope's name should be added as an early civil rights hero whose contribution helped launch the legal momentum for the first national twentieth-century civil rights organization to focus on test case litigation.[40]

The delegates' negativity and arguable lack of appreciation in the *Pope* case stemmed in part from nonlawyers' lack of awareness of the tortuous path on which most litigation proceeds. But their disenchantment extended to other matters as well. Another major source of dissatisfaction at the 1907 membership meeting concerned the Niagara Movement's organizing model. Delegates spoke about the need for a larger local presence, a goal impeded by the cautious rules about approving full-membership applications that had been put in place to prevent the organization from becoming infiltrated by Washington spies. Reverend Waldron emerged as an advocate of change in the organization's membership vision. Like Ransom, Waldron was an adherent of social gospel ministry and an avowed democratic socialist. He wanted a people's mass organization, not a stuffy assemblage of the race's talented tenth. What the Niagara Movement needed to do, Waldron argued, was to reach the common people—to get to the masses "just as the Irishmen do when their countrymen arrive" in this country. The delegates adopted this suggestion as a resolution. He also agreed to take a larger leadership role, accepting appointment as Niagara Movement treasurer for the year. Bulkley, who had formerly held this role, agreed to serve as temporary treasurer to assist him at the beginning of his term. Like other ambitious but disgruntled leaders before him, Waldron would soon grow sufficiently impatient with the Niagara Movement to channel his energies to new organizations. This process would help move the civil rights leadership community toward founding the NAACP as a new initiative bringing together all of the disparate organizational efforts taking place by the close of a new century's first decade.[41]

The aspect of the 1907 Boston meeting that the Niagara Movement's internal woes most affected involved the discussion of approving the Massachusetts chapter's certified election roster. This matter was minor in comparison to the problems of alleged voting irregularities within the AAC. But the Niagara Movement was a younger and more fragile organization than the AAC had been at the time of its internal electoral troubles, so that dissension from within the Niagara Movement, coupled with the Bookerite threat from without, proved harder for the Niagara Movement to weather. After Trotter made his new charges that the chapter had illegally elected certain members, Du Bois had proposed a written ballot election to determine the final membership of the Massachusetts branch. This election had resulted in the chapter's members once again approving all members currently on its list. But this still did not satisfy Trotter. During the business meeting Du Bois even offered to resign his leadership post in order to put any allegations of management irregularities behind the organization. The delegates, however, rejected this solution, most likely realizing that without Du Bois's organizing energy the Niagara Movement would surely collapse. Instead, the members voted to appoint a committee to look into the allegations of wrongdoing, and the meeting adjourned with no definitive resolution of the conflict yet in sight. Even worse, the matter hit the press. As Ovington lamented to Du Bois, "How happy Washington must be over this. I can see him rubbing his hands with glee."[42]

That fall Bentley, who leaned toward Trotter in the dispute, wrote to Du Bois suggesting that another executive committee meeting be held on neutral ground in Chicago or elsewhere in the Midwest. McGhee told Du Bois that he agreed with this proposal. Morgan opposed taking up the Massachusetts matters again, but Du Bois in the end decided to send a letter calling an executive committee meeting to take up the problem of the "Massachusetts trouble [that] has spread from a local coolness to a cause of nation-wide dissension in our ranks." The executive committee thus met in Cleveland, Ohio, approved all of Du Bois's actions in Massachusetts, and yet again confirmed the full list of members in that state. But the momentum generated in the period following the successful 1906 Harper's Ferry meeting had been irretrievably disturbed.[43]

Niagara Movement Lessons

Although the Niagara Movement continued to meet for two more years, and although some local chapters remained active, such as the one in Washington, DC, where Rev. Waldron, Carrie Clifford, Ida Bailey, and others led with their enthusiasm, the Niagara Movement gradually faded as a key organization on the national scene. Its most important leaders moved on to other projects and could no longer be found promoting the Niagara Movement as the proper organizational vehicle for building national civil rights momentum. Even Du Bois, clearly stunned by the rapid collapse of his arduously constructed work, turned toward other projects, especially his long-standing idea of founding a magazine that could serve as the publication organ for the national civil rights organizing effort he envisioned. In this project, too, Du Bois would at first meet with frustration, largely due to a lack of sufficient financing, but in the end would find the role best suited to his enormous strengths.

Figure 9.2 W.E.B. Du Bois at Niagara delegates meeting, 1907 (Special Collections and University Archives, University of Massachusetts at Amherst Library).

The Niagara Movement's implosion taught Du Bois important lessons that would serve him well in the future. First, it pointed out the fallacy of his "talented tenth" organizing model. Du Bois had believed he could avoid the cooptation of his organization by being choosey about whom to admit. He urged the branches to elect only "the choicest spirits" for membership and not "the craven, the sycophant and the compromising." But he had not counted on the facts of human nature that can lead even those of the highest social status to stoop to petty bickering. Nor had he recognized the fact that the character trait of maintaining high moral principles frequently resides uncomfortably close to less desirable traits, such as difficulty with compromise and understanding others' viewpoints.

Even more problematically, as others have explored, Du Bois's notion of the talented tenth rested on old-fashioned ideas about the correlation between social class and high character that would soon become outmoded under the more egalitarian sensibilities of a new century. Even though the Niagara Movement's "talented tenth" members had earned rather than simply inherited their socially elite position, they were not inherently, as Du Bois believed, the natural leaders of their race. Indeed, Du Bois's very noticeable tendency toward social snobbery resided rather uncomfortably with his developing socialist politics long into his future life. The leader's intellectual brilliance did not preclude him from the usual human flaw of personal inconsistency; if anything, the size of his genius also amplified the scale of his contradictions.

Second, Du Bois had realized the importance of having a full-time salaried organizer to staff a national organization. Like other national organization leaders before him such as Alexander and Fortune, Du Bois had learned the hard way that under completely volunteer staffing a national organization would struggle to handle the time-sensitive demands of coaxing a nationwide effort in a coherent direction. A person devoting full-time attention to the organization would be more able to react in a timely manner to the inevitable brush fires that would occur as members' personalities rubbed against each other and other small crises threatened to flare.

A third lesson Du Bois drew from his experience leading the Niagara Movement concerned the strengths and weakness of his own personality. Du Bois was always much more an ideas man than a people person, and he had been blindsided by how quickly the petty personality clashes that plagued the Boston branch grew into a national internal crisis. As he confided to Ovington in the midst of the "Massachusetts trouble," he found this kind of situation to be "one of the unpleasant things to 'leadership' " and wished himself "very heartily out of this kind of work, because it does not really belong to me, I should like to give my time to writing; nevertheless I am going to try to do my duty."[44] His Niagara Movement experience thus taught him that he was best at handling the vision side of building a national protest movement, and during the next stage of his life, continuing until he resigned from the NAACP in 1934, his prodigious organization-building skills would be focused on developing and articulating the big ideas for that organization; he would leave field organizing primarily to others.

The Horizon

In the meantime, Du Bois had seized on the importance of developing a magazine that would serve as a propaganda organ for the Niagara Movement. He had started with *The Moon* in 1905. After *The Moon* collapsed for lack of financial backing, Du Bois began again with a new magazine, this one called *The Horizon*. Working with his trusted colleague Hershaw and fellow founding Niagara Movement member and printer F. H. M. Murray, Du Bois and his fellow editors began producing pithy writing on the political and civil rights matters of the day. They created a board of directors that included Waldron, Hawkins, Henry Bailey, and Du Bois, and eventually expanded their list of guarantors to more than twenty men, most of them Niagara Movement members. The three editors aimed to make the publication a serious and sustainable one that could attract financial backing despite Washington's continuing efforts to thwart projects in which Du Bois was involved.

During the same period Milholland of the Constitution League, together with Barber, proposed issuing a periodical along the same lines. Du Bois wrote to them to urge that there be no more divided efforts and that all the interested parties instead agree to unite in one strong periodical. The paper would be a "literary digest of all things concerning the negro race" and would include contributions from "the best writers of both races." The founders estimated that they would need to obtain capital of $25,000, and Milholland undertook to help raise this fund, though nothing much came of this effort. Nevertheless, *The Horizon* lasted for three and a half years, and through it Du Bois and the Niagara Movement developed a template that would contribute to the early NAACP's success, especially with regard to its publication, *The Crisis*, which Du Bois would begin editing in late 1910.[45]

Each of *The Horizon*'s principals controlled the content of one of the three sections in which it was organized. Du Bois's section, titled "Overlook," went first and contained a mix of original reporting and excerpts deemed of special note from other magazines. Favorite topics included political ideology—including Du Bois's thoughtful 1907 essays announcing his turn toward socialism, in which he sounded every bit like Fortune and the young Ransom before him; Africa and racial justice issues in other parts of the world; attacks on the Bookerites; and miscellaneous reporting on racial justice organizing, including the Georgia Equal Rights Convention, assembled in 1906 to advocate educated manhood suffrage and other civil rights issues in that state, in which Du Bois was for a time involved. Hershaw's "Out-Look" section followed, frequently containing precise and valuable reports about new civil rights cases, in which the careful lawyer admonished readers about the importance of attending to legal developments so they did not pass by without a mobilized response as had happened too frequently in the past. Murray's "In Look" section closed each issue and focused on issues of special relevance to the race, including new literature and national news. Each issue opened and closed with literary quotations that the editors chose from vastly disparate sources ranging from the great classics to feminist writers to the insights of current and past race leaders.

The Horizon clearly catered to the highly educated class in both content and style. It took pains to be aesthetically pleasing in its art nouveau illustrations and clean format, and indeed looked more like a literary than a news magazine. Its first volumes used a standard cover illustration of the back of a delicate woman of indecipherable race gazing out at a horizon intended to symbolize the race divide; later editions would feature portraits of figures ranging from John Brown to contemporary race leaders, who would more provocatively look the reader in the eye from the covers. Du Bois would retain much the same format for *The Crisis,* including the eye-catching cover illustrations and attention to aesthetic detail in his layout and art deco typeface. But *The Crisis* also frequently bore cover illustrations that portrayed the common person and piqued interest—or even sometimes brazenly provoked—in this manner, signaling a change in Du Bois's conception of his publishing mission and audience.

A survey of the contents of *The Horizon* reflects the growing momentum toward law-focused civil rights organizing. At the same time, *The Horizon* continued to attend to the vast array of social issues relevant to the struggle for racial justice.[46] In producing eloquent and impassioned prose, Du Bois was freed of the petty personality conflicts that marked the arena of mundane human affairs. The Niagara Movement's internal woes thus received only the barest mention in Du Bois's 1907 *Horizon* article on the Niagara Movement, after which he published its address to the nation. In it Du Bois singled out six issues of particular salience in a year full of "wrong and discrimination," including the Atlanta massacre, where the governor of Georgia was "stained by the blood of innocent black workingmen who fell," and the Brownsville affair, in which President Theodore Roosevelt had swaggered "roughshod over the helpless black regiment whose bravery made him famous." Sounding themes almost unchanged from the founding days of the AAL (though he did not point this out), Du Bois demanded on behalf of the Niagara Movement freedom from labor peonage, a free and fair ballot, denial of representation to states who denied citizenship rights, federal legislation forbidding exclusion of persons from interstate cars on account of race or color, and schooling for every child, at national expense if necessary. Finally, Du Bois called on the race to help defeat Roosevelt or Taft (depending on who won the Replication presidential nomination) and to instead vote with the white laboring classes, while also admonishing labor to "remember the cause of labor is the cause of black men and that the black man's cause is labor's own." In subsequent communiqués, Du

Figure 9.3 Cover page from August 1908 issue of the *Horizon* magazine (UCLA).

Figure 9.4 Cover page from March 1912 issue of *The Crisis* (New York Public Library).

Bois again repeatedly admonished *The Horizon*'s readers to abandon Taft and the Republican party and to vote for the democratic populist candidate, William Jennings Bryan. Bryan's record on race matters, Du Bois argued, showed some signs for hope in contrast to Taft's dismal performance on Brownsville and other matters.[47]

As Du Bois's organizing energies switched to helping create the NAACP, his reporting switched focus too. In *The Horizon* he would announce with approval the first meetings of the National Negro Committee and then would offer words of advice to both the white philanthropists who were moving in to contribute their social and financial capital to a project that had begun decades before and to the African American activists who had been long at this work:

> Hitherto there has been in this country a strange, to some, almost inexpli-
> cable hiatus between the cause of Negro uplift and other great causes of
> human advance. If one met the workers for women's rights, prison reform,
> improvement in housing, consumers leagues, social settlements, universal
> peace, socialism—almost any of the myriad causes for which thinkers and
> doers are today toiling, one met persons who usually either knew nothing
> of the Negro problem or avoided it if they did know. On the other hand
> Negroes have long been working on the theory that the Negro problem is
> separate and distinct from other social problems in America, and [needed]
> to be settled by peculiar remedies. Today both sets of social workers are
> awakened to their mistake...Social workers who called [the] conference,
> like Jane Addams,...Florence Kelly, Oswald Garrison Villard, Charles
> Edward Russell, Lillian D. Wald, William English Walling and others are
> today realizing that there is in America today no human problem of advance
> and uplift which does not in a more or less subtle way involve the Negro
> American...So too, the Negroes who responded eagerly to the call are
> beginning to learn that the Negro problem is simply a problem of poverty,
> ignorance, suffrage, women's rights, distribution of wealth, and law and
> order among both blacks and whites, and that to attack any of these evils
> properly involves close cooperation with the great reform forces of the day.[48]

Here, of course, Du Bois was exaggerating for the sake of a point: T. Thomas Fortune had seen the struggle for racial justice as inextricably intertwined with other great reform movements back in 1883. What Du Bois was offering, however, was a vision of connection among social reform movements and issues, and between "social work" and political activism; this vision would help inspire the NAACP's founding and subsequent sense of its mission. He also could not have failed to realize that this blueprint connected racial justice activists' work to funding networks available to progressive white social reformers whose allegiance might be wooed away from Booker T. Washington.[49]

The End of the Niagara Movement

After 1907 the death of the Niagara Movement was relatively painless—a kind of fading away without further discord. By the end of 1907 its new treasurer, Waldron, wrote to members reporting that $2,650 in dues were owed, the treasury had only $5 in it, and the organization was in debt to Du Bois for $90.83, to McGhee for $155.95 for legal services rendered, and to the local counsel who had helped on the *Pope* case, an attorney named C. I. Sims, for $240, putting the Niagara Movement's total debt at $486.78.[50]

By 1908 the lines of division between previously feuding organizations were fading. In DC, AAC President Walters joined the Niagara Movement as an associate member, and the call for the Niagara Movement's 1908 meeting invited all who sympathized with the organization's objectives, including the members of the Afro-American Council, the National Negro American Political League, and other similar associations. That meeting took place in Oberlin, Ohio, on August 31 and September 1 and 2; according to the Niagara Movement's official statement, about fifty delegates, representing eleven states, attended.[51]

The year 1908 was a watershed for civil rights organizing. The Brownsville affair was still very much the focus of national attention, as reflected in frequent coverage in *The Horizon* and other publications. Waldron, Alexander, and Trotter had formed the National Negro League and were organizing to oppose Taft's presidential bid, emphasizing that his dismal role in the Brownsville affair predicted a negative future record on civil rights. Nevertheless, many of the Niagara Movement's usual stalwarts failed to show at its 1908 annual meeting. Waldron's absence most deeply disappointed Du Bois. Ovington, too, wrote to Du Bois explaining that it would not be possible for her to leave New York City but that she was still taking part in the "Federation of Colored Women's Clubs" and remembered with great fondness "singing John Brown at Harpers Ferry and encouraging winning rights of manhood for every Negro." McGhee likewise wrote that he could not attend because he was deeply involved in other work.[52]

The Oberlin gathering's business meetings focused on matters such as removing the requirement that branch secretaries be current on their dues and voting to lower dues from five dollars to two dollars per year; in exchange, the Niagara Movement hoped that members would pay their back dues. The treasurer's report showed that money coming into the Niagara Movement's account totaled $64.87, while a separate "Jim Crow Car" fund had raised $98.87. Energy around the Niagara Movement's substantive agenda continued, however, with the Niagara Movement's most loyal members continuing to serve in leadership roles. Department reports included discussion of the successful prosecution of a "Reid" Pullman Car Company case (for which records have not been located). McGhee had agreed in absentia to assume responsibility as head of the Civil and Political

Rights Department, while W. H. Richards became head of Legal Defense. Wright remained head of Crime, Rescue, and Reform, and the head of the Economic Opportunity Department remained from 1906, while Gertrude Morgan stayed on as leader of the "Women's auxiliary."[53]

The Niagara Movement had one more annual meeting, this time in Sea Isle City, New Jersey, in 1909. This one was billed as a "quiet outing to Sea Isle City," with its theme being a focus on "concentration of effort through race organizations." Du Bois acknowledged his disappointment in the Niagara Movement's actual accomplishments but urged activists to keep at their work. And some work was clearly continuing: Richard Wright reported that he had been involved in organizing an "association of colored mechanics," and Mason Hawkins reported that he had written to college men who had graduated from Harvard urging them to form junior Niagara Movement local chapters—an organizing strategy the NAACP would later duplicate. McGhee could not be present, he explained, because he was hard at work battling against the rise of school segregation in St. Paul, but sent along an illuminating report reflecting his thoughts after five years of attempting to spearhead the Niagara Movement's test case litigation efforts.[54]

McGhee began this report rather defensively and inaccurately—or perhaps confusing the several national organizations whose legal affairs he had directed—with the claim that "ours is the only organization of Negroes that can boast of having actually carried our cause to the Supreme Court, prosecuted an action in the Federal Court and both with success." During the last year, however, McGhee explained, this department had been "unable to do anything owing to lack of funds except to offer advice and assistance in preparation of briefs that have come to us." He hoped a possible North Carolina case might raise the question of legality of that state's new constitution in a new form and in a manner that "we believe will put the question to the court so it cannot so easily dodge it."[55]

There was room also for finger-pointing at competitor organizations. McGhee characterized the AAC's Louisiana *Gaines* case, this time fairly accurately, as "terribly prepared." Moreover, he argued, the bishops should have gotten better lawyers to challenge the railroads in the cases they had prosecuted before the ICC. Concluding his report, McGhee offered a frustrated defense of the legal work the Niagara Movement had attempted to accomplish:

> But has not the whole race been doing the self same thing, neglecting to take proper steps to contest the question of our rights in the courts? Until the advent of the Niagara Movement the cases affecting these cherished rights, with but few exceptions, had been presented by counsel that did not have the questions at heart...the principles involved have not been made the thing of all importance.[56]

Of course, this was the very criticism that had been leveled against the strategy that had been attempted in the *Pope* case (and the *Ryanes* case before it), and McGhee would unfortunately die before he could see his hard-earned insights produce success in subsequent test cases. What was most obvious, McGhee concluded, is that "looking to the future we are not discouraged; indeed we have much reason for encouragement." Nonetheless, "the one thing we most need is a fund so we may prepare cases and present them under the best and most favorable conditions." Thus the Niagara Movement's experiment with test case litigation, building from the AAC and developing additional lessons to be in turn passed on to the early NAACP, ended with this acknowledgement of the heavy financial requirements of sponsoring test case litigation. [57]

Atlanta and New York City; Founding the National Urban League

This book has been examining how national civil rights organizations developed and for this reason has focused on national-level activity. But investigating the sources of that activity also requires looking at how national organizations built on resources existing at the local level. This chapter begins with a focus on the relationship between local conditions and national organization building at the turn of the twentieth century in two major cities: Atlanta and New York City. These cities were, of course, only two of the many sites of local activism that fed into early twentieth-century national organization-building efforts, but they were important ones, especially for understanding the origins of the two great flagship national organizations founded in 1910 to advance racial justice goals—namely, the NAACP and the National Urban League. Key founders of these two associations came from these major cities. Comparing activists' very different local experiences in these cities, one in the South and the other in the North, shows how diverse locally shaped strains of activism contributed to different models for national organization building in the early twentieth century. Political conditions in Atlanta, which included frequent lynchings and disfranchisement, blocked avenues for political and civil rights reform. But Atlanta's stark economic separatism also created opportunities for, and interest in, alternative institution building in the private realm, run by and for African Americans. New York City presented more open political conditions. At the same time, its integrated economy embodied structural features that subordinated African Americans in the lowest employment rungs. These differing conditions created a variety of avenues for reform. Both New York City and Atlanta supported strategies that focused on social welfare goals, as in the New York City–based early NUL as well as Atlanta's Neighborhood Union. But New York City offered possibilities of fruitful work focused on political and civil rights issues that Atlanta did not. The early NAACP and its very active local committee in New York City focused on these avenues for reform.

After examining and comparing the different emphases of turn-of-the-century local activism in Atlanta and New York City, this chapter looks at how that activism flowed into the founding of the preeminent national organization devoted to the economic and social welfare aspects of racial justice in the early twentieth century—namely, the National Urban League. The National Urban League eventually grew from its New York City beginnings in the 1910s to a powerful national organization that played a key role in advancing racial justice in the first half of the twentieth century. Although sometimes dismissed as the NAACP's more conservative cousin, the National Urban League in fact pioneered far-reaching, sociologically oriented approaches to solving problems of racial injustice, including structural employment subordination as well as housing, health, and social welfare work.[1] At its beginning, however, the NUL developed an internal "logic" that took social welfare issues largely out of the realm of reform activism and instead defined them as matters requiring a professional cadre of social service workers devoted to individual services work. This chapter looks at how predecessor organizing efforts contributed to the National Urban League's founding agenda and how that agenda then moved in directions that temporarily split national racial justice initiatives into specializations that separated social welfare from political and civil rights work.

Du Bois's Work in Atlanta

Du Bois's laborious work to build the Niagara Movement often took place from his desk at Atlanta University, where he served as a professor of history and economics and pioneered the emerging discipline of African American sociology. The Niagara Movement was but one of many projects that took up his time. As his biographer David Levering Lewis explains, Du Bois was an extreme workaholic. These work habits caused him to virtually abandon at an emotional level his wife, Nina Gomer, in the inhospitable Southern city to which he had taken her after their marriage in 1896. A shy person to begin with, Nina's isolation was compounded by the couple's principled refusal to use Atlanta's segregated streetcars. Traveling downtown from the neighborhood near the university where the Du Boises lived required two miles of walking, and there would have been little to do there anyway since the "respectable" establishments a woman of Nina's class status would feel comfortable visiting barred African Americans. There were no department stores to shop in without enduring racial insult, no restaurants at which to dine.[2]

Even after their son Burghardt was born in 1897, Du Bois reportedly worked almost around the clock. Then Atlanta's segregation had tragic consequences for Burghardt as well. When he was two years old he fell ill, and his parents could not find a doctor nearby to treat him due to Atlanta's race-segregated medical system. Burghardt died on May 24, 1899. The death of her young son compounded Nina's social withdrawal, and the couple's marriage became further strained. The two spent much time apart, and Nina did not become very involved in the social reform efforts occurring around her, devoting her attention instead to raising a daughter, Yolanda, born three years later—whom Du Bois also reportedly interacted with little, except through correspondence when she was older.[3]

Du Bois's coping mechanism for both personal tragedy and political oppression was to throw himself ever more intensely into his work. In his Atlanta years, this work included a dozen studies and associated conferences exploring various aspects of African American life at the turn of the century. In the twelve years he spent at Atlanta University, Du Bois produced at least one study per year on topics such as the "College Bred Negro," "The Negro Common School," and "Efforts for Social Betterment among Negro Americans," which provided information about political and social welfare organizing often used by scholars.[4] He sent these reports, referred to as "Atlanta bulletins," to his former Harvard professor, philosopher William James. Like his pragmatist mentor, Du Bois believed, during this Progressive-era period of his thought, that careful inquiry could itself help bring about social change by inducing others to respond to the scholar's illumination of facts and presentation of rational analysis.[5] In keeping with other classical pragmatists, Du Bois understood an inextricable connection between thought and action, and he saw his activist commitments and his scholarship as linked in this way.[6] Du Bois's various Atlanta University studies spanned hundreds of pages of text, accompanied by charts, graphs, and data tabulations. His conferences brought together respected authorities on the topics under study, including figures such as Jane Addams, who came to one 1908 conference on the "Negro family" and contributed a paper to that study report.[7]

The Atlanta conference that perhaps had the most immediate political impact was Du Bois's fourth investigation, titled "The Negro in Business." Du Bois organized a conference related to this study at Atlanta University on May 30 and 31, 1899 (only days after Burghardt's death). Participants in the conference passed a series of resolutions that called on African Americans to patronize businesses that members of their own race owned, proposed business leagues "in every town and hamlet," and envisioned "the gradual federation" of these into state and then national organizations. His close friend John Hope, who would later join him in founding the Niagara Movement, was a conference participant. A particularly brutal lynching of a farmer named Sam Hose in a community on the outskirts of Atlanta only a month before served as a graphic reminder of the limits on African Americans' open assertion of rights.

Hope decided to focus on intrarace economic development in his conference paper. He began by noting that whites had accumulated capital on the basis of the work of African American laborers, but now those same laborers were being squeezed out of most employment sectors due to race discrimination. Hope argued that with this coming of the Jim Crow era, African Americans should "take some if not all of the wages [and] turn it into capital." This could help protect African

Americans' employment by developing jobs that came from African American sources. He explained that, as an academic rather than a businessperson, he did not believe that material wealth was the touchstone of "highest development and manhood." Nevertheless, he did believe that such "highest development" required "a material foundation." Thus, he urged, those involved in developing African American businesses should think of themselves as doing crucial work in elevating the race.[8]

This conference led Du Bois and Washington, still several years away from their public falling out, to work together to create the National Negro Business League, founded in 1900. As the conference illuminated, even civil rights radicals like Du Bois and Hope saw that any racial advancement strategy required multiple prongs; neither economic empowerment nor civil and political rights advancement could be achieved without the other. Although these multiple strands of a concerted strategy became less tightly woven together as various groups began to specialize in particular aspects of the racial justice agenda, race activists of the era viewed economic advancement and gains in political and civil rights as interconnected. Southerners, especially, worried about the white backlash that could result from public militancy, as Booker T. Washington's public stances reflected. But activists throughout the country held generally shared understandings of the need for multifaceted strategies combining efforts on the many relevant dimensions of economic, political, and civil rights as aspects of the racial justice struggle.

Du Bois's Local Political Work

Du Bois's self-conception during his Atlanta years focused on his role as scholar, but he joined in local organizing initiatives as well. In 1900 Du Bois, Hope, and other African American educators petitioned against proposals in the Georgia legislature to divide school funds based on the amount of taxes different races paid.[9] In 1902 Du Bois and others fought against the whites-only policy instituted at the "public" library Andrew Carnegie built for the city. Still another political commitment Du Bois made was to the Georgia Equal Rights Convention (GERC), founded in early 1906 in the wake of the Niagara Movement's successful kickoff the summer before.[10] The GERC's members included Georgia-based Niagara Movement men such as Du Bois, Hope, and Barber, as well as former AAC leader Judson Lyon, who had also joined the Niagara Movement. The GERC lasted only a year, but it held a well-attended statewide convention, at which speakers emphasized many themes similar to those of the Niagara Movement, especially "manly" insistence on equal civil rights.

Like the early Niagara Movement, all GERC members were men, though it viewed itself as representing both the men and the women of the race. Like the Niagara Movement, its statement of principles spanned a wide array of eloquently articulated concerns, including racial inequality in funding education, the new slavery of peonage labor, the convict lease system, the exploitation of African American laborers generally, Jim Crow in transportation and public accommodations, and the scourge of lynchings. It spoke out against disfranchisement, which took the form not only of new state legislation but also the cumulative poll tax. These steep taxes had partially achieved black disfranchisement in Georgia in the 1890s, by imposing prohibitive barriers to voting on low-paid African American laborers. The GERC delegates protested the oppressive and unfair enforcement of vagrancy laws, the lack of African American representation on juries, and the cruel and excessive punishment of African American criminal defendants. Careful to renounce any interest in social association with whites, they emphasized that their claims addressed legal rights only and ended with a call for hard work to promote economic progress and African American businesses. Summing up their future goals, they wrote: "We must agitate, complain, protest and keep protesting against the invasion of our manhood rights; we must besiege the legislature, carry our cases to the courts and above all organize these million brothers of ours into one great fist which shall never cease to pound at the gates of Opportunity until they fly open."[11]

Atlanta's Economic and Political Conditions

The GERC's priorities stemmed from the economic, social, and legal conditions in the state. In many parts of Georgia's agricultural belt, where cotton was the main product, African Americans outnumbered whites, or nearly did so. After emancipation, whites had moved quickly to replace the institution of slavery with other oppressive institutions, including peonage labor and tenancy farming. In the period between 1880 and 1900, a majority of Georgia's black citizens remained engaged in agriculture, but African Americans had begun to move from Georgia's agricultural areas to the cities in order to escape these rural conditions. Jobs in cities were scarce, and black unemployment was high. Even African Americans with manual skills as blacksmiths, masons, and carpenters rarely found work in the skilled trades, which had typically provided the route to economic and class advancement for less advantaged whites. Most white trade unions refused African Americans the membership cards necessary to get work in the city, and the few that allowed such membership did so on highly discriminatory terms, including requiring segregated locals, higher dues, and denying apprenticeships to black workers. Only a few independent black craft unions existed, and these were isolated and rare and lacked strength to protect their members' ability to secure work in the trades.

White labor unions also ensured that African Americans did not move into manufacturing jobs. In 1897, for example, the white women's workers at Atlanta's Fulton Bag and Cotton Mill struck to protest the hiring of African Americans at the plant, and management readily accepted their demand. Similar strikes took place at other mills, with similar results. The railroad unions were even worse, as the murderous 1909 Georgia railway strike, in which dozens of African Americans were injured or killed by whites striking to maintain whites-only jobs, attested.[12]

This racial caste system forced most African Americans, especially women, into domestic service, so that fully one-third of Georgia's black population in 1900 was engaged in this occupation, mostly in white homes. Higher-paying jobs involved doing personal service work for commercial enterprises as porters, janitors, and waiters. The limited routes to economic advancement that did exist were through business ownership and the professions. In the 1870s African American business-men had racially mixed clienteles, especially in groceries and barbershops, but the rise of Jim Crow wiped this out. In Atlanta, much earlier than in other cities such as Chicago, African American business success rested exclusively on the loyalty of a large African American consumer community.

Similarly, the most successful professional pursuit in Atlanta was medicine, aided by the community norm, propelled in part by a segregated medical system, that patients should patronize health care providers of their own race. Lawyers had a harder time because potential clients perceived, not incorrectly, that whites con-trolled the justice system. Only a handful of African American lawyers practiced in the entire state—fewer than ten until World War I, most of whom made their primary living in real estate, insurance, and claims collection.[13]

In turn, economic separatism influenced the ideological model Atlanta's race leaders espoused.[14] Segregation had economic benefits for African American busi-nesspeople and thus, in economic terms at least, was not an unmitigated evil. As in other cities, African Americans who acquired significant assets and wealth often did so through real estate investments in African American communities or the provi-sion of capital and insurance to African American businesses.[15]

Not only the economic landscape of Atlanta but also the political landscape shaped organizing directions. By 1890 the national political scene looked dismal for black Georgians. The Republican Congress had repudiated campaign pledges to pass federal laws to protect and advance the objectives of Reconstruction. The Lodge Federal Elections Bill, which would have protected African Americans' right to vote, had failed, and the Blair Federal Aid to Education Bill, which would have improved schools, was also effectively defeated. At the same time, a succession of presidents had grown increasingly silent about African American civil and political rights.[16]

On the state level, the agrarian Populist movement had previously provided some notes of optimism for African Americans' political future but then had turned viciously antiblack. In the 1880s Populist alliances seeking to seize back power from the industrial conglomerates such as railroads, industry, and capital markets in the North had arisen and flirted with encouraging the black vote. Populists orga-nized a Colored Farmers' Alliance, and in 1890 various alliances merged into the Populist Party, which called for reforms such as government loans to farmers, public ownership of railroads and communications, and free silver. Its rhetoric emphasized how divisions among the little people kept them divided so that the capitalists could have their way over them.[17] The Colored Alliance directed its political support away from the Republicans, who were backing away from their commitments to African Americans, and toward the third-party Populists.[18] But this support did not end up paying political dividends, and the Populists began to eschew race equality as well.

The career of Georgia Populist demagogue Tom Watson illustrates the trajectory of African Americans' fate with the Georgia Populists. Elected to Congress as a Democrat in 1890, Watson quickly renounced that party and espoused Populism instead. His early Populist rhetoric catered to blacks and whites alike. Races attended his political rallies together, and Watson was known to call on white audience members to swear to protect African American constitutional rights. In 1891 he supported the election of African Americans to the party's campaign committee and made promises to support antilynching legislation.[19] But by the early 1890s the Populists were also supporting disenfranchising legislation being introduced in the Georgia legislature. In 1891 the state legislature enacted a statute that required railroads to provide separate coaches for blacks and whites and authorized city streetcars to separate the races as fully as feasible.[20] The Atlanta City Council adopted an ordinance providing for streetcar segregation, and its African American community responded with the 1892 streetcar boycott, which failed after some members of the African American elite, such as AME bishop Henry M. Turner, continued to use the streetcar system.[21]

The Georgia legislature also passed legislation to allow all-white state primaries and to strengthen the convict lease system. In 1892 the Populists again asked for and expected the black vote, but they did not get it in any overwhelming numbers. Watson lost his congressional seat to a Democrat and also lost the special election his opponent offered after Watson charged that there had been massive voter fraud. Claims flew that the Democrats had manipulated the black vote, and Watson began to engage in race-baiting tactics when speaking to whites, suggesting, as one historian has argued, "a pattern of duplicity" in which Watson simultaneously tried to play to "white supremacy and Black aspirations."[22] By 1894 Watson had shifted his position still further to become a virulently antiblack demagogue (along with being anti-Semitic and anti-Catholic as well). Instead of calling for solidarity on the basis of class or relationship to capital, Watson exploited the gains to be had in calling for solidarity on race lines.

All political parties realized that the large black population in the state potentially provided African Americans with political power. Even with the significant disfranchisement caused by the poll tax passed in Georgia immediately after Reconstruction, blacks could serve as the swing vote in some Georgia elections.[23] The solution was to disenfranchise African Americans as thoroughly as possible, using a combination of tactics including all-white primaries, property and poll tax requirements, and literacy and "understanding" tests. But better-off, educated

African Americans remained participants in Atlanta politics until the early 1890s.[24] This situation ended after an all-black ticket for city offices, representing some of the wealthiest and most prominent African Americans in Atlanta, ran against the all-white primary ticket but was solidly defeated.[25] Afterward, Atlanta's African Americans saw their best tactic as demanding representation on party committees, under the implicit threat that, if they were not represented, they would cast their support to candidates of the other party in the general election.[26] This potential presented all parties with the specter of unpredictable results and further increased the volatility of Atlanta's political situation.[27]

The so-called Progressive era ushered in various other antiblack measures aimed at "improving" government in Atlanta as well, including strengthening vagrancy laws in order to permit rounding up African Americans from the city's streets and cracking down on prostitution and vice in African American parts of the city.[28] Restaurants and bars imposed segregation rules, and barbershops designated whether they served white or black customers, further enforcing the city's economic and social segregation. Hospitals refused to treat African Americans, office building elevators were labeled white-only, city parks and the zoos were segregated, and public and private libraries were closed to African Americans.[29] It was in the midst of this Jim Crow Atlanta that Washington delivered his famous accommodationist speech at the 1895 Atlanta Exposition, having vowed to himself, according to his classic biographer, "not to say anything that would give undue offense to the South" while also staying true to his views that African Americans in the South must make economic and social progress even under an apartheid political system.[30]

The use of disfranchisement and segregation to give tangible expression to a racial caste system did not exhaust whites' strategies for opposing African Americans' achievement of full citizenship status. Extralegal means of enforcing the racial caste system were also popular. Georgia ranked second only to Mississippi in numbers of lynchings. Sites of African American strength and organizing, such as churches and fraternal lodges, were frequently bombed and burned.[31] One particularly brutal lynching involved the mob murder of Sam Hose in 1899 in Palmetto, a community near Atlanta. Hose, a black farmer, had killed a white farmer after an argument. A mob first beat Hose to death and then burned him at the stake in front of two thousand townspeople, who fought for scraps of his flesh as souvenirs and exhibited his charred knucklebones in the window of a local store. Du Bois identified this incident as the turning point in his realization that he could no longer act as a "calm, cool and detached scientist while Negroes were lynched, murdered and starved."[32]

At the time of the GERC's 1906 convention, Georgia's complex politics were becoming even more vitriolic as Hoke Smith, a Democratic lawyer allied with Tom Watson, began to use racist rhetoric in his campaign for governor. Just a month after the Niagara Movement's second annual meeting at Harpers Ferry, the powder keg of racial animosity mixed with political demagoguery exploded in a three-day race riot in Atlanta. In its aftermath, top GERC leaders faced the danger of being lynched just as Max Barber had. Du Bois, who had been away during the riot studying peonage in Alabama, returned a few days later. Sickened by what he saw but assured that his immediate family was all right, he left town again to finish his study. He published a stirring piece about the horror of the event, written in religious tones that were deeply evocative at a spiritual level but abstract enough to avoid censure. After 1906 Du Bois declined to lend his name to or continue to participate in local efforts to oppose the disenfranchising provisions included in Georgia's soon-to-be-enacted new state constitution.[33]

Indeed, after 1906 all of the GERC's leaders dramatically moderated their approach, though some continued their local civic engagement.[34] They renamed the GERC the Colored Association in order to avoid any mention of equal rights.[35] Another organization, called the Georgia Suffrage League, continued to work on disfranchisement. In 1907 Hoke Smith's proposed grandfather clause amendment to the Georgia constitution passed the state legislature, which then scheduled it for a voter referendum in 1908. Despite the Georgia Suffrage League's attempt to oppose the measure, it met with easy voter ratification—a result that was all the more inevitable because most African American voters were already disenfranchised by the cumulative poll tax.[36] The grandfather clause did, however, make disfranchisement even more thorough: African American male voter registration dropped from more than 28 percent in 1904 to less than 4 percent in 1910.[37] Given these political and social conditions, a strategy of militantly advocating for manhood rights was not only futile but also highly dangerous.

This blockage in the political and civil rights sphere did not, however, stop Atlanta's race activist leaders from exercising agency. Instead, it channeled that agency in directions supported by the city's economic separatism. As August Meier and others have explained, Atlanta became a model for an intrarace uplift approach to economic and social progress. Rather than knocking at the doors of white society, Atlanta's African American community set out to develop its resources internally. To be sure, the 1906 Atlanta riot had shown the fallacy of investing in economic progress without protection for political and civil rights. But community self-help to rebuild after the riot presented a strategy for racial advancement, however precarious, and could be carried out even while avenues for political and civil rights reform remained closed. Atlanta's African American women's clubs provided much of the key leadership. Prominent in these efforts was Lugenia Burns Hope.

Lugenia Burns Hope

A detailed study of Lugenia Burns Hope's life by Jacqueline Anne Rouse offers insight into this important social reformer. Like her husband, John Hope, Lugenia Burns Hope had mixed-race ancestry. Her white grandfather on her father's side was William Burns, secretary of the state of Mississippi in the 1850s, who had lived openly with an African American wife and five children in Natchez, Mississippi. Lugenia Burns Hope was born in 1871 in St. Louis, Missouri, after her parents moved there. Her family then moved to Chicago, where her family's difficult financial circumstances forced her to abandon her education after several years of high school. She found work as a bookkeeper—first for a charitable organization, whose evening educational programs for working girls she managed along with other duties, and then as the personal secretary to a prominent white Chicago society woman and social reformer who was active at Hull House. Lugenia Burns Hope assisted in this Hull House work and formed the goal of initiating similar work herself someday. In 1897 she married John Hope, whom she had met at a ball held during the 1893 Chicago Exposition, and moved with him to Atlanta. There Du Bois, quickly learning of her interest and prior experience in social work, involved her in his conference on the welfare of African American children. Through this participation Burns Hope met Gertrude Ware, a kindergarten training schoolteacher at Atlanta University and sister of the institution's president, and they soon formed a plan to establish free kindergartens and preschools in Atlanta for African American children left unattended when their mothers went to work.[38]

A group called the Gate City Kindergarten Association took up this plan, and Lugenia became its fund-raising committee chair. Through the largesse of one of Atlanta's most successful African American businessmen—Alfonso Herndon, who made his money in insurance and was also one of the Niagara Movement's founders—the association was able to buy a large building to use as a school and playground. Herndon also funded a teacher position for the kindergarten and paid for the daily milk delivery. In time the project grew to become a day care center and five kindergartens throughout the city. Burns Hope wanted the project to grow even more ambitious by taking on the task of establishing neighborhood centers throughout the city, but her organization's board turned down this request. Not one to be daunted by a setback, she rallied faculty wives and other middle-class African American women in Atlanta to form a new group to press for improvements in the almost nonexistent recreational services available to African American children. This group eventually created facilities for playgrounds on the campus of Atlanta Baptist, where John Hope was president. Burns Hope also began working on providing social work services in Atlanta's poor African American communities.[39]

During the 1906 riot, she and her group of faculty wives turned the city's African American college campuses into safe havens for persons seeking shelter. The crisis, she later reported, further strengthened her racial solidarity and reform resolve. By 1908 Burns Hope had founded a settlement project in Atlanta named the Neighborhood Union, which had as its objective the moral, social, intellectual, and religious uplift of the neighborhoods in which it established branches. Its membership comprised both educated middle-class women, including many faculty wives, and working-class women. Burns Hope was elected its first president. She would continue to work with this group for decades to come. Its first initiatives included organizing women volunteers to survey neighborhoods and visit families, supporting women and girls in families, and ridding neighborhoods of so-called fallen women, who were perceived as a bad example for young girls. The union's motto was "Burn, Bury, and Beautify," and its projects soon extended beyond providing private supports to taking on social and political campaigns of relevance to the city, including advocating for African American police officers and better police protection in African American communities, promoting voter registration, improving city facilities for African Americans, and protesting segregation and race discrimination.[40]

Meeting and marrying John Hope took Burns Hope out of a life of economic struggle and paid secretarial work and transferred her into the social class of the Southern educated professional elite. But her prior paid employment also equipped her with strong administrative experience, giving her the personal resources to make the most of the opportunities her new status offered. Burns Hope became a sought-after leader on the national stage of the women's club movement, although her frequent travels in this role were against her husband's wishes. Her national involvements led her to form ties with leaders involved in founding the National Urban League, and its leaders regarded her as an important Atlanta ally.

There was a definite tension between the two organizations, too, as she sought to maintain the autonomy of her organization.[41] In the early 1910s Atlanta was more of a stronghold for social welfare organizing than for the NAACP. By the late 1910s the NAACP would gain traction in Atlanta; both John and Lugenia Burns Hope would become leaders of that effort.[42] At the beginning of the new century, however, economic empowerment appeared a more promising route to racial advancement than a local focus on political and civil rights equality demands.[43]

Du Bois in New York City

Du Bois was geographically anchored to Atlanta because of his academic position there, but the trauma of the Sam Hose lynching, followed by the Atlanta riot, left him increasingly alienated from that city. Atlanta's generally oppressive social and political conditions led Du Bois to turn increasing amounts of his attention and energy elsewhere. He spent his summers in Boston; New York City was also a frequent travel destination. There Du Bois attended and served as secretary at a meeting in 1903 with figures such as social reformer William Bulkley, professor and ethicist Felix Adler, and others to discuss strategies for bettering race conditions. In 1904 he negotiated with Washington before and after the Carnegie-funded meeting of race leaders that took place in the city, which led to the formation of the Committee of Twelve. Du Bois gave that plan a brief chance before resigning once it became clear that Washington would thoroughly control it. Instead Du Bois turned to other organizing work occurring in New York City, where the diversity and richness of reform activity meant that no one leader could fully control what was going on.

Even if he was not consciously thinking of devising an escape route from the South, Du Bois's organizing attention became increasingly focused on the work of Northern activists who were combining political and civil rights advocacy with social welfare work. This offered a model for organizing that most appealed to his own vision. One such activist who came to Du Bois's attention was Mary White Ovington, his age peer who worked in settlement houses for African Americans and was pioneering the new role of white egalitarian race supporter, just as Du Bois was pioneering the role of scholar-activist. Their correspondence started a friendship that would help support them both over many years of mutual involvement in the NAACP. Ovington cast Du Bois as her tutor on race matters. At the same time, she attempted to persuade him to share her own firm opinions, especially as to the virtues of democratic socialism.[44] Du Bois at first kept his distance, understandably skeptical of yet another white do-gooder reformer. He wrote back, however, seeming to sense enough sincerity in Ovington's enthusiasm to merit his attention. The two fell into a comfortable epistolary friendship reflecting what was for the times an unusual intellectual exchange across both race and gender lines.

Du Bois and Ovington

In early correspondence Ovington courted Du Bois intellectually, explaining that she had received a fellowship to study economic opportunities for young African American men and women in New York City and had plans to do social work among them; since Du Bois knew "more of social work probably than anyone else" she would like to request his assistance. Ovington had at this point acted as head worker and lived at the Greenpoint Settlement serving white immigrants in Brooklyn for seven years, so she was no newcomer to settlement work. But she had decided, after hearing Booker T. Washington lecture in New York City in 1903, to concentrate her future social work on African Americans. Using her settlement movement connections, she obtained the fellowship funding to study the social and economic conditions facing African Americans of all classes in the city. Ovington explained that a committee of advisers, all but one of whom were "Columbia men," including Edwin Seligman, Franz Boas, and anthropologist Livingston Farrand, was overseeing her work. The funding for it had grown out of the 1903 meeting at which Du Bois had served as secretary. Moreover, Du Bois was to her "one of our [best] modern writers." Therefore, although they had never met, she hoped he could be persuaded to give her his assistance.[45]

Du Bois replied by sending her copies of his Atlanta bulletins. Ovington in turn made a financial contribution for this work, which seemed to warm Du Bois's attitude considerably.[46] In the next months, Ovington reported to Du Bois on the investigation she was undertaking. To research recreational and employment opportunities, she had been able to accompany Jessie C. Sleet, an African American visiting nurse who was also publishing reports about her nursing work.[47] (Sleet, Ovington, Bulkley, and Wilford H. Smith all worked together on a New York antituberculosis committee aimed at African American communities as well, further attesting to the dense overlap of reform networks in the city at the time.) In her travels through the city Ovington observed many small business undertakings; she wondered whether a settlement might teach work skills aimed at these neighborhood employment possibilities, such as shoemaking. In a later initiative, she approached Felix Adler about opening doors for young African Americans in Jewish offices because she believed Jews have "less prejudice than other folk here." Ovington also visited Victoria Earle Matthew's White Rose Mission and watched Miss Sleet lead a girls club meeting at another settlement. Ovington put together a small advisory committee composed of Sleet and two African American men involved in social work to review her findings so that she could gain from "their wider experience" and "know better the significance of what I see."[48]

As Ovington's confidence grew she needed less guidance from Du Bois on her sociological investigation; she would eventually publish it as an outsider's study of various aspects of African American life in New York City. Her letters to Du Bois now tended to share news rather than report as a pupil. Describing her attendance at many reform committee efforts, Ovington described working with William Bulkley, whom she now viewed as one of the men having "more intelligent knowledge of social work than any other." She was equally impressed with Dr. William Henry Brooks, who was the founding pastor of St. Mark's United Methodist Church in New York City, where he ran an "institutional" church supporting a variety of social missions. Ovington would later recruit both Bulkley and Brooks for the committee that would found the NAACP.[49]

Ovington was soon off on a cross-country trip, stopping in Chicago to visit Celia Wooley's Frederick Douglass Center and Jane Addams's Hull House, where she dined with Rev. Wright, the Niagara Movement founding member who had assisted Ransom at the ICSS. She was delighted that Hull House supporter and University of Chicago professor Sophonisba Breckinridge was "such a glorious radical," which she had found "a complete surprise"—Breckinridge would later join both the National Urban League and the NAACP's governing boards.[50] Du Bois invited Ovington to attend his tenth annual Atlanta University conference, asking her to speak at an annual "Mother's meeting," which, he explained, "is a small assembly of 100–200 women of the more intelligent class."[51] Ovington spoke on a panel on "Child Study and the Kindergarten," along with Gertrude Ware, the Atlanta kindergarten movement advocate. This type of work served as an important point of commonality between Atlanta and New York City; social work activism in both cities was firmly rooted in women's organizations. Another New York City activist on the panel was Frances Kellor, whom Ovington would soon work with through NUL-affiliated organizations. A fourth member was Mary Evans Wilson of Boston, whose husband, Butler Wilson, would become head of the Boston NAACP branch.

After her visit Ovington candidly wrote to Du Bois of finding Atlanta "just a little worse than anyone would be able to imagine" and the university too strict toward its students, though she realized she should "face the fact of the greater difficulties they will meet than other young people, and the need they will have of a Puritan ability to endure hardness." She praised Ware's kindergarten efforts and appreciated how much harder her work was "in a city where there is no strong public sentiment for social betterment." Ovington guiltily thought of New York City in contrast, where she would "feel myself living in a land of milk and honey if I wasn't endeavoring to help the most neglected folk in it."[52]

Ovington managed the improbable feat of gaining Du Bois's support through a combination of assertive charm and sincerity. But she also had something to offer back, in the form of detailed information about what was happening in the interracial activist circles in New York City into which she was gracefully inserting herself. She may also have offered Du Bois a glimpse of a possible path out of Atlanta. She wrote enthusiastically to Du Bois about new organizing efforts going on in which she, Bulkley, and Brooks were involved. In May 1906 she reported that Bulkley had been "the prime mover" of a new organization intended to bring together prominent African Americans and a few white people to improve the economic condition of African Americans in New York. A wealthy white businessman active in reform circles, William Jay Schieffelin, would be chair; Bulkley would be executive secretary. Others involved included Dr. Verna Morton-Jones, an African American physician who ran the Lincoln Settlement in Brooklyn, and Brooklyn lawyer D. Macon Webster, who represented business clients and would later be appointed as the only African American lawyer on the NAACP's Legal Committee.[53] In this letter Ovington was describing the coming together of another new organization that would soon be called the Committee for Improving the Industrial Condition of Negroes in New York City (CIICN), one of several that would later merge to become the National Urban League.

By 1907 Ovington had moved into a tenement called the Tuskegee, located in the African American district of San Juan Hill.[54] She and John Milholland had convinced Andrew Carnegie's business partner, Henry Phipps, to construct this building. Phipps did not want its purpose to extend to social work, however, so Ovington had started a social work project with Dr. Morton-Jones at the Lincoln Settlement House in Brooklyn, which Morton-Jones headed. The Lincoln Settlement had started as an extension of Lillian Wald's Henry House and offered a health clinic, day nursery, free kindergarten, health lectures, and vocational and recreational classes and clubs in an African American community. It later became part of the National Urban League. Collaboration between Morton-Jones and Ovington would continue into the future as both played active roles in the CIICN and other organizations that eventually merged to form the NUL. Morton-Jones joined the NAACP's board of directors and served on its executive committee, frequently as the only African American woman at these meetings, Ovington would later recall.

Like many others, Morton-Jones was also active in women's clubs and had joined the Niagara Movement as soon as its membership policies permitted her to do so.[55]

Cosmopolitan Club Scandal

In April 1908 Ovington wrote with anticipation to Du Bois about a restaurant dinner being planned for an organization called the Cosmopolitan Club, which sought to bring together a racially mixed group of New York City progressives to hear speakers and discuss the issues of the day. Ovington was particularly excited about the list of speakers, which she believed was to include Reverdy Ransom.[56] Other speakers included socialist John Spargo and editors Oswald Garrison Villard of the *Evening Post* and Hamilton Holt of the *Independent*. Ovington little realized at the time that the modest dinner gathering she was anticipating would become the source of a major national scandal. On the night of the dinner reporters, rumored to have been sent by Washington, burst into the Cosmopolitan room in an attempt to photograph what they had been told would be the shocking scene, to some eyes, of white women dining next to African American men. Newspapers far from the city reported on the incident. According to the *Alexandria Gazette* of Virginia, the scene involved "a dozen white girls, clad in shimmering gowns, some of them in décolleté, with negroes on each side of them"; the paper deemed the event the worst of "all the abhorrent banquets ever held in this country." In South Carolina, the notorious antiblack Populist senator Benjamin Tillman used the incident to proclaim in a newspaper in his state that "the best way to eliminate the suggestion of social equality is to remove political equality" by repealing the Reconstruction amendments. The *Washington Times* and the *New York Evening World* reported on interviewing Ovington the next day at her home in the Phipps model housing, where "she is the only white tenant in the big negro tenement." Ovington expressed her view that there had been nothing wrong with the incident and tried to downplay the issue of intermarriage, which had been highlighted in news reports that took a speaker's comments out of context. In the end she could not quite pull off her attempt at public relations repair: "I do not believe in intermarriages of the races—at least not at present...I don't believe there is any reason to talk about it. Ultimately all the nations of the world will intermarry, but those things work themselves out." Even Ovington's elderly parents received obscene hate mail. In his next letter Du Bois conveyed his sympathies to Ovington, hoping that the incident had not "hurt her good work."[57]

By 1908 the "good work" in which Ovington was participating was coalescing into several major social welfare organizations. Learning as she went while contributing her enthusiastic energy and gaining access in part through her social standing, Ovington played an active role in several of these groups, though she would later concentrate her efforts on the NAACP. These various social welfare organizations springing up in New York City were responding to the particular conditions they encountered there. Some of these were similar to Atlanta's, but others were quite different.

Social and Economic Conditions in New York City

Like Atlanta's, New York City's race-related problems were pressing and severe. Unlike Atlanta, however, legally inscribed Jim Crow did not present their most obvious manifestation. Instead, the constrictions on African Americans' opportunities were caused by structural oppression brought about through a host of factors including employment discrimination that both employers and unions imposed. The results of race oppression were nevertheless often similar, manifesting themselves in statistics revealing that African Americans were concentrated in the least lucrative employment spheres and faced oppressive living conditions in housing, health, education, and social services. A survey conducted by George Edmund Haynes, soon to become director of the National Urban League, gave a clear picture. Haynes found that in 1890 a large majority of African American wage earners were engaged in domestic and personal service. There were, however, small numbers of bookkeepers and accountants and slightly larger numbers of draymen (wagon drivers), teamsters, and workers engaged in manufacturing, mechanical pursuits, and, among women, dressmaking. By 1905 some positive developments had taken place: Now only about 40 percent of African American male workers in New York City were engaged in domestic and personal service, 8 percent were in manufacturing and mechanical pursuits, and 20 percent were in trades. Among women, however, about 90 percent were still in domestic and personal service, fewer than 6 percent were in manufacturing and mechanical pursuits, mostly dressmaking and garment work, and less than 1 percent worked in trades. There was increasing evidence of union organization among African American workers, including in carpentry and mechanics, though there were few skilled trades in which African Americans were union members. Haynes further found that the typical African American business was in retail. These businesses were small in both size and number of employees and were facing increasingly severe competition from white-owned firms with greater access to capital.[58]

These conditions, as well as activists' sociological approach to understanding them, shaped the focus of their work. In New York City this work was often aimed, as in the case of Bulkley's industrial education school, at attempting to dismantle the barriers imposed by employer and union discrimination, which kept African Americans from rising into skilled employment sectors. The presence of more collective union activity in New York City, but at the same time less consumer solidarity, put the focus on working-class jobs rather than business entrepreneurism.

Other aspects of the social and economic landscape confronting African Americans in early twentieth-century New York City were also in some ways similar to and in other ways different from Atlanta. Both cities were experiencing the in-migration of rural African Americans, but this phenomenon (not yet at the levels of the Great Migration, which started around 1918) was different in New York City, both because of the greater scale of that metropolis and because of the greater distance from home of African American migrants who had traveled from the rural South to this great Northern city. Social workers quite correctly viewed these travelers, often young women, as particularly vulnerable to exploitation. These Victorian-era reformers were quick to pick up on this image of feminine, youthful weakness and made it their highest priority to attempt to deliver young female migrants out of the city's dangers, usually by escorting them to settlement houses staffed by trustworthy volunteers.[59]

The White Rose Mission and National League for the Protection of Colored Women

One of the organizations pioneering this work was the White Rose Mission, founded in 1897 by African American journalist and club woman Victoria Earle Matthews. White Rose workers met young women arriving in the city's ports of entry and offered them safe and "respectable" lodging in the mission's settlement house, along with job training, employment placement, and other social services.[60] Although Matthews died in 1907 at the age of forty–six of a tuberculosis-related condition, the White Rose Mission continued to operate, offering travelers' aid and temporary lodging as well as employment training, clubs, and other typical settlement services. In 1907 its volunteers met five hundred steamers, assisted 250 girls coming from these ships, and provided lodging to more than 300 girls in all—statistics that, while arguably only scratching the surface of the problems it was seeking to address, stacked up favorably in comparison to what bigger, nationally oriented organizations were later able to accomplish. Reverend Brooks and Rev. Clayton Powell, both soon to become board members of the early NAACP, sat on its board of directors along with an impressive list of other prominent social reformers.[61]

In 1905 a new organization seeking to extend the model of the White Rose Mission's work on a national basis came on the scene. Its name was the National League for the Protection of Colored Women (NLPCW), and it would become another predecessor organization of the National Urban League. One of the NLPCW's founders was the forceful Frances Kellor, a white woman who held a law degree from Cornell and had also studied sociology at the University of Chicago.[62] Kellor had become interested in the plight of young African American women who were migrating to large cities and falling victim to unscrupulous employment practices, including being channeled into prostitution. She published a book on this subject in 1904 and set up the NLPCW as a vehicle to attack this problem.[63] Matthews appears to have been pushed aside to some extent at this juncture. As her friend Fortune pointed out from the pages of *The Age*, "White men and women have entered the same field of work" as Matthews, "as much for the notoriety and profit to be got out of it as for the good to be accomplished." Rather than seeking to cooperate with the White Rose Mission, "they have striven to crush it out, because they were not allowed to dominate it." Fortune continued by warning that charity controlled by others "ennobles nothing that it touches" and urged African Americans to keep control of this work themselves.[64]

Kellor remained general secretary of the NLPCW for five years. Sarah Willie Layten, president of the Women's Convention of the National Baptists and founder of the California Federation of Colored Women's Clubs, now lived in Philadelphia and served as the NLPCW's cofounder. It thus started with offices in New York City and Philadelphia. By 1910 it had expanded into eight more cities, although it is unclear how much work some of its branches accomplished. Its records show that, in New York City, it continued to rely on White Rose Mission social workers to meet new arrivals at the city's ports and provide shelter, employment assistance, and training to young women workers. When Kellor left the NLPCW to become an investigator for the New York State Bureau of Industries and Immigration, Layten took over as the NLPCW's general secretary. Its board of directors included many Booker T. Washington supporters, including Ruth Standish Baldwin, wife of Long Island Railroad Company president William Henry Baldwin Jr.; Schieffelin, who also helped found and sat on the board of the CIICN and would later serve on the board of the NAACP; and Fred Moore, the Tuskegee machine operative who headed the National Negro Business League and became editor of *The Age* after ousting Fortune in 1907. All of these figures would later transfer to become members of the NUL board.

The Committee for Improving the Industrial Condition of Negroes in New York City

The second of the National Urban League's predecessor organizations was the CIICN, the organization whose founding meeting Ovington took part in and described to Du Bois in her 1906 correspondence.[65] With Bulkley as its prime mover, the CIICN devoted itself to helping African American workers acquire the skills and training they needed to find better employment and employers willing to offer it. As well as making potential employees aware of employment opportunities, the CIICN "hoped to educate whites about black capabilities and enlist their help in improving industrial conditions for blacks." In early 1907 the CIICN's executive committee included a mix of more radical figures, including Bulkley, Brooks, and Ovington, along with pro-Washington stalwarts, including two Tuskegee-affiliated

African American lawyers, Charles W. Anderson and Wilford H. Smith. Smith headed a legal committee, Brooks headed a public meetings committee, and Ovington chaired a committee on neighborhood work. She also served on two additional committees, one on tradesmen and another on employment.[66]

By 1911 the CIICN's governing board and other committees had evolved to become far leaner and also to tilt in a more conservative direction. A comparison of that year's list of CIICN leaders with those of the NLPCW suggests that the two organizations' leaders were basically engaged in a game of musical chairs, with many of the same figures involved in both group's governing bodies but in varying roles. The cast of characters on the CIICN's letterhead included many involved in the NLPCW and the groups it worked with: Schieffelin was chair; Kellor was on its Neighborhood Work Committee; and Mary L. Stone, a white reformer who had served in various capacities on the board of the White Rose Mission, was on its General Committee, as was Ovington, who now held only this position. On the Executive Committee sat Fred Moore, along with Ruth Baldwin, Brooks, and Webster. Bulkley still served as the CIICN's vice chair.

An account of how and why the CIICN developed as it did involves excavating a previously unnoticed back story: Initially Bulkley had hoped to move this impressively credentialed, top-heavy organization in activist directions but he found himself unable to do so. It seems that Bulkley had hoped to tap into the social capital and financial resources the CIICN's wealthy white board members possessed but to retain African American activists' control over the organization's direction. Bulkley was trying, in other words, to heed Fortune's advice from the pages of *The Age* that African American activists should retain leadership over the proliferation of new organizations being established to help the race.

In an effort to carry out this strategy, Bulkley called a meeting at his high school of only the African American members of the exploratory committee that had formed to found the CIICN in April 1906. In this smaller meeting, Bulkley recommended dividing into a wide array of subcommittees. His vision for these committees was an activist one: A committee on public meetings would arrange for meetings in the churches, especially African American ones, to enlighten congregants as to their needs and opportunities; a committee on employment would investigate not only African Americans' training for craft jobs but also the attitudes of employers and labor organizations; and a legal committee would research laws affecting African American employment and stand ready to protect these workers in their "rights as a working man."[67]

Thus at the next general organizing meeting held a month later, Bulkley had done his background organizing work and could confidently offer a polished series of recommendations, under which the organization would split into a series of subcommittees to address each facet of the problems identified—much like the Niagara Movement had done the year before, though he did not point this out. In the following months, Bulkley, along with chair of the public meetings committee Rev. Brooks, proceeded to plan a series of meetings to be held in African American churches in Manhattan and Brooklyn, as well as one large meeting to be held in one of the big ballrooms in the city. Bulkley, as "the author of the movement," planned to speak at every meeting "to outline the ideas which he has at heart." Each meeting would be carefully balanced to include one white and one African American speaker, so that the resulting picture would be one of cooperation and mutuality rather than of continued race-based domination. The goal of these meetings, Bulkley envisioned, would be to "place firmly in the minds of the masses of African Americans of New York," both the urgency of acquiring skills for employment and the possibility that avenues for using these skills could be opened. Bulkley explained that the organization "has the aim of breaking down color caste in gainful occupations in New York."[68]

Differing Organizational Visions

Bulkley's vision for the CIICN was that of an activist organization that would reach out to the working-class masses and gradually dismantle the racial caste system in employment. But this was not the only organizational vision in play within the CIICN. There were at least several others, and different members of the governing body probably held in their own minds varying combinations of these alternative visions of the organization's purposes. One of these other visions, just as Fortune predicted, was based on wealthy white charity—in other words, on the idea that the more fortunate should offer assistance to those far less fortunate than themselves. Another vision involved Tuskegee-style accommodationism; it sought to design social welfare programs in such a way as to politically mollify and thus attract the financial support of wealthy, politically moderate whites. This vision fit well with the philanthropic paternalism of some of the CIICN's well-off white patrons, as Washington's great success in fund-raising from this same group for Southern vocational schools already attested. Washington wanted to use the same model for social welfare work in New York City, and he recognized that Bulkley's community self-empowerment model potentially posed a threat to these plans. Washington wrote to his ally Charles Anderson about the need to ensure that the "important organization" the CIICN represented not be taken over by militants such as "Bulkley and his crowd."[69]

However, another approach had arrived on the scene as well, in the form of the vision of professionalism that George Edmund Haynes injected as he took over the NLPCW in 1908. Haynes became active in the CIICN as well. At the time Haynes was pursuing his doctorate through the University of Chicago's sociology department and the New York School of Philanthropy (which would later become the New York School of Social Work of Columbia University).

Figure 10.1 George E. Haynes (New York Public Library).

The general mission for the NLPCW and CIICN Haynes envisioned involved increasing the efficiency of the social welfare work being carried out for African Americans through a multitude of organizations in New York City. Influenced by his graduate school training, Haynes wanted to achieve greater professionalization of such work by placing it in the hands of well-trained social workers who were African American themselves. He believed this objective could be realized by unifying the various social welfare organizing efforts taking place in New York City under one central organization.

On his arrival on the New York City social welfare organizing scene, Haynes resolutely set out to achieve this objective. He succeeded admirably in doing so, bringing together the main organizations and personalities working in New York City through a lengthy process that would require, as one observer put it, "great patience and tact."[70] Haynes's interim plan for how the main organizations doing social welfare work in the city could be successfully merged involved first creating yet another organization, this one to be called the Committee on Urban Conditions among Negroes (CUCN). In 1908 many of the people involved in the NLPCW and the CIICN met to form this organization with the purpose of merging the NLPCW and the CIICN as well as consolidating their fund-raising and other public appeals.[71] The CUCN gradually accomplished this, leaving the National League on Urban Conditions among Negroes, or NUL, as the new consolidated structure.

Founding the National Urban League

Thus the end of the twentieth century's first decade saw many actors involved in racial justice organizing moving toward greater organizational consolidation; this occurred both among civil rights organizations, such as the AAC and the Niagara Movement, and among organizations focused on social welfare issues. This process led to increased specialization of organizations that focused on these two realms of racial justice work as well. Organizational consolidation among groups with similar focuses thus had the additional consequence of producing increased divergence between the missions of the various remaining associations.

The CUCN was officially established in 1910, and it is usually to this date that the founding of the National Urban League is attributed, although it would actually take several more years of negotiations and gradual integration of the organizational functions of the NLPCW, CIICN, and CUCN before they would unite fully under the name of the NUL. Recounting the many incremental steps involved in this eventual unification need not detain us here; for the purposes of this account, the relevant trajectory concerns Haynes arriving and taking over as director. The key question is how his vision and his work to achieve it stamped the NUL's character in its early years. Haynes believed in efficiency and professionalization; he also believed in achieving organizational goals at a very high standard of professional success. His first goal as CUCN director was fund-raising to support a professionally staffed organization.

From the start Haynes, with the help of board members, targeted large donors. This was made easier because of various board members' ties to the same set of wealthy benefactors as Washington had previously cultivated—indeed, some of the CUCN's key board members, such as Ruth Baldwin, wife of William Baldwin Jr., the president of the Long Island Railroad, were among Washington's chief financial backers. Once Haynes came on board at the CUCN and began systematically guiding board members in fund-raising, large checks began to roll in the door. These contributions in turn supported budget goals that included far more paid staff than did the early NAACP's more militantly political profile.

A few examples illustrate the sources of the NUL's early financial support. Wall Street lawyer Paul Cravath—who had not long before advised Washington and Wilford Smith on contesting Pullman car segregation—made repeated contributions of $150 (worth several thousand dollars today).[72] Another lawyer with a Wall Street address, Alfred T. White, yearly contributed $900 jointly with his sisters and offered matching funds that increased his contribution to $1,500 in at least one year.[73] These were large contributions for the time. The top corporate lawyers who sat on the NAACP's first legal committee came nowhere near matching them but seemed to instead regard their main contribution to be the donation of their valuable time in legal services.

If lawyers were financially generous to the infant NUL, New York City's financiers and businessmen far exceeded their largesse. Paul Sachs, with the authorization of his father, Samuel Sachs, head of Goldman, Sachs and Co., gave a total of $1,500 over three years and promised to add more to create matching incentives. John D. Rockefeller Jr. one year pledged $1,000 outright and several thousand more in matching funds if fund-raising goals were met. That same year Sears, Roebuck and Co. founder Julian Rosenwald contributed $2,000. He then vowed to pay 20 percent of the organization's annual budget, projected at the time to rise to $25,000 in five years.[74] (Around the same time, Rosenwald made a single $2,000 contribution to the NAACP.) NUL historian Nancy J. Weiss calculates that gifts from these three men accounted for more than 40 percent of the NUL's budget in its first years.[75]

The NUL, in short, focused itself under Haynes's professional direction on what would today be called a corporate-sector fund-raising strategy, an option readily available to it given the identities of its board members. But with this fund-raising focus, the NUL necessarily needed to communicate organizational purposes that would appeal to wealthy donors. Gone in the documents prepared in 1913 with this goal in mind were any references to the mass meetings among African American workers that Bulkley had envisioned when he founded the CIICN. In place of this image, the NUL emphasized the goal of cultivating "the trained Negro social worker" and listed service provision, including traveler's aid; "discouraging the mixing of the good and the bad" in tenements; and placing social workers in paid positions as its chief accomplishments. Its future goals were to develop a "nucleus of sixteen workers as a competent staff with good office routine and records," to train them "to efficient methods," and to promote a "system of graduate training"—which would in turn have the additional benefit of producing professional work for African American college graduates.[76]

In the terms used by social movement theorists, the NUL and the NAACP soon evolved different organizational "logics." The NUL sought wealthy, more conservative donors and undertook projects that could be made to sound appealing to them, while the NAACP began developing a grassroots orientation and a mass-based, small-donor fund-raising model to match. The two organizations' leaders were aware that this divergence helped both organizations: The NUL could pursue wealthy donors without scaring them away with militant civil rights talk, while the NAACP could target its message to the rising masses. But the subject matters of the two organizations' primary focus also diverged, and that divergence appeared less clearly thought out or strategically controlled.[77]

The NUL's "Logic" of Social Service to Individuals

The NUL's activities in its early years were diverse—even scattered—but can be generally classified under the mission of providing assistance to individuals to help them improve their economic and social circumstances by offering services such as housing, vocational placement and training, probation counseling, and a multitude of other interventions. For all its efficiency and the amount of money the NUL spent, the volume of services it actually dispensed was not great, especially once it started trying to spread its resources over several cities in pursuit of its ambitious national aspirations. In 1913, for example, it reported handling 128 new preventative cases in one month (with follow-up in 66 additional old cases). Twenty-four employment positions had been obtained, and the housing bureau had certified eighteen new houses as meeting acceptable living standards, for a total of twenty-three tenements.[78] As Haynes acknowledged to board chair Ruth Baldwin, "I agree fully with you that the results so far achieved have been rather at too high a unit cost and it will be my endeavor from now on to increase the ratio of results to cost."[79]

This focus on individual service provision did not meet with the approval of some members of the consolidated NUL board, especially those who had founded their organizations with a very different vision of what they might achieve. Thus, at the same time that Haynes was writing to Baldwin about the need to reduce "unit costs," he was also writing to NUL board members about an "attitude of opposition" that figures like Bulkley and Brooks displayed. Haynes believed that this attitude "goes back to the old Industrial Committee attitude and pride and feeling of independence." As if to appease Bulkley, Ruth Baldwin made a special donation for urgently needed supplies to his industrial school. The NUL's treasurer, L. Hollingsworth Wood, then sought to intervene to control how Mrs. Baldwin's funds would be spent, leading to a letter of polite complaint from Bulkley. Bulkley, a steady and self-disciplined advocate, did not let whatever differences he had with the NUL's direction drive him off its board, on which he remained active throughout the period this book covers. But such self-restraint must have come at some internal cost.[80]

The NUL's Issue Priorities

The NUL's board, which drew equal numbers of members from each of its constituent organizations, continued to boast many prominent names familiar as Washington supporters, including Ruth Baldwin, Wood, Cravath, Sachs, and Moore. It retained many less conservative members as well, including Bulkley, Columbia professors Edwin Seligman and Felix Adler, Sophonisba Breckenridge, Ruth's nephew Roger Baldwin (later head of the ACLU), and others.[81] A number of these figures were also lending their names and efforts to the new NAACP. Thus the overall picture of New York City race activism in the early 1910s was not one of a schism between more militant civil rights work and more staid social welfare work; instead, overlapping groups worked on both projects. At the same time, the dominant tenor of the work in these two spheres had unmistakably diverged. As historian of the early NUL Nancy J. Weiss correctly observes based on her comprehensive comparative analysis of leaders of the two organizations, despite much overlap, there was "considerable difference in ideology between those who supported the Urban League and those who joined the NAACP.... [T]he most advanced members of the NAACP were considerably more radical than their counterparts in the League."[82]

Weiss takes this contrast still further in proposing that the NUL "eschewed" any form of legislative action. She claims that, in contrast to the NAACP's court and legislative work:

> The Urban League in its early decades eschewed the legislative process. It never considered seeking congressional action to make equal employment opportunity the law of the land, or to give blacks access to a wider range of housing or to give them the right to use public parks and playgrounds. Instead, it tried to change individual practices in different businesses or cities by private, individual persuasion.... This emphasis on private practices rather than public laws set the Urban Leaguers apart from the settlement workers and most of their progressive colleagues.[83]

In so describing the NUL, Weiss correctly captures its general tenor but does not explore the reasons the NUL—or the NAACP, for that matter—failed to ask for legislative fixes to problems of racial discrimination in the realm of private-sector business activity such as employment and housing. Those reasons lie in the legal context and doctrine of the era, which could not have easily supported legal theories that declared private-sector discrimination illegal in matters such as employment and housing. Nor does Weiss point to any evidence that the NUL affirmatively rejected legislative strategies. To the contrary, close scrutiny of its early board meeting minutes shows that it did occasionally work for legislation; it was just that the legislative initiatives it focused on were aimed at transferring some of the burden of supporting its social welfare projects to public institutions. In this respect the NUL's strategy was, not surprisingly, much like that of the NACW affiliates. The NUL sought to experiment with ways to improve economic and social welfare conditions for African Americans and, once having found programs that worked, to push for government funding for them.

The projects on which the NUL focused reflected a mix of strategies that arose from its specific history. To the leaders involved, the activities reflected not a hodgepodge of priorities but a common mission of serving those in need. They also reflected strong efforts to persuade both large corporations and government institutions to take a more active role in racial justice issues. A major part of the work involved providing individual services, but another aspect of the early NUL's work, which it inherited primarily from the CIICN, involved conducting surveys on employer attitudes about hiring and promoting African Americans in various occupational sectors, including commuter railroads, the building trades, and mercantile establishments. An initiative undertaken in cooperation with the Methodist Episcopal Church had approached the Metropolitan Insurance Company in an attempt to secure jobs for African Americans as agents and collectors "in districts largely inhabited by Negroes." The NUL also worked to promote the organization of associations or unions in various occupational sectors, including elevator operators and public porters.

In still another facet of his work, Haynes undertook to meet with the executive council of the AFL. This meeting represented yet another of the many attempts race justice activists unsuccessfully made during this period to develop lines of communication and cooperation with the trade union movement (but at the same time would lay important groundwork that would bear fruit in a later era). Haynes wrote a report to his board about his efforts, in which he put the possibilities of future cooperation in positive terms but explained that the members of the group with which he had met "seemed somewhat disinclined to take any definite action on this first appearance before them" and that he "therefore decided not to ask them to do any definite thing."[84]

Another focus of activity involved intervention in New York City's criminal justice system, continuing the work initially undertaken primarily for girls but extending it to boys and young men as well. Thus the NLPCW board had first asked the courts to appoint workers affiliated with the NLPCW as regular probation officers. As a next step it asked for public funding for these positions. On the recommendation of an affiliated neighborhood club, the NLPCW board agreed to help open a temporary detention home for delinquent girls; a few months later, the board resolved to ask the judges of the court why the pretrial investigation work these probation officers were required to do "should not be done by the State and at the State's expense" and also to seek an "appropriation by the City for such work." It further resolved to ask New York City's Episcopal bishop to assist in "pressing such appeals to the legislature," as well as "to ask the City for support in expanding the accommodations" open for housing delinquent girls.[85] A similar strategy of gradually seeking to enlist public funding characterized other efforts as well, such as setting up a playground in Harlem and then inducing the City Department of Parks to take responsibility for its maintenance.[86]

Other projects took the form of investigations, such as one to probe the treatment accorded African American physicians and patients in hospitals in the greater New York area. Another involved researching and publishing a list of "respectable" tenements—which engendered much debate about whether interested real estate investors should be approached for funding assistance. Leaders ended up rejecting the idea due to conflict of interest concerns. Another investigation involved inspecting dance halls, and still another investigating an African American legal aid society that claimed to "guarantee protection and legal services in the case of arrest." Here the investigators concluded that the enterprise was "a commercial scheme to bring revenue to its promoters," which should be "discouraged as being against the best interest of the respectable" African American. The NUL even dabbled in community legal education, sponsoring a lecture course on the rights of landlords and tenants.[87]

The direction of the NUL's organizational growth resulted largely from historical contingency just as its issue agenda did. Its main expansion efforts involved seeking to establish a presence in other cities where it had good connections, but here as with the total amount of services provided, growth was slow and difficult. The NUL sought to organize local affiliates where it knew of enthusiastic local leaders, and it found such leaders in disparate places, including St. Louis and Talladega College in Alabama, the locations of its first two chapters, as well as Baltimore; Louisville; Newport News, Virginia, where many African American shipyard workers were employed; and both Savannah and Augusta, Georgia, where local enthusiasm led the national board to allocate resources in the form of extended visits from associate director E. K. Jones. At the same time, it made no attempt to gain grassroots membership; its organizational model was very much a traditional one for the era, which rested on gathering small, elite groups of leading community figures.[88]

The presence of Burns Hope's imposing Neighborhood Union in Atlanta required a special strategy. There Haynes placed one of his best former student "fellows" in a teaching position at Atlanta's Morehouse College (headed at the time by Burns Hope's husband), with the charge that this NUL fellow work with the Neighborhood Union to gradually bring it officially within the NUL. This process was not smooth; Burns Hope had ideas of her own about how neighborhood social services organizations should be run and was hesitant to become swallowed by the NUL, though she was very willing to, and did, cooperate extensively with it.[89]

The NUL avoided Boston altogether. The "bellicose attitude" of African Americans there led it to conclude that it was "wise not to attempt organization there at this time." It likewise found it difficult to gain traction in Washington, DC, despite Kelly Miller's efforts to help. It did set up a chapter at Howard University, where Miller taught. In Chicago, the board voted to lend aid to a local settlement effort. Boston, Washington, DC, and Chicago would be bastions of early NAACP local chapter building; at first local leaders' energies tended to be funneled in the direction of this national organizing effort (though this picture would soon change as conditions evolved to support ever more activity on a range of fronts). Similarly, the Hopes became prominent supporters of the NAACP's Atlanta chapter once it got going in the later 1910s.

The NUL, in short, did not operate under a particularly well-defined, big-picture strategy either on substantive issues or organizational growth. Nor did its individual service provision focus point it toward grand strategic thinking about big-picture reform. Indeed, given the many conservatives on its governing board, ideas promoting broad political reform would probably have been controversial. But as Weiss trenchantly notes in her classic treatment of the NUL's history, using a largely case-by-case approach to fix social welfare problems that arose out of large-scale, social-structural forces did not prove particularly effective in improving the lives of the majority of African Americans who lacked economic resources.[90] The NUL's work was helpful to particular individuals, itself a laudable goal. But under the NUL's dominant ideology, that work lacked the political valence that had made it part of an effort to achieve broadscale social reform when deployed by organizations like Ransom's ICSS, Church Terrell's NACW, or Bulkley's CIICN as he originally envisioned it.

To be sure, just as activists specializing in civil rights advocacy never thought of law reform in the simplistic, "legal liberalist" terms they are sometimes accused of adopting, the activists involved in the early NUL never agreed that a depoliticized, professionalized form of social work would be their organizational goal. Haynes's vision was based in a commitment to intrarace self-help. He sought to nurture new generations of professionals in a discipline he was in the process of inventing from the funded position he obtained in 1910 on the faculty of Fisk University. Haynes envisioned this new social work discipline as one that combined rigorous sociological training with fieldwork and service to the race. His extensive course syllabi and class notes, carefully preserved at Fisk University, reflect the prototype of courses that would later emerge as the field of Afro-American studies. Haynes was a pragmatist, but he was no accommodationist. Always polite to the wealthy white leaders who supported the NUL, Haynes also looked for opportunities to gently nudge along their sensibilities by guiding them to see the social forces that produced the world of racial subordination they observed.[91]

In short, like all stories, the story of the early NUL is complex and full of contestation—sometimes at levels that require probing to uncover. But even with this complexity appreciated, it is indisputably fair to say that the dominant organizational ideology of the early NUL was very far from the radical activist thinking of leaders like Ransom, Du Bois, or the young Fortune—or even from the vision of moderate progressive race leaders like Bulkley. The reasons for the NUL's early development in apolitical, relatively conservative directions were sound in many respects, allowing the NUL to attract the wealthy white support that a more militant approach would have scared away. However, the consequences of this approach were also significant, especially in defining the early twentieth-century model for pursuing the social welfare goals that had long been an important part of the overall national racial justice organizing project.

11

Founding the NAACP: Building the Organization, 1908–1915

This chapter takes us close to the end of the story this book tells—to the denouement, at which many of the figures encountered over the course of the preceding chapters came together to contribute to founding and setting the course for the early NAACP. Most historical accounts of the NAACP's achievements begin well after this founding period. None carefully traces the bridges from past to future that late nineteenth- and turn-of-the-twentieth-century national racial justice organizations and leaders provided. These leaders, as I show, provided ideas that propelled the NAACP through its infancy.[1] The following account focuses on this neglected aspect of the NAACP's early history, stripping away other aspects that, although interesting, can be investigated by reading other descriptions.[2]

Ripe Conditions for a New Organizing Effort

Many factors contributed to creating the conditions for founding a new racial justice organization at the end of the first decade of the twentieth century. Most important, national civil rights organizing confronted a major obstacle in Booker T. Washington's stranglehold on potential sources of funding for ambitious national legal initiatives. The funding sources Washington had carefully cultivated and solidly controlled, which were based in wealthy white philanthropist heads of major corporations, could be channeled toward charitable efforts that appeared non-threatening to the overall legal and political structure, such as the early National Urban League. But Du Bois and his Niagara Movement colleagues had not been able to tap such funding sources to support their efforts, and without such financial backing their projects could not survive. This was so even though there were well-to-do white progressives who appeared ready for more insistent forms of protest. These included Constitution League founder John Milholland, a moderately wealthy businessman, and Oswald Garrison Villard, newspaper editor and heir to the white side of the abolitionist legacy as the grandson of William Lloyd Garrison. The problem was that these potential contributors wanted to direct as well as fund any organizations in which they became involved.

Had it not been for the dire need for substantial financial backing that could match the large national organizing ambitions Du Bois and his compatriots held, the NAACP might never have been born—at least not as a synthesis of decades of African American racial justice organizing experience coupled with social capital and funds provided by white progressives. Not only Fortune but many of the top national African American civil rights leaders of the period emphasized the importance of African Americans taking the primary leadership role in directing efforts aimed at improving African Americans' welfare in the nation. But the need for major funding sources to support a national organizing agenda also loomed large in these leaders' calculations. A hard-nosed realism convinced Du Bois that opportunities for major funding required coalescing with white progressives. This was perhaps his underlying point in urging the Niagara Movement's backers to support the NAACP in one of his last articles in *The Horizon,* though he did not put it quite that way.[3]

Standard accounts of the NAACP's founding emphasize the fortuity of the NAACP's specific beginnings, which occurred in a series of personal encounters among a small group of white progressives in New York City. These accounts underplay the long-developing conditions that produced an environment ripe for an effort to create a new biracial national organizing initiative. The Carnegie-funded 1904 conference had failed to produce a lasting organization, due in part to Du Bois's suspicions that Washington would thoroughly dominate the group's agenda. At the same time, Du Bois had repeatedly confronted the obstacles presented by Washington's tight lock on most sources of white philanthropic assets. Du Bois realized that he needed to build an alternative funding base, and it was most likely this reality that led him to throw his energies into the organizing initiative that produced the NAACP. Standard accounts tend to privilege the role whites played in the NAACP's founding but generally fail to recognize that these efforts would have been for naught if Du Bois had not delivered the base he controlled. Put most simply, that base was his Niagara Movement constituency, composed of the subset of members of the African American "talented tenth" leadership class who were willing to take professional and personal risks to support more insistent racial justice advocacy.

As the standard accounts typically recite, the immediately precipitating event underlying the NAACP's founding was the race riot that occurred in Springfield, Illinois, in the summer of 1908. Much like the riot that had taken place two years before in Atlanta, the violence in Springfield was initially spurred by false reports of black-male-on-white-female sexual assault. White resentment of African American economic and citizenship gains also provided an important underlying cause. As in Atlanta, initial incidents of violence grew into a multiday rampage in which whites attacked African American businesses and homes. Innocent citizens were brutally murdered, and property destruction was widespread. What was different about the 1908 riot, however, was that it took place in the North—in the town of Abraham Lincoln's birth, no less.[4]

William English Walling, a wealthy, Southern-born writer who dabbled in a variety of progressive reform causes, was visiting the area with his wife, the Russian-born radical Anna Strunsky. Both Walling and Strunsky were socialists with an interest in writing about social injustice. The pair had little prior involvement with race issues in the United States, but they were shocked by what they saw and heard as they investigated the events in Springfield and inquired into the attitudes of whites they interviewed there. Walling wrote an extensive report about the riot for the abolitionist-founded New York City newspaper *The Independent,* which was widely read by progressive reformers. Under the title "The Race War in the North," Walling described the riot in detail and warned that few seemed to understand the seriousness of the racial hatred spreading throughout the country. Walling closed with a query as to what "large and powerful body of citizens" would step up to the task of addressing this situation.[5]

On reading Walling's article, the indomitably energetic Ovington immediately contacted him to propose meeting to discuss Walling's suggestion that progressively minded citizens be brought together to address the country's worsening racial situation. In January 1909 such a meeting took place in Walling's small New York City apartment with only three persons in attendance: Walling, Ovington, and social worker Henry Moskowitz, a long-standing friend of Walling's who had worked with him in the past on settlement house movement and labor reform projects. Ovington was the most sophisticated about interracial organizing due to her work with the New York City social welfare organizations that merged to become the NUL. She quickly proposed that African American leaders be included in future meetings, and suggested extending invitations to two such clergymen she knew from her reform work: Bishop Walters, leader of the AAC, and Rev. William Henry Brooks, pastor of St. Marks Methodist Episcopal Church in New York City, who sat on the CIICN's board. Walling added to this list of invitees his friends Florence Kelley, with whom he had worked at Hull House, and Lillian Wald, with whom he had helped found the Women's Trade Union League. The group also invited Oswald Garrison Villard and muckraking journalist Charles Edward Russell. Russell was another of Walling's socialist friends, who had recently published a well-respected exposé of the convict and peonage labor systems in the South. This expanded group decided to call itself the National Negro Committee (NNC) and soon grew to nearly two dozen members.[6] Thus a fortuitous series of encounters produced just the right circumstances to set off a new organizing alignment at a particular historical moment.

Building the Leadership Coalition

In choosing its members, the NNC strove to build a coalition that would reflect the wide range of progressive reformers who might be motivated to work together on promoting greater racial fairness at the start of a new century. Included were many figures already familiar to this story, including Walters, Du Bois, Waldron, Church Terrell, and Bulkley. Bulkley displayed his characteristically excellent attendance while offering wise advice and his extensive contacts. Du Bois traveled from Atlanta to attend meetings. Bishop Walters, though a less frequent attendee, lent his credentials and contacts, and added his voice of experience on the key matter of institutional design, as further discussed below. Socialist minister Rev. Waldron, formerly of the Niagara Movement and founder of the National Negro American Political League (NNAPL), took part, as did fellow DC resident Mary Church Terrell.

Church Terrell had remained a Roosevelt supporter and held back from joining outspoken protest organizations until the president's conduct in the Brownsville affair of 1906 finally led her to a more outspoken stance. Through her involvement in the Constitution League, Church Terrell had publicly protested Roosevelt's actions in firing an entire regiment of African American soldiers with no due process whatsoever, as well as the unconvincing apologies Booker T. Washington had made on the president's behalf. When Washington learned that she was taking part in the NNC, he warned her husband in none-too-veiled terms of the potential political consequences to him of his wife's involvement in a clearly anti-Tuskegee organizing initiative. But Terrell supported his wife's decision, and she continued to participate in the NNC, even lending her name to the public call for the NAACP's founding.[7] Her path of gradually increasing militancy exemplified the changing mood among even moderate race activist leaders, who were ready to try a new, more forceful approach.

The NNC's organizers sought to bring white religious progressives into the fold as well. Unitarian minister John Haynes Holmes, also a board member of the early NUL, became an active member of the NNC, as did Rabbi Stephen S. Wise, founder of a breakaway branch of reform Judaism. Walling, Ovington, Russell, and Villard appointed themselves the group's leaders, with Walling and Russell alternating in the position of chair and Ovington serving as recording secretary. Villard agreed to chair the conference the group decided to organize.

A First Organizing Conference in 1909

The NNC's goal for its first organizing conference was to introduce a wider audience of potential supporters to the idea of forming a new national interracial organization to address racial justice issues.[8] The committee decided on New York City as the location for such a conference and May 31 and June 1 as its scheduled dates. The goal of this conference, as Walling would later explain, was "to establish a relation between organizations already in existence as well as among individuals who, while working for the colored population primarily in some other direction, were also firmly decided to stand for the Negro's political and civil rights."[9] The NNC, in other words, was seeking to work with already mobilized activists and organizations to promote race-related political and civil rights issues—not to supplant the social welfare activism that was simultaneously taking place but to augment it with

an organization focused on the political and civil rights dimensions of the multifaceted problem of racial justice in the United States. With this objective in mind, the
members of the NNC efficiently split into subcommittees to accomplish the tasks
of planning the program, writing a platform and resolutions for the conference,
and developing a list of invitees. That list read like a virtual "who's who" of activists
already mentioned in this narrative.[10]

A key question involved how to handle Booker T. Washington. He obviously
could be expected to disapprove of the NNC's plans to build a militant civil rights
organization, but its organizers knew they could not simply ignore him. Villard took
on the job of communicating with him. In the fall of 1908 Washington had written to Villard seeking funds for a proposed test case to challenge peonage labor in
Alabama—a case that Washington would secretly support and that would produce
an important win in 1911 before the U.S. Supreme Court in *Bailey v. Alabama*,
which declared peonage labor illegal under the Thirteenth Amendment's prohibition against involuntary servitude.[11] Villard had written back at that time to decline
the request for a contribution but had noted that he was thinking along similar
lines. As Villard explained, this was "precisely the kind of a case for which I want
my endowed 'Committee for the Advancement of the Negro Race,' " which could
"instantly handle any similar discrimination against the negro, and carry the case, if
necessary, to the higher court."[12] In the context of planning the NNC's conference,
Villard halfheartedly renewed these overtures regarding possible collaboration,
extending a lukewarm personal invitation to Washington to attend and outlining the committee's vision of a "permanent organization" that would have "a press
bureau, a bureau of study and investigation ... ; a legal bureau to take up any case of
crime against the negro; a political bureau to contend against political wrongs; an
educational bureau to raise funds for distinctively negro institutions, etc., etc." The
plan, Villard further explained, was that this committee would "absorb the association for the industrial improvement of the [N]egroes in this city [i.e., the CIICN]
and also, perhaps, the Constitution League." Villard expressed his appreciation for
"the delicacy" of Washington's position but hoped to gain Washington's "sympathetic interest" even if "you do not desire to become closely allied with us."[13] Not
surprisingly, when the meeting took place in May 1909, neither Washington nor his
close allies were present.

A printed record of the public sessions of the NNC's 1909 conference allows
close scrutiny of its substance and tone. Two dozen scheduled speakers, sixteen of
whom were white and eight of whom were African American, submitted papers
and spoke.[14] This latter group included many of the NNC members by now well
familiar by virtue of their other organizational leadership roles—including Du Bois,
Bulkley, Waldron, Walters, and Wells Barnett.

The conference opened on May 31, 1909, in New York City's Cooper Union Hall.
The goal of the morning session, as its chair explained, was to move unenlightened
whites away from their "ignorant position" that "the Negro is essentially inferior,

something less than fully human, half a brute, and incapable of reaching the standard of civilization."[15] The first two speeches focused on the "scientific" evidence that persons of African descent were not biologically inferior. Columbia University anthropology professor and physician Livingston Farrand, an associate of Franz Boas, gave the first substantive speech, summarizing this scientific evidence and offering the rather convoluted conclusion that "it is absolutely unjustifiable to assert that there is trustworthy evidence for the view that marked differences of mental capacity between different races exist; that if they exist they are certainly of a much slighter extent than would appear from hasty observation," but that "on the other hand it is equally unjustifiable to assert that no differences exist."[16] A second speech, delivered by a professor of neurology and vertebrate zoology at Cornell University, was well intended but quite bizarre. Following pages of quotes from scientists who argued for the theory of innate biological differences between the races, and including photos and charts comparing the brain sizes and weights of African Americans and orangutans, baboons, and white murders, this speaker concluded that the "average brain-weight of obscure American Negroes is a little ... less than that of obscure American whites," and with "Negroes more frequently than with whites does there occur prefrontal deficiency," but "[m]any Negro brains weigh more than the white average, and many white brains weigh less that the Negro average" and "[s]ome white brains present [deficiencies] of the prefrontal lobe, and some Negro brains do not." [17] It is hardly surprising that, when the business meeting discussions began later that day, the African Americans who had sat through the day's proceedings were in a less than cheerful mood.

The proceedings then turned to political science, with progressive Columbia economist Edwin R. A. Seligman offering shorter and more tactful remarks, although they, too, fell short of insisting on absolute equality among the races. Emphasizing "the necessity of distinguishing between the individual and the group and the danger of making unduly broad generalizations," Seligman suggested that "there is nothing more tragic in the whole of human experience than the lot of that American Negro, cultivated, refined gentleman, who at the same time is thrown into the cauldron and fused with a mass of his unhappy and more unfortunate brethren." Nevertheless, Seligman added, "we can expect to see the elevation of the great mass come about only very, very slowly."[18]

Next the philosopher John Dewey spoke briefly "to express my sympathy with the purpose of this gathering." Dewey was friends with Jane Addams and Florence Kelley, having spent much time at Hull House when he lived in Chicago in the mid-1890s. In 1905 Dewey had moved to New York City to accept a position at Columbia University, where he was a key figure in helping the early American legal realists think philosophically about the relationship between politics, society, and law. Dewey was a social friend of Lillian Wald's and not surprisingly found his white-race progressive friends drawing him into the NAACP's founding proceedings.[19] In contrast to the speakers who had preceded him, Dewey plainly asserted that science showed that "there is no 'inferior race' " and therefore that "the members of a race so-called should each have the same opportunities of social environment and personality as those of a more favored race." Emphasizing the importance of equality in opportunities in education, Dewey argued that, "from a strictly scientific standpoint" and "leaving out all sentimental and moral considerations," it should be seen as the "responsibility of society as a whole today to see to it that the environment is provided which will utilize all of the individual capital that is being run into it." He further proposed that "a society that does not furnish the environment and education and opportunity of all kinds…is not merely doing an injustice to that particular race and those particular individuals but is doing an injustice to itself by depriving itself of that social capital."[20]

As I have argued elsewhere, the modesty of Dewey's speech belies its significance. Dewey was gently but plainly suggesting that race reform required white Americans to rid themselves of race prejudice, as manifested in a host of key institutions, including education. Dewey would remain active on NAACP committees addressing federal educational funding issues through the 1910s, although this fact is not often recognized. Dewey's thought was important to early twentieth-century racial justice advocacy not because he was in the vanguard of theorizing cutting-edge ideas for committed activists, but because he did important rear-guard work. Over the next several decades he developed ideas about the importance of diversity and cultural pluralism in education and political life in the United States which helped move white moderates in a more racially progressive direction.[21]

If the goal of the opening session was to cater to whites who knew very little about race matters, the goal of the later sessions was to engage progressive reformers who were well versed on issues of political economy. A session titled "Politics and Industry" began to invoke the democratic socialist concepts favored by figures such as Du Bois, Kelley, Ovington, Ransom, Russell, Waldron, Walling, and many other politically progressive race reform activists of the period. Du Bois opened with a speech that encapsulated the ideas underlying the important gathering. He began with a primer sketching the landscape of African American civil rights activity. Du Bois acknowledged that many observers thought that "the Negroes of the land are divided into two great parties—one asking no political rights but giving all attention to economic growth and the other wanting votes, higher education and all rights." Du Bois characterized this idea as "wrong and mischievous," however, for several reasons. First, he pointed out, there was "no such division of opinion among Negroes as is assumed. They are practically a unit in their demand for the ballot." Instead, the real division was on whether "frank agitation," on the one hand, or "influence and diplomacy," on the other hand, should be used to achieve this goal. He attributed the latter strategy to "an organized political machine which dictates the distribution of offices among black men," thus obviously referring to Washington and the Tuskegee machine. In contrast, Du Bois continued, those opposing this group "hold that this kind of political development by secrecy and machine methods is both dangerous and unwholesome and is not leading toward real democracy." Moreover, he explained, segueing to the central theme of his presentation, "it is encouraging a coming economic conflict which will threaten the South and the Negro race."[22]

Du Bois's second point made a similar observation about alleged differences in activists' views about the importance of economic development. Du Bois pointed out that virtually all leaders understood "the tremendous importance of economic uplift among Negroes." But, he argued, sounding a theme that would continue in subsequent speakers' presentations, economic advancement and citizenship rights must be understood to be inextricably connected. He explained the importance of equal citizenship rights to hope, self-esteem, and the avoidance of industrial conflict between African Americans and working-class whites. This conflict, Du Bois perceived, "accentuates race prejudice": From the perspective of poor working-class whites, it "seems an insult if the whole nation hates and pours contempt on a particular category of people that they should be working beside me." Thus, Du Bois argued, the "first result of denial of civil rights is industrial hatred and jealousy." Moreover, he pointed out, "if white workers have the vote and blacks not so, white workers can enforce their feelings of prejudice and repulsion."[23]

Du Bois went on to describe the problems of structural exclusion of African Americans from desirable employment sectors caused by the actions of unions and employers. The corresponding reaction of African American workers, forced to underbid white workers on wages and to work as strikebreakers in order to obtain employment, further exacerbated cycles of labor violence and animosity. Du Bois concluded by predicting that "the Negro problem" would not be settled until "you give black men the power to be men, until you give them the power to defend that manhood," including achieving the day when "the Negro casts a free and intelligent vote in the South."[24]

Many of the whites who spoke at the founding conference were similarly committed to political viewpoints that reflected progressivism merging into socialism of a mild democratic sort. Thirty years had passed since Fortune had read and been inspired by Henry George, John Ruskin, Karl Marx and the English socialists, but the NAACP's founders had read many of the same works and were committed to many of the same ideas. Walling, for example, shared Du Bois's emphasis on economic class in his remarks. As a Southerner by birth, Walling described with firsthand knowledge "two Souths, those who employ negro labor and those who compete with it." Walling argued that the "white workingmen must be persuaded that their only permanent welfare is cooperation with colored fellowworkers and that opposition must inevitably lead to total demoralization of all organized effort of both classes."[25]

In the ensuing discussion period, Trotter agreed, tying together economic conflict and disfranchisement in his remarks from the floor.[26] Reverend Waldron added his thoughts as well, opining that "unless something is done to change things, the poor white man not only of the South, but particularly of the South, is going to feel the pinch of the shoe just as much as the Negro." In a paper Waldron delivered later in the day, he called on the Negro to "make common cause with the working class which to-day is organizing and struggling for better social and economic conditions." He noted that the "old slave oligarchy maintained its ascendency largely by fixing a gulf between the Negro slave and white free laborer" and argued that the "Negro, being a laborer, must see that the cause of labor is his cause."[27] Former *Voice of the Negro* editor Max Barber spoke from the floor, arguing that if "[you] tell me that economics and industry are going to solve this problem, I think you are radically wrong," and that if "you will give a man the right to vote" and "if he will see that the proper man goes to Congress, a man who will see that American citizens are protected in their rights, then you will get these other things."[28]

Russell's remarks from the floor captured the speakers' impression on the audience. He noted that, even though "I think I have been a pretty close observer, I can tell you that what I have heard to-day has opened up an entirely new horizon to me." As Russell explained, "I have been following my colored brother with sympathy, with all my heart, because my father was an abolitionist," but "I am bound to say that I have had more education on this question since ten o'clock this morning, than I have had before in all the rest of my life."[29]

Bulkley also delivered a speech, voicing his perspective based in his own reform commitments focused on opening opportunities in employment. He, too, focused on the problems of labor and economics, pointing to the "unjust industrial restrictions" placed "upon us as a people," and addressed its many manifestations, such as the 1909 Georgia railroad strike then under way, in which white railroad unions had demanded the exclusion of African Americans from all but the least desirable jobs. To force their demand, the white railway workers had gone on strike and engaged in acts of violence, including murders of African American workers. The state's governor had refused to intervene, instead expressing support for the aims of the strikers.[30] Using this situation as a backdrop for his remarks, as did other speakers, Bulkley attacked the structures under which there are "classes of skilled labor which it is not permitted a Negro to enter." He further noted that "even certain vocations which belonged almost exclusively to the Negroes ever since the days of slavery are fast being closed against them," thus "keeping within the bounds of unskilled labor those who might do credit in the ranks of skilled labor." Expressing his characteristically progressive optimism about the future, Bulkley outlined his view of the required strategy going forward, which would focus both on improved education and on creating increased economic and employment opportunities by appealing to employers to voluntarily hire more African Americans.[31]

Still other speeches emphasized the requirements for building a successful organization in the aftermath of the conference. Wells Barnett began with the pointed observation that "[t]here is a kind of talking that does not accomplish anything, and there is a sort of talking that does, that makes for the beginning of great things," leaving hanging the implicit question as to which of these "two kinds of talking" the conference would turn out to be about. She also raised the question of fund-raising and the deficiencies prior organizations had suffered in that regard. The next day she presented a thundering speech on lynching, in which she endorsed Albert Pillsbury's draft legislation to make lynching a federal crime. Wells Barnett closed by urging a new national organization to make antilynching work a top priority and to set up a bureau to coordinate work on this issue, outlining steps the NAACP would indeed soon undertake.[32]

The next day's morning session similarly concentrated on both organizational and substantive priorities. Bishop Walters served as this session's chair. Echoing the AAC's substantive agenda, he explained that "[t]he need of the hour is the creation of a healthy public sentiment in favor of the enforcement of the Fourteenth and Fifteenth Amendments to the federal Constitution. We should hold public meetings in different sections of the country, and have the best informed men... prepare papers and discuss subjects bearing on the problem." Notably, Walters did not discuss bringing legal challenges but instead proposed forming a publication bureau, a lecture bureau, and a coordinated effort to generate political pressure by splitting "the vote of the black man between the two great parties."[33]

Following Walters, Pillsbury spoke at length to emphasize the importance of the antidisfranchisement struggle. He urged passage of legislation the AAC had previously championed that would have lowered disfranchising states' voting strength in proportion to the percentage of their male populations denied voting rights, as specifically called for in the Fourteenth Amendment.[34] John Milholland's speech emphasized his favorite themes, focusing on the Georgia railway situation and also on the educational funding issues he had long championed and would continue to push within the early NAACP.[35]

The conference's final session took place that afternoon. Villard now took the podium to outline an ambitious immediate pragmatic action plan. In this closing speech, Villard presented a program for organizing a strong permanent body to grow out of the conference. Borrowing lines from his 1906 speech before the AAC in which he had endorsed that group's legal action platform, Villard urged that a new national organization establish a "political and civil rights bureau" that "would bend its energies to bringing about enforcement of the Fourteenth and Fifteenth Amendments" and to "obtaining court decisions upon the disenfranchising laws and other discriminatory legislation." Villard assured his audience that, with the right connections, a sponsoring board "would have no difficulty in raising" large sums and proposed that the organization set as one of its goals to "have at its disposal sufficient money to employ the highest legal talent obtainable and to pay the heavy cost of carrying up to the Supreme Court case after case." With such resources available to sustain a legal assault, Villard envisioned that the Court, which he characterized as "that shifting and evasive body," would finally be "compelled to decide whether there shall be two degrees of citizenship in this country."[36]

Villard noted that other organizations were also working for "the civil and political rights of the Negro," including the Niagara Movement, the Constitution League, and various legal aid organizations in New York City. Nonetheless, he argued, the race needed a "strong central legal bureau able to employ the ablest counsel." He also emphasized the need to take on particular cases as a means of combating lynchings. He then described, more briefly, a host of other priorities for a new organization, calling for establishing both an education bureau and an industrial bureau, which would work on issues such as labor relations, the creation of job opportunities, housing in both rural and urban areas, the acquisition of land, and assistance to African Americans who were emigrating from the South. Finally, pointing to the child labor, environmental, and public health antituberculosis campaigns as models, Villard closed by suggesting that all such "great crusades" required a national committee and publicity bureau.[37]

The resolutions the 1909 conference attendees adopted echoed these priorities. They outlined three "first and immediate steps," namely: "(1.) That the Constitution be strictly enforced and the civil rights guaranteed under the Fourteenth Amendment be secured impartially to all"; "(2.) That there be equal educational opportunities for all and in all the States, and that public school expenditure be the same for the Negro and white child"; and "(3.) That in accordance with the Fifteenth Amendment the right of the Negro to the ballot on the same terms as other citizens be recognized in every part of the country." The resolutions further "denounce[d] the ever-growing oppression of our 10,000,000 colored fellow citizens" and stated that the "systematic persecution of law-abiding citizens and their disfranchisement on account of their race alone is a crime that will ultimately drag down to an infamous end any nation that allows it to be practiced, and it bears most heavily on those poor white farmers and laborers whose economic position is most similar to that of the persecuted race." Along with action on the issues of the persecution of organized workers, peonage, enslavement of prisoners, and disfranchisement of "large bodies of whites in many Southern States," the resolutions demanded "for the Negroes, as for all others, a free and complete education." In other words, in their chosen priorities, topics, focus, and tone, these resolutions closely resembled Fortune's AAL's platform, drafted almost two decades earlier.[38]

In these public declarations the conference organizers thus conveyed a sense of continuity with the past efforts of the AAL, the AAC, and the Niagara Movement, as well as a tone of optimism and unity. Behind the scenes, however, a different mood prevailed. The organizers could not "wire" the gathering's business meetings the same way they could the public speakers' sessions. The more spontaneous discussion that emerged in the business meetings was full of tension as two groups on opposite sides of the era's deep racial divide sought to negotiate the terms by which they might begin to work more closely together. From the perspective of the more suspicious long-time activists such as Wells Barnett, Trotter, and Waldron, the white newcomers appeared to be trying to take over. Vocal in this skepticism, they appeared contrarian and argumentative to the whites, who saw themselves as the beneficent helpers of a less fortunate race. Villard conveyed this perspective in a confidential account to his uncle, Francis J. Garrison. Garrison served as Villard's mentor. He was Villard's mother's brother and thus the youngest son of William Lloyd Garrison. As Villard related to his uncle, in his view some of the African American delegates, especially Waldron and Trotter, had displayed an attitude marked by "wrangling," "open suspicion," and "ill conceived hostility." Villard acknowledged, "I suppose we ought really not to blame these poor people who have been tricked so often by white men, for being suspicious." Nevertheless, exhausted at the end of the conference, as many of the central organizers reported feeling, Villard confessed that he and Walling had considered backing out altogether at one point when the delegates seemed unable to make headway in the business meetings.[39]

Indeed, neither Villard nor Walling lasted long in major leadership roles in the organization that was thus painfully born in May 1909. In 1911 Walling resigned his office due to an embarrassing paternity-suit scandal. In 1913 Villard resigned from his position as chair of the board after clashing with Du Bois, though he retained a role on the board as treasurer. Ovington, after trying hard to persuade Villard not to take this step, expressed her view of Villard's action quite bluntly, stating that "to me it means a confession to the world that we cannot work with colored people unless they are our subordinates."[40]

Not only participants remained skeptical of the NNC's prospects based on the interpersonal difficulties they encountered in negotiating a merging of efforts. The father of national civil rights organization building, T. Thomas Fortune, voiced his own criticism from afar. Reporting on the NNC conference for the now-Tuskegee-controlled *Age* as a guest contributor, Fortune started with the proposition that it is a "safe and sane position to take that any conference for the uplift of the Negro...is good in conception." Thus starting with the positive, Fortune reported that Du Bois was the "most learned" speaker at the conference, Bulkley the "most eloquent," and Waldron and Trotter "the most talkative" of the attendees. Fortune noted the prominent talk about labor conditions, especially the recent Georgia labor strike. He described his friend Wells Barnett as having been full of figures on lynching that never lied and Gertrude Mossell, whom he seemed to like less well, as having argued that the African American should "stand behind himself." In his usual cynical fashion, Fortune quipped that Mossell would soon learn that the African American instead "stands before himself," where he is bound to "stumble and fall." Fortune also criticized white Chicago race reformer Celia Woolley's claim that the "present greatest need of the Negro in this country is the discriminating friendship of the white man." "I do not think so," Fortune responded, "and I have had thirty-five years of working and thinking to do so. I think the present greatest need of the Negro in this country is the discriminating friendship of the Negro." Summing up his overall impression, Fortune described the gathering as marked by confusion, a mood of talking rather than doing, and a "white cloud of disgust" that hung over the debates.[41]

A few weeks later, Fortune did not hesitate to find still more reasons to criticize the naivety of the white newcomers who were attempting to lead a new national organizing effort. Writing again from the front page of *The Age,* Fortune lectured newcomer Walling for what he saw as his mistaken approach in denouncing Booker T. Washington for failing to champion "social equality" between the races. Walling's criticism of Washington, Fortune argued, overlooked the important distinction race activists had long carved between "social privileges," not reachable by law, and "civil rights," inseparable from citizenship. Fortune explained that, since Walling had been a chief moving spirit of the recent conference "who appeared to have at heart the good of the Negro people,... it is worthwhile to correct his errors lest he stumble and fall in the good work" he had undertaken.[42]

This exchange highlighted a shifting discourse about race as the NAACP came on the scene. In earlier years, savvy race activists, including figures with great rhetorical sophistication such as Du Bois, Fortune, Straker, and Congressman White, had always taken great care to emphasize that they had no desire to achieve so-called social equality with whites. This was the coded term used to refer to the specter of cross-racial social mixing, especially among young people and persons of different sexes, which whites found particularly threatening because it could lead to interracial sexual attraction and consensual sex (somehow all the more threatening in spite of, or perhaps because of, the obviously widely occurring phenomenon of coerced sex perpetuated by white men on African American women). Now newcomers with their talk of social equality were unnecessarily hitting this raw nerve, as Fortune saw it, and he strived to point out their insensitivity to the subtleties of what he viewed as effective discourse about citizenship rights in the context of race.

Fortune's negativity did little, however, to impede the NNC from declaring its first meeting a great success. The turnout had been high, many attendees had left with a new commitment to engage in racial justice work, and a critical mass of prominent supporters—including potential funders—seemed willing to move forward. Du Bois had endorsed the new effort from the pages of *The Horizon,* and Washington had not been able to mount any degree of effective opposition. The NNC's steering committee wasted no time gathering to plan a second meeting to build on the momentum generated by the first. This time its foremost priority was to choose a central substantive topic for an action program.

The NNC's Second Conference, 1910

In planning for a second conference, the NNC unanimously resolved to highlight disfranchisement as its key immediate action item. It planned the program highlights accordingly. To speak on the legal issues involved in the antidisfranchisement struggle, it turned to longtime AAC advisor on these issues Albert E. Pillsbury. The committee also decided to invite as a speaker Boston attorney and respected U.S. Supreme Court advocate Moorfield Storey, who had recently expressed interest in handling cases. Complementing these two august legal experts' speeches would be personal testimony from educated African Americans who had been refused the right to cast ballots. Finally, the NNC invited former congressman and AAC vice president George White to lend the session the benefit of his political experience.[43]

The organizers also initially envisioned the subject of "The Negroes and Trade Unions" as a separate agenda item that would build on the attention this topic had received at the first conference. Walling chaired a subcommittee that considered this proposal. Walling's ties to the trade union movement, including to AFL leader Samuel Gompers, for whom he would later work as an advisor, made him an excellent choice to pursue this important topic. But Walling reported to the program committee that his subcommittee had decided that the relationship between trade unionists and race activists should not be separately addressed at the next NNC meeting. Although a "point of vital importance," Walling explained, the subcommittee had discovered that there "would be at present no possibility of securing prominent labor men as speakers" and that to deal with the matter "from the outside" would do little good. Walling instead suggested that the meeting deal with the substitute topic of "the effects of disfranchisement on the working man." This motion carried.[44] Walling, in other words, had learned a lesson that Fortune, Ransom, Du Bois, Haynes, and others had already discovered—namely, that the desire for coalition building across race lines based on class solidarity and mutual interests in economic justice at the time flowed in one direction only. Race justice advocates saw the common economic concerns uniting working-class persons regardless of race and hoped to pursue the strategic organizing possibilities associated with these overlapping interests. But the deep racism affecting many—though not all—trade union leaders during the nadir period blocked such avenues of political coordination.[45] Racial justice advocates pursued cross-race alliances with leaders of a number of reform movements, including the settlement house movement and white women's consumer- and labor-related reform organizations. They could not, however, unite with trade unionists during this historical period.

The steering committee discussed other outreach strategies and developed a several-pronged plan. Mary Maclean, a white socialist who worked as a staff writer for the New York Times and would soon assist Du Bois as an investigator, contributor of articles, and occasional volunteer managing editor for The Crisis, noted the need to do press outreach to African American newspapers. Bulkley volunteered to lend his knowledge to Maclean by working with her on this endeavor.[46] Another plan involved conducting outreach to progressive religious institutions. The committee resolved to hold some of the conference sessions in African American churches and others in white ones.[47] The NNC asked Unitarian minister John Haynes Holmes to call on New York City's religious leaders of all denominations to preach on disfranchisement and also to invite them to attend the upcoming meeting.[48] Rabbi Wise moved that a similar initiative be undertaken with a special focus on African American churches, to include a letter jointly signed by Holmes and Brooks inviting the African American ministers of the city not only to preach about disfranchisement but also to attend the next conference.[49] At least one return letter from a rabbi accepted the offer and offered support.[50]

With religious institutions and African American press outlets thus identified as key targets for membership recruiting (much as the AAC had done), the organizing committee recognized an additional need to gain support from the moneyed and socially privileged progressives who made New York City their home. This was a population to which the AAL, AAC, and Niagara Movement had not had ready access—especially because of Washington's tightly controlled fund-raising monopoly on wealthy progressives interested in contributing to race advancement work. But the NNC's white leaders moved in social circles that brought them in contact with such potential donors. Thus another key target group, as invitation subcommittee chair Ovington explained, were "business men and lawyers." Ovington asked all steering committee members to make a special effort to identify persons in this category for invitations.[51]

The committee's planning came together in a second NNC meeting, held from May 12 through May 14, 1910. The official program of the NNC Second Annual Conference announced its focus as "the various phases of the Negro Problem from the point of view of disfranchisement, such as the effects of disfranchisement upon the courts, upon the citizen at the ballot box, in the industrial field, in education, etc." The representation of African Americans on the NNC's official Committee of Forty (really only thirty-eight) had grown to approximately 30 percent and included the familiar names of many longtime national activists. These Committee of Forty members included Bishop Walters, Dr. Bulkley, Maria Baldwin, Archibald Grimké, Wells Barnett, Dr. Bentley, R. R. Wright Jr., Lafayette Hershaw, Church Terrell, Rev. Waldron, and Du Bois. Still others on the committee were whites who had lent support to the AAC, Niagara Movement, NACW, CIICN, ICSS, and other similar national and regional efforts in years past, including figures such as Jane Addams, John Dewey, Ovington, Pillsbury, and Celia Parker Woolley. An appointing committee, composed of Ovington, Villard, and Bulkley, had designed this lineup. These names signaled to those with activist experience that the NNC was not a brand new organization but a merging of various strains of activism that had been going on for years.[52]

Again, eyewitness accounts, newspaper reports, and preserved documents allow detailed reconstruction of the substance and import of the second NNC conference. Writing one of the many letters to his uncle that provide key historical evidence of the inner workings of the group that would become the NAACP, Villard reported that the second meeting had been more focused and harmonious than the first. Although the turnout at the second meeting was much lower than at the first, the speeches had been on the whole "on a much higher level." Villard, a political moderate, was the furthest to the right of the figures in the NNC's inner leadership circle and confessed to his uncle that he had disapproved of Clarence Darrow's "radical talk," finding him to be an "outright demagogue." Nevertheless, Villard was as high about the second conference as he had been low and exhausted after the first. He explained that the benefit of Darrow's speech had been that it "gratified the extreme radicals and Socialists among us" and that "most of the ardent workers who are really accomplishing something, Miss Ovington, Miss [Frances] Blascoer [then organizational secretary], Walling, Mrs. MacLean, etc., are all Socialists." Villard further reported that Moorfield Storey and Pillsbury had spoken well despite a "note of hopelessness and pessimism" in Pillsbury's address. (Pillsbury's involvement in the AAC's disfranchisement litigation battle explained his pessimism, a fact that Villard, a relative newcomer, could not fully appreciate.) Kelly Miller, the young, up-and-coming professor at Howard University whom Du Bois had failed to woo into the Niagara Movement, was "charming and witty." Du Bois's paper was "excellent," and Wells Barnett and Church Terrell had also spoken "admirably."[53]

Even *The Age* reported favorably and at length on this second conference. This newspaper called out for special mention a speech Rev. Ransom had made and quoted at length from Wells Barnett's address, which had detailed the facts and presented an updated analysis of the nation's record of lynchings. *The Age* also published the full text of official resolutions adopted at the meeting. These yet again read very much like those the AAC and the AAL before it had routinely articulated: The NNC had resolved that "the Constitution be strictly enforced and the civil rights guaranteed under the Fourteenth Amendment be secured impartially to all"; that "there be equal education opportunities for all and in all the states, and that public school expenditure be the same for the Negro and the white child"; and that "in accordance with the Fifteenth Amendment the right of the Negro to the ballot on the same terms as other citizens be recognized in every part of the country."[54]

Looking back on 1910 a few years later, Ovington saw this year as the watershed moment in founding a new national organization with the ingredients necessary for future growth. Most important in Ovington's view was securing funds for Du Bois's position as editor of *The Crisis*, which allowed him to move to New York City to become a full-time presence within the new organization's office. In this way, Ovington explained, drawing on her personal recollections, "we were brought closely in touch with an organization of colored people, formed in 1905 at Niagara and known as the Niagara Movement," which had "attempted a work of legal redress along very much the lines" the NAACP wanted to work. The Niagara Movement, Ovington further explained, had already "conducted important civil rights cases and had in its membership" lawyers such as W. Ashbie Hawkins, who transferred their efforts to the NAACP's early test case litigation. Moreover, as Ovington—herself a transitional Niagara Movement-to-NAACP figure—observed, the two organizations' "platforms were practically identical," and many "of the most prominent members of the Niagara Movement thus brought their energy and ability into the service of the Association, and eight are now serving on its Board of Directors."[55]

The momentum that would propel the NAACP to become one of the great social change organizations of the twentieth century had begun to grow. With the combined energies of longtime African American activists with decades of experience in racial justice organizing, mixed with the enthusiasm of several dozen whites who were also experienced in reform organization building but relative newcomers to the field of racial justice, promising new synergies developed. Even the wariest old-time activists, such as Wells Barnett, gave the new initiative a chance, at least at first. Attending the executive session meeting immediately following the 1910 conference, Wells Barnett recommended publishing and distributing the proceedings of the second conference as widely as possible. She further urged attention to fund-raising, suggesting that each member of the national committee be asked to pledge to raise at least $100 toward the new organization's expenses.[56]

These steps toward publicizing the organization, recruiting new members, and fund-raising to support issue work began. With them would come at first slow but steady and then more rapid progress in building a solid organization. The steering committee had enough confidence about the future to vote to authorize the hiring of two full-time employees, a director of research and publication—the position Du Bois would assume—and a separate office of secretary. This position would be held up until 1919 by a succession of white women reformers with socialist inclinations (the ones whom Villard praised so highly to his uncle for their dedicated work) who traveled from city to city to organize membership outreach and coordinate various branches' activities.[57]

The most important goal the second NNC meeting achieved was a formal resolution to form a permanent organization. After much discussion, the group decided to call this permanent organization the NAACP. It further resolved to find more persons of color to add to its expanded list of figurehead leaders, which it now referred to as its Committee of One Hundred. These members of the Committee of One Hundred included the obvious major leaders of national African American organizations such as Du Bois, Walters, Church Terrell, and Bulkley, who were already members of the NNC. To these were added other names by now familiar to this story, which were likewise drawn from the national leadership ranks of the organization's predecessors. These figures included former Niagara Movement lawyers Justin Carter and George Crawford, newspaper editor Harry Smith, Chicago activist Charles Bentley, and women's club leaders Carrie Clifford and Josephine Yates.[58]

By June 1911 the NAACP had filed and obtained its first certificate of incorporation and elected as the leaders of its first board of directors Moorfield Storey as president, Bishop Walters and John Milholland as vice presidents, Villard as chair of the board of directors, Ovington as secretary, and Du Bois as director of publicity and research. Most Committee of One Hundred members transferred to become general members of the board, and the NAACP was thus officially born.[59]

There had already been debate within the NNC about where the national organization should be located. The political and personal ramifications of this decision were not lost on the experienced activists involved. Church Terrell, long savvy about the political implications of such decisions based on her strategic success in geographically manipulating the founding location of the NACW, had suggested Washington, DC, as the location for the NCC's 1910 conference. Bulkley had spoken in favor of remaining in New York City. At that time, the general sense of the meeting, which was dominated by New Yorkers, was not surprisingly to concur with Bulkley.[60] Following the 1910 meeting Waldron had again proposed moving the next meeting to the nation's capital. Again this motion was "laid on the table."[61] By 1911 the NAACP laid this issue to rest when it officially designated New York City as its permanent headquarters in its articles of incorporation.

All of these were important steps in shaping the future character of a new permanent organization, but the biggest question the committee faced was how to organize the relationship between local chapters and the national headquarters. This was crucial to the organization's future success, as the experienced activists involved in its founding realized. The organization needed both to take advantage of the potential political power that organizing members at the local level could harness and to retain enough central control to rein in local enthusiasm and direct it in a coordinated and unified fashion. Fortunately, several members of the NNC steering committee had just the right experience to tackle this problem. They did so by drawing on lessons they had learned in their prior leadership posts within the NAACP's predecessors.

Defining the Relationship between Locals and the National Office

During the period in which the NNC steering committee was planning its second organizing meeting, it appointed a special subcommittee to deal with the important matter of designing the membership structure for a permanent organization. The appointees to this committee were Walters, the former longtime leader of the AAC, and Du Bois, the Niagara Movement's founder. Villard also placed himself on this important committee. Walters and Du Bois saw eye to eye on questions of the organization's design, and Villard listened to and was persuaded by what they had to say. But Villard also received conflicting advice from his uncle, who spoke from the perspective of an earlier generation of white abolitionists. Villard's epistolary discussions with "Uncle Frank" provide valuable evidence of the contrasting perspectives of these two generations of racial justice advocates.

Both Walters and Du Bois had their own difficult experiences in leading transition-period, top-heavy organizations still fresh in their minds. They urged the NAACP to build a national network rooted in the strength of local membership organizations. Villard appeared to agree, but in doing so he met with resistance from Francis Garrison and his friends. This group of old-school abolitionists held abiding suspicions about grassroots organizing plans. Garrison thus urged adoption of an organizational structure that would prevent local branches from obtaining too much power. The initial plan proposed in part followed Garrison's advice: A national association would be formed, composed of a national committee of one hundred members. From this national committee an executive committee of thirty members would be elected, composed of fifteen members from New York City and fifteen members who resided elsewhere. The national organization's activities would include public meetings in various cities; investigations; data collection on "questions that interest us," such as "peonage, public education, lynching, injustices in the courts, etc."; and publicity, all of which would be supported by a permanent, full-time field-worker. But the subcommittee on organization realized that tapping local enthusiasm was crucial. Accordingly, the subcommittee proposed that the best way of building support would be to tap membership in "those places where we have already secured a foothold"—namely, cities in which racial justice organizing had been going on for decades, such as Chicago, Philadelphia, and Washington, DC.[62]

Most important, the committee on permanent organization proposed a plan for membership. As first proposed, the organization would have only the big-name figures listed on its Committee of One Hundred as actual members. Those wishing to lend support as auxiliary members could choose among several membership price points, paying either the hefty dues of $100 to gain the privilege of voting at and attending all meetings and receiving all publications free of cost, or dues figure of $10 per year, which granted basically the same auxiliary membership privileges but fewer free publications. At an even lower financial burden, auxiliary members could pay at the $2 level, which would entitle them to a copy of the annual proceedings and a vote in officer elections but would allow them to attend only public, but not private, organizational meetings. The NNC steering committee soon approved this plan, after adding a $500 lifetime donor level as well as an associate membership option, at $1, with no voting privileges, at Wells Barnett's suggestion. The committee also created a membership category for groups such as church lodges and clubs, much as the AAC and Niagara Movement had done before it.[63]

But this plan did not fully resolve the issue of the relationship between local members and the national organization. At first Villard proposed that local members should belong directly to the national body—though it would also "be well to form local groups throughout the country which would take the nature of vigilance committees." All of the organization's important work, however, would be conducted through the central New York City executive committee. Where local committees were established, membership dues would be paid two-fifths to the local and three-fifths to the national association.[64]

This plan for a national organization, which focused on big-name national members but also built in part on the strength of local chapters, enjoyed the support of Du Bois, Waldron, Walters, and others. Still, an older, Boston-based generation steeped in the traditions of abolitionism feared the grant of power and funds to local affiliates. Thus Garrison wrote to his nephew Villard cautioning that he and others "shrink very much from so elaborate machinery for the branches as you are providing for" out of concern that it could "weaken" the organization's prestige and ability to act quickly. This group wanted all memberships and most of the contributions to flow directly to the parent organization. "Uncle Frank" pointed to the model of other Progressive-era reform organizations, such as those on "child labor and labor legislation," which were "centralized in New York." This, Garrison argued, was the model it would be most prudent to follow.[65]

In writing back to his uncle, Villard politely expressed the New York City contingent's disagreement. Activists there had already organized a strong local chapter and felt that relying on a national organization that met irregularly "and is asleep part of the time" would cause "members to drift away from the work." It would be better, Villard argued to his elder mentor, to keep local members constructively engaged. Moreover, Villard noted, "Dr. Du Bois feels very strongly upon that point as I do, and he, as you know, has much experience in similar organizations."[66] Villard further reported a few days later that "the Chicago people want their own organization and control of their own cause. That is the rock upon which at least two organizations which Du Bois helped to get up went to pieces."[67] In the end, Ovington, ever the mediator, reported to the annual meeting that the split of membership fees between the local and the national organization would remain unchanged and urged all of the activists to continue working to strengthen the national organization.[68]

Building an Organization of Strong Local Branches

The fees structure as finally approved thus allowed for funding local chapters as well as national organization building. With such a structure in place local-chapter organization building took off, especially in areas that had previously been strongholds for earlier associations' organizing efforts. Leaders in those communities simply shifted their activist energies to the NAACP. Thus the NAACP's predecessors not only passed on to the infant organization ideas wrought from experience, but also contributed particular individuals who possessed the skills and commitment to build the organization's chapters at the local level.[69] In *The Crisis*, Du Bois explained what activities these local NAACP chapters should undertake, listing more than a dozen ambitious tasks that national headquarters wanted them to carry out. These included watching for hostile and discriminatory legal developments in legislation, administration of law, or injustice in the courts; monitoring the "barometer of racial discrimination" in their region by noting new efforts at discrimination, reporting them, and opposing them, such as by attending to behavior by police and charities; pursuing "good test cases" before the courts and obtaining "strong decisions" in them; and working for new laws and ordinances. Other suggested tasks were to keep African Americans in school and then in good colleges or technical training programs, open libraries and museums to African Americans, promote health and healthful habits, and pursue the opening of more occupational opportunities for African American youth.[70] All of this might have been a very tall order, but experienced hands relished this work, especially because the goals and strategies sounded familiar to those who had been involved in turn-of-the-century race justice organizing long before the NAACP arrived on the scene.

It thus was not surprising that many of the experienced figures involved in earlier organizing efforts provided the energy for the NAACP's earliest local branch activities. These branches existed in the very places in which earlier organizations had been strong: New York City, Washington, DC, Chicago, and Boston. (Philadelphia was also strong, though its leaders remained loyal to Milholland's Constitution League, which was resisting being swallowed up by the NAACP, and they were viewed as somewhat obstructionist as a result.[71]) Smaller cities, such as St. Paul, where McGhee played a local branch leadership role until his untimely death in 1915, also made sizeable contributions.

The study of local branch growth and activity cannot detain us for too long so late in this story, but a few highlights bear mention in order to illustrate the transmission of identifiable, experienced activists' commitments from earlier organizations to the new NAACP.[72] Active in the DC branch, for example, were Du Bois's friend and Niagara Movement supporter Carrie Clifford; Niagara Movement activist Milton Waldron, who served as the branch's first president until he was usurped by Archibald Grimké in 1913; and Mary Church Terrell, who also sat on the national board and sometimes lectured for the NAACP. The DC branch's activities included congressional monitoring and lobbying, raising funds, and fighting local discrimination. Archibald Grimké represented the association at congressional hearings seeking to oppose segregation and anti-intermarriage bills, and mass meetings carried the NAACP's message to churches, lodges, and neighborhoods.[73]

In Chicago, Bentley served on the national committee and played an active role in the local branch. This branch fought against state anti-intermarriage and Jim Crow car bills and formed a vigilance committee to investigate an arson that had recently occurred. Another Chicago committee worked to amend the state civil rights laws to cover cemeteries and hospitals.[74] In early 1912 this branch agreed to host the 1913 annual meeting. Its members launched into ambitious planning, with Jane Addams agreeing to serve as honorary chair and Hull House serving as the location for organizing meetings. Wells Barnett chaired the reception committee, and Dr. Bentley chaired the committee on speakers.[75]

Boston's active branch members included many familiar names, such as Maria Baldwin and Mrs. M. A. McAdoo of the Niagara Movement Women's Committee; Josephine St. Pierre Ruffin of the NACW; and Monroe Trotter, Clement Morgan,

ELLIOTT.   COLUMBUS, OHIO.

Figure 11.1 Carrie Clifford, member of the Niagara Movement and the Washington, DC, branch of the NAACP, n.d. (Moorland-Spingarn Research Center, Howard University).

and Butler Wilson, all formerly of the Niagara Movement. Branch president Wilson noted that it "had in its membership a large number of sons and daughters of the abolitionists" and that its work had included seeking the indictment of a white man who had committed an outrageous assault on an African American "servant girl" and fighting the offensive name given a paint color by a department store. The branch worked on issues such as segregation in housing, hospitals, and the YMCA, and received reports from national secretary Blascoer about the national legal redress committee's work.[76]

Also from New England, George Crawford, former Niagara Movement loyalist, sat on the national NAACP board and was active in the New Haven, Connecticut, branch.[77] In 1914 *The Crisis* carried a summary of the work of many other active NAACP chapters that existed in cities in which civil rights organizing had been long ongoing as well, including Cleveland, Kansas City, Minneapolis, and St. Paul. Notably absent was Atlanta, where the young Walter White, later to become the NAACP's great executive secretary, began organizing a local chapter in 1916.[78]

In New York City, national headquarters leaders played a large local role. Constitution League lawyer Gilchrist Stewart (son of McCants Stewart, who had handled Fortune's 1891 test case) initially served as local counsel but was then largely squeezed out of this position. Charles Anderson and Rev. Brooks, also active in the NUL, joined the local New York City committee, which was known as the Vigilance Committee. Bishop Walters did, too, and at the same time served as a vice president of the NAACP national board.[79] Walters's NAACP leadership tenure was relatively short lived, however, despite the importance of his early contribution to shaping the organization's design. In 1913 he clashed with Villard over how forceful to be in opposing President Wilson's federal workforce segregation policies. Villard accused Walters, who had campaigned for Wilson, of having indicated his acquiescence to such segregation to officials in the Wilson administration; Walters took deep offense and resigned.[80]

New York City remained a hotbed of activist experimentation with a strong civil rights focus. As it explained in its report to the annual meeting that year, this branch, finding that there was already in the city "a strong organization dealing with the social economy of the Negro" and deeming it inappropriate to "infringe on the work projected by this society," had decided not to deal with "the economic and industrial and kindred conditions already preempted by the [NUL]" but instead to focus on "the civil and social rights" of African Americans. It saw itself as thus addressing the problem that many people "are willing to aid in improving the economic status of the Negro [and] can understand the claims of social service and welfare work in the interests of the lowly" but "view with alarm all attempts to give such a race the strength and self-respect which come, not from charity, but from equality of rights." The New York City branch vowed that it "is with this more difficult problem, and with this more unpopular mode of approach to its solution" that it had decided to "almost exclusively concern itself."[81]

With this objective in mind, its vigilance committee searched for cases of racial injustice to prosecute. It organized evenings during which groups of "testers" visited theaters to ascertain compliance with the city's ordinance prohibiting discrimination in public accommodations; theaters that barred African American customers then found themselves facing lawsuits, which attorneys cooperating with the vigilance committee filed against them. Another tactic involved visiting bars in mixed-race groups and banging on the table with beer mugs if the members of the group were not promptly served, as Arthur Spingarn later recalled. In so doing these groups were uncannily reenacting acts similar to those underlying Fortune's test case for the AAL, filed back in 1891.[82]

Local branches formed in many other mid-sized cities and towns throughout the country as well, including in the South.[83] By the end of 1912, a year and a half after its official incorporation, the NAACP's annual report boasted of ten branches and a membership of 1,100, up from three branches and 330 members the year before. It had appointed May Childs Nerney as executive secretary. She had traveled to Detroit to interest activists in affiliating with the NAACP and had learned that activists there had already formed themselves into a vigilance committee that was litigating public accommodations discrimination cases based on the state's civil rights statute (which AAL activists had succeeded in passing decades before). The New York Vigilance Committee had likewise won a public accommodations discrimination case against an opera house, handled by lawyer Gilchrist Stewart.[84]

At the beginning of 1915, the annual meeting approved a new constitution and bylaws with a membership fee structure that allowed full membership at the $1 level (one-half what it had been before) and threw in a free yearly subscription to *The Crisis* at the membership fee of $2 a year. The organization now had six thousand members and fifty locals and branches.[85] Six months later, national membership was at seventy-five hundred persons.[86] The advantages of strong local chapters with growth bolstered by affordable mass membership fees were becoming increasingly clear.

The organization's growth soon began to take off even more rapidly. Secretary Nerney's report at the end of that year described a membership of 9,416, with sixty-three chapters, whose memberships ranged from 1,100 in the District of Columbia to 45 in El Paso, Texas. For the first time, the national organization had a positive bank balance, though its finances remained precarious as the possibility of a larger budget created greater programmatic ambitions as well.[87] In short, with the NAACP's adoption of an organizational structure rooted in building local organizational strength to a far greater extent than earlier transition-period national organizations had been, an early twentieth-century model for national race justice advocacy was launched. That model rested on the dual tenets of strong national control and direction, on the one hand, supported by the power base of vibrant local activism, on the other.

Building the NAACP's Legal Agenda, 1910–1915

The early 1910s saw not only the crucial first steps in the NAACP's organizational development but also the birth of its law-focused agenda. The NAACP's first successful cases were not the impressive test cases of popular memory; instead, they were a handful of criminal justice matters involving individual defendants against whom grave procedural wrongs had been committed. No big legal victories were secured in these cases, but the starkness of the injustice done the defendants stirred the conscience of even the most conservative of the NAACP's founding leaders and spurred them to direct scarce funds toward more legal work.

First Criminal Defense Matters

One of the NAACP's first legal undertakings was to defend Steve Green, a tenant farmer in Arkansas who left his land after his landlord drastically raised his rent. The landlord angrily told Green he should not expect to find any more work in the county, but Green found work with a neighbor. When his former landlord discovered Green working for someone else, he shot Green in the neck, leg, and arm. Green ran away, got his rifle at home, and, when his landlord tracked him down, Green shot and killed him. With the help of friends, Green then fled to Chicago, where someone turned him over to the police.[1]

Ida Wells Barnett brought the situation to the NAACP's attention, and Chicago activists raised funds to bring a habeas corpus petition on Green's behalf. The NAACP's leaders used their social and political connections to help in other ways as well: Villard placed a story about the case in his *Evening Post,* and Du Bois publicized the case in *The Crisis.* The court granted the habeas petition on grounds of a technical error in the extradition process, and supporters were then able to take Green to Canada for safety. Another positive result came from the lesson the case taught relative newcomers to racial justice work. As Joel Spingarn's wife recalled, it was the Steven Green case that first interested her husband in the NAACP's work.[2]

Another very early legal matter involved the defense of Pink Franklin, a South Carolina sharecropper whom the NAACP and other activists were able to save from execution and eventually to free from prison. Franklin's employer charged him with breaking his labor contract because he left his job before the end of his employment term. Some time afterward, a police officer burst into Franklin's home, in the middle of the night and without announcing his purpose, to serve a warrant based on this charge. Franklin shot and killed the intruder. Despite these facts strongly supporting a claim of self-defense, Franklin was convicted of murder by a local jury and sentenced to death. When the case came before the state supreme court on appeal, Franklin lost again. Villard, who had been closely tracking the case, wrote of this result as a "terrible blow" that would "encourage the whole South to go ahead with its peonage business." Villard wrote to Booker T. Washington in an attempt to persuade him to appeal to President Taft on the matter. Washington responded with the advice that no one outside South Carolina could be of much service and that Villard should consider retaining "one of the strongest white lawyers" or a minister influential with whites there to approach the state's governor on Franklin's behalf.[3]

The members of the NNC executive committee then discussed the case at their November 1910 meeting. Their hope was to find a lawyer or other person of sufficient stature to intervene with the governor to commute Franklin's death sentence. Villard also attempted to approach President Taft. The political pressure the NAACP generated through a number of routes finally convinced the South Carolina governor to commute Franklin's sentence from death to life imprisonment. Du Bois praised the governor for his brave act in *The Crisis* and vowed that the association would continue its efforts to secure Franklin's release from prison. In 1915 the NAACP secured Franklin's release on parole.[4]

Other similar efforts in the NAACP's first years included seeking to commute the death sentences of two juvenile defendants in light of their young age. In another case involving a defendant named Thomas Williams, the organization succeeded in having murder charges dismissed through a habeas petition. In short, rather than outlining plans to begin pursuing high-impact test cases right away, the first pages of *The Crisis* and the early NAACP board minutes are instead full of references to the organization's aid in individual criminal justice matters. These cases viscerally triggered the instincts of the NAACP's new white leaders to oppose injustice. Put otherwise, these urgent criminal legal matters helped to focus the organization's still-developing race conscience in legal directions.[5]

Dividing Subject Matter Jurisdiction with the National Urban League

At around the same time that the NAACP was first developing its legal agenda, it and the organizations that were engaged in the process of merging to become the NUL began to discuss how they might best work together. It was not clear how the vast landscape of race-related matters requiring urgent attention should be tackled: There was an enormous amount to do but only a few organizations with national ambitions available to coordinate national campaigns on all of these pressing issues. These discussions led to an agreement, left quite informal but still adhered to in the two organizations' first years, which leaders of the NAACP and the NUL reached at a joint meeting in early 1911. Not all of the documents memorializing this meeting still survive, but it is still possible to ascertain that the meeting resulted after someone on the CUCN's board of directors brought up the "matter of the relationship" between it and the NAACP, pointing out that there might be "some overlapping in the work" of the organizations. At its next meeting, the CUCN board chair reported "a satisfactory outcome of a conference between a special committee" of the CUCN, consisting of Seligman, Wood, and another board member, and a special committee of the NAACP, composed of Du Bois, Ovington, and Maclean. This committee had met at the NAACP's offices and negotiated a written agreement as follows:

1. That the National Association for the Advancement of Colored People shall in its local New York branch occupy itself principally with the political, civil and social rights of the colored people, while the Committee on Urban Conditions shall occupy itself primarily with questions of philanthropy and social economy.
2. That these two committees interchange monthly reports of their activities and plans.

W.E.B. Du Bois, chairman.

In other words, the two organizations (or set of organizations in the case of the still-coalescing NUL) agreed to divide up the vast realm of racial justice issues into two spheres. One sphere would involve civil and political rights, to be approached through legal strategies, in which the NAACP was already developing a specialized expertise as it recruited lawyers to help advise it in the legal matters in which it had become involved. The other would address economic and social welfare objectives, which the NUL would handle through its specialty of social work. This effort involved matters such as private institution building, along the lines of NACW affiliates' long-standing work, as well as encouraging industry leaders to take voluntary action and support race advancement efforts financially, methods at which Washington had excelled.[6]

Mary White Ovington later recounted that she and others at the NAACP had initially "gasped at having so large a field of 'advancement' taken out of our program." But, as she further pointed out, it worked out that "nothing could have been more fortunate." Ovington continued: "We could not have raised money for 'philanthropy' as successfully as an organization with a less militant program, and securing employment [in other words, recruiting employers to voluntarily open jobs to African Americans, as the NUL sought to do] is a business in itself." Thus, Ovington explained, "the two national organizations divided the field, working together from time to time as action demanded."[7]

Of course, "divid[ing] the field" could not occur nearly as neatly as the two organizations' leaders envisioned, and this jurisdiction-dividing agreement did not solve
the problem of splitting the field for long. In late 1913 the NAACP national board
voted to appoint Arthur Spingarn to head a new committee—"one of its most important"—with the charge to "confer with the Urban League regarding the relation of
their work to" the NAACP's.[8] That committee, which included Du Bois, Maclean,
and Ovington, met in 1914 with Seligman, Wood, and Haynes of the NUL and
again agreed that the NAACP and its New York City branch would occupy themselves "principally with the Political, Civil, and Social rights of the colored people,"
while the NUL "shall occupy itself primarily with the questions of philanthropy and
social economy."[9]

But this agreement did not work out very well; as Secretary Nerney would
explain in her 1915 reflections presented in her report to the board after extensive travels throughout the country, "the majority of colored people are not interested in legal disabilities as much as in securing an economic opportunity," and
"it is evident that our organization cannot be kept alive without our encroaching
on the social-economic field and laying down immediately a definite and practical program for our branches." Thus Nerney recommended creating committees
in each NAACP branch that would "make persistent effort to secure professional
and industrial opportunity for colored people. These committees should try not
only to reach leading manufacturers, business and professional men, but also labor
unions."[10] Leaders of the two organizations communicated often as they passed matters back and forth and worked out cooperative arrangements on particular issues,
such as improving housing conditions in Harlem, which involved both legal and
institution-building strategies.[11] Moreover, as Mary Church Terrell and others were
already starting to see, attacking race discrimination by private-sector employers
through both legal and voluntary strategies was to become important to the economically focused thrust of a multidimensional racial justice agenda. Legal attacks
on private-sector employment discrimination could not begin in earnest until avenues for legal change in that arena opened with the end of the *Lochner* era, when the
U.S. Supreme Court finally disavowed its jurisprudence that defined regulation of
the private employment relationship as unconstitutional under a natural law "freedom of contract" ideology.[12] That doctrinal shift, coupled with the other social and
economic changes of the 1930s, permitted the birth of private-sector employment
antidiscrimination law, as I have written about in other work. By then, the NUL
would be immersed in legal reform as its sociologist leaders invented the concept of
structural employment discrimination and otherwise contributed to the invention
of employment antidiscrimination doctrine.[13]

In the early period of the NUL's and the NAACP's first decade, however, the
NUL's voluntarist strategies involved recruiting willing employers to step up their
hiring and advancement of African American workers. Those efforts laid down
important precatory principles of racial inclusiveness in employment that would

later become legal mandates. At the same time, the NAACP focused on developing the law-focused work for which it had agreed to assume responsibility under its jurisdiction-dividing plan with the NUL.

Forming a National Legal Committee

Charged with mounting the legal side of a national campaign to improve race conditions in the country, the NAACP's national headquarters undertook to organize the resources necessary to carry out this task. To do so it sought to set up and fund the legal redress committee Villard had been proposing along the lines of the similar AAC committee he had learned about in preparing for his 1906 speech before that organization's annual meeting. In February 1911—the same month the NAACP agreed to divide the territory of race justice matters and strategies with the NUL— the executive committee voted to form such a legal committee. By April it had appointed thirteen members, most of whom were successful white business lawyers from New York City. Only one was African American: D. Macon Webster, a prominent New York City business attorney, who was regarded as an ally of Washington's but respected within the NAACP for his judgment and legal skill. When Albert Pillsbury communicated through Villard that he was willing to take NAACP cases to the Supreme Court without charge, the executive committee politely described this offer as "the most valuable donation the Association has received" and voted to include Pillsbury's name as an honorary legal committee member as well.[14]

William Wherry Jr., a white New York City lawyer who was counsel to Villard's *Evening Post,* assumed leadership of the group, initially called the Legal Redress Committee. Wherry was an energetic public interest advocate with broad interests. His other public service activities included establishing a lawyer's referral service to provide legal services to moderate-income persons as well as advocating for utility rate reform.[15] By the January 1912 annual meeting, Wherry was reporting on at least five cases in hand, ranging from an unjustifiable police shooting and a criminal libel to a lynching, a wage discrimination case, and a case arising from the dynamiting of homes occupied by African Americans on a block of traditionally white residences in Kansas City. Wherry urged the legal committee to begin strictly disciplining itself in choosing among the many cases referred to it and recommended that it lay down a general policy of taking on only those cases that specifically raised race discrimination issues; those that came to it simply because an African American was involved should be referred to legal aid bureaus. Wherry further recommended that the NAACP permanently establish a legal committee that included both lawyers and laypersons. This committee's task would be to determine which cases to take on and then to generally oversee their handling under a policy of selecting only cases that centrally involved "the Negro question." Wherry further proposed employing a staff counsel whose function it would be to investigate facts and develop reports for presentation to the legal committee and then to arrange for proper prosecution of cases the legal committee decided to accept.[16]

That same month, wealthy Chicago businessman Julius Rosenwald donated $2,000 for a legal redress fund. Wherry's law firm associate C. Ames Brooks had been serving as "of counsel" to the legal committee, but by November, with this money in hand, the NAACP had hired a recent white Harvard Law School graduate named Chapin Brinsmade to serve as paid staff counsel. Brinsmade had been working in Wherry's law offices and made up in energy for what he lacked in experience. The lengthy reports Brinsmade began submitting to the board on the Legal Bureau's work discussed widely disparate matters such as lobbying for the nondiscriminatory distribution of funds for agricultural education in the South, championing Judge Terrell's reappointment to the District of Columbia bench, and defending an African American cavalry soldier convicted of a crime on insufficient evidence. Another report focused on various approaches being used to fight discrimination against federal civil service workers.[17]

At the end of 1912 the NAACP's annual report explained that "Legal Redress" was one of the three main areas of its focus (the other two were the closely related matters of "Organization" and "Publicity"). The "advisory" aspects of legal redress were the responsibility of the members of the Legal Redress Committee, while the "machinery for carrying out details" included both African American and white investigators and attorneys.[18] Wherry remained official legal counsel, and Brinsmade its one paid legal staff. The NAACP sought to raise extra money from branches to continue to fund this position but ultimately was not successful, requiring Brinsmade to be let go in 1914.[19]

First Test Cases

In 1913 the association's legal work focused on matters in North Carolina, Virginia, and Baltimore, Maryland, where it was attempting to test the constitutionality of segregation ordinances. The case being fought by the Baltimore local branch, "under the guidance of an able attorney, W. Ashbie Hawkins"—the former Niagara Movement lawyer—was showing particularly "good prospects for a victory."[20] Hawkins wrote about the Baltimore situation in *The Crisis*, explaining that demographic shifts in housing there were leading to increased racial tension as the composition of neighborhoods changed. After an African American lawyer who had graduated from Yale University purchased a desirable house on a so-called white block, the city's legislature had passed an ordinance mandating that only blacks could live on neighborhood blocks deemed to have "51%" or more black residents, and only whites on blocks with 51% or more white residency." Hawkins pointed out the pernicious and illogical results of such an ordinance, including that white residents suddenly found themselves "illegally" residing in homes they had long owned. He stated his intent to organize a test case to challenge the statute and called on NAACP members for support.[21] And Hawkins soon litigated just such a case, first winning a motion to block the eviction of an African American church on a "white" street and then an opinion striking down the entire ordinance based on its punitive and irrational consequences.[22]

Hawkins's victory would become the template for the NAACP's test case several years later in Louisville, Kentucky, which provided the national organization with its second major symbolic Supreme Court victory in *Buchanan v. Warley,* which declared residential segregation ordinances of this type illegal.[23] That result would not eradicate residential segregation but merely shifted the techniques used to accomplish this end toward private restrictive covenants. Here, though, as in other court victories, wins—however symbolic—boosted sprits and reinforced nondiscrimination principles as the appropriate ideal toward which activists were motivated to strive.

The same year that Hawkins was fighting residential segregation ordinances in Baltimore, the association began organizing a chapter to mount the same kind of challenge in Louisville. Because of the legal opportunity offered there, it continued to pursue this organizing plan despite some initial setbacks when the local population proved less than enthusiastic. Here legal opportunity drove organizing goals just as local organizing strength sometimes drove legal initiatives. The NAACP's leaders became increasingly aware of the opportunities for local membership growth presented by test case possibilities.[24]

Another Maryland matter that branch successfully pursued involved the defeat of a proposed grandfather clause voting provision there. In addition, just before it hosted the organization's 1914 annual conference, the Baltimore chapter won a struggle to defeat a state Jim Crow streetcar proposal. Soon after that it reported that it had won a case challenging a criminal indictment against a passenger who had refused to take a seat in a Jim Crow car on a railroad line. Thus Baltimore, home of the first postbellum civil rights test case initiatives of its Brotherhood of Liberty, continued in this tradition by experimenting with a host of such test case initiatives under the auspices of the early NAACP.[25]

Still other legal matters pursued in other regions included work on race discrimination by a white railroad union and on several potential Jim Crow car cases, including the NAACP's opposition to the nomination to the Supreme Court of a judge who had voted unfavorably in the *McCabe v. Atkinson, Topeka and Santa Fe Railway Company* case.[26] *McCabe* had upheld Jim Crow sleeping and dining cars where there was insufficient demand for separate first-class cars for African American travelers. William Harrison, the African American lawyer who had been handling the case in Oklahoma, had written to the NAACP asking for its assistance as the case headed for the U.S. Supreme Court, and Moorfield Storey had initially indicated some willingness to become involved in it. After reviewing the record, however, Storey declined to appear because the challenge had been filed before setting up the facts so that someone had actually suffered discrimination under the statute being challenged.[27]

As Storey predicted, the U.S. Supreme Court declined to consider the case on the merits because the plaintiffs had not shown sufficient personal injury. With the case thus lost, Du Bois harshly criticized Harrison for failing to bring in other "more experienced attorneys" despite the warning he had received to "associate with himself the best legal talent of the country so that his case might be adequately presented."[28] But later scholars view *McCabe* far less harshly than Du Bois did. As leading constitutional law scholar Benno Schmidt has pointed out, in *dicta* the *McCabe* Court stated that "if facilities are provided, substantial equality of treatment of persons traveling under like conditions cannot be refused."[29] Schmidt maintains that this statement, perhaps easier to include because it did not involve a merits disposition, presented one of the first chinks in the armor of the legal ideology that ignored the grave constitutional harm of legally mandated segregation.[30] Here Du Bois's intellectual elitism won out over his racial solidarity with grassroots African American lawyers who were attempting to push the legal envelope that encased segregation, albeit with less sophisticated case theories than the early NAACP wanted to countenance.

McCabe was but one of the cases the national office considered assisting in, and in that case it did agree to pay the costs of the appeal on Harrison's request.[31] As the AAL, AAC, and Niagara Movement had done before it, the national office of the NAACP monitored and sometimes assisted with such local cases involving discrimination in public accommodations. The New York branch also handled several public accommodations discrimination cases on its own.[32]

Nor was segregation the only focus of the national office's legal activity. The national organization sent investigators to lynchings and sought to generate public outcry through reports in newspapers and magazines. And, as in its very first cases involving defendants Green and Franklin, it sought to investigate, bring political pressure to bear, and provide legal representation in several criminal cases involving unjust prosecutions of African American defendants, sometimes with success.[33]

Defensive Battles and Proactive Initiatives

The new organization's busy legal activity extended far beyond handling cases to encompass a broad range of legal matters. Especially important given political conditions were efforts to combat pernicious new state and federal legislative proposals. The early NAACP also undertook the many dimensions of antilynching advocacy that had so preoccupied its predecessors. As these organizations had done many times before, the NAACP presented an antilynching resolution to President Taft; a Washington, DC–based contingent including Waldron, Archibald Grimké, Church Terrell, and Carrie Clifford took on this task. The early NAACP also tracked lynching statistics and attempted to take action in specific cases by intervening with executive branch officials of various states. It also sought to work with local politicians and pursued any other potentially promising redress routes.[34]

As had the AAC, the NAACP attempted to maintain a presence in Washington, DC, in order to monitor and fight the many federal developments threatening to move the country in a regressive direction on race issues. In 1913 the association retained an expert to monitor every bill introduced in the House and Senate in Washington, recognizing that "without the careful watching of an expert" the discriminatory proposals being put forward there with increasing frequency could be "railroaded through at any moment." By 1914 *The Crisis* was publishing evaluations of the overall voting records of each member of Congress on civil rights issues.[35]

The early NAACP sought to fight against pernicious initiatives at the state and local levels as well. Thus much of its earliest law-related work took a defensive posture as the organization frantically sought to head off the many anti–civil rights initiatives brewing at the national, state, and local levels. As its 1913 Annual Meeting report explained, "The past year has been characterized by a flood of discriminatory legislation—anti-intermarriage bills, 'Jim Crow' bills, segregation ordinances in cities and segregation in the Federal departments at Washington. Everywhere we have witnessed efforts to officialize caste."[36]

Most discouragingly, the NAACP witnessed the introduction of segregation in federal government employment. President Woodrow Wilson undertook this initiative after his election in 1912, much to the disappointment of NAACP national leaders who had hoped for much better from Wilson based on his campaign promises.[37] The NAACP's efforts to protest the situation at high government levels went nowhere. This greatly disappointed Villard, who fruitlessly attempted to use his social capital to persuade Wilson and his top aides on this issue. Finally, in 1913 William Monroe Trotter, who had left the NAACP along with Ida Wells Barnett to devote attention to an African American–led organization called the National Equal Rights League, organized a delegation to the president to protest his segregationist federal employment policies. Trotter's blunt words to the president led Wilson to eject him from his office. Old guard NAACP members such as Francis Garrison worried that this incident had set back the cause, but the NAACP's more grassroots membership clearly approved of Trotter's bravery, sending an early warning signal to the NAACP that militancy in the face of blatant racial injustice would be expected from the organization's leaders if they were to continue to claim the premiere leadership role in national race advocacy in years to come.[38]

The early NAACP often drew on the social capital of its most prominent members to intervene in incidents of discrimination by quasi-public bodies that dispensed important social privileges. When the American Bar Association refused admission to three African American lawyers—one of whom was Boston NAACP president Butler Wilson—the NAACP protested through the voice of prominent

ABA member Moorfield Storey and succeeded in winning these candidates' admission—though future applicants of color continued to be excluded for several decades.[39]

This defensive work under conditions of escalating racism throughout the country would have provided more than enough of a legal agenda for the NAACP, but the organization was determined to develop a proactive legal agenda as well. In early 1911 it vowed to take up once again the issue of federal aid to education, which had been a key project of the AAL years before.[40] It also drafted antilynching legislation and introduced it in Congress even though its chances of advancing were slim to nonexistent there.[41]

Yet another early affirmative initiative, this one a particular pet project of Villard's, involved a proposal Villard carefully outlined to President Woodrow Wilson to revive the idea of a national race commission to study the race question in the United States. This proposal provided for a presidentially appointed body to investigate the sociological, political, and legal status of African Americans. Villard and other NAACP insiders first began to think about this plan in 1911, but the idea took more concrete form after DC branch member Lafayette Hershaw sent a letter to Du Bois in late 1912. Hershaw, formerly a key AAC activist who helped spearhead its DC-based legislative and lobbying initiatives, wrote to his good friend and former Niagara Movement colleague Du Bois to forward a newspaper clipping announcing Congress's recent creation of a national commission on industrial relations. Drawing on his memory of the AAC's prior effort to establish such a commission on race questions, Hershaw suggested that a commission like the one newly proposed could also "inquire into many of the conditions in the South and in the country at large which the N.A.A.C.P. seeks to deal with," such as the "ballot, education, housing conditions, hours of labor, organization of labor, exclusion from labor unions, exclusion from employment in the industries, etc." Hershaw politely concluded: "I make this suggestion in the hope that it may be considered with a view to taking such action as may seem wise and feasible."[42] An NAACP correspondent soon replied: "My dear Mr. Hershaw: ... We are very much interested in your suggestion and will take it up with the officers of the Association at the next Board Meeting."[43] Soon afterward, new board Chair Joel Spingarn wrote to Secretary Nerney: "I have your note in regard to the proposed commission on the negro in mind for some time, and meant to speak to you about it last night." Spingarn suggested gathering together "a small conference of all types of men interested in the question" and enclosed a draft definition of the scope of the commission as "(a) To investigate the present status of the negro in the United States; (b) To contrast this status with that of fifty years ago ... ; (c) to indicate the obstacles to progress in the past and the future; (d) to make practical suggestions to his future welfare."[44] A few days later Ovington wrote to Villard, now treasurer of the board, with a similar suggestion, enthusiastically proposing the following: "Could we not call the commission 'A Commission to Investigate the Status of the Negro in the United States'?

That would include the conditions we want studied, the franchise, the courts, segregation, education and mob law, and it would study them from the fundamental view point of American citizenship."[45] An unsigned memo dated a few days earlier asked Villard's view about "Hershaw's suggestion on the Industrial Commission" and urged that "all our efforts" be concentrated "on the proposed Race Commission." Villard approved the proposal with a handwritten okay.[46] Soon handsome bound copies of "A Proposal for a National Race Commission to be appointed by the President of the United States, as suggested by the NAACP" were printed, which Villard offered to the president in May 1913.

Much to Villard's frustration, this proposal went nowhere. Instead, Wilson's policies regarding race segregation in the federal civil service moved ever more alarmingly in the wrong direction. Villard wrote to his uncle expressing his desire to draft an emphatic protest to the president: "I hate to make the protest at this time when the project of the National Commission is under way, but I am inclined to think that this is the more important duty."[47]

Once again, a proposal for a national commission to investigate race in the United States went nowhere. But the line of transmission of the idea—focused on the need to elevate to national consciousness the empirically collected facts regarding race relations in the nation, along with analysis of underlying reasons—extended back to the AAC and, more specifically, to Hershaw's work for its DC branch. Eventually such ways of approaching the analysis of race relations would become incorporated in national policy as the civil rights era dawned. For the time being, however, in the midst of the nadir period, a sociological vision of the complex underpinnings of racial injustice continued to be passed from generation to generation of race activists, without yet catching fire in the public's or policymakers' consciousness.

Assessing Early Achievements

By the end of 1913 the race commission idea had effectively died for lack of executive branch interest. But other efforts of the association had born more fruit. The NAACP's 1914 annual report laid out its central achievements and priorities on the legal front. The NAACP's list of activities that local chapters generated reads strikingly like the work the AAL and AAC had undertaken in previous decades. The NAACP had achieved an "improved Civil Rights Law" in New York State, though "it still falls short of being the model statute which we had hoped to send forth for imitation to the legislature of all the states." It had "no definite victories to record in the courts of New York during the past year," but other branches had more success. First on this list was the Baltimore branch, where Hawkins had achieved yet another favorable outcome in "acquitting George Howe, a colored man who shot into a mob bombarding his house." The Baltimore branch had also defeated a state Jim Crow car bill. Detroit, continuing a long-standing tradition stretching back to AAL-sponsored cases, "fought fourteen cases of discrimination in theatres and won four." Other local branches had filed cases and obtained some successes as well. "Undoubtedly the most important work of the year has been the Association's vigilance and activity in opposing hostile legislation in Washington." Two paid monitors "keep in close touch with New York Headquarters and with the District of Columbia Branch, which acts as a Congressional Committee and takes the lead in the local campaign against hostile bills." The report closed with congratulations to its membership that "despite the overwhelming Southern majority in Congress, not a single bill which was directly on its face intended to humiliate or repress colored men and women was permitted to pass during the year 1914." It suggested, not implausibly, that "if this Association had never existed it is almost certain that some or all of these bills would have passed," and gave the credit to the DC chapter, which "has been on the firing line in all this work," so that "all men owe it a debt of gratitude for what it has accomplished." That chapter, of course, derived its energy and expertise from the presence of many members who had performed similar roles for the AAC and the Niagara Movement.[48]

A First U.S. Supreme Court Victory

The NNC's first substantive priority had been to continue the legal fight against disfranchisement, but it was several years before those early ambitions found a test case vehicle. Of particular historical significance, as it would turn out, was the NAACP's decision to file an amicus brief in a grandfather clause test case emerging from Oklahoma, which the U.S. Justice Department was developing under the theory that state officials had conspired to violate the Fifteenth Amendment.[49] *The Crisis* had been carefully tracking the case, but little else was happening. When Harry Smith argued in the *Cleveland Gazette* that a national organization seeking to help African American people should be pressing more forcefully on the three issues of disfranchisement, interstate Jim Crow cars, and lynching, Du Bois replied from the pages of *The Crisis* with a plea for patience. Du Bois's perspective, based on his long, frustrating experiences with attempts to successfully pursue test cases within both the AAC and the Niagara Movement, led him to go so far as to lecture Smith, whose activist experience was even more long-standing. As Du Bois wrote: "But the *Gazette* should know that cases before the Supreme Court are delicate matters. It does not do to rush into court with any haphazard case.... Theoretically, it would seem very easy to settle such matters. Practically, it is very hard, but we propose to keep at it." Du Bois concluded, somewhat defensively, as follows:

> Some folk seem to imagine that the walls of caste and prejudice in America will fall at a blast of the trumpet, if loud enough. Consequently, when an association like the [NAACP] does something, they say querulously: "But

nothing has happened." They ought to say: Nothing has yet happened, for that is true and that is expected. If in fifty or a hundred years *The Crisis* can point to a distinct lessening of disfranchisement, and undoubted reduction of lynching, and more decent traveling accommodations, this will be a great, an enormous accomplishment.... What is possible to-day and to-morrow and every day is to keep up necessary agitation, make unfaltering protest, fill the courts and legislatures and executive chambers, and keep everlastingly at the work of protest in season and out of season.[50]

Du Bois's one-hundred-year projection proved unduly pessimistic, even though there was little basis for greater optimism at the time he wrote. The case that would begin to suggest more possibility on the level of symbolic victory if not real change on the ground was *U.S. v. Guinn*. When the case reached the U.S. Supreme Court in 1913, the Boston abolitionist and prominent corporate lawyer Moorfield Storey agreed to argue it on the NAACP's behalf as amicus curiae, or "friend of the court."

The *Guinn* case was argued in the fall of 1913 but not decided until the summer of 1915.[51] By that time, Moorfield Storey had been elected NAACP vice president (along with Milholland, Archibald Grimké, Mary White Ovington, and others); Joel Spingarn had become chair of the board, following Villard's resignation; and Arthur Spingarn, Joel's brother, had taken over as legal committee chair, a position he would retain and conscientiously fulfill until the 1940s. In his early years, Arthur Spingarn frequently combined his role as legal advisor with that of spokesperson at mass meetings organized to generate enthusiasm and funds for test cases.[52] When the Court finally announced its decision holding that the grandfather clause at issue was unconstitutional, the NAACP's leaders were jubilant. This victory in *Guinn* became the NAACP's first U.S. Supreme Court success. Its importance did not lie so much in any significant change in the law that it accomplished since the clause it invalidated had already done its exclusionary work. Oklahoma soon replaced it with another disfranchising device, the all-white primary, which the NAACP and the U.S. Department of Justice failed to follow up on with a new challenge. Instead, its significance was symbolic but important nevertheless. To the NAACP's potential allies and membership base, *Guinn* showed that test case litigation before the U.S. Supreme Court might indeed bring long-wished-for victories on key matters of legal principle. It could be used to bring new members to the organization as well. The line of transmission for this antidisfranchisement litigation campaign clearly went from the AAC to the early NAACP, having started with Pillsbury's involvement in advising the AAC in 1901 and continuing through Villard's enthusiasm in hearing about and praising the AAC's litigation initiatives in 1906. This in turn contributed to the NNC's adoption of antidisfranchisement work as its top substantive priority and meeting theme in 1910, then culminating in Pillsbury and Storey contributing their legal services pro bono to carry on this legal campaign through the association's amicus brief in *Guinn*.

Du Bois was now as high about the future as he had been low about it in respond-ing to Harry Smith two years before, characterizing *Guinn* in *The Crisis* as the "most important race decision since the Dred Scott holding." The Court had, as Du Bois saw it, announced that "a Negro not only has a constitutional right to vote, but to have his vote counted." Du Bois forecast—wildly overoptimistically this time—"it is believed that the Negro once more may become a potent factor in the community in the Southland, wherever he may reside."[53]

In the same late summer issue of *The Crisis* Du Bois wrote of the NAACP's plans for yet another test case to challenge a residential segregation ordinance in Louisville. This case, based on Hawkins's earlier work in Maryland, would end up reaching the U.S. Supreme Court as *Buchanan v. Warley* in 1917, providing the NAACP with its second win before the high Court. By mid-1915, although the story of the NAACP was just beginning, the story of its tentative infancy was drawing to a close.

Conclusion

This book began with T. Thomas Fortune's 1891 founding of the National Afro-American League. Fortune envisioned the AAL as a national organization that would tackle racial injustice on many fronts, using a variety of strategies. He saw litigation as a vehicle for defending the civil and political rights promised in the nation's founding documents and in the Reconstruction-era amendments to its constitution. He saw federal legislation as the appropriate means of guaranteeing that all citizens received an adequate public education to ensure a good chance at life and prepare them for the responsibilities of political citizenship. Fortune was a democratic socialist, and he saw the end goal of racial justice activism as achieving a fair distribution of social and economic resources for all persons regardless of race. He believed that, in the long term, alliances between race and labor activists could be built to produce such change through majoritarian, democratic processes.

Fortune's AAL attracted activists with like-minded views, such as lawyer and political theory writer Augustus Straker, but deterred others with more conservative views and/or personal political ambitions. As a result of this and other factors, especially difficulties in raising funds, the AAL collapsed at a national level after only a few years of existence. Bishop Alexander Walters's 1898 call to rebuild the AAL, now called the Afro-American Council, revived the idea of building a permanent national organization to work against racial injustice. But his organizing vision had some differences reflecting the changing tenor of the times. Walters envisioned the AAC as an umbrella organization that could hold within it leading citizens with a wide variety of political perspectives. Accordingly, its action agenda focused on pragmatic issues requiring immediate attention—ones on which everyone could agree. The AAC thus concentrated on fighting for political and civil rights in the face of the ever-worsening racial conditions of the nadir period. It sought to oppose waves of hostile state legislation disfranchising African American male voters and imposing Jim Crow in transportation and public accommodations throughout the south, as well as to counter the growing epidemic of lynchings and other forms of brutal racial violence. Fortune's vision of a national organization that would spearhead work on the social welfare and economic aspects of achieving racial justice was not so apparent within the AAC, but this was not because the AAC's leaders did not care about these issues. To the contrary, all of the main activists within the AAC were very much concerned about the social welfare and economic uplift of African American communities—if anything, they saw these issues as even more important than the frustrating battle in which they were engaged on political and civil rights. The problem was not a lack of concern about the social and economic dimensions of racial justice but instead, I have argued, one of fundamental disagreement about appropriate strategies and ultimate visions. The conservatives within the AAC—most notably, Booker T. Washington, who was at the height of his political power—believed that African Americans' long-term economic interests lay in forging alliances with the white capitalist class as against working-class laborers. The radicals within the AAC, including Reverdy Ransom, followed a bit later by W.E.B. Du Bois and others, adhered to the early Fortune's democratic socialist vision and believed in the potential for broadscale economic reform brought about through cross-race alliances within the working class.

Another important aspect of racial justice activism at the cusp of the twentieth century involved the social service and private institution-building work of the National Association of Colored Women. The NACW worked on these social welfare and economic uplift concerns through projects aimed at literally constructing the material institutions for a social welfare state within the space of African American communities. This plan was not a thoroughly separatist one, however; NACW activists always understood that the general institutions of government should be required to step up to their responsibilities of supporting these projects.[1] Thus, I have argued, NACW activists were also pursuing law-related goals; their focus was on redefining the line between the public and the private as a means of combating policies that were generally hostile to the well-being of African American citizens.

This work to shift the bounds of government responsibility to include the social and economic well-being of racial outsiders did not often achieve success. But activists recognized it as a first step toward constituting a social reality that could undergird further change. Similarly, key leaders in the NACW's "brother" organization, the AAC, were well aware by the early years of the twentieth century that their legislative and litigation work would go nowhere unless they could gain greater power in the political sphere. This was the import of Jesse Lawson's sociological summit in 1903—changing conditions required changing strategies, and the old equal rights paradigm of the abolitionists needed to give way to new ideas that better fit the political environment of the nadir period.

Turn-of-the-century race activists were, in other words, far from naive legal liberals who believed that the nation's courts would impose justice despite the contrary forces of political power. At the same time, however, these leaders would not have embraced the "hopelessness theory" that scholars such as Michael Klarman and Gerald Rosenberg have articulated. This theory questions whether test case litigation is ever an effective tool in bringing about social change.[2] Test case litigation certainly did not lead to any significant change in the time period at issue here. Even the few test cases that were successful, such as *Carter v. Texas* (jury discrimination), *Rogers v. Alabama* (juries), *U.S. v. Guinn* (grandfather clauses), and *Buchanan v. Warley* (residential segregation ordinances), showed that wins in court would not produce "change on the ground," so to speak. Nevertheless, the activists who helped sponsor these cases believed that legal reform strategies, fought through both test cases *and* legislative initiatives, were important for different but no less crucial reasons. They recognized that, in the intricate dance of constructing social understandings through interactions between institutions and ideas, legal debates and victories mattered to the overall flow of discourse and change. A legal campaign created a goal for activists' work; a win provided important symbolic affirmation of the righteousness of the cause. Even losses spurred additional productive effort, as shown, for example, by activists' work for Northern and Midwestern state civil rights statutes after the Court's 1883 decision in the *Civil Rights Cases* invalidated civil rights legislation at the federal level.[3]

The multifaceted action priorities of the 1905 Niagara Movement further demonstrate the robust mix of litigation, legislation, and social welfare objectives that characterized national racial justice organizing at the turn of the twentieth century. In that organization, too, radicals fed up with Washington's attempts to control the AAC sought to attack racial injustice through a mix of strategies and on multiple fronts. The Niagara Movement's organizing model had not yet achieved the correct formula for organization-building success. That formula, as Du Bois and others would recognize too late, required open membership policies that could encourage large-scale, grassroots participation. But in its action agenda the Niagara Movement delivered to the NAACP a well-developed substantive program and strategy plan that had been in use and in the process of refinement since Fortune first wrote the AAL's initial platform.

The NAACP's founding, half a decade after Du Bois created the Niagara Movement, took up the law side of a campaign for racial justice, but it did not take on all of the Niagara Movement's social welfare and economic objectives. This was, again, not because the NAACP's founders, many of whom were democratic socialists or like-minded progressives, did not consider social welfare and economic justice matters of at least as much importance as political and civil rights issues. Instead, the years at the close of the twentieth century's first decade saw a trend toward specialization among social reform organizations. The early NAACP concentrated on its area of expertise—namely, test case litigation and legislative reform—and agreed to leave social welfare and economic uplift issues to the National Urban League, whose leadership strength and special expertise were in the kind of private, voluntarist institution building and advocacy work that the NACW's chapters and other projects, such as social settlements and institutional churches, also promoted. The early 1910s thus saw a coupling of political and civil rights with litigation and legislative reform, on the one hand, and social welfare and economic issues with voluntarist institution building in the private sphere, on the other. Again, this tentative and always unstable division of responsibility took place not out of a sense of a hierarchy or priority with regard to these issues but instead out of a sense of the need to focus effort. Hard experiences had shown the high degree of determination and sophistication that would be required to tackle tough, intractable issues with any hope for success.

Explaining Why National Organizing Developed as It Did

A question presented is *why* national racial justice organizing developed along these lines. Any explanation must point to many variables: some legal, some political, and some residing in the agency of the activists involved. As we have seen, turn-of-the-century race activist organizations in the United States focused primarily on legislation and litigation for civil and political rights objectives and on voluntarist strategies in the private realm for their equally important social welfare priorities. Part of the explanation as to why they adopted these particular strategies goes back to the nineteenth-century jurisprudential dichotomy between civil and political rights, on the one hand, and "social" nonrights on the other. This jurisprudential dichotomy, discussed in chapter 3, carved a distinction between "public," legally regulable matters and "private," nonregulable concerns. The U.S. Supreme Court carved these dichotomies in decisions like the *Civil Rights Cases,* as well as in the line of opinions that culminated in the Court's decision in *Lochner v. New York,* which held that the state could not regulate the terms of employment contracts in order to protect worker safety because doing so interfered with employers' and employees' natural rights to "freedom of contract."[4] Although some white women's reform groups of the era, such as Florence Kelley's National Consumers League (NCL), pressed ahead with legislative and litigation strategies to achieve social welfare goals despite the problems these legal precedents posed, racial justice advocates faced more severe constraints on their strategic options.[5] Not only did African American men throughout the South face broadscale disfranchisement, stripping them of their potential electoral power, but the powerful trade union movement, led by Samuel Gompers and his American Federation of Labor, was becoming increasingly race prejudiced as this historical period progressed.[6] Other political forces as well, as we have seen—including outspoken racists in the Democratic party (Tillman, Hoke, Watson, and many others), the lily-white Republicans, and reactionary elements in the white press—vehemently opposed efforts to improve the social welfare or economic status of African American citizens, just as they were also opposing the grant of civil and political rights equality.

In contrast, as many feminist scholars have pointed out, white women reform leaders enjoyed class and race privileges that allowed them the benefits, among many other advantages, of close access to men in positions of political power. Moreover, they could often count on the sympathies of state legislatures in pursuing their objectives. It was all well and good, in other words, for upper-class white women to ask for social welfare protections, mainly for women, portrayed as more fragile and thus as requiring "special protection" (as well as for some male members of the working class, it should also be noted). But race activists in this political period were starting from no such comparable political position that would have allowed challenge to the basic jurisprudential categories that defined which "rights" law could reach.[7]

Other political factors shaped the direction of turn-of-the-century racial justice activism as well. As we have seen, opponents of legal protections for African Americans relentlessly employed a hostile rhetoric of illegitimate "special rights" to denounce all legal efforts to protect citizens on the basis of race. This was—and continues to be—a favorite tactic of opponents of measures aimed at African Americans' advancement.[8] In the period under consideration here, this was so even though civil rights leaders emphasized that what they were asking for was the *same* treatment as everyone else—they just were not getting it, as, for example, under statutes that forced African American riders to move to less preferential seating in trains and streetcars or barred them from voting because their grandfathers had neither fought in the Civil War nor been entitled to vote before it. Even when race leaders advocated for *non*discriminatory treatment, they were criticized for seeking special protection.

Another route of attack accused African Americans of at bottom seeking "social" equality—in other words, of wanting to be accepted into whites' voluntary social orderings and arrangements. Here, too, civil rights leaders in this period went to great pains to explain that social equality was not what they were asking for; they simply wanted equal access to the public or quasi-public goods and resources, such as accommodations, dining, and entertainment. Civil rights foes continued to raise this bugaboo of social equality, however, not for the purpose of rational argument but to inflame irrational fears. In light of these dual drumbeats of political attack, based on special treatment and social equality, African American leaders assiduously continued to note at every turn that what they were asking for was *equality* of treatment, and with respect to *legal* status only. In other words, they felt the need to emphasize that their legal demand was for a nondiscrimination principle without more.

The fact that racial justice advocates were acutely sensitive to the political booby trap for African Americans of even appearing to be asking for special favors from the state enhanced their wariness about attempting to achieve social welfare goals through legal mandates. But this was not the only cause of their wariness. African American advocates were also skeptical—to a far greater degree than the women of the NCL—about the potential benefits of state intervention through law in any case. This skepticism arose from their outsider perspective. Numerous examples of law operating in the post-Reconstruction period showed it to be acting primarily to advance the interests of those with power and to oppress African Americans' interests. Jim Crow and voter disfranchisement laws were examples, but a host of other statutes curtailed employment opportunities, subjected African Americans to peonage labor, upheld exploitative tenancy farming arrangements, and generally employed law as an explicit mechanism of racial subordination in many other ways as well.[9] Such observations of the operation of law gave leaders little reason to conclude that legal strategies would produce better outcomes than would strategies that kept the advancement of African Americans' interests within community leaders' hands. In this respect, the literature on black nationalism and economic separatism helpfully intersects with legal civil rights history.[10] A strategy that looked to law to enhance social welfare necessarily regarded legal institutions as generally beneficent means to achieve social reform, but racial justice activists during the period at issue here were unlikely to put much faith in law for these purposes. Turn-of-the-century race activists believed in the potential efficacy of law for some matters—primarily those encompassed under a natural law theory of fundamental political and civil rights. They were less likely to see law as useful for other objectives, such as the promotion of the social welfare of African American communities. For these reasons as well, African American activists focused on fighting for civil and political equality through law but resolved to use voluntary measures, operating outside general legal mandates, to achieve social welfare and economic advancement objectives.[11]

African American women's exclusion from white women's activist networks likewise led them to form separate organizations dedicated to the hybrid civil rights and social welfare agenda that was of concern to African American women.[12] In turn, this exclusion of African American women reformers from white women's reform networks had consequences for the development of social policy in the United States in the early twentieth century. A by now large literature examines the influence of white women's reform activism, including the Progressive-era statutory reform and litigation experiments of the NCL, in setting the stage for and later contributing to the development of the social welfare state of the New Deal.[13] This literature also critiques the ways in which these reformers' state-building achievements bore the marks of their gendered—as well as race- and class-based—origins. Robyn Muncy, for example, points to the "danger inherent in the relatively closed system built by female reformers in the Progressive era" and notes that "both class and race were aspects of this restriction," resulting in what she terms a "dominion" that was "fraught with the arrogance of power."[14] Linda Gordon concludes that white women's influence on the development of welfare policy supported ideas—such as means testing, insulting invasions of privacy, and a charity rather than an entitlement-based rationale—that African American women tended to disfavor. Many other scholars have similarly pointed out a myriad of additional ways in which the racially exclusionary organization of civil society institutions, such as labor unions, not coincidentally mapped onto the exclusory consequences for African Americans of legislation such as the Fair Labor Standards Act, which explicitly exempted employers in the domestic service and agricultural sectors, where most African Americans workers were employed, or the Wagner Act, which empowered racially exclusionary unions to protect their members' interests against those of racial outsiders.[15]

Building on these insights, I have sought to explore from a legal scholar's perspective the ways that African American and white reform networks not only influenced the institutions of the social welfare state in different ways but also accessed and conceived of the benefits and drawbacks of the institutions of *law* in dissimilar ways. Attending to these differences can reveal additional important insights that help illuminate the relationship between law and social movement organizations, including questions about what law reform strategies are perceived as potentially useful by differently situated groups and why. Thus, I have suggested, an analysis of how and when activist networks use law and what kind of law they use for what purposes should take into account the socially situated nature of their options and choices. For example, the use of standard avenues of legal reform, including legislation *or* test case litigation, presupposes a certain degree of political power and public acceptance. Some situations may require other avenues, such as institution building in relatively more private spaces, to create a reality on the ground that presents the conditions for gaining sufficient political power to launch law reform initiatives (or, alternatively, not to choose this path).

It is easy to regard institution building in the private sector as an alternative to, or at least as something other than, law reform. I have argued, however, that it may also be an *aspect* of law reform and should be analyzed as such rather than being divided from and cast away as a subject for law and social movement analysis. Activist work in the intersections between what is viewed as law and "not law" may serve, as in the example of the NACW's hybrid work on social welfare and civil rights, to push change in law, such as by altering understandings as to the proper allocation of public welfare responsibilities between the state and nongovernment actors.[16] Moreover, I have suggested, who gets to make law and what kind of law they get to make has important consequences. These are questions that should be further explored in law and social movement scholarship, as, indeed, insightful social movement theorists have already begun to point out.[17]

I have thus far argued that a combination of legal and political factors accounts for why early twentieth-century racial justice activism took the particular directions that it did. These factors are well accounted for under political opportunity theory, which posits that social reform organizations target reform efforts based on the dual considerations of (1) where problems exist and (2) where opportunities for transformation appear possible. This explanation works to explain why activists did not try to use legal strategies for social welfare objectives—namely, because there was very little chance of success given both specific legal doctrine and general political circumstances. But it does not explain why these activists *did* use legal strategies for some matters even when their chances for success were minimal. As we have seen,

racial justice activists resolutely fought for several kinds of affirmative federal legislation, such as the Blair education bill and the White antilynching proposal, even
though their chances for success on these fronts were close to nonexistent given
national political conditions. Other factors must account for these choices. These
factors, I suggest, lie in the agency of the activists. Put otherwise, they arise in ideas
generated in activists' interaction with their environment regarding appropriate law
reform objectives outside considerations of political feasibility. Not only did activists persist in bringing test case litigation despite their very low win rate, but they
also lobbied for many years, as we have seen, for the federal Blair bill, which would
have provided federal funding to Southern states to improve education, thus supporting what many abolitionists saw as a fundamental right to adequate education
for all; for the Crumpacker resolution, which would have reduced Southern electoral representation to reflect the disfranchisement of African American voters, thus
enforcing the explicit language of the Fourteenth Amendment; for the antilynching proposals of Congressman George White and others, which would have made
lynching a federal crime akin to treason; and for the Irwin bill to investigate the
political, social, and economic conditions African Americans were facing. As the
nadir period arose and progressed, it became increasingly clear that none of these
proposals had any hope of being enacted into law, but racial justice advocates still
viewed it as crucial to press for this legislative agenda despite their low chances of
success and the charges that were inevitably made against them on special legislation grounds. No explanation other than the force of their convictions can account
for these acts. Race activists persevered, in other words, because they held beliefs,
grounded in an evolving but still enduring natural law ideology, that their cause was
just under the nation's founding documents. This ideology was another key factor
that kept racial justice activism going even in the nadir period. Political opportunity
certainly shaped the direction and successfulness of their social reform activism,
but it cannot fully account for why it arose and endured—and, even more, developed and transformed through decades of experience so that its transfer to later
generations could support the birth of a movement.

Situating Early Activism within Civil Rights Historiography

We thus leave the story of early twentieth-century racial justice activism at its very
beginning. A great deal happened afterward, of course, which this conclusion cannot even begin to summarize. Nonetheless, the interested reader will find a growing literature in legal history and related disciplines that is adding great richness
to scholars' understanding of the wealth of experimentation that took place with
respect to both goals and strategies for racial justice activism over the course of the
twentieth century—or over the "long civil rights movement," as some like to say.[18]

In light of the legal focus of my study, I primarily highlight in this short summary literature that speaks most closely to the legal aspects of civil rights history, but in so doing I do not mean to give short shrift to a great many other important works in this vein.

In this field of legal history scholarship, Risa Goluboff has led the way in encouraging new lines of investigation, showing that the NAACP was continuing to litigate matters related to economic justice well into the 1940s.[19] As Goluboff explains, in the 1930s and 1940s:

> civil rights law barely resembled the field as we now know it. In particular, both laypeople and legal professionals included not only the rights with which we associate the term today but also collective labor rights to governmentally provided economic security and affirmative rights to material and economic equality. Contemporaries saw an explicit connection between discrimination and economics, rights and reform, individual entitlement and government obligation. Lawyers who took the cases of black workers treated as civil rights issues labor-based and economic harms as well as racial ones, and they placed responsibility for rights protection within government as well as in opposition to it.[20]

Goluboff focuses primarily on NAACP and U.S. Department of Justice litigation efforts aimed at economic rights issues. Other legal scholars have taken Goluboff's discoveries still further by investigating the NAACP's initiatives focused on legal tribunals other than courts. Sophia Lee, for example, shows how the NAACP pursued charges before the National Labor Relations Board in order to promote recognition of unions' legal duty not to discriminate on the basis of race. She explains that the NAACP's decision to pursue this route was motivated not only by legal considerations but also by Labor Director Herbert Hill's political perspectives. Hill wanted to work with the labor movement whenever possible and to encourage African American union membership because he "viewed the labor movement, not litigation, as the preferred vehicle for producing" change in African American workers' situation. The NAACP "sought to facilitate class-based collective action." Lee shows how the NAACP's carefully orchestrated labor strategy under Hill in the 1950s produced, after much effort and perseverance, a major administrative law victory when the NLRB announced an expansive reading of the state action doctrine in a key NLRB case.[21] For a time at least, this victory prompted the NLRB to vigorously enforce the proscription against labor union race discrimination. In later years, the Board's vigilance decreased, frustrating Hill and causing the NAACP's workplace constitutionalism to "fade out" by the late 1970s. But Lee's research shows that the NAACP's strategies in the 1950s and 1960s encompassed the goal of securing desirable, well-paid employment, and thus economic advancement, for African American workers.[22]

Carol Anderson's *Eyes off the Prize* shows the NAACP's efforts to use the principles of international human rights law to pursue its domestic civil rights agenda.[23] Although this NAACP campaign suffered defeat due to a lack of sufficient support by key actors, including Eleanor Roosevelt, Anderson's work shows yet another creative and bold experiment in varied methods of using law to bring about improved racial justice, this time employing an international human rights paradigm.

Historian Nancy MacLean's focus is on the work of the NAACP and other civil rights groups in the 1960s and after to open jobs for African American workers. This was work the NUL had started to tackle in the 1910s using voluntarist strategies; Title VII of the Civil Rights Act of 1964 now provided help in the form of a federal employment antidiscrimination mandate. MacLean's point, too, is to correct for what she aptly calls the "airbrush[ing] from popular memory the long struggle for economic inclusion," and she concludes her important book with a reminder of the need to continue to recognize that equal citizenship rights are not enough to achieve racial justice in the face of growing economic inequality.[24]

Kenneth Mack's work, as well, explicitly takes on the legal liberalism paradigm, focusing on the identity that elite African American lawyers crafted through their very presence in the courtroom and daily law office practice.[25] Tomiko Brown-Nagin's scholarship, too, has emphasized the importance of socioeconomic class issues to civil rights activists' strategies.[26] In tracing the clash of perspectives between a new generation of radical lawyers and other militants who led the SNCC's direct-action sit-ins in Atlanta in the 1960s on the one hand and older generations of activist lawyers on the other, Brown-Nagin demonstrates that neither of these generations held views about the relationship between courts and social change resembling the legal liberalist caricature. Her story is instead far more complex and interesting, exploring not only intergenerational conflict but also class and gender differences within the movement. Brown-Nagin's initial focus is on Atlanta from the 1940s through the direct-action protests of the 1950s and 1960s. She then continues her examination of activism in that city through the 1970s, depicting the African American women involved in welfare rights organizing and analyzing the relationship of that work to the civil rights activism that came before it.[27]

Still another important legal scholar's voice is that of Athena Mutua, who argues for conceiving of "the civil rights era" as beginning in the 1930s and continuing to pursue a still-unfinished radical agenda. Mutua concludes that:

> the abbreviated story of the civil rights movement cuts it off from its roots in the protest activism of the 1930s and its wings in the black power movement. In doing so it not only excludes a host of people involved in the movement, people who passed their traditions on to future generations, but it guts the movement of its central message and goal of a broad egalitarian democratic order. That is, the movement recognized that both slavery and Jim Crow, as well as today's oppressive racial isolation, were

not just racial systems meant to oppress and offend human dignity but also economic systems meant to facilitate the exploitation of black labor, to deny black material well-being, and to assist the few in hoarding the resources created by the many including th[ose] created by black people as a whole.[28]

Work exploring alternate strands of civil rights activism abounds in various academic disciplines, including treatments less focused on law. In her important article on the long civil rights movement, Jacqueline Dowd Hall notes the work of Robert Korstad on "civil rights unionism," which "highlights the conjunction of race and class interests," and Martha Biondi's work on race activism in New York City in the 1940s, as well as Glenda Gilmore's deeply researched book on the influence of the Communist Party on civil rights organizing.[29] Eric Arnesen and many others have researched anticommunist civil rights leaders who focused on economic empowerment through labor unionism, as he discusses vividly in his important critique of the long civil rights movement concept.[30]

Thomas Jackson traces the ways in which Martin Luther King Jr. was working to connect ideas about racial justice with ideas about substantive economic justice.[31] In addition, Nikhil Pal Singh argues that the standard narrative of the civil rights movement "fails to recognize the historical depth and heterogeneity of black struggles against racism, narrowing the political scope of black agency and reinforcing a formal, legalistic view of black equality."[32] Focusing on the 1930s and after, Singh points to an internationalist group of black intellectuals who analyzed the connections between colonialism and racism and further notes that "blacks were the one political constituency that consistently supported the expansion of social as well as civil rights, or the development of a full-employment welfare-state in the United States."[33]

In short, recent scholarship has been making it increasingly clear that rich strains of thought and activism existed throughout the history of the racial justice movement, strains that sometimes connected law with economic and social welfare concerns, class analysis and awareness, and the articulation of rights discourses embracing far more than a negative nondiscrimination principle. This book has traced some of those strands through a foundational period of debate among racial justice activists in the late nineteenth and early twentieth centuries. It has demonstrated that, although these strands are complex and by no means continuous—or even remembered—across generations, their roots are as deep as talk about racial equality. In so doing the book joins many other works in demonstrating that critiques that cast legal liberalism as the dominant paradigm for racial justice activism are based on a myth—a myth that threatens to perniciously influence visions of the future by placing restrictive blinders on views of the past.[34] Awareness of a far richer, experimentalist past can point the way to a similarly rich, experimentalist future, one that continues to embrace ambitious objectives and refuses to be constrained by the awareness that some important goals, especially the development and application of law-related techniques to lessen economic inequality, have not yet been met. In thinking ahead to the future of civil rights law and policy, it may be that these unattained but nevertheless historically prominent goals most require continued attention.

ACKNOWLEDGEMENTS

Writing this book has been a slow-burning joy over a period of about a dozen years. Along the way I have incurred many more interpersonal debts than I can ever acknowledge or even recall. At crucial junctures I received invaluable support from senior figures in my field, including Rick Abel, Robert Gordon, Lani Guinier, David Wilkens, and Gregory Williams.

Three faculty colleagues endured the most intensive exposure to this project in reading and offering extensive comments on substantial portions of the manuscript, book proposal, and/or related presentations: Darren Hutchinson, Binny Miller, and Robert Tsai; I could not have had better fortune than to end up with such professional friends. Nancy Polikoff and Brenda Smith offered both many insightful comments on the project and especially helpful personal support. Lewis Grossman generously shared his legal history expertise. Jamin Raskin, especially, as well as Angela Davis, Bob Dinerstein, Lia Epperson, Andy Popper, and others, provided advice on the book's title. A great many of my faculty colleagues, who I am told are too numerous to list, cheered me on; I am very lucky to work in such a supportive peer environment.

The colleague who has lived with this project most intimately for the longest period is Deputy Director of the Law Library Adeen Postar, who repeatedly performed research miracles. Interlibrary Loan Manager Y. Renée Talley-Cuthbert likewise deserves my deepest thanks. Mukarrama Freeman-Terrell offered invaluable technical assistance and problem-solving skills for many years, as well as unflagging enthusiasm. Among numerous contributions, she printed and organized hundreds of historical newspapers articles and found them at least as interesting as I did.

During the many years it has taken me to finish this research I have been aided by generations of law student research assistants (or "dean's fellows" as we call them at WCL). These include Matt Acocella, Farhan Ali, Walekewon Belgay, Aaron Brand, Prudence Cho, Danielle Combes, Ryan Hatley, Megan Hu, Matt Hill, Chavette

Jackson, Tiffany Kelley, Whitney Mancino, Joe Richardson, Michaela Spero, Kevin Stein, Kathy Tuznick, and Erin Zacuto. I cannot express enough thanks for their intelligent and energetic work. All of these researchers contributed in unique, invaluable ways at different stages of this book's slow progress, but as I finalize this I am especially cognizant of Erin Zacuto's unflaggingly cheerful support while working intensively on the book's technical aspects.

I also benefited from chances to present this project at various stages of its completion at the Baldy Center at SUNY Buffalo, Fordham University Law School, Georgetown University Law Center, George Washington University Law School, University of California at Irvine Law School, University of California at Los Angeles Law School, University of Miami Law School, Smith College, Stanford Law School, Texas Wesleyan Law School, and the Washington College of Law. In addition, I received excellent feedback at a 2012 Law and Society panel organized and chaired by Robert W. Gordon; a 2012 International Legal Ethics Conference in Banff, Canada; a 2011 American Society of Legal History panel chaired by Mary Dudziak; a 2011 National Science Association–funded interdisciplinary conference at Ohio University, organized by Katherine Sullivan, Julie Novkov, and Priscilla Yamin; a 2009 American Society for the Study of African American Life and History panel organized by Shawn Leigh Alexander; a 2009 Organization of American Historians panel organized by Jay Driskell; and a 2008 conference on John Dewey organized by John Shook at the Center for Inquiry in Amherst, NY. At these events and others, a multidisciplinary community of generous scholars offered me helpful feedback, including but not limited to the persons already mentioned, as well as Scott Cummings, Adrienne Davis, Martha Fineman, Catherine Fisk, V. P. Franklin, Jason Gilmer, David Fort Godshalk, Bruce Green, Desmond King, Lynn Mather, Marnie Mahoney, Ann McGinley, Russell Pearce, Jim Pope, Carla Pratt, Paul Ortiz, Rogers Smith, Ann Southworth, Patricia Strach, Shauhin Talesh, Lillian S. Williams, Victoria Wolcott, and Jim Wooten. In 2008 Shawn Leigh Alexander generously offered enthusiastic comments on my draft article, which stated this project's main thesis,[1] and Jay Driskell generously offered his wide-ranging knowledge and insights in reading several chapters in draft. Rhys Conlon offered wonderful expert assistance in the photo research and permissions process. I am also grateful to David McBride at Oxford University Press and the multiple thoughtful anonymous reviewers he recruited at various stages of the book's development for excellent advice on manuscript improvements.

Funding ended up being very crucial to this book's completion. The early travel research for this book was all personally financed, but in the final year the Ruth Landes Fund offered the most wonderful assistance possible by way of a generous research grant that allowed me to complete my "must do" research travel itinerary and devote a full-time summer and half-time semester to finishing the book. Without this support from the Ruth Landes Fund, I doubt this book would have seen the light of day.

Billie Jo Kaufman, WCL Dean for Library and Information Services, followed with another generous grant to support the inclusion of illustrations in this book; that generous financial assistance is also deeply appreciated. For many summers WCL Dean Claudio Grossman awarded me summer research stipends and research assistantship support that helped this project progress. Dean Grossman is also responsible for setting the tone at my institution that defines inquiry into the conditions supporting the advancement of social justice as a worthwhile scholarly focus.

Librarians and curators of manuscript collections around the country made the research for this book possible. All of the archives I visited, listed in the Bibliography, offered highly professional and courteous assistance. I regret that I did not always record the names of the librarians who assisted me but extend my deepest gratitude to them. Among these many individuals who made special efforts on my behalf were the librarians at Fisk University; Dr. Ida E. Jones, assistant curator at the Moorland Spingarn Center at Howard University; William W. Lefevre, reference archivist for the Labor and Urban Affairs Archive at Wayne State University; Diana Franzusoff Peterson, manuscript librarian at Haverford College's Special Collections; and Adrienne Cannon, manuscript specialist at the Library of Congress. Librarians at Wilberforce University's archives provided invaluable documents through interlibrary loan. Independent scholar Daniel Weinfeld shared with me his transcriptions of T. Thomas Fortune's autobiographical articles in the *Norfolk Journal and Guide*.

This project benefited not only from resources reflecting activist experiments of the past but also from living examples of activism in the present and future. I started my professional life as a community organizer and later worked as a lawyer in the Justice Department Civil Rights Division and then as a union-side labor lawyer. The many activists I have met along the way continue to inspire me with their example. Since entering law teaching I have had the privilege of being inspired by numerous students committed to various forms of forward-looking social justice activism, as well a host of other individuals I have met in various other ways while doing this research, all of whom remind me that the activism I examine in this book is very much an ongoing, ever-creative process.

Most personally important during the years in which I was working on this book was the family center of my life: my son, Joshua, who has taught me many deep lessons; my mother, Gloria, who taught me to be tough and to care about fairness; and my father, Jack, whose intellectual curiosity and erudition gave me an important early role model. My spouse, Henry Friedman, gave me enormous personal support through these years—not to mention also reading every word of this manuscript, often many times over. This book is dedicated to him in recognition of the justice-seeking values he so steadfastly embodies.

NOTES

Preface

1. A representative sampling of this literature includes Mark Tushnet, *The NAACP's Legal Strategy against Segregated Education, 1925–1950* (Chapel Hill: University of North Carolina Press, 1987); Kenneth W. Mack, *Representing the Race: The Creation of the Civil Rights Lawyer* (Cambridge, MA: Harvard University Press, 2012); Risa Goluboff, *The Lost Promise of Civil Rights* (Cambridge, MA: Harvard University Press, 2007); Sophia Z. Lee, "Hotspots in a Cold War: The NAACP's Postwar Workplace Constitutionalism, 1948–1964," *Law and History Review* 26 (2008): 327–78; Tomiko Brown-Nagin, *Courage to Dissent: Atlanta and the Long History of the Civil Rights Movement* (New York: Oxford University Press, 2011); Serena Mayeri, *Reasoning from Race: Feminism, Law, and the Civil Rights Revolution* (Cambridge, MA: Harvard University Press, 2011).

2. These debates are well summarized in Jeanne Woods and Hope Lewis, *Human Rights and the Global Marketplace: Economic, Social and Cultural Dimensions* (Ardsley, NY: Transnational Publishers, 2004), and Henry J. Steiner, Philip Alston, and Ryan Goodman, *International Human Rights in Context: Law, Politics, Morals*, 3rd ed. (New York: Oxford University Press, 2008), 263–374.

3. Cf. Michael C. Dorf and Charles F. Sabel, "A Constitution of Democratic Experimentalism," *Columbia Law Review* 98 (1998): 267–473 (describing the general tenets of democratic experimentalism, including its emphasis on the decentralization of power and allowing local actors to develop their own solutions rather than having large public bureaucracies dictating them); Charles F. Sabel and William H. Simon, "Destabilization Rights: How Public Law Litigation Succeeds," *Harvard Law Review* 117 (2004): 1015–1101 (describing how public law reform litigation is moving toward the use of experimentalist methods emphasizing negotiation and problem solving rather than court-ordered dictates); see also Susan Sturm, "Second Generation Employment Discrimination: A Structural Approach," *Columbia Law Review* 101 (2001): 458–598 (exploring how a backdrop of legal rules can create incentives for local problem solving without resort to courts).

4. On interactionism in social movement theory, see David A. Snow and Sarah A. Soule, *A Primer on Social Movements* (New York: W.W. Norton, 2010), 51; Doug McAdam, *Political Process and the Development of Black Insurgency, 1930–1970*, 2nd ed. (Chicago: University of Chicago Press, 1999), xiv, 12, 40.

5. Susan D. Carle, "Theorizing Agency," *American University Law Review* 55 (2005): 307–93. For discussions of the need to better appreciate human agency within social movement theory,

See, e.g., David S. Meyer, "Protest and Political Opportunities," *Annual Review of Sociology* 30 (2004): 125 (noting that critics of political opportunity theory have argued that it runs the danger of neglecting the importance of activists' agency); Aldon Morris, "Reflections on Social Movement Theory: Criticisms and Proposals," *Contemporary Sociology* 29 (2000): 445, 446 (arguing that "current theories continue to misspecify the central role that human agency plays in social movements").

6. Emma Lou Thornbrough, *T. Thomas Fortune: Militant Journalist* (Chicago: University of Chicago Press, 1972); Emma Lou Thornbrough, "The National Afro-American League, 1887–1908," *Journal of Southern History* 27 (1961): 494–512; Patrick H. Carroll, "*The 1905 Niagara Movement Attendants: An Interpretative Analysis of Their Lives and Ideologies*" (bachelor's thesis, College of the Holy Cross, 1980).

7. See, e.g., Alexander, Shawn Leigh, *An Army of Lions: The Civil Rights Struggle before the NAACP* (Philadelphia: University of Pennsylvania Press, 2012); Cornelius L. Bynum, "An Equal Chance in the Race for Life: Reverdy C. Ransom, Socialism, and the Social Gospel Movement, 1890–1920," *Journal of African American History* 93 (2008): 1–20; Jay Driskell, "First Class Citizens," unpublished manuscript, Jan. 2013 draft; Blair L. M. Kelley, *Right to Ride: Streetcar Boycotts and African American Citizenship in the Era of Plessy v. Ferguson* (Chapel Hill: University of North Carolina Press, 2010); Robert J. Norrell, *Up from History: The Life of Booker T. Washington* (Cambridge, MA: Belknap Press, 2009); R. Volney Riser, *Defying Disfranchisement: Black Voting Rights Activism in the Jim Crow South, 1890–1908* (Baton Rouge: Louisiana State Press, 2010).

8. See, e.g., Bettye Collier-Thomas, *Jesus, Jobs and Justice: African American Women and Religion* (New York: Alfred A. Knopf, 2010); Glenda E. Gilmore, *Gender and Jim Crow: Women and the Politics of White Supremacy in North Carolina, 1896–1920* (Chapel Hill: University of North Carolina Press, 1996); Evelyn Brooks Higginbotham, *Righteous Discontent: The Women's Movement in the Black Baptist Church, 1880–1920* (Cambridge, MA: Harvard University Press, 1993); Deborah Gray White, *Too Heavy a Load: Black Women in Defense of Themselves, 1894–1994* (New York: W. W. Norton, 1999); see also Wanda A. Hendricks, *Gender, Race, and Politics in the Midwest: Black Club Women in Illinois* (Bloomington: Indiana University Press, 1998); Anne Meis Knupfer, *Toward a Tenderer Humanity and a Nobler Womanhood: African American Women's Clubs in Turn-of-the-Century Chicago* (New York: New York University Press, 1996); Jacqueline Anne Rouse, *Lugenia Burns Hope: Black Southern Reformer* (Athens: University of Georgia Press, 1989).

Introduction

1. On these first and second stages of success in opposing racial disfranchisement, see Richard M. Valley, *The Two Reconstructions: The Struggle for Black Enfranchisement* (Chicago: University of Chicago Press, 2004).

2. I use the somewhat awkward qualifier "intended to have long-term status" to distinguish these first permanent national organizations of the late nineteenth century from the earlier convention movement, which involved periodic gatherings to discuss a range of racial justice issues, including both economics and civil rights, but without intent to create an ongoing, permanent organization. For a general description of the African American convention movement, see August Meier, *Negro Thought in America, 1880–1915* (Ann Arbor: University of Michigan Press, 1963), 4–10; Robert L. Factor, *The Black Response to America: Men, Ideals, and Organization from Frederick Douglass to the NAACP* (Reading, MA: Addison-Wesley, 1970), 49–56.

3. Rayford W. Logan, *The Negro in American Life and Thought: The Nadir, 1877–1901* (New York: Dial Press, 1954); Rayford W. Logan, *The Betrayal of the Negro from Rutherford B. Hayes to Woodrow Wilson* (New York: Collier Books, 1965), 11–12 (noting the debate about dating the nadir period and arguing that it extended into the 1920s).

4. For example, Doug McAdam, in his foundational work on political opportunities theory in the social movements genre, examines the origins of the American civil rights movement and argues that forceful civil rights activism started to emerge only in the 1930s, when social and political conditions began changing in ways that allowed mobilization. See Doug McAdam, *Political Process and the Development of Black Insurgency, 1930–1970*, 2nd ed. (Chicago: University of Chicago Press, 1999), 71. McAdam argues that social movements may survive despite hostile environmental conditions but that such examples are "rare" because without "sufficient environmental 'receptivity' " they are unlikely to "survive long enough to be recognized as movements" (xxxiii). My study, in examining the deeper historical antecedents of the movement McAdam studied in a later period, suggests instead that in hostile environments social change activists convinced of the righteousness of their cause may experiment with and improve on their ideologies and strategies, as well as engage in change-related but non-state-centered activity, such as voluntary institution building in the private sphere. These activities can sustain organizing momentum and build internal resources that permit later success despite still improbable odds once somewhat more receptive conditions arise. For a general discussion of political opportunities theory, as well as challenges to that theory, see David S. Meyer, "Protest and Political Opportunities," *Annual Review of Sociology* 30 (2004): 125, 132–45.

5. In the vocabulary of social movement theory, these efforts generated the collective "meaning making" on which later efforts relied. See McAdam, *Political Process and the Development of Black Insurgency*, xxxii. There are other reasons to study social movement "failures" as well, but this study's focus is on how repeated failures were crucial to later success. For an example of the deep insights that can be gained from studying failed social movements, see Robert Tsai, "America's Forgotten Constitutions: Visions of Power and Community after the Founding," Forthcoming, Harvard University Press, 2014.

6. See, e.g., Mark Tushnet, *The NAACP's Legal Strategy against Segregated Education*; Kenneth W. Mack, "Rethinking Civil Rights Lawyering and Politics in the Era before *Brown*," *Yale Law Journal* 115 (2005): 256–354 (exploring civil rights lawyering in the periods between World War I and World War II); Kenneth W. Mack, *Representing the Race* (focusing mostly on post–World War I lawyers); Risa Goluboff, *The Lost Promise of Civil Rights* (discussing the 1930s and 1940s); Sophia Z. Lee, "Hotspots in a Cold War," 327–78 (discussing the 1940s and 1950s); Tomiko Brown-Nagin, *Courage to Dissent* (covering the period between 1940 and 1980); Serena Mayeri, *Reasoning from Race* (examining the 1960s and 1970s).

An analogous trend in the discipline of U.S. history emphasizes the concept of the "long civil rights movement," again dating its start to the 1930s. See, e.g., Jacquelyn Dowd Hall, "The Long Civil Rights Movement and the Political Uses of the Past," *Journal of American History* 91 (2005): 1235 (dating the beginning of the civil rights movement to "the liberal and radical milieu of the late 1930s").

7. See, e.g., McAdam, *Political Process and the Development of Black Insurgency* (focusing on the 1930s and after).

8. Eric Arnesen makes a powerful argument along these lines in "Reconsidering the 'Long Civil Rights Movement,' " *Historically Speaking* 10(2) (April 2009): 31–34 (presenting counterarguments to the long civil rights movement concept). See also Shawn Leigh Alexander, *Army of Lions*, xiv (arguing that early "individuals and organizations and their activities did not constitute a movement in the sense that scholars understand the post–World War II American civil rights movement").

9. See McAdam, *Political Process and the Development of Black Insurgency*, 71, 85.

10. Social movement scholar Verta Taylor, writing primarily about the feminist movement, critiques the tendency of scholars of the social movements of the 1960s to promote an "immaculate conception" view of their origins, under which those movements are seen to have "emerged out of nowhere." To refute those views, Taylor traces how women's organizations that existed between the periods of first- and second-wave feminism held the ideas of that movement in "abeyance." Taylor defines this term as "a holding process by which movements

sustain themselves in nonreceptive political environments and provide continuity from one stage of mobilization to another." Verta Taylor, "Social Movement Continuity: The Women's Movement in Abeyance," *American Sociological Review* 54 (1989): 761–75. In a similar way, the turn-of-the-century civil rights organizations I study here preserved the ideas of the abolitionists and passed them on to later generations. But they also actively tested and transformed those ideas to meet new political and social circumstances, as I will show in detail as the book's narrative unfolds.

11. Similarly, historians continue to debate whether even the civil rights activism of the 1930s and 1940s deserves this classification. See, e.g., Arnesen, "Reconsidering the 'Long Civil Rights Movement.'"

12. See, e.g., Thornbrough, "The AAL," 512 ("the program of the NAACP, both in its objectives and methods, was essentially the program which Fortune had conceived for the Afro-American League twenty years earlier."); see also Robert C. Smith, *Encyclopedia of African American Politics* (New York: Facts On File, 2003), 70, 71 (describing the generally held understanding of a trajectory of civil rights organizing efforts from the AAL and the Niagara Movement to the NAACP).

13. In the vocabulary of social movement theory, the research questions I investigate are the following: "[W]hy do challenges take the forms that they do? What does the interaction between challengers and target tell us about the nature of domination in society? [and] Under what conditions do challenges originate, survive, and succeed?" See Elizabeth A. Armstrong and Mary Bernstein, "Culture, Power, and Institutions: A Multi-Institutional Politics Approach to Social Movements," *Sociological Theory* 26 (2008): 74, 76.

14. See, e.g., Jack M. Balkin, "Brown as Icon," in *What* Brown v. Board of Education *Should Have Said: The Nation's Top Legal Experts Rewrite America's Landmark Civil Rights Decision*, ed. Jack M. Balkin (New York: New York University Press, 2001), 3, 12 ("In the half century since *Brown*, it is clear that although the elimination of Jim Crow has done much good, blacks as a group still lag behind whites in many of the most important social measures of well-being and success—household income, infant mortality, life expectancy, educational opportunity, and employment levels"). As leading legal historian Kenneth Mack explains, legal liberalism's core elements include "courts as the primary engines of social transformation; formal conceptual categories such as rights and formal remedies such as school desegregation decrees, as the principal mechanisms for accomplishing that change; and a focus on reforming public institutions (or, in some versions, public and private institutions without much distinction) as a means of transforming the larger society." Mack, "Rethinking Civil Rights Lawyering," 258.

15. See, e.g., Goluboff, *Lost Promise* (detailing NAACP campaigns in the 1930s and 1940s to litigate economic rights issues); Brown-Nagin, *Courage to Dissent* (exploring generations of racial justice organizing spanning classic civil rights and welfare justice goals); Mayeri, *Reasoning from Race* (exploring myriad and overlapping strategies of 1960s' activist lawyers on both race and gender issues); Mack, "Rethinking Civil Rights Lawyering" (emphasizing race uplift and self-help aspects of African American civil rights lawyers' work in the interwar period); Lee, "Hotspots in a Cold War" (exploring the NAACP's use of administrative law strategies to pursue workers' rights issues). This literature is discussed in further detail in the conclusion.

16. Thus, for example, although I initially planned a full chapter on John Milholland and the Constitution League, space considerations forced me to relegate this interesting figure to a lengthy footnote in chapter 5 as well as short discussions in other parts of the text. Other national organizing attempts that were more ephemeral or tangential to the development of law-related early twentieth-century racial justice strategies likewise receive only passing mention, though they fully deserve more complete analysis in a work with different aims. Another painful choice forced by space limits involved restricting my discussion of the many international connections that influenced the leaders and organizations I write about here. I do mention these in passing, but that topic merits more extensive treatment in a work with a different focus as well.

17. I am not the first to notice this. As I discuss in further detail in chapter 4, a new generation of revisionist historians of the African American experience have been advancing various arguments in support of new understandings of race activism in this historical period.
These include Shawn Leigh Alexander, "We Know Our Rights and Have the Courage
to Defend Them" (PhD diss., University of Massachusetts at Amherst, 2004); see also
Alexander, *Army of Lions* (later book version of his dissertation; because the book came
out after these chapters were substantially completed I generally cite to his dissertation);
Blair L. M. Kelley, *Right to Ride: Streetcar Boycotts and African American Citizenship in the
Era of Plessy v. Ferguson* (Chapel Hill: University of North Carolina Press, 2010); Robert J.
Norrell, *Up from History: The Life of Booker T. Washington* (Cambridge, MA: Belknap Press,
2009); R. Volney Riser, *Defying Disfranchisement: Black Voting Rights Activism in the Jim
Crow South, 1890–1908* (Baton Rouge: Louisiana State Press, 2010), and earlier disserta-
tion candidate George Mason Miller, " 'A This Worldly Mission': The Life and Career of
Alexander Walters (1858–1917)" (PhD diss., State University of New York at Stony Brook,
1984). Some of this work (namely that of Alexander, Norell, and Riser) seeks to improve
Washington and his allies' reputations, while others' work seeks to show that race activists
during this period were testing the boundaries of the possible despite Washington's often
pernicious influence (Kelley, Miller). As I further explain in chapter 4, my views are closest
to Kelley's and Miller's.

Chapter 1

1. Paul Ortiz, *Emancipation Betrayed: The Hidden History of Black Organizing and White Violence
in Florida from Reconstruction to the Bloody Election of 1920* (Berkeley: University of California
Press, 2005), 23–24; Michael Newton, *The Invisible Empire: The Ku Klux Klan in Florida*
(Gainesville: University Press of Florida, 2001), 22–23; *Testimony of Emanuel Fortune Taken
by the Joint Select Committee to Inquire into the Condition of Affairs in the Late Insurrectionary
States: Miscellaneous and Florida, U.S. Congress* (Washington, DC: Government Printing
Office, 1872), 94–101.
2. Emma Lou Thornbrough, *T. Thomas Fortune: Militant Journalist* (Chicago: University of
Chicago Press, 1972), 17.
3. The basics of Fortune's early biography are from Thornbrough, *T. Thomas Fortune*, 1–22.
4. T. Thomas Fortune, "After War Times, Part 23," *Norfolk Journal and Guide*, Dec. 3, 1927, 16.
5. A small literature has begun to develop on Ransom, most of it focusing on his theological and institution-building contributions to the AME Church. The most comprehensive
work on Ransom is Calvin S. Morris, *Reverdy C. Ransom: Black Advocate of the Social Gospel*
(Lanham, MD: University Press of America, 1990). A shorter summary version can be found
in Calvin S. Morris, "Reverdy Ransom, the Social Gospel and Race," *Journal of Religious
Thought* 41 (1984): 7–21. Other helpful recent treatments include Cornelius L. Bynum, "An
Equal Chance in the Race for Life: Reverdy C. Ransom, Socialism, and the Social Gospel
Movement, 1890–1920," *Journal of African American History* 93 (2008): 1–20 (examining how
Ransom brought "progressive social science methodologies and reform initiatives to bear on
the problems confronting African Americans migrating to industrial centers"), and Annetta L.
Gomez-Jefferson, *The Sage of Tawawa: Reverdy Cassius Ransom, 1861–1959* (Kent, OH: Kent
State University Press, 2003). Gomez is the daughter of one of Ransom's mentees, Bishop
Joseph Gomez, and contributes invaluable insights into Ransom's contributions to the AME
Church. Another scholar whose work helped me understand Ransom is Terrell Dale Goddard,
"The Black Social Gospel in Chicago, 1896–1906: The Ministries of Reverdy C. Ransom and
Richard R. Wright, Jr.," *Journal of Negro History* 84 (1999): 227–46. An older work exam-
ining some valuable primary material is Donald Albert Drewett, "Ransom on Race and
Racism: The Racial and Social Thought of Reverdy Cassius Ransom—Preacher, Editor, and

Bishop in the African American Methodist Episcopal Church, 1861–1959" (PhD diss., Drew University, 1988). Ransom's social ministry work is helpfully examined in Michele Andrea Bowen-Spencer, "The Institutional Church and Social Settlement, 1900–1904: Reverdy C. Ransom's Church for the Black Masses" (master's thesis, University of North Carolina at Chapel Hill, 1994).

6. Reverdy C. Ransom, *The Pilgrimage of Harriet Ransom's Son* (Nashville: Sunday School Union, 1949), 15; Morris, *Reverdy C. Ransom,* 15.

7. Morris, *Reverdy C. Ransom,* 25–27.

8. Ransom, *Pilgrimage,* 30–32. For Ransom's account of his days at Wilberforce, see Reverdy C. Ransom, *School Days at Wilberforce* (Springfield, OH: New Era, 1892).

9. On Oberlin's record in educating African American students, see W. E. Bigglestone, "Oberlin College and the Negro Student, 1865–1940," *Journal of Negro History* 56 (1971): 198–219; James Oliver Horton, "Black Education at Oberlin College: A Controversial Commitment," *Journal of Negro Education* 54 (1985): 477–99; Cally L. Waite, "The Segregation of Black Students at Oberlin College after Reconstruction," *History of Education Quarterly* 41 (2001): 344–64.

10. Ransom, *Pilgrimage,* 33. It is possible to track this incident in contemporaneously published accounts in Oberlin sources. See Bigglestone, "Oberlin College," 200–201, and accompanying notes; Waite, "Oberlin College after Reconstruction," 352–55, and accompanying notes.

11. Ransom, *Pilgrimage,* 39.

12. On the social gospel movement, see generally Ralph E. Luker, *The Social Gospel in Black and White: American Racial Reform, 1885–1912* (Chapel Hill: University of North Carolina Press, 1991).

13. Morris, *Reverdy C. Ransom,* 64.

14. Ibid., 30.

15. Ransom, *Pilgrimage,* 35; Ransom, *School Days.*

16. Ransom, *Pilgrimage,* 45; Jessie Carney Smith, ed., *Notable Black American Women,* vol. 2 (Detroit: Gale Research, 2003), 542. Emma Ransom's work eventually led to the naming of a YWCA residence building in New York City in her honor (ibid.).

17. Ransom, *Pilgrimage,* 49.

18. Morris, *Reverdy C. Ransom,* 103–104.

19. Ibid., 104; Ransom, *Pilgrimage,* 69.

20. Ransom, *Pilgrimage,* 67.

21. David A. Gerber, *Black Ohio and the Color Line, 1860–1915* (Urbana: University of Illinois Press, 1976), provides a rich account of late nineteenth-century African American politics in Ohio. On Cleveland and Harry S. Smith, see especially ibid., 122, 128–29, 135, 175, 251–54. On Smith's role in the Niagara Movement, see Patrick H. Carroll, "The 1905 Niagara Movement Attendants: An Interpretative Analysis of their Lives and Ideologies" (bachelor's thesis, College of the Holy Cross), 108. Smith was also a member of the NAACP's Committee of 100. Morris, *Reverdy C. Ransom,* 133.

22. Rayford W. Logan and Michael R. Winston, eds., *Dictionary of American Negro Biography* (New York: W. W. Norton, 1982), 564–65.

23. Morris, *Reverdy C. Ransom,* 120.

24. Some of the speeches in this program are collected in John Henry Barrows, ed., *The World's Parliament of Religions: An Illustrated and Popular Story of the World's First Parliament of Religions held in Chicago in connection with the Columbian Exposition of 1893,* 2 vols. (Chicago: Parliament, 1893), 1056, 1068, 1101 (contains addresses of social gospel adherents such as Professor Richard T. Ely and Rev. Washington Gladden, as well as Bishop Benjamin W. Arnett and Fanny Barrier Williams, both specifically speaking to race issues). On the transatlantic character of both the social gospel and settlement house movements, see generally Daniel T. Rodgers, *Atlantic Crossings: Social Politics in a Progressive Age* (Cambridge, MA: Harvard University Press, 1998), 63–65.

25. Morris, *Reverdy C. Ransom,* 12 (quoting reports of Ransom's colleague that the Parliament of Religions was where "Ransom fell under the influence of the social gospel and advocates such as Jane Addams and Reverend Graham Taylor").

26. On Addams, Taylor, and other white settlement house leaders' support of Ransom's work in Chicago, see Ransom, *Pilgrimage,* 104.

27. To distinguish Mary Church Terrell from her husband, Robert Terrell, who also plays a role in this narrative, I refer to her as Church Terrell.

28. Waite, "Oberlin College after Reconstruction," 362.

29. Beverly Washington Jones, "Quest for Equality: The Life of Mary Eliza Church Terrell, 1863–1954" (PhD diss., University of North Carolina, Chapel Hill, 1980), 14.

30. On Mary Church Terrell generally see Beverly W. Jones, "Mary Church Terrell and the National Association of Colored Women, 1896–1901," *Journal of Negro History* 67 (1982): 20–33.

31. See generally Constance McLaughlin Green, *The Secret City: A History of Race Relations in the Nation's Capital* (Princeton: Princeton University Press, 1967), 17.

32. Ibid., 133.

33. Mary Church Terrell, "Society among the Colored People of Washington, D.C.," *Voice of the Negro* 1 (1904): 150–56; "Christmas at the White House," ibid., 593–600; "The Social Functions during Inauguration Week, *Voice of the Negro* 2 (1905): 237–42.

34. Mary Church Terrell, "Peonage in the United States: The Convict Lease System and Chain Gangs" (1906), draft in Mary Church Terrell Papers, MCTPLOC, later published in *Nineteenth Century* 62 (August 1907), 306–22.

35. Mary Church Terrell, *Voice of the Negro* 2 (1905): 182, 186.

36. Mary Church Terrell, *A Colored Woman in a White World* (New York: G. K. Hall, 1996), 18.

37. Mary Church Terrell, "The Mission of the Meddler," *Voice of the Negro* 2 (1906): 566, 568.

38. See, e.g., Jane Addams, *"The Subjective Value of Social Settlements"* (n.d., reprint New Haven, CT: Research Publications, 1977) (bemoaning the results when "cultivated people" do not involve themselves with "a certain portion of the population," from which "all social advantages are persistently withheld").

39. See, e.g., MWOP, "Financial Records, 1915" (showing estimated income from stock of $510 and rental income of $850, along with a gift from her brother of $500 and salary of $305. Her total estimated budget for the year, including small amounts of income from writing and food donations, was $2,500).

40. Victor Michael Glasberg, "The Emergence of White Liberalism: The Founders of the NAACP and American Racial Attitudes" (PhD diss., Harvard University, 1971), 44 (quoting correspondence).

41. James Boylan, *Revolutionary Lives: Anna Strunsky and William English Walling* (Amherst: University of Massachusetts Press, 1998), 265–66.

42. For an example of Ovington's romantic essentialist tendencies, see Mary White Ovington, *Half a Man: The Status of the Negro in New York* (New York: Hill and Wang, 1969, first published 1911 by New York: Longmans, Green), 125 (describing Italians' "finer feeling for beauty and wholesome gaiety," Jews' "great intellectual achievements," and African Americans' "happy spontaneity"). Citations refer to the Hill and Wang edition. Compare W.E.B. Du Bois, "The Conservation of Races," *Occasional Papers,* no. 2 (published by American Negro Academy, 1897), 9 ("The English nation stood for constitutional liberty and commercial freedom; the German nation for science and philosophy; the Romance nations stood for literature and art; and [each of] the other race groups [is] striving, each in its own way, to develop for civilization its particular message, its particular ideal").

43. On Ovington's background, see Charles Flint Kellogg, "Introduction," in Ovington, *Half a Man,* xi, xii; Carolyn Wedin, *Inheritors of the Spirit: Mary White Ovington and the Founding of the NAACP* (New York: John Wiley and Sons, 1998), 56–57, 70, 277–78.

44. Mary W. Ovington to W.E.B. Du Bois, Aug. 8, 1906, NMA, W.E.B. Du Bois Library, Special Collections, at http://www.library.umass.edu/spcoll/dubois/?page_id=896 (hereinafter NMA).

45. In 1914, in the midst of his struggles with Villard, Du Bois wrote to Ovington, "your unfailing and unselfish devotion to our cause has been a beacon light spreading hope when every other light seemed dim." W.E.B. Du Bois to Mary White Ovington, Nov. 5, 1914, MWOP. On the tense early relationships within the NAACP national office, see Charles Flint Kellogg, *NAACP* (Baltimore: Johns Hopkins Press, 1967), 89–115.

46. See, e.g., David Levering Lewis, *W.E.B. Du Bois: Biography of a Race, 1868–1919* (New York: Henry Holt, 1993); Adolph L. Reed Jr., *W.E.B. Du Bois and American Political Thought: Fabianism and the Color Line* (New York: Oxford University Press, 1997); Manning Marable, *W.E.B. Du Bois: Black Radical Democrat* (Boston: Twayne, 1986).

47. Biographical information on Bulkley comes from J. W. Gibson and W. H. Crogman, *Progress of a Race: or, The Remarkable Advancement of the American Negro, from the Bondage of Slavery, Ignorance, and Poverty to the Freedom of Citizenship, Intelligence, Affluence, Honor and Trust* (Miami: Mnemosyne, 1969; first published 1902 by J. L. Nichols), 529–30. Citations refer to the Mnemosyne edition; Margaret Peckham Motes, *Free Blacks and Mulattos in South Carolina: 1850 Census* (Baltimore: Clearfield Press, 2000), 31; Michele V. Ronnick, "Abstract: William Lewis Bulkley (1861–1933): The First African American to Earn a Doctorate in Latin" (unpublished), apaclassics.org/images/uploads/documents/abstracts/Ronnick_38. pdf; "Colored School Principal: William L. Bulkley to Be Nominated to Public School No. 80," *NYT*, Feb. 18, 1901; Gilbert Osofsky, "Progressivism and the Negro: New York: 1900-1915," *American Quarterly* 16 (1964): 153–68.

48. William L. Bulkley, "The School as a Social Center," *Charities* 15 (Oct. 7, 1905): 76–78; William L. Bulkley, "The Industrial Condition of the Negro in New York City," *Annals of the American Academy of Political and Social Science* 27 (1906): 128–34; Osofsky, "Progressivism," 164 (citing "A Slave Boy, Now a Professor," *Success*, April 8, 1899, and *NYA*, July 22, 1909).

Chapter 2

1. See, e.g., John Mercer Langston, "Citizenship and the Ballot," in *Freedom and Citizenship: Selected Lectures and Addresses* (Washington, DC: Rufus H. Darby, 1883), 99 (hereinafter Langston, *Lectures*).

2. John Mercer Langston, *From the Virginia Plantation to the National Capitol; or, the First and Only Negro Representative in Congress from the Old Dominion* (Hartford: American Publishing, 1894), 104–13.

3. Ibid., 125.

4. On Langston's life until 1865, see generally William Cheek and Aimee Lee Cheek, *John Mercer Langston and the Fight for Black Freedom, 1829–65* (Urbana: University of Illinois Press, 1989).

5. Rayford W. Logan, *Howard University: The First Hundred Years, 1867–1967* (New York: New York University Press, 1968), 79–80.

6. Langston, "Citizenship and the Ballot," in *Lectures*, 100.

7. Linda Przybyszewski, *The Republic according to John Marshall Harlan* (Chapel Hill: University of North Carolina Press, 1999), 81–7, 114–15 (discussing this late nineteenth-century tax-onomy of rights).

8. Slaughter-House Cases, 83 U.S. 36, 51–56 (1872) (describing the privileges and immunities of citizens of the United States as only those fundamental to the citizens of all free governments).

9. The Civil Rights Cases, 109 U.S. 3 (1883).

10. Przybyszewski, *Republic According to Harlan*, 99–100.

11. Ibid., 81–117.

12. Langston, "Equality before the Law," in *Lectures*, 154 (delivered at Oberlin College in 1874).

13. Langston, "Eulogy on Charles Sumner," in *Lectures*, 178 (delivered at Howard University on Apr. 24, 1874).

14. Ibid., 178–79.

15. 163 U.S. 537 (1896).

16. See, e.g., Elaine Kaplan Freeman, "Harvey Johnson and Everett Waring, a Study of Leadership in the Baltimore Negro Community, 1880–1900" (master's thesis, George Washington University, 1968), 24 (discussing Rev. Johnson of the Brotherhood of Liberty's faith in law as the best strategy to promote African American citizenship rights).

17. Thornbrough, *T. Thomas Fortune*, 37.

18. Ibid., 41.

19. See, e.g., "Eleven Men Murdered—Is the White South Civilized?" *NYA*, Mar. 21, 1891.

20. Philip S. Foner, *Organized Labor and the Black Worker, 1619–1973* (New York: Praeger, 1974), 47–63.

21. See, e.g., Mrs. N. F. Mossell, "Our Women's Department," *NYA*, May 8, 1886.

22. See, e.g., "Mr. Fortune of the West: Glances at Indianapolis and Chicago," *NYA*, Aug. 11, 1888 (describing meeting Wells); T. Thomas Fortune, "Afro-American Women," *NYA*, Apr. 25, 1891 (describing African American women's accomplishments as physicians and other professionals and concluding that "women are taking care of themselves"); "Woman Suffragists," *NYF*, Dec. 20, 1884 (report of Frederick Douglass's speech at a state women's suffrage convention); "Madam Marie Selika: Woman's Suffrage Convention," *NYF*, Nov. 7, 1885 (describing a women's suffrage convention in Boston presided over by Archibald Grimké); "The Nation's Capital," *NYG*, Sept. 13, 1884 (reporting that "Belva A. Lockwood, one of the most distinguished lawyers at the capital," had accepted the women's rights nomination for president). See also Paula J. Giddings, *Ida: A Sword among Lions* (New York: Amistad, 2008) 151, 231–32 (describing Fortune's support for Wells's career).

23. "Prejudice against Jews," *NYF*, July 23, 1887 (sympathizing with the indignant feelings of Jews about discrimination they faced).

24. See, e.g., "Mr. Downing on Ireland: What Irishmen Have Done for Freedom," *NYF*, Jan. 9, 1886.

25. Archibald Grimké was a prominent lawyer who never became active in the AAL or the AAC but offered often-incisive independent commentary while pursuing a diplomatic career. See Dickson D. Bruce, *Archibald Grimké: Portrait of a Black Independent* (Baton Rouge: Louisiana State University Press, 1993).

26. T. Thomas Fortune, *Black and White: Land, Labor, and Politics in the South* (New York: Washington Square Press, 2007, first published 1884 by Fords, Howard, and Hubert), 72. Citations refer to the Washington Square Press edition.

27. See John Ruskin, *Unto This Last and Other Writings*, ed. Clive Wilmer (London: Penguin Press, 1985, 1994). First printed 1862 in *Cornhill Magazine*.

28. Fortune, *Black and White*, xxxii.

29. Fortune called on African Americans to break away from the Republican Party, which had betrayed them both during and after Reconstruction. He also saw that the Democratic Party was no friend to African Americans; what was needed was political independence so that African Americans could make politicians work for their votes (ibid., 69–79). This was a theme to which Fortune would return repeatedly in the pages of his paper, and one that likewise shaped his organizational plan for the Afro-American League (AAL).

    The debate about higher education concerned the respective virtues of classical higher education, emphasizing languages, the classics, and rhetoric, versus what was often referred to as "industrial" education, centered on more practical, often manual or vocational, skills. This is one of the points of disagreement often cited in summarizing the clash between Booker T. Washington and W.E.B. Du Bois. It is possible to make too much of this disagreement, however, since in actuality all significant race organizations took care to formally endorse both educational routes. Fortune brought a personal vehemence to the topic, though it is hard to see why any personal bitterness about his own educational experiences underlay his views. His exposure at Howard University to a classical education, emphasizing rhetoric, elocution, and classical languages, helped prepare him for his own subsequent career as a journalist— although his manual typesetting skills were also essential. Fortune may have been writing less out of personal experience than out of sympathetic identification with many of his cohorts' frustration at finding themselves continually thwarted by discrimination from success in professional careers. As Fortune argued, "I maintain that any education is false which is unsuited to the condition and the prospects of the student. To educate him for a lawyer when there are no clients, for medicine when the patients, although numerous, are too poor to give him a living income, to fill his head with Latin and Greek as a teacher when the people he is to teach are to be instructed in the *a b c's*—such education is a waste..." (Fortune, *Black and White*, 47).

Opponents of industrial education sometimes argued that advocating vocational training was equivalent to admitting African American inferiority and entitlement to a less advanced form of education than that which white students could routinely expect. But that was far from Fortune's point. To Fortune, there was nothing degrading about being a member of the laboring class; rather, it was there that human dignity rested. Those who deserved to be looked at askance, as members of a "peculiar" class that "stand off by themselves," were those few African Americans who had higher educations and elitist aspirations. Ibid., 38 (emphasis omitted). Fortune's profession (though certainly not his income) placed him in this elite class of intellectuals, but his allegiance rested with laborers.

30. These lawsuits against transportation providers to protest ill treatment asserted a variety of legal theories, including common-law doctrines that required common carriers to transport all passengers willing to pay, admiralty law, the Interstate Commerce Act (enacted in 1887), and federal civil rights statutes (enacted in 1868 and 1875). Fortune followed these developments and discussed cases with great interest. Scholarly work documenting the frequency of, and various case theories underlying, these lawsuits includes David S. Bogen, "Precursors of Rosa Parks: Maryland Transportation Cases between the Civil War and the Beginning of World War I," *Maryland Law Review* 63 (2004): 721, 723–34; Patricia Hagler Minter, "The Failure of Freedom: Class, Gender, and the Evolution of Segregated Transit Law in the Nineteenth-Century South," *Chicago-Kent Law Review* 70 (1995): 993–1009; Barbara Y. Welke, "When All the Women Were White, and All the Blacks Were Men: Gender, Class, Race, and the Road to *Plessy*, 1855–1914," *Law and History Review* 13 (1995): 261–316; and Joseph R. Palmore, "The Not-So-Strange Career of Interstate Jim Crow: Race, Transportation, and the Dormant Commerce Clause, 1878–1946," *Virginia Law Review* 83 (1997): 1733–1817.
31. "Mr. Justice Harlan's Opinion of Civil Rights," *NYG*, Nov. 24, 1883.
32. 106 U.S. 629 (1882).
33. 109 U.S. 3 (1883).
34. 106 U.S. 583 (1883).
35. 92 U.S. 542 (1875).
36. Eric Foner, *Reconstruction: America's Unfinished Revolution, 1863–1867* (New York: Harper and Row, 1988), 437.
37. Cruikshank, 92 U.S. at 548, 554, 555 (emphasis added).
38. United States v. Reese, 92 U.S. 214, 215, 220 (1875).
39. United States v. Harris, 106 U.S. 629, 629–30 (1882).
40. Ibid., 634, 644, 641.
41. See, e.g., "Civil Rights Laws," *NYG*, Feb. 3, 1883; "Is There Any Law for the Negro?," *NYG*, Feb. 17, 1883; "The Ku-Klux Law," *NYG*, Jan. 27, 1883.
42. Civil Rights Cases, 109 U.S. 3, 3–5, 9 (1883). On the significance of gender in these "ladies' car" cases, see generally Welke, "When All the Women Were White."
43. Civil Rights Cases, 109 U.S. at 14.
44. Ibid. The Court would reach that question, again with results adverse to the civil rights cause, in *Plessy v. Ferguson*, 163 U.S. 537 (1896).
45. Civil Rights Cases, 109 U.S. at 20, 22, 24, 25.
46. Ibid., 36 (Harlan, J., dissenting).
47. Ibid., 39.

48. "Between Two Fires," *NYG*, Oct. 27, 1883.

49. For a thorough discussion of the responses of many African American statesmen, journalists, and other leaders to the *Civil Rights Cases*, see Marianne L. Engelman Lado, "A Question of Justice: African-American Legal Perspectives on the 1883 *Civil Rights Cases*," *Chicago-Kent Law Review* 70 (1995): 1123–95.

50. "The Civil Rights Decision," *NYG*, Oct. 20, 1883.

51. Pace v. Alabama, 106 U.S 583, 584 (1883).

52. 163 U.S. 537 (1896).

53. Pace, 106 U.S. at 585.

54. "The Southern Problem," *NYG*, Mar. 3, 1883.

55. "Troubled Waters," *NYG*, Mar. 3, 1883; "Social Disorders," *NYG*, Mar. 3, 1883 ("[W]e were the stepping stones of ambitious men who treated us with contempt when we could no longer be used as tools."); "The Civil Rights Decision" (the Republican party has "tried the faith of the colored man. It has gradually stripped him of all the rights which had been given to him for his valor," while the Democratic party is "a narrow-minded, corrupt, bloody fraud").

56. Daniel W. Crofts, "The Black Response to the Blair Education Bill," *Journal of Southern History* 37 (1971): 41–65; Allen J. Going, "The South and the Blair Education Bill," *Mississippi Valley History Review* 44 (1957): 267–90.

57. Going, "Blair Education Bill," 275.

58. Crofts, "The Black Response," 43; Going, "Blair Education Bill," 273–90.

59. Crofts, "The Black Response," 53 (reporting the surprise of one egalitarian white congressman on discovering that African American Baptist ministers with whom he met in Washington, DC, supported segregated education). On the separate schools debate, see "Mixed or Separate Schools: Lack of Business Enterprise by Race Journals," *NYF*, May 29, 1886 (opposing the position of a speaker at the Bethel Literary Society in Washington, DC, who had advocated separate schools). A good summary of late nineteenth-century African American intellectuals' debate on this question is in Meier, *Negro Thought*, 48–49.

60. See Fortune, *Black and White*, 70–71.

61. "Status of the Race: Mr. Fortune before the United States Senate Committee on Education and Labor," *NYG*, Sept. 22, 1883.

62. "The Blair Education Bill," *NYF*, Jan. 1, 1887.

63. "Status of the Race."

64. See, e.g., "Rambles in the South: Industrial Slavery in South Carolina," *NYF*, May 16, 1885 (condemning the system of "industrial slavery" in South Carolina); lead editorial, *NYF*, Dec. 3, 1886 (discussing the "southern labor question"); lead editorial, *NYF*, Sept. 18, 1886 (analyzing states' enactment of laws to keep "industrial slaves' noses to the grindstone"); "Victorious Strikers," *NYF*, Feb. 19, 1887 (reporting on a strike of guano workers in Alabama); "The Rich and the Poor," *NYG*, Dec. 29, 1883 (describing as "among the most difficult problems" this issue of how millions of industrious African American laborers in the South "are to be protected against deliberate robbery, and robbery viler still because clothed in the garb of legislative enactment"); "Infamies of the Southern Convict Lease System," *NYG*, Feb. 2, 1884 ("[W]e unhesitatingly pronounce the penal systems of the twelve Southern States which practice the 'Convict Lease System' as an open violation of the 13th article of the Federal Constitution").

65. "The Rich and the Poor."

66. See, e.g., "Labor Upheavals," *NYF*, Mar. 20, 1886 (reporting on the Knights of Labor and maintaining that "colored men all over the Union are rapidly becoming affiliated with the organization," a fact "[w]e predicted…in 'Black and White,' but we did not expect so speedy a consummation of [our] prediction"); "Colored Knights of Labor in Arkansas," *NYF*, July 17, 1886 (reporting on a Knights of Labor strike in Arkansas and tying it to an analysis of peonage labor as a "virtual continuation of the slave system"); *NYF*, Oct. 9, 1886 (the Knights of Labor "took Southern prejudice, arrogance and intolerance by the throat and gave it the most furious shaking it has had since the war" and refused "to sanction the discrimination made against

their colored fellow-member"); "Boston's Labor Movement: The True Lesson of Judge Ruffin's Funeral," *NYF,* Dec. 11, 1886 (reporting on a Knights of Labor meeting in Boston).

67. See, e.g., "The Economic and Civil Conditions North and South," *NYF,* Feb. 12, 1887 (stating that the time will come "when the white and black masses of the South will recognize that they have mutual interests"). By the end of the decade, labor confrontations had grown increasingly violent, and Jim Crow had infected the white-led labor movement just as it had the rest of the country. Fortune began to publish critical reports about race prejudice within the labor movement but continued to express hope that the labor movement would take a turn in a positive direction. See, e.g., M. W. Caldwell, "Civil Rights in Tennessee: Manifestations of Prejudice in Nashville," *NYA,* July 5, 1890, 3 (reporting on the "ludicrous discrimination" of the railroad unions).

68. See "Pernicious Labor Teachings," *NYF,* May 1, 1886.

69. "Some Crude Notions of Capital and Labor," *NYF,* May 22, 1886. For a cross-generational exploration of the Stewart family, see Albert S. Broussard, *African-American Odyssey: The Stewarts, 1853–1963* (Lawrence: University Press of Kansas, 1998). T. McCants Stewart was an energetic, peripatetic race leader with whom Fortune remained in touch throughout his life. Stewart had been born of free but not elite parents in Charleston, South Carolina, in 1853. After attending an American Missionary Association school, he enrolled at Howard University in 1869 but left in 1873 to enroll instead at the University of South Carolina, where he obtained both his BA and law degrees in 1875. He then practiced law, taught in a state agricultural and mechanical school, and in 1878 began theological training at Princeton. Leaving before completing the degree, Stewart was ordained as an AME minister in 1880 and granted a prestigious assignment as the pastor of the Bethel AME church in New York City that same year.

By 1882, Stewart had begun a lifelong intermittent connection with the nation of Liberia, accepting a position as a professor at Liberia College. Three years later he was back in New York City, having fallen out with the school's administration. In 1886 Stewart obtained admission to the New York bar and set up a law practice in the financial district, receiving frequent favorable profiles and reports in his close friend Fortune's newspaper. See, e.g., "Resumes His Law Practice: T. McCants Stewart to Practice Law Again," *NYF,* Jan. 9, 1886; "Mr. Stewart's Practice," *NYF,* Feb. 5, 1887. Stewart was also a frequent contributor to and editorialist in Fortune's papers and in 1887 became for a time a copublisher as well. An engaging speaker, Stewart spent a good deal of time traveling to various literary societies and other gatherings to lecture on his experiences in Liberia and his views on intraracial cooperation. See, e.g., untitled announcement, *NYF,* Feb. 27, 1886 (publicizing a Stewart lecture on "The Necessity of co-operation among Africo-Americans"); "Brooklyn Literary Union: Lawyer Stewart's Lecture on Co-operation," *NYF,* Oct. 23, 1886 (describing Stewart's talk on the need for race pride).

Although Stewart and Fortune agreed on many subjects, they did not see eye to eye on all matters. One such difference involved labor unions, as already discussed; another involved the two men's views about African repatriation. Fortune disapproved of the Back-to-Africa movement, believing that African Americans' future lay in the United States, whereas Stewart retained a lifelong attachment to Liberia. Despite his first unsuccessful experience there, Stewart returned to Liberia in 1906 and established a law practice in Monrovia. In 1906 he was asked to revise Liberia's statutes and completed this task that year and then again in 1911. In 1912 he became an associate justice of the Liberian Supreme Court, but in 1914 he was removed from that position, apparently for refusing to condone corruption by the country's president and legislature. He left Liberia, living for periods after that in London and the Virgin Islands and traveling frequently to the United States. On his death in 1923 he was, at his request, buried with the Liberian flag. Broussard, *African-American Odyssey,* 88, 90, 92, 100.

70. Editorial, *NYF,* Nov. 13, 1886.

71. See Du Bois, "The Conservation of Races" (arguing that African Americans should maintain a separate identity, along with separate educational, business, and cultural institutions, while also demanding equal civil and political rights); August Meier, "Negro Class Structure and

Ideology in the Age of Booker T. Washington," *Phylon* 23 (1962): 258, 260 (describing the ideology of race "uplift" as arising from "the shift in the economic basis of the Negro bourgeoisie"); John Dittmer, *Black Georgia in the Progressive Era: 1900–1920* (Urbana: University of Illinois Press, 1977), 35, 59 (discussing separatism in Georgia); Mark R. Schneider, *Boston Confronts Jim Crow, 1890–1920* (Boston: Northeastern University Press, 1997) (describing the rise of Jim Crow in New England).

72. On the difference between the Knights of Labor and trade unionism, see Foner, *Organized Labor*, 56 ("The reform program of the Knights stressed land reform, increased education, and workers' cooperatives, matters of minor interest to the national trade unions, which concentrated on higher wages, shorter hours, and improved working conditions").

73. James Green, *Death in the Haymarket: A Story of Chicago, the First Labor Movement and the Bombing that Divided Gilded Age America* (New York: Pantheon Books, 2006), 145–91. The Haymarket riot involved a massive strike in Chicago that ended in multiple deaths of civilians and police officers after unknown persons threw a bomb into the crowd. It marked the culmination of a growing wave of strikes called primarily by the craft union movement to force employers to grant an eight-hour day and other labor concessions.

74. "The Futility of Strikes and Boycotts," *NYF*, May 8, 1886.

75. See Ida B. Wells-Barnett, "Mob Rule in New Orleans," in *Southern Horrors and Other Writings: The Anti-Lynching Campaign of Ida B. Wells, 1892–1900*, ed. Jacqueline Jones Royster (Boston: Bedford/St. Martins, 1997), 158.

76. See Foner, *Organized Labor*, 78 n.†.

77. See, e.g., "Shall We Help Ireland?" *NYF*, Jan. 9, 1886 (arguing that, like the Irish, African Americans should strike back rather than "run[ning] like a deer").

Chapter 3

1. See Thornbrough, *T. Thomas Fortune*, 105–106 (describing an 1884 speech by Fortune calling for a new national organization); Alexander, *Army of Lions*, xviii and xxxiiin42 (describing several 1884 articles making this proposal); "A Proposed Afro-American National League," *NYF*, May 28, 1887 (making a detailed proposal); see generally Emma Lou Thornbrough, "The National Afro-American League, 1887–1908," *Journal of Southern History* 27 (1961): 494–512 (describing Fortune's process in coming up with the idea for the league).

2. "Proposed Afro-American National League."

3. "The Afro-American League," *NYF*, June 4, 1887.

4. Ibid.

5. Ibid.

6. On the multiple national organizing efforts initiated at the time, see "The Negroes Divided," *WB*, Dec. 14, 1889 ("it has now come to light that three different sets of men have issued calls for national conventions"). On the national and state African American convention movement, see Meier, *Negro Thought*, 4–10 (describing various conventions). As Meier notes, the focus of these conventions swung between civil rights issues in some meetings and economic advancement and labor issues in others (ibid., 8–9). On Fortune's plans for his proposed organization's priorities, see "Education in the South," *NYG*, Sept. 15, 1883; "The Proposed Conference," *NYG*, Feb. 16, 1884.

7. "Shall We Help Ireland?" *NYF*, Jan. 9, 1886.

8. "Equal Rights League," *NYF*, June 19, 1886.

9. Jones v. United States, 137 U.S. 202 (1890); Rev. W. M. Alexander, *The Brotherhood of Liberty: Or Our Day in Court, Including the Navassa Case* (Baltimore: Printing Office of J. F. Weishamrel, 1891) (pamphlet describing the Brotherhood of Liberty's campaigns); Henry J. McGuinn, "Equal Protection of the Law and Fair Trials in Maryland," *Journal of Negro History* 24 (1939): 143, 151–53 (describing the Brotherhood's work in the Navassa case). See generally Freeman, "Harvey Johnson and Everett Waring."

10. The 1883 *Civil Rights Cases* led to many efforts in the North to pass state civil rights protections, and some local and regional groups affiliated with the AAL took part in these efforts. On the successful initiatives of civil rights activists in Northern states to pass state legislation in the wake of the 1883 *Civil Rights Cases,* see generally Leslie H. Fishel Jr., "The Genesis of the First Wisconsin Civil Rights Act," *Wisconsin Magazine of History* 49 (Summer 1966): 324–33. Examples of reports of cases filed under such statutes include "Ohio's Civil Rights Law," *CG,* Nov. 30, 1898 (describing a jury verdict in favor of a plaintiff in a case filed under Harry Smith's civil rights law); "Civil Rights Case," *WB,* June 5, 1897 (describing a case a DC lawyer filed against an eating saloon under an 1873 statute); "Teach Them the Law," *Illinois Record,* May 7, 1898, 2 (describing several cases filed under an Illinois state law prohibiting discrimination by innkeepers).

11. Joseph S. Davis, letter to the editor, "Baltimore Lawyer's View of the Case," *NYF,* July 16, 1887.

12. See, e.g., "A League in Rhode Island," *NYA,* Dec. 24, 1887 (Rhode Island); "An Afro-American League," *NYF,* June 11, 1887 (Boston); "In Readiness for Chicago," *NYA,* Dec. 28, 1889 (New Jersey, Pennsylvania, Illinois, and Ohio); "Kansas State Convention," *NYF,* Oct. 8, 1887 (Kansas); "League Project Booming," *NYA,* Nov. 16, 1889 (Syracuse, San Francisco, Washington, DC, New York, and Knoxville); "League Sentiment Growing," *NYA,* Nov. 9, 1889 (Minnesota and Philadelphia); "New London Notes," *NYF,* Oct. 1, 1887 (New London); "Now for Chicago Leaguers," *NYA,* Dec. 7, 1889 (Cleveland); "The Afro-American League," *NYF,* July 9, 1887 (hereinafter "The Afro-American League, July 9, 1887") (Louisville); "The Afro-American League," *NYF,* June 25, 1887 (hereinafter "The Afro-American League, June 25, 1887") (Baltimore).

13. "League Sentiment Growing." On McGhee see Paul D. Nelson, *Fredrick L. McGhee: A Life on the Color Line, 1861–1912* (St. Paul: Minnesota Historical Society Press, 2002), 131–32.

14. "Now for Chicago Leaguers."

15. Fortune published many letters and columns supporting his call for creating the league but published some criticism and dissent as well. See, e.g., ibid. (the *Christian Monitor* believed league organizing should slow down, whereas the *Bee,* a Washington, DC–based African American newspaper, wanted an equal rights league, an idea to which Fortune would "not consent"); "The Afro-American League," *NYF,* June 25, 1887 (publishing a letter urging the organization of state leagues before calling a national convention); "The Afro-American League," *NYF,* July 2, 1887 (publishing an article arguing that the evils the league wished to address were not amenable to political treatment); "The Florida Facts," *NYF,* Aug. 13, 1887 (league idea opposed in Florida).

16. J. C. Price, "The Afro-American League," *NYA,* Oct. 11, 1890.

17. "Importance of the League Meeting," *NYA,* Jan. 4, 1890.

18. See "The League Convention," *NYA,* Feb. 1, 1890 (reporting that the "uproar which the newspapers chronicled…was of a mild character, the result rather of the desire of each delegate to have something to say than a disposition to be boisterous" and describing how a "gavel had not been secured for the chairman," so that a delegate had "contributed to the humor of the situation by handing [Fortune] a hayseed looking umbrella").

19. Ibid.

20. See Thornbrough, "National Afro-American League," 499.

21. "A.C.E.R. Association," *DP,* Feb. 14, 1890.

22. "Opinion Divided in Boston," *NYA,* Feb. 15, 1890: "Endorsing the Lodge Bill"; "The American Citizens' Civil Rights Association," *NYA,* Feb. 15, 1890, 2 (urging union of the AAC and Civil Rights Association).

23. "A League in Rhode Island," *NYA,* July 11, 1891 (Rhode Island league); "Personal and League Notes," *NYA,* June 6, 1891 (Nebraska and Minnesota state leagues); "Personal and League Notes," *NYA,* May 30, 1891 (Harrisburg, Pennsylvania, convention); "Civil and Public Rights," *NYA,* Apr. 12, 1890 (New York civil rights legislation drafted by supporters of the New York league); "Insurance Discrimination," *NYA,* May 17, 1890 (Albany league's progress on insurance legislation); "New York State League," *NYA,* May 9, 1891 (state AAL convention at which

Fortune spoke); "The Civil Rights Measure," *NYA*, Apr. 26, 1890 (reporting on the hotel industry's opposition to the Albany league's work on antidiscrimination legislation as well as introduction of another bill banning discrimination in insurance); "The New York League on Deck," *NYA*, Mar. 1, 1890 (discussing the New York league's work with a committee on Civil Rights); "Work of the Albany League," *NYA*, Mar. 28, 1891 (insurance bill passes); "Insurance Bill Signed," *NYA*, Apr. 11, 1891.

24. "The Life Insurance Discriminations," *NYA*, March 29, 1890; "Insurance Discrimination," *NYA*, May 17, 1890, 4.

25. "The New York State League," *NYA*, May 31, 1890.

26. "Counsel to the State League," *NYA*, June 14, 1890.

27. "Insurance Discrimination."

28. "The Insurance Bill Passed," *NYA*, Mar. 21, 1891, 2; "Work of the Albany League," *NYA*, Mar. 28, 1891, 4.

29. "Insurance Bill Signed. Analysis of the Influences that Secured its Passage—An Argument for Division," *NYA*, Apr. 11, 1891.

30. "A Brutal Police Outrage," *NYA*, June 7, 1890, 1.

31. "Civil Rights in New York State," *NYA*, June 14, 1890.

32. "The Southern Problem Transferred," *IF*, June 14, 1890 (an Indianapolis paper noting that the "New York problem is the same as the Georgia problem" and "[w]e hope to see the affair thoroughly ventilated in the courts"); "The Press on the Outrage," *NYA*, June 21, 1890, 2 (quoting the *Brooklyn Sentinel:* "Make It a Test Case, Bro. Fortune").

33. See, e.g., "Fortune Prosecution Fund," *NYA*, June 5, 1890 (listing contributions totaling $53 to a prosecution fund"); E. L. Thornton, "Fortune Prosecution Fund," *NYA*, Sept. 13, 1890; "Fortune Prosecution Fund," *NYA*, Aug. 9, 1890 (listing contributions totaling $82.62 deposited with Stewart); "Make It a Test Case," *IF*, June 28, 1890, 3 (urging the AAL to make the Fortune incident a test case); "Establishing a Precedent," *IF*, June 28, 1890, 4 (urging readers to contribute even small sums "if you cannot spare more" to assist in the Fortune test case); "The Press on the Outrage," *NYA*, June 21, 1890, 2 (reporting on press coverage of Fortune's case).

34. "Raise a Million Dollars," *NYA*, July 5, 1890, 3.

35. See, e.g., "Justice," *NYA*, Nov. 14, 1891; "The League Wins Again," *DP*, Nov. 13, 1891, 8; "Congratulations," *NYA*, Nov. 21, 1891; "The Fortune Verdict," *IF*, Nov 21, 1891, 4 ("The Fortune verdict is a gleam of light through a dark sky, a harbinger of better things."); see *IF*, July 16, 1892 (reporting on the New York court's affirmance of the lower court judgment).

36. See, e.g., William C. Nell, "At the Cradle of Liberty," *NYA*, Aug. 9, 1890; William C. Nell, "Boston's National League," *NYA*, July 19, 1890 (both reporting on Boston meetings).

37. "Ohio's Civil Rights Law," *CG*, Nov. 30, 1895.

38. "Enter Suit," *CG*, Nov. 30, 1895, 2.

39. "Afro-American League," *DP*, Jan. 10, 1890.

40. Ferguson v. Gies, 82 Mich. 358, 363, 9 L.R.A. 589 (1890).

41. "Afro-American League," *DP*, Jan. 10, 1890 (reporting on founding meeting and the *Litt* lawsuit); [no title], *DP*, Aug. 12, 1892 (announcing new incidents of public accommodations discrimination in Michigan and Ohio and urging, "Why not at once organize Afro American Leagues, or resuscitate the old ones, not for play or dilly-dallying, but for work?").

42. Fishel, "First Wisconsin Civil Rights Act," 327.

43. Ibid., 328.

44. Ibid., 332. "A Just Ruling," *DP*, July 25, 1890 (describing the outcome of the *Howell v. Litt* case and crediting the victory to the AAL); "Afro-American Leaguers: Good Work Done in Wisconsin for the Race," *DP*, Sept. 26, 1890; "Enter Suit," *CG*, Sept. 26, 1891 (reporting on facts in *Green* and lamenting that the AAL "has been allowed to die" in Ohio).

Another similar lawsuit involved plaintiff Simpson Younger in Kansas City, Missouri. That suit, pursued primarily on a contracts theory, failed, and there is no obvious evidence that it was related to the AAL's organizing efforts. "No Redress in Law," *DP*, Feb. 14, 1890; "An Important Decision in a Civil Rights Case," *Times-Picayune*, Feb. 4, 1890.

45. "Personal and Pertinent. Notes upon the League Convention—The Infamy of the 'Jim Crow' Car," *NYA*, July 25, 1891; see *DP*, July 3, 1891, 4 (noting that the Tennessee law would be hard on delegates traveling to the AAL convention and urging the AAL to bring a test case against it).

46. See *DP*, July 3, 1891, 4 ("pity it is that the National [AAL] is not strong enough to test the constitutionality" of Tennessee's separate-car law); "Afro-American: Claims," *DP*, July 17, 1892 (reporting that the Louisiana high court had returned a verdict favorable to Heard and opining that it was "unfortunate" that the local branches did not respond to the national AAL's call for fund-raising to push the claims further). On Heard's similar case before the Interstate Commerce Commission two years before see "A Civil Rights Case," *St. Paul Daily Globe*, Apr. 11, 1889, 4; William H. Heard v. Georgia R.R. Co., 1 I.C.C. Reports 428 (1888). He filed suit before the I.C.C. again the next year. See Heard v. Georgia R.R., 3 ICC 111 (1889).

47. "A Pullman Sleeper Outrage," *NYA*, Aug. 8, 1891, 2; *CG*, Aug. 15, 1891, 2 (reporting on the Heard incident and Heard's affiliation with the AAL); "First Blood for the League," *NYA*, Sept. 5, 1891, 2; *DP*, Sept. 11, 1891, 4, 6; "Two Blows and Each a Victory," *State Capital*, Sept. 12, 1891 (published in Springfield, Illinois).

48. See *NYA*, Oct. 10, 1891, 2.

49. See *CG*, Sept. 9, 1891, 2.

50. See *DP*, Sept. 18, 1891, 4; *CG*, Nov. 21, 1891, 2. The *Gazette* soon joined the *Plaindealer* in wondering where the Heard settlement money had ended up. See "Rev. Heard and that $500," *CG*, Nov. 14, 1891; see also *IF*, Nov. 21, 1891 (quoting the *Gazette*'s argument that people should not contribute to the Heard case against the Nashville railroad until he contributed the settlement money—incorrectly quoted as $500—to the AAL); *CG*, Nov. 21, 1891 (reporting on a letter from Heard explaining that the settlement had been for $250 and that he had received none of this money).

51. See *NYA*, Oct. 31, 1891 (quoting a Galveston newspaper).

52. "The Heard Case," *NYA*, Sept. 19, 1891; "A Vote of Thanks," *DP*, Oct. 1, 1891; "The League and the Heard Case," *NYA*, Oct. 3, 1891 (publishing various letters of thanks from prominent figures and newspapers).

53. See *NYA*, Oct. 10, 1891, 2. Minnesota had generated another test case as well, in a matter that may have been related to the AAL. A local activist, William Hazel, filed a lawsuit after he was denied accommodations at the Astoria and Clarendon hotels. Hazel was at first hostile to the AAL because he believed the organization had done nothing significant, but it appears that he ended up agreeing that his lawsuit should be a test case for the state group that cooperated with the AAL. In 1891 Hazel pursued a second suit against a different restaurant, producing an out-of-court settlement, and a few years later his wife sued the same restaurant again and won a verdict of $25. McGhee handled both cases. Nelson, *Life on the Color Line*, 171.

54. See Hardy v. East Tennessee, Virginia and Georgia Railway Co., C.C.S.D. Tenn. (1891). "That Tennessee Law—L. E. Hardy Will Test His Constitution Rights to the End," *IF*, Aug. 1, 1891, 9 (stating that the Hardy test case "will be carried to the Supreme Court of the United States"); "Minnesota Speaks," *St. Paul Appeal*, Aug. 29, 1891 (describing in detail the St. Paul organizing meeting); *DP*, Sept. 4, 1891 (announcing Minnesota plans to push a test case based on Hardy's treatment); *DP*, Sept. 18, 1891 (discussing the Heard and Hardy cases together); Nelson, *Life on the Color Line*, 32–34 (describing McGhee's efforts in this case and his frustration at the AAL's lack of successful fund-raising for it).

55. See, e.g., American Bar Association Model Rules of Professional Conduct 1.16 (setting strict limits on a lawyer's freedom to drop a case once the lawyer has accepted a client representation even when the client lacks money to pay the lawyer's bills). I am grateful to Catherine Fisk and Ann Southworth for this observation.

56. Nelson, *Life on the Color Line*, 39–49.

57. For a description of the short-lived National Federation of Colored Men, which focused its efforts on lobbying the Republican Party to include antilynching and disfranchisement planks in its platform, see Alexander, *Army of Lions*, 70–71, 73.

58. On Straker's biography see Dorothy Drinkard Hawshawe, "David Augustus Straker, Black Lawyer and Reconstruction Politician, 1842–1908" (PhD diss., Catholic University of America, 1974).

59. On Fortune's influence on Grimké, see Bruce, *Archibald Grimké*, 56–57 ("Fortune's book and, through it, Henry George's were clearly identifiable sources for Grimké").

60. D. Augustus Straker, *The New South Investigated* (1888, repr., New York: Arno Press, 1973). Citations refer to the Arno Press edition.

61. Ibid. ("the defeated Southerner needed moral elevation...from gross social and political darkness, to the knowledge of the light of a new civilization.... In this changed condition, stagnation marked the South..."); ibid., 107 ("the very vitals of their progress are being eaten out by their own prejudice"); ibid., 176 ("It is the voice of capital that makes back seats for Negroes and churches and theaters, and provides Jim Crow cars for colored ladies and gentlemen on the railroad, and refuses them admittance into public places of accommodation in our South Land").

62. Ibid., 18 ("social government" of the South prior to the Civil War kept "the poor whites in the South in the state of serfdom and the Negro in a state of total subjection and ignorance"); ibid., 86 ("poor wages, bad laws and race prejudice, arising from social distinction[,]...have produced the present social condition of the South"); ibid., 90 (discussing the "oppression of capital against labor"; asserting that "[t]he outgrowth of this oppression is to establish two classes, a superior and inferior one in the South, as it is in the North, East and West, with this difference, that in the South the social condition is largely characterized by the caste prejudice of former condition and color, and this enters into and shapes laws and prescribes an ostracism"); ibid. (arguing that "[i]t is the land power in the South that makes back seats for Negroes in theatres and in hotels, on railroad cars and in steamboats, nay, even in churches"; that "[i]t is capital that keeps the poor white man of the South and the Negro in a state of servitude"; and that "[i]t is capital as represented chiefly by land" that makes the law handle murder in the South differently depending on the races of the perpetrator and the victim); ibid., 184 ("it is capital and its oppression of labor that disfranchises thousands of colored voters in the South").

63. Ibid., 24 ("the next step of importance was the education of the masses. The Negro needed education to fit him for his new responsibilities of citizen and voter; the poor whites needed education to fit them for the new condition of the South, which for the first time had presented an opportunity for all alike to rise in the scale of human progress. But this movement towards the education of the Negro, found great opposition from the native whites, who, lacerated in feeling and debased in pride, saw in the education of the Negro the total oblivion of the former rule of an aristocratic class"); ibid., 43 ("the South needs more education for the masses, and money to carry it on.... The chief need of the South today is higher education for the masses, which should be enjoyed by all alike."); ibid., 45 (arguing for passage of the Blair bill); ibid., 69 (more discussion of the Blair bill).

64. Ibid., 45; see also ibid., 159 ("If the Southern States are not to be aided in the education of the citizen, then Congress should provide a National free school, wherein every citizen of the United States may avail himself of an education"). For a contemporary continuation of this argument regarding the federal government's robust responsibility for education from a civil rights perspective, see Lia B. Epperson, "Legislating Inclusion," *Harvard Law and Policy Review* 6 (2012): 801–14; Lia B. Epperson, "Equality Dissonance: Jurisprudential Limitations and Legislative Opportunities," *Stanford Journal of Civil Rights and Civil Liberties* 7 (2011): 213–38.

65. Straker, *New South Investigated*, 85 (discussing Henry George's ideas about shared property and offering a "more practical plan of an equal share of profit between capital and labor" as a start); ibid., 91 (describing George as explaining the causes of the great disparities between

rich and poor "more clearly than any other political economist known to me"); ibid., 185 (lauding George's "profound work" concerning "the true rights and relationship between capital and labor").

66. Ibid., 67 (pejoratively describing "the rapid tendency of a large class of foreigners to establish disorder and anarchy in our midst"); ibid., 98 (pejoratively describing race discriminatory trade unions "as inciting just such resistance as Communism and Anarchism produce."); ibid., 176 ("I say to oppressed labor, strike on, not by mobs and bombs, but through organization dedicated to reform—reform in which the work will be not destruction, but construction" [emphasis omitted]).

67. Ibid., 96.

68. Ibid., 97 ("This discriminating process in the use of available labor, is the curse of every spot on which it is found. It has its origin in what is known in America as 'trades unions,' whose ostensible object is to protect labor against the oppression of capital, but whose hidden purpose is to shut and keep shut the doors of industry against a class of people on account of their race, color, past condition.... These societies have not the claim to the respect or sympathy... some show the Knights of Labor."); ibid., 186 (criticizing the selfish motives of labor organizations that discriminate on the basis of race).

69. Ibid., 100 (emphasis in original).

70. Ibid., 100, 128–29.

71. Ibid., 127.

72. Ibid., 101.

73. Ibid., 49.

74. Ibid., 114.

75. Ibid., 67 ("Let [the African American citizen] rise in his might, and demand this right which is his just due as an American citizen."); ibid., 116, 123 (discussing suffrage rights for both African Americans and women).

76. Ibid., 125.

77. I am grateful to Adolph L. Reed Jr. for helping me see this point through a talk he gave at the Washington College of Law on September 23, 2008.

78. See, e.g., Archibald H. Grimké, "Modern Industrialism and the Negroes of the United States," *Occasional Papers*, no. 12 (published by the American Negro Academy, 1908).

79. "The League," *NYA*, Oct. 11, 1890; "Apathy in the League," *NYA*, Dec. 6, 1890.

80. "What's the Matter with the League?" *NYA*, Mar. 14, 1891.

81. See "The League Very Much Alive," *NYA*, Aug. 29, 1891.

82. Thornbrough, "National Afro-American League," 501.

83. The continuation of local and regional activity following the demise of the national AAL was not well appreciated until Shawn Leigh Alexander proved this point in Alexander, "We Know Our Rights," 69–89.

84. Conversation with Shawn Alexander, fall 2008.

85. W.E.B. Du Bois, "The Lash," in *Writings in Periodicals Edited by W.E.B. Du Bois: Selections from the Horizon*, ed. Herbert Aptheker (White Plains, NY: Kraus Thomson Organization, 1985), 16. First published May 1907 in *The Horizon: A Journal of the Color Line* (May 1907).

Chapter 4

1. For the origins of the well-accepted distinction between the so-called civil rights radicals and conservatives in this period, see Meier, *Negro Thought*, 171–75.

2. "Fred Douglass Dead," *WP*, Feb. 21, 1895, 1.

3. Booker T. Washington, "Southern Prisons," *NYF*, Apr. 17, 1886.

4. Louis R. Harlan, *Booker T. Washington: The Making of a Black Leader, 1856–1901* (New York: Oxford University Press, 1972), 219–20 (hereinafter Harlan I).

5. On Du Bois's initial support of Washington, including his favorable views of his 1895 Atlanta speech, see Marable, *W.E.B. Du Bois*, 43. On Smith's remarks, see Harlan I, 226 (quoting *CG*, Nov. 2, 1895). The Texas commenter's article is in *WE*, November 1895, 8–9.

6. Harlan I, 223.

7. Harlan describes Washington's generous work and advice to educational institutions other than his own in Louis R. Harlan, *Booker T. Washington: The Wizard of Tuskegee, 1901–1905* (New York: Oxford University Press, 1983), 128–29, 197–200 (hereinafter Harlan II).

8. Ibid., 133–36.

9. Benjamin R. Justesen, *Broken Brotherhood: The Rise and Fall of the National Afro-American Council* (Carbondale: Southern Illinois Press, 2008), 83. For a description of the nature and extent of Washington's influence with white politicians and philanthropists, see Meier, *Negro Thought*, 112–16.

10. Mark R. Schneider, "*The Colored American* and *Alexander's*: Boston's Pro-Civil Rights Bookerites," *Journal of Negro History* 80 (1995): 157–69.

11. Riser provides an example of the former approach; Shawn Alexander is an example of the later perspective. Compare Riser, *Defying Disfranchisement*, 96, 107–108 (arguing that Washington was powerful and the AAC was disorganized and inconsequential), with Alexander, "We Know Our Rights," 214–89 (arguing that the AAC dominated civil rights work independently of Washington).

12. Meier notices this, though he does not in my view do enough to explore its implication. See Meier, *Negro Thought*, 168 ("the anti-Bookerites tended to lean toward economic radicalism— toward Bryanism, interracial trade unionism, and socialism").

13. Harlan I, 39–44.

14. Ibid., 109.

15. Morris, *Reverdy C. Ransom*, 64.

16. See, e.g., Reverdy C. Ransom, "The Negro and Socialism," in *Making the Gospel Plain: The Writings of Bishop Reverdy C. Ransom*, ed. Anthony B. Pinn (Harrisburg: Trinity Press, 1999), 183, 186 (hereinafter *Ransom Writings*).

17. Ibid., 186.

18. Ibid., 189.

19. Reverdy C. Ransom, *The Industrial and Social Conditions of the Negro: A Thanksgiving Sermon, Speech before the Bethel AME Church, Chicago, Ill.*, 3 (Nov. 26, 1896). Pamphlet. Chicago: Conservator Print.

20. Ibid., 7.

21. Ibid., 7, 8–9.

22. Ibid., 10–11; 163 U.S. 537 (1896).

23. For a description of these members of Chicago's social elite, which overlapped considerably with the congregants of Ransom's church, see Willard B. Gatewood, *Aristocrats of Color: The Black Elite, 1880–1920* (Fayetteville: University of Arkansas Press, 2000), 122–26.

24. See Helen Buckler, *Daniel Hale Williams: Negro Surgeon* (New York: Pitman, 1968).

25. See Reverdy C. Ransom, "First Quadrennial Report of the Pastor and Warden of the Institutional Church and Social Settlement, May 1904" (hereinafter "ICSS Report"), Wilberforce University Archives, Reverdy Ransom Manuscript Collection; Buckler, *Daniel Hale Williams*, 221 (describing Alice Williams's extensive involvement in the ICSS); Morris, *Reverdy C. Ransom*, 107.

26. Gatewood, *Aristocrats of Color*, 123 (quoting Alice Williams's statement that "I'd rather stay home and read a book" than "mingle with ill-bred people"); Addams, "Subjective Value of Social Settlements" (explaining that a major motive of social settlements was to bring the "social energy and accumulation of civilization to those portions of the race which have little").

27. See Ida B. Wells, *Crusade for Justice: The Autobiography of Ida B. Wells*, ed. Alfreda M. Duster (Chicago: University of Chicago Press, 1970), 239–40 (quoting newspaper account of the satin, crepe, and orange blossoms at Wells's wedding).

28. Wells Barnett wrote enthusiastically about Ransom's leadership of Bethel AME and the many programs he developed there in Ida B. Wells Barnett, "Rev. R. C. Ransom, D.D.," *Christian Recorder* 47 (Jan. 25, 1900).

29. Ibid., 249–50; Giddings, *Ida,* 383–84.

30. See, e.g., Jacqueline Anne Rouse, *Lugenia Burns Hope: Black Southern Reformer* (Athens: University of Georgia Press, 1989); Steve Kramer, "Uplifting Our 'Downtrodden Sisterhood': Victoria Earle Matthews and New York City's White Rose Mission, 1897–1907," *Journal of African American History* 91 (2006): 243–66.

31. See generally Elisabeth Lasch-Quinn, *Black Neighbors: Race and the Limits of Reform in the American Settlement House Movement, 1890–1945* (Chapel Hill: University of North Carolina Press, 1993). Lasch-Quinn explores the negative racial attitudes of white settlement house movement reformers and their frequent exclusion of African Americans and argues that these aspects of the movement weakened and eventually defeated its potential.

32. See Allen F. Davis, *American Heroine: The Life and Legend of Jane Addams* (New York: Oxford University Press, 1973), 42 (describing how Jane Addams's first exposure to mission work, through visits to African American mission endeavors, was the experience that lifted her out of her postcollege depression and gave her life its meaning and direction).

33. Addams, though one of the most supportive white progressives of her time on African American issues, was by no means free of race prejudice, as scholars have explored. See, e.g., Lasch-Quinn, *Black Neighbors,* 14 (discussing Addams's racial attitudes as shown in her statements and conduct); Giddings, *Ida,* 430–31 (discussing a debate between Wells Barnett and Addams after Addams wrote an article assuming " 'for argument's sake,' " that lynchings resulted from black men committing rape).

34. Morris, *Reverdy C. Ransom,* 109.

35. On the National Urban League leaders' promotion of the professionalization of social work in the later 1910s, see Nancy J. Weiss, *The National Urban League* (New York: Oxford University Press, 1974), 66, 112. Weiss argues that the National Urban League's brand of race uplift through social work lacked the more dynamic political aims that characterized both African American and white settlement house work (ibid., 87).

36. Gatewood, *Aristocrats of Color,* 182-86 (describing the Manasseh Society and the complex issue of skin tone among the African American leadership elite).

37. "Aid Aim of New Church," *CT,* July 9, 1900, 3; Ransom, *Pilgrimage,* 103–105.

38. Bowen-Spencer, "Institutional Church and Social Settlement," 25.

39. Goddard, "Black Social Gospel in Chicago," 227, 239–40. Wright would go on to an important career of his own as an AME minister and sociologist and would participate with Ransom in the Niagara Movement and the NAACP (ibid.).

40. "Dedicate New Church Today," *CT,* Oct. 20, 1900, 3. Fallow shared Ransom's pro-labor views. See, e.g., "Pastors Talk of Strikes," *CT,* Aug. 4, 1902, 15; "Clergymen Pray Unions May Win," *CT,* Aug. 8, 1904 (reporting on Fallows's pro-labor speeches during Chicago labor conflicts).

41. For a short biographical summary, see *BTW Papers,* vol. 3, 505n1. In 1904 Gunsaulus spoke at a forum along with Wright and Wells Barnett to state that he believed that African Americans and whites stood on a plane of absolute social equality. "Regards Negro as Equal," *CT,* Nov. 21, 1904. This view as to African Americans' social equality was considerably more egalitarian than that of figures such as Addams, Taylor, Florence Kelley, and most other racially progressive whites at the time.

42. "Dedicate New Church Today."

43. Ransom, *Pilgrimage,* 86, 88, 104. See, e.g., Harris Winesap to Jane Addams, Oct. 19, 1900, in Jane Addams Papers, series 1, supplement, microformed on Swarthmore College Peace Collection, r. 3, fr. 1679; ibid., r. 3, fr. 1680 (enclosing letter from Monroe N. Work [Oct. 15, 1900]).

44. Reverdy C. Ransom, "First Quadrennial Report of the Pastor and Warden of the Institutional Church and Social Settlement to the Twenty-Second Session of the General Conference

and to the Connectional Trustees of the African Methodist Episcopal Church, convened at Quinn Chapel, Chicago, Illinois," May 1904, unpublished report, Reverdy Ransom Papers, Wilberforce University Archives.

45. Drewett, "Ransom on Race and Racism," 126, quoting Reverdy Ransom, "The Institutional Church a Great Thing, But Extremes Must Be Avoided," *Southern Christian Recorder* 12 (May 30, 1901): 3.

46. Ibid.

47. See, e.g., "Kindergartens for Colored Children," *CT*, Oct. 27, 1900, 16 (reporting on a speech at the ICSS by the founder of the only school for African American kindergarten workers in Washington, DC); "Inquiry on City Negroes," *CT*, July 14, 1902, 4 (reporting on a convention to undertake an inquiry into the condition of the African American population of Chicago, which convened at the ICSS); "Negroes Talk of Crime," *CT*, July 15, 1902, 11 (reporting further on the convention, including a discussion of Emma Ransom's findings on conducting home visits to African Americans residing near the ICSS and the need for night schools and kindergartens and on remarks by Mrs. L. A. Davis, national organizer of the federation of African American women's clubs); "Negro Rescue Work Here Harder than in South," *CT*, May 26, 1903, 3 (reporting on a meeting on "negro rescue work" at which Chicago juvenile probation officer Mary McDonald and others spoke).

48. Irving Stone, *Clarence Darrow for the Defense* (1941, repr., New York: Signet, 1973), 109–22, 197, 531. Citations refer to the Signet edition (describing Darrow's friendly relations with African Americans and with Ransom in particular). Ransom, *Pilgrimage*, 113; Morris, *Reverdy C. Ransom*, 80. Darrow would later become a member and cooperating attorney for the NAACP.

49. See, e.g., "Blame Lynching on Governor," *CT*, June 15, 1903, 1 (reporting on a mass meeting held at the ICSS to protest recent lynchings); "Must Insist on Rights," *CT*, June 29, 1903, 2 (describing Ransom's speech at the ICSS denouncing lynching and urging African Americans to assert their legal and political rights).

50. Ransom, *Pilgrimage*, 114 (describing his involvement in race-related mediation of a Chicago strike); Eric Arnesen, "Specter of the Black Strikebreaker: Race, Employment, and Labor Activism in the Industrial Era," *Labor History* 44 (2003): 319, 321–25 (analyzing race dynamics in Chicago labor strikes of the industrial era).

51. Mark H. Haller, "Policy Gambling, Entertainment, and the Emergence of Black Politics: Chicago from 1900 to 1940," *Journal of Social History* 24 (1991): 719–20.

52. "Forces Arising to Crush Policy," *CT*, May 3, 1903, 1.

53. Ibid., 724.

54. "Blast Answers Policy Crusade," *CT*, May 4, 1903, 1; "A Bad Time for Policy Kings," *CT*, May 4, 1903, 2.

55. "Policy Men See Writing on Wall," *CT*, May 3, 1903, 1–2 ("Ransom said yesterday that no threats would deter him from pressing the crusade. He will preach on policy next Sunday evening at the same place" while carrying a "revolver" under his Bible); "Scores Policy; Pistol Near By," *CT*, May 11, 1903, 3.

56. "Policy Men See Writing on Wall," 1; "Policy Trials Put Off," *CT*, May 12, 1903, 7; "Policy Swindler Near Surrender," *CT*, May 6, 1903, 1; "King of Policy Leaves the City," *CT*, May 7, 1903, 4; "Policy Agents Growing Bold," *CT*, June 17, 1903, 7; "Forces Arising to Crush Policy," 2.

57. See, e.g., Elizabeth Dale, " 'Social Equality Does Not Exist among Themselves, nor among Us': *Baylies v. Curry* and Civil Rights in Chicago, 1888," *American Historical Review* 102 (1997): 311, 319, 328–30 (discussing Morris's successful representation of Josephine Curry, a middle-class African American businesswoman, in a civil rights action against a white-owned theater that refused to seat her and her husband).

58. "Blast Answers Policy Crusade," 4.

59. See, e.g., "Get Speeches, Few Pictures," *CT*, May 1, 1900, 6 (reporting on a meeting at which both Ransom and Morris spoke).

60. See Nelson, *Life on the Color Line*, 9.

61. Ransom, *Pilgrimage*, 115.

62. Bryan Bach, "Edward H. Morris: Dean of Chicago's African American Lawyers, 1858–1943" (student paper, American University Washington College of Law, 2008) (on file with author).

63. On McGhee's life and early death caused in part from overwork, see Nelson, *Life on the Color Line*. Early death from overwork, as well as mental health issues caused by the stress and sacrifices imposed by intense commitment to racial justice activism, marked the lives of a number of other race justice activists of the era, including not only McGhee and Fortune but also Trotter, who appears to have ended his own life, according to his biographer Stephen Fox, and Barbara Pope, the NM's test case plaintiff, as further described in chapter 9. Stephen R. Fox, *The Guardian of Boston: William Monroe Trotter* (New York: Atheneum, 1970), 271–72.

64. Ransom, *Pilgrimage*, 135.

65. Ibid. On Jourdain, see Carroll, "Niagara Movement," 29–33; Sherman Beverly, "The Emergence of Black Political Power in Evanston: The Public Career of Edwin B. Jourdain, Jr., 1931–1947" (PhD diss., Northwestern University, 1973), 52–57 (discussing the background of Edwin Jourdain Sr.).

66. On Reverend Scott's blending of political activism with social gospel ministry to the poor in work that resembled Ransom's, see Carroll, "Niagara Movement," 23–28. On one of Ransom's Faneuil Hall speeches, see Ransom, *Pilgrimage*, 143–49, 171 (quoting a newspaper account describing Ransom's oratory as the "climax and the sensation of . . . the whole celebration").

67. See Reverdy C. Ransom, "The Atlanta Riot: A Philippic on the Atlanta Riot, delivered in Faneuil Hall, Boston, Massachusetts" (Sept. 28, 1906), in *The Spirit of Freedom and Justice: Orations and Speeches* (Nashville: A.M.E. Sunday School Union, 1926), 117 (hereinafter *Orations*). In that speech, Ransom again pointed out the connection between political rights and economic security:

> The Negro's greatest present need is not money and property, it is not even education; it is a voice in the community through the exercise of the franchise with which to make himself secure . . . . The Negro's chief protection in the south today is poverty. If he were to largely engage in mercantile pursuits, having shops, stores and banks, the mob would find a ready pretext to assail him in order to loot, to plunder and to steal. (ibid., 119–20)

68. Morris, *Reverdy C. Ransom*, 111.

69. See Weiss, *National Urban League*, 26. For Ransom's speech at the 1910 National Negro Committee meeting, see Reverdy C. Ransom, "Democracy, Disfranchisement and the Negro," in *Orations*, 42.

70. On this phase of his life, see Gomez-Jefferson, *Sage of Tawawa*, 175–219.

Chapter 5

1. Alexander Walters, *My Life and Work* (New York: Fleming H. Revell, 1917), 98–99, http://docsouth.unc.edu/neh/walters/walters.html; "Bishop Walters' Action," *Richmond Planet*, Nov. 12, 1898, 2.

2. Walters, *My Life and Work*, 2.

3. Ibid.

4. Benno C. Schmidt Jr., "Principle and Prejudice: The Supreme Court and Race in the Progressive Era: Part 1: The Heyday of Jim Crow," *Columbia Law Review* 82 (1982): 444, 463, citing C. Vann Woodward, *The Strange Career of Jim Crow* (New York: Oxford University Press, 1955), 146.

5. Louisville, New Orleans, & Texas Ry. Co. v. Mississippi, 133 U.S. 587 (1890). The fact that the state's highest court had interpreted the statute in question to apply only to *intra*state travel

allowed the Court to distinguish this case from its precedent in *Hall v. De Cuir,* 95 U.S. 485 (1877), which had struck down a Reconstruction-era Louisiana statute that prohibited race discrimination in transportation. The Court in *De Cuir* held that Louisiana's effort during this era to enforce the dictates of the Reconstruction-era amendments through state legislation violated the Commerce Clause's reservation to Congress of the exclusive power to regulate interstate commerce. Later, race justice advocates would attempt to use the unsettled question regarding states' power to enforce Jim Crow statutes against passengers engaged in *inter*state travel as an area in which they could push for a civil rights doctrinal win. Indeed, Niagara Movement founding member William H. H. Hart won one of the few cases disapproving Jim Crow transportation on this very issue, as discussed further in chapter 8.

6. Plessy v. Ferguson, 163 U.S. 537, 548 (1896).
7. Council v. Western & A.R.R., 1 ICC 339 (1887); Heard v. Georgia RR, 1 ICC 428 (1888); Heard v. Georgia RR, 3 ICC 111 (1889).
8. Kelley, *Right to Ride,* 7–8, 35–40.
9. See generally Welke, "When All the Women Were White."
10. Ida B. Wells Barnett, *The Memphis Diary of Ida B. Wells,* ed. Miriam Decosta-Williams (Boston: Beacon Press, 1995), 56–57; Kelley, *Right to Ride,* 15–32 (antebellum lawsuits). In 1885, for example, the Brotherhood of Liberty sponsored a successful test case on behalf of three women of "unobjectionable character and conduct" who were refused proper first-class sleeping accommodations after purchasing first-class tickets for a night steamboat trip on the Chesapeake Bay. See The Sue, 22 F. 843 (D. Md. 1885) (granting $100 damage awards to each of the three plaintiffs); see also McGuinn v. Forbes, 37 F. 639 (D. Md. 1889) (rejecting a lawsuit by "an educated colored clergyman" against a steamboat for failing to allow a first-class ticketholder to sit at the dinner table).
11. This analysis follows Michael Perman, *Struggle for Mastery: Disfranchisement in the South, 1888–1908* (Chapel Hill: University of North Carolina Press, 2001), 248 (most states enacted separate-cars laws in "close relation to their drive for disfranchisement").
12. Ibid., 6, 26. For a discussion of these cases and other illustrative incidents, see chapter 2.
13. On the disfranchising effects of poll taxes, see Perman, *Struggle for Mastery,* 29, 58, 313–14.
14. Riser, *Defying Disfranchisement,* 14.
15. Ibid., 18.
16. 170 U.S. 213 (1898).
17. Riser, *Defying Disfranchisement,* 47–55.
18. "Mr. Fortune Declines to Call a Meeting of the Afro-American League," *WB,* Aug. 27, 1898.
19. "The Afro-American Council," *St. Paul Appeal,* Sept. 24, 1898.
20. Ibid.
21. The delegates at first rejected Fortune's ruling from the chair, but they then sustained it on a second vote, after which the inquirer left the room. Cyrus Field Adams, *The National Afro-American Council* (Washington, DC: C. F. Adams, 1902), 5 (hereinafter *AAC Internal History*).
22. Walters, *My Life and Work,* 105–106; *AAC Internal History,* 5–6.
23. *AAC Internal History,* 5–6.
24. "The Afro-American Council," *St. Paul Appeal,* Sept. 24, 1898.
25. "Bishop Walters' Action," *Richmond Planet,* Nov. 12, 1898.
26. "What Must We Do to Be Saved?" *Christian Recorder,* Dec. 29, 1898 (publishing Walters's address); "Aims to Help Negro: Opening Sessions of Afro-American Council," *WP,* Dec. 30, 1989 (reporting on evening public meetings attended by more than a thousand men and women); "Two Noisy Sessions: Plenty of Excitement at the Afro-American Council," *WP,* Dec. 31, 1899; "Colored Men in Session: A Large Meeting in Washington to Protest Southern Outrages," *NYT,* Dec. 30, 1898 (discussing the AAC meeting as a reaction to recent race riots in Wilmington, North Carolina).
27. The full text of this section provides that:

when the right to vote at any election for the choice of electors for President and Vice President of the United States, Representatives in Congress, the Executive and Judicial officers of a State, or the members of the Legislature thereof, is denied to any of the male inhabitants of such State, being twenty-one years of age, and citizens of the United States, or in any way abridged, except for participation in rebellion, or other crime, the basis of representation therein shall be reduced in the proportion which the number of such male citizens shall bear to the whole number of male citizens twenty-one years of age in such State.

28. *AAC Internal History*, 22–25; "Two Noisy Sessions," *WP*, Dec. 31, 1898; "Colored Men in Session," *NYT*, Dec. 30, 1898.
29. "Negroes Call at White House," *WP*, Jan. 1, 1899.
30. On Clinton's advocacy on behalf of women's rights see Bettye Collier-Thomas, *Jesus, Jobs, and Justice: African American Women and Religion* (New York: Alfred A. Knopf, 2010), 95. For general biographical information, see Frank Lincoln Mather, ed., *Who's Who of the Colored Race*, vol. 1 (1915; repr., Detroit: Gale Research, 1976), 69; "Bishop G. W. Clinton," *CA*, May 19, 1900. Clinton was born enslaved in Lancaster, South Carolina, in 1859, graduated from the University of South Carolina after taking a "junior classical course" in 1878, taught in Lancaster for twelve years, and then obtained a divinity degree from Wilberforce University in 1894, after which he was elected bishop in 1896.
31. On White's life and political viewpoints, see Benjamin R. Justesen, *George Henry White: An Even Chance in the Race of Life* (Baton Rouge: Louisiana State University, 2001).
32. On Lyons, see J. Clay Smith Jr., *Emancipation: The Making of the Black Lawyer* (Philadelphia: University of Pennsylvania Press, 1993), 197. On Lyons's fall from grace in Washington's eyes, as well as Washington's political punishment of him and others, see Marable, *W.E.B. Du Bois*, 58.
33. See Ann Field Alexander, *Race Man: The Rise and Fall of the "Fighting Editor," John Mitchell Jr.* (Charlottesville: University of Virginia Press, 2002), 107–108. By 1902 Mitchell had moved into the banking and insurance industries and was less willing to speak out in support of Hayes's court challenges to Virginia's newly adopted constitutional disfranchising provisions (ibid., 103, 117).
34. "Will Not Be Suppressed: T. Thomas Fortune Tells Why He Did Not Go to the White House," *WP*, Jan. 2, 1889.
35. See "The National Council," *St. Paul Appeal*, Aug. 26, 1899 (list under "Executive Committee"). Justesen states that this was in accordance with a formal AAC policy. Justesen, *Broken Brotherhood*, 43.
36. *AAC Internal History*, 31.
37. "Colored Men in Session."
38. "A Great Gathering," *Christian Recorder*, Aug. 10, 1899.
39. *AAC Internal History*, 12–14.
40. George Mason Miller persuasively argues this point in his dissertation on Walters's life. See Miller, "This Worldly Mission," 12–13. Miller criticizes in particular Meier's accusation that Walters underwent "kaleidoscopic changes in ideological expression and bewildering alliances with the proponents and opponents of Booker T. Washington" (ibid., quoting August Meier, *Negro Thought*, 218).
41. Miller, "This Worldly Mission," 22–26.
42. These facts concerning Walters's biography come from Miller's very helpful unpublished dissertation.
43. Alexander, "We Know Our Rights," 145.
44. See generally Justesen, *Broken Brotherhood*, and Alexander, *Army of Lions*.
45. "Take Up Negro's Rights," *CT*, Aug. 14, 1899, 9.
46. *AAC Internal History*, 15; "Program," *Christian Recorder*, Aug. 3, 1899.
47. "Colored Men in Session," *CT*, Aug. 18, 1899, 5.

48. The AME Zion Church was a separate institution from the AME, founded in New York City in 1821. See generally Anthony B. Pinn, *The African American Religious Experience in America* (Westport, CT: Greenwood Press, 2006), 129–31. Both churches began when the African American Methodists broke away from the white Methodist Episcopal Church because of increasingly strained relations based on racial subordination within that church (ibid.).

49. "Convention Opens Today," *Chicago Inter Ocean*, Aug. 14, 1899.

50. Giddings, *Ida*, 413.

51. See "To Aid Negro Race," *Chicago Inter Ocean*, Aug. 19, 1899.

52. "The Afro-American Council," *NYT*, Aug, 15, 1899.

53. "Take Up Negro's Rights," *CT*, Aug. 14, 1899, 9 (reporting that a "great fight" was being anticipated between radicals and conservatives over resolutions denouncing President McKinley).

54. "Want Negro Vote Used," *CT*, Aug. 19, 1899, 12; "Try Political Move," *Chicago Inter Ocean*, Aug. 19, 1899; Alexander, "We Know Our Rights," 193.

55. "Closes in a Tumult," *Chicago Inter Ocean*, Aug. 20, 1899, 5; see also Alexander, "We Know Our Rights," 194; "Did Not Score Washington," *Chicago Inter Ocean*, Aug. 25, 1899 (letter of Reverdy Ransom explaining his criticisms of Washington).

56. T. Thomas Fortune to Booker T. Washington, June 1, 1899, *Booker T. Washington Papers 1889–1900*, ed. Louis R. Harlan and Raymond W. Smock, vol. 5 (hereinafter *BTW Papers*).

57. This is the account given in "Negro Leader Is Upheld," *CT*, Aug. 20, 1899, 4; see also Harlan I, 264–65. Ransom later explained his actions in a letter to the editor: "I arose at the urgent request of Mrs. Booker T. Washington to move that her name be stricken from the programme of the National Afro-American Council." Reverdy Ransom, "Editorial, Did Not Score Washington," *Chicago Inter Ocean*, Aug. 25, 1899, 6. Ransom denied calling Washington "a traitor, or a trimmer, or a coward, as everyone who was present when I spoke well knows," stating that it was possible that those words might have been uttered by someone else in the audience. Ransom further wrote the following: "It may have been unwise for me to have referred to Mr. Washington at all; but I certainly did not do so with any intention either to misrepresent him or do him harm; but…I felt that if he had any message to convey to the council, or desired to exercise any control over its deliberations, he should have come into our midst. We had met to deliberate upon our social, industrial, educational, financial, and civil conditions; we needed the help of our best and wisest minds" (ibid.).

58. *BTW Papers*, vol. 5, 175–76.

59. "Want Negro Vote Used" (reporting on Ransom's resolution calling for the appointment of a committee to confer with the leaders of organized labor to bring about a cessation of discrimination and to meet with the National Labor Bureau to lay before it the condition of African American laborers).

60. Ibid. The resolution provided: "That the attitude of trades unions and nearly all forms of organized labor toward negro workingmen is both short-sighted and cruel. The divine right to work ought not to be taken from any people: we recommend that a committee be appointed to wait upon the labor leaders and the national industrial commission and seek by every effort to bring about between white and black laborers that spirit of fraternity and co-operation which is to the best interests of both" ("Closes in a Tumult").

61. "Negro Leader Is Upheld."

62. See "Convention Opens Today," *Chicago Inter Ocean*, Aug. 17, 1899; "To Aid Negro Race," *Chicago Inter Ocean*, Aug. 18, 1899.

63. For these letters and the *New York Times* newspaper article, see *BTW Papers*, vol. 5, 175–81.

64. According to one newspaper account, Du Bois stated that "[t]he spirit of this gathering was not represented at all in the remarks of Mr. Ransom and I deeply regret that anything of the kind took place," and that Washington is "one of the greatest men of our race" ("Closes in a Tumult").

65. Lewis, *Biography of a Race*, 229–30.

66. Reverdy Cassius Ransom to Booker T. Washington, Aug. 31, 1899, *BTW Papers,* vol. 5, 194 ("I felt…that we should have had the benefit of your presence, but it may be doubtless true that reasons which influenced your judgment to remain away were the wisest and the best").

67. See *IF,* July 14, 1900, quoting the *Chicago Conservator.* Cited in Thornbrough, "National Afro-American League," 494, 504.

68. "National Afro-American Council," *CA,* June 16, 1900, and July 28, 1900; "N.A.-A.C.," *St. Paul Appeal,* July 7, 1900.

69. Ransom, *Pilgrimage,* 85.

70. W.E.B. Du Bois, "Of Mr. Booker T. Washington and Others," in *The Souls of Black Folk* (New York: Modern Library, 1996).

71. See Fox, *Guardian of Boston,* 46–62.

72. Justesen, *Broken Brotherhood,* 64 (noting the relative success of revenue raised from this meeting).

73. *AAC Internal History,* 9.

74. "Afro-American Convention," *NYT,* Aug. 8, 1900, 3.

75. "N.A-A.C.," *St. Paul Appeal,* July 7, 1900, 1.

76. Justesen, *Broken Brotherhood,* 92 (noting low turnout at this meeting).

77. "Great Council Meeting," *CA,* Mar. 30, 1901.

78. Emmett Scott to Booker T. Washington, Aug. 13, 1901, *BTW Papers,* vol. 6, 186–87.

79. *AAC Internal History,* 11.

80. Emmett J. Scott to Booker T. Washington, Aug. 13, 1091, *BTW Papers,* vol. 6, 186.

81. For a lively and colorful account of the meeting and McGhee's role in it see Nelson, *Life on the Color Line,* 96–111. For the call for the meeting and its planned schedule of speakers, see "Annual Meet," *CG,* June 14, 1902, 4.

82. "Outlook of a Race," *St. Paul Globe,* July 10, 1892, 2; "N.A.A.C.," *Indianapolis Appeal,* July 19, 1902, 1.

83. "N.A.A.C.," *St. Paul Appeal,* July 9, 1902, 1–2.

84. "Learning How to Work," *St. Paul Appeal,* July 11, 1902.

85. Justesen describes these shenanigans well. Justesen, *Broken Brotherhood,* 112–13.

86. Scott to Booker T. Washington, July 17, 1902, quoted in Thornbrough, "National Afro-American League," 504, and Nelson, *Life on the Color Line,* 106.

87. "Outlook of a Race," *St. Paul Globe,* July 10, 1902; "Learn How to Work," *St. Paul Globe,* July 11, 1902.

88. Lewis, *Biography of a Race,* 299.

89. Justesen, *Broken Brotherhood,* 111, 113.

90. *WB,* July 26, 1902, quoted in Thornbrough, "National Afro-American League," 505n24.

91. [No title], *CA,* Nov. 8, 1902.

92. "Afro-American Council's Mistake," *Broad Ax,* July 26, 1902.

93. "Plan of Council Organization," *St. Paul Appeal,* Dec. 12, 1902, and Jan. 24, 1903.

94. "Advice to Blacks," *AC,* Dec. 12, 1902.

95. "The National Afro-American Council," *St. Paul Appeal,* Feb. 14, 1903.

96. "Object to Drawing the Color Line," *St. Paul Globe,* Dec. 11, 1903.

97. Walters's leadership is an example of Marshall Ganz's observation that leaders' strategic capacities, including their "repertoires as well as the organizational context within which they operate," is a resource that is sometimes underappreciated by social movement scholars; this factor, for example, helps explain why some organizations "with poor resource endowments" do much better than could be predicted under resource mobilization theory. See John L. Campbell, "Where Do We Stand? Common Mechanisms in Organizations and Social Movements Research," in *Social Movements and Organization Theory,* ed. Gerald F. Davis et al. (New York: Cambridge University Press, 2005), 41, 63–64 (citing Ganz and others).

The example of Walters points to the observations of many social movement scholars that African American churches provided an important base for the civil rights struggle in the United States. In the era examined here, churches provided material support in several specific respects. One was in providing salaries and institutional legitimacy to ministers, such as Walters, who then devoted considerable time to civil rights organizing activity—a valuable material resource, just as Atlanta University's salary to Du Bois similarly provided material support to his organizing activities. Other specific aspects of such backing were in furnishing not only a physical location for mass turnout and planning meetings but also a network of social justice sympathizers who could be readily mobilized for fund-raising and issue work. On the general proposition that African American churches served as an important base for civil rights organizing, discussing later periods, see McAdam, *Political Process and the Development of Black Insurgency,* xiii, xxv.

98. "Hayes Stirs His Race," *WP,* Jan. 27, 1903; "Negroes against Violence," *NYT,* Feb. 1, 1903.

99. "Negroes Hostile to B. T. Washington," *NYT,* July 3, 1903; T. Thomas Fortune to Booker T. Washington, July 7, 1903, *BTW Papers,* vol. 7, 200; "Afro-American Council," *CA,* July 11, 1903, 1.

100. "Afro-American Council," *CA,* July 11, 1903, 1; "Speaks for Peace," *WP,* July 3, 1903; "Negroes on Lynching," *NYT,* July 4, 1903.

101. For more on Trotter's unsuccessful effort to organize this national group, see Fox, *Guardian of Boston,* 82.

102. "Returns from Afro-American Council," *St. Paul Globe,* July 7, 1903.

103. "McGhee Reminds Bishop Walters of Bad Faith That Killed Afro-American Council and Advises Niagara Movement," *WB,* Aug. 12, 1905.

104. Justesen, *Broken Brotherhood,* 137, quoting *CG,* July 11, 1903.

105. "Afro-American Council," *CA,* July 11, 1903; "Negroes Talk of Bolt," *NYT,* Aug. 7, 1903.

106. Justesen, *Broken Brotherhood,* 142, 234n5; Thornbrough, "National Afro-American League," 258n8, citing J. Douglas Wetmore to Booker T. Washington, Mar. 4 and May 19, 1904; Booker T. Washington to J. Douglas Wetmore, Apr. 16 and May 19, 1904; T. Thomas Fortune to Emmett Jay Scott, Mar. 26 and Mar. 28, 1904, *BTW Papers,* microfilm ed., LOC.

107. Alexander, "We Know Our Rights," 387–88.

108. "Call for Meeting," *St. Paul Appeal,* Aug. 27, 1904.

109. "The Afro-American Council: Bishop Walters Calls upon the Old Guard to Rally," *NYA,* July 27, 1905; "Call for Meeting of National Afro-American Council," *WB,* Aug. 5, 1905.

110. "Niagara Movement," *Broad Ax,* Aug. 5, 1905.

111. Ibid., Aug. 12, 1905, reprinting text without date from the *St. Louis Advance.*

112. "Afro-American Council," *IF,* Aug. 12, 1905.

113. See Logan and Winston, *Dictionary of American Negro Biography,* s.v. "Johnson, James Weldon"; J. Clay Smith, *Emancipation,* 278–80.

114. James Weldon Johnson, *Along This Way: The Autobiography of James Weldon Johnson* (New York: Viking Press, 1933), 76, 138, 141.

115. "Another Test of the Avery Law," *Florida Times-Union,* July 20, 1905; "Making Progress," *Idaho Statesman,* Aug. 15, 1905 (describing the success of the test case against the Jim Crow streetcar law pursued by an African American law firm).

116. State v. Patterson, 50 Fla. 127, 132–33, 39 So. 398 (1905).

117. This general account draws in part from Shira Levin, " 'To Maintain Our Self-Respect': The Jacksonville Challenge to Segregated Street Cars and the Meaning of Equality, 1900–1906," *Michigan Journal of History* (Winter 2005), unpaginated, n. 86, http://www.umich.edu/~historyj/issues.html.

118. Patterson v. Taylor, 51 Fla. 275, 40 So. 493 (1906); Crooms v. Schad, 51 Fla. 168, 40 So. 497 (1906).

119. Cf. Welke, "When All the Women Were White"; Kenneth W. Mack, "Law, Society, Identity, and the Making of the Jim Crow South: Travel and Segregation on Tennessee Railroads,

1875–1905," *Law and Social Inquiry* 24 (1999): 377–409 (noting this gendered aspect of courts' transportation segregation cases).

120. See, e.g., "1906 Would Be a Happier Year," *IF,* Jan. 6, 1906 (listing among many developments that would make the year better, "if the people would rally around J. Douglas Wetmore and the African American Council in their efforts to wipe out jim crow street cars in leading Southern cities").

121. "Jim-Crowism in the South," *WB,* Aug. 12, 1905, 1; *IF,* May 5, 1906, 1 (announcing Wetmore's move to New York and describing his "brilliant record in knocking a hole through the jim-crow car laws of Florida" and his plans to practice law and "continue the warfare upon the discriminations enforced against colored passengers").

122. Booker T. Washington to Emmett Jay Scott, Mar. 23, 1905, *BTW Papers,* vol. 8, 223. By 1908 Wetmore had moved to New York City, and Washington's spies were reporting that he was taking part in meetings denouncing Washington. See, e.g., Charles William Anderson to Booker T. Washington, Oct. 2, 1908, *BTW Papers,* vol. 9, 633–34 (reporting on such a meeting in Wetmore's offices and a subsequent large gathering at Ransom's church, where Wetmore denounced Washington for his failure to speak out after the Brownsville incident). Wetmore, unaware of Washington's concealed enmity toward him, sought Washington's support for his attempts to achieve public office, but Washington used his influence to block any such appointment. See, e.g., Booker T. Washington to William Loeb Jr., Apr. 6, 1909, *BTW Papers,* vol. 10, 87 (opposing Wetmore's appointment to a U.S. assistant district attorney position and stating that "Wetmore was one of the most persistent and dirty of President Roosevelt's abusers").

Wetmore did some spying for Washington of his own, reporting in 1906, for example, about Mary Church Terrell's critical comments about the style of race leadership that "tells dialect stories," "advises the race not to retaliate," and "counsels the race to acquire only an inferior sort of education"—remarks that, Wetmore reported, Church Terrell later told him were intended to "unshirt" Washington. Charles William Anderson to Booker T. Washington, Dec. 11, 1906, *BTW Papers,* vol. 13, 519.

Wetmore was also the subject of criticism based on rumors that he passed socially as white, and in his later life he does appear to have crossed the color line, turning up in the 1930 census with his race designated as white and as married to a white woman half his age. See Levin, "To Maintain Our Self-Respect," unpaginated, n. 86.

123. "Afro-American Council Protests against Wrongs," *NYA,* Oct. 11, 1905.

124. "Eighth Annual Meeting of the Afro-American Council," *St. Paul Appeal,* Sept. 9, 1905; "Negro's Appeal," *WB,* Dec. 9, 1905 (reporting on the AAC's activities, including letters to railroads protesting discriminatory practices).

125. "Let Us Organize Our Strength," *NYA,* July 12, 1906, 4.

126. "The Afro-American Council," *IF,* Oct. 20, 1906; see also "Afro-American Council," *Topeka Plaindealer,* Oct. 26, 1906, 8 (providing additional details, including that "a noble band of women" served the delegates lunch and dinner).

127. Oswald Garrison Villard, "The Aims of the Afro-American Council," *CA,* Nov. 1906, 349–53.

128. Milholland and his Constitution League present an interesting story that had to be cut from the book due to space considerations. A well-presented biography of Milholland is Brian W. Blaesser, "John E. Milholland" (senior thesis, Brown University, 1969). A reading of Milholland's diaries reveals him to be a devout social gospel adherent who believed it was his duty to use the financial proceeds of his business success to help fund racial justice activism. He believed that God would show him the path this work should take and, perhaps as a result of this idea system, he tended to lack savvy in his political dealings as an activist. Milholland resented Oswald Garrison Villard and appeared to assume that his funds should guarantee him a large role in the NAACP when it was formed, only to find himself largely shunted to the side—except insofar as he might be expected to make large financial contributions. Around this time Milholland's business prospects dimmed—partly as a result of Booker T. Washington's lobbying against him with federal bureaucrats. Washington, who distrusted

Milholland's militancy and tendency to "go off half-cocked" (as many, including Villard, also described him), maneuvered to have canceled the contracts with the U.S. Postal Service on which the success of Milholland's pneumatic tube business heavily depended. After some involvement in the early NAACP's efforts on national funding for education, Milholland's earlier racial justice activity waned on the national racial justice scene. But he, like many others, deserves mention in a story about individuals who acted against their immediate self-interest to help nurture a critical early stage of national civil rights organization building.

On Milholland's substantial financial contributions to turn-of-the-century civil rights advocacy, which often took the form of paying to rent large meeting spaces for mass turnout protest events but also included lobbying and other activities, See, e.g., *IF*, Feb. 6, 1904, 4 (Constitution League has agreed to fund test of legality of Virginia disfranchisement measure); *Olympia Record*, Feb. 2, 1906, 6 (huge Cooper Union Constitution League meeting of three thousand persons, at least four-fifths African American, to protest disfranchisement in the South); *Salt Lake Telegram*, Feb. 2, 1906, 2 (highlighting Church Terrell's "violent" remarks (which others characterized as merely passionate and overly lengthy) at this Cooper Union meeting); *Dallas Morning News*, Feb. 3, 1906 (report on Cooper Union meeting); Milholland diary, Jan. 5, 1906, JMP (describing this Cooper Union meeting as "the greatest event in my life"); ibid., Jan. 12, 1906 (stating that the meeting "has shaken my faith in Booker T. Washington to the very foundations" due to his agents' effort to undermine it); "Equality of Suffrage," *Wichita Searchlight*, Feb. 24, 1906 (describing the Constitution League's plans for a series of meetings in both the North and the West to agitate for equal suffrage); *Philadelphia Inquirer*, Feb. 27, 1906, 16 (mass meeting under the Constitution League's auspices to be held at the Academy of Music); *Fort Worth Star Telegram*, Nov. 22, 1906, 1 (Constitution League Cooper Union meeting to protest Brownsville incident). Milholland also funded the salary of a Constitution League staff counsel, the young lawyer Gilchrist Stewart (son of T. McCants Stewart), and sent Stewart to Brownsville to investigate and then write a report on the facts regarding the innocence of the soldiers dishonorably discharged there. See, e.g., *Washington Herald*, Nov. 29, 1906, 3; "Evidence on Brownsville," *New York Daily Tribune*, Dec. 12, 1906. A prominent anti–Tammany Hall Republican, Milholland campaigned to convince the Republican Party to include antilynching planks in its platforms and lobbied for federal education funding and antidisfranchisement legislation. See, e.g., Milholland diary, Sept. 23, 1960, JMP; Blaesser, "John Milholland," 13–16, 19, 43. On his social gospel beliefs and how he meshed them with what he called "the Crusade for Justice for the Negro," See, e.g., Milholland diary, JMP, at the following dates: Oct. 8, 1906; Oct. 22, 1906; Dec. 13, 1906 (writing about seeing "God's blessing" to "do things in the Master's Eye"); Dec. 30, 1906 ("calling upon God to help me to our cause for the Negro"); Dec. 31, 1906 (describing "part of my life work" as "rousing this Nation to the danger that confronts it in consequence of its indifference to Constitutional revelations" and of his feeling "that He approves of the effort and that He stands back of the man who fights for Truth!"). On his views about Villard and the early NAACP, See, e.g., Milholland diary, June 1, 1909, JMP ("Villard's Committee has made a sad mistake" because he "did not consult with me après to make up").

129. See, e.g., "Barber Took to His Heels," *NYA*, Oct. 25, 1906.

130. See Blaesser, "John E. Milholland," 82; Milholland diary, Nov. 18, 1906, JMP; Mary Church Terrell, "The Disbanding of the Colored Soldiers," *The Voice of the Negro* 3 (1906): 554–58; Mary Church Terrell, "A Sketch of Mingo Saunders," *The Voice of the Negro* 4 (1907): 128–31. Church Terrell undertook public speaking engagements on the issue as well. See, e.g., *Richmond Planet*, Dec. 22, 1906, 6. In the theoretical terms used by social movement theorists, Brownsville was a relatively small-scale but nevertheless significant "transformative event." See Aldon Morris, "Reflections on Social Movement Theory: Criticisms and Proposals," *Contemporary Sociology* 29 (2000): 452 (noting that political process theorists such as McAdam and Sewell formulated the "transformative event" concept to capture the fact that some events produce important turning points in collective action campaigns); see also

Lewis M. Killian, "Organization, Rationality and Spontaneity in the Civil Rights Movement,"
American Sociological Review 49 (1984), 770, 782 (noting "the feeling states and the cognitions
which sometimes cause individuals to throw caution to the winds" and act in the face of great
or unknown odds).

131. "Ministers Score Roosevelt," *CG*, Nov. 24, 1906, 1 ("In our churches here Sunday sermons
were preached attacking President Roosevelt for disbanding the three companies of the
Twenty-fifth infantry...").

132. On the concept of destabilizing events in social movements theory, see Doug McAdam and
W. Richard Scott, "Organizations and Movements," in Davis et al., *Social Movements and
Organization Theory* (Cambridge, UK: 2005): 18, 4–40.

133. "Negro Soldiers to Sue on Roosevelt's Order," *NYT*, Nov. 17, 1906.

134. "Going to the Courts," *Savannah Tribune*, Nov. 24, 1906, 1.

135. "Urges Uprising of Blacks: Negro Bishop Attacks Roosevelt and Urges Resort to War," *Broad
Ax*, Mar. 9, 1907.

136. See *Broad Ax*, June 15, 1907.

137. "Afro-American Council: Most Successful Meeting in the History of the Organization," *WB*,
July 6, 1907, 1.

138. "Afro-American Council Protests against Wrongs," *NYA*, Oct. 11, 1906; "Failure of the
Afro-American People to Organize" (ibid.).

139. "Afro-American Council Protests against Wrongs," *NYA*; "Council Ends Best Session," *NYA*,
Oct. 18, 1906.

140. See "Negroes Roused by Anti-Taft Orator," *Grand Forks Herald*, June 12, 1908, 3.

Chapter 6

1. A recent, largely persuasive account criticizing the AAC's handling of this test case is Riser,
Defying Disfranchisement, 95–100.

2. On the development of this norm and an assessment of its pros and cons as a model for pub-
lic interest legal representations, see Susan D. Carle, "Re-Envisioning Models for Pro Bono
Lawyering: A Comparative Study of the Early NAACP and the National Consumers League,"
American University Journal of Gender, Social Policy, & the Law 9 (2001): 81–96.

3. See, e.g., "A Million for Defense: Immense Protective Fund Started by the Council," *NYF*, Aug.
25. 1906, 1 (describing "monster mass meetings" in New York and plans for a benefit sponsored by entertainers to raise funds for a one-million-dollar permanent defense fund for test
cases to challenge disfranchising constitutions); "Testing the Grandfather Clause," *WB*, Aug.
18, 1906 (announcing the AAC's plans to prepare and raise financial support to file a case
that would test "so directly that the Federal Supreme Court cannot evade it," the Grandfather
Clause's constitutionality under the Fifteenth Amendment).

4. "Afro-American Council—A Resume of Its History, Object and Advancement for Unbelievers,"
IF, Dec. 29, 1900 (appealing to all denominations, colleges, newspapers, and literary societies
that support equal rights to send contributions to aid the Louisiana test case); "The Louisiana
Constitution," *WP*, Mar. 30, 1899 (announcing the AAC's plans to push the matter to the U.S.
Supreme Court); "Proclamation Observed," *Christian Observer*, June 8, 1899 (reporting on a
call for prayer meetings by Walters and other ministers acting on behalf of the AAC); "The
Council at Work," *CA*, Jan. 6, 1900 (describing the appointment of committees within the
AAC to push Congressman White's antilynching bill, support the Crumpacker bill reduc-
ing representation in states that disfranchised male citizens, and devise means of testing the
Louisiana law); "Afro-Americans Will Test the Suffrage Clause of the Louisiana Constitution,"
Idaho Daily Statesman, Mar. 5, 1900, 1.

5. "Lynching and Civil Rights," *NYT*, June 18, 1900.

6. "Chips," *Broad Ax*, Feb. 23, 1901.

7. "The Council's Meet," *CG*, June 22, 1901, 1 (outlining expenses incurred and funds needed and urging delegates at upcoming meetings to contribute funds for legal fees in the Louisiana case); [no title], *Springfield Daily Republican*, June 10, 1901, 6 (same).

8. See Jesse Lawson to Booker T. Washington, Feb. 9, 1900, *BTW Papers*, vol. 5, 436; Jesse Lawson to Booker T. Washington, Oct. 3, 1900, *BTW Papers*, vol. 5, 647–48; Jesse Lawson to Booker T. Washington, Oct. 3, 1900, *BTW Papers*, vol. 5, 647–48; Jesse Lawson to Booker T. Washington, Oct. 8, 1900, *BTW Papers*, vol. 5, 651–52; Alexander Walters to Booker T. Washington, June 27, 1901, *BTW Papers*, vol. 6, 160.

9. Booker T. Washington to Francis Jackson Garrison, Feb. 27, 1900, *BTW Papers*, vol. 5, 450–51 (asking whether Garrison "might like to help us find persons in Boston who would consider it a pleasure to contribute" to a test case concerning "the Louisiana Election Law" being handled by a "number of responsible colored men"); Booker T. Washington to Francis Jackson Garrison, Mar. 11, 1900, *BTW Papers*, vol. 5, 458 (responding to a reply from Garrison that asked for more details by explaining that "as near as we can get at the matter now it will require $2,000 to take the case up through the Supreme Court"); see also Richard Price Hallowell to Booker T. Washington, Mar. 2, 1900, ibid. (sending a $20 check "to help along an effort to have the Louisiana Election Law tested before the United States Supreme Court" and adding that "[m]oney spent for such purposes is too often expended injudiciously, but as this is to go through your hands I have no hesitation on that account"). Hallowell was a Quaker merchant and banker who had been an active abolitionist and women's rights supporter. See ibid., 94n5 (providing biographical information).

10. Emmett Jay Scott to Booker T. Washington, Aug. 13, 1901, *BTW Papers*, vol. 6, 186 ("In making his report, Mr. Lawson did not use your name, but the initials X.Y.Z. Whenever they were called cheers were given").

11. See, e.g., "Alabama to Disfranchise the Negro," *Broad Ax*, Apr. 8, 1899 (noting the threat to voting rights in Alabama and opining as follows: "The time is not far distant when Booker T. Washington will be repudiated as the leader of our race, for he believes that only the mealy-mouthed negroes like himself should be permitted to participate in politics").

12. Harlan I, 294–303.

13. Robert Norrell's biography of Washington makes a persuasive case that in his political involvements Washington was pushing to the edge of what whites in the South would tolerate without placing the Tuskegee Institute in danger. Norrell, *Up from History*.

14. Harlan II, 134.

15. See, e.g., Jay Driskell, "First-Class Citizens."

16. Constitution of the State of Louisiana, as adopted in Convention at the City of New Orleans, May 12, 1898 (New Orleans: H. J. Hearsey, Convention Printer, 1898).

17. *BTW Papers*, vol. 5, 648n1 (biographical note on Birney); Alcée Fortier, ed., *Louisiana: Comprising Sketches of Parishes, Towns, Events, Institutions, and Persons* (Madison, WI: Century Historical Association, 1914), 382–83 (biographical information on Romain).

18. Petition-Mandamus, July 12, 1901, and Amended Petitions-Mandamus, Ryanes v. Gleason, July 21, and Aug. 1, 1901 (copies on file with author).

19. State ex rel Ryanes v. Gleason, no. 65432, Division "E," Judgment, Honorable W. B. Somerville, Judge, Aug. 23, 1901 (unpublished, on file with author). In a complicated decision, the court parsed the parties' various arguments. It held that, contrary to Gleason's arguments, it possessed jurisdiction to hear the case but then pointed out, among other items, two problems it viewed as lethal to Ryanes's petition. First, Ryanes would not be entitled to the writ of mandamus he was requesting even if Section 5 were unconstitutional, as he alleged, because he was not entitled to vote in any event under either the Section 3 (literacy) or Section 4 (property) qualifications provisions, which he was not challenging. Second, Ryanes had failed to prove that there were any white voters who had registered under Section 5 of Article 197 who could not have also registered under sections 3 or 4. Thus, the court concluded, citing *Williams*

v. Mississippi, 170 U.S. 213 (1898), Ryanes had failed to demonstrate that unconstitutional discrimination on the basis of race had occurred.

20. See *Portland New Age*, May 31, 1902, 5; "Call for Meeting of National Afro-American Council at St. Paul," *Wisconsin Weekly Advocate*, June 12, 1902, 4; "Annual Meet," *CG*, June 14, 1902, 4.

21. According to Ryanes's petition, these figures showed that the total African American registration for all wards in the Orleans parish for the year 1897 was 3,086 out of a total of 29,411, or 10.5 percent, but by November 2, 1899, after the effective date of the new registration requirements, the total African American registration for the parish was a mere 1,368 out of a total of 38,964, or a total of only 0.9 percent. Ryanes ran into problems when he was cross-examined on the stand, however, because he had to admit that he could not name any white voters who had been entitled to register solely by virtue of Section 5 of Article 197—in other words, Ryanes could not show that the grandfather clause was qualifying whites to vote who otherwise would have been ineligible under the literacy and property qualification requirements. Registrar Gleason testified that he could produce no list of white voters registered solely by virtue of Section 5 because his office's practice was to allow all who could register through Section 5 to do so even if they also could have availed themselves of Sections 3 or 4 because they were literate or owned sufficient property.

22. State ex rel Ryanes v. Gleason, no. 67606, Division "C," Opinion of Honorable John St. Paul, July 28, 1902 (unpublished, on file with author). More specifically, the appeals court held that it lacked jurisdiction because state law granted no specific right of appeal to a person seeking to challenge the denial of an alleged right to register as a voter, and Ryanes had not alleged that the matter in dispute involved $200 or more in damages, which would have been required for him to avail himself of the state's general law allowing for appeals to the high court (ibid.).

23. Fredrick L. McGhee to Booker T. Washington, Apr. 5, 1902, *BTW Papers*, vol. 6, 435.

24. For Pillsbury's self-reported biography, see *Memoirs of the Judiciary and the Bar of New England for the Nineteenth Century*, ed. Leonard A. Jones and Conrad Reno, vol. 2 (Boston: Century Memorial, 1901), 162–65. For an example of his legal advocacy on the constitutionality of federal antilynching legislation, see Albert E. Pillsbury, "A Brief Inquiry into a Federal Remedy for Lynching," *Harvard Law Review* 15 (1902): 707–13.

25. Albert E. Pillsbury to Booker T. Washington, July 30, 1901, *BTW Papers*, vol. 6, 182–83.

26. Voter registrars also insisted on proof difficult to obtain whenever men of color asserted a right to vote under these clauses. See Wilford Smith, "The Negro and the Law," in *The Negro Problem: A Series of Articles by Representative American Negroes of Today* (New York: James Pott, 1903).

27. See Giles v. Harris, 189 U.S. 475, 483 (1903); Constitution of the State of Alabama, as adopted by the Constitutional Convention, Sept. 3, 1901 (Montgomery, AL: Brown Printing, 1901).

28. On Washington's efforts to persuade the Alabama constitutional delegates not to proceed with disfranchising measures, see Riser, *Defying Disfranchisement*, 115–24; Harlan I, 288–303.

29. Max Bloomfield has conducted in-depth research into the details and economics of Smith's Galveston practice. See "From Deference to Confrontation: The Early Black Lawyers of Galveston, Texas, 1895–1920," in *The New High Priests: Lawyers in Post–Civil War America*, ed. Gerard W. Gawalt (Westport, CT: Greenwood Press, 1984), 151, 155, 158–61.

30. Carter v. Texas, 177 U.S. 442 (1900). I found no evidence of any link between Smith and the AAC. Riser convincingly argues that Smith's work was entirely independent of and invisible to the AAC. Riser, *Defying Disfranchisement*, 107.

31. 177 U.S. at 444.

32. Smith, for example, led the legal strategy through which Washington succeeded in having his adversary William Monroe Trotter serve an eighteen-month jail sentence after participating in disrupting a National Negro Business League meeting in Boston at which Fortune was the featured speaker. He also attempted to buy stock in Trotter's *Guardian* and force it into bankruptcy. In addition, in a 1911 public scandal in which Washington was accused of lurking near

a red-light district on the mistaken belief that a white woman who lived there was a prostitute, Smith was one of two lawyers Washington called to his side. After Washington's death, Smith worked for Marcus Garvey and his United Negro Improvement Association, resigning just months before Garvey was federally prosecuted for allegedly embezzling funds. See generally Riser, *Defying Disfranchisement*, 102.

33. Wilford Smith, "Negro and the Law," 159, 139.
34. Michael J. Klarman, *From Jim Crow to Civil Rights: The Supreme Court and the Struggle for Racial Equality* (New York: Oxford University Press, 2004), 117–35, 152–58.
35. Ibid., 146–48, 153–54, 156–59.
36. August Meier, "Toward a Reinterpretation of Booker T. Washington," *Journal of Southern History* 23 (1957): 220, 222; Louis R. Harlan, "The Secret Life of Booker T. Washington," *Journal of Southern History* 37 (1971): 393, 398.
37. On Giles's biography, see Riser, *Defying Disfranchisement*, 150–51.
38. Giles v. Teasley, 193 U.S. at 147.
39. "Filipino" (Wilford Smith) to Booker T. Washington, June 1, 1902, *BTW Papers*, vol. 6, 481–84. Riser describes Smith's outstanding abilities in strategically framing his cases to force the Court to give them merits consideration. See Riser, *Defying Disfranchisement*, 165–70.
40. This provision, referred to as § 1979 in Holmes's opinion, is now known as § 1983 and continues to be a key provision for civil rights litigators.
41. See Richard H. Fallon Jr. et al., *Hart & Wechsler's The Federal Courts and the Federal System*, 6th ed. (New York: Foundation Press, 2009), 162 (describing the severability doctrine); See, e.g., Ayotte v. Planned Parenthood of N. New England, 546 U.S. 320, 330 (2006) ("We try not to nullify more of a legislature's work than is necessary, for we know that a ruling of unconstitutionality frustrates the intent of the elective representatives of the people").
42. Giles v. Harris, 189 U.S. at 493.
43. Giles v. Teasley, 193 U.S. 146 (1904).
44. 177 U.S. 442 (1900).
45. Booker T. Washington to Wilford H. Smith, Feb. 2, 1904, *BTW Papers*, vol. 7, 423.
46. Prominent law and social movement theorist Michael McCann has frequently made this point in the contemporary context, emphasizing the importance of the "mobilization opportunities" offered when activists invoke legal symbols and normative claims in courts even when doing so does not result in judicial approval. In his study, however, wins were more affirming than losses, and wins perceived as important victories were the most productive of further mobilization. See, e.g., Michael W. McCann, *Rights at Work: Pay Equity and the Politics of Legal Mobilization* (Chicago: University of Chicago Press, 1994), 12; see also Michael W. McCann, "Reform Litigation on Trial," *Law and Social Inquiry* 17 (1992): 715, 723–24 (refuting claims that courts do not produce social change by pointing out the enormous symbolic importance of shifts in legal consciousness that can be produced by court victories, such as the importance of *Brown* to civil rights activists' perceptions of what kind of social change might be possible with more agitation).
47. Klarman, *From Jim Crow to Civil Rights*, 43 ("Between 1904 and 1935, the Court did not reverse the conviction of even one black defendant on the ground of race discrimination in jury selection, even though blacks were universally excluded from southern juries").
48. Wilford H. Smith to Booker T. Washington, Feb. 26, 1904, *BTW Papers*, vol. 7, 452; see also Booker T. Washington to Wilford H. Smith, Mar. 3, 1904, *BTW Papers*, vol. 7, 455–56; Wilford H. Smith to Booker T. Washington, Mar. 31, 1904, *BTW Papers*, vol. 7, 480. Here Smith seemed to be offering Washington the option of continuing to use legal tactics to at least keep a "challenge alive" under conditions in which other options were not feasible. McCann notes this as an important use of legal challenges in his classic refutation of Gerald Rosenburg's "hollow hope" thesis about the futility of using courts to create social change. See McCann, "Reform Litigation on Trial," 740n56.
49. Riser, *Defying Disfranchisement*, 243, 245.

50. See, e.g., Charles William Anderson to Booker T. Washington, May 13, 1903, *BTW Papers,* vol. 7, 138–41 (report by a Washington spy on a meeting to plan a suffrage convention in New York City the next month, at which Hayes had "ridicule[d] the manner in which Smith conducted his case" and "insinuated that Smith was not a lawyer").

51. Riser, *Defying Disfranchisement,* 188.

52. See Jones v. Montague, 194 U.S. 147 (1904); Selden v. Montague, 194 U.S. 153 (1904).

53. Brickhouse v. Brooks, 165 F. 534 (4th Cir. 1908).

54. See, e.g., Alexander, *Army of Lions,* 166.

55. See, e.g., *CG,* June 3, 1905, 2 (complaining that "[s]ince the unfortunate change of control in the council we have not heard a word" about the test case challenging the constitutionality of the Louisiana constitution).

56. See Carle, "Re-Envisioning Models for Pro Bono Lawyering," 81–96 (discussing elite lawyer-dominated models of public interest litigation in the early twentieth century).

57. Some still remain, such as many states' prohibitions on ex-felon voting. See Michelle Alexander, *The New Jim Crow* (New York: New Press, 2010), 2, 153–56 (arguing that ex-felon disfranchisement, among many other criminal justice institutions, reflects the continuation of a Jim Crow regime).

58. 238 U.S. 347 (1915).

59. For more on how the early NAACP used *Guinn* for organization-building purposes, see Susan D. Carle, "Race, Class, and Legal Ethics in the Early NAACP (1910–1920)," *Law and History Review* 20 (2002): 97, 117.

60. See Klarman, *From Jim Crow to Civil Rights,* 85–86. After the Court handed down *Guinn,* the Oklahoma legislature enacted a new transparent subterfuge that automatically qualified as voters all those who had voted in the 1914 general election, but required those who had not registered to vote in that election to register to vote within a twelve-day window extending from April 30 to May 11, 1916. The Court eventually struck down this new disfranchising device in *Lane v. Wilson,* 307 U.S. 268 (1939).

61. See, e.g., "To Help the Council," *CA,* Apr. 28, 1900 (reporting on "efforts last evening of the committee of energetic and race-loving young ladies who gave an entertainment in aid of the Afro-American Council").

62. "To Share His Burden," *WP,* Jan. 25, 1903 (reporting on a large public meeting held in conjunction with the AAC's executive committee meeting in Washington, DC, at which Virginia attorney James Hayes and others spoke about testing the constitutionality of disfranchising legislation in the South).

63. An excellent and extensive general literature focusing on these early cases from a legal perspective includes C. Matthew Hill, " 'We Live Not on What We Have': Reflections of the Birth of the Civil Rights Test Case Strategy and Its Lessons for Today's Same-Sex Marriage Litigation Campaign," *National Black Law Journal* 19 (2006): 175, 179–87 (discussing the Brotherhood of Liberty's sponsorship of *The Sue* test case); Bogen, "Precursors of Rosa Parks," 721–51 (focusing on Maryland, a key location for these cases); Mack, "Law, Society, Identity, and the Making of the Jim Crow South," 377–409 (focusing on the rise of *de jure* segregation on Tennessee railroads); Welke, "When All the Women Were White," 261–315 (discussing the intermeshing of race, gender, and class dimensions in Jim Crow car cases); Minter, "Failure of Freedom," 993–1008 (uncovering and analyzing late nineteenth-century transportation segregation cases). On early test cases challenging Jim Crow in the antebellum North, see Kelley, *Right to Ride,* 15–33.

64. See Mark Elliott, *Color-Blind Justice: Albion Tourgée and the Quest for Racial Equality from the Civil War to* Plessy v. Ferguson (New York: Oxford University Press, 2006), 262–95; Harvey Fireside, *Separate and Unequal: Homer Plessy and the Supreme Court Decision That Legalized Racism* (New York: Carroll and Graf, 2004).

65. "An Appeal for Funds by the Legal and Legislative Bureau of the National Afro-American Council," *Broad Ax,* Apr. 16, 1904.

66. W.E.B. Du Bois to Booker T. Washington, Dec. 4, 1902, *BTW Papers*, vol. 6, 605.

67. Ibid. For examples of these appeals, see "Money Needed," *St. Paul Appeal*, Dec. 5, 1903, cited in Justesen, *Broken Brotherhood*, 233n65; "Send Your Subscription," *St. Paul Appeal*, Apr. 30, 1904, 2; May 14, 1904, 2; May 21, 1904, 2.

68. See, e.g., Booker T. Washington to Robert Todd Lincoln, Jan. 1903, *BTW Papers*, vol. 7, 3 (enclosing a report of bad treatment of an African American college graduate on a Pullman car and urging that the matter be settled in such a way as to not humiliate passengers); Emmett Jay Scott to E. Donaldson, May 4, 1903, *BTW Papers*, vol. 7, 137 (Scott's personal report of bad treatment forwarded to Washington); Booker T. Washington to Robert Todd Lincoln, Oct. 28, 1903, *BTW Papers*, vol. 7, 312 (another entreaty on the general issue of humiliating treatment of African American passengers on Pullman trains); Booker T. Washington to William Henry Baldwin Jr., Oct. 28, 1903, *BTW Papers*, vol. 7, 313 (urging Baldwin to bring pressure to bear on Lincoln); Booker T. Washington to James Napier, Nov. 2, 1903, *BTW Papers*, vol. 7, 324 (discussing appointment of a committee to seek a meeting with Lincoln); William Henry Baldwin Jr. to Booker T. Washington, Mar. 19, 1900, *BTW Papers*, vol. 5, 46–68 (reporting on his discussions with railway companies in the South and urging that no test case be made and that the companies work out ways to avoid state legislation instead); Booker T. Washington to Lucia True Ames Mead, June 19, 1906, *BTW Papers*, vol. 9, 32 (dismissing a report that Reverdy Ransom was badly treated on a Pullman as instead being the result of Ransom's intoxication and arguing that bad treatment of African Americans was uncommon).

69. Meyer, "Protest and Political Opportunities," 139.

70. On the difference between standard institutional politics and social movement strategies, see McAdam, *Political Process and the Development of Black Insurgency*, xxx–xxxi, xxxvi (noting a period of unsuccessful negotiation between state and nonstate elites prior to the development of popular social movements); ibid., 16–18 (defining ordinary or institutionalized politics as "rational group-action in pursuit of substantive political goals" and arguing that social movements are not so much characterized by nonrational action as by politically excluded groups' inability to exercise "influence through institutionalized means"); ibid., 22–24, 25 (discussing resource mobilization theorists' focus on excluded political actors' dedication to rationally advancing their political goals and distinguishing public interest lobbies from the efforts of excluded groups that involve recourse to "noninstitutional forms of political participation"). The cusp of the twentieth century saw the AAC's legislative arm wavering between standard institutional politics and "challenger" approaches, but being pushed toward the latter strategy as a result of its inability to influence policy through the standard political avenues.

71. On the Lodge bill and its demise, see Perman, *Struggle for Mastery*, 39–41.

72. See Jeffry A. Jenkins, Justin Peck, and Vesla M. Weaver, "Between Reconstructions: Congressional Action on Civil Rights, 1891–1940," *Studies in American Political Development* 24 (2010): 57, 61–62.

73. 34 *Cong. Rec.* 748 (1901); "Ballot Laws in the South," *CA*, Dec. 6, 1899.

74. See [no title], *CA*, Nov. 8, 1902 (urging Congress to take up the Crumpacker resolution).

75. See, e.g., T. Thomas Fortune to Booker T. Washington, Nov. 20, 1899, *BTW Papers*, vol. 5, 269–70 (expressing his opinion that a reduction in Southern electoral representation would not, in the end, benefit African American voters).

76. "Ballot Laws in the South." But see *CG*, Nov. 24, 1900 (opposing the *Denver Statesman*, the *Chicago Conservator* [the Barnetts' paper], and all other papers that urged passage of the Crumpacker bill and arguing instead that the constitutionality of disfranchising measures should be tested in court).

77. Perman, *Struggle for Mastery*, 225, 228–29.

78. House Commission to Inquire into the Condition of the Colored People, H. Rep. no. 2194, 57th Cong., 1st Sess., 1902. See also 35 Cong. Rec. 5786 (1902) (introduction of the AAC's petition praying for the creation of a commission, referred to the Committee on Education and Labor).

79. House Commission to Inquire into the Condition of the Colored People, part 2, 1–2.

80. "Cry from Macedonia," *Richmond Times,* Jan. 31, 1899, 4.

81. See Darren Hutchinson, "Racial Exhaustion," *Washington University Law Review* 86 (2009): 917–74.

82. *BTW Papers,* vol. 6, 447n1–2 (biographical note on Murray and on the background to the Irwin bill).

83. "Learn How to Work," *St. Paul Globe,* July 11, 1902.

84. *Who's Who of the Colored Race,* s.v. "Lawson, Jesse"; *BTW Papers,* vol. 3, 570 (biographical note); see *CA,* Dec. 8, 1900, 11; See, e.g., "The Light of History: Prof. Jesse Lawson's Review of Thirty Years," *CA,* Feb. 8, 1902.

85. "Race Problem Inquiry: National Sociological Society's Appeal to Congress," *NYT,* Nov. 13, 1903 (describing the society's sessions).

86. National Sociological Society, *How to Solve the Race Problem: The Proceedings of the Washington Conference on the Race Problem in the United States* (Washington, DC: Beresford, Printer, 1904).

87. Ibid., 5.

88. Ibid., 40.

89. Ibid., 130.

90. Ibid., 134.

91. Ibid., 253.

92. Ibid., 139.

93. For a summary of the literature on political destabilization as a social movement strategy, see McAdam, *Political Process and the Development of Black Insurgency,* 42.

94. National Sociological Society, *How to Solve the Race Problem,* 141.

95. Ibid., 145.

96. Ibid., 226.

97. Ibid., 264.

98. "Race Problem Inquiry."

99. David Augustus Straker, *Negro Suffrage in the South* (Detroit: Published by author, 1906).

100. House Committee on Interstate and Foreign Commerce, *Hearings on the Bills to Amend the Interstate Commerce Law,* 57th Cong., 1st sess., 1902, 437–53.

101. "Appeal for Rights," *WP,* Mar. 11, 1902; "Discussed Jim Crow Cars," *WP,* Apr. 15, 1902.

102. See generally Daniel W. Crofts, "The Warner-Foraker Amendment to the Hepburn Bill: Friend or Foe of Jim Crow?" *Journal of Southern History* 39 (1973): 341–58.

103. Miller and Grimké, "How the Warner Foraker Amendment Was Killed," *NYA,* Aug. 2, 1906.

104. Crofts, "Warner-Foraker Amendment," 353.

105. 33 Cong. Rec. 1017, 1021 (1900).

106. See 33 Cong. Rec. 2153 (1900).

107. George White on the floor of Congress, Feb. 23, 1900, 33 Cong. Rec. 2151 (1900).

108. See Justesen, *White,* 213–29.

109. Justesen, *Broken Brotherhood,* 64–65, 93.

110. Justesen, *White,* 389. After failing in an effort of several years' duration to secure a DC political appointment, White retired to Philadelphia, where he practiced law and became deeply involved in a land-improvement company and the establishment of a school, through which efforts he hoped to create the kind of intentional African American community that participants at the NSS conference had discussed (ibid., 400–404).

111. On the NAACP's campaign to promote passage of federal antilynching legislation, see Robert L. Zangrando, *The NAACP Crusade against Lynching, 1909–1950* (Philadelphia: Temple University Press, 1980). Much later these efforts gave birth to a distant cousin—federal anti-hate crime legislation enacted in 1968 and expanded in 2009. On the legislative history of federal antihate crimes legislation, see Rebecca Dansky, "Strengthening and Expanding Federal Hate Crimes Law in the 21st Century" (student paper, American University Washington College of Law, 2009, on file with author).

112. McAdam, *Political Process and the Development of Black Insurgency,* 89.

113. See generally Mary Frances Berry, *My Face Is Black Is True: Callie House and the Struggle for Ex-Slave Reparations* (New York: Alfred A. Knopf, 2005).

114. "Hanna Aids Ex-Slaves," *NYT,* Feb. 5, 1903 (the AAC "denounced the ex-slave pension project").

115. Berry, *My Face Is Black Is True,* 170–250.

116. See "Mob Rule in New Orleans: Robert Charles and His Fight to the Death," in *Southern Horrors and Other Writings,* 158. For a harrowing account of the Charles murder, see Joel Williamson, *The Crucible of Race: Black-White Relations in the American South since Emancipation* (New York: Oxford University Press, 1984), 201–209.

117. Alexander, *Army of Lions,* 167.

118. "Afro-American Proclamation," *Christian Recorder,* May 11, 1899; "Proclamation Observed," *Christian Recorder,* June 8, 1899; "Appeal against Lynching: Afro-Americans Ask Fair and Impartial Trials in the South," *NYT,* June 11, 1899. See also "Negroes Must Resist," *Broad Ax,* May 9, 1899 (describing Walters's address before a large New Jersey audience). For a graphic description of the Sam Hose lynching, see Williamson, *Crucible of Race,* 204–205.

119. See Alexander, *Army of Lions,* 161–62.

120. "Day of Prayer for Negroes," *NYT,* Oct. 3, 1906; "The Day for Prayer," *WB,* Aug. 18, 1906.

121. On AAC meetings with McKinley, see Justesen, *Broken Brotherhood,* 83. Justesen offers a comparative discussion of the track records of McKinley and Roosevelt with respect to appointments of African Americans to political office, with Roosevelt's total of fifteen such appointments in his first six months in office stacking up unfavorably against McKinley's appointment of 179 African Americans in his first six months (ibid., 123).

122. *AAC Internal History,* 10.

123. See "Civil Rights Cases," *CA,* Dec. 2, 1899, 5; see also Alexander, "We Know Our Rights," 431, 21–211, 229.

124. See, e.g., "Rev. L. G. Jordon before the Afro-American Council," *Alexander's Magazine* 3: 96–100 (Dec. 15, 1906); see also Alexander, "We Know Our Rights," 416.

Chapter 7

1. See Dorothy C. Salem, "*The NACW*" (PhD diss., Kent State University, 1986), 13 (refuting "Meier's claim that civil rights and protest activities were 'rather rare'" in black women's clubs), citing Meier, *Negro Thought,* 135. This work became the basis for Salem's important study, *To Better Our World: Black Women in Organized Reform, 1890–1920* (Brooklyn, NY: Carlson, 1990).

2. I am grateful for Jay Driskell for helping me see this point more clearly. See Driskell, "First Class Citizens," 11n8.

3. A recent exploration of the history of these many clubs, concentrating primarily on religious organizations, is Collier-Thomas, *Jesus, Jobs, and Justice,* 264–68. A classic work is Higginbotham, *Righteous Discontent.* Other major works on the African American club women's movement in general, and the NACW in particular, which were especially helpful to this particular project include Giddings, *Ida;* Elizabeth Lindsay Davis, *Lifting as They Climb* (New York: G. K. Hall, 1996); Floris Barnett Cash, *African American Women and Social Action: The Clubwomen and Volunteerism from Jim Crow to the New Deal, 1896–1936* (Westport, CT: Greenwood Press, 2001); Knupfer, *Toward a Tenderer Humanity;* Cynthia Neverdon-Morton, *Afro-American Women of the South and the Advancement of the Race, 1895–1925* (Knoxville: University of Tennessee Press, 1989); Lynda F. Dickson, "The Early Club Movement among Black Women" (PhD diss., University of Colorado, 1982); White, *Too Heavy a Load,* 1–110. These works generally do not explore in depth the central question of this project concerning the relationship between the women's club movement and the development of ideas about how to use law for social change, with the important exception of Dorothy Roberts's work on the role of African

American club women in the development of welfare policy in the United States. See Dorothy Roberts, "Black Club Women and Child Welfare: Lesson for Modern Reform," *Florida State Law Review* 32 (2005): 957–72.

4. Dickson, "Early Club Movement," 61. By 1925 the NACW had three hundred thousand members (ibid.).

5. Giddings, *Ida*, 348, 359–60; "Some Information concerning Jacks, the Letter Writer," *WE*, July 1895, 2–3. Ruffin's call is reprinted in Davis, *Lifting as They Climb*, 14.

6. For example, many African American women's clubs enthusiastically supported the temperance movement and the projects of the Women's Christian Temperance Union (WCTU). See, e.g., "Minutes of the Third Biennial Meeting of…the NACW," St. Louis, Mo., July 1904, 23, NACWP (Texas club report of work in connection with the WCTU). But the WCTU's leaders were known to express racially pernicious views, especially on the issue of lynching, which they frequently blamed on black male sexual violence against white women. See "Lady Somerset and Miss Willard Confess of Themselves Apologists for Lynching," *WE*, Aug. 1895, 17 (quoting and criticizing an article by WCTU leaders blaming lynching in the United States on unpunished sex crimes). Another example of white women's race prejudice involved the National Federation of Women's Club's refusal to seat Josephine Ruffin at its 1900 annual convention as a delegate from an African American women's club. See *NACWN*, Feb. 1901, 2–3 (discussion of this incident); *NACWN*, Feb. 1902, 2–3 (further discussion of the incident).

   Despite these actions, NACW leaders did not completely cut off ties with white women's clubs, appreciating the existence of some common bonds due to shared issues of gender subordination. See Collier-Thomas, *Jesus, Jobs, and Justice*, 81 (noting NACW's determination that interracial alliances were necessary to accomplish its goals). Thus the goals of women's reform activism on the two sides of the race divide sometimes dovetailed and sometimes diverged. Progressive white women sometimes spoke at NACW conventions, and Jane Addams invited NACW representatives to Hull House. Mary Church Terrell, "The Second Convention of the NACW," Sept. 2, 1899, 3, Speeches and Writings File, MCTPLOC (discussing the meeting of NACW delegates with residents of Jane Addams's Hull House).

   For more examples of the strained but continuing interrelation between African American and white women reformers, See, e.g., *NACWN*, Jan. 1901, 2–3 (letter from Elizabeth Cady Stanton criticizing white women's clubs that refused African Americans' membership); "Minutes of the Fourth Biennial Meeting…of the NACW," Detroit, Michigan, July 1906, 10, Conventions, NACWP (discussion of an NACW memorial service held for Susan B. Anthony); ibid., 18 (motion supporting the extension of the YWCA's work "among our women"); Mary Church Terrell, "The Progress of Colored Women," n.d., circa 1904, 4, Speeches and Writings File, MCTPLOC ("In their earnest endeavor to work out their own salvation Colored women have been generously aided and encouraged by their more fortunate sisters of the dominant race, many of whom are broad in their views on the race problem, just and kind in their treatment of their sisters of a darker hue and strong in their determination to render them any assistance in their power"); Mary Church Terrell, "The Strongest for the Weakest," n.d. [circa 1904], 10, Speeches and Writings File, MCTPLOC (noting the importance of white female antislavery societies to emancipation).

7. Mary Church Terrell, "Address Delivered at the National Council of Women Convention," Apr. 9, 1905, 2, Speeches and Writings File, MCTPLOC. This quote captures a classic example of identity formation and category formation as aspects of the rise of a social movement. See generally Doug McAdam, Sidney Tarrow, and Charles Tilly, *Dynamics of Contention* (Cambridge, UK: Cambridge University Press, 2004), 126, 132, 143. McAdam et al. argue that identities become "political" primarily when they involve "relations to government" (ibid., 132). Note that here, however, the politicization of identity occurs in relation to the organizations of civil society.

8. Mary Church Terrell, "History of the Colored Women's League," MCTPMS, box 102–103, f. 59, 3.

9. Logan and Winston, *Dictionary of American Negro Biography*, 535, s.v. "Ruffin, Josephine St. Pierre"; "A Leader of Colored Women," *CT*, June 17, 1900, 24 (giving biographical details about Ruffin's high social standing and elite background following her rejection from the General Federation of Women at its 1900 Milwaukee convention).

10. Kate Dossett makes a similar point in observing that women's clubs were more comfortable than male leaders in spanning both integrationist and separatist strategies. See Kate Dossett, *Bridging Race Divides: Black Nationalism, Feminism, and Integration in the United States, 1896–1935* (Gainesville: University Press of Florida, 2008), 6.

11. On Kelley and Milholland as early female lawyer-activists, see Susan D. Carle, "Review Essay: Gender in the Construction of the Lawyer's Persona," 22 *Harvard Women's Law Journal* (1999), 253–66; Linda J. Lumsden, *Inez: The Life and Times of Inez Milholland* (Bloomington: Indiana University Press, 2004), 62–91.

12. See generally Kenneth Mack, "A Social History of Everyday Practice: Sadie T. M. Alexander and the Incorporation of Black Women into the American Legal Profession, 1925–1960," *Cornell Law Review* 87 (2002): 1405, 1417; J. Clay Smith, ed., *Rebels in Law: Voice in History of Black Women Lawyers* (Ann Arbor: University of Michigan Press, 1998), 13–15. A handful of earlier African American women lawyers were often barred from bar admission and faced even worse discrimination than did their male counterparts. See, e.g., Rosalyn Terborg-Penn, *African American Women in the Struggle for the Vote, 1850–1920* (Bloomington: Indiana University Press, 1998), 38–39 (discussing the experience of Mary Ann Shadd Cary, an African American women's suffrage activist and the first woman student at Howard Law School shortly after it was founded, who was not permitted to graduate because DC law prohibited women from bar admission).

13. Jacqueline Jones, *Labor of Love, Labor of Sorrow: Black Women, Work, and the Family from Slavery to the Present* (New York: Basic Books, 1985), 143–44.

14. As Ruffin once put it, espousing the civil rights militancy characteristic of Boston activists, "If laws are unjust, they must be continually broken until they are killed or altered." Collier-Thomas, *Jesus, Jobs, and Justice*, 433.

15. On the discriminatory barriers to African American women's access to careers in law prior to the 1920s, see Kenneth W. Mack, "A Social History of Everyday Practice: Sadie T. M. Alexander and the Incorporation of Black Women into the American Legal Profession, 1925–1960," *Cornell Law Review* 87 (2002): 1405, 1407–17.

16. "History of the Bethel Literary and Historical Association," n.p., 15, 20, in BLSP.

17. Beverly Washington Jones, "Quest for Equality," 76.

18. "History of Bethel Literary," 17, 20.

19. Beverly Washington Jones, "Quest for Equality," 17–18; Giddings, *Ida*, 28–32. Another biography that enhanced my understanding of Wells Barnett is Linda O. McMurry, *To Keep the Waters Troubled: The Life of Ida B. Wells* (New York: Oxford University Press, 1998).

20. Ibid., 34–38.

21. Wells Barnett, *Memphis Diary*, 150 (entry for July 13, 1887).

22. See, e.g., Church Terrell, *Colored Woman*, 163 ("I did not have the knack (or whatever it is) of inducing newspaper men to give me write-ups").

23. Wells Barnett, *Autobiography*, 47–52; Church Terrell, *Colored Woman*, 105, 108.

24. On Barnett's commitment to his wife's public activities, see Wells Barnett, *Autobiography*, 352, 311; Alfreda M. Duster, introduction to *Autobiography*, xxii (Duster, who was Wells Barnett's daughter, reflects on the egalitarian relationship between her parents and on her father's support for her mother's public engagements). On Robert Terrell's similar support for his wife, see Church Terrell, *Colored Woman*, 158, 194, 397.

25. Wells Barnett, *Autobiography*, 279–83; see also ibid., 251–52 (describing her feelings about motherhood).

26. *NACWN*, Apr. 1900, 1 (Woman's Era Club report attacking the conduct of the national convention).

27. W. E. Burghardt Du Bois, "Two Negro Conventions," *Independent*, Sept. 7, 1899, 2425–27 (comparing the AAC and the NACW, among other organizations, and assessing the relative advantages and disadvantages of forming national organizations by accreting already existing local bodies as opposed to forming new ones).

28. Collier-Thomas, *Jesus, Jobs, and Justice*, 288.

29. "Report of the Women's Loyal Union of New York and Brooklyn," reprinted in "A History of the Club Movement among the Colored Women of the United States" (hereinafter "NACW Internal History"), 1902, 13, in part I, NACWP; see also ibid., 65 (reiterating that this affiliate was organized in 1892 for "the advocacy of that justice which is the divine right of man."); *NACWN*, Apr. 1900, 3 (reporting that this group's literature committee had arranged for the publication and circulation of an important leaflet containing AAC leader Jesse Lawson's "Address to the People of the United States").

30. See "Third Annual Convention of the Colorado State Federation of Colored Women's Clubs," June 1906, attachments, NACWP; "NACW Internal History," 13 (report of Women's Club of Jefferson County).

31. *WE*, June 1896, 5 (report of a newly formed Women's Auxiliary Club); "NACW Internal History," 116 (report of the Woman's Era Club); *NACWN*, Nov. 1899, 2–3 (report of the Progressive Circle of the Kings' Daughters); *NACWN*, Oct. 1904, 2 (report of the Dearborn Center). On the religious motivation of many women's clubs and their connection to the ideas of the social gospel movement, see generally Collier-Thomas, *Jesus, Jobs, and Justice*, 192–96.

32. See "The Yearly Report of the Women's Club of Atlanta, Ga.," in Minutes of the NACW in Nashville, Tennessee, Sept. 1897, NACWP (reporting that its members, "filled with the spirit of Christ," intended to "help save the race from immorality & vice [and] to put forth every effort to prevent the young from going astray"); *NACWN*, May 15, 1897, 1 (reporting that Tuskegee Institute teachers traveled to nearby plantations to conduct lessons in "home making" for plantation women and children); "NACW Internal History," 72 (report of the Phyllis Wheatley Circle of Greenville, Mississippi, on organizing a girl's school to teach sewing, mending, cooking, painting, and needlepoint); ibid., 108 (Women's Uplifting Club of Eufaula, Alabama, plans to establish a "woman's home for orphan and erring girls"); *NACWN*, Nov. 1900, 4 (Women's Mutual Improvement Club of Knoxville, Tennessee, report on opening five rooms of housing for "the friendless" and "helpless," staffed by both white and African American volunteers); *NACWN*, Oct. 1904, 2 (report of the Ladies Sewing Circle of Louisville, Kentucky, on providing clothing and shoes for the residents of an orphans' home).

33. Works noting the political and civil rights objectives of African American women's organizations include Collier-Thomas, *Jesus, Jobs, and Justice*, 261, 277, 280, 298, and Salem, "NACW," 13, 39, 74. A classic example of the benefits of studying women's and men's activism together is Gilmore's *Gender and Jim Crow*.

34. "NACW Internal History," 6, 9, 48–49 (containing minutes of Boston 1895 meeting and NFAA 1896 meeting in Washington, DC).

35. Ibid., 50–51.

36. *WE*, Oct. and Nov. 1896. It was clear that the African American women's club movement would be overtly and resolutely political even at the National Colored Women's Congress convened in conjunction with the 1895 International Exposition in Atlanta. This Women's Congress condemned the convict lease system and called upon "the legal authorities of the states where the convict lease system is in force, to at least make proper provision for the separation of the sexes." It insisted that the white-led WCTU, in which many African American women were active, express "less equivocal" attitudes about lynching and color prejudice generally; called on "Southern legislators, in the name of the common womanhood, to adopt a first and second class fare [system], so that the womanhood of the race may be protected from every outrage and insult" of the separate car system; and condemned "every form of lawlessness and miscarriage of justice," concluding with a demand for "the equal enforcement of the law for all classes of American citizens" (*WE*, Jan. 1896, 2–3). The insistent tone of these resolutions contrasts

with the conciliatory approach of Booker T. Washington's address delivered at the same event, as Glenda Gilmore has observed. Gilmore, *Gender and Jim Crow,* 26. The theoretical literature on social change movements has proposed, on the basis of cross-cultural study, that women's organizations can sometimes take more confrontational stands than men's organizations without being perceived as presenting as great a threat to the existing social order. See, e.g., Mira Marx Ferree and Carol McClurg Mueller, "Feminism and the Women's Movement: A Global Perspective," in *The Blackwell Companion to Social Movements,* ed. David Snow, Sarah Soule, and Hanspeter Kriesi (Malden, MA: Blackwell, 2005), 576, 578–79 (observing that in Chile and East Germany, women's networks enjoyed greater protection and moral leverage in challenging dictatorships than did men's networks and hypothesizing that women's frequent invisibility as political actors sometimes renders them less threatening than men).

37. *NACWN,* June 1899, 3.
38. "What Colored Women Have Done," *NACWN,* Nov. 1900, 1, 3. Earlier examples of attention to Jim Crow transportation include *NACWN,* Sept. 1898, 2 (discussing Jim Crow railroad legislation in South Carolina).
39. "Third Address to the National Association of Colored Women, Delivered in Buffalo, New York, 1901," at 9, 11, MCTPLOC, microfilm edition, Speeches and Writings Files (hereinafter MCT, "Third NACW Address").
40. *NACWN,* Oct. 1904, 1.
41. "Minutes of the Fourth Convention of the NACW," July 1904, 25, NACWP.
42. MCT, "Third NACW Address," 6.
43. *NACWN,* Apr. 1900, 4; letter from Harriet Taylor Upton, NAWSA, to Mary Church Terrell, Nov. 4, 1902 (enclosing life membership certificate), MCTPLOC, 1902 correspondence. Church Terrell's papers contain many folders of clippings related to the women's suffrage movement. See also Collier-Thomas, *Jesus, Jobs, and Justice,* 258 (discussing the interest of African American religious women's groups in the female suffrage issue).
44. African American women's suffrage work is well researched in Terborg-Penn, *Struggle for the Vote.*
45. *WE,* Nov. 1895, 6; ibid., 11 (editorial arguing that African American women especially needed suffrage).
46. *WE,* Jan. 1896, 11. For more on Layten, her views on the "new woman movement," and the many leadership roles she played within the NACW through the 1920s, see Collier-Thomas, *Jesus, Jobs, and Justice,* 273–74, 292. Knupfer points out that not all NACW activists were in favor of the vote. Knupfer, *Toward a Tenderer Humanity,* 6.
47. Mary Church Terrell, "The Progress of Colored Women," n.d., circa 1914, 2, Speeches and Writings File, MCTPLOC. This quote also highlights the international awareness of Church Terrell and other NACW leaders. As did other organizations of the era, the NACW worked to develop bonds with women's organizations in other countries, including both organizations of women of color around the world and predominantly white European women's organizations. In 1904 it sent representatives to the International Congress of Women in Germany. There Church Terrell was the only U.S. delegate to deliver her remarks in German as well as English, and Mary Washington participated on behalf of the NACW as well. See *NACWN,* Jan. 1901, 1 (reporting on the NACW's admission to the International Council of Women); Mary Church Terrell, "Address to Be Delivered at the International Congress of Women in Berlin," June 15, 1904," Speeches and Writings File, MCTPLOC; "Minutes of the Fourth Biennial Meeting...of the NACW," Detroit, Mich., 1906, 18, Minutes, NACWP (motion of Mary Church Terrell requesting that an NACW organizer form women's clubs in Liberia and begin an organization like the NACW in Africa to produce an International Association of Colored Women); "Minutes of the Fifth Biennial Meeting...of the NACW," Aug. 1908, 30, Minutes, NACWP (resolution of representatives of women's clubs in the United States, Liberia, and Bermuda giving expression to their mutual aims).
48. "NACW Internal History," 93; *WE,* Aug. 1895, 16–17.

49. *WE*, Oct. 1895, 11; ibid., Nov. 1895, 13.

50. *NACWN*, Nov. 1899, 4.

51. Knupfer, *Toward a Tenderer Humanity*, 57–58.

52. *NACWN*, Apr. 1900, 3.

53. Knupfer, *Toward a Tenderer Humanity*, 44, 56–59.

54. In 1901 the NACW elected as its second president university professor Josephine Silone Yates. Resolutions addressing the political and civil rights issues of the day, including Jim Crow, lynching, convict leasing, and women's suffrage, continued at its biennial national conferences. In 1906 the NACW elected Lucy Thurman, a leading figure in the AME Church and an ardent temperance organizer, as its third president. As the decade came to a close, women's clubs continued to engage in political activity through the formation of civic leagues in both the North and the South as the national battle for women's suffrage heated up. For more on Lucy Thurman, see Collier-Thomas, *Jesus, Jobs, and Justice*, 282.

55. See, e.g., Dossett, *Bridging Race Divides* (noting that a close reading of Margaret Murray Washington's speeches "reveals the degree to which she had a different agenda from that of her husband").

56. *WE*, Oct. 1895, 19 (report of Texas editor Cora L. Smith, suggesting that "[t]here are few women who would not marry under favorable circumstances, but in this age one cannot accept what her grandmother or great-grandmother was proud to take" and that "[t]he one good thing the new woman has done for us is to emancipate us and give us employment in every field of labor, so that if our wandering half fails to join us on this side of the river Styx we are so busy that we fail to note the omission"). Examples of attention to women in business and the professions include *NACWN*, May 1899, 3 (articles supporting the advancement of women in politics and in the professions "without regard to sex"); *NACWN*, Nov. 1899, 2 (reprinting a newspaper article reporting on the progress of women in the real estate business); "Minutes of the Fourth Biennial Meeting...of the NACW," July 1906, 6, 23, NACWP (listing and summarizing a scheduled symposium on "The Afro-American Woman in the Professions"); "Seventh Biennial Convention of the NACW, July 1910," 3, NACWP (listing a scheduled paper on "The Influence of Professional Women on the Young").

57. See, e.g., Mary Church Terrell, "President's First Address to the NACW," Sept. 15, 1897, n.p., in Speeches, MCTPLOC ("the work which we hope to accomplish can be done better...by the mothers, wives, daughters and sisters of our race than by the fathers, husbands, brothers and sons."); Mary Church Terrell, "The Duty of the NACW to the Race," Aug. 1899, 7, Speeches, MCTPLOC ("If I were called upon to state in a word where I thought the organization should do its most effective work, I should say unhesitatingly—in the home. The purification of the home must be our first consideration and care"). See generally Eileen Boris, "The Power of Motherhood: Black and White Activist Women Redefine the Political," *Yale Journal of Law and Feminism* 2 (1989–90): 25–49.

58. "Remarks Made at the Dinner Given by the Women's Henry George League," Feb. 18, 1905, 6, in Speeches, MCTPLOC.

59. Higginbotham, *Righteous Discontent*, 14. Higginbotham goes on to show how this "deliberate, highly self-conscious concession to hegemonic values" served the important end of allowing poor black women to define themselves "outside the parameters of prevailing racist discourses" (ibid., 192); Kevin Gaines, *Uplifting the Race: Black Leadership, Politics, and Culture in the Twentieth Century* (Chapel Hill: University of North Carolina Press, 1996), 2–3, 82; see also Cash, *African American Women and Social Action*, 4 (discussing and critiquing Gaines's thesis); Dossett, *Bridging Race Divides*, 11 (arguing that "respectability was not simply the prerogative of the middle classes, imposed upon the poor," but was sometimes based on " 'community consensus and cross-class participation' ") (further citations omitted).

60. Rouse, *Lugenia Burns Hope*, 16.

61. Church Terrell, *Colored Woman*.

62. Kramer, "Uplifting Our 'Downtrodden Sisterhood,'" 243, 245–49; Knupfer, *Toward a Tenderer Humanity*, 81.

63. Examples of fund-raising for facilities construction work include *WE*, Feb. 1895, 11 (Louisiana report on asylum construction leading to a "magnificent structure...perfect in every detail which pertains to modern improvements" and "new and comfortable quarters" for "poor little folks"); "Minutes of the Second Convention of the NACW, Chicago, Ill.," 1899, 9 (report of Memphis, TN, club's purchase of twenty-five acres of land for a home for orphans); *NACWN*, Apr. 1902, 3 (Missouri club's report about purchasing a piece of property for the St. Louis Colored Orphans Home, housing thirty-five children).

64. W.E.B. Du Bois, *Efforts for Social Betterment among Negro Americans*, Atlanta University Publication no. 14 (Atlanta: Atlanta University Press, 1909), 42 (quoting Josephine S. Yates), cited in Andrew Billingsley and Jeanne M. Giovannoni, *Children of the Storm: Black Children and American Child Welfare* (New York: Harcourt Brace Jovanovich, 1972), 50; Salem, *To Better Our World*, 68–71 (describing many examples of women's groups that started old-age homes).

65. Du Bois's study of African American social work included an interview with Elizabeth McDonald, founder of a Chicago orphanage, who reported that she had established a home for fifty-six children and two mothers in her own private home, supporting the project through public speaking and nominal charges to some of the children's parents. Du Bois, *Efforts for Social Betterment*, 80, cited in Billingsley and Giovannoni, *Children of the Storm*, 53–54; see also ibid. (detailing examples of other orphanages). Du Bois described numerous additional examples of orphanages as well; see Du Bois, *Efforts for Betterment*, 77–87. Atlanta club woman Carrie Steele, born an orphan herself, founded a home for orphans and then convinced the city to purchase it and take over its management under the direction of an African American board of trustees. Neverdon-Morton, *Afro-American Women of the South*, 143–44; Salem, *To Better Our World*, 82–23.

66. Knupfer does a particularly good job of detailing this kind of fund-raising work as it took place in the Chicago area to support the opening of the Provident Hospital and the Phyllis Wheatley Home to provide a safe environment for young girls new to the city. Knupfer, *Toward a Tenderer Humanity*, 37.

67. On day nursery programs, See, e.g., Mary Church Terrell, "The Progress and the Problem of the Colored Woman," n.d, circa 1914, 14, in Speeches, MCTPLOC (describing progress in founding day nurseries, "of which there is an imperative need" due to the many "[t]housands of our wage-earning mothers...obliged to leave their children all day, while they go out to work").

68. Knupfer, *Toward a Tendered Humanity*, 106 (noting the vocational importance of dressmaking); Gilmore, *Gender and Jim Crow*, 160-61 (noting the collateral benefits of sewing circles in producing clothing for those who needed it).

69. See, e.g., *WE*, Jan. 1896, 14 (report on recognition given the excellence of a sewing school run by Miss Carrie Syphax within the industrial department of African American public schools in Washington, DC); Mary Church Terrell, "President's First Address to the NACW," Sept. 15, 1897, 14, Speeches and Addresses File, MCTPLOC (daring delegates to work for "the establishment of industrial schools, in connection with the public school system, so that our boys and girls may be given trades"); Mary Church Terrell, "The Duty of the [NACW] to the Race," Aug. 1899, 6, Speeches and Addresses File, MCTPLOC (calling for the establishment of training schools for domestic science and nursing); *NACWN*, Nov. 1900, 1, 3 (Church Terrell's report that clubs all over the country were being urged to establish schools of domestic science in which girls could be trained to be skilled domestics, which would "do more toward solving the labor question as it affects our women than by any other means...in our power to employ"); Knupfer, *Toward a Tenderer Humanity*, 90–91 (describing Matthews's White Rose Mission).

70. Paula Giddings, *When and Where I Enter: The Impact of Black Women on Race and Sex in America* (New York: Bantam Books, 1984), 100.

71. Billingsley and Giovannoni, *Children of the Storm,* 57.

72. Neverdon-Morton, *Afro-American Women of the South,* 142.

73. See, for example, Mrs. Dr. C. H. Phillips, "A Plea for the New Education," *NACWN,* June 1899, 11 (calling for the establishment of kindergartens as an integral part of the public school system throughout the states); "Why the [NACW] Should Devise Means of Establishing Kindergartens," *NACWN,* Nov. 1899, 1 (outlining the push for kindergartens); ibid., 2 (reporting that the Washington, DC, Women's League opened six kindergartens "in connection with the public schools of Washington, D.C."); *NACWN,* Jan. 1900, 2 (report from Atlanta on kindergarten successes in various regions); "First Free Kindergarten for Colored Children," *NACWN,* Nov. 1900, 4 (report on free kindergartens established in Southern states); "Kindergarten Work in Rome, Ga.," *NACWN,* Feb. 1902, 3 (report on a kindergarten established with few resources); "Minutes of the Third Biennial Meeting...of the NACW, St. Louis, Mo.," July 1904, 13, Conventions, NACWP (report of Mrs. Hablee Campbell, superintendent of the Department of Kindergarten Work, urging delegates to attend a kindergarten class in session during the convention); see also Knupfer, *Toward a Tenderer Humanity,* 43 (detailing nine such kindergartens supported by the Chicago Federation of Colored Women's Clubs in 1902 and twelve by 1903).

74. On the difference between African American and white women's work experience, see generally Jacqueline Jones, *Labor of Love.*

75. "Do We Need Reformatories?" *NACWN,* Feb. 1900, 1, 3 (reporting on juvenile reformatories operating in various states and arguing they were much better for juveniles than prisons); "Minutes of the Fourth Biennial Meeting...of the NACW, Detroit, Mich.," July 1906, 4, Conventions, NACWP (paper on "the Juvenile Court"); ibid., 17 (describing this paper as explaining the short national history of the juvenile court system and urging women to visit these courts to "see that these children get justice"); ibid., 30 (appointing a superintendent of the NACW's "National Department of Juvenile Work"); "Minutes of the Fifth Biennial Meeting...of the NACW," Aug. 1908, 5, Conventions, NACWP (announcing scheduled symposium on "Juvenile Court Work"); ibid., 16 (discussion of the content of this symposium, which focused on the "horrors of prison life for little Negro children" and "the fact that in so many cases the charges against the children were so minor that they could not be called a crime but the children were kept in custody because they had no one to speak in their behalf").

76. Knupfer, *Toward a Tenderer Humanity,* 63–80.

77. See, e.g., *WE,* June, 1895, 2 (Victoria Earle Matthews's report on a New York conference involving presentations by physicians and nurses "demonstrating to the public the great progress made by this class of our professional men and women"); *NACWN,* April 1902, 3 (describing varied activities of the Afro-American Women's Club Visiting Nurse Association); "Minutes of the Fifth Biennial Meeting...of the NACW, Brooklyn, NY," Aug. 1908, 21, Conventions, NACWP (paper presented on "What We Can Do to Lower the Rate of Mortality"); Seventh Biennial Convention of the NACW, July 1910, 3 (symposium on health and hygiene, including topics such as the antituberculosis crusade, physical defects in children, and hookworm and pellagra, a vitamin-deficiency disease); see also Rouse, *Lugenia Burns Hope,* 71 (discussing antituberculosis work in Atlanta); see also Neverdon-Morton, *Afro-American Women of the South,* 146 (discussing Lugenia Burns Hope's organizational work related to community health in Atlanta).

78. Salem, *To Better Our World,* 76.

79. Ibid., 108.

80. On Lugenia Burns Hope's social survey work in Atlanta, see chapter 10. On tenement inspection work led by Chicago club woman Dr. Carrie Golden, see Knupfer, *Toward a Tenderer Humanity,* 49.

81. "Address of Josephine St. P. Ruffin, President of Conference," reprinted in Davis, *Lifting as They Climb,* 17; Mary Church Terrell, "The Duty of the National Association of Colored Women to

the Race," Aug. 1899, Speeches and Addresses File, MCTPLOC. For other examples of the frequent expression of these concerns about employment, see Mary Church Terrell, "The Progress of Colored Women," n.d., circa 1914, 9, 18, Speeches and Writings File, MCLPLOC (describing "flagrant discrimination against Colored youth, particularly against the girls, [tht] must be abhorrent to all fair-minded people, no matter how great their prejudice against Colored people may be"); Mary Church Terrell, "Third Address to the NACW," Buffalo, NY, 1901, 12, Speeches and Addresses File, MCTPLOC (need to "knock on the gates of labor"); Mary Church Terrell, "Difficulties of Negroes in the United States, A Word about Lynching," Nov. 3, 1905, 2–3, Speeches and Addresses File, MCTPLOC (describing labor union exclusion); ibid., 4 (describing employer race discrimination in hiring and pay); ibid., 5, 12 (describing morale effects of pervasive employment discrimination); *NACWN*, Apr. 1899, 1 (paper read by Mrs. Carrie Fortune (T. Thomas's wife) discussing the importance of working to enlarge the occupations available to African American women and offering training to prepare them for work, and contrasting their situation with that of white women, whose opportunities were increasing while black women's were narrowing); "Minutes of the Fifth Biennial Meeting…of the NACW," Aug. 1908, 15, NACWP (reporting on a symposium on working girls held at the convention, including remarks of Baptist women's leader Layten about prejudice encountered by "Negro girl servants"); "Minutes of the Fifth Biennial Meeting…of the NACW," Aug. 1908, 30, NACWP (expressing the mutual aims of women's clubs in the United States, Liberia, and Bermuda to give greater attention to the needs of "working girls"). On the NACW's efforts to gather survey data on the labor situation of African Americans, see "Minutes of the Fourth Biennial Meeting…of the NACW," Detroit, MI, 1906, 16, Conventions, NACWP (report from NACW Department of Social Sciences on mailing questionnaires to more than 150 clubs, producing a "very full report of social conditions" among African Americans in the country). I discuss the NAACP and the National Urban League's successful campaign to enact the first state employment antidiscrimination law covering private-sector employers in Susan D. Carle, "A Social Movement History of Title VII Disparate Impact Analysis," *Florida Law Review* 63 (2011): 251, 270–86.

82. For an excellent synthetic discussion of the concept of legal consciousness in the context of social movements theory, see Edelman et al., "On Law, Organizations, and Social Movements," 661–63.

83. Du Bois saw this in his study of civic institution building of many types in African American communities in the turn-of-the-century period. As Du Bois wrote: "That *organization is the first step in nation making*, and that a nation can rise in the scale no higher than its womanhood, are principles which have come to be looked upon by the sociologists and all students of the development of humanity as self-evident truth." Du Bois, *Efforts for Social Betterment*, 80, cited in Billingsley and Giovannoni, *Children of the Storm*, 50 (emphasis supplied).

Chapter 8

1. "A Proposed Platform for the Conference at Buffalo," July 1905 folder, NMA; "NM First Annual Meeting" (typewritten list of attendees), NMA.

2. Fox, *Guardian of Boston*, 31–66. Du Bois later recounted that the unfairness of Trotter's jail sentence was an impetus for his founding of the Niagara Movement. W.E.B. Du Bois, *The Autobiography of W.E.B. Du Bois* (New York: International Publishers, 1968), 138.

3. Fox, *Guardian of Boston*, 22–28, 80, 211–12, 266–68.

4. Thornbrough, *T. Thomas Fortune*, 296–312 (describing these events through abundant documentary evidence).

5. See, e.g., "The Niagara Movement," *Voice of the Negro* 2 (1905): 522.

6. David Fort Godshalk, *Veiled Visions: The 1906 Atlanta Race Riot and the Reshaping of American Race Relations* (Chapel Hill: University of North Carolina Press, 2005), 84–114.

7. See Reverdy C. Ransom, "The Atlanta Riot," in *Orations*, 117–21.

8. See, e.g., "Barber Took to His Heels," *NYA*, Oct. 25, 1906.

9. J. Max Barber, "The Philadelphia Negro Dentist," *Crisis* 7 (1914): 179–81.

10. See W.E.B. Du Bois, "The Cultural Missions of Atlanta University," *Phylon* 3, no. 2 (Second Quarter 1942): 105, 110–11.

11. Lewis, *Biography of a Race*, 223–24, 383, 387.

12. Ibid., 242–46.

13. "A Proposed Platform for the Conference at Buffalo," n.d., circa July 1905, NMA.

14. Fox, *Guardian of Boston*, 103.

15. For examples of Du Bois's emphasis on manhood rights, see W.E.B. Du Bois, "The Niagara Movement," *Voice of the Negro* (Sept. 1905): 619–22, reprinted in *W.E.B. Du Bois Speaks: Speeches and Addresses, 1890–1910* (New York: Pathfinder, 1970), 144, 148; "The Growth of the Niagara Movement," *Voice of the Negro* 3 (1906); 43–45 (describing the Niagra Movement as a "thoughtful, dignified attempt to unite in one National organization men who think alike" and welcoming to it "intelligent, manly men who are not afraid to stand up and be counted").

16. W.E.B. Du Bois to Miss Anna Jones, Jan. 23, 1906, in W.E.B. Du Bois Correspondence Files, WEBDBP.

17. Du Bois's talented tenth concept is familiar to most students of African American history, but law professors who may not be as cognizant of it can read W.E.B. Du Bois, "The Talented Tenth," in *Negro Problem*, 30–75.

18. The Committee of Twelve has already been well explored by historians. See, e.g., Harlan II, 63–83.

19. W.E.B. Du Bois to Messrs. Grimké and Miller, Mar. 21, 1905, in *The Correspondence of W.E.B. Du Bois*, vol. 1, *Selections, 1877–1934*, ed. Herbert Aptheker (Amherst: University of Massachusetts Press, 1973), 105–106; W.E.B. Du Bois to Archibald Grimké and Kelly Miller, Aug. 13, 1905, in ibid., 112–13.

20. See, e.g., Robert H. Terrell, "A Glance at the Past and Present of the Negro" (speech delivered at Church's Auditorium before the Citizen's Industrial League of Memphis, TN, Sept. 22, 1903) (published by Press of R. L. Pendleton, 1903) 11, 14 ("It is a popular thing nowadays to say that the ballot was given the Negro too soon…I know not by what system of reasoning these conclusions are reached"; "Our enemies succeeded for a long time in making the country believe that the black man was lynched only for the unspeakable crime. The record has always belied this charge").

21. See Killian, "Organization, Rationality, and Spontaneity in the Civil Rights Movement," 782 (arguing that social movements theory must recognize, but not treat as irrational, the "feeling states and cognition which sometimes cause individuals to throw caution to the winds").

22. See Clifford J. Plummer to BTW, July 16, 1906, *BTW Papers*, vol. 8, 328–29 (assuring Washington, erroneously as it turned out, that no meeting of Niagara men near Buffalo, New York, had taken place).

23. "Constitution and By-Laws of the Niagara Movement, as adopted July 12 and 13, 1905, at Buffalo, N.Y.," NMA.

24. "Programme," Niagara Movement, July 11–July 14, 1905, NMA.

25. Ibid.

26. Niagara Movement, General Secretary, Membership Letter no. 1, Sept. 13, 1905; Membership Letter no. 2, Oct. 7, 1905, NMA.

27. Membership Letter no. 3, Nov. 1, 1905, NMA.

28. Membership Letter no. 1.

29. Logan and Winston, *Dictionary of American Negro Biography*, 452, s.v., "Morgan, Clement G."; Carroll, "Niagara Movement," 20–21.

30. On John Hope's biography see Ridgely Torrence, *The Story of John Hope* (New York: Macmillan, 1948); *New Georgia Encyclopedia*, s.v. "Hope, John," accessed July 24, 2012, http://www.georgiaencyclopedia.org/nge/Article.jsp?id=h-855.

31. "Lafayette McKeen Hershaw," *Journal of Negro History* 30 (1945): 462–64; *BTW Papers*, vol. 6, 345n2 (biographical note on Hershaw).

32. See, e.g., W.E.B. Du Bois to Oswald Garrison Villard, Mar. 24, 1905, reprinted in *BTW Papers*, vol. 8, 224 (listing evidence concerning Washington's manipulation of the African American press, including charges that he published against Hershaw); Charles W. Anderson to Booker T. Washington, May 27, 1907, *BTW Papers*, vol. 9, 274 (reporting on conversation with President Roosevelt in which Anderson accused Hershaw of being the source of anti-Roosevelt attacks); Lewis, *Biography of a Race*, 219, 319.

33. Lafayette M. Hershaw, "The Status of the Free Negro prior to 1860," unnumbered, American Negro Academy, reprinted in *The American Negro Academy Occasional Papers 1–22* (New York: Arno Press, 1969), 39–47; Lafayette M. Hershaw, "Peonage," Occasional Papers no. 15, American Negro Academy (Washington, DC, 1915), reprinted in ibid., 4–13.

34. Carroll, "Niagara Movement," 106.

35. On Jourdain see ibid., 29–31; Beverly, "Emergence of Black Political Power in Evanston," 53–57.

36. See Logan and Winston, *Dictionary of American Negro Biography*, s.v. "Wilson, Butler R[oland]."

37. Kenneth W. Mack, "The Role of Law in the Making of Racial Identity: The Case of Harrisburg's W. Justin Carter," *Widener Law Journal* 18 (2008–2009): 1–22; *Pennsylvania Negro Business Directory, 1910* (Harrisburg, PA: James H. W. Howard and Son, 1910), 81; Carroll, "Niagara Movement," 114–15.

38. On McGhee as the source of the idea for the NM, see Du Bois, "Niagara Movement," 619. For McGhee's Niagara Movement activities and reports, See, e.g., Minutes of NM Meeting, Aug. 17, 1906, NMA; Minutes, Aug. 18, 1906, NMA; Secretaries and Committees of the Niagara Movement, Apr. 1, 1907, NMA; Membership Letter no. 4, Apr. 10, 1907, NMA; Fredrick L. McGhee to W.E.B. Du Bois, June 1, 1907, NMA.

39. Nelson, *Life on the Color Line*, 167, 194, 198–200; Omar Hamid Ali, "*Black Populism in the New South, 1886–1898*" (PhD diss., Columbia University, 2003), 238.

40. Nelson, *Life on the Color Line*, 149–52.

41. These facts capturing the flavor of McGhee's life are drawn from Nelson's detailed and convincing biography.

42. Lafayette M. Hershaw, "William H. H. Hart," *Journal of Negro History* 19 (1934): 211–13; Carroll, "Niagara Movement," 51–53; Logan and Winston, *Dictionary of American Negro Biography*, 294–95, s.v. "Hart, William H. H."

43. Hart v. State, 100 Md. 595 (1905).

44. Carroll, "Niagara Movement," 125–130.

45. This model of a clean dichotomy between pro bono and for-profit legal work arose later in the twentieth century. Contemporary scholars of the legal profession such as Ann Southworth and Scott Cummings have argued for the importance of developing a more multifaceted image of public-interest lawyering that appreciates the importance of fee-for-services arrangements in helping fill unmet legal services needs. See, e.g., Ann Southworth and Scott Cummings, "Between Profit and Principle: The Private Public Interest Firm," in *Private Lawyers and the Public Interest: The Evolving Role of Pro Bono in the Legal Profession*, ed. Robert Granfield and Lynn Mather (New York: Oxford University Press, 2009), 183–210; see also Susan Carle, "Re-Valuing Lawyering for Middle-Income Clients," *Fordham Law Review* 70 (2001–2002): 719–46 (arguing that fee-for-service work for clients with modest means should be regarded as having a public-interest aspect).

46. For his biographer's attempt to track down these and other civil rights cases and track their dispositions, see Nelson, *Life on the Color Line*, 168–76.

47. See, e.g., Fredrick L. McGhee, "To the Fifth Annual Conference, Niagara Movement, Sea Isle City, N.J.," Aug. 14, 1909, NMA.

48. See Dale, "Social Equality Does Not Exist among Themselves."

49. See chap. 5, n. 7.

50. "The Niagara Movement, Second Annual Meeting," NMA (flyer calling for meeting attendance).

51. See *Alexandria Gazette*, Aug. 8, 1906, 2; *Alexandria Gazette*, Oct. 16, 1906, 3; "Woman Ejected: Sues Road," *Washington Herald*, Jan. 20, 1907, 4.

Chapter 9

1. Max Barber, "The Niagara Movement at Harper's Ferry," *Voice of the Negro* 3 (1906): 402, 408; Minutes of Meeting, Aug. 17, 1906, NMA; Carroll, "Niagara Movement," 123–24 (summarizing biographical sources on Diggs); Printed Programme, *The Niagara Movement Second Annual Meeting* (Washington, DC: Murray Bros., 1906), NMA; Angela Jones, *African American Civil Rights: Early Activism and the Niagara Movement* (Santa Barbara, CA: Praeger, 2011), 218; William H. Ferris, *The African Abroad*, vol. 2 (New Haven, CT: Tuttle, Morehouse and Taylor, 1913; Johnson Reprint Corp., 1968), 794. Citations refer to the Johnson edition; "The Niagara Movement," *WB*, Aug. 25, 1906, 1.

2. Reverdy S. Ransom, "The Spirit of John Brown," reprinted in *Ransom Writings*, 92–102 (all emphases in the original).

3. On the Brotherhood of Liberty, see chap. 2. Minutes of Meeting, Aug. 17, 1906, NMA (summary of reports of Committees on Education, Health, and Legal Defense); Mather, *Who's Who of the Colored Race*, 273–74, s.v. "Waldron, John Milton" (Waldron biography); Bruce, *Archibald Grimké*, 185–86 (describing Waldron's clash with Hershaw and ouster from NAACP DC branch leadership).

4. Barber, "Niagara Movement at Harpers Ferry," 406–407.

5. Niagara Movement Minutes, Aug. 18, 1906 (10 a.m.), NMA; Niagara Movement Minutes, Aug. 18, 1906 (9:30 p.m.), NMA.

6. Barber, "Niagara Movement at Harpers Ferry," 410.

7. Du Bois, *Autobiography*, 250–51. The address was also published in the *Washington Bee*. See "Niagara Movement," 2.

8. "Women and the Niagara Movement," NMA; "Women and the Niagara Movement, Circular no. 2," NMA.

9. "Dues Paid: Full Members" (1906), NMA; "Associate Members" (1906), NMA.

10. See Angela Jones, *African American Civil Rights*, 197 (noting the need for more biographical information about Niagara Movement women members).

11. See Darlene Clark Hine, ed., *Black Women in America: An Historical Encyclopedia* (Brooklyn, NY: Carlson, 1993), 261–62; National Institute of Medicine, "Changing the Face of American Medicine: Celebrating America's Women Physicians," at http://www.nlm.nih.gov/changingthefaceofmedicine/physicians/biography_66.html; Salem, *To Better Our World*, 77 (recounting anecdote about Cole's correction of Du Bois's study).

12. See generally Jessie Carney Smith, *Notable Black American Women*, 137, 139. On the Cook and Appo families, see Gatewood, *Aristocrats of Color*, passim. On Cook's club work, See, e.g., "Washington Letter," *WE*, Mar. 24, 1894.

13. Jessie Carney Smith, *Notable Black American Women*, 105–107; "Proceedings of the Executive Committee, which met August, 1900, in Detroit Michigan," Dec. 1900, *NACWN*, 1 (recording Clifford's election as secretary and her report to the delegates); Minutes of the Fourth Biennial Meeting of the NACW, 24, Conventions, NACWP (reporting on Clifford's loss of election for vice president); Dolen Perkins-Valdez, " 'Atlanta's Shame': W.E.B. Du Bois and Carrie Williams Clifford Respond to the Atlanta Race Riot of 1906," *Studies in the Literary Imagination* 40 (2007): 133–51.

14. Alexander, *Army of Lions*, 127, 331n119.

15. Salem, *To Better Our World*, 34, 70, 155; "Elizabeth Carter Brooks," Office of Institutional Diversity, Bridgewater State University, at http://www.bridgew.edu/hoba/Brooks.cfm; Kellogg, *NAACP*, 305 (listing members of the first NAACP General Committee). Later in her

life, Carter married Bishop William Sampson Brooks and moved with him to Texas, but when he died four years later she returned to New Bedford, where she became head of the NAACP's Bedford branch and presided over the NAACP's regional conference. In 1921 Carter was also a founding member of the International Council of Women of the Darker Races of the World. Salem, *To Better Our World,* 236.

16. [No title], *Friends' Intelligencer and Journal* 47 (Sept. 13, 1890): 592 (reporting on Gould's appointment to Livingstone College); Elizabeth McHenry, *Forgotten Readers: Recovering the Lost History of African American Literary Societies* (Durham, NC: Duke University Press, 2002), 223, 229–38 (providing a detailed examination of Gould's role as a literary commentator); William B. Gould IV, *Diary of a Contraband: The Civil War Passage of a Black Soldier* (Stanford, CA: Stanford University Press, 2002), xxi, 45 (describing the Gould family history).

17. McHenry, *Forgotten Readers,* 172, 218.

18. Maria Baldwin School webpage, "Maria Baldwin Biography," http://www.cpsd.us/BAL/history_baldwin.cfm; Angela Jones, *African American Civil Rights,* 55.

19. African American Studies at Beinecke Library, Yale University (biographical information accompanying this collection), accessed May 31, 2013. http://beinecke.library.yale.edu/about/blogs/african-american-studies-beinecke-library/2010/02/09/orpheus-m-and-mattie-allen-mcadoo.

20. W.E.B. Du Bois to Mary White Ovington, Oct. 30, 1906, MWOP.

21. Announcement of Address by W.E.B. Du Bois at the Shiloh Baptist Church, Sept. 30, 1907, 3, NMA (listing members of Niagara Movement's DC branch).

22. "Cromwell, John Wesley," in Mather, *Who's Who of the Colored Race,* 81; "Notes," *Journal of Negro History* 12 (1927): 563–66; Adelaide M. Cromwell, *Unveiled Voices, Unvarnished Memories: The Cromwell Family in Slavery and Segregation, 1692–1972* (Columbia: University of Missouri Press, 2007), 89.

23. On the acclaim Pope received for her literary efforts, See, e.g., "A New Literary Star," *Broad Ax,* June 26, 1897; "The Book World," *St. Paul Appeal,* Feb. 10, 1900. On reporting of her social activities, See, e.g., *WB,* Aug. 31, 1895, 7; *WB,* Aug. 29, 1896, 5. Special thanks to Adeen Postar for helping me in the arduous task of uncovering Pope's short stories, originally published in the *Waverly Magazine.* Although a digitized version of these documents available online is incorrectly copied, the stories can be obtained from the Library of Congress, where they are stamped as part of (the AAC's own) Daniel A. Murray Collection of African American Literature. Their titles are "The New Woman," "A Social Mishap," "Cornelia," and "Campbell's Experiment." On the importance of expanding the range of "material artifacts" used to tell the story of the long civil rights movement to include literary production, see Christopher Metress, "Making Civil Rights Harder: Literature, Memory, and the Black Freedom Struggle," *Southern Literary Journal* 40 (Spring 2008): 138, 141, 148.

24. Anita Hackley-Lambert, *F. H. M. Murray: First Biography of a Forgotten Pioneer for Civil Justice* (Fort Washington, MD: Hackley-Lambert Enterprise, 2006), 71, 75, 85, 126 (describing Delilah Murray as serving on the Niagara Movement's 1906 women's organizing committee); 144.

25. Connie Park Rice, "Pioneer Women: The 'Ladies' of the Niagara Movement," *Association for the Study of African American Life and History Black History Theme Magazine* (2005), 42.

26. "Ida Dean Bailey," *Horizon* 3 (March 1908): 2–3; "A Farewell Message to Our Race," ibid., 20–21.

27. Rice, "Pioneer Women," 37, 41. The complex mix of Du Bois's often progressive political commitments on gender issues and his sometimes less enlightened conduct with respect to gender in his personal affairs has been the topic of much insightful scholarship. See, e.g., Susan Gillman and Alys Eve Weinbaum, eds., *Next to the Color Line: Gender, Sexuality, and W.E.B. Du Bois* (Minneapolis: University of Minnesota Press, 2007); Lewis, *Biography of a Race,* passim.

28. "Secretaries and Committees of the Niagara Movement" (dated Apr. 1, 1907), NMA; Carle, "Race, Class, and Legal Ethics in the Early NAACP," 97, 103 (Hawkins's role in the early NAACP).

29. "Secretaries and Committees of the Niagara Movement."

30. "Verdict for One Cent," *Alexandria Gazette,* June 5, 1907, 3; "Put Off Train, Paid a Cent," *Washington Times,* June 5, 1907, 12.

31. W.E.B. Du Bois, Membership Letter no. 4, Apr. 10, 1907, NMA.

32. W.E.B. Du Bois Letter to "Colleagues," May 16, 1906 (reproducing letter from Clement Morgan dated May 13, 1906), NMA.

33. Niagara Movement Department of Civil Rights, Departmental Letter no. 1, Apr. 15, 1907, NMA.

34. W.E.B. Du Bois, "A Brief Resume of the Massachusetts Trouble in the Niagara Movement," n.d., NMA. Some historians have claimed that the person to whose membership Trotter objected was Mrs. Archibald Grimké (based on one of Du Bois's accounts of Trotter's 1906 opposition to a "Mrs. Grimké"), but Archibald Grimké had been a widower since 1898, so this cannot be correct. "Mrs. Grimké" must refer to Charlotte Forten Grimké, the wife of Archibald's brother, Francis Grimké, a Presbyterian minister based in Washington, DC. The certified election results from the September poll confirming the Massachusetts chapter's membership roster list "A. H. Grimké" as an approved member, further confirming that Trotter's objections in 1907 were to Archibald, whom he openly disliked. Niagara Movement, Massachusetts Branch, "The undersigned have counted...," NMA. On Trotter's dislike of the Grimkés, including Charlotte, see Bruce, *Archibald Grimké,* 198–99 (noting that Trotter's failure to acknowledge Charlotte Grimké's 1914 death exacerbated the animosity between him and Archibald).

35. W.E.B. Du Bois, "Brief Resume of the Massachusetts Trouble." On the relationship between Trotter and Forbes, see Clement G. Morgan to W.E.B. Du Bois, May 31, 1927, in *Du Bois Correspondence,* 355.

36. This tendency of those of a more radical bent to sympathize with Trotter is reflected in a letter from Ovington to Du Bois in which she asked him about the Boston troubles and confided that she had grown to admire Trotter and "greatly hoped he would win, since Mr. Morgan, while very pleasant, has great vanity, and that often blinds a man's judgment." Mary White Ovington to W.E.B. Du Bois, Oct. 8, 1907, NMA. Horizon editor F. H. M. Murray was also a close friend of Trotter's, who served as the DC collection agent for *The Guardian* and took his side. See F. H. M. Murray to "[Niagara Movement] Colleague," Oct. 29, 1907; Geraldine Trotter to F. H. M. Murray, July 13, 1914, General Correspondence Files, FHMMP.

37. "Minutes," Aug. 27, 1907, 3, NMA.

38. Ibid.

39. *Alexandria Gazette,* Sept. 7, 1980, 3; *Washington Times,* Sept. 7, 1908, 9; WB, Sept. 12, 1908, 1, 5.

40. On Giles's employment status after filing his lawsuit, see Riser, *Defying Disfranchisement,* 226–27; on Trotter's death, see Fox, *Guardian of Boston,* 271–72.

41. Minutes, Afternoon Meeting, Aug. 27, 1908, NMA.

42. Mary White Ovington to W.E.B. Du Bois, Oct. 8, 1907, NMA.

43. W.E.B. Du Bois, "Communication, General Secretary to the Executive and Sub-executive committee in the mid-winter Conference Assembly," NMA.

44. W.E.B. Du Bois to Mary White Ovington, Oct. 14, 1907, MWOP.

45. W.E.B. Du Bois to the Guarantors of *The Horizon,* Mar. 12, 1909, in *Du Bois Correspondence,* 144–45.

46. Illustrative examples of Du Bois's most frequent topics include "Socialist of the Path" and "Negro and Socialism," *Horizon* 1 (Feb. 1907): 7–8; "Africa," *Horizon* 1 (April 1907): 6; " 'Whining' Again," *Horizon* 1 (July 1907): 22–23 (criticizing Bookerites); "The Foreign View," *Horizon* 2 (Oct. 1907): 4 (discussing international perspectives). A few representative examples of Hershaw's legal journalism include "Chinese Exclusion," *Horizon* 2 (Dec. 1907): 13–14; "Separate Car Agitation," *Horizon* 2 (March 1980): 9–10; "The Suffrage in Maryland," *Horizon* 5 (Nov. 1909): 3; "A New Black Law," *Horizon* 5 (Feb. 1910): 6; "A New Dred Scott Decision," *Horizon* 6 (June 1910): 5–6; "The Latest Separate Car Case—Again," *Horizon* 6 (June 1910): 10.

47. "Niagara," *Horizon* 2 (Sept. 1907): 4 (noting that "[t]his year" critics had dwelled on the theme of "Disruption," saying "we could not stand, our doom was written in the stars"); "Address," ibid., 5–6; "Taft," *Horizon* 3 (June 1908): 3–5; "The Negro Voter," *Horizon* 4 (July 1908): 4–7; "Negro Vote," *Horizon* 4 (Aug. 1908): 1–5; "The Negro Vote: Talk Number Four," *Horizon* 4 (Sept. 1908): 4–6.

48. "National Negro Conference," *Horizon* 5 (Nov. 1909): 1.

49. In the vocabulary of social movement theory, Du Bois's interest in seeking an alliance with outsider elites who did not fully share the commitments of the Niagara Movement's members was an attempt to "routinize resource input" despite his awareness of the potential trade-offs between "benefits obtained and costs incurred" through this strategy. McAdam, *Political Process and the Development of Black Insurgency,* 27.

50. J. Milton Waldron Letter beginning "Dear Fellow member" (1908), NMA.

51. "Niagara Movement" (1908), NMA.

52. W.E.B. Du Bois to Rev. Waldron, Sept. 3, 1908, NMA; Mary White Ovington to W.E.B. Du Bois, Aug. 29, 1908, NMA.

53. "Niagara Movement: Inter-State Committees" (1908); "Cash Accounts of the Niagara Movement," NMA.

54. F. M. McGhee, Sect., Legal Dept., "To the Fifth Annual Conference, Niagara Movement, Sea Isle City, NJ," Aug. 14, 1909, NMA.

55. Ibid.

56. Ibid.

57. Ibid.

Chapter 10

1. Classic organizational histories of the early NUL include Weiss, *The NUL;* Guichard Parris and Lester Brooks, *Blacks in the City: A History of the National Urban League* (Boston: Little, Brown, 1971); and Moore, *A Search for Equality.* On the NUL's role in pioneering structural approaches to employment subordination, see Carle, "A Social Movement History of Title VII Disparate Impact Analysis," 270–86.

2. On these aspects of the Du Bois's life in Atlanta, see Lewis, *Biography of a Race,* 212, 344–45.

3. Ibid., 227–28, 345.

4. Ibid., 378.

5. Cf. ibid., 366.

6. For an exploration of Du Bois's ideas during his years at Atlanta University, see Adolph L. Reed, *W.E.B. Du Bois and American Political Thought,* 48, 50.

7. Lewis, *Biography of a Race,* 377–78.

8. W.E.B. Du Bois, ed., *The Negro in Business* (Atlanta: Atlanta Bulletin, 1899), http://www.library.umass.edu/spcoll/digital/dubois/dubois4.pdf, 50, 56, 57–60.

9. For a general discussion of Du Bois's civic activism projects in Atlanta prior to 1906, see Elliott Rudwick, *W.E.B. Du Bois: Voice of the Black Protest Movement* (Chicago: University of Chicago Press, 1982), 54–55.

10. On the GERC, see generally Dominic J. Capeci Jr. and Jack C. Knight, "W.E.B. Du Bois's Southern Front: Georgia 'Race Men' and the Niagara Movement, 1905–1907," *Georgia Historical Quarterly* 83 (1999): 479–507; Godshalk, *Veiled Visions,* 73–74, 181–85; Jay Driskell, "First Class Citizens."

11. See Georgia Equal Rights Convention, held in Macon Georgia, Feb. 13–14, 1906, WEBDBP; "A Call to the Colored Men & Women of Georgia," 3–4, 10–12, WEBDBP; "Address of the First Meeting of the Georgia Equal Rights Convention," 13–16, WEBDBP.

12. Dittmer, *Black Georgia,* 33–34.

13. Ibid., 37.

14. Dittmer, *Black Georgia,* 27; Meier, *Negro Thought,* 153–54.

15. Dittmer, *Black Georgia*, 43.

16. August Meier, "The Negro and the Democratic Party, 1875–1915," *Phylon* 17 (1956): 173, 175.

17. Jack Abramowitz, "The Negro in the Populist Movement," *Journal of Negro History* 38 (1953): 257, 261.

18. William H. Chafe, "The Negro and Populism: A Kansas Case Study," *Journal of Southern History* 34 (1968): 404.

19. R. Jean Simms-Brown, "Populism and Black Americans: Constructive or Destructive?" *Journal of Negro History* 65 (1980): 349, 351; C. Van Woodward, *Tom Watson: Agrarian Rebel* (Savannah: Beehive Press, 1973 reissue, 1938), 190.

20. Acts and Resolutions of the General Assembly of the State of Georgia, 1890–1891 (Atlanta, 1891), cited in Clarence A. Bacote, "Negro Proscriptions, Protests, and Proposed Solutions in Georgia, 1880–1908," *Journal of Southern History* 25 (1959): 471, 473.

21. See generally August Meier and Elliott Rudwick, "The Boycott Movement against Jim Crow Streetcars in the South, 1900–1906," *Journal of American History* 55 (1969): 756, 769.

22. Charles Crowe, "Tom Watson, Populists, and Blacks Reconsidered," *Journal of Negro History* 55 (1970): 99, 112.

23. Francis M. Wilhoit, "An Interpretation of Populism's Impact on the Georgia Negro," *Journal of Negro History* 52 (1967): 116, 119.

24. Eugene J. Watts, "Black Political Progress in Atlanta: 1868–1895," *Journal of Negro History* 59 (1974): 268.

25. Ibid., 285.

26. Ibid., 276.

27. On African American men's involvement in Atlanta politics and patronage, see Allison Dorsey, *To Build Our Lives Together: Community Formation in Black Atlanta, 1875–1906* (Athens: University of Georgia Press, 2004), 140–46.

28. Crowe, "Tom Watson," 246.

29. Dittmer, *Black Georgia*, 20–21; Lewis, *Biography of a Race*, 227.

30. Harlan I, 216.

31. Dittmer, *Black Georgia*, 56–57.

32. Du Bois, *Autobiography*, 222, quoted in Lewis, *Biography of a Race*, 226.

33. Capeci and Knight, "W.E.B. Du Bois's Southern Front," 491, 504–505.

34. Ibid., 492 ("Georgia's race men en masse abandoned Niagaran tendencies, profoundly aware that their terra firma had become a bloody battleground").

35. Ibid., 497.

36. Dittmer, *Black Georgia*, 102.

37. Godshalk, *Veiled Visions*, 183.

38. Rouse, *Lugenia Burns Hope*, 18, 20–40. To distinguish Lugenia Burns Hope from her spouse, John Hope, I refer to her as Burns Hope.

39. Ibid., 28–30. On Herndon's involvement with the NM's founding, see Carroll, "The Niagara Movement," 104–105.

40. Rouse, *Lugenia Burns Hope*, 45, 65, 66–69, 89.

41. See E. K. Jones to L. Hollingsworth Wood, Mar. 24, 1913, LHWP (discussing "Mrs. John Hope, Leader of the Atlanta Organization which has become affiliated with us"). On the relationship between Burns Hope and the NUL and its Atlanta chapter through the 1920s, see Salem, *To Better Our World*, 190–95; Godshalk, *Veiled Visions*, 251–52.

42. Rouse, *Lugenia Burns Hope*, 51–52; J. Driskell, "First Class Citizens" (chapter 3 on the Neighborhood Union).

43. See Kimberley Johnson, *Reforming Jim Crow: Southern Politics and State in the Age before Brown* (New York: Oxford, 2010), 10. Johnson makes the important argument that, during the Jim Crow era throughout the South, African American reformers were working on pragmatic alternatives that accepted neither Du Bois's nor Washington's approaches but instead sought creatively to improve conditions of life given the avenues for agency that were available at the time.

44. Mary White Ovington to Du Bois, Sept. 20, 1906, WEBDBP ("I hope you are going to vote the socialist ticket"); Mary White Ovington to W.E.B. Du Bois, Apr. 13, 1907, WEBDBP (Ovington expressing the hope that she would be invited to speak on socialism at the NM meeting that summer); Mary White Ovington to W.E.B. Du Bois, Aug. 29, 1908, NMA ("There is a working man's party in the country. How can the Negro belong with any other?").

45. Mary White Ovington to W.E.B. Du Bois, Oct. 7, 1904, WEBDBP. On the background to Ovington's fellowship funding, see Kellogg, "Introduction," in Ovington, Half a Man, xv.

46. Mary White Ovington to W.E.B. Du Bois, Nov. 4, 1904, WEBDBP; W.E.B. Du Bois to Mary White Ovington, Nov. 8, 1904, MWOP (asking whether he had been "entertaining a Millionaire unawares").

47. See, e.g., Jessie C. Sleet, "In the Day's Work of a Visiting Nurse," Charities 15 (Oct. 1905): 73–74. On Sleet (whose married last name was Scales) and her work, see Karen Buhler-Wilderson, No Place like Home: A History of Nursing and Home Care in the United States (Baltimore: Johns Hopkins University Press, 2001), 95–97. On the membership of the New York City antituberculosis committee, see "Committee on the Prevention of Tuberculosis among Negroes, New York," Charities 15 (Oct. 1905): 5.

48. Mary White Ovington to W.E.B. Du Bois, Oct. 7, 1904, WEBDBP; Mary White Ovington to W.E.B. Du Bois, Oct. 27, 1904, WEBDBP.

49. See Ovington, Half a Man; Mary White Ovington to W.E.B. Du Bois, Apr. 11, 1905, WEBDBP. On Rev. William Brooks and his institutional church work, see Maude K. Griffin, "The Negro Church and Its Social Work—St. Mark's," Charities 15 (Oct. 7, 1905): 75–76. Du Bois shared Ovington's assessment of Bulkley, describing him as "a fine man" in later correspondence. W.E.B. Du Bois to Mary White Ovington, June 7, 1906, MWOP.

50. Mary White Ovington to W.E.B. Du Bois, Jan. 9, 1905, WEBDBP; Mary White Ovington to W.E.B. Du Bois, June 27, 1905, WEBDBP.

51. W.E.B. Du Bois to Mary White Ovington, May 13, 1905, MWOP.

52. W.E.B. Du Bois to Mary White Ovington, [no date, circa March 1905], WEBDBP; Mary White Ovington to W.E.B. Du Bois, June 27, 1905, WEBDBP; W.E.B. Du Bois, ed., A Select Bibliography of the Negro American, (Atlanta: Atlanta University Press, 1905), 5, http://www.library.umass.edu/spcoll/digital/dubois/dubois10.pdf.

53. Mary White Ovington to W.E.B. Du Bois, May 20, 1906, WEBDBP. On Webster's clients, see J. Clay Smith, Emancipation, 400 (Webster's clients included Lord & Taylor and the Tiffany companies). On his involvement on the NAACP's first legal committee, see chapter 12 and Carle, "Race, Class, and Legal Ethics in the Early NAACP," 112–13.

54. For a description of the living conditions in San Juan Hill at the time, see Marcy S. Sacks, Before Harlem: The Black Experience in New York City before World War I (Philadelphia: University of Pennsylvania Press, 2006), 76–82.

55. For a biographical summary of Morton Jones, see Hine, ed., Black Women in America, 656–57. On Ovington's work at the Lincoln Settlement, see Kellogg, "Introduction," in Ovington, Half a Man, xviii–xix.

56. Mary White Ovington to W.E.B. Du Bois, Apr. 24, 1908, WEBDBP. Reverend Diggs, another social gospel minister, in fact spoke at the dinner.

57. [No title], Alexandria Gazette, Apr. 29, 1908, 2; " 'Equals' of Negro Raise Big Turmoil: New York Police Fear Trouble from Mixed Dinner," Washington Times, Apr. 29, 1906, 9; "Millionaire's Daughter Proud of Negro Friends," Evening World, Apr. 28, 1989, Final Results Edition; Wedin, Inheritors of the Spirit, 98–99; W.E.B. Du Bois to Mary White Ovington, May 14, 1908, WEBDBP.

58. George Edmund Haynes, The Negro at Work in New York City: A Study in Economic Progress (New York: Arno Press, 1968; New York: Longmans, Green, 1912), 69, 74, 77, 82–83, 108, 124. Citations refer to the Arno Press edition. A study by Du Bois at around the same time found similar trends and also counted a total of ten African American lawyers in the city, twenty physicians, and at least ninety persons in civil service, as well as one school principal

and fewer than forty African American teachers in public schools. Du Bois wrote that the "center" of African American life in the city was "still the church" and that community life also supported building associations, hospitals, and homes for orphans and the aged, all conducted entirely by African Americans and mainly supported by them. W.E.B. Du Bois, *The Black North in 1901: A Case Study* (New York: Arno Press, 1969; 1901), 10, 16.

59. Cf. Victoria W. Wolcott, *Remaking Respectability: African American Women in Interwar Detroit* (Chapel Hill: University of North Carolina Press, 2001) (discussing black women migrants to Detroit after World War I and club women's social work aimed at helping them).

60. See Kramer, "Uplifting Our 'Downtrodden Sisterhood,' " 243, 245–49; Cheryl Waites, "Victoria Earle Matthews: Residence and Reform," in *African American Leadership: An Empowerment Tradition in Social Welfare History*, ed. Iris B. Carlton-LaNey (Washington, DC: NASW Press, 2001), 1–16; " 'To Embalm Her Memory in Song and Story': Victoria Earle Matthews and Situated Sisterhood," in *"We Are Coming": The Persuasive Discourse of Nineteenth-Century Black Women*, ed. Shirley W. Logan (Carbondale: Southern Illinois University Press, 1999), 127–51.

61. Annual Report of the White Rose Working Girls' Home, for the year ending Dec. 31, 1907, 1, 4, 6, WRMP; Annual Report for the Year Ending Dec. 31, 1912, White Rose Industrial Association, 1, WRMP.

62. For a recent treatment of Kellor as a nonconforming gender identity pioneer, see John Kenneth Press, *Founding Mother: Frances Kellor and the Creation of Modern America* (New York: Social Books, 2012), iv. Kellor, who came from a poor background, is another example of an early female activist law school graduate (ibid., 23, 51).

63. Frances Kellor, *Out of Work: A Study of Employment Agencies, Their Treatment of the Unemployed, and Their Influence upon Homes and Business* (New York: Putnam, 1904).

64. "Shall White Agencies Dominate Our Charity Work?" *NYA*, Dec. 28, 1905, 4. Ovington, too, complained about Kellor, writing to Du Bois that work Kellor had published on the causes of African American crime had so insulted an unnamed African American collaborator of Ovington's that this woman had refused to work with Ovington any longer. Mary White Ovington to W.E.B. Du Bois, Sept. 8, 1905, WEBDBP. Kellor's prolific writings prove Ovington's point. Kellor attributed the causes of crime to social influences rather than innate biology, but her descriptions nevertheless reek of offensive bias. To take one randomly selected passage of a great many that could be quoted, Kellor wrote the following:

> There are few or no truly great negro criminals. They are notorious and dangerous, but there is no criminal genius.... Negroes are notorious thieves, but they remain months and years in stockades that would not hold ordinary northern safe-blowers twenty-four hours.... This deficiency in organization and great criminals shows that the race may be inferior, but is not necessarily possessed of a greater criminal *sense*. Frances Kellor, *Experimental Sociology, Descriptive and Analytical: Delinquents* (New York: Macmillan, 1901), 31.

65. "Permanent Organization Formed at Dr. Bulkl[e]y's School," *NYA*, Apr. 26, 1906 ("The ladies and gentlemen whom Prof. W. L. Bulkl[e]y invited to a conference at Public School 40 last Friday night resolved themselves into a permanent organization to consider the political, economic and social condition of the Afro-American").

66. Letter on CIICN letterhead to W.E.B. Du Bois, June 13, 1907, WEBDBP.

67. "To Win Industrial Chances—Leaders of Both Races Form Permanent Committee: Will Try to Open Up Avenues of Employment in Skilled Trade," *NYA*, May 17, 1906.

68. "Industrial Campaign: Bulkley's Committee to Hold Series of Meetings: Both Races to Help," *NYA*, July 12, 1906.

69. Booker T. Washington to Charles W. Anderson, Oct. 1, 1907, BTWP, Box 35, cited in Weiss, *The NUL*, 321n32.

70. L. Hollingsworth Wood, "The Urban League Movement," *Journal of Negro History* 9 (1924): 117, 119. A Quaker, Wood was involved in many reform projects and at various points served as treasurer or assistant treasurer of the CUCN and the NUL.

71. CUCN, "Annual Report for 1910–11," NLPCW Minutes Folder, "LHWP; "Announcement, 1911–12 (ibid., LHWP).

72. Paul Cravath to Ruth Baldwin, Nov. 11, 1910, NUL Correspondence, 1910–1917, LHWP; Paul Cravath to L. Hollingsworth Wood, Sept. 29, 1911, NUL Correspondence, 1910–1917, LHWP; Paul Cravath to Dear Sir [Booker T. Washington], Dec. 9, 1903, WEBDBP (re: "Pullman Palace Car Company" analysis).

73. Alfred T. White to Ruth Baldwin, Oct. 27, 1911, NUL Correspondence, 1910–1917, LHWP; E. K. Jones to L. Hollingsworth Wood, Jan. 30, 1913, NUL Correspondence, 1910–1917, LHWP.

74. Paul J. Sachs to Ruth Baldwin, May 6, 1912, NUL Correspondence, 1910–1917, LHWP; Steve Mumfries to L. Hollingsworth Wood, July 25, 1912 (ibid.); E. K. Jones to Wood, July 12, 1912 (ibid.); Julius Rosenwald to Paul Sachs, June 30, 1914 (ibid.).

75. Weiss, *The NUL*, 82.

76. "Brief Statement of the Work of the [NUL]," National Urban League, folder 20, LHWP; see also Bulletin of the [NUL], Jan. 1913 (briefer printed version of the organization's goals) (ibid.).

77. For the literature on competing logics in social movement organizations, see generally Edelman et. al, "On Law, Organizations, and Social Movements," 661.

78. "To the Members of the Executive Board of the [NUL]," Apr. 24, 1913 (signed by E. K. Jones), National Urban League, Correspondence, 1910–1917, LHWP.

79. George E. Haynes to Ruth Baldwin, May 22, 1913, Correspondence, GHP.

80. E. K. Jones to L. Hollingsworth Wood, Feb. 13, 1913, National Urban League, Correspondence, 1910–1917, LHWP (forwarding contribution from Baldwin for Bulkley's school); William Bulkley to L. Hollingsworth Wood, Feb. 19, 1913 (ibid.) (discussing conflict about Wood's attempt to direct how funds should be spent); George E. Haynes to L. Hollingsworth Wood, May 5, 1913 (ibid.) (discussing problem of Bulkley's and others' attitude); George E. Haynes to Ruth Baldwin, May 5, 1913 (ibid.) (describing former Industrial Committee members' concerns that the NUL should not be so nationally focused and reporting that "we are trying to whip them into line" and that Brooks had assured that "if we do not crowd them too much they will come into full harmony").

81. "Brief Statement of the Work of the NUL."

82. Weiss, *The NUL*, 56.

83. Ibid., 88.

84. See CIICN Board Minutes, Nov. 3, 1909, Minutes Folder, GHP (reporting to executive committee of the CIICN on an employer survey in which some railway lines were found to be very supportive of the CIICN's goals and others gave unsatisfactory answers); CUCN Minutes, Dec. 23, 1912, Minutes Folder, GHP; Minutes of NUL Executive Board, Feb. 7, 1912, Minutes Folder, GHP; Minutes of CIICN Board, Feb. 4, 1913, Minutes Folder, GHP (report on a comparative investigation of the positions of porters in various railways, which raised questions by board members of the legality of employment contracts that may have contained special conditions for African American employees); Report of Associate Director E. K. Jones, Oct. 8, 1913, Reports and Recommendations Folder, GHP (discussing work with elevator operators', hallmen's, and public porters' associations). Many of the meeting minutes of organizations associated with the NUL are also available at NULP.

85. NLPCW Board Minutes of Mar. 4, 1912, Jan. 6, 1913, Minutes Folder, GHP; NUL Executive Board Meeting, Jan. 8, 1913, Minutes Folder, GHP.

86. Minutes of the NUL Executive Board, Apr. 3, 1912, Minutes Folder, GHP.

87. Minutes of the NUL Executive Board, Apr. 3, 1912, Minutes Folder, GHP; Director's Report for Period between Oct. 1 and Feb. 1, 1911, Minutes Folder, GHP; Minutes of NUL Regular

Monthly Meeting, May 1, 1912, Minutes Folder, GHP; Report of the CUCN, Sept. 1912, Minutes Folder, GHP; Report of the CUCN, Sept. 1912, Reports and Recommendations Folder, GHP.

88. See, e.g., Report of Director, June–July 1913, Folder 20, Reports and Recommendations, GHP.
89. On Lugenia Burns Hope and the Neighborhood Union's relationship with the Atlanta and National Urban Leagues in the post–World War I period, see Salem, *To Better Our World,* 190–91, 194; Godshalk, *Veiled Visions,* 251–52.
90. Other scholars have argued, correctly in my view, that the NUL's leaders did have a socio-structural vision of the problems they were confronting. See, e.g., Touré F. Reed, *Not Alms but Opportunity: The Urban League and the Politics of Racial Uplift, 1910–1950* (Chapel Hill: University of North Carolina Press, 2008), 4–5, citing Jesse Thomas Moore Jr., *A Search for Equality: The National Urban League, 1910–1961* (University Park: Pennsylvania State University Press, 1981), 32–34, 54–60 (noting that historians in a different "camp" from Weiss have emphasized that "the League's social-work focus stressed structural…remedies for inequality"). Leaders such as Haynes and others after him were well-trained sociologists after all, and Haynes's writing is replete with analyses of the sociostructural forces at work in creating the urban conditions affecting African Americans. The NUL's understanding of the problem thus displayed ample awareness of the operation of structural forces, but its proposed strategies for addressing it did not directly involve large-scale, structural reform. The NUL's focus on voluntarist strategies and its interest in attacking structural problems were not nec-essarily incompatible, however; later sociologist leaders of the NUL plausibly believed that the best way to achieve structural change was to attack attitudes through employer education and persuasion. See Carle, "Social Movement History of Title VII Disparate Impact Analysis," 279–81.
91. For an example of Haynes's politeness in this regard, See, e.g., George E. Haynes to Roger Baldwin, May 19, 1911, Correspondence Folders, GHP; Roger Baldwin Jr. to George E. Haynes, May 17, 1911, Correspondence Folders, GHP (seeking to reassure Baldwin that the woman who sat through Baldwin's lecture on the "moral conditions" among African Americans with a "bowed head" was not "expressing disapproval" but was merely "bashful"). For an example of Haynes "nudging along" Baldwin's sensibilities, See, e.g., George E. Haynes to Roger Baldwin, Apr. 7, 1913, and Apr. 22, 1914, Correspondence Folders, GHP (suggesting that, rather than confining his talk to the subject of "delinquency" among African Americans, Baldwin might expand his topic to discuss the "relation of the municipality or the state to social betterment").

Chapter 11

1. In the vocabulary of social movements theory, the NAACP drew from the resources of already existing institutions to produce a national organization with strategic and ideological sophisti-cation, along with experienced leadership and local membership bases. Cf. McAdam, *Political Process and the Development of Black Insurgency,* xxxv (arguing that movements always arise from transforming existing collectives "into a vehicle of collective protest."); ibid., 15 ("as numerous studies attest, it is within established interactional networks that social movements develop"); see also Anthony Oberschall, *Social Conflict and Social Movement* (Englewood Cliffs, NJ: Prentice-Hall, 1973), 125 (mobilization occurs through the recruiting of already highly organized groups); Jo Freeman, "The Origins of the Women's Liberation Movement," *American Journal of Sociology* 78 (1973): 792–811 (attributing the rise of second-wave femi-nism to the preexistence of national networks of like-minded people).
2. The classic general account of the NAACP's founding and early years remains Kellogg, *NAACP.* Another classic description that focuses on the NAACP's legal work starting in the 1920s is Tushnet, *NAACP's Legal Strategy against Segregated Education, 1925–1950.* A lively recent treatment that starts with the NAACP's founding is Patricia Sullivan, *Lift Every Voice: The*

NAACP and the Making of the Civil Rights Movement (New York: New Press, 2009). Many other excellent works investigate later periods, as discussed further in the Conclusion.

3. See "National Negro Conference," *Horizon* 5 (Nov. 1909): 1.

4. For a detailed account of the Springfield riot see Roberta Senechal, *The Sociogenesis of a Race Riot: Springfield, Illinois, in 1908* (Urbana: University of Illinois Press, 1990).

5. William English Walling, "The Race War in the North," *Independent* (1908): 529–34; Mary White Ovington, "How the National Association for the Advancement of Colored People Began," *Crisis* 8, no. 4 (1914): 184–88. On Walling's interests, background, and travel to Springfield with Strunsky, see James Boylan, *Revolutionary Lives*, 151–57; Kellogg, *NAACP*, 9–12.

6. Ovington, "How the National Association for the Advancement of Colored People Began," 184–85; Boylan, *Revolutionary Lives*, 157–58. On Russell's background in investigating race conditions in the South and his initial involvement in founding the NAACP, see Robert Miraldi, *The Pen Is Mightier: The Muckraking Life of Charles Edward Russell* (New York: Palgrave Macmillan, 2003), 154–68. Like Walling, Russell did not remain at the core of the NAACP's leadership for long.

7. Booker T. Washington to Robert H. Terrell, Apr. 27, 1910, *BTW Papers*, vol. 10, 325 ("To have Mrs. Terrell's name appear on a program where the opposition is in charge [referring to the second NNC annual meeting] naturally makes it harder for your friends to help you when the time comes").

8. Minutes of the First Meeting of all of the members of the National Negro Conference, undated [March 1909], NAACPP, Part I, Meetings of the Board of Directors (hereinafter, Minutes, NAACPP).

9. William English Walling, "Preface," in *Proceedings of the National Negro Conference,* ed. William Loren Katz, 5–6 (New York: 1909; New York: Arno Press, 1969) (citations refer to Arno Press edition; hereinafter *1909 NNC Proceedings*).

10. Familiar names on this list include Ida Wells Barnett, J. Max Barber, Rev. William Henry Brooks, William Bulkley and Mary Bulkley, Carrie Clifford, George Haynes, L. M. Hershaw, Dr. Verna Morton-Jones, Charles Moore, Nathan Mossell and Gertrude Mossell, John Milholland, Albert Pillsbury, Reverdy Ransom and Emma Ransom, William Monroe Trotter, J. Milton Waldron, Elizabeth Walton, D. Macon Webster, J. Douglass Wetmore, Celia Parker Woolley, and Rev. R. R. Wright Jr. "Conference on the Status of the Negro," [n.d.], FHMMP.

11. 219 U.S. 219 (1911). On Washington's assistance in the *Bailey* case, see Factor, *Black Response to America*, 232, 245n16.

12. Booker T. Washington to Oswald G. Villard, Sept. 7, 1908, Correspondence Files, OGVP; Oswald G. Villard to Washington, Sept. 10, 1908, Correspondence Files, OGVP.

13. Villard to Washington, May 26, 1909, Correspondence Files, OGVP.

14. James M. McPherson, introduction to *1909 NNC Proceedings*, 1.

15. "Address of William Hayes Ward," *1909 NNC Proceedings*, 9, 10.

16. Livingston Farrand, "Race Differentiation—Race Characteristics," *1909 NNC Proceedings*, 14, 21.

17. Burt G. Wilder, "The Brain of the American Negro," *1909 NNC Proceedings*, 22, 39.

18. Edwin R.A. Seligman, "Address," *1909 NNC Proceedings*, 67, 68–69.

19. See Susan D. Carle, "John Dewey and the Early NAACP: Developing a Progressive Discourse on Racial Injustice, 1909–1921," in *Dewey's Enduring Impact*, ed. John R. Shook and Paul Kurtz (New York: Prometheus Books, 2011), 249–62. On the important connections between Dewey and the early American legal realists see John Henry Schlegel, *American Legal Realism and Empirical Social Science* (Durham: University of North Carolina Press, 1995), 24–25, 57–58, 68–69 (tracing the ways in which Dewey's pragmatic philosophy was a center-piece of early legal realist consciousness). For readers from disciplines other than law, I will clarify that the legal realists were very different from the philosophical realists. The legal realists saw law as socially constructed and largely a product of political and psychological forces.

Dewey's thought thus had an indirect but important influence on some of the lawyers who would seek to make social change through law by assisting the NAACP, such as legal realist Karl Llewellyn, who would lend his support to the NAACP. See Mark Tushnet, *Making Civil Rights Law: Thurgood Marshall and the Supreme Court, 1956-61* (New York: Oxford University Press, 1994), 148, 333n21, 346n36 (examples of Llewellyn's peripheral involvement in the NAACP).

20. John Dewey, "Address,"*1909 NNC Proceedings*, 71, 72-73.

21. Carle, "John Dewey and the Early NAACP," 257-58.

22. W.E.B. Du Bois," Politics and Industry," *1909 NNC Proceedings*, 79, 80-82.

23. Ibid., 81, 83, 84.

24. Ibid., 87-88.

25. William English Walling, "The Negro and the South," *1909 NNC Proceedings*, 98, 101.

26. "Discussion," *1909 NNC Proceedings*, 114.

27. Ibid., 110; J. Milton Waldron, "The Problem's Solution," *1909 NNC Proceedings* 159,164-65.

28. "Discussion," *1909 NNC Proceedings*,115-16; see also Gaines, *Uplifting the Race*, 66 (analyzing Barber's remarks).

29. "Discussion," *1909 NNC Proceedings*,114, 115.

30. See Dittmer, *Black Georgia*, 30-32 (describing Georgia railway strike).

31. William L. Bulkley, "Race Prejudice as Viewed from an Economic Standpoint," *1909 NNC Proceedings*, 89, 91, 94, 97.

32. "Discussion," *1909 NNC Proceedings*, 118-19; Ida Wells Barnett, "Lynching Our National Crime," *1909 NNC Proceedings*, 174, 178. On the NAACP's later campaign against lynching, see Zangrando, *NAACP Crusade against Lynching.*

33. Bishop A. Walters, "Civil and Political Status of the Negro," *1909 NNC Proceedings*,167, 172

34. Albert E. Pillsbury, "Negro Disfranchisement as It Affects the White Man," *1909 NNC Proceedings*, 180, 188-95.

35. John Milholland, "Address," *1909 NNC Proceedings*, 127-28.

36. Oswald G. Villard, "The Need of Organization," *1909 NNC Proceedings*, 197, 202-203.

37. Ibid., 201, 204, 205.

38. "Resolutions," *1909 NNC Proceedings*, 222-24.

39. Oswald G. Villard to Francis Garrison, June 4, 1909, and June 7, 1909, Correspondence Files, OGVP.

40. Mary White Ovington to Oswald Villard, Nov. 25, 1913, Correspondence Files, OGVP.

41. "Conference Confusion," *NYA,* June 10, 1909, 1, 3.

42. "Mr. Walling's Lamentation," *NYA,* June 24, 1909, 1.

43. Minutes of NNC Meeting, Nov. 8, 1909, WEBDBP; Subcommittee on Plans and Organization, undated announcement (1909), WEBDBP; "The National Negro Committee Invites You to Attend the Sessions of Its Second Annual Conference" [1910], WEBDBP.

44. Minutes, NNC, Dec. 13, 1909, NAACPP; Kellogg, *NAACP,* 35 (describing Walling's association with Gompers).

45. On the work of one white trade union leader, Michael Donnelly, to build a racially inclusive union in the meat-packing industry, see Alma Herbst, *The Negro in the Slaughtering and Meat-Packing Industry in Chicago* (1932; New York: Arno Press, 1971), 21-22. Pagination is from original edition.

46. Minutes of Special Meeting of the NNC, May 5, 1910, NAACPP. On Mary Maclean see Kellogg, *NAACP,* 37, 45n66, 52, 145, 151, 212-13; Oswald G. Villard to Francis J. Garrison, May 17, 1910, OGVP (identifying Maclean as one of the socialist women who were the organization's most ardent workers). Maclean won high praise from all of her NAACP colleagues for her work, and they greatly mourned her untimely death in 1912. See Minutes of NAACP Board Meeting, Aug. 6, 1912, NAACPP (Maclean's death "a terrible loss to the Association").

47. Not coincidentally, these organizations provided a key base of support for passage of the first state statute banning race and religious discrimination in private-sector employment in New York State several decades later. See Carle, "Social Movement History of Title VII Disparate Impact Analysis," 276–77.
48. Minutes, NNC, Feb. 14, 1910, NAACPP.
49. Minutes of a Special Meeting of the NNC, Apr. 7, 1910, NAACPP.
50. Minutes of a Special Meeting of the NNC, May 5, 1910, NAACPP.
51. Special Meeting of the NNC, Apr. 21, 1910, NAACPP.
52. National Negro Committee Second Annual Conference Program, 1910, WEBDBP; Kellogg, *NAACP*, 34 (listing members of appointing committee). For a well-researched examination of the social identities of the NAACP's white leaders at this stage of its history, see William Stueck, "Progressivism and the Negro: White Liberals and the Early NAACP," *Historian* 38 (Nov. 1975): 58–78.
53. Oswald G. Villard to Francis J. Garrison, May 17, 1910, Correspondence, OGVP.
54. "National Negro Conference," *NYA*, May 19, 1910, 5.
55. Ovington, "How the National Association for the Advancement of Colored People Began."
56. Minutes of Executive Session, May 14, 1910, NAACPP.
57. Minutes of Executive Committee Meeting, May 25, 1910, NAACPP.
58. Minutes of the Executive Committee, June 7, 1910, NAACPP.
59. Waiver of Notice of First Meeting of Incorporation and other documents dated between May 25 and June 11, 1911, NAACPP; Minutes of First Meeting of NAACP Board of Directors, June 20, 1911, NAACPP; Minutes of the Meeting of the Executive Committee, Jan. 4, 1912, NAACPP.
60. Minutes of the NNC, Nov. 8, 1909, NAACPP.
61. Minutes of Executive Session, May 14, 1910, NAACPP.
62. Report of the Preliminary Committee on Permanent Organization (undated), attached to Minutes of Special Meeting of the NNC, May 5, 1910, NAACPP.
63. Minutes of Executive Session, May 14, 1910, 2, NAACPP; Minutes of Executive Committee Meeting, May 25, 1910, NAACPP.
64. Minutes of the Executive Committee, Nov. 29, 1910, 1–2, NAACPP.
65. Francis J. Garrison to Oswald G. Villard, Apr. 5, 1911, Correspondence, OGVP; Garrison to Villard, Apr. 8, 1911, Correspondence, OGVP.
66. Oswald G. Villard to Francis J. Garrison, Apr. 7, 1911, Correspondence, OGVP.
67. Oswald G. Villard to Francis J. Garrison, Apr. 10, 1911, Correspondence, OGVP.
68. NAACP Minutes of the Meeting of the Board of Directors, Dec. 3, 1912, NAACPP; Annual Meeting Minutes, Jan. 21, 1913, 10, NAACPP (Ovington reporting that the apportionment of membership fees raised by local branches would be left unchanged and "for one more year at least every effort should be made to strengthen the central organization").
69. See Taylor, "Social Movement Continuity" (describing a similar process in which experienced activists moved into key organizing positions as second-wave feminism got going).
70. "Editorial," *Crisis* 6, no. 31 (May 1913): 26–29.
71. On the tension arising from the question of the Constitution League's continued existence after the NNC's founding, See, e.g., Minutes of a Special Meeting of the NNC, Apr. 7, 1910, NAACPP.
72. In the vocabulary of social movement theory, "the existence of established organizations within the movement's mass base insures the presence of recognized leaders who can be called upon to lend their prestige and organizing skills to the incipient movement." McAdam, *Political Process and the Development of Black Insurgency*, 45.
73. NAACP Annual Meeting Minutes, Jan. 21, 1913, 7, NAACPP (DC branch report including suggestion for a paid congressional lobbyist); Annual Meeting Minutes, Feb. 12, 1915, 4, NAACPP (DC report on extra funds raised and focus on fighting hostile measures in Congress); "The Women's Committee," *Crisis* 5, no. 5 (March 1913) (report that Carrie

Clifford would head a committee to raise $1,000 "to make *The Crisis* beautiful" and encourage African American art). Walters and Waldron left the NAACP at around the same time, and the internal political maneuvering that underlay these developments was tinged with long-standing hostilities stretching back to the Niagara Movement. See, e.g., F. H. M. Murray to William Trotter, Sept. 22, 1913, General Correspondence Files, FHMMP (expressing anger and suspicion about the internal politics related to Waldron's ouster).

74. "A Year's Work," *Crisis* 8, no. 3 (July 1914): 140–46 (synopses of branches' activities that year).

75. "The NAACP," *Crisis* 3 (Feb. 1912): 157–59.

76. Minutes of a Meeting of the Members of the Friends of the NAACP, May 10, 1911, included in Board of Directors Meetings folder for 1911, NAACPP (Boston meeting minutes and list of attendees); NAACP Annual Meeting Minutes, Jan. 12, 1913, NAACPP (Boston branch activities); NAACP Board of Director Minutes, Nov. 6, 1913, NAACPP (reporting that a Boston YMCA discrimination case had been successfully handled); NAACP Annual Meeting Minutes, Feb. 12, 1915, NAACPP (Boston branch presented check for extra funds raised by Mrs. Butler Wilson and Mrs. Francis Garrison through their sponsorship of musicals and other events); "A Year's Work," 141. On Butler Wilson's background and Niagara Movement membership, see Schneider, *Boston Confronts Jim Crow,* 136–37. A later internal history listed as additional early accomplishments the Boston branch's successful intervention to prevent the suspension of an African American girl from school for erroneous reasons, its campaign to pressure the Massachusetts Bar Association to object to the exclusion of African American lawyers, mass meetings to protest federal employment segregation, and opposition to the racist film "Birth of a Nation." Robert C. Hayden, *Boston's NAACP History, 1910–1982* (Boston: Boston Branch NAACP, 1982).

77. NAACP Board of Directors Meeting Minutes, Nov. 6, 1913, NACCPP; Minutes of Meeting of Board of Directors, Nov. 6, 1913, 2, NAACPP (Crawford's activity in New Haven).

78. Kenneth Robert Janken, *White: The Biography of Walter White, Mr. NAACP* (New York: New Press, 2003), 23.

79. See Arthur Spingarn to Charles Anderson, June 27, 1913, General Correspondence, 1913–1915, ASP; Gilchrist Stewart to Arthur Spingarn, Aug. 1, 1913, General Correspondence, 1913–1915, ASP.

80. See NAACP Board of Directors Executive Committee Meeting, Mar. 7, 1911, 2, NAACPP (Walters as Vigilance Committee vice president); NAACP Board of Directors Meeting Minutes, Nov. 6, 1913, NAACPP (Walters's resignation from the board accepted, and Archibald Grimké appointed in his place); Oswald Villard to Archibald Grimké, Nov. 11, 1913, AGP (discussing Walters's alleged statements); Miller, "This Worldly Mission," 316, 359, 380–85 (detailing Walters's campaign efforts for Wilson and his subsequent attempts to persuade Wilson to appoint African Americans to office, and arguing that the Wilson administration set Walters up as part of its retreat on race issues).

81. NAACP Third Annual Report, Jan. 1913, NAACPP.

82. On the use of testers to detect discrimination in theatres, See, e.g., Meeting of the Board of Directors, Apr. 4, 1912, 2, NAACPP (report of Joel Spingarn on New York City branch activities). Arthur Spingarn's recollection of visiting bars to protest discrimination by "smashing glasses on the floor" is recounted in Farnsworth Fowle, "Arthur Spingarn of the NAACP Is Dead," *NYT,* Dec. 2, 1971, 1, 50. The New York City chapter pursued saloon discrimination cases through legal means until mid-1915. See Minutes of Board of Directors Meeting, July 12, 1915, 3 (reporting that the case of *Gibbs v. Arras* [170 A.D. 897 (NY App. Div. 1915)] would be the last saloon case the NAACP would bring; in the future it planned to reserve its efforts for restaurant and theater discrimination). New York's highest court later overturned the judgment for Mr. Gibbs, deciding that saloons were not covered entities under the New York Civil Rights Law forbidding public accommodations discrimination. Gibbs v. Arras Bros., Inc., 222 N.Y. 332 (1918).

83. For examples of the organization of such branches, see Minutes of Board of Directors Meeting, Feb. 4, 1913, NAACPP (applications of branches in Washington, Topeka, and St. Joseph); Minutes of Board of Directors Meeting, Mar. 11, 1913, NAACPP (accepting

branch applications for Lynchburg, Virginia, and Howard University); Minutes of Board of Directors Meeting, June 3, 1913, NAACPP (Muskogee and Oklahoma City branch applications); Minutes of Board of Directors Meeting, Dec. 2, 1913, NAACPP (branch applications approved for Cleveland, Providence, and Talladega); Minutes of Board of Directors Meeting, Nov. 6, 1913, NAACPP (report of successful meeting of Portland branch); Minutes of NAACP Annual Meeting, Feb. 12, 1915, NAACPP (Des Moines, Iowa, branch report on fighting state anti-intermarriage bill); Minutes of Board of Directors Meeting, May 10, 1915, 3, NAACPP (eight new branches in Illinois and Indiana had been formed, almost all of which included white members); ibid., 4 (applications from Lincoln University and local branches in Montana and Washington State considered).

84. "The NAACP," *Crisis* 3 (Feb. 1912): 203–205.

85. Minutes of the NAACP Annual Meeting, Feb. 12, 1915, 2, NAACPP.

86. Minutes of Board of Directors Meeting, June 14, 1915, 2, NAACPP.

87. NAACP Minutes of the Board of Directors, 1916, NAACPP; "Report of the Secretary," Annual Meeting Report, 27, NAACPP.

Chapter 12

1. "Steve Green's Story," *Crisis* 1, no. 1 (Nov. 1910), 14.

2. Ibid.; Oswald Garrison Villard to Francis J. Garrison, Oct. 17, 1910, Correspondence, OGVP; Kellogg, *NAACP*, 62–63 and n. 71. On Spingarn's recollections of the importance of the Green case to his affiliation with the NAACP, see Sullivan, *Lift Every Voice*, 20.

3. "The Pink Franklin Case," *Crisis* 1, no. 1 (Nov. 1910): 14; "Pink Franklin," *Crisis* 1, no. 2 (Dec. 1910): 26; Oswald Garrison Villard to Francis J. Garrison, June 1, 1910, Correspondence, OGVP; Oswald Garrison Villard to Booker T. Washington, Aug. 4, 1910, Correspondence, OGVP; Booker T. Washington to Oswald Garrison Villard, Aug. 9, 1910, OGVP.

4. Meeting of the NNC Executive Committee, Nov. 29, 1910, NAACPP; "Pink Franklin's Reprieve," *Crisis* 1, no. 4 (Feb. 1911): 15–16 (letter from assisting attorney Charles J. Bonaparte); "Pink Franklin," *Crisis* 1, no. 4 (Feb. 1911): 17; Kellogg, *NAACP*, 157–62; Kenneth W. Goings, *The NAACP Comes of Age: The Defeat of Judge John J. Parker* (Bloomington: Indiana University Press, 1990), 12.

5. Executive Committee Meeting, April 11, 1911, NAACPP; Minutes of Executive Committee Meeting, Jan. 3, 1911, NAACPP; See, e.g., Executive Committee Meeting, June 6, 1911, NAACPP (Lakewood unlawful arrest case resolved as reported in *The Crisis*).

6. Minutes of the Meetings of the CUCN, Nov. 7, 1910, Feb. 6, 1911, and Mar. 31, 1911, Minutes Folder, GHP. An interview with Du Bois and text of letter from him to Haynes on this subject, which is cited in Weiss, *The NUL*, 329n45, could not be located in the L. Hollingsworth Wood Papers when I visited them in July 2012.

7. Mary White Ovington, *The Walls Came Tumbling Down*, 111–12 (New York: Harcourt, Brace: 1947).

8. May Childs Nerney to Arthur Spingarn, Nov. 18, 1913, General Correspondence, 1913–1915, ASP.

9. Undated [1914] document signed "W.E.B., Chairman," in General Correspondence, 1913–1915, ASP.

10. Draft report by May Childs Nerney, dated Dec. 6, 1915, 1–2, in General Correspondence, 1913–1915, ASP.

11. See, e.g., May Childs Nerney to Eugene K. Jones, June 20, 1914, Administrative File, 1885–1949, Subject File, 1905–1914, Box I: C384, National Urban League, 1914–1939, NAACPP (NAACP's seeking information on the NUL's work on questions of African American children's attendance in New York City public schools, the location of these schools, possible differential enforcement of truancy regulations at those schools, and efforts to give these children industrial training and education); May Childs Nerney to Eugene K. Jones, June 29, 1914 (ibid.) (discussing problems with NAACP's organizing in relation to legal cases in Louisville and Richmond and inviting Jones to drop by her office as "we could both profit by a frank discussion of the whole matter"); Hallie B. Craiginell [NUL secretary for women's work] to May Childs Nerney,

July 10, 1914 (ibid.) (reporting on the disposition of a child welfare matter referred to the NUL by the NAACP); May Childs Nerney to Eugene K. Jones, July 15, 1914 (ibid.) (discussing NAACP lawyer Brinsmade's investigation into housing segregation in Harlem, leading to his recommendation that a mortgage company be set up to provide loans on African American property and suggesting that the NAACP's legal committee and a committee from the NUL meet jointly to continue to pursue the matter); Secretary to Miss Nerney to Eugene K. Jones, Nov. 1, 1915 (ibid.) (thanking Jones for his kind offer to assist the NAACP in Louisville and looking forward to hearing further about the possibility of cooperating with the NAACP there); John T. Clark to "Gentlemen" [of the NAACP], Dec. 6, 1915, replied to by May Childs Nerney to "Gentlemen" [at the NUL], Dec. 11, 1915 (ibid.) (rejecting a case the NUL referred to the NAACP, involving the collection of a loan as it did not involve "discrimination on account of color"); Roy Nash [acting NAACP secretary] to Eugene K. Jones, Apr. 13, 1915 (ibid.) (asking whether the NUL might be able to investigate conditions at an orphanage that had been brought to the NAACP's attention). This correspondence continues with increasing frequency into 1916 and after. See also Minutes of the Meeting of the Board of Directors, Nov. 6, 1913, 2, NAACPP (reporting that Arthur Spingarn was to chair and appoint the members of a committee to confer with the NUL about the relation of their work to the NAACP).

12. See, e.g., West Coast Hotel v. Parrish, 300 U.S. 379 (1937) (upholding the constitutionality of a state minimum wage law for women on the ground that "recent economic experience has brought into strong light... [t]he exploitation of a class of workers who are in an unequal position with respect to bargaining power"); NLRB v. Jones & Laughlin Steel Co., 301 U.S. 1 (1937) (upholding the constitutionality of the National Labor Relations Act as a legitimate exercise of Congress's power to regulate interstate commerce).

13. Carle, "Social Movement History of Title VII Disparate Impact Analysis," 279–85.

14. Meeting of the Executive Committee, Feb. 7, 1911, NAACPP; Executive Committee Meeting, Apr. 11, 1911, NAACPP. I discuss the members of this first legal committee in further detail in Carle, "Race, Class, and Legal Ethics in the Early NAACP," 97–146.

15. See, e.g., August Meier and Elliott Rudwick, Along the Color Line (Champaign: University of Illinois Press, 1976), 163n27; William M. Wherry Jr., Public Utilities and the Law (New York: N. L. Brown, 1928).

16. Executive Committee Meeting Minutes, Nov. 14, 1911, NAACPP; Crisis 3, no. 4 (Feb. 1912): 157–59.

17. Oswald Garrison Villard to Francis J. Garrison, Jan. 29, 1912, Correspondence, OGVP; Minutes of the Meeting of the Board of Directors, Feb. 6, 1912, NACCPP; NAACP Third Annual Report, Jan. 1913, 8, NAACPP; "Our New Legal Bureau," Crisis (Jan. 1914): 139–40; Chapin Brinsmade, "Our Legal Bureau," Crisis (Easter 1913): 291–92; Chapin Brinsmade, "Our Legal Bureau," Crisis 8, no. 43 (May 1914): 34–36; Minutes of Board of Directors' Meeting, Mar. 3, 1914, 2, NAACPP (Brinsmade's report on legal matters to the board); Minutes of Board of Directors' Meeting, Apr. 28, 1914, 3, NAACPP (Brinsmade's report about organizing mass meeting in Louisville and other matters).

18. NAACP Third Annual Report, Jan. 1913, 6–7, NAACPP.

19. Minutes of Board of Directors Meeting, July 1, 1913, 1, NAACPP (letters sent from national headquarters asking branches for $100 each to fund this lawyer position; initial favorable replies received from ten).

20. NAACP Third Annual Report, Jan. 1913, 7, NAACPP; Board of Directors Meeting Minutes, July 1, 1913, 1, NAACPP (report on hearing before Maryland Supreme Court).

21. W. Ashbie Hawkins, "A Year of Segregation in Baltimore," Crisis 3, no. 1 (Nov. 1911). For more on Hawkins, see J. Clay Smith, Emancipation, 146–47 and 181n199; Garrett Power, "Apartheid Baltimore Style: The Residential Segregation Ordinances of 1910–13," Maryland Law Review 42 (1983): 289, 305, 311–13.

22. "Courts," Crisis 3, no. 5 (March 1912): 189; "Baltimore Segregation," Crisis 6, no. 33 (July 1913); 127–28. The case was State v. Gurry, 121 Md. 534, 88 A. 546 (1913).

23. 245 U.S. 60 (1917).

24. Minutes of Board of Directors Meeting, Feb. 2, 1915, NAACPP (discussing Arthur Spingarn's work to bring together the Louisville case and organize a local NAACP branch to sponsor it).

25. "Judicial Decisions," *Crisis* 1, no. 2 (Dec. 1910): 6; "The Maryland Decision," *Crisis* 1, no. 2 (Dec. 1910), 12 (reporting on victory in U.S. Circuit Court on Maryland disfranchisement matter); [no title], *Crisis* 1, no. 5 (Mar. 1911): 7 (reporting on second favorable decision in a test case filed against registration clerks who refused African Americans' registration); "Disfranchising Voters in Maryland," *Crisis* 3, no. 4 (Feb. 1912): 160–65; Minutes of Board of Directors Meeting, June 3, 1913, NAACPP; "Baltimore," *Crisis* 8, no. 1 (May 1914), 33; *Crisis* 8, no. 47 (Sept. 1914), 219; "State of Maryland v. Jenkins" file, ASP (including copy of Hawkins's brief).

26. 235 U.S. 151 (1914).

27. For the chain of correspondence about the *McCabe* case between attorney Harrison and Storey, Brinsmade, and others in the national office, see "McCabe v. Atchison, Topeka and Santa Fe RR" file, ASP.

28. "In Court," *Crisis* (Jan. 1915): 137–38.

29. *McCabe,* 235 U.S. at 161.

30. Benno C. Schmidt Jr., "Principle and Prejudice," 444, 485, 492–93.

31. See William Harrison to Moorfield Storey, Aug. 12, 1913, "McCabe v. Atchison, Topeka & Santa Fe R.R." file, ASP (asking for court costs for the case to be paid by NAACP); William Harrison to NAACP, Aug. 23, 1913 (ibid.) (repeating this request); Mary Childs Nerney, "Memo for Mr. Turner," Sept. 5, 1913 (ibid.) (asking for a check to be drawn from the Legal Redress fund to pay these costs).

32. NAACP Executive Committee Meeting, Oct. 16, 1911, 1, NAACPP (Du Bois report on two public accommodations discrimination cases in New York City); NAACP Minutes of the Meeting of the Board of Directors, June 4, 1912, 1, NAACPP (Wherry report on lynching investigation and public accommodations cases); Arthur Spingarn to Charles Studin, Dec. 18, 1912, General Correspondence File, 1913–1915, ASP (discussing theater discrimination case); Board of Directors Meeting Minutes, Aug. 6, 1912, 1, NAACPP (legal work on segregation statutes and discriminatory labor contracts); Board of Directors Meeting Minutes, Sept. 3, 1912, 1, NAACPP (more on same issues); Board of Directors Meeting, Apr. 1, 1913, 1, NAACPP (considering prosecution of Chicago hotel for turning away large delegation of African American club women).

33. See, e.g., Executive Committee Meeting, Apr. 11, 19199, 1, NAACPP (discussing efforts to secure a commutation of death sentence for two African American youths in New Jersey); Minutes of Annual Meeting of the Members of the NAACP, Jan. 3, 1916, 9–11, NAACPP (discussing cases involving African American men accused of crime in which the NAACP had intervened where "color discrimination" could be proved).

34. Executive Committee Meeting, June 6, 1911, 4, NAACPP (Livermore, Kentucky; Lake City, Florida; and Oklahoma lynchings protested through letters to governors); Meeting of the Executive Committee, Nov. 14, 1911, 2, NAACPP (Coatesville lynching investigation by Maclean; motion to approve funding for one-half of lawyer's fee); Minutes of the Meeting of the Board of Directors, July 2, 1912, 2, NAACPP (Georgia lynching investigation); Minutes of the Meeting of the Board of Directors, Aug. 6, 1912, 1, NAACPP (investigation completed; funders to receive letter describing progress); Minutes of the Meeting of the Board of Directors, Oct. 1, 1912, and Nov. 12, 1912, NAACPP (more on Coatesville lynching); Third Annual Report, Jan. 1913, 9–11, NAACPP (assessing the organization's contribution to this matter though no conviction was obtained).

35. "NAACP," *Crisis* (Dec. 1913): 88; "Where Does Your Congressman Stand?" *Crisis* 9, no. 49 (Nov. 1914): 19–24.

36. Third Annual Report, 8–9, NAACPP; see also Minutes of Annual Meeting, Feb. 12, 1915, NAACPP (highlighting the organization's success in opposing hostile legislation in Congress); Executive Committee Meeting, Mar. 7, 1911, 2, NAACPP (opposing Massachusetts proposed

bill against intermarriage); Board of Directors Meeting Minutes, Feb. 4, 1913, 2, NAACPP (report on anti-intermarriage bills in New York, Kansas, Michigan, and other states); Board of Directors Meeting Minutes, Mar. 11, 1913, 1–2, NAACPP (the association opposed anti-intermarriage bills in DC, Illinois, Wisconsin, New York, Ohio, California, and Iowa and defeated them in several states).

37. There is an ample general literature on race activists' response to these developments during the Wilson administration, so I do not delve into it in great detail so late in this narrative. See, e.g., Nancy J. Weiss, "The Negro and the New Freedom: Fighting Wilsonian Segregation," *Political Science Quarterly* (1969): 61–79; Henry Blumenthal, "Woodrow Wilson and the Race Question," *Journal of Negro History* 48 (1963): 1–21; Nicholas Patler, *Jim Crow and the Wilson Administration: Protesting Federal Segregation in the Early Twentieth Century* (Boulder: University Press of Colorado, 2007); Sullivan, *Lift Every Voice,* 28–33; Kellogg, *NAACP,* 161–75.

38. This incident is well described in Fox, *Guardian of Boston,* 179–87. According to Fox, the National Equal Rights League was earlier called the National Independent Political League (ibid.).

39. Board of Directors Meeting Minutes, Mar. 5, 1912, 2, NAACPP; NAACP Third Annual Report, Jan. 1913, 21, NAACPP.

40. Minutes of Board of Directors Executive Committee Meeting, Jan. 3, 1911, 2, NAACPP; Board of Directors Minutes of Meeting, Mar. 5, 1912, NAACPP (reporting on discussions of committee set up to work on federal aid to education issues and documenting John Dewey's participation in this committee); Board of Directors Meeting Minutes, Jan. 7, 1913, 2, NAACPP.

41. Arthur Spingarn to Samuel Scott, Oct. 4, 1914, General Correspondence, 1913–1915, ASP; Arthur Spingarn to Samuel Scott, Oct. 30, 1914, General Correspondence, 1913–1915, ASP; Arthur Spingarn to May Childs Nerney, Nov. 29, 1914, General Correspondence, 1913–1915, ASP.

42. L. M. Hershaw to W.E.B. Du Bois, Dec. 23, 1912, "Race Commission" folder, OGVP.

43. Carbon copy draft letter, Villard to L. M. Hershaw, Dec. 31, 1912, "Race Commission" folder, OGVP.

44. J. E. Spingarn to May Childs Nerney, Jan. 13, 1913, Race Commission folder, OGVP.

45. Mary White Ovington to Villard, Jan. 18, 1913, Race Commission folder, OGVP.

46. "Memo for Mr. Villard," Jan. 15, 1913, Race Commission folder, OGVP.

47. Oswald Garrison Villard to Francis J. Garrison, May 13, 1913, OGVP; Oswald Garrison Villard to Francis J. Garrison, July 17, 1913, OGVP. For a blow-by-blow description of the demise of the National Race Commission proposal, see Kellogg, *NAACP,* 159–69.

48. Fifth Annual Report of the NAACP," reprinted in *Crisis* 9, no. 6 (Easter 1915): 288–93.

49. Guinn v. United States, 238 U.S. 347, 354 (1915).

50. "The Oklahoma Decision," *Crisis* 2, no. 3 (July 1911): 104; Board of Directors Minutes, Oct. 7, 1913, 2, NAACPP (reporting that Storey's brief had been filed for the association).

51. *Guinn,* 238 U.S. 347 (1915).

52. See, e.g., May Childs Nerney to Arthur Spingarn, Dec. 10, 1913, General Correspondence, 1913–1915, ASP; Arthur Spingarn to May Childs Nerney, Oct. 7, 1913, General Correspondence, 1913–1915, ASP.

53. "The Grandfather Decision," *Crisis* (Aug. 1915): 171, 173.

Conclusion

1. Cf. Dossett, *Bridging Race Divides,* 14 (pointing out that by the late 1930s African American women had a firm belief that their institutions "should have equal access to resources and state provisions" though "integration could and should wait"). I realize that this project has butted up against a large and important literature on the history of the ideologies of black nationalism and economic separatism, of which Dossett's book is but one recent thoughtful example. The literature on black nationalism and separatism examines a set of questions somewhat

different from those here, which centrally concern how activists developed ideas about how to distinguish between legal and nonlegal problems and racial justice strategies, but it is helpfully related nonetheless. As I have pointed out along the way, there certainly were nationalists involved in the activist work this book recounts, such as AME bishop Henry Turner, who unsuccessfully sought to have the AAL endorse an Africa migration resolution as described in chapter 3. But here and in other instances, the AAL and later the AAC and the Niagara Movement rejected nationalism and instead emphasized legal equality and equal citizenship rights in the United States—along with *social* racial self-sufficiency. In a later period, nationalist ideologies would become more politically salient—indeed, as already pointed out, Wilford Smith would become Marcus Garvey's personal lawyer much as he had been Washington's.

2. The basic debate on this question is captured in David. A. Schultz, ed., *Leveraging the Law: Using the Courts to Achieve Social Change* (New York: Peter Lang, 1998).

3. Cf. McCann, *Rights at Work*, 277–310 (arguing that the battle for pay equity, though unsuccessful, produced important changes in legal consciousness).

4. 198 U.S. 45 (1905).

5. In the language of social movement theory, these activists responded to the "political opportunity structure" presented by their social and historical context. See Meyer, "Protest and Political Opportunities," 128–29 (discussing the body of social movement literature that has developed and applied the political opportunity structure concept).

6. Bernard Mandel, "Samuel Gompers and the Negro Workers, 1886–1914," *Journal of Negro History* 40 (1955): 34, 53–60.

7. This is a general point that scholars of the African American and white women's reform groups of the era have often made. See generally Linda Gordon, ed., *Women, the State, and Welfare* (Madison: University of Wisconsin Press, 1990); Gilmore, *Gender and Jim Crow*.

8. See, e.g., "Cry from Macedonia," *Richmond Times*, Jan. 31, 1899 (denouncing the AAC's proposal for a commission to inquire into the conditions facing African Americans in the country on the ground that this reflected ideas that "the [negro] is the special ward of the nation, and that the nation should take care of him, looking after him in the several states and compelling the States to do this and that, for him," when in fact "the government should not have favorites"); see also Hutchinson, "Racial Exhaustion" (tracing variations on this rhetoric as used in different historical periods).

9. David E. Bernstein, *Only One Place of Redress: African Americans, Labor Regulations, and the Courts from Reconstruction to the New Deal* (Durham: Duke University Press, 2001) is replete with examples of such legislation.

10. Here I use the definition of black nationalism offered by Wilson Jeremiah Moses: "If there is one *essential* quality of black nationalism, however, it is the feeling on the part of black individuals that they are responsible for the welfare of other black individuals, or of black people as a collective entity, simply because of a shared racial heritage and destiny." Wilson Jeremiah Moses, *The Golden Age of Black Nationalism, 1850–1925* (New York: Oxford University Press, 1978); see also Michael C. Dawson, *Black Visions: The Roots of Contemporary African American Political Ideologies* (Chicago: University of Chicago Press, 2001), 85–134.

11. This point follows one Christopher Tomlins and William Forbath have made in analyzing Samuel Gompers's distaste for utilizing the courts for labor law reform, given his overwhelming negative experiences with courts' use of antilabor injunctions to shut down union activity prior to the New Deal. See Christopher L. Tomlins, *The State and the Unions: Labor Relations, Law, and the Organized Labor Movement in America, 1880–1960* (New York: Cambridge University Press, 1985), 62–63; William E. Forbath, *Law and the Shaping of the American Labor Movement* (Cambridge, MA: Harvard University Press, 1991), 128–30. Scholars have also shown that Gompers *did* favor legislative reform on issues such as prohibition of child labor and minimum wage regulation. See, e.g., Meagan Hu, "Revisiting Samuel Gompers' Views on Using Law to Pursue Social Reform," student paper, American University Washington College of Law, 2010 (on file with author). In an analogous way, African American activists

had ambivalent views about the strategic possibilities offered by traditional law reform techniques during the period. Their misgivings were for different reasons and produced different outcomes. On the one hand, they saw courts as a venue for articulating formal equality claims and the federal legislature as a venue for some kinds of law reform objectives, such as education funding. On the other hand, they did not regard courts or legislatures as a generally promising avenue for enhancing the social welfare of an unpopular minority.

12. Thus, for example, as Deborah Gray White has noted, "the race problem . . . inherently included the problems of poverty." See Linda Gordon, "Black and White Visions of Welfare: Women's Welfare Activism, 1890–1945," *Journal of American History* 78 (1991): 559, 580 (quoting an unpublished paper by White). See also White, *Too Heavy a Load,* 24 (noting that the NACW, which "became the black woman's primary vehicle for race leadership," "saw a set of interlocking problems involving race, gender, and poverty, no one of which could be dealt with independently"). Linda Gordon, further pursuing this insight, concludes on the basis of her comparative study of African American and white women's welfare reform networks during the Progressive and New Deal eras that these two groups of women conceived of welfare in different ways and that these differences should "alter somewhat our understanding of what welfare *is.*" Gordon, "Black and White Visions of Welfare," 562.

13. See, e.g., Alice Kessler-Harris, *In Pursuit of Equity: Women, Men, and the Quest for Economic Citizenship in 20th-Century America* (New York: Oxford University Press, 2001); Gwendolyn Mink, *The Wages of Motherhood: Inequality in the Welfare State, 1917–1942* (Ithaca, NY: Cornell University Press, 1995); Julie Novkov, *Constituting Workers, Protecting Women: Gender, Law, and Labor in the Progressive Era and New Deal Years* (Ann Arbor: University of Michigan Press, 2001); Kathryn Kish Sklar, *Florence Kelley and the Nation's Work: The Rise of Women's Political Culture, 1830 1900* (New Haven: Yale University Press, 1995); Theda Skocpol, *Protecting Soldiers and Mothers: The Political Origins of Social Policy in the United States* (Cambridge, MA: Harvard University Press, 1992).

14. Robyn Muncy, *Creating a Female Dominion in American Reform, 1890–1935* (New York: Oxford University Press, 1991), 162–65.

15. Weiss, *The NUL,* 273–75; Paul Frymer, *Black and Blue: African Americans, the Labor Movement, and the Decline of the Democratic Party* (Princeton: Princeton University Press, 2008), 28–29 (documenting the unsuccessful joint effort by the NAACP and the NUL in the 1930s to persuade Congress to modify the proposed Wagner Act to mitigate its racially exclusionary features); Nancy MacLean, *Freedom Is Not Enough: The Opening of the American Workplace* (Cambridge, MA: Harvard University Press, 2006): 17 ("The New Deal . . . wrote inequality into its component policies, from labor standards and work relief to housing and Social Security").

16. For an interesting discussion of the use that civil rights activists made of the law/not law distinction in a much later period, see Christopher W. Schmidt, "Conceptions of Law in the Civil Rights Movement," *UC Irvine Law Review* 1 (2011): 641–76.

17. See, e.g., Armstrong and Bernstein, "Culture, Power, and Institutions," 80, 82 (noting the importance of exploring why actors make the decisions they do about strategies and goals and what insights these investigations offer into the "nature of domination" in society).

18. On the concept of the long civil rights movement, see the literature cited in footnotes 6 through 8 of the Introduction.

19. Goluboff, *Lost Promise.* Goluboff especially emphasizes the NAACP's interest in these years in developing litigation theories to boost economic as well as political and civil rights (ibid., 6, 13, 14).

20. Ibid., 5.

21. Hughes Tool Co., 147 N.L.R.B. 1573 (1964).

22. Lee, "Hotspots in a Cold War," 327–78.

23. Carol Anderson, *Eyes off the Prize: The United Nations and the African American Struggle for Human Rights, 1944–1955* (New York: Cambridge University Press, 2003).

24. MacLean, *Freedom Is Not Enough,* 341, 347.

25. See, e.g., Mack, *Representing the Race,* 7–9 (arguing that these elite African American lawyers "constructed race"); Mack, "Rethinking Civil Rights Lawyering and Politics in the Era before *Brown*" (contesting the legal liberalism view of civil rights lawyering and arguing that black lawyers' focus in the interwar period was primarily on developing successful everyday practices and promoting intrarace advancement).

26. See, e.g., Tomiko Brown-Nagin, "Race as Identity Caricature: A Local Legal History Lesson in the Salience of Intra-Racial Conflict," *University of Pennsylvania Law Review* 151 (2003): 1913–76 (analyzing the intersection of race and class issues in civil rights activists' strategic decisions about test case litigation).

27. Brown-Nagin, *Courage to Dissent.*

28. Athena D. Mutua, "Restoring Justice to Civil Rights Movement Activists?: New Historiography and the 'Long Civil Rights Era,' " unpublished paper, University at Buffalo Law School, State University of New York, 2008, available through SSRN.

29. Glenda Gilmore, *Defying Dixie: The Radical Roots of Civil Rights, 1919–1950* (New York: W. W. Norton, 2008).

30. Arnesen, "Reconsidering the 'Long Civil Rights Movement,' " 33–34 (praising the important scholarly work of Beth Tompkins Bates and others).

31. Thomas F. Jackson, *From Civil Rights to Human Rights: Martin Luther King, Jr., and the Struggle for Economic Justice* (Philadelphia: University of Pennsylvania Press, 2007) (exploring Martin Luther King Jr.'s efforts to reclaim and further develop ideas connecting racial and economic justice).

32. Nikhil Pal Singh, *Black Is a Country: Race and the Unfinished Struggle for Democracy* (Cambridge, MA: Harvard University Press, 2004), 6.

33. Ibid., 48, 54.

34. See Susan D. Carle, "How Myth-Busting about the Historical Goals of Civil Rights Activism Can Illuminate Paths for the Future," *Stanford Journal of Civil Rights and Civil Liberties* 7 (2011): 167–95. Cf. Larry Isaac, "Movement of Movements: Culture Moves in the Long Civil Rights Struggle," *Social Forces* 87 (2008): 33, 56 (arguing for the importance of analyzing the "forgetting" that has taken place in producing the "dominant consensus story" of the civil rights movement).

Acknowledgements

1. See Carle, Susan D. "Debunking the Myth of Civil Rights Liberalism: Visions of Racial Justice in the Thought of T. Thomas Fortune, 1880–1890" *Fordham Law Review* 77 (2009): 1479–1533.

BIBLIOGRAPHY

Manuscript Collections

FISK UNIVERSITY SPECIAL COLLECTIONS LIBRARY
Haynes, George Edmund. Papers (GHP).

HARVARD UNIVERSITY, HOUGHTON SPECIAL COLLECTIONS
Villard, Oswald Garrison. Papers (OGVP).

HAVERFORD COLLEGE LIBRARY, QUAKER AND SPECIAL COLLECTIONS
Wood, L. Hollingsworth. Papers (LHWP).

LIBRARY OF CONGRESS, WASHINGTON, DC
National Association for the Advancement of Colored People. Papers (NAACPP).
National Association of Colored Women. Papers (NACWP).
National Urban League. Papers (NULP).
Spingarn, Arthur. Papers (ASP).
Terrell, Mary Church. Papers (MCTPLOC).
Washington, Booker T. Papers (BTWP).

MOORLAND-SPINGARN RESEARCH CENTER, HOWARD UNIVERSITY, WASHINGTON, DC
Bethel Literary Society. Papers (BLSP).
Grimké, Archibald. Papers (AGP).
Murray, Freeman Henry Morris. Papers (FHMMP).
Spingarn, Joel E. Papers (JSP).
Terrell, Mary Church. Papers (MCTPMS).

SCHOMBURG CENTER FOR RESEARCH IN BLACK CULTURE, NEW YORK PUBLIC LIBRARY, NEW YORK CITY
Fortune, T. Thomas. Papers.
Matthews, Victoria Earle. Papers (VMP).
White Rose Mission, NYC. Papers (WRMP).

TICONDEROGA HISTORICAL SOCIETY, TICONDEROGA, NY

Milholland, John. Papers (JMP).

W.E.B. DU BOIS RESEARCH LIBRARY, UNIVERSITY OF MASSACHUSETTS AT AMHERST

Du Bois, W.E.B. Papers (WEBDBP).
Niagara Movement Archives. Also available online (NMA).

WALTER P. REUTHER LIBRARY, WAYNE STATE UNIVERSITY

Ovington, Mary White. Papers (MWOP).

WILBERFORCE UNIVERSITY ARCHIVES

Ransom, Reverdy C. Papers.

Historical Newspapers and Magazines

Alexander's Magazine
Alexandria Gazette
Atlanta Constitution (AC)
Broad Ax
Chicago Conservator
Chicago Inter Ocean
Chicago Tribune (CT)
Christian Observer
Christian Recorder
Cleveland Gazette (CG)
Colored American (CA)
Crisis
Dallas Morning News
Denver Statesman
Evening World (New York)
Florida Times-Union
Fort Worth Star Telegram
Friends' Intelligencer and Journal
Grand Forks Herald
Horizon
Idaho Daily Statesman
Idaho Statesman
Illinois Record
Independent
Indianapolis Appeal
Indianapolis Freeman (IF)
National Association (of Colored Women) Notes (NACWN)
New York Age (NYA)
New York Daily Tribune
New York Freeman (NYF)
New York Globe (NYG)
New York Times (NYT)
Norfolk Journal and Guide
Olympia Record
Philadelphia Inquirer

Plaindealer (Detroit) (DP)
Plaindealer (Topeka)
Portland New Age
Richmond Planet
Richmond Times
Salt Lake Telegram
Savannah Tribune
Southern Christian Recorder
Springfield Daily Republican
St. Paul Appeal
St. Paul Globe
State Capital
Times-Picayune
Washington Bee (WB)
Washington Herald
Washington Post (WP)
Washington Times
Wichita Searchlight
Wisconsin Weekly Advocate
Woman's Era (WE)
Voice of the Negro (VN)

Cases, Government Documents, and other Legal Materials

42 U.S.C. § 1983.
Acts and Resolutions of the General Assembly of the State of Georgia, 1890–1891 (Atlanta, 1891).
Ayotte v. Planned Parenthood of Northern New England, 546 U.S. 320 (2006).
Bailey v. Alabama, 219 U.S. 219 (1911).
Brickhouse v. Brooks, 165 F. 534 (C.C.E.D. Va. 1908).
Buchanan v. Warley, 245 U.S. 60 (1917).
Carter v. Texas, 177 U.S. 442 (1900).
Civil Rights Cases, The, 109 U.S. 3 (1883).
Constitution of the State of Alabama, as adopted by the Constitutional Convention, Sept. 3, 1901 (Montgomery, AL: Brown Printing, 1901).
Constitution of the State of Louisiana, as adopted in Convention at the City of New Orleans, May 12, 1898 (New Orleans: H. J. Hearsey, Convention Printer, 1898).
Council v. Western & A.R.R., 1 ICC 339 (1887).
Crooms v. Schad, 51 Fla. 168, 40 So. 497 (1906).
Cumming v. Board of Education of Richmond County, 175 U.S. 528 (1899).
Ferguson v. Gies, 82 Mich. 358, 9 L.R.A. 589 (1890).
Gibbs v. Arras Bros., 170 A.D. 897, 154 N.Y.S. 1123 (N.Y. App. Div. 1915).
Gibbs v. Arras Bros., 118 N.E. 857, 222 N.Y. 332 (1918).
Giles v. Harris, 189 U.S. 475 (1903).
Giles v. Teasley, 193 U.S. 146 (1904).
Guinn v. United States, 238 U.S. 347 (1915).
Hall v. De Cuir, 95 U.S. 485 (1877).
Hardy v. East Tennessee, Virginia & Georgia Railway Co., C.C.S.D. Tenn. (1891).
Hart v. State, 100 Md. 595, 60 A. 457 (Md. Ct. App. 1905).
Heard v. Georgia R.R., 1 ICC 428 (1888).
Heard v. Georgia R.R., 3 ICC 111 (1889).
Hughes Tool Co., 147 N.L.R.B. 1573 (1964).
Jones v. Montague, 194 U.S. 147 (1904).

Jones v. United States, 137 U.S. 202 (1890).

Lane v. Wilson, 307 U.S. 268 (1939).

Lochner v. New York, 198 U.S. 45 (1905).

Louisiana *ex rel.* Ryanes v. Gleason, No. 65432, Division "E," Judgment, Honorable W. B. Somerville, Aug. 23, 1901 (unpublished, on file with author).

Louisiana *ex rel.* Ryanes v. Gleason, No. 67606, Division "C," Opinion of Honorable John St. Paul, July 28, 1902 (unpublished, on file with author).

Louisville, New Orleans & Texas Railway Co. v. Mississippi, 133 U.S. 587 (1890).

McCabe v. Atkinson, Topeka and Sante Fe Railway Co., 235 U.S. 151 (1914).

McGuinn v. Forbes, 37 F. 639 (D. Md. 1889).

NLRB v. Jones & Laughlin Steel Co., 301 U.S. 1 (1937).

Pace v. Alabama, 106 U.S. 583 (1883).

Patterson v. Taylor, 51 Fla. 275, 40 So. 493 (1906).

Plessy v. Ferguson, 163 U.S. 537 (1896).

Selden v. Montague, 194 U.S. 153 (1904).

Slaughter-House Cases, 83 U.S. 36 (1872).

State v. Gurry, 121 Md. 534, 88 A. 546 (1913).

State v. Patterson, 50 Fla. 127, 39 So. 398 (1905).

Sue, The, 22 F. 843 (D. Md. 1885).

Testimony of Emanuel Fortune Taken by the Joint Selection Comm. to Inquire into the Condition of Affairs in the Late Insurrectionary States: Miscellaneous and Florida, United States Congress (Washington, DC: Government Printing Office, 1872).

United States v. Cruikshank, 92 U.S. 542 (1875).

United States v. Harris, 106 U.S. 629 (1882).

United States v. Reese, 92 U.S. 214 (1875).

U.S. Congress. 33 *Cong. Rec.* 1012–22 (1900).

———. 33 *Cong. Rec.* 2111–74 (1900).

———. 34 *Cong. Rec.* 672–751 (1901).

———. 35 *Cong. Rec.* 5785–840 (1902).

———. House. Committee on Interstate and Foreign Commerce. *Hearings on the Bills to Amend the Interstate Commerce Law (H.R. 146, 273, 2040, 5775, 8337, and 10930).* 57th Cong., 1st sess., 1902. Government Printing Office.

———. House. Commission to Inquire into the Condition of the Colored People. *House Report no. 2194.* 57th Cong., 1st sess., 1902.

West Coast Hotel v. Parrish, 300 U.S. 379 (1937).

Williams v. Mississippi, 170 U.S. 213 (1898).

Books and Published Monographs

Adams, Cyrus Field. *The National Afro-American Council.* Washington, DC: C. F. Adams, 1902.

Alexander, Ann Field. *Race Man: The Rise and Fall of the "Fighting Editor," John Mitchell Jr.* Charlottesville: University of Virginia Press, 2002.

Alexander, Michelle. *The New Jim Crow.* New York: New Press, 2010.

Alexander, Shawn Leigh. *An Army of Lions: The Civil Rights Struggle before the NAACP.* Philadelphia: University of Pennsylvania Press, 2012.

Alexander, Rev. W. M. *The Brotherhood of Liberty: Or Our Day in Court, Including the Navassa Case.* Baltimore: Printing Office of J. F. Weishamrel, 1891.

American Bar Association. *Model Rules of Professional Conduct.* American Bar Association, 2012.

Anderson, Carol. *Eyes off the Prize: The United Nations and the African American Struggle for Human Rights, 1944–1955.* New York: Cambridge University Press, 2003.

Aptheker, Herbert, ed. *The Correspondence of W.E.B. Du Bois.* Vol. 1, *Selections, 1877–1934.* Amherst: University of Massachusetts Press, 1973.

Barrows, John Henry, ed. *The World's Parliament of Religions: An Illustrated and Popular Story of the World's First Parliament of Religions held in Chicago in connection with the Columbian Exposition of 1893.* 2 vols. Chicago: Parliament, 1893.

Bernstein, David E. *Only One Place of Redress: African Americans, Labor Regulations, and the Courts from Reconstruction to the New Deal.* Durham: Duke University Press, 2001.

Berry, Mary Frances. *My Face Is Black Is True: Callie House and the Struggle for Ex-Slave Reparations.* New York: Alfred A. Knopf, 2005.

Billingsley, Andrew, and Jeanne M. Giovannoni. *Children of the Storm: Black Children and American Child Welfare.* New York: Harcourt Brace Jovanovich, 1972.

Boylan, James. *Revolutionary Lives: Anna Strunsky and William English Walling.* Amherst: University of Massachusetts Press, 1998.

Broussard, Albert S. *African-American Odyssey: The Stewarts, 1853–1963.* Lawrence: University Press of Kansas, 1998.

Brown-Nagin, Tomiko. *Courage to Dissent: Atlanta and the Long History of the Civil Rights Movement.* New York: Oxford University Press, 2011.

Bruce, Dickson D. *Archibald Grimké: Portrait of a Black Independent.* Baton Rouge: Louisiana State University Press, 1993.

Buckler, Helen. *Daniel Hale Williams: Negro Surgeon.* New York: Pitman, 1968.

Buhler-Wilderson, Karen. *No Place like Home: A History of Nursing and Home Care in the United States.* Baltimore: Johns Hopkins University Press, 2001.

Cash, Floris Barnett. *African American Women and Social Action: The Clubwomen and Volunteerism from Jim Crow to the New Deal, 1896–1936.* Westport, CT: Greenwood Press, 2001.

Cheek, William, and Aimee Lee Cheek. *John Mercer Langston and the Fight for Black Freedom, 1829–65.* Urbana: University of Illinois Press, 1989.

Collier-Thomas, Bettye. *Jesus, Jobs, and Justice: African American Women and Religion.* New York: Alfred A. Knopf, 2010.

Cromwell, Adelaide M. *Unveiled Voices, Unvarnished Memories: The Cromwell Family in Slavery and Segregation, 1692–1972.* Columbia: University of Missouri Press, 2007.

Davis, Allen F. *American Heroine: The Life and Legend of Jane Addams.* New York: Oxford University Press, 1973.

Davis, Elizabeth Lindsay. *Lifting as They Climb.* New York: G. K. Hall, 1996.

Davis, Gerald F., Doug McAdam, W. Richard Scott, and Mayer N. Zald, eds. *Social Movements and Organization Theory.* New York: Cambridge University Press, 2005.

Dawson, Michael C. *Black Visions: The Roots of Contemporary African American Political Ideologies.* Chicago: University of Chicago Press, 2001.

Dittmer, John. *Black Georgia in the Progressive Era: 1900–1920.* Urbana: University of Illinois Press, 1977.

Dorsey, Allison. *To Build Our Lives Together: Community Foundations in Black Atlanta, 1875–1906.* Athens: University of Georgia Press, 2004.

Dossett, Kate. *Bridging Race Divides: Black Nationalism, Feminism, and Integration in the United States, 1896–1935.* Gainesville: University Press of Florida, 2008.

Du Bois, W.E.B., ed. *The Negro in Business.* Atlanta: Atlanta Bulletin, 1899. http://www.library.umass.edu/spcoll/digital/dubois/dubois4.pdf.

———. *The Black North in 1901: A Case Study.* 1901. Reprint, New York: Arno Press, 1969.

———. *The Souls of Black Folk.* 1903. Reprint, New York: Modern Library, 1996.

———, ed. *A Select Bibliography of the Negro American.* Atlanta: Atlanta University Press, 1905. http://www.library.umass.edu/spcoll/digital/dubois/dubois10.pdf.

———. *Efforts for Social Betterment among Negro Americans.* Atlanta University Publication no. 14. Atlanta: Atlanta University Press, 1909.

———. *The Autobiography of W.E.B. Du Bois.* New York: International Publishers, 1968.

———. *W.E.B. Du Bois Speaks: Speeches and Addresses, 1890–1910.* New York: Pathfinder, 1970.

Duster, Alfreda, ed. *Crusade for Justice: The Autobiography of Ida B. Wells*, by Ida B. Wells Barnett, xiii–xxxii. Chicago: University of Chicago Press, 1970.

Elliott, Mark. *Color-Blind Justice: Albion Tourgée and the Quest for Racial Equality from the Civil War to Plessy v. Ferguson.* New York: Oxford University Press, 2006.

Factor, Robert L. *The Black Response to America: Men, Ideals, and Organization from Frederick Douglass to the NAACP.* Reading, MA: Addison-Wesley, 1970.

Fallon, Richard H., Jr., Daniel J. Meltzer, David L. Shapiro, Henry M Hart Jr., Herbert Wechsler, and John F. Manning. *Hart and Wechsler's The Federal Courts and the Federal System,* 6th ed. New York: Foundation Press, 2009.

Ferris, William H. *The African Abroad, or, His Evolution in Western Civilization: Tracing His Development under Caucasian Milieu.* 2 vols. New York: Johnson Reprint Corp., 1968. First published 1913 by Tuttle, Morehouse and Taylor.

Fireside, Harvey. *Separate and Unequal: Homer Plessy and the Supreme Court Decision That Legalized Racism.* New York: Carroll and Graf, 2004.

Foner, Eric. *Reconstruction: America's Unfinished Revolution, 1863–1867.* New York: Harper and Row, 1988.

Foner, Philip S. *Organized Labor and the Black Worker, 1619–1973.* New York: Praeger, 1974.

Forbath, William E. *Law and the Shaping of the American Labor Movement.* Cambridge, MA: Harvard University Press, 1991.

Fortier, Alcée, ed. *Louisiana: Comprising Sketches of Parishes, Towns, Events, Institutions, and Persons.* Madison, WI: Century Historical Association, 1914.

Fortune, T. Thomas. *Black and White: Land, Labor, and Politics in the South.* New York: Washington Square Press, 2007. First published 1884 by Fords, Howard, and Hubert.

Fox, Stephen R. *The Guardian of Boston: William Monroe Trotter.* New York: Atheneum, 1970.

Frymer, Paul. *Black and Blue: African Americans, the Labor Movement, and the Decline of the Democratic Party.* Princeton: Princeton University Press, 2008.

Gaines, Kevin. *Uplifting the Race: Black Leadership, Politics, and Culture in the Twentieth Century.* Chapel Hill: University of North Carolina Press, 1996.

Gatewood, Willard B. *Aristocrats of Color: The Black Elite: 1880–1920.* Fayetteville: University of Arkansas Press, 2000.

Gerber, David A. *Black Ohio and the Color Line, 1860–1915.* Urbana: University of Illinois Press, 1976.

Gibson, J. W., and W. H. Crogman. *Progress of a Race: or, The Remarkable Advancement of the American Negro, from the Bondage of Slavery, Ignorance, and Poverty to the Freedom of Citizenship, Intelligence, Affluence, Honor and Trust.* Miami: Mnemosyne, 1969. First published 1902 by J. L. Nichols. Page references are to the 1969 edition.

Giddings, Paula J. *When and Where I Enter: The Impact of Black Women on Race and Sex in America.* New York: Bantam Books, 1984.

———. *Ida: A Sword among Lions.* New York: Amistad, 2008.

Gillman, Susan, and Alys Eve Weinbaum, eds. *Next to the Color Line: Gender, Sexuality, and W.E.B. Du Bois.* Minneapolis: University of Minnesota Press, 2007.

Gilmore, Glenda E. *Gender and Jim Crow: Women and the Politics of White Supremacy in North Carolina, 1896–1920.* Chapel Hill: University of North Carolina Press, 1996.

———. *Defying Dixie: The Radical Roots of Civil Rights, 1919–1950.* New York: W. W. Norton, 2008.

Godshalk, David Fort. *Veiled Visions: The 1906 Atlanta Race Riot and the Reshaping of American Race Relations.* Chapel Hill: University of North Carolina Press, 2005.

Goings, Kenneth W. *The NAACP Comes of Age: The Defeat of Judge John J. Parker.* Bloomington: Indiana University Press, 1990.

Goluboff, Risa. *The Lost Promise of Civil Rights.* Cambridge, MA: Harvard University Press, 2007.

Gomez-Jefferson, Annetta L. *The Sage of Tawawa: Reverdy Cassius Ransom, 1861–1959.* Kent, OH: Kent State University Press, 2003.

Gordon, Linda, ed. *Women, the State, and Welfare.* Madison: University of Wisconsin Press, 1990.

Gould, William B., IV. *Diary of a Contraband: The Civil War Passage of a Black Soldier.* Stanford, CA: Stanford University Press, 2002.

Green, Constance McLaughlin. *The Secret City: A History of Race Relations in the Nation's Capital.* Princeton: Princeton University Press, 1967.

Green, James. *Death in the Haymarket: A Story of Chicago, the First Labor Movement and the Bombing That Divided Gilded Age America.* New York: Pantheon Books, 2006.

Hackley-Lambert, Anita. *F. H. M. Murray: First Biography of a Forgotten Pioneer for Civil Justice.* Fort Washington, MD: Hackley-Lambert Enterprise, 2006.

Harlan, Louis R. *Booker T. Washington: The Making of a Black Leader, 1856–1901.* New York: Oxford University Press, 1972.

———. *Booker T. Washington: The Wizard of Tuskegee, 1901–1905.* New York: Oxford University Press, 1983.

———, et al. *The Booker T. Washington Papers: 1889–1900.* 14 vols. 1972. Repr., Urbana: University of Illinois Press, 2000.

Hayden, Robert C. *Boston's NAACP History, 1910–1982.* Boston: Boston Branch NAACP, 1982.

Haynes, George Edmund. *The Negro at Work in New York City: A Study in Economic Progress.* New York: Arno Press, 1968. First published 1912 by Longmans, Green.

Hendricks, Wanda A. *Gender, Race, and Politics in the Midwest: Black Club Women in Illinois.* Bloomington: Indiana University Press, 1998.

Herbst, Alma. *The Negro in the Slaughtering and Meat-Packing Industry in Chicago.* New York: Arno Press, 1971. First published 1932 by Houghton Mifflin.

Higginbotham, Evelyn Brooks. *Righteous Discontent: The Women's Movement in the Black Baptist Church, 1880–1920.* Cambridge, MA: Harvard University Press, 1993.

Hine, Darlene Clark, ed. *Black Women in America: An Historical Encyclopedia.* Brooklyn, NY: Carlson, 1993.

Jackson, Thomas F. *From Civil Rights to Human Rights: Martin Luther King, Jr., and the Struggle for Economic Justice.* Philadelphia: University of Pennsylvania Press, 2007.

Janken, Kenneth Robert. *White: The Biography of Walter White, Mr. NAACP.* New York: New Press, 2003.

Johnson, James Weldon. *Along This Way: The Autobiography of James Weldon Johnson.* New York: Viking Press, 1933.

Johnson, Kimberley. *Reforming Jim Crow: Southern Politics and State in the Age before Brown.* New York: Oxford, 2010.

Jones, Angela. *African American Civil Rights: Early Activism and the Niagara Movement.* Santa Barbara, CA: Praeger, 2011.

Jones, Jacqueline. *Labor of Love, Labor of Sorrow: Black Women, Work, and the Family from Slavery to the Present.* New York: Basic Books, 1985.

———. *See also* Royster, Jacqueline Jones.

Jones, Leonard A., and Conrad Reno, eds. *Memoirs of the Judiciary and the Bar of New England for the Nineteenth Century,* vol. 2. Boston: Century Memorial, 1901.

Justesen, Benjamin R. *George Henry White: An Even Chance in the Race of Life.* Baton Rouge: Louisiana State University, 2001.

———. *Broken Brotherhood: The Rise and Fall of the National Afro-American Council.* Carbondale: Southern Illinois Press, 2008.

Katz, William Loren, ed. *Proceedings of the National Negro Conference, 1909.* 1909. Reprint, New York: Arno, 1969.

Kelley, Blair L. M. *Right to Ride: Streetcar Boycotts and African American Citizenship in the Era of Plessy v. Ferguson.* Chapel Hill: University of North Carolina Press, 2010.

Kellogg, Charles Flint. *NAACP.* Baltimore: Johns Hopkins Press, 1967.

Kellor, Frances. *Experimental Sociology, Descriptive and Analytical: Delinquents.* New York: Macmillan, 1901.

———. *Out of Work: A Study of Employment Agencies, Their Treatment of the Unemployed, and Their Influence upon Homes and Business.* New York: Putnam, 1904.

Kessler-Harris, Alice. *In Pursuit of Equity: Women, Men, and the Quest for Economic Citizenship in 20th-Century America.* New York: Oxford University Press, 2001.

Klarman, Michael J. *From Jim Crow to Civil Rights: The Supreme Court and the Struggle for Racial Equality.* New York: Oxford University Press, 2004.

Knupfer, Anne Meis. *Toward a Tenderer Humanity and a Nobler Womanhood: African American Women's Clubs in Turn-of-the-Century Chicago.* New York: New York University Press, 1996.

Langston, John Mercer. *Freedom and Citizenship: Selected Lectures and Addresses.* Washington, DC: Rufus H. Darby, 1883.

———. *From the Virginia Plantation to the National Capitol; or, the First and Only Negro Representative in Congress from the Old Dominion.* Hartford: American Publishing, 1894.

Lasch-Quinn, Elisabeth. *Black Neighbors: Race and the Limits of Reform in the American Settlement House Movement, 1890–1945.* Chapel Hill: University of North Carolina Press, 1993.

Lewis, David Levering. *W.E.B. Du Bois: Biography of a Race, 1868–1919.* New York: Henry Holt, 1993.

Logan, Rayford W. *The Negro in American Life and Thought: The Nadir, 1877–1901.* New York: Dial Press, 1954.

———. *The Betrayal of the Negro from Rutherford B. Hayes to Woodrow Wilson.* New York: Collier Books, 1965.

———. *Howard University: The First Hundred Years, 1867–1967.* New York: New York University Press, 1968.

———, and Michael R. Winston, eds. *Dictionary of American Negro Biography.* New York: W. W. Norton, 1982.

Luker, Ralph E. *The Social Gospel in Black and White: American Racial Reform, 1885–1912.* Chapel Hill: University of North Carolina Press, 1991.

Lumsden, Linda J. *Inez: The Life and Times of Inez Milholland.* Bloomington: Indiana University Press, 2004.

Mack, Kenneth. *Representing the Race: The Creation of the Civil Rights Lawyer.* Cambridge, MA: Harvard University Press, 2012.

MacLean, Nancy. *Freedom Is Not Enough: The Opening of the American Workplace.* Cambridge, MA: Harvard University Press, 2006.

Marable, Manning. *W.E.B. Du Bois: Black Radical Democrat.* Boston: Twayne, 1986.

Mather, Frank Lincoln, ed. *Who's Who of the Colored Race,* vol. 1. 1915. Reprint, Detroit: Gale Research, 1976.

Mayeri, Serena. *Reasoning from Race: Feminism, Law, and the Civil Rights Revolution.* Cambridge, MA: Harvard University Press, 2011.

McAdam, Doug. *Political Process and the Development of Black Insurgency, 1930–1970,* 2nd ed. Chicago: University of Chicago Press, 1999.

———, Sidney Tarrow, and Charles Tilly. *Dynamics of Contention.* Cambridge, UK: Cambridge University Press, 2004.

McCann, Michael W. *Rights at Work: Pay Equity and the Politics of Legal Mobilization.* Chicago: University of Chicago Press, 1994.

McHenry, Elizabeth. *Forgotten Readers: Recovering the Lost History of African American Literary Societies.* Durham, NC: Duke University Press, 2002.

McMurry, Linda O. *To Keep the Waters Troubled: The Life of Ida B. Wells.* New York: Oxford University Press, 1998.

Meier, August. *Negro Thought in America, 1880–1915.* Ann Arbor: University of Michigan Press, 1963.

———, and Elliott Rudwick. *Along the Color Line.* Champaign: University of Illinois Press, 1976.

Mink, Gwendolyn. *The Wages of Motherhood: Inequality in the Welfare State, 1917–1942.* Ithaca, NY: Cornell University Press, 1995.

Miraldi, Robert. *The Pen Is Mightier: The Muckraking Life of Charles Edward Russell.* New York: Palgrave Macmillan, 2003.

Moore, Jesse Thomas, Jr. *A Search for Equality: The National Urban League, 1910–1961.* University Park: Pennsylvania State University Press, 1981.

Morris, Calvin S. *Reverdy C. Ransom: Black Advocate of the Social Gospel.* Lanham, MD: University Press of America, 1990.

Moses, Wilson Jeremiah. *The Golden Age of Black Nationalism, 1850–1925.* New York: Oxford University Press, 1978.

Motes, Margaret Peckham. *Free Blacks and Mulattos in South Carolina: 1850 Census.* Baltimore: Clearfield Press, 2000.

Muncy, Robyn. *Creating a Female Dominion in American Reform, 1890–1935.* New York: Oxford University Press, 1991.

National Sociological Society. *How to Solve the Race Problem: The Proceedings of the Washington Conference on the Race Problem in the United States.* Washington, DC: Beresford Printer, 1904.

Nelson, Paul D. *Fredrick L. McGhee: A Life on the Color Line, 1861–1912.* St. Paul: Minnesota Historical Society Press, 2002.

Neverdon-Morton, Cynthia. *Afro-American Women of the South and the Advancement of the Race, 1895–1925.* Knoxville: University of Tennessee Press, 1989.

Newton, Michael. *The Invisible Empire: The Ku Klux Klan in Florida.* Gainesville: University Press of Florida, 2001.

Norrell, Robert J. *Up from History: The Life of Booker T. Washington.* Cambridge, MA: Belknap Press, 2009.

Novkov, Julie. *Constituting Workers, Protecting Women: Gender, Law, and Labor in the Progressive Era and New Deal Years.* Ann Arbor: University of Michigan Press, 2001.

Oberschall, Anthony. *Social Conflict and Social Movement.* Englewood Cliffs, NJ: Prentice-Hall, 1973.

Ortiz, Paul. *Emancipation Betrayed: The Hidden History of Black Organizing and White Violence in Florida from Reconstruction to the Bloody Election of 1920.* Berkeley: University of California Press, 2005.

Ovington, Mary White. *The Walls Came Tumbling Down.* New York: Harcourt, Brace, 1947.

———. *Half a Man: The Status of the Negro in New York.* New York: Hill and Wang, 1969. First published 1911 by Longmans, Green. Page references are to the 1969 edition.

Parrish, Guichard, and Lester Brooks. *Blacks in the City: A History of the National Urban League.* Boston: Little, Brown, 1971.

Patler, Nicholas. *Jim Crow and the Wilson Administration: Protesting Federal Segregation in the Early Twentieth Century.* Boulder: University Press of Colorado, 2007.

Pennsylvania Negro Business Directory, 1910: Industrial and Material Growth of Negroes of Pennsylvania. Harrisburg, PA: James H. W. Howard and Son, 1910.

Perman, Michael. *Struggle for Mastery: Disfranchisement in the South, 1888–1908.* Chapel Hill: University of North Carolina Press, 2001.

Pinn, Anthony B., ed. *Making the Gospel Plain: The Writings of Bishop Reverdy C. Ransom.* Harrisburg: Trinity Press, 1999.

———. *The African American Religious Experience in America.* Westport, CT: Greenwood Press, 2006.

Press, John Kenneth. *Founding Mother: Frances Kellor and the Creation of Modern America.* New York: Social Books, 2012.

Przybyszewski, Linda. *The Republic according to John Marshall Harlan.* Chapel Hill: University of North Carolina Press, 1999.

Ransom, Reverdy C. *School Days at Wilberforce.* Springfield, OH: New Era, 1892.

———. *The Spirit of Freedom and Justice: Orations and Speeches.* Nashville: A.M.E. Sunday School Union, 1926.

———. *The Pilgrimage of Harriet Ransom's Son.* Nashville: Sunday School Union, 1949.

Reed, Adolph L., Jr. *W.E.B. Du Bois and American Political Thought: Fabianism and the Color Line.* New York: Oxford University Press, 1997.

Reed, Touré F. *Not Alms but Opportunity: The Urban League and the Politics of Racial Uplift, 1910–1950.* Chapel Hill: University of North Carolina Press, 2008.

Riser, R. Volney. *Defying Disfranchisement: Black Voting Rights Activism in the Jim Crow South, 1890–1908.* Baton Rouge: Louisiana State Press, 2010.

Rodgers, Daniel T. *Atlantic Crossings: Social Politics in a Progressive Age*. Cambridge, MA: Harvard University Press, 1998.

Rouse, Jacqueline Anne. *Lugenia Burns Hope: Black Southern Reformer*. Athens: University of Georgia Press, 1989.

Royster, Jacqueline Jones, ed. *Southern Horrors, and Other Writings: The Anti-Lynching Campaign of Ida B. Wells, 1892–1900*. Boston: Bedford/St. Martins, 1997.

———. *See also* Jones, Jacqueline.

Rudwick, Elliott. *W.E.B. Du Bois: Voice of the Black Protest Movement*. Chicago: University of Chicago Press, 1982.

Ruskin, John. *Unto This Last, and Other Writings*, edited by Clive Wilmer. London: Penguin Press, 1985, 1994. First printed 1862 in *Cornhill Magazine*.

Sacks, Marcy S. *Before Harlem: The Black Experience in New York City before World War I*. Philadelphia: University of Pennsylvania Press, 2006.

Salem, Dorothy C. *To Better Our World: Black Women in Organized Reform, 1890–1920*. Brooklyn, NY: Carlson, 1990.

Schlegel, John Henry. *American Legal Realism and Empirical Social Science*. Durham: University of North Carolina Press, 1995.

Schneider, Mark R. *Boston Confronts Jim Crow, 1890–1920*. Boston: Northeastern University Press, 1997.

Schultz, David. A., ed. *Leveraging the Law: Using the Courts to Achieve Social Change*. New York: Peter Lang, 1998.

Senechal, Roberta. *The Sociogenesis of a Race Riot: Springfield, Illinois, in 1908*. Urbana: University of Illinois Press, 1990.

Singh, Nikhil Pal. *Black Is a Country: Race and the Unfinished Struggle for Democracy*. Cambridge, MA: Harvard University Press, 2004.

Sklar, Kathryn Kish. *Florence Kelley and the Nation's Work: The Rise of Women's Political Culture, 1830–1900*. New Haven: Yale University Press, 1995.

Skocpol, Theda. *Protecting Soldiers and Mothers: The Political Origins of Social Policy in the United States*. Cambridge, MA: Harvard University Press, 1992.

Smith, J. Clay, Jr. *Emancipation: The Making of the Black Lawyer*. Philadelphia: University of Pennsylvania Press, 1993.

———, ed. *Rebels in Law: Voice in History of Black Women Lawyers*. Ann Arbor: University of Michigan Press, 1998.

Smith, Jessie Carney, ed. *Notable Black American Women*, vol. 2. Detroit: Gale Research, 2003.

Smith, Robert, ed. *Encyclopedia of African American Politics*. New York: Facts On File, 2003.

Snow, David A., and Sarah A. Soule. *A Primer on Social Movements*. New York: W. W. Norton, 2010.

Steiner, Henry J., Philip Alston, and Ryan Goodman. *International Human Rights in Context: Law, Politics, Morals,* 3rd ed. New York: Oxford University Press, 2008.

Stone, Irving. *Clarence Darrow for the Defense*. New York: Signet, 1973. First published 1941 by Doubleday, Doran.

Straker, David Augustus. *Negro Suffrage in the South*. Detroit: Published by author, 1906.

———. *The New South Investigated*. New York: Arno Press, 1973. First published 1888 by Ferguson Printing.

Sullivan, Patricia. *Lift Every Voice: The NAACP and the Making of the Civil Rights Movement*. New York: New Press, 2009.

Terborg-Penn, Rosalyn. *African American Women in the Struggle for the Vote, 1850–1920*. Bloomington: Indiana University Press, 1998.

Terrell, Mary Church. *A Colored Woman in a White World*. New York: G. K. Hall, 1996.

Terrell, Robert H. *A Glance at the Past and Present of the Negro*. Washington, DC: Press of R. L. Pendleton, 1903. Originally delivered at Church's Auditorium before the Citizen's Industrial League of Memphis, Tenn., September 22, 1903.

Thornbrough, Emma Lou. *T. Thomas Fortune: Militant Journalist*. Chicago: University of Chicago Press, 1972.

Tomlins, Christopher L. *The State and the Unions: Labor Relations, Law, and the Organized Labor Movement in America, 1880–1960*. New York: Cambridge University Press, 1985.

Torrence, Ridgely. *The Story of John Hope*. New York: Macmillan, 1948.

Tushnet, Mark. *The NAACP's Legal Strategy against Segregated Education, 1925–1950*. Chapel Hill: University of North Carolina Press, 1987.

———. *Making Civil Rights Law: Thurgood Marshall and the Supreme Court, 1956-61*. New York: Oxford University Press, 1994.

Valley, Richard M. *The Two Reconstructions: The Struggle for Black Enfranchisement*. Chicago: University of Chicago Press, 2004.

Walters, Alexander. *My Life and Work*. New York: Fleming H. Revell, 1917. http://docsouth.unc.edu/neh/walters/walters.html.

Wedin, Carolyn. *Inheritors of the Spirit: Mary White Ovington and the Founding of the NAACP*. New York: John Wiley and Sons, 1998.

Weiss, Nancy J. *The National Urban League*. New York: Oxford University Press, 1974.

Wells Barnett, Ida B. *Crusade for Justice: The Autobiography of Ida B. Wells*, edited by Alfreda M. Duster. Chicago: University of Chicago Press, 1970.

———. *The Memphis Diary of Ida B. Wells*, edited by Miriam Decosta-Williams. Boston: Beacon Press, 1995.

Wherry, William M., Jr. *Public Utilities and the Law*. New York: N. L. Brown, 1928.

White, Deborah Gray. *Too Heavy a Load: Black Women in Defense of Themselves, 1894–1994*. New York: W. W. Norton, 1999.

Williamson, Joel. *The Crucible of Race: Black-White Relations in the American South since Emancipation*. New York: Oxford University Press, 1984.

Wolcott, Victoria W. *Remaking Respectability: African American Women in Interwar Detroit*. Chapel Hill: University of North Carolina Press, 2001.

Woods, Jeanne, and Hope Lewis. *Human Rights and the Global Marketplace: Economic, Social and Cultural Dimensions*. Ardsley, NY: Transnational Publishers, 2004.

Woodward, C. Vann. *The Strange Career of Jim Crow*. New York: Oxford University Press, 1955.

———. *Tom Watson: Agrarian Rebel*. Savannah: Beehive Press, 1973 reissue, 1938.

Zangrando, Robert L. *The NAACP Crusade against Lynching, 1909–1950*. Philadelphia: Temple University Press, 1980.

Articles and Short Publications

Abramowitz, Jack. "The Negro in the Populist Movement." *Journal of Negro History* 38 (1953): 257–89.

Addams, Jane. "The Subjective Value of Social Settlements." N.d., circa 1892. Reprint New Haven, CT: Research Publications, 1977.

Armstrong, Elizabeth A., and Mary Bernstein. "Culture, Power, and Institutions: A Multi-Institutional Politics Approach to Social Movements." *Sociological Theory* 26 (2008): 74–99.

Arnesen, Eric. "Specter of the Black Strikebreaker: Race, Employment, and Labor Activism in the Industrial Era," *Labor History* 44 (2003): 319–35.

———. "Reconsidering the 'Long Civil Rights Movement.'" *Historically Speaking* 10, no. 2 (April 2009): 31–34.

Bacote, Clarence A. "Negro Proscriptions, Protests, and Proposed Solutions in Georgia, 1880–1908." *Journal of Southern History* 25 (1959): 471–98.

Balkin, Jack M., ed. "Brown as Icon." In *What Brown v. Board of Education Should Have Said: The Nation's Top Legal Experts Rewrite America's Landmark Civil Rights Decision*, 3–28. New York: New York University Press, 2001.

Barber, J. Max. "The Niagara Movement at Harper's Ferry." *Voice of the Negro* 3 (1906): 402–11.

Bigglestone, W. E. "Oberlin College and the Negro Student, 1865–1940." *Journal of Negro History* 56 (1971): 198–219.

Bloomfield, Max. "From Deference to Confrontation: The Early Black Lawyers of Galveston, Texas, 1895–1920." In *The New High Priests: Lawyers in Post–Civil War America*, edited by Gerard W. Gawalt, 151–70. Westport, CT: Greenwood Press, 1984.

Blumenthal, Henry. "Woodrow Wilson and the Race Question." *Journal of Negro History* 48, no. 1 (1963): 1–21.

Bogen, David S. "Precursors of Rosa Parks: Maryland Transportation Cases between the Civil War and the Beginning of World War I." *Maryland Law Review* 63 (2004): 721–51.

Boris, Eileen. "The Power of Motherhood: Black and White Activist Women Redefine the Political." *Yale Journal of Law and Feminism* 2 (1989–90): 25–49.

Brown-Nagin, Tomiko. "Race as Identity Caricature: A Local Legal History Lesson in the Salience of Intra-Racial Conflict." *University of Pennsylvania Law Review* 151 (2003): 1913–76.

Bulkley, William Lewis. "The School as a Social Center." *Charities* 15 (October 7, 1905): 76–78.

————. "The Industrial Condition of the Negro in New York City." *Annals of the American Academy of Political and Social Science* 27 (1906): 128–34.

Bynum, Cornelius L. "An Equal Chance in the Race for Life: Reverdy C. Ransom, Socialism, and the Social Gospel Movement, 1890–1920." *Journal of African American History* 93 (2008): 1–20.

Campbell, John L. "Where Do We Stand? Common Mechanisms in Organizations and Social Movements Research." In *Social Movements and Organization Theory*, edited by Gerald F. Davis, Doug McAdam, W. Richard Scott, and Mayer N. Zald, 41–68. New York: Cambridge University Press, 2005.

Capeci, Dominic J., Jr., and Jack C. Knight. "W.E.B. Du Bois's Southern Front: Georgia 'Race Men' and the Niagara Movement, 1905–1907." *Georgia Historical Quarterly* 83 (1999): 479–507.

Carle, Susan D. "Review Essay: Gender in the Construction of the Lawyer's Persona." 22 *Harvard Women's Law Journal* (1999): 239–73.

————. "Re-Envisioning Models for Pro Bono Lawyering: A Comparative Study of the Early NAACP and the National Consumers League." *American University Journal of Gender, Social Policy, & the Law* 9 (2001): 81–96.

————. "Re-Valuing Lawyering for Middle-Income Clients." *Fordham Law Review* 70 (2001–2002): 719–46.

————. "Race, Class, and Legal Ethics in the Early NAACP (1910–1920)." *Law and History Review* 20 (2002): 97–146.

————. "Theorizing Agency." *American University Law Review* 55 (2005): 307–93.

————. "Debunking the Myth of Civil Rights Liberalism: Visions of Racial Justice in the Thought of T. Thomas Fortune, 1880–1890." *Fordham Law Review* 77 (2009): 1479–1533.

————. How Myth-Busting about the Historical Goals of Civil Rights Activism Can Illuminate Paths for the Future." *Stanford Journal of Civil Rights and Civil Liberties* 7 (2011): 167–95.

————. "John Dewey and the Early NAACP: Developing a Progressive Discourse on Racial Injustice, 1909–1921." In *Dewey's Enduring Impact*, edited by John R. Shook and Paul Kurtz, 249–62. New York: Prometheus Books, 2011.

————. "A Social Movement History of Title VII Disparate Impact Analysis." *Florida Law Review* 63 (2011): 251–300.

Chafe, William H. "The Negro and Populism: A Kansas Case Study." *Journal of Southern History* 34 (1968): 402–406.

Crofts, Daniel W. "The Black Response to the Blair Education Bill." *Journal of Southern History* 37 (1971): 41–65.

————. "The Warner-Foraker Amendment to the Hepburn Bill: Friend or Foe of Jim Crow?" *Journal of Southern History* 39 (1973): 341–58.

Crowe, Charles. "Tom Watson, Populists, and Blacks Reconsidered." *Journal of Negro History* 55 (1970): 99–116.

Dale, Elizabeth. " 'Social Equality Does Not Exist among Themselves, nor among Us': *Baylies vs. Curry* and Civil Rights in Chicago, 1888." *American Historical Review* 102 (1997): 311–39.

Dorf, Michael C., and Charles F. Sabel. "A Constitution of Democratic Experimentalism." *Columbia Law Review* 98 (1998): 267–473.

Du Bois, W.E.B. "The Conservation of Races." *Occasional Papers*, no. 2 (1897): 5–15. Published by American Negro Academy.

———. "The Talented Tenth." In *The Negro Problem: A Series of Articles by Representative American Negroes of Today*, edited by Booker T. Washington and W. E. Burghardt Du Bois, 30–75. New York: James Pott, 1903. Facsimile of the first edition, LaVergne, TN: Kessinger, 2009.

———. "The Niagara Movement." *Voice of the Negro* 2 (September 1905): 619–22.

———. "The Growth of the Niagara Movement." *Voice of the Negro* 3 (1906): 43–45.

———. "The Cultural Missions of Atlanta University." *Phylon* 3, no. 2 (Second Quarter 1942): 105–15.

———. "The Lash." In *Writings in Periodicals Edited by W.E.B. Du Bois: Selections from the Horizon*, compiled and edited by Herbert Aptheker, 16. White Plains, NY: Kraus-Thomson Organization, 1985. First published May 1907 in *The Horizon: A Journal of the Color Line*.

———. "Of Mr. Booker T. Washington and Others." In *The Souls of Black Folk*, 43–61. New York: Modern Library, 1996.

Edelman, Lauren B., Gwendolyn Leachman, and Doug McAdam. "On Law, Organizations, and Social Movements." *Annual Review of Law and Social Science* 6 (2010): 653–85.

Epperson, Lia B. "Equality Dissonance: Jurisprudential Limitations and Legislative Opportunities." *Stanford Journal of Civil Rights and Civil Liberties* 7 (2011): 213–38.

———. "Legislating Inclusion." *Harvard Law and Policy Review* 6 (2012): 801–14.

Ferree, Mira Marx, and Carol McClurg Mueller. "Feminism and the Women's Movement: A Global Perspective." In *The Blackwell Companion to Social Movements*, edited by David Snow, Sarah Soule, and Hanspeter Kriesi, 576–607. Malden, MA: Blackwell, 2005.

Fishel, Leslie H., Jr. "The Genesis of the First Wisconsin Civil Rights Act." *Wisconsin Magazine of History* 49 (Summer 1966): 324–33.

Fortune, T. Thomas. "After War Times, Part 23." *Norfolk Journal and Guide*, Dec. 3, 1927, 16.

Freeman, Jo. "The Origins of the Women's Liberation Movement." *American Journal of Sociology* 78 (1973): 792–811.

Goddard, Terrell Dale. "The Black Social Gospel in Chicago, 1896–1906: The Ministries of Reverdy C. Ransom and Richard R. Wright, Jr." *Journal of Negro History* 84 (1999): 227–46.

Going, Allen J. "The South and the Blair Education Bill." *Mississippi Valley History Review* 44 (1957): 267–90.

Gordon, Linda. "Black and White Visions of Welfare: Women's Welfare Activism, 1890–1945." *Journal of American History* 78 (1991): 559–90.

Griffin, Maude K. "The Negro Church and Its Social Work—St. Mark's." *Charities* 15 (Oct. 7, 1905): 75–76.

Grimké, Archibald H. "Modern Industrialism and the Negroes of the United States." *Occasional Papers*, no. 12 (1908): 3–18. Published by American Negro Academy.

Hall, Jacquelyn Dowd. "The Long Civil Rights Movement and the Political Uses of the Past." *Journal of American History* 91 (2005): 1233–63.

Haller, Mark H. "Policy Gambling, Entertainment, and the Emergence of Black Politics: Chicago from 1900 to 1940." *Journal of Social History* 24 (1991): 719–39.

Harlan, Louis R. "The Secret Life of Booker T. Washington." *Journal of Southern History* 37 (1971): 393–416.

Hershaw, Lafayette M. "Peonage." *Occasional Papers*, no. 15. (1915): 1–13. Reprinted in *The American Negro Academy Occasional Papers 1–22* (New York: Arno Press, 1969).

———. "William H. H. Hart." *Journal of Negro History* 19 (1934): 211–13.

———. "The Status of the Free Negro prior to 1860." Papers of the American Negro Academy. Reprinted in *The American Negro Academy Occasional Papers 1–22* (New York: Arno Press, 1969), 39–47.

Hill, C. Matthew. " 'We Live Not on What We Have': Reflections on the Birth of the Civil Rights Test Case Strategy and Its Lessons for Today's Same-Sex Marriage Litigation Campaign." *National Black Law Journal* 19 (2005–2006): 175–202.

Horton, James Oliver. "Black Education at Oberlin College: A Controversial Commitment." *Journal of Negro Education* 54 (1985): 477–99.

Hutchinson, Darren. "Racial Exhaustion." *Washington University Law Review* 86 (2009): 917–974.

Isaac, Larry. "Movement of Movements: Culture Moves in the Long Civil Rights Struggle." *Social Forces* 87 (2008): 33–63.

Jenkins, Jeffery A., Justin Peck, and Vesla M. Weaver. "Between Reconstructions: Congressional Action on Civil Rights, 1891–1940." *Studies in American Political Development* 24 (2010): 57–89.

Jones, Beverly Washington. "Mary Church Terrell and the National Association of Colored Women, 1896–1901." *Journal of Negro History* 67 (1982): 20–33.

Kellogg, Charles Flint. "Introduction," in *Half a Man: The Status of the Negro in New York*, by Mary White Ovington, xi–xxiii. New York: Hill and Wang, 1969.

Killian, Lewis M. "Organization, Rationality and Spontaneity in the Civil Rights Movement." *American Sociological Review* 49 (1984): 770–83.

Kramer, Steve. "Uplifting Our 'Downtrodden Sisterhood': Victoria Earle Matthews and New York City's White Rose Mission, 1897–1907." *Journal of African American History* 91 (2006): 243–66.

Lado, Marianne L. Engelman. "A Question of Justice: African-American Legal Perspectives on the 1883 *Civil Rights Cases*." *Chicago-Kent Law Review* 70 (1995): 1123–95.

"Lafayette McKeene Hershaw." *Journal of Negro History* 30 (1945): 462–64.

Lee, Sophia Z. "Hotspots in a Cold War: The NAACP's Postwar Workplace Constitutionalism, 1948–1964." *Law and History Review* 26 (2008): 327–78.

Levin, Shira. " 'To Maintain Our Self-Respect': The Jacksonville Challenge to Segregated Street Cars and the Meaning of Equality, 1900–1906." *Michigan Journal of History* (Winter 2005), unpaginated. http://www.umich.edu/~historyj/issues.html.

Logan, Shirley W., ed. " 'To Embalm Her Memory in Song and Story': Victoria Earle Matthews and Situated Sisterhood." In *"We Are Coming": The Persuasive Discourse of Nineteenth-Century Black Women*, 127–51. Carbondale: Southern Illinois Press, 1999.

Mack, Kenneth W. "Law, Society, Identity, and the Making of the Jim Crow South: Travel and Segregation on Tennessee Railroads, 1875–1905." *Law and Social Inquiry* 24 (1999): 377–409.

———. "A Social History of Everyday Practice: Sadie T. M. Alexander and the Incorporation of Black Women into the American Legal Profession, 1925–1960." *Cornell Law Review* 87 (2002): 1405–74.

———. "Rethinking Civil Rights Lawyering and Politics in the Era before *Brown*." *Yale Law Journal* 115 (2005): 256–354.

———. "The Role of Law in the Making of Racial Identity: The Case of Harrisburg's W. Justin Carter." *Widener Law Journal* 18 (2008–2009): 1–22.

Mandel, Bernard. "Samuel Gompers and the Negro Workers, 1886–1914." *Journal of Negro History* 40 (1955): 34–60.

McAdam, Doug, and W. Richard Scott. "Organizations and Movements." In *Social Movements and Organization Theory*, edited by Gerald F. Davis, Doug McAdam, W. Richard Scott, and Mayer N. Zald, 4–40. New York: Cambridge University Press, 2005.

McCann, Michael W. "Reform Litigation on Trial." *Law and Social Inquiry* 17 (1992): 715–43.

McGuinn, Henry J. "Equal Protection of the Law and Fair Trials in Maryland." *Journal of Negro History* 24 (1939): 143–66.

Meier, August. "The Negro and the Democratic Party, 1875–1915." *Phylon* 17 (1956): 173–91.

———. "Toward a Reinterpretation of Booker T. Washington." *Journal of Southern History* 23 (1957): 220–27.

———. "Negro Class Structure and Ideology in the Age of Booker T. Washington." *Phylon* 23 (1962): 258–66.

———, and Elliott Rudwick. "The Boycott Movement against Jim Crow Streetcars in the South, 1900–1906." *Journal of American History* 55 (1969): 756–75.

Metress, Christopher. "Making Civil Rights Harder: Literature, Memory, and the Black Freedom Struggle." *Southern Literary Journal* 40 (Spring 2008): 138–50.

Meyer, David S. "Protest and Political Opportunities." *Annual Review of Sociology* 30 (2004): 125–45.

Minter, Patricia Hagler. "The Failure of Freedom: Class, Gender, and the Evolution of Segregated Transit Law in the Nineteenth-Century South." *Chicago-Kent Law Review* 70 (1995): 993–1009.

Morris, Aldon. "Reflections on Social Movement Theory: Criticisms and Proposals." *Contemporary Sociology* 29 (2000): 445–54.

Morris, Calvin S. "Reverdy Ransom, the Social Gospel and Race." *Journal of Religious Thought* 41 (1984): 7–21.

"The Niagara Movement." *Voice of the Negro* 2 (1905): 522–59.

"Notes." *Journal of Negro History* 12 (1927): 563–66.

Osofsky, Gilbert. "Progressivism and the Negro: New York, 1900–1915." *American Quarterly* 16 (1964): 153–68.

Ovington, Mary White. "How the National Association for the Advancement of Colored People Began." *Crisis* 8, no. 4 (1914): 184–88.

Palmore, Joseph R. "The Not-So-Strange Career of Interstate Jim Crow: Race, Transportation, and the Dormant Commerce Clause, 1878–1946." *Virginia Law Review* 83 (1997): 1733–1817.

Perkins-Valdez, Dolen. " 'Atlanta's Shame': W.E.B. Du Bois and Carrie Williams Clifford Respond to the Atlanta Race Riot of 1906." *Studies in the Literary Imagination* 40 (2007): 133–51.

Pillsbury, Albert E. "A Brief Inquiry into a Federal Remedy for Lynching." *Harvard Law Review* 15 (1902): 707–13.

Power, Garrett. "Apartheid Baltimore Style: The Residential Segregation Ordinances of 1910–13." *Maryland Law Review* 42 (1983): 289–328.

Ransom, Reverdy C. *The Industrial and Social Conditions of the Negro: A Thanksgiving Sermon, Speech before the Bethel AME Church, Chicago, Ill.* (November 26, 1896). Pamphlet. Chicago: Conservator Print.

Rice, Connie Park. "Pioneer Women: The 'Ladies' of the Niagara Movement." *Association for the Study of African American Life and History Black History Theme Magazine* (2005): 37–43.

Roberts, Dorothy. "Black Club Women and Child Welfare: Lessons for Modern Reform." *Florida State University Law Review* 32 (2005): 957–72.

Sabel, Charles F., and William H. Simon. "Destabilization Rights: How Public Law Litigation Succeeds." *Harvard Law Review* 117 (2004): 1015–1101.

Schmidt, Benno C., Jr. "Principle and Prejudice: The Supreme Court and Race in the Progressive Era: Part 1: The Heyday of Jim Crow." *Columbia Law Review* 82 (1982): 444–524.

Schmidt, Christopher W. "Conceptions of Law in the Civil Rights Movement." *UC Irvine Law Review* 1 (2011): 641–76.

Schneider, Mark R. "*The Colored American* and *Alexander's*: Boston's Pro-Civil Rights Bookerites." *Journal of Negro History* 80 (1995): 157–69.

Simms-Brown, R. Jean. "Populism and Black Americans: Constructive or Destructive?" *Journal of Negro History* 65 (1980): 349–60.

Sleet, Jessie C. "In the Day's Work of a Visiting Nurse." *Charities* 15 (Oct. 1905): 73–74.

Smith, Wilford. "The Negro and the Law." In *The Negro Problem: A Series of Articles by Representative American Negroes of Today*, edited by Booker T. Washington and W. E. Burghardt Du Bois, 125–59. New York: James Pott, 1903. Facsimile of the first edition, LaVergne, TN: Kessinger, 2009.

Southworth, Ann, and Scott Cummings. "Between Profit and Principle: The Private Public Interest Firm." In *Private Lawyers and the Public Interest: The Evolving Role of Pro Bono in the Legal Profession*, edited by Robert Granfield and Lynn Mather, 183–210. New York: Oxford University Press, 2009.

Stueck, William. "Progressivism and the Negro: White Liberals and the Early NAACP." *Historian* 38 (November 1975): 58–78.

Sturm, Susan. "Second Generation Employment Discrimination: A Structural Approach." *Columbia Law Review* 101 (2001): 458–598.

Taylor, Verta. "Social Movement Continuity: The Women's Movement in Abeyance." *American Sociological Review* 54 (1989): 761–75.

Terrell, Mary Church. "Christmas at the White House." *Voice of the Negro* 1 (1904): 593–600.

———. "Society among the Colored People of Washington, D.C." *Voice of the Negro* 1 (1904): 150–56.

———. "Service Which Should Be Rendered the South." *Voice of the Negro* 2 (1905): 182–86.

———. "The Social Functions during Inauguration Week." *Voice of the Negro* 2 (1905): 237–42.

———. "The Disbanding of the Colored Soldiers." *Voice of the Negro* 3 (1906): 554–58.

———. "The Mission of the Meddler." *Voice of the Negro* 2 (1906): 566–68.

———. "Peonage in the United States: The Convict Lease System and Chain Gangs." *Nineteenth Century* 62 (1907): 306–22.

———. "A Sketch of Mingo Saunders." *Voice of the Negro* 4 (1907): 128–31.

Terrell, Robert H. "A Glance at the Past and Present of the Negro." Speech delivered at Church's Auditorium before the Citizen's Industrial League of Memphis, TN, September 22, 1903. Published by Press of R. L. Pendleton, 1903.

Thornbrough, Emma Lou. "The National Afro-American League, 1887–1908." *Journal of Southern History* 27 (1961): 494–512.

Waite, Cally L. "The Segregation of Black Students at Oberlin College after Reconstruction." *History of Education Quarterly* 41 (2001): 344–64.

Waites, Cheryl. "Victoria Earle Matthews: Residence and Reform." In *African American Leadership: An Empowerment Tradition in Social Welfare History*, edited by Iris B. Carlton-LaNey, 1–16. Washington, DC: NASW Press, 2001.

Walling, William English. "The Race War in the North." *Independent* (1908): 529–34.

Watts, Eugene J. "Black Political Progress in Atlanta: 1868–1895." *Journal of Negro History* 59 (1974): 268–86.

Weiss, Nancy J. "The Negro and the New Freedom: Fighting Wilsonian Segregation." *Political Science Quarterly* (1969): 61–79.

Welke, Barbara Y. "When All the Women Were White, and All the Blacks Were Men: Gender, Class, Race, and the Road to *Plessy*, 1885–1914." *Law and History Review* 13 (1995): 261–316.

Wells Barnett, Ida B. "Mob Rule in New Orleans." In *Southern Horrors and Other Writings: The Anti-Lynching Campaign of Ida B. Wells, 1892–1900*, edited by Jacqueline Jones Royster, 158–208. Boston: Bedford/St. Martins, 1997.

Wilhoit, Francis M. "An Interpretation of Populism's Impact on the Georgia Negro." *Journal of Negro History* 52 (1967): 116–27.

Wood, L. Hollingsworth. "The Urban League Movement." *Journal of Negro History* 9 (1924): 117–26.

Unpublished Theses, Dissertations, and Student Papers

Alexander, Shawn Leigh. "We Know Our Rights and Have the Courage to Defend Them." PhD diss., University of Massachusetts at Amherst, 2004.

Ali, Omar Hamid. "Black Populism in the New South, 1886–1898." PhD diss., Columbia University, 2003.

Bach, Bryan. "Edward H. Morris: Dean of Chicago's African American Lawyers, 1858–1943." Student paper, American University Washington College of Law, 2008. On file with author.

Beverly, Sherman. "The Emergence of Black Political Power in Evanston: The Public Career of Edwin B. Jourdain, Jr., 1931–1947." PhD diss., Northwestern University, 1973.

Blaesser, Brian W. "John E. Milholland." Senior thesis, Brown University, 1969.

Bowen-Spencer, Michele Andrea. "The Institutional Church and Social Settlement, 1900–1904: Reverdy C. Ransom's Church for the Black Masses." Master's thesis, University of North Carolina at Chapel Hill, 1994.

Carroll, Patrick H. "The 1905 Niagara Movement Attendants: An Interpretive Analysis of Their Lives and Ideologies." Bachelor's thesis, College of the Holy Cross, 1980.

Dansky, Rebecca. "Strengthening and Expanding Federal Hate Crimes Law in the 21st Century." Student paper, American University Washington College of Law, 2009. On file with author.

Dickson, Lynda F. "The Early Club Movement among Black Women." PhD diss., University of Colorado, 1982.

Drewett, Donald Albert. "Ransom on Race and Racism: The Racial and Social Thought of Reverdy Cassius Ransom—Preacher, Editor, and Bishop in the African American Methodist Episcopal Church, 1861–1959." PhD diss., Drew University, 1988.

Driskell, Jay. "First Class Citizens: Rights, Respectability and the Making of Modern Black Politics." Unpublished manuscript, Jan. 2013 draft.

Freeman, Elaine Kaplan. "Harvey Johnson and Everett Waring, a Study of Leadership in the Baltimore Negro Community, 1880–1900." Master's thesis, George Washington University, 1968.

Glasberg, Victor Michael. "The Emergence of White Liberalism: The Founders of the NAACP and American Racial Attitudes." PhD diss., Harvard University, 1971.

Hawshawe, Dorothy Drinkard. "David Augustus Straker, Black Lawyer and Reconstruction Politician, 1842–1908." PhD diss., Catholic University of America, 1974.

Hu, Meagan. "Revisiting Samuel Gompers' Views on Using Law to Pursue Social Reform." Student paper, American University Washington College of Law, 2010. On file with author.

Jones, Beverly Washington. "Quest for Equality: The Life of Mary Eliza Church Terrell, 1863–1954." PhD diss., University of North Carolina, Chapel Hill, 1980.

Miller, George Mason. " 'A This Worldly Mission': The Life and Career of Alexander Walters (1858–1917)." PhD diss., State University of New York at Stony Brook, 1984.

Mutua, Athena D. "Restoring Justice to Civil Rights Movement Activists?: New Historiography and the 'Long Civil Rights Era.' " Unpublished paper, University at Buffalo Law School, State University of New York, 2008, available through SSRN.

Ronnick, Michele Valerie. "Abstract: William Lewis Bulkley (1861–1933): The First African American to Earn a Doctorate in Latin." Unpublished. apaclassics.org/images/uploads/documents/abstracts/Ronnick_38.pdf.

Salem, Dorothy C. "The NACW." PhD diss., Kent State University, 1986.

Tsai, Robert. "America's Forgotten Constitutions: Visions of Power and Community after the Founding." Forthcoming, Harvard University Press, 2014.

Internet Sources

Bridgewater State University, Office of Institutional Diversity, "Elizabeth Carter Brooks." Last modified November 17, 2004. http://www.bridgew.edu/hoba/Brooks.cfm.

Maria L. Baldwin School, "Maria L. Baldwin Biography." Accessed October 30, 2012. http://www.cpsd.us/BAL/history_baldwin.cfm.

National Institute of Medicine, s.v. "Dr. Rebecca J. Cole." Accessed October 30, 2012. http://www.nlm.nih.gov/changingthefaceofmedicine/physicians/biography_66.html.

New Georgia Encyclopedia, s.v. "John Hope." Accessed July 24, 2012. http://www.georgiaencyclopedia.org/nge/Article.jsp?id=h-855.

"Orpheus M. and Mattie Allen McAdoo Papers," African American Studies at Beinecke Library, Yale University (biographical information accompanying announcement of the availability of this collection). Accessed May 31, 2013. http://beinecke.library.yale.edu/about/blogs/african-american-studies-beinecke-library/2010/02/09/orpheus-m-and-mattie-allen-mcadoo.

INDEX